CZECHOSLOVAKIA

VRATISLAV BUSEK and NICOLAS SPULBER
Editors

Published for the
MID-EUROPEAN STUDIES CENTER of the
FREE EUROPE COMMITTEE, INC., by

Atlantic Books

FREDERICK A. PRAEGER
NEW YORK

STEVENS & SONS LIMITED
LONDON

First published in the United States of America in 1956 by
FREDERICK A. PRAEGER, INC., *Publishers, 150 East 52nd Street*
New York, 22, N. Y.

This is VOLUME NUMBER *19*
of Praeger Publications in Russian History and World Communism

Library of Congress Catalog Card Number 57-9333
Printed in the United States of America

Published in Great Britain by
Atlantic Book Publishing Co. Ltd.
of 119 & 120 Chancery Lane, London

Distributed in Great Britain by
Stevens and Sons Limited of
119 & 120 Chancery Lane, London

FOREWORD

The Mid-European Studies Center, a unit of the Free Europe Committee, Inc. (formerly the National Committee for a Free Europe), was founded in the summer of 1950 principally to help maintain the intellectual traditions and cultural heritage of the peoples of Central and Eastern Europe now under Communist control, to assist exiles of scholarly competence to continue their work against Communist tyranny, and to increase the fund of information available on this area, which is a *terra incognita* for even educated Americans. The Center has completed and published a large number of studies, and has probably been the principal research institute in the world concentrating on East-Central Europe.

This volume, *Czechoslovakia under the Communists,* is one of a series of seven. The series was conceived in the spring of 1954 by Mr. Stetson S. Holmes, then Director of the Mid-European Studies Center, by Mr. Jacob B. Hoptner, then Director of Research of the Mid-European Studies Center, and by Dr. Stephen Fischer-Galati, then a staff member. It was organized as a joint project of refugee scholars and of American specialists, and it was hoped that the volumes would not only increase the fund of information, but would also help define the boundaries of our knowledge and the areas in which research and analysis were most needed. The books are designed to provide thorough, accurate, and well-organized information on Albania, Bulgaria, Czechoslovakia, Hungary, Poland, Romania, and Yugoslavia since they have been under Communist rule. Eastern Germany and the Baltic states, Lithuania, Latvia, and Estonia, all important parts of the Soviet empire in East-Central Europe, were omitted because the Center lacked both the personnel and the materials for volumes on these states.

The series is a massive project, which the Mid-European Studies Center is particularly well qualified to prepare and to publish. As the research division of the Free Europe Committee, it possesses a small but highly-qualified staff of experts on this area. Some of these specialists lived for years in East-Central Europe, were educated there, and held important positions in cultural, political, and government life; others have American academic training. In addition, the

Center has developed close relations with specialists on this area teaching in American colleges and universities or working in research institutions. Finally, the Free Europe Committee, of which the Center is a part, has the largest collection of materials available in the non-Communist world, particularly on developments within the last six years.

However, this material is often fragmentary. Moreover, Communist data must be examined with great care, because all Communist material has a political purpose. In addition, little analysis has been made anywhere in the world of recent developments in East-Central Europe, so that there are few secondary studies available. In a sense, each chapter of each volume—in other words, the 150 chapters in the series—represents pioneer research, with all the faults and weaknesses from which such research suffers. This explains why each volume contains quantities of useful information, but lacks generally the kind of analysis one would find in studies of areas where American research has had a longer and richer tradition.

Dr. Fischer-Galati at the beginning was entrusted with the administration and direction of the series. He prepared the outline for the seven volumes, selected the original contributors, reviewed most of the preliminary drafts, and managed the enterprise generally until he accepted appointment as assistant professor of history at Wayne University in the summer of 1955. At that time, I assumed the editorship, with Mr. Paul Sivak my invaluable support on this volume. All the resources of the Center were mobilized to complete the series by the summer of 1956.

When the editorial process was begun by the Center's staff and by the editors of the individual volumes, we discovered that some chapters were excellent, but that others failed to meet the standards set for the work as a whole, because of the wide variety of training, experience, and political points of view of the authors. It also became clear that many important and interesting issues and problems had not been included in the general outline. Consequently, within a limited budget and period of time, some additional chapters were added, and substantial editing, revising, and, in some cases, complete rewriting of other chapters were undertaken. This task was assumed and completed with skill and diligence by the staff of the Mid-European Studies Center.

The difficulties were all grievously compounded when, as the various volumes were nearing completion, the flow of information from the Soviet Union and from the countries under Communist control suddenly increased sharply. In some cases, the new data constituted the first solid information on important aspects of the economies of these countries; in other cases, the new information supplemented or replaced estimates derived from many scraps of information. All this information had to be carefully analyzed and incorporated. Just as this task was being completed, the Twentieth Congress of the Soviet Communist Party, and the extraordinary attacks on Stalin and Stalinism which accompanied and followed it, brought considerable revisions and additions to some sections of the books, particularly those dealing with the Communist Party and biographies of Communist leaders.

This volume reflects the state of American scholarship, and of Western scholarship generally, on developments within Communist Czechoslovakia. Its authors and editors have sought to ensure that it be an accurate and objective description and analysis of what has happened in Czechoslovakia under Communist rule. The manuscript was delivered to the publisher in June 1956, so that it reflects data available at that time, although minor additions and revisions were made later as new information became available.

The editor of the political, social, and cultural parts of this volume, Dr. Vratislav Busek, born in Prague in 1897, was educated at the Faculty of Law at Charles University in Prague, from which he obtained an L.L.D. and in which he started his academic career as docent of canon law. He was later Professor of Canon Law and Roman Law at the Faculty of Law at the Comenius University in Bratislava in Slovakia, at the Masaryk University in Brno in Moravia, and at Charles University in Prague in Bohemia. He was successively Dean of the Faculty of Law and President at Comenius University. He has written approximately a hundred books, pamphlets, articles, and reviews in his special field, as well as innumerable articles about public affairs. He was a member of the parliamentary committee of experts preparing the draft of the new Czechoslovak Constitution to be published in the year 1948. For his democratic convictions and activities, he was placed in a concentration camp by the Gestapo for three years, and later he was compelled to flee his native country after the Communist *coup d'état* in 1948. In exile, he worked with the Centre National de la Recherche Scientifique in Paris and was a lecturer in history at Seton Hall College. Since July 1950, he has been a scriptwriter for Radio Free Europe. His most recent work is *Pouceni z unoroveho prevratu* (The Lesson of the February Coup).

The editor of the economic section, Dr. Nicolas Spulber, is Associate Professor of Economics at Indiana University and a member of the staff of the Institute of East European Studies at that university. He was born in Romania and was educated both in Europe and in the United States, to which he came in 1948. He received the Halle Fellowship from the Graduate Faculty of the New School for Social Research, and continued his graduate studies both at that institution and at the Russian Institute of Columbia University. He obtained his

Ph.D. from the New School. After two years as Research Associate in the Center for International Studies at the Massachusetts Institute of Technology, and as Lecturer at the French University of New York (Ecole Libre des Hautes Etudes), he joined Indiana University in 1954, first as a Lecturer, then as an Associate Professor. Dr. Spulber has contributed numerous articles to American and European economic journals. He is the author of *The Economics of Communist Eastern Europe* and is now completing a study of national income in the countries under Soviet control.

Robert F. Byrnes

PREFACE

The greatest challenge in editing a volume on Czechoslovakia under Communist rule is to maintain a proper balance between the long historical evolution and Western tradition of the country and the very short revolutionary situation which has developed since the Communist *coup d'état* in February 1948. Moreover, while the literature and the documentary material for the period before 1948 are rich, it has been very difficult to obtain solid evidence about the past eight years.

This volume has undergone many changes since it was first initiated. The editors, who assumed their responsibilities only in 1955, had to work within a general outline and framework adopted in 1954. Even though the volume has been revised considerably during the past year, it proved impossible to carry out some of the desired additions and reorganizations.

We would like to thank Mr. Pavel Korbel, Mr. Alois Rozehnal, Mr. Vladislav Brdlik, Mr. Vojtech Vagassky, Mrs. Milada Souckova, and Mrs. Jane Feierabend for their most valuable and friendly assistance. It is also our fond duty to thank the staff members of the Mid-European Studies Center, who performed an extremely difficult assignment in helping to prepare this volume for publication. Miss Lyn Kuckenberg edited the entire volume with grace and care. Professor Robert F. Byrnes, who had the thankless task of making excisions from the contributions of the authors, did this with undisputed competence and tact.

Nicolas Spulber
Vratislav Busek

CONTENTS

Appendix

MAPS

NOTE

The American equivalents of continental measures used in this volume are as follows:

1 kilometer (km.)–0.62 mile
1 square kilometer (km^2)–0.386 square mile
1 hectare (ha.)–2.47 acres
1 kilogram (kg.)–2.20 lbs. avoirdupois
1 quintal–220.46 lbs. avoirdupois
1 hectoliter–2.84 U. S. bushels

References to "tons" indicate metric tons (1 metric ton–1.1023 short tons).

The following symbols have been used in the tables:

Dots (. . . .) indicate that data are not available.

A dash (–) indicates that the amount is nil or negligible.

East-Central Europe Under the Communists

CZECHOSLOVAKIA

Part I. Geography and Demography

1. THE LAND

Abraham Melezin

Area and Boundaries

Czechoslovakia now consists of the Czech lands (Bohemia and Moravia-Silesia) and Slovakia. Ruthenia was ceded to the Soviet Union in June 1945. Czechoslovak territory, comprising 140,508 square kilometers (54,250 square miles) during the interwar period, was reduced to 127,827 square kilometers (49,354 square miles) in 1945. Her boundaries were reduced from 4,111 kilometers (2,554 miles) in 1938 to 3,641 kilometers (2,262 miles) in 1945, as shown in Table 1.

Table 1. Political Boundaries in 1938 and 1945

	1938		1945	
Boundary with	in kilometers	in per cent	in kilometers	in per cent
Germany	1,545	37.6	905[a]	24.8
Poland	984	23.9	1,390	38.2
Hungary	832	20.2	678	18.6
Austria	549	13.4	570	15.7
Romania	201	4.9	—	—
Soviet Union	—	—	98	2.7
Total	4,111	100.0	3,641	100.0

Source: Ceskoslovensko v mapach (Czechoslovakia in Maps) (Prague, 1954), p. 6.

[a] Of which 549 kilometers with East Germany.

The most significant boundary changes after World War II related to the frontiers with Germany and Poland. The short frontier with West Germany is Czechoslovakia's only link with the free world. The prewar boundary with Romania no longer exists. It has been replaced by a frontier with the Soviet Union.

Note: This chapter is based partly on material compiled by Dr. Vladislav Brdlik.

Czechoslovakia's frontiers are mostly mountainous, but many passes and valleys form excellent gateways, which make the country easily accessible. The Soviet frontier runs mostly along the low Carpathian ranges, and the Polish along the Carpathians and the Sudetes. The frontier with Germany links the mildly elevated mountains, such as Krusne Hory, Cesky Les, and Sumava. The Austrian border extends south of the Sumava Mountains, running through the southern parts of the Bohemian peneplain, and partly along the Morava River. The Danube and its tributary, the Ipel, comprise a part of the Hungarian frontier, which cuts through the hills of the Slovak Ore Mountains and the Karst, and continues east through the plains of Slovakia.

Czechoslovakia is completely landlocked, with over 300 kilometers separating her northwest frontier from the nearest Baltic seaport of Szczecin. The distance from her southwest border to Trieste on the Adriatic is also over 300 kilometers, and the distance to the Danube Delta is over 600 kilometers.

Structure and Relief

The physical features of Czechoslovakia are heterogeneous, due to the presence of both Hercynian and Alpine elements. The two main elements, the Bohemian Massif and the Carpathians, are separated by a zone of subsidence, occupied by the upper Oder and Morava rivers, which provide a channel of communication between the southern and northern parts of Central Europe. Moving from west to east, the main geographical components of Czechoslovakia are the Bohemian Square, the Moravian Depression, and the Carpathian System.

The Bohemian Square. This region consists of old Hercynian mountains with an enclosed plateau. The complex is often called the Bohemian Massif. This rigid structural element stopped the wave of Alpine folding, but, in the process, the old peneplainized area was broken up, uplifted, and surrounded by an elevated rim on its fringes. This elevated rim is marked by a fault line and is tilted in a northern direction. The area forms the most stable and compact core of the Hercynian system in Central Europe. Composed of ancient crystalline rocks, mainly granites and gneisses, it has dislocated Paleozoic sedimentary elements, preserved in the syncline of the central part of the Massif. Erosional forces reshaped the rim into a mountain system consisting of three main components: the Sudetes, the highest mountain chain; the Krusne Hory (the Ore Mountains); and the Sumava Mountains. These are further subdivided into several small ranges, groups, and massifs.

The Sudetes occupy the northeastern part of the Bohemian Massif. They are structurally complicated and form six main ranges: the Jesenik, the Orlicke, the Bystricke, the Jilove, the Krkonose, and the Jizerske mountains. All run parallel to each other, and are divided by tectonic, graben-like depressions. Cretaceous sandstones and marls and Permian slates are penetrated by extrusives. The ranges, which are partly narrow ridges and partly dome-like elevations, reach their extreme altitudes in the north. The highest summits are Snezka (5,258 feet) and Sisak (4,940 feet). The Sudetes form a wide barrier, defined by a fault-like scarp in the Krkonose Mountains. Traces of local glaciation, found in the Krkonose, appear in the form of small cirques and corries. Lakes are rather uncommon. The upland topography is generally represented by mature forms, such as rounded summits and broad, shallow river valleys. Most of the important intermontane basins of this area are in Poland.

The Krusne Hory rise steeply above the central depression and are gently tilted in the northwest. A sharply defined straight fault scarp creates the impression that the horst is limited from the south by a graben. The central part of the far western region was downfaulted, forming inner and outer ridges, known respectively as the Krusne Hory and the Cisarsky Les mountains. The trough is now occupied by the Ohre River, a tributary of the Labe (Elbe), and an important communication route. The ranges are composed of old crystalline rock, considerably dissected by streams. The elevations reach over 3,280 feet, attaining a height of 4,080 feet at the summit of Mount Klinovec. The lower Cisarsky Les mountain ranges seldom exceed a height of 3,000 feet. The foothills of the Krusne Mountains are covered by Tertiary sediments, overlain in the east by Tertiary effusives of the Doupovske Hills and the Stredohori. The volcanic activity lasted through the Pliocene, leaving many thermal springs (such as Karlovy Vary, Teplice, Marianske Lazne) noted for their curative properties. The Labe cuts the Stredohori and later the Krusne Hory in a tectonic depression of Cretaceous sandstones. Similar erosional features, identified as "Saxonian Switzerland," are found in Czechoslovakia as well as in Germany. The gorge of the Labe is ancient, antedating the era when the Bohemian Massif was uplifted. Several basins, the Cheb, Falknov, and Zatec, were created due to erosional work of the Ohre River. The Zatec basin represents a fertile rolling country, while the clayish soils overlying the Tertiary rocks of the Cheb and Falknov basins are poorly suited to farming.

The southwestern part of the elevated rim is known as the Sumava Mountains. Its hilly ranges, known as the Cesky Les, join the Krusne Mountains. This part of the Bohemian Massif is not very impressive, but the mountains in the southeast are higher, attaining an elevation of 4,780 feet at Mount Javor. A mature upland topography of rounded summits creates a monotonous landscape. The sedimentary components were largely eroded, exposing the crystalline core. The uplifted area falls steeply along a southwest fault line, facing the Bavarian Forest Mountains. Evidence of local glaciation is provided by small cirques and lakes.

The well defined rim of the Massif is less pronounced in the southeastern part. The Moravian Heights comprise a mildly elevated fringe of the central peneplain. They are considerably lower than other rim mountains, reaching 2,739 feet at Mount Javorice. The area is crossed by several passes.

The central part of the Bohemian Massif, a plateau-like tectonic depression built of crystalline rock, granites, and gneisses is surrounded by the aforementioned ranges. Dislocated Paleozoic strata of the synclinal part and the sandstone ranges of Brdy resemble Apallachian folding with its symmetric parallel alignment. Other parts are composed of dislocated Silurian, Devonian, and Carboniferous strata. Sedimentary strata of Cretaceous origin are found in the northern part. Here, along the Labe River, soft Cretaceous marls were eroded away, creating the plain of Polabi. Polabi is a subsidence area mantled by loess, with scattered monadnocks breaking up the monotonous landscape. The southern part of Bohemia consists of the upland basins of Trebon, drained by Luznice River, and Ceske Budejovice, drained by the upper Vltava. The basins of the northern part of the plateau include the Kladno, Labe, and Plzen (Pilsen). Convergence of rivers, deposits of coal, and fertile soils account for the economic importance of this region.

The Moravian Depression. This area is enclosed between the Moravian Heights and western Carpathians. It is a tectonic depression which connects the lowlands of the south and north, forming a corridor between Hungary and Silesia. The Moravian Heights are easily accessible through lower areas stretching athwart the plateau, such as the gate of Trebova. The gate, located where the river systems of Labe and Morava are separated by a small swamp, reaches the height of 1,466 feet. It is crossed by a railroad connecting Prague and Brno. The easternmost part of the Moravian Heights, north of Brno, has a distinct karst topography developed during the Paleozoic. The spectacular gorge of Macocha, the Katerinske caves, and the Masaryk Dome are notable features.

The Moravian Gate in the northern part of the Depression is one of the most important gateways of Central Europe. It constitutes a frontier between the Hercynian and the Alpine systems, and a link between the Northern European Plain and southern lowlands. This depression facilitated the northward movement of Miocene seas, and later, the southward movement of the continental ice sheet. The Silesian Plateau, with its rich coal deposits, is located north of the Moravian Gate. In the south lies the Morava basin, formed during the Tertiary and covered with a thick mantle of loess. The abrupt ridges of Chriby Plateau and Pavlovske Hills break up the monotony of the lower part of the basin.

In the east, Moravia is limited by the Carpathian ranges of Bile Karpaty (White Carpathians) and the Javorniky Mountains.

The Carpathian System. The Carpathians extend through northern Slovakia, starting near the Danube as the Little Carpathian range. Built of crystalline slates and limestones, they attain heights of 2,496 feet. In the north, the Little Carpathians are joined by the White Carpathians, rising to 3,175 feet at Mount Javorina, and by the Javorniky range, reaching 4,205 feet at Mount Smrk. Further north are the Bezkydy Mountains, which turn east, forming the first Carpathian bow. These outer ranges of the Carpathians are composed of Flysch. Their mature monotonous landscape of mildly elevated ranges is dissected by numerous river valleys. Such passes as the Vlara (928 feet) and the Jablunka (1,807 feet) facilitate communication. The piedmont areas consist of low hills separated by wide valleys.

The Orava and the Vah valleys separate the outer Carpathians from the inner crystalline zone. Several intermontane basins, the Liptov, Turiec, Poprad, and Hornad, separate the Carpathians into fragments. The High and the Low Tatra mountains, built of a crystalline rock in the core, and of Triassic limestones in the outer slopes, have a typical Alpine landscape with traces of glaciation in the form of cirques, small lakes, and moraines. These rugged, steeply-sloped mountains rise above 1,500 meters (4,920 feet). Several peaks reach elevations over 2,000 meters (6,560 feet). Mount Gerlach, which is the highest, reaches 8,735 feet.

The southern part of the Carpathian bow is defined by fractures, marked by the volcanic hills of Slovenske Krusnohorie (Slovak Ore Mountains). These dome-like elevated ranges are characterized by steep slopes facing the lowlands.

Finally, a typical region is formed by the Slovak lowlands. These are mostly northern fringes of the Danube Basin, known as Little Alfoeld or parts of the Big Alfoeld in the east, where they are considerably smaller (Ipel and Kosice basins). The lowlands, drained by the tributaries of the Danube, and covered by fertile loess soils, are important agricultural regions.

The surface configuration of Czechoslovakia, characterized by mild elevations and low mountains is indicated in Table 2, which shows the distribution of hypsometric layers.

Table 2. Distribution of Hypsometric Layers

Elevation above Sea Level	Per Cent of Total Area
(in meters)[a]	
0 - 200	13.63
200 - 300	16.75
300 - 500	31.69
500 - 750	26.28
750 - 1,000	7.98
1,000 - 1,250	2.37
1,250 - 1,500	0.94
above 1,500	0.36

Source: State Statistical Office, *Statistical Digest of the Czechoslovak Republic, 1948* (Prague, 1948).

[a] 1 meter=3.280833 feet.

Climate

The climate of Czechoslovakia is defined as a humid, moderate, continental type with cool summers. It is mainly influenced by Atlantic air masses. Except for the high areas, which have a mountainous climate, the country is marked by considerable climatic variations from west to east. The influence of fragmented relief is responsible for "local" climates, particularly in the Bohemian Square region.

Pressure and Winds

The low pressure system of the Atlantic affects Czechoslovakia throughout the year. Westerly winds account for almost 60 per cent of all winds. Easterly winds, which account for about 25 per cent, are connected with the Asiatic winter high pressure center extending into Central Europe. Generally, Czechoslovakia has low wind velocities and somewhat stagnated air movements caused by the surrounding mountain ranges and hills. The most important local wind is the foehn, which occurs in northeastern Bohemia, and in the piedmont areas of the Carpathians. It raises temperatures and causes winter thaws.

Temperature

The mean annual temperature of Czechoslovakia ranges from 43 to 50 degrees Fahrenheit. It is lower in the isolated mountain areas, especially in the Tatras and the Sudetes. Isothermic lines reflect the fragmentation of relief.

The warmest parts of the country are the basins and lowlands such as the Polabi in Bohemia, the Moravian plains, and the lowlands along the Danube and Tisa. The Polabi basin is warmer than southern Bohemia, and the lowlands of Slovakia are warmer than the plains of the western part of the country. Due to fragmentation of relief, cold and hot pockets are found in Bohemia and Moravia. In the mountains, the northern slopes, which are exposed to the moderating westerly and northwesterly winds, are warmer than the southern slopes. Spring is generally cooler than autumn. Temperature ranges in the eastern parts reflect more continental features. Temperature variations are greater in spring than in autumn.

Precipitation

A close correlation between rainfall and topography is evident in Czechoslovakia. Rainfall varies not only with elevation, but also with the degree of exposure of areas, situation on windward or leeward sides, and shelter from winds. These account for a rather unusual distribution of precipitation, which increases toward the east. Furthermore, in the eastern parts of the country, rainfall is never as scarce as in some of the western basins. The summer maximum is more pronounced in the lowlands, but the distribution of rainfall tends to be more uniform with increasing altitudes. The lowlands exposed in the south, particularly Moravia and the Danubian plain, have a second maximum in October as a result of Mediterranean influences.

Generally, elevations up to 250 meters (820 feet) have the least precipitation (up to 24 inches), and the leeward locations even less (under 20 inches). Although the western parts have less rainfall, aridity is more common in the east (Danubian lowland), due to the seasonal distribution of rainfall.

The more elevated hilly regions and piedmont areas receive up to 34 inches of rainfall, and the mountains have as much as 50-55 inches. The lower, but westwardly situated Sumava Mountains receive as much precipitation as the higher Tatra Mountains, chiefly due to Atlantic influences.

The average number of days with snowfall amounts to 45 in the west and only to about 27 to 30 days in the east. The snow cover lasts 70 to 80 days, though longer in the mountains. It is more stable in Slovakia than in Bohemia due to more uniform winter temperatures.

Climatic Regions

Although Czechoslovakia is a country of local climates, with considerable differences in a relatively small area, several climatic regions may be distinguished.

Climates of Mountain Regions. This group can be divided into the zones of high mountains and of lower mountains. The zone of high mountains, rising above 5,250 feet, is characterized by a relatively small temperature range. Average temperatures are never above 50 degrees Fahrenheit and often fall below 14 degrees. Precipitation is mostly in the form of snow, which falls steadily over a long winter. The second zone includes the lower mountains, ranging from 2,300-5,250 feet in altitude. Summer temperatures are generally between 50 and 65 degrees. Winter lasts up to six months, and the annual precipitation exceeds 40 inches, with a maximum in June.

Transitional Climates. The main subdivisions of this group are piedmont, central Bohemian, and intermontane basins and valleys. Piedmont climates have an average annual temperature of 43 to 47 degrees, and precipitation up to 34 inches. They are exposed to local winds and the foehn. The central Bohemian climate is complicated by numerous basins and valleys. It resembles the piedmont type in its thermal conditions, but has less rainfall, more severe winters, cooler summer nights, and frequent fogs. The intermontane basins and valleys have a mean annual temperature ranging from 42 to 46 degrees; annual rainfall amounts to 20-24 inches in Bohemia and 24-32 inches in Slovakia. Local winds and frequent temperature inversions during the winter are among the most typical features.

Climates of Lowlands. These are found in the Moravian and Danubian lowlands. The principal factor is the Mediterranean influence, which brings a second rainfall maximum in the fall. The Moravian sub-zone is milder than the Danubian, which is warmer, more continental, and arid due to hot summers.

Hydrography

Rivers

Czechoslovakia's location athwart the main European divide explains the drainage pattern of her rivers. The systems of the Labe and Oder drain toward the north and, together with the basin of the Vistula, cover an area of some 59,000 square kilometers. The remaining part of the country belongs to the Danubian system, which drains into the Black Sea. Most of the rivers of Czechoslovakia are short; the three major rivers, Labe, Oder, and Danube, continue into other Central European countries.

Bohemia constitutes a hydrographic unit with a centripetal pattern around the Vltava-Labe. Similarly, Moravia forms a distinct hydrographic region with an axis along the Morava River. The Danubian system does not represent a unit, as many tributaries tend to flow parallel in their upper courses and converge near the confluence with the Danube.

Most Bohemian and Moravian rivers follow turbulent middle courses and tend to flow in narrow, gorge-like valleys. Danubian tributaries are generally rapid, carrying sediments which form large alluvial fans. This creates an obstacle to navigation.

The Czechoslovak sector of the Danube is 172 kilometers (107 miles) long. Although the river is fed by Alpine glaciers, there is considerable difference between high and low water levels. In May, the average flow is twice as voluminous as in November. Averaging 10 feet in depth, the Danube poses several navigation problems due to a high volume of sediments which require dredging. In winter, the river freezes, and small river barges are threatened by floating ice. The main tributaries of the Danube are the Morava, the Vah with the Nitra, the Hron, the Ipel, and the tributaries of the Tisa, of which the Hornad is most important. Most rivers are not regulated, and, notwithstanding the protection of forests in their upper courses, floods are often disastrous. The main value of the rivers is their hydroelectric potential.

The Labe River extends over 364 kilometers (226 miles) in Czechoslovakia. It originates in the Krkonose Mountains, about 4,560 feet above sea level. The average flow in the spring is three times as voluminous as in the fall; this also applies to its main tributary the Vltava. Both rivers are navigable in their lower reaches, but freeze up to sixty days a year. Certain parts of their flows are regulated to secure sufficient depth for river craft. The length of major rivers is given in Table 3.

Lakes

A complex of small lakes is found in central Bohemia in the area of the Trebon and Budejovice basins. These occupy small kettle-like depressions formed in heavy impermeable clay deposits of Tertiary origin. Many serve as fish ponds. A number of small lakes of glacial origin are found in the mountains. These include the Certovo and Cerne Jezero in the Sumava Mountains, and Strbske and Popradske Pleso in the Carpathians.

Table 3. Length of Selected Rivers

Basin	River	Length in Czechoslovakia
		(in kilometers)
Labe (Elbe)	Labe	364
	Jizera	164
	Vltava	430
	Luznice	208
	Sazava	220
	Berounka	247
	Ohre	256
Oder	Oder	132
	Opava	114
	Moravica	102
Vistula	Poprad	108
Danube	Danube	172
	Morava	365
	Becva	118
	Dyje	263
	Jihlava	180
	Vah	391
	Orava	112
	Nitra	232
	Hron	276
	Ipel	89
	Slana	98
	Hornad	168
	Laborec	130

Soils

In general, Czechoslovakia has fertile soils, suitable for extensive cultivation of grain and industrial crops. The heterogeneous character of bedrock and the diversified relief have influenced the country's soil mantle. Climatic conditions also contribute to the mosaic of soil patterns. Podzolic and brown forest are the most common types of soil. Smaller areas are covered by chernozem, alluvial, and humus-carbonate soils. Mountainous stony soils prevail in higher altitudes, while peat soils and salines dot the lowlands and mountains.

The distribution of soils in Bohemia and Moravia resembles two concentric zones surrounding Polabi and the Moravian Lowland. The core of each zone consists of fertile chernozem soils formed on loess. This core is surrounded by fertile brown forest soils on rolling regions found in central Bohemia and southern Moravia. These are in turn succeeded by podzols, which cover considerable areas in Bohemia, Silesia, and northern Moravia. Finally, the bordering uplands and mountains are covered by stony, thin mountainous soils.

The residual soils of Bohemia and part of those of Moravia are formed on Paleozoic, and, to a lesser extent, on Mesozoic and Tertiary bedrock. This explains the difference in their composition. The non-residual soils, loess and alluvials, are less common but of greater economic value.

The distribution of soils in the eastern part of the country is influenced by relief, rainfall, and temperature. Southern Slovakia has a belt of chernozem soils between the lower Vah and Hron rivers. These are surrounded by a zone of brown forest soils which intrude north in the river valleys. Podzols are found on the margins, while mountainous soils prevail in higher regions.

Alluvial soils appear along the Danube and in the Tisa basin in eastern Slovakia. Peat soils are common north of Bratislava, on the fringes of Liptov-Poprad basins, and further north in the Bezkydy near the Polish frontier. Patches of saline soils are found on Great Rye Island (Vel'ky zitny ostrov), further north between Galanta and Nove Zanky, and in a few scattered localities along the Hungarian border.

Natural Vegetation

Altitude and climate tend to determine the natural vegetation of Czechoslovakia. The peneplainized uplands of Hercynian mountains are covered by high moor associations in which sphagnum moss, heaths, cotton grass, dwarf birch, and knee pine predominate. The mountains above the timber line, extending up to 4,250-4,600 feet in the west, and to about 5,400 in the east, are covered with Alpine meadows. Anemones, oxslip, larkspur, foxglove, and thistle are common in this area.

Czechoslovakia is among the most forested countries of Europe. A zone of forests extends below the Alpine meadows and moors. The woodland is sparser in lower altitudes. In altitudes above 1,000 meters (3,280 feet), forests cover over 60 per cent of the surface, while in lower regions of 650-1,600 feet, forests account for 15 per cent of the area. Forested areas are denser in the east, covering about 34 per cent of Slovakia and 30 per cent of Bohemia and Moravia.

The upper forest zones have a variety of tree species, while in lower regions, the forest is more uniform, consisting of spruce, beech, and fir. The lower zones have a mixed forest, with spruce, beech, fir, oak, maple, ash, and elm species. Spruce covers most of the forested areas of Slovakia. Beech is also found in abundance. Oak has suffered from deforestation due to its association with fertile soils.

As to composition, coniferous forests generally account for about 70 per cent of the country's woodland, with spruce accounting for about 45 per cent. The forests of Slovakia, which are compact and cover large areas, are particularly suited for exploitation.

In the lowlands, a steppe-type vegetation predominates. Trefoil, sea-plantan, goose-foot, and the reed are common. Other species include cocksfoot, carex, broom grass, milfoil, and milk-vetch.

Transition areas between the lowlands and plateaus are covered by a prairie-like zone, where patches of deciduous forest are intruded by Pannonian vegetation (fescue grass, mignonettes, trefoil, sage and verbena). Man has largely destroyed the natural vegetation, displacing it by crops and younger forests which dominate the landscape.

Human Site

Administrative Division

The binational state of Czechoslovakia is divided into 19 administrative regions *(kraj)*. The average area of a region is 5,000-6,000 square kilometers with a population of 500,000-600,000. The regions are distributed among the provinces in the following manner:

Bohemia, 8 regions: Praha (Prague), Ceske Budejovice, Plzen, Karlovy Vary, Usti nad Labem, Liberec, Hradec Kralove, and Pardubice;

Moravia, 5 regions: Jihlava, Brno, Olomouc, Gottwaldov, and Ostrava;

Slovakia, 6 regions: Bratislava, Nitra, Banska Bystrica, Zilina, Kosice, and Presov.

Each region is divided into 12-15 districts *(okres)*, with further subdivisions into rural and urban communities.

Economic-Geographical Division

Czechoslovakia has long-established and well-defined economic regions, based on the country's natural and human resources. The economic divisions are marked by a considerable amount of regional specialization in both agriculture and industry.

The country may be divided into two contrasting parts, the Czech lands (Bohemia and Moravia-Silesia) and Slovakia. The two parts differ in their physical site, relationship between agriculture and industry, and social structure. The Czech lands are generally industrialized in both their urban and rural communities. Underdeveloped areas include the Czech-Moravian Heights, the forefront zone of the Sumava Mountains, the south Bohemian lake region, the plateau of Brdy, and sub-Carpathian Moravia. Slovakia is less developed than the Czech lands, and industrialization is limited to a few centers. The underdeveloped areas of Slovakia are located in the east and north.

Contrasting physical, agricultural, and industrial factors tend to divide the Czech lands into seven, and Slovakia into four, subregions. The western subregions may be grouped as follows:

1. The Ostrava, Liberec-Hradec, and Krusne mountains' subregions, characterized by extensive industrial development. The most highly industrialized of these is the Ostrava subregion, known as the Black country.
2. The Prague and Moravian industrial-agricultural subregions. These areas consist mainly of large industrial centers surrounded by extensive agricultural areas, based on the most fertile soils of the country.
3. Plzen, an isolated industrial subregion in the center of a typical agricultural area.
4. The Budejovice-Jihlava subregion, characterized by agricultural-industrial development. Agriculture prevails over industry in secondary centers.

Slovakia may be divided into four subregions:

1. The Danubian subregion, with extensive agriculture, and increasing light industry.
2. The northwestern subregion, an agricultural area in the process of intensive industrialization.
3. The south-central subregion, an agricultural and industrial area, based on mining, metallurgy, and forestry.
4. Eastern Slovakia, an agricultural area, with developing industry based on natural resources and power.

The size and demographic indices of the economic regions are given in Table 4.

Table 4. Selected Indices of Economic-Geographical Subregions, by District, 1950

bregion and District	Area (in square kilometers)	Population (in thousands)	Inhabitants per Square Kilometer	Per Cent of Population Employed in Industry	Per Cent of Population Employed in Agriculture
ague					
Prague	9.7	2078	214	38.4	20.9
Pardubice	4.2	435	103	34.5	27.9
dejovice-Jihlava					
Ceske Budejovice	9.0	510	57	28.2	32.5
Jihlava	6.6	436	66	28.7	38.3
zen	7.9	567	72	36.2	26.7
usne Mountains					
Usti nad Labem	4.1	646	156	....	....
Karlovy Vary	4.6	312	68	....	....
berec-Hradec					
Liberec	4.2	497	118	49.1	16.3
Hradec	5.2	571	110	38.8	22.7
oravia					
Brno	7.4	966	130	36.9	22.0
Gottwaldov	5.1	614	120	37.2	22.7
Olomouc	6.2	607	98	39.6	28.3
strava	4.5	819	182	52.3	11.8
anubian					
Bratislava	7.5	862	115	....	....
Nitra	7.9	710	89	....	....
orthwestern					
Zilina	8.3	525	64	....	....
entral-Southern					
Banska Bystrica	9.3	502	54	....	....
astern Slovakia					
Kosice	7.5	479	64	31.1	39.8
Presov	8.5	460	54	13.8	71.9

Source: I. M. Maergoiz, *Chekhoslovakia* (Czechoslovakia) (Moscow, 1954), pp. 30-302, *passim*.

Agricultural Regions

Agriculture is highly diversified, and considerable variation occurs within short distances. The country may be divided into six agricultural regions.

1. A region of sugar beets, grain, and extensive livestock raising corresponds with areas of fertile loess and chernozem soils, such as the Moravian plains, Polabi, and the lower Vltava and Ohre basins. Sugar beets are the leading crop, occupying about 15 per cent of the cultivated area. Winter wheat, barley, and truck farming are also important. Animal husbandry, mainly cattle raising, is based on fine pastures and by-products of agricultural industry.

2. A region of grain, sugar beets, and livestock raising, with pockets of highly specialized crops (such as grapes and tobacco), covers most of the Czechoslovak portion of the Danubian lowlands. The leading grains are wheat, barley, and corn. Livestock breeding is less developed than in the Moravian plains and the Labe-Vltava and Ohre basins, but there is a high percentage of draft animals.

3. A grain, potato, and livestock region is identified with podzolic soils in Bohemia, western Moravia, and most of the areas situated between the altitudes of 1,300 and 2,600 feet. Potatoes, which are the leading crop, occupy over 15 per cent of cultivated area. Rye and oats are partly displaced by fodder, industrial crops, and wheat. Cattle, hogs, and sheep are raised in these regions which generally possess natural pastures.

4. A grain and cattle region is largely confined to the lowlands around the river Tisa. Wheat is the major grain crop. Natural meadows and pastures, which cover up to 25 per cent of the total area, favor animal husbandry.

5. The dairying region is identified with the rim mountains of the Bohemian Massif. About one half of agricultural land is natural pasture. The other half is primarily under fodder crops such as grass, beets, and oats. The most common small grain is rye.

6. A mountainous region of beef cattle and sheep raising is found in the Carpathians. Natural pastures, Alpine meadows, and seasonal migration of animals are its noted feature. Potatoes, barley, and oats are grown on patches of suitable soils.

Generally, the intensity of land cultivation diminishes toward the east. Recent efforts to change this pattern are evident in the intensified cultivation of industrial and fodder crops. This change would increase the value of agricultural produce, and stabilize livestock economy by lessening its dependence on natural fodder areas. The pattern of land use shown in Table 5 reflects the shift from grain farming between

1937 and 1948. In 1953, the share of grain crops was to be further reduced to 50 per cent, while that of industrial crops was to increase to 9 per cent.

Table 5. Pattern of Agricultural Land Use, 1937 and 1948 (in per cent of total agricultural land)

Crop	1937		1948	
Grain	61.2		57.1	
Rye and wheat		31.7		30.1
Industrial	4.3		5.4	
Sugar beets		3.2		3.4
Potatoes	13.6		11.2	
Fodder	18.9		23.0	
Grass		16.1		20.0
Other	2.0		3.3	

Source: Ibid., p. 117.

Industrial Regions

Industry first developed in areas where fuel, raw materials, water, and power were plentiful. Industrial centers clustered around the coal mines in northwestern and central Bohemia and northeastern Moravia-Silesia. The textile industry grew in the mountainous northeastern regions of the Czech lands where water and manpower were abundant; the glass, porcelain, and ceramics industry developed near glass sand, kaolin, and clay deposits, particularly in northwestern Bohemia. Since many raw materials had to be imported, some industries, such as cotton spinning, woolen goods, and edible fats production, developed along the Danube or Labe rivers, near their natural supply routes.

The industrial regions are generally characterized by a high population density, a concentrated network of railroads and highways, and a high degree of electrification. The country may be divided into nine industrial regions: northwest Bohemian, Prague-Plzen, northeast Bohemian, east Bohemian, south Bohemian, northeast Moravian-Silesian, central Moravian, west Moravian, and Slovakian.

Northwest Bohemian Region. This region, bordered in the north by the Krusne Hory, stretches from the westernmost point of Czechoslovakia up to the Labe River. Industrial production is based on high grade deposits of brown coal, kaolin, clay and other minerals. The region's principal industrial products include synthetic motor fuels, chemical products, iron ware and machinery, glass, fine ceramic ware, crockery, fireproof and insulating tiles, bricks, lime, and cement. Large thermoelectric plants are located at Trmice, Nove Sedlo, and Ervenice.

Prague-Plzen Region. This region embraces both the wide vicinity of the capital and the region between the two cities. The heart of the region is the Kladno-Rakovnik bituminous coal basin and the smaller Plzen Basin. Industrial manufacture includes heavy machinery, automobiles, railroad cars and locomotives, armaments, bricks, lime, cement, and ceramic products. Electrotechnical industry and manufacture of steel are also important. Smaller establishments produce paper, plywood, furniture, optical instruments, clothing, furs, inorganic chemicals, and edible fats. Thermoelectric generating plants are located near Prague and Plzen.

Northeast Bohemian Region. This region stretches from the right bank of the Labe River on the west to the Orlicke Hory in the east. In the north, it is bordered by the Sudetes; in the south, it extends to Jaromer, Turnov, and Nova Paka. The most important sources of energy in this region are the fast flowing mountain streams, harnessed to produce electricity for industrial establishments. The region is poor in raw materials, with the exception of glass sands near Turnov. Characteristic industries are textiles, paper, and glass. Agricultural, textile, and metal working machinery are also produced on a small scale.

East Bohemian Region. This region centers on both banks of the Labe River up to the northeast Bohemian region. In the east, it is bordered by the Orlice River flowing into the Labe; in the west, it touches both banks of the Labe, extending beyond the city of Kolin. Situated in the fertile lowlands of the Labe, it is characterized by well-developed sugar, alcohol, and coffee substitute industries. Shoes, textiles, artificial fertilizers, agricultural machinery, and chemical products are also manufactured. Oil refineries are located in Pardubice and Kolin. Electricity is the main source of energy in this region.

South Bohemian Region. This region is the least developed in Bohemia and has no outstanding industrial centers comparable to those of the other regions. Solid fuel resources are relatively scarce, but the power potential of the Vltava River is now being developed through the construction of several hydroelectric dams. Characteristic industries of this region are industrial alcohol distilleries, lumber and wood manufacture (telephone poles, railroad ties, plywood, building lumber), paper manufacture, and graphite pencils. Other industries include manufacture of woolen textiles, glass hollow ware, chemicals, matches, ceramics, kitchenware, textile machinery, and pearl buttons.

Northeast Moravian-Silesian Region. This region comprises all Opava and Tesin (Teschen) regions of Silesia, and that part of north and northeast Moravia which stretches approximately from the upper Becva River to the upper Morava River. The important Ostrava and Karvina bituminous coal mines are located in the eastern part of this region. Iron and steel manufacture, centered in Ostrava, Trinec, and Kuncice is the largest industry. Machine production, including manufacture of cars, trucks, railroad cars, textile and sewing machinery, is the largest in Czechoslovakia. Textile, paper, cement, and lime industries are also important.

Central Moravian Region. This region stretches along both banks of the central and lower Morava River and its tributaries. Situated largely in a fertile lowland, its industries include sugar refining, industrial alcohol, malt and coffee substitutes, as well as a large woodworking industry and lime and cement works. The heart of this region is the triangle formed by the cities of Olomouc-Prostejov-Prerov. These cities have iron and steel foundries, armament factories, and electrical and agricultural machine industries. Gottwaldov (formerly Zlin) is the center of the shoemaking industry in Czechoslovakia. Manufacture of ready-to-wear clothing and glass working are also important. Power in this region is largely provided by the thermoelectric station in Zabreh and by a network of hydroelectric stations.

West Moravian Region. This region is located in the basins of the Svitava, Svratka, Jihlava, and Dyje rivers. Woodworking industries, iron foundries, shoemaking, and ready-to-wear clothing manufacture comprise the characteristic industries of this area. Armament industry, iron and steel foundries, rolling mills, and machine building industry are located in and around Brno, the most important industrial center. Large cement works, limestone quarries, china factories, and the manufacture of fireproof ceramics, glass, and paper are also found in this region.

Slovakia. Until recently, this region lagged considerably in industrial development and as yet has no large industrial centers. Traditional industries are lumber, paper, and chemicals. Textile mills, metalworking, lime and cement works, fine ceramics, hollow glass ware, and clothing manufacture are also represented. While agriculture remains the most important part of the Slovak economy, industry, especially heavy industry, has progressed rapidly in recent years.

2. POPULATION

Demographic Factors

Distribution and Density

On March 1, 1950, the date of the latest census, Czechoslovakia's reported population was 12,338,000. The latest official estimate puts the total as of July 1, 1955 at 13,089,000 (United Nations, *Population and Vital Statistics Reports* [New York, April 1956], p. 20).

The country extends over 49,354 square miles—approximately the area of the state of New York. It occupies 2.6 per cent of the area and has 3.1 per cent of the population of Europe west of the Soviet Union. Density of population, amounting to 250 persons per square mile in 1950, was about one fifth above the average for Europe; estimated density, as of July 1, 1955, was about 265 persons per square mile.

Czechoslovakia was established as an independent republic in 1918, mainly from parts of the former Austro-Hungarian monarchy, to which a small section of Prussian Silesia was added. During the interwar period, the Republic was divided into four provinces: Bohemia and Moravia-Silesia in the west; Slovakia and Ruthenia in the east. After the Munich Pact in September 1938, Germany occupied and incorporated into the Reich the periphery of the two western provinces, which included most of the ethnic Germans of Czechoslovakia as well as many Czechs. During the following six months, the dismemberment of the Republic was completed by Germany, Hungary, and Poland. Germany proclaimed the remainder of western Czechoslovakia the Protectorate of Bohemia and Moravia, while Slovakia retained nominal independence.

After World War II, the pre-Munich boundaries of Czechoslovakia were restored. However, in June 1945, Ruthenia and a small section of Slovakia were ceded to the Soviet Union, which thereby gained direct access to Hungary. The ceded territory extended over about 4,900 square miles and had a population of some 800,000. In the peace treaty with Hungary, Czechoslovakia acquired three villages on the right bank of the Danube opposite Bratislava, with 24 square miles and a prewar population of about 3,000 persons, which were added to Slovakia in 1947.

The three remaining provinces of postwar Czechoslovakia—Bohemia, Moravia-Silesia, and Slovakia—were abolished as administrative units in 1948 and replaced by nineteen regions *(kraje)*. Thirteen of these regions, corresponding to the former provinces of Bohemia and Moravia-Silesia, are officially designated as Czech regions, while six regions comprise what was the province of Slovakia and are referred to as Slovak regions.

Since the 1950 census gave only the total population of Czechoslovakia, no geographic or other breakdowns are available for that year. Consequently, for postwar data we must rely on population surveys taken in the Czech regions on May 22, 1947 and in the Slovak regions on October 4, 1946. While it has been possible to adjust the more important information on the Slovak regions to the 1947 data, additional details were available for the Czech regions only. Table 1 shows the area, 1947 population, and population density of the former provinces and of the new administrative regions of Czechoslovakia.

Table 1. Area, Population, and Population Density, by Provinces and by Regions, 1947

Provinces and Regions	Area in Square Miles	Population	Persons per Square Mile
Provinces			
Bohemia	20,101	5,627,200	280
Moravia-Silesia	10,351	3,135,200	303
Slovakia	18,902	3,402,300	180
Total	49,354	12,164,700	246[a]
Czech regions			
Brno	2,876	934,400	325
Ceske Budejovice	3,463	493,700	143
Gottwaldov	1,972	593,600	301
Hradec Kralove	1,986	552,800	278
Jihlava	2,568	422,500	165
Karlovy Vary	1,768	299,600	169
Liberec	1,636	479,900	293
Olomouc	2,399	585,000	244
Ostrava	1,747	790,300	452
Pardubice	1,636	423,000	259
Plzen	3,045	549,900	181
Praha (Prague)	3,756	2,014,900	536
Usti nad Labem	1,600	622,700	389
Total, Czech regions	30,452	8,762,400	288[a]

Table 1. (con't.)

Provinces and Regions	Area in Square Miles	Population	Persons per Square Mile
Slovak regions			
Banska Bystrica	3,577	490,300	137
Bratislava	2,903	819,000	282
Kosice	2,887	448,300	155
Nitra	3,076	702,900	229
Presov	3,266	439,300	135
Zilina	3,193	502,500	157
Total, Slovak regions	18,902	3,402,300	180[a]

Source: State Statistical Office, *Zpravy statniho uradu statistickeho, 1949* (Reports of the State Statistical Office) (Prague, 1949), p. 4, Table 1.

Note: Columns may not add up to totals because of rounding. Density of population computed before rounding.

[a] Average.

The Czech regions comprised 62 per cent of the area and 72 per cent of the 1947 population of the Republic; the Slovak regions 38 per cent of the area and 28 per cent of the inhabitants. Population density was much higher in the Czech regions than in the Slovak regions: 288 persons per square mile in the former as compared with 180 persons per square mile in the latter. The region of Prague (Praha), which includes the capital of Czechoslovakia, was the largest, most populous, and most densely settled of the nineteen regions.

The administrative regions are subdivided into districts *(okresy)*, and these in turn into localities *(obce)*. The number of localities in Czechoslovakia in 1947 was 15,055, of which 11,695 were in the Czech regions and 3,360 in the Slovak regions. The average locality in Czechoslovakia is a rather small unit, extending over only 3.3 square miles.

Table 2 presents the distribution of localities and of their 1947 population by number of inhabitants. A slight majority of the population resided in rural areas, defined in official statistics as those localities with less than 2,000 inhabitants. In the Czech regions, the rural population comprised 48.5 per cent of the total, while in the Slovak regions it comprised 57.8 per cent. It should be noted, however, that in the Czech regions, only localities with less than 500 inhabitants had a majority of their labor force employed in agriculture. The correlation between the size of the locality and the propor-

Table 2. Distribution of Localities, by Size Class, 1947

Number of Inhabitants	Number of Localities	Total Population	Per Cent of Total Population
Less than 200	4,391	559,400	4.6
200-500	5,581	1,806,000	14.8
500-1,000	2,939	2,028,000	16.7
1,000-2,000	1,343	1,828,400	15.0
2,000-5,000	592	1,781,400	14.6
5,000-10,000	125	846,900	7.0
10,000-20,000	53	742,500	6.1
20,000-100,000	26	905,400	7.4
100,000 and over	5	1,666,800	13.7
Total	15,055	12,164,700	100.0

Source: State Statistical Office, *Zpravy statniho uradu statistickeho, 1948,* pp. 31-32, Table 3.

Note: Columns may not add up to totals because of rounding. Percentages computed before rounding.

tion of economically active population engaged in agriculture in 1947 is demonstrated by the following figures (Czech regions only):

Number of Inhabitants	Per Cent in Agriculture
Less than 200	76.2
200-500	61.4
500-1,000	44.5
1,000-2,000	31.0
2,000-5,000	16.5
5,000-10,000	7.2
10,000-20,000	5.4
20,000-100,000	3.3
100,000 or more	1.7

Source: State Statistical Office, *Zpravy statniho uradu statistickeho, 1948,* pp. 103-105, Table 9.

These percentages include unpaid family workers and are comparable with other statistics on the economically active population. No data have been found for the Slovak regions, where the proportion of agricultural workers in the labor force is much higher than in the Czech regions.

In 1947, localities with 10,000 or more inhabitants comprised 32.0 per cent of the population of the Czech regions, but only 15.2 per cent in the Slovak regions. For the largest cities with more than

100,000 inhabitants, the corresponding ratios were 17.1 per cent and 5.1 per cent, respectively. There were four such cities in the Czech regions (Prague, Brno, Ostrava, and Plzen) and only one in the Slovak regions (Bratislava).

In the Czech regions, population density in the various size classes of rural localities ranged from 78 to 300 persons per square mile, while among the classes of urban places, it ranged from 515 to 7,438 persons per square mile. In the capital city of Prague, population density in 1947 was 13,880 persons per square mile, compared with an average of 7,517 persons for all cities with more than 50,000 inhabitants in the United States (1950).

Sex and Age

The population of Czechoslovakia in 1947 consisted of about 5,909,000 males and 6,256,000 females, corresponding to a sex ratio of 94.4 males per 100 females. As shown in Table 3, males were more numerous than females among children and youth under 20 years, while the opposite was true at later ages.

Table 3. Age-Sex Distribution of the Population, 1947

Age Group	Males	Females	Total	Per Cent of Total Population	Males per 100 Female
0-4	582,100	562,800	1,144,900	9.4	103.4
5-9	471,100	456,500	927,600	7.6	103.2
10-14	445,400	435,500	880,900	7.3	102.3
15-19	512,900	504,700	1,017,600	8.4	101.6
20-24	524,500	543,800	1,068,300	8.8	96.4
25-29	409,200	422,300	831,500	6.8	96.9
30-34	394,300	414,400	808,600	6.7	95.1
35-39	505,100	519,300	1,024,400	8.4	97.3
40-44	466,100	484,200	950,300	7.8	96.3
45-49	414,400	446,100	860,400	7.1	92.9
50-54	315,300	372,400	687,700	5.7	84.7
55-59	249,200	304,000	553,100	4.6	82.0
60-64	208,800	261,300	470,100	3.9	79.9
65-69	164,100	206,800	370,900	3.1	79.3
70-74	119,700	154,200	273,900	2.3	77.6
75-79	73,700	94,000	167,700	1.4	78.3
80-84	31,900	45,100	77,000	0.6	70.8
85 and over	11,300	18,800	30,100	0.2	60.3
Not stated	9,400	10,000	19,400	—	—
Total	5,908,500	6,256,200	12,164,700	100.0	94.4

Source: State Statistical Office, *Zpravy statniho uradu statistickeho, 1948*, pp. 43-44, Table 1.

Note: Because of rounding, rows and columns may not add up to totals. Derived figures computed before rounding.

The overall sex ratio of the population was much closer to equilibrium in Czechoslovakia than in a number of other European countries, notably those which suffered heavily in World War II:

County	Males per 100 Females
Czechcslovakia (1947)	94.4
France (1950)	92.9
Yugoslavia (1948)	92.6
Hungary (1949)	92.5
United Kingdom (1951)	92.2
Poland (1949)	90.9
Federal Republic of Germany (1950)	88.2
Austria (1951)	86.6

The age structure of the population in 1947, presented in Table 3, shows the marked contractions between 25 and 35 years and again between 5 and 15 years of age; this reflects the decline in the birth rate during World War I and during the depression.

More than two thirds (68.2 per cent) of the population of Czechoslovakia in 1947 were within the economically active or labor force age range, conventionally defined as 15-64 years. Less than one fourth (24.2 per cent) were children under 15 years of age, and only 7.6 per cent were 65 years old or older. This age distribution, as shown in Table 4, is similar to that of other European countries.

Table 4. Age Distribution in Selected European Countries (in per cent)

Country	Under 15	15-64	65 and over
France (1950)	21.7	66.5	11.8
United Kingdom (1951)	22.5	66.7	10.8
Austria (1951)	23.2	66.7	10.1
Federal Republic of Germany (1950)	23.5	67.2	9.3
Czechoslovakia (1947)	24.2	68.2	7.6
Hungary (1949)	24.6	67.6	7.8
Poland (1949)	28.4	66.5	5.1
Yugoslavia (1948)	32.1	62.2	5.7

Source: United Nations, *Demographic Yearbook* (New York), various issues.

The age structure of the Czech regions and of the Slovak regions reveals the "West European" demographic pattern of the former and the "East European" character of the latter. This structure is indicated below (in percentages):

Age Group	Czech Regions	Slovak Regions
Under 15	22.8	28.2
15-39	38.7	40.2
40-64	30.6	25.0
65 and over	7.9	6.6

The customary urban-rural differences in age structure were likewise found in Czechoslovakia. Since cross-tabulations by age and size of locality are lacking, the following comparison is limited to the four largest cities of the Czech regions, on the one hand, and the remainder of the Czech regions on the other (in percentages):

Age Group	Four Largest Cities	Remainder of Czech Regions
Under 15	18.2	23.8
15-64	75.1	68.0
65 and over	6.7	8.2

Source: State Statistical Office, *Zpravy statniho uradu statistickeho, 1948,* pp. 43-44, Table 3.

The high percentage of persons of labor force age in the cities (75.1 per cent) reflected the influx from smaller towns and rural areas and the comparatively low birth rates of the urban population.

Population Change

The population of Czechoslovakia in 1947 was approximately equal to the number of inhabitants of the same territory in 1900, and the 1950 population was only 1.5 per cent larger. As shown below, there was almost no increase between the censuses of 1910 and 1921—the period which included World War I and the influenza epidemic of 1918/19—and there was a loss of almost 2,450,000 from 1939 to 1947.

Year[a]	Population[b]
1900	12,159,000
1910	13,000,000
1921	13,003,000
1930	13,998,000
1939	14,612,000
1947	12,165,000
1950	12,338,000
1955	13,089,000

Sources: 1900-1930 and 1947, State Statistical Office, *Zpravy statniho uradu statistickeho, 1948,* pp. 31-32, Table 1; 1939, United States Bureau of the Census, *The Population of Czechoslovakia* (Washington, D. C., 1953) Series P-40, No. 3; 1950, United Nations, *Demographic Yearbook 1955*, p. 109; 1955, United Nations, *Population and Vital Statistics Reports, loc. cit.*

[a] Census figures are used for all years, except 1939 and 1955 which are estimates.

[b] Population figures refer to present territory only. However, prior to 1950, they do not include the Bratislava bridgehead which, in 1941, had a population of less than 4,000.

The major factor contributing to the decline from 1939 to 1947 was the expulsion of the great majority of the ethnic German population of Czechoslovakia under the Potsdam Agreement. Some 250,000 persons, according to an official estimate, lost their lives as a result of the war and German occupation of the country. This figure includes 110,000 death within Czechoslovakia and 140,000 abroad, largely in German concentration camps. At least 60 per cent of these were Jews. Minor outward movements of ethnic and/or religious minorities (Magyars, Jews) and of political dissidents were, in part, balanced by the return of former emigrants from abroad.

The regional distribution of population change in recent times can be studied only in terms of a comparison between 1930 and 1947, since regional data are not available for other years. The decline amounted to 18 per cent in the Czech regions, while the population of the Slovak regions increased 2.4 per cent. All of the Czech regions participated in the decline, except Gottwaldov (formerly Zlin) where industrial development, centered primarily in shoe factories, resulted in a small increase. The loss was relatively greatest in the three northwestern regions bordering on Germany (Karlovy Vary, Usti nad Labem, and Liberec), ranging from 30 to 52 per cent. In these regions and in other frontier areas, the decline of population was the direct result of the expulsion of the Germans. In the interior of the country, where comparatively few Germans had lived, it reflected the movement of Czechs to the lands and factories vacated by the Germans. Because of this double shift, only one third of the combined 1947 population of the three northwestern regions, and less than 15 or even 10 per cent in many districts, lived in the same locality where they had resided in May 1945, as compared with almost four-fifths in the remainder of the Czech regions and about 90 per cent in the solidly ethnic Czech districts of the interior.

Vital Statistics

In her pattern of birth and death rates, Czechoslovakia (like Hungary) occupies a position between Western and Eastern Europe, though somewhat closer to the former. At the beginning of the twentieth century, as shown in Table 5, the birth rate in what is now Czechoslovakia stood near 35 per 1,000 population, the death rate near 24. By the end of World War I, a considerable decline in both rates had taken place. During the period 1921-25, a birth rate of 26.3 and a death rate of 15.9 per 1,000 were recorded. The decline continued to the middle thirties, when the birth rate reached a minimum near 16, while the death rate levelled off at about 13 per 1,000. Since then, the birth rate has increased somewhat irregularly.

Table 5. Vital Statistics of Czechoslovakia, 1901-1954
(per 1,000 population)

Years	Births	Deaths	Natural Increase
1901-05	34.7	24.2	10.5
1906-10	32.3	21.6	10.7
1911-13	29.1	20.2	8.9
1921-25	26.3	15.9	10.4
1926-30	22.4	15.0	7.4
1931-35	18.8	13.6	5.2
1936	16.6	13.0	3.6
1937	16.3	13.1	3.2
1938	16.7	13.2	3.5
1939	18.6	13.3	5.3
1940	20.6	14.0	6.6
1941	20.1	14.0	6.1
1942	19.7	14.4	5.3
1943	21.5	14.0	7.5
1944	22.0	15.0	7.0
1945	19.5	17.8	1.7
1946	22.7	14.1	8.6
1947	24.2	12.1	12.1
1948	23.4	11.5	11.9
1949	22.1	11.7	10.4
1950	23.3	11.5	11.8
1951	22.8	11.4	11.4
1952	22.2	10.6	11.6
1953	21.2	10.5	10.7
1954	20.5	10.4	10.1

Sources: State Statistical Office, *Statisticka rocenka republiky Ceskoslovenske* (Statistical Yearbook of the Czechoslovak Republic) (Prague, various volumes); 1946-54, United Nations, *Demographic Yearbook* (New York, 1955).

In the five years 1946-50, an average birth rate of 23.2 per 1,000 was attained, roughly equal to that prevailing two decades earlier. This comparatively high level coincided with a postwar increase in marriages. For the years 1946-50, the marriage rate was 10.8 per 1,000 population, compared with 8.8 during the decade 1926-35. By 1954, the marriage rate had declined again to 7.9, and the birth rate to 20.5 per 1,000 population.

The death rate increased during the war years to a peak of 17.8 per 1,000 in 1945, when Czechoslovakia became a battleground. Subsequently, it declined rapidly below its prewar level, averaging 11.6 during 1948-50 and 10.8 during 1952-54. As a result of these divergent trends in natality and mortality, the rate of natural increase —excess of births over deaths—rose from 3.2 per 1,000 population in 1937 to 12.1 per 1,000 in 1947. Since then it has declined, amounting to 10.1 per thousand in 1954.

The vital rates of Czechoslovakia are compared with those for selected countries in Western and Eastern Europe during the period 1951-54 in Table 6. The intermediate position of the Czechoslovak birth rate is apparent.

Table 6. Vital Statistics of Selected European Countries, Average 1951-1954
(per 1,000 population)

Country	Births	Deaths	Natural Increase
Austria	14.8	12.0	2.8
Federal Republic of Germany	15.6	10.6	5.0
United Kingdom	15.7	11.4	4.3
France	19.0	12.4	6.6
Hungary	21.4	11.3	10.1
Czechoslovakia	21.3	10.5	10.8
Yugoslavia	28.9	11.7	17.2
Poland (1950)	30.5	11.6	18.9

Source: United Nations, *Demographic Yearbook 1955*, p. 616.

Birth rates have been markedly lower in the Czech regions than in the Slovak regions. The difference has been reduced over the past 30 years, but is still apparent in the latest available statistics. During the earlier part of the period, there was also a parallel difference in death rates. However, this had virtually disappeared by 1946-50. Vital statistics of Czech and Slovak regions for the period 1921-50 are shown in Table 7.

It should be noted, however, that the average age of the population is higher in the Czech regions than in the Slovak regions, and that this tends to raise the overall death rate in the former area relative to that in the latter.

Table 7. Vital Statistics of Czech and Slovak Regions, Five-Year Averages, 1921-1950 (per 1,000 population)

Years	Birth Rate		Death Rate		Natural Increase	
	Czech Regions	Slovak Regions	Czech Regions	Slovak Regions	Czech Regions	Slovak Begions
1921-25	23.6	35.4	14.9	19.0	8.7	16.4
1926-30	19.9	30.4	14.2	17.6	5.7	12.8
1931-35	16.6	25.6	13.1	15.1	3.5	10.5
1936-40	16.1	22.8	13.2	13.9	2.9	8.9
1941-45	19.2	24.8	14.6	16.3	4.6	8.5
1946-50	22.0	26.2	12.2	12.3	9.8	13.9

Sources: State Statistical Office, *Statisticka rocenka republiky Ceskoslovenske,* various issues; United States Bureau of the Census, *The Population of Czechoslovakia.*

Infant mortality, considered by many one of the most sensitive indicators of the state of public health and social well-being, declined from more than 150 deaths under one year of age per 1,000 live births during the period 1921-25 to less than 90 per 1,000 in 1946-50.

Years	Infant Mortality
1921-25	153.5
1926-30	144.2
1931-35	124.8
1936-40	108.1
1941-45	113.0
1946-50	88.2

Sources: United Nations, *Demographic Yearbook,* and State Statistical Office, *Statistica rocenka republiky Ceskoslovenske,* various volumes.

In 1951, the infant mortality declined to 73.4 and in 1952 to 56.0. Since then, it has fallen sharply to 45.0 in 1953 and 37.0 in 1954. This is by far the lowest infant mortality rate reported in the Central European area, and it is lower than the corresponding rate in the Federal Republic of Germany (46.2), and only very slightly higher than that in France (36.4).

Migration

Prior to World War I, migration from the territories now constituting Czechoslovakia flowed primarily to the capitals of the Austro-

Hungarian monarchy of which these territories were a part. This internal migration ceased with the break-up of the monarchy. Its magnitude can be estimated from the numbers of persons born in Czechoslovakia who were enumerated in Austria and Hungary during the interwar period. Around 1930, such persons totalled 442,000 and 238,000 respectively, together almost 5 per cent of the population of Czechoslovakia. Among these migrants many spoke German or Magyar as their mother tongue, but even those who were ethnic Czechs or Slovaks tended to be well assimilated into their new environment.

Next in importance as a country of destination was the United States, where the following numbers of foreign-born from Czechoslovakia were reported in the dicennial censuses:

1920	362,000
1930	492,000
1940	320,000
1950	278,000

These figures are probably low since many older foreign-born persons from Czechoslovakia claimed Austria as their place of birth. During the decade 1921-30, about 102,000 immigrants from Czechoslovakia were admitted to the United States.

When the Republic was dismembered in 1938, not only foreign troops but thousands of German and Hungarian officials and their families moved in to administer the newly acquired territories. Subsequently, more than 500,000 Czechs and Slovaks were employed in German war industries, some voluntarily and others as forced labor. Most of these returned to their homes after the war.

The migrations of the war period were dwarfed by the movements of people in the early postwar years. The event of greatest demographic importance was the expulsion of the Germans. About 2,400,000 were transferred to Germany under the terms of the Potsdam Agreement; about 600,000 had fled with the retreating German forces in 1945. About 800,000 Ruthenians were ceded to the Soviet Union. In addition, some 92,000 Magyars were expelled from Czechoslovakia during the years 1945-47, while 63,000 ethnic Slovaks were received from Hungary under an agreement with that country. An estimated 55,000 Jews had survived the war; by 1950 all but 16,000 had emigrated.

To compensate for the loss of manpower, especially of skilled workers, caused by the expulsion of the Germans, the postwar government of Czechoslovakia has tried to persuade former emigrants to return. The extent to which these efforts have been successful cannot be accurately determined, but it appears that only some 30,000 responded. The number of political refugees who left Czechoslovakia after February 1948, when the Communist Party came into control was estimated at 50,000 in mid-1952. Comparatively few have been able to leave since that time.

Social and Economic Factors

Ethnic Groups

Czechoslovakia's population was ethnically more heterogeneous during the interwar period than it is today. The dominant nationalities were the Czechs and Slovaks, both branches of the western Slavs. They were never shown separately in official statistics, since they were considered as one nationality, though their languages were slightly different. The Czechs lived primarily in the interior of Bohemia and Moravia-Silesia, but during the interwar period substantial numbers of them migrated to the eastern provinces of the Republic to serve as administrators and school teachers as well as to engage in business. Other Slavic-speaking groups were the Ruthenians, residing in the eastern parts of Slovakia and in Ruthenia, who spoke a form of Ukrainian, and a small Polish minority in a limited area in the north of Moravia-Silesia. The most important non-Slavic group were the Germans, whose compact settlement occupied much of the peripheral zones of Bohemia and Moravia-Silesia, bordering on Germany and Austria. (This area is sometimes erroneously referred to as the Sudetenland; in proper usage, the latter term denotes only the area of the Sudeten Mountains, a series of mountain ranges on the northeastern border of the Czech lands.) Other Germans lived in scattered *Sprachinseln* (language islands) in the interior of Czechoslovakia. Magyars were numerous in Slovakia and Ruthenia. In the eastern provinces, there were also many Jews who spoke Yiddish, German, or Hungarian and reported themselves in the census as being of Jewish nationality. In Bohemia and Moravia-Silesia, on the other hand, most adherents of the Jewish faith spoke Czech or German and reported themselves as belonging to these groups.

Since 1945, the great majority of the Germans and many of the Magyars have been expelled, while Ruthenia has been ceded to the Soviet Union. Most Jews were either killed by the Germans during World War II or have emigrated. As a result, the population of the Republic has come to consist almost entirely of Czechs and Slovaks.

There are no official census statistics on nationality in Czechoslovakia after 1930. Table 8 presents the 1930 figures of the official census. The second column shows the estimates for May 1947 made by the United States Bureau of the Census. These figures generally conform with those based on Miroslav Blazek's semi-official estimates for 1950 in the *Hospodarska geografie Ceskoslovenska* (Economic Geography of Czechoslovakia), shown in the third column.

Table 8. Nationality Groups in Czechoslovakia, 1930, 1947, and 1950 (in thousands)

Nationality	1930	1947	1950[a]
Czechs	9,722	11,090	8,428
Slovaks			2,838
Germans	3,305	250	.... [b]
Magyars	604	600	580
Ruthenians	118	100	161
Poles	100	110	.... [b]
Jews	110	50	.... [b]
Others	46		333
Total	14,004[c]	12,200	12,340

Sources: 1930, official census of 1930; 1947, estimates of May 1947 of the United States Bureau of the Census; 1950, Miroslav Blazek, *Hospodarska geografie Ceskoslovenska* (Economic Geography of Czechoslovakia) (Prague, 1954).

[a] Estimates.

[b] Figures for Germans, Poles, and Jews were not separately reported, and are included in the category "Others."

[c] Including 6,000 persons in the small section of Slovakia ceded to the Soviet Union in 1945.

The number of Germans in Czechoslovakia in 1939 was approximately 3,500,000, all but a few thousand of whom lived in the present territory of the Republic. Assuming a natural increase and war losses proportionate to those of Germany, the corresponding total in 1948 would have been about 3,400,000. At that time, the number of ethnic German refugees in the Federal Republic of Germany, the Soviet Zone of occupation, and Berlin, who had been residents of Czechoslovakia in 1939, together with their children, was approximately 2,700,000. Another 150,000 or so were in Austria. It is doubtful whether unrecorded deaths can explain the discrepancy between the projected total of Germans and the numbers reported for 1948.

The number of Magyars in present-day Czechoslovakia, projected from 1930 to 1948, would seem to be at least 670,000. During the period 1945-47, about 92,000 persons of that nationality are known to have left Czechoslovakia. War losses and unrecorded emigration are unlikely to have been of significant magnitude.

Ethnic Czechs and Slovaks, on the other hand, appear to have increased more rapidly than could be expected on the basis of the numbers of births and deaths and of migratory movements, which are either known or can be estimated within fairly narrow limits. The conclusion seems warranted, therefore, that substantial numbers of persons formerly classified as belonging to the various minority nationalities—probably including many individuals of mixed parentage—now consider themselves or are considered by the government to be Czechs or Slovaks.

Religious Affiliation

Data on religious affiliation of the people of Czechoslovakia, like those on nationality, have not been published since 1930. A breakdown of Czechoslovakia's population by religious denominations for 1921 and 1930 will be found in Chapter 7.

Literacy

While those former Austrian provinces which became the western portion of Czechoslovakia had long enjoyed an excellent system of public schools, educational services were less satisfactory in the Hungarian counties, later constituting the eastern part of the Republic. As a result, a marked west-east differential in regard to literacy prevailed during the interwar period. According to the census of 1930, approximately 1.5 per cent of the population of the Czech regions, ten years old and over, was unable to read and write, a figure close to the irreducible minimum. In the Slovak regions, the percentage of illiterates was 8.5 per cent. (The German and Jewish populations, both highly literate and both almost entirely absent from present-day Czechoslovakia, have been omitted from the calculation of these percentages.)

The percentage of illiterates in 1930 was highest among the elderly and aged. By 1950, illiteracy was probably reduced to about 1 per cent in the Czech regions and less than 4 per cent in the Slovak regions.

The Labor Force

According to the census of 1947, the economically active population or labor force of Czechoslovakia numbered 5,852,000 or slightly less than one half of the total population. It consisted of 3,793,000 males (65 per cent) and 2,059,000 females (35 per cent). Economically active males amounted to 86.0 per cent of the male population 15 years old and over, while economically active females equalled 42.9 per cent of the female population 15 years old and over. The corresponding ratios for the United States, including troops and others abroad (1950), were 80.5 per cent and 29.5 per cent, respectively. The percentage of economically active persons in Czechoslovakia was higher than in the United States because of the much greater numbers of unpaid family workers in Czechoslovakia, most of whom helped on farms. Exclusion of unpaid family workers from the labor force reduces the economically active males in Czechoslovakia to 80.0 per cent of the male population 15 years and over, compared with 79.3 per cent in the United States. Economically active females are reduced even more markedly to 23.9 per cent, far below the corresponding ratio of 28.6 per cent in the United States.

Table 9 shows the 1947 distribution of the entire labor force by major industry groups for the Czech and Slovak regions. In Czecho-

Table 9. Economically Active Population of Czech and Slovak Regions, by Major Economic Sector, 1947
(in thousands and in percentages of total)

Economic Sector	Males	Females	Czech Regions	Slovak Regions	Total
Agriculture, forestry, and fishing	1,123.2	1,084.0	1,216.3	990.9	2,207.3
Per cent	29.6	52.6	29.2	59.0	37.7
Mining	133.0	9.6	126.2	16.4	142.6
Per cent	3.5	0.5	3.0	1.0	37.7
Manufacturing, handicrafts, and construction	1,506.2	536.2	1,670.9	371.5	2,042.3
Per cent	39.7	26.0	40.1	22.1	34.9
Commerce, banking, and insurance	244.5	132.5	317.9	59.2	377.0
Per cent	6.4	6.4	7.6	3.5	6.4
Transportation	261.0	24.9	221.5	64.4	285.9
Per cent	6.9	1.2	5.3	3.8	4.9
Public administration and services	422.1	162.4	454.1	130.4	584.5
Per cent	11.1	7.9	10.9	7.8	10.0
Professions	20.1	11.2	25.6	5.7	31.3
Per cent	0.5	0.5	0.6	0.3	0.5
Personal and domestic service	75.4	85.1	123.1	37.4	160.5
Per cent	2.0	4.1	3.0	2.2	2.7
Others, not stated	7.8	13.1	16.4	4.5	20.9
Per cent	0.2	0.6	0.4	0.3	0.4
Total	3,793.4	2,059.0	4,172.0	1,680.4	5,852.4
Per cent	100.0	100.0	100.0	100.0	100.0

Source: State Statistical Office, *Zpravy statniho uradu statistickeho, 1948*, pp. 50-53, Table 2.

Note: Because of rounding, rows and columns may not add up to totals. Percentages computed before rounding.

slovakia as a whole, agriculture, with its subsidiaries accounted for three-eighths of the economically active population; manufacturing, handicrafts, and construction, together with mining, accounted for another three-eighths; and all other activities comprised the remaining fourth of the total. The percentage of the labor force employed in agriculture was substantially greater in Czechoslovakia than in the United States or in highly industrialized European countries, such as the United Kingdom, Belgium, the Netherlands, or the Federal Republic of Germany. However, it was smaller than in Italy, Poland, Hungary, or Yugoslavia. A comparison of the economically active population engaged in agriculture in selected European countries is shown by the following figures:

Country and Year	Per Cent
United Kingdom (1951)[a]	4.9
Belgium (1947)	12.1
United States (1950)	12.2
Netherlands (1947)	19.3
Federal Republic of Germany (1950)	23.2
Austria (1951)	32.3
France (1946)	36.5
Czechoslovakia (1947)	37.7
Hungary (1949)	46.9
Italy (1951)	40.0
Poland (1950)	57.6
Yugoslavia (1948)	78.3

[a] Excluding Northern Ireland.

As shown in Table 9, the agricultural labor force of Czechoslovakia included a larger proportion of the economically active females (52.6 per cent) than of the males (29.6 per cent). The only other employment groups with higher percentages of females than of males were the domestic and personal services and the small residual category. In the Czech regions, only 29.2 per cent of the labor force was employed in agriculture, against 59.0 per cent in the Slovak regions. For each non-agricultural group, the percentage was higher in the Czech regions than in the Slovak regions, the relative differences being most marked in mining and commerce.

The 1947 labor force of Czechoslovakia consisted of 1,126,000 employers and self-employed persons (19.2 per cent), 1,174,000 unpaid family workers (20.1 per cent), and 3,552,000 wage and salary earners, including apprentices (60.7 per cent). In agriculture, the family farm predominated, with 83.3 per cent of the economically active population classified as employers, self-employed, or unpaid family workers. In the non-agricultural labor force, an even higher proportion (87.3 per cent) were wage and salary earners.

No official data are available concerning the changes undergone by the economically active population of Czechoslovakia since the census of 1947. According to the computations of the research staff of the Free Europe Press, a drop in agricultural manpower of more than 450,000 was registered during the period 1948-53. This source estimates the number of economically active individuals in the major economic sectors in 1953 as follows:

Sector	Number of Persons
Agriculture	1,743,000
Manufacturing (excluding handicrafts)	1,788,000
Construction	321,000
Transportation	397,000

Part II. The Government and the Party

3. THE CONSTITUTIONAL SYSTEM

Stephen Kocvara

The First Republic, 1918-1938

The independence of the Czechs and Slovaks from the Austro-Hungarian Empire was proclaimed in Prague on October 28, 1918, by the Czech National Committee, representing the Czech political parties. Two days later, representatives of the Slovak political parties assembled in Turciansky Svaty Martin and declared the Slovak nation part of the Czechoslovak nation. On May 8, 1919, the Central National Council of the Ruthenians declared in Uzhorod that Ruthenia should join Czechoslovakia as an autonomous territory. These proclamations laid the formal foundation for the Czechoslovak Republic, a state composed of Czechs, Slovaks, Ruthenians, and of large national minorities, especially German and Magyar. Of the territories granted to this state by the peace treaties of Versailles, Saint-Germain, and Trianon at the close of World War I, only Bohemia and Moravia-Silesia were previously joined in a state within the framework of the medieval Bohemian Kingdom. Slovakia and Ruthenia had previously been integral parts of Hungary. Nevertheless, there was a strong cultural and political bond between the Czechs and Slovaks.

On November 13, 1918, the Constituent National Assembly in Prague passed a Provisional Constitution which was later replaced by the Constitution of February 29, 1920. Along with democratic institutions, the Constitution provided for the protection of the rights of ethnic minorities, in accordance with international obligations undertaken by the Czechoslovak Republic. On February 29, 1920, Constitutional Law No. 122 was passed, securing the rights of the ethnic and religious minorities. This Constitution provided for representative democracy, in which the legislature was, in principle, superior to the executive. The people were to be the ultimate source of all governmental power.

The 1920 Constitution

Preamble. This Constitution, like the Constitution of the United States, was preceded by a preamble stating that the Czechoslovak nation desired:

> to consolidate the perfect unity of our nation, to establish a reign of justice in the Republic, to assure the peaceful development of our native Czechoslovak land, to contribute to the common welfare of all citizens of this State, and to secure the blessings of liberty to coming generations . . . since we desire to take our place in the family of nations as a culturally developed, peace-loving, democratic, and progressive member.

Legislative Power. Legislative power was vested in a National Assembly for the whole Republic, with the exception of an autonomous legislature for Ruthenia. It was responsible for legislation in matters concerning "language, education, religion, local government, and other matters delegated by the laws of the Republic." The National Assembly was composed of the Chamber of Deputies (300 members) and the Senate (150 members). The members of the Chamber were elected for a term of six years and those of the Senate for eight years through universal, equal, and direct franchise, by secret ballot, and on the basis of proportional representation. A bill passed by the Chamber of Deputies could become law against the will of the Senate, but not conversely. Only the Chamber of Deputies could pass a vote of no confidence in the Cabinet, which, thereupon, was bound to tender its resignation to the President of the Republic.

Executive Power. Executive power was vested in the President and the Cabinet. The President was elected for a term of seven years by the National Assembly. No one could be elected for more than two successive terms except the first President, Thomas G. Masaryk, who remained in office from 1918 to 1935.

The President represented the Republic in international relations, was Commander in Chief of the Army, was authorized to appoint and dismiss members of the Cabinet as well as to dissolve the Parliament, to appoint university professors, higher judges, civil servants, and to commission army officers of higher rank. The Cabinet was responsible for the exercise of the presidential functions and for his official pronouncements. Every presidential act was to be countersigned by the member of the Cabinet who was responsible for its execution. If the President were unable to execute the duties of his office, the Cabinet was to exercise his functions and could entrust specific functions to the Prime Minister.

The members of the Cabinet were appointed by the President usually from among the leaders of the political parties. The Cabinet was responsible to the Chamber of Deputies. If the Chamber, upon a motion signed by not less than one hundred deputies, passed a vote of no confidence or refused to pass a vote of confidence proposed by the Cabinet, the Cabinet was bound to tender its resignation to the

President. The jurisdiction of the Cabinet included, among other powers, presentation of bills to the National Assembly; issuance of decrees to implement laws passed by the National Assembly; promulgation of measures concerning all political matters; appointment of judges, civil servants, and commissioned army officers above certain grades, as well as submission of proposals to the President for the appointment of high officials. Administrative power in the new state was held by the Cabinet while the administrative machinery was run by trained civil servants, subordinate to the Cabinet.

Executive power in Ruthenia was vested in a governor appointed by the President of the Republic on the nomination of the Cabinet. The Constitution required that civil servants in Ruthenia be selected from the population of Ruthenia, whenever possible.

Local Administration. A system of self-government prevailed on the local administrative level. Representative bodies, elected by the population, enjoyed considerable independence in local matters and formulated their budgets. Such representative bodies existed on all administrative levels: in communities, counties, and provinces. There were four provinces *(zeme)* in 1938: Bohemia, Moravia-Silesia, Slovakia, and Ruthenia.

Judicial Power. This branch of the government was separate from, and independent of, the executive. No one could be tried except by a court whose jurisdiction was established by law. In the exercise of their judicial functions, the judges were bound only by law. A judge was appointed for life and could not be transferred, dismissed, or retired against his will except if a new court organization were set up for a time specified by law or on the grounds of a conviction in a disciplinary action. Civil cases were tried by civil courts and by courts of arbitration. Criminal cases were tried by criminal courts, providing that such trials were not reserved to military courts or to administrative authorities by special law. There was one Supreme Court and one Supreme Administrative Court for the whole Republic. Civil and criminal cases were tried by district courts, regional courts, courts of appeals (high courts), and the Supreme Court.

Minority Rights. The rights of ethnic, religious, and racial minorities were protected by the Constitution. The minorities could establish and administer philanthropic, religious, and social institutions in which they could use their own language and worship according to their creed. The ethnic minorities were assured the privilege of instruction in their own languages in public schools, and the right to use their language before any administrative or judicial agency in districts where they represented at least 20 per cent of the population.

In communities and counties where over half of the population were of an ethnic minority, self-government was wholly in their hands. Where an ethnic minority comprised less than half the population, their share in self-government was secured by the principle of proportional representation, upon which the electoral laws were based.

Ethnic minority groups shared all other civil and political rights equally with the rest of the population. Following the stabilization of conditions after World War I, representatives of some political parties of the German minority became members of the Cabinet, and their political clubs in the National Assembly participated in government coalitions. In 1935, the parliamentary representation of all the national minorities voted for the coalition candidate for presidency.

Civil Rights. All citizens and residents of the Czechoslovak Republic were to enjoy complete security of life and liberty, regardless of their origin, nationality, language, race, or religion. Every citizen could select his residence, acquire property, and engage in business. Expropriation was possible only on the basis of law. Inviolability of the domicile, secrecy of the mails, freedom of the press, and the rights of peaceable assembly, of association, and of petition were guaranteed. Freedom of opinion, conscience, and religion were also assured.

Democracy and the political rights of citizens were secured by the traditional freedoms and by independence of the political parties, liberal electoral laws, responsibility of the Cabinet to the National Assembly, an independent judiciary, and by self-government in local administration. Political parties could be established without any restrictions. Various national and social groups were represented by their own political parties (in the last pre-Munich general elections in 1935, for example, sixteen political parties campaigned). There was an Electoral Court, which decided disputes arising from elections, and a Constitutional Court, which was competent to decide questions relating to the constitutionality of laws. Encroachments by the administration were subject to judicial review. A Supreme Administrative Court had jurisdiction in "all cases in which the plaintiff stated that his right was violated by an illegal decision of, or a measure taken by, an administrative (executive) authority." In exercising their judicial authority, courts were bound only by duly promulgated laws (acts of legislature) and had the authority to refuse the enforcement of administrative ordinances and decrees, including those issued by the Cabinet, whenever they considered them at variance with law.

In social legislation, pre-Munich Czechoslovakia was among the leading countries in Europe. The enactment of an eight-hour working day (Law of December 19, 1918, No. 91) was among the first statutes of the Republic, and the law on social insurance (Law of October

9, 1924, No. 221) served as a model for other European legislatures. An extensive land reform was also carried out.

1938-1945

The Autonomy of Slovakia and Ruthenia

After the Munich Pact (September 30, 1938) and the Vienna Arbitrage (November 2, 1938), neither of which were ratified by Parliament, the Constitution was amended by Law Nos. 299 and 328 of November 22, 1938, concerning the autonomy of Slovakia and Ruthenia. In contrast with the Declaration at Turciansky Svaty Martin in 1918, which stated that there was a single Czechoslovak nation, and which became the fundamental principle of the 1920 Constitution, the preamble of Law No. 299 spoke of "the agreement between the two sovereign wills of the two nations equal in rights [i.e. the Czechs and the Slovaks]."

Slovakia was declared an autonomous part of the Republic. A Slovak Diet and Cabinet were established. The Slovak legislative power resided in the Slovak Diet, although some of this power was delegated to the Czechoslovak National Assembly. In certain matters concerning Slovakia, however, the passage of laws required the vote of a majority of the Slovak deputies. The consent of the Slovak Diet was needed for ratification of international agreements concerning Slovakia. The Diet, composed of 63 members, was elected on December 18, 1938, on a single ticket.

The executive power in Slovakia was exercised by the Slovak Cabinet appointed by the President of the Republic. The Cabinet was a part of the National (Czechoslovak) Cabinet, but it was also responsible to the Slovak Diet. To indicate that the National Cabinet must have the confidence of the majority of the Slovak nation, one third of the deputies of the National Assembly elected in Slovakia could call for a vote of no confidence in the National Cabinet.

A separate Slovak Supreme Court and Slovak Supreme Administrative Court were established. Slovak recruits were to be assigned to military formations located in Slovakia.

Law No. 328 of 1938 on the autonomy of Ruthenia was based on principles similar to those of Law 299 relating to Slovakia. However, this constitutional reconstruction had a short life. Under pressure from Germany, the Slovak Diet declared Slovakia an "independent" state on March 14, 1939. The Ruthenians followed suit the next day. On March 15, 1939, Germany occupied the Czech lands, transforming them into a German protectorate, while Ruthenia was occupied by Hungary on March 18.

The Government in Exile

In 1938, following the Munich Pact, President Benes resigned and left the country. Many politicians and other citizens followed him. After the outbreak of World War II, the Czechoslovak exiles established the Czechoslovak National Committee in Paris, which was recognized by the French government in November 1939 and by the government of the United Kingdom in December 1939, as representing the Czechoslovak people and authorized to establish a Czechoslovak army abroad. In June 1940, this Committee moved to London, where, on July 9, 1940, it established the Czechoslovak State Organization Abroad, consisting of the President of the Republic, a Cabinet, and a State Council appointed by the President. The government of the United Kingdom recognized this provisional state organization on July 21, 1940. Full recognition of the government in exile and of its President, Edward Benes, was granted on July 18, 1941. Recognition by the Soviet Union, the United States, and other governments followed. The Munich Pact was repudiated by the Allied governments. The government in exile acted on the basis of Czechoslovak pre-Munich laws, and new legislation was carried out by presidential decrees, issued on the basis of Cabinet proposals with the cooperation of the State Council.

1945-1948

The President and some members of the government in exile returned home via Moscow in March 1945. On April 4, 1945, at Kosice (in eastern Slovakia), the President formed a new Cabinet, including representatives of the Communist Party. The President's negotiations with the Communists resulted in the formation of a common platform of the liberal parties and the Communists, which was published on April 5, 1945, and later named the Kosice Program.

The program provided for the election of a Provisional National Assembly and, later, of a Constituent Assembly for the whole country. The Constituent National Assembly was to draft and adopt a new constitution. However, the Kosice Program itself disposed of some of the most fundamental constitutional issues. While it pledged to safeguard all the usual constitutional rights and freedoms, it also declared that the Cabinet would ban some political parties, including the Agrarian Party which had been the strongest political party in the country prior to 1938. People's Committees were to take over the administration of the country on all levels up to the Cabinet. Retributory justice was to be administered by people's tribunals on the basis of *ex post facto* decrees, ostensibly directed against the Nazi collaborationists and traitors.

State control of large sectors of the economy was stipulated in the Kosice Program: "The entire financial and credit system, the key industrial and insurance enterprises, natural and energy resources are to be placed generally under the control of the state, and at the service of reconstruction of the national economy and the revival of production and commerce." This part of the Kosice Program was implemented by Presidential decrees proposed by the Cabinet and issued by the President before the Provisional National Assembly convened, which approved them *ex post facto* on March 28, 1946.

The basic principles of the structure of the Republic were also revised by the Kosice Program:

> Recognizing that the Slovaks should be masters in their own land as the Czechs are in their native land and that the Republic shall be reconstructed as a common state of the Czechs and Slovaks, enjoying equal rights, the Cabinet shall demonstrate this recognition in important political acts of the state. [The Cabinet] shall treat the Slovak National Council which shall be based on the People's Committees in communities and counties, not only as a representative of the Slovak nation, distinct from that of the Czechs, but also as the bearer of state power (legislative as well as executive) in the territory of Slovakia in accordance with the special agreement between the Slovak National Council on the one hand, and the President of the Republic and the Czechoslovak Cabinet in London [in 1944] on the other. The Cabinet, as the central Cabinet of the Republic, shall carry out the common state tasks in the closest cooperation with the Slovak National Council and the Board of Slovak Commissioners as the executive agency of the Slovak National Council.[1]

This part of the Kosice Program was implemented by two Prague agreements between the Cabinet and the Slovak National Council (June 2, 1945 and April 11, 1946) and the agreement of June 27, 1946 between the political parties of the Czech National Front and the Slovak National Front.

Under the first agreement, in national (Czechoslovak) matters, the President, upon proposal by the Cabinet and in agreement with the Slovak National Council, exercised the legislative power by means of his decrees. These national matters involved "the principal national economic, socio-cultural, and administrative-political issues," and the decrees and laws, passed later by the legislature, were to be enforced

[1] This refers to the governmental organs set up during the 1944 Slovak uprising.

generally by the Cabinet. In Slovakia however, they were forced through the Board of Slovak Commissioners, whic sponsible to the Cabinet. Residual legislative power in Slc exercised by the Slovak National Council, whose jurisd embraced civil service personnel. The executive power, wh served to the National Cabinet, belonged to the Slovak National Council. The Commissioners enjoyed final jurisdiction in administrative matters, except when these were reserved to members of the National Cabinet. The Supreme Administrative Court was to be transferred to the Slovak capital of Bratislava. The jurisdiction of the highest judicial tribunals of Czechoslovakia was to extend to the whole Republic. Each tribunal was to have two presidents, one of whom was to be a Slovak.

The second and third agreement expanded the jurisdiction of some of the national constitutional organs to Slovakia, and limited the power of the Slovak National Council and the Board of Slovak Commissioners. The government setup during the transition period, 1945-48, was an attempt at coexistence with the Communists, but the failure of this effort was apparent almost from the beginning. The period ended with the Communist *coup d'état* on February 25, 1948.

The Constitution of 1948

After the Communist *coup d'état* in February 1948, the constitutional structure of the state was changed to correspond to the Soviet theory of state. Accordingly, the Communist Party assumed a monopoly of political power and all restrictions on the government were withdrawn. Western democratic devices restricting the power of government, such as the separation of the legislative, executive, and judicial powers, the doctrine of checks and balances, and the principle of rule by law, were rejected by the Communists.

A new Constitution (Law of 1948, No. 150, *Sbirka zakonu a narizeni republiky Ceskoslovenske* [Collection of Laws and Decrees] was adopted by the Constituent National Assembly on May 9, 1948. The text of the Constitution of 1948 affords only limited material for the study of the constitutional system of present day Czechoslovakia. Some of its provisions conceal rather than reveal the true situation. Several provisions adapted from the old Constitution seem to outline the features of a parliamentary regime, but these are ineffective because of other provisions designed to nullify them and because of individual laws and decrees issued in disregard of the Constitution.

General Constitutional Provisions

The Constitution consists of three parts: Declaration, Fundamental Articles, and Specific Provisions. The Declaration affirms the determination to "insure ourselves [the Czechoslovak people] of peaceful progress toward socialism." This statement is of far reaching importance for administrative authorities and judges, since the individual provisions of the Constitution must be interpreted "in the spirit of the whole and of the principles upon which it is based" (Section 171). In the message introducing the constitutional draft, the Fundamental Articles are described as containing the essence of the political theory of the Czechoslovak state. The principles stated in this section are developed in the Specific Provisions and will be discussed with these.

Legislative Power

The Constitution states that the "supreme organ of legislative power is the National Assembly" (Article V). However, the National Assembly meets seldom and then only for short sessions of one or two days. From December 12, 1952 to September 1953, the Assembly met only seven times. The Assembly elects the Presidium, a committee of 24 members, which theoretically has broad legislative powers during the interim periods between the sessions of the Assembly. The Cabinet, defined as "the supreme agency of governmental and executive power" (Article VII), exercises in fact, all legislative authority. Thus, Law No. 241 of 1948 on the first Five-Year Plan allowed the Cabinet "to redefine the tasks assigned by the plan" (Section 41) and "to take measures necessary for the accomplishment of tasks prescribed by the Five-Year Plan, including such measures as would otherwise require a legislative act" (Section 42). Likewise, Constitutional Law No. 47 of May 18, 1950 authorized the Cabinet to create and abolish ministries and other agencies of public administration and to define their jurisdiction. Thus, the major issues of public life are shifted from the legislative to the administrative branch. The Collection of Laws and Decrees for 1951 lists 21 laws and 74 Cabinet decrees; for 1952, 39 laws and 69 Cabinet decrees; and for 1953, 16 laws and 70 Cabinet decrees. The Cabinet, sitting "in council," has the power to issue decrees "in implementation of an individual law, within its limits" (Section 90). The Cabinet may further delegate its power to individual ministers.

The ruling function of the Communist Party is emphasized by the [illegible] that major policy decisions are officially published as joint res-[illegible]ions of the Communist Party and the Cabinet or of the Central [illegible]mittee of the Party and the Cabinet. Neither the Constitution nor any other law provides for this procedure. A similar practice has been followed in the Soviet Union since 1932.

Executive Power

The executive power is exercised by the President and the Cabinet. In this respect, the provisions of the 1948 Constitution are similar to those of the 1920 Constitution. However, the similarity is merely formal since the multi-party system has been replaced by the Communist Party monopoly, and no separation of powers exists between the legislative and executive branches of the government.

Election of Deputies

According to Article IV of the Constitution, the representative bodies are elected by universal, equal, direct, and secret suffrage. However, the electoral laws implementing this provision deprive the voter of the right to choose his candidate, and the right of founding political parties has been suppressed. Of the six existing political parties, two are Communist and the remaining four are Communist dominated. The independence of the non-Communist parties was destroyed by the use of a single ticket in elections and by the method of nominating candidates, which is completely controlled by the Communist Party through the National Front. According to Law Nos. 14 and 27 of 1954, the right of nomination belongs exclusively to the National Front, "representing the union of toilers, peasants and working intelligentsia, the fighting bloc of the Communist Party of Czechoslovakia, the Revolutionary Trade Union Movement, the Czechoslovak Youth League, the Czechoslovak Socialist Party, the Czechoslovak People's Party, the Party of the Slovak Rebirth, the Freedom Party, and other organizations of the working people." All these organizations are dominated by the Communist Party.

The complete supremacy of the Communist Party over all other political organizations is demonstrated by the fact that resolutions on basic policies of the country are passed and promulgated by the Central Committee of the Communist Party and the Cabinet rather than by the Cabinet and all the political parties.

Local Government

The functions of local government and of self-government are exercised by the People's Committees in each community (village, town, city), county, and region. Sections 123–133 of the Constitution deal with the People's Committees. These constitutional provisions have been subsequently implemented and amended by numerous legislative acts.

Law Nos. 12, 13, and 14 of 1954 provide that the People's Commiteees are elected by the people, but the right of nomination lies exclusively with the National Front. Members of the Committees are revocable by their electors, but only on a motion of the National Front. The Communists claim that the formation of the People's Committees has achieved a higher type of democracy, because the people now participate directly in both legislative and executive functions on the local level. In fact, the People's Committees are local agencies of the state, and subordinate to the Cabinet.

It is provided that "the People's Committees shall direct and control the work of their councils, departments, and other organs . . . ," but it is also stated that "People's Committees shall be controlled by the Cabinet . . ." and that "a lower People's Committee shall be controlled by a higher People's Committee and shall be responsible to it." Resolutions of the Cabinet are binding upon the People's Committees at all levels, and resolutions of a higher Committee are binding upon subordinate Committees. The Cabinet and the higher People's Committees have the right to amend or abolish resolutions of the subordinate People's Committees. The law stipulates that "the Council of a People's Committee shall be its executive organ. It shall be elected from among its members. The Councils of the People's Committees shall be subordinate to the Cabinet and, at the same time, a Council shall be subordinate both to its People's Committee and to the Council of the higher People's Committee." Similar hierarchical subordination applies to the administrative departments of the Councils of the People's Committees and to the chiefs of these departments. Each of these chiefs is responsible to his own Council and to the chief of the corresponding department of a higher People's Committee. The chiefs of departments of the regional People's Committees are responsible to the Cabinet Minister in charge of a particular branch of administration.

The statutes of March 1954, which amended the constitutional provisions (Law No. 12), replaced by the laws implementing these provisions (Law No. 13) and regulated the elections of the People's Committees (Law No. 14), were enacted by the government in an effort to tighten its control over the People's Committees. Although the Communist Party has controlled the People's Committees since 1945, a March 1954 Cabinet report, introducing a bill for the transfer of jurisdiction over the People's Committees from the Ministry of the Interior to the Cabinet, complained that the People's Committees enacted arbitrary and illegal acts, violated discipline and the "people's democratic legality," failed to unite the workers, peasants, and the working intelligentsia, acted in the spirit of local patriotism and pre-Comn views, lost contact with the working people, and did not comply the "principles of Marxism-Leninism."

Judicial Power

The third branch of the government is the judiciary. The Constitution stipulates that the courts discharge their power through professional and lay judges (Section 140). The judges must pledge by oath that they will render decisions pursuant to socialist legality for the benefit of the working people, and that they will guard the secrecy of official information. In a commentary on the 1950 Criminal Code, socialist legality was defined as "the precise application and observation of such laws as are in accordance with the will of the working class and of the toilers," its aim being "to crush the people's enemies and to protect and strengthen the dictatorship of the working class in order to construct socialism and later communism . . ." (*O obecne casti trestniho zakona* [On the General Provisions of the Criminal Code], Prague, 1951, p. 32).

The Constitution and most of the laws relating to the judiciary were amended or abolished by a series of laws of October 1952 (Law Nos. 64-69, *Collection*) by which the courts and the administration of justice were, in effect, subordinated to the Cabinet.

These laws established two categories of courts: ordinary and special courts. The first category consists of the Supreme Court, regional courts, and people's (district) courts; the second category consists of military courts and courts of arbitration which handle disputes between governmental agencies engaged in business. There are two classes of judges: professional and people's (lay) judges. Theoretically, both types are elected, though at present they are appointed. The first duty of the courts is to protect the social and political system of the Republic, socialist construction, and socialist ownership. They are to see that the laws and other legal provisions are applied in the interest of the working people. Judges must declare on oath that they will abide not only by laws but also by orders. Thus, they are not allowed to examine either the constitutionality of laws or the legality of administrative orders.

The Supreme Court is authorized to order any court to submit any civil or criminal case for review by the Supreme Court or to have it transferred to another court for decision. The President of the Supreme Court has the right to preside over any bench of the Supreme Court. In this way, the independence of the courts is effectively diminished. The people's judges are appointed by the Cabinet or the People's Committees. Only citizens "loyal to the government and devoted to the principles of the People's Democratic order," i.e. Communists or those willing to cooperate with the Communists, may be appointed people's judges.

The most effective organ of government control over the judiciary is the Procurator General, who is responsible to the Cabinet. He has supervisory power over the application of laws and other legal provisions by ministries, governmental agencies, courts (including the Supreme Court), people's committees, public institutions, public officials, and private individuals. He must safeguard, enforce, and strengthen social legality "by safeguarding the social and governmental system of the Republic, socialistic construction, and socialist ownership, as well as the interests of the working people against enemies and disturbers of their constructive efforts; by safeguarding the combat efficiency and discipline of the armed forces; by strengthening the authority of commanders and contributing to the defense of the country; by rearing citizens to perform all duties and to abide by the laws, other legal provisions, and rules of socialist common life" (Law of 1952, No. 65, *Collection*).

The Procurator General has the right to protest against decisions and measures of administrative authorities and may appeal against the final decision of the courts. It is the duty of every citizen to call his attention to any illegal act. The Procurator General is entitled to participate in the sessions of the People's Committees, of their organs, and of other agencies of the administration, arbitration boards, and of the Cabinet when it deals with his protest.

The Procurator General replaced the Supreme Administrative Court. Subordinate to the Procurator General are regional and district procurators and their deputies, and military procurators appointed by him.[2]

Slovak Governmental Agencies

Part Five of the Constitution deals with the Slovak government agencies. The Constitution states that the organ of legislative power in Slovakia is the Slovak National Council, consisting of 100 members elected in Slovakia for six years (Article IX). The Council may exercise this power only in matters enumerated in the Constitution (Section 96), which do not require a uniform national regulation but are of special concern to Slovakia (Section 94). However, even in these matters, the final word rests with the Prague Cabinet. The

[2] Law No. 66 of 1952 concerning the courts' organization has been amended by Law No. 66 of 1956. Law No. 65 of 1952 concerning the Procurator General has been amended by Law No. 65 of 1956 by which his powers have been extended.

Premier, whose signature is required for each act, may submit those acts "which he deems to infringe upon the Constitution or a constitutional act or which are inconsistent with the uniform economic plan or the budget act" to the Cabinet, which renders a final decision within two months (Section 110).

The administration of Slovakia is in the hands of a Board of Commissioners. Although it is stated in the Constitution that the members of this Board are responsible to the Cabinet and to the Slovak National Council (Article IX), the detailed provisions stipulate that the Commissioners are appointed and recalled by the Cabinet (Sections 114 and 117). There are no provisions which enable the Council to force the resignation of a Commissioner, whose duty "to abide by the directives and instructions of the Cabinet" and of the individual ministers is emphasized.[3]

Right of Ownership and the Economic System

The general provisions of the 1948 Constitution guarantee limited private ownership, but this guarantee is greatly weakened by other clauses and laws, and is disregarded in practice.

Government Enterprises. Though the Constitution stipulates that means of production may be owned privately (Section 146), it assigns the following branches of the economy to exclusively national ownership: mineral resources and their extraction; sources of natural energy and power plants; foundries; natural therapeutic sources; the production of goods serving the health of the people; enterprises with more than 50 employees (excluding the undertakings of People's Cooperatives); banks and insurance institutions; public rail transport and regular road and air transport; postal services, public telegraph services, and telephone services; broadcasting, television, and motion pictures (Section 148).

Private Ownership. The field left to private enterprise is thus highly restricted. Section 8 of the 1948 Constitution provides that "within general statutory limits, every citizen may acquire real and other property anywhere within the territory of the Czechoslovak Republic and carry on gainful activity there," and Section 158 states that "private ownership of small and medium enterprises employing up to 50 persons is guaranteed. . . ." Nevertheless, in 1950 the Cabinet reported to the National Assembly that "by means of the legislation on na-

[3] Part five of the Constitution has been amended by Constitutional Law No. 33 of 1956, which broadened to some extent the jurisdiction of Slovak governmental agencies.

tional administration, confiscation, and nationalization, and partly also through retributory measures, the victorious working people have deprived the big bourgeoisie of its economic basis." The "retributory measures" included forced labor camps which held many thousands of small tradesmen whose shops were nationalized. Other small entrepreneurs were ruined by taxes. In 1951, the Minister of Finance reported that the state budget had "an additional important function, namely to support the development of the socialist enterprise and to eliminate the remnants of capitalism. . . ." The President of the Republic reported in his 1951 New Year's message that "the small trades have been almost completely nationalized on a socialist basis . . ." (*Rude pravo* [Red Right], January 3, 1951).

A plan for communal enterprises was devised to eliminate the private enterprises which remained after nationalization. The laws of 1948 and 1950, as amended by Law No. 105 of 1953, provide that communal enterprises, like national enterprises, are owned by the state. The People's Committees can thus force small entrepreneurs to give up their businesses and to join communal enterprises. In recent years, all but an insignificant fraction of industrial output has been produced by state enterprises.

Economic Plans as Vehicles of Socialization. The law on the first Five-Year Plan (Law of 1948, No. 241, *Collection*) aimed directly at the elimination of private enterprise. According to the Constitution, the state directs all economic activity (Section 162), and it is the duty of individuals and corporate bodies to adapt their economic activities to the state economic plan (Section 164). With regard to contracts, the new Civil Code provides that "competent authorities may impose obligations in accordance with the needs of economic planning . . . ; if the needs of economic planning so require, the competent authorities may change obligations flowing from legal relations important for the fulfillment of the uniform economic plan," and under the same conditions obligations may be cancelled (Law of 1950, No. 141, *Collection*).

Confiscation of Savings. According to Section 158 of the Constitution, "personal property of citizens is inviolable. This provision specifically refers . . . to savings derived from personal labor." In spite of this, the entire national debt was repudiated and all bank accounts accumulated prior to November 1, 1945, were cancelled under the Law of May 30, 1953 (Law No. 41, *Collection*). The savings of the population were thus confiscated.

Restriction of Land Ownership. The Constitution guarantees "private ownership of land to farmers who till the land themselves . . .

up to the limit of 50 hectares" (Section 159). Nevertheless, smaller holdings were taken under the pretext that the owners did not personally till the land, or that they were traitors or collaborators. By applying various coercive means, the government compels farmers to join collective farms.

Some farmers are classified as "the village rich," or, by the Russian term "kulak." According to a joint declaration of the Communist Party and of the Cabinet, the village rich represent a danger because they are members of the most numerous capitalist class. Farmers who own smaller acreage, and at the same time, are innkeepers, millers, grocers, butchers, carters, grape growers, or vegetable growers, even if they are not practicing their trade, are also included in the category of village rich.

Shortly after the Communist coup, a campaign to drive the village rich out of economic life was begun. In 1952, a Cabinet resolution declared: "The Cabinet calls on all groups forming the National Front of the Czechs and Slovaks . . . to mobilize all their members for the struggle against the sworn enemy of the working people . . . against the village rich, and to induce the farmers to join the Uniform Agricultural Cooperatives to till the land collectively" (*Uredni list* [Official Gazette], February 14, 1952). A Cabinet Decree of November 4, 1952, ordered that the delivery quotas of the village rich exceed by 10 per cent those imposed upon other producers with the same acreage. If the quotas are not met, the farm is seized by the government and allocated to an agricultural cooperative. This decree was later replaced by other similar measures. Excessive quotas are a common means to force independent farmers to join collective farms.

Protection of Family and Youth. Sections 10 and 11 of the Constitution proclaim that "the state shall ensure that the family be a sound foundation for the development of the nation . . . ," and that children shall be ensured " special care and protection. . . ." Nevertheless, the government issued regulations denying rationed goods to housewives who are not employed and who care for their children at home. The People's Committees were authorized to deny ration cards to women who have children and live in the country near a nursery or crèche and who do not work on the collective farm, and to women who live in a town where there is a labor shortage and who do not join a working group.

Education

Sections 12, 13, and 14 of the Constitution provide that "the state shall ensure that everyone shall receive education and training in accordance with his natural abilities and with a view toward the needs of the community. . . . All schools shall be state schools. Basic education shall be compulsory, uniform, and free. . . . All education and all instruction shall be provided so as not to be inconsistent with the people's democratic order. . . ."

These provisions form the basis of the present discriminatory practices in education. In 1953, the principals of secondary schools were instructed by the Ministry of Education not to recommend "children of the village rich, the bourgeoisie, former highly placed members of the bureaucracy, and traitors of the working people for study in institutions of higher learning" (*Vestnik Ministerstva skolstvi* [Bulletin of the Ministry of Education], IX, Part 3 [Jan. 31, 1953], 23-25). Another order of the Ministry of Education states that the background of students admitted to institutions of higher education must warrant "the expectation that they will develop into an intelligentsia which will be linked to the working class by its origin and its upbringing."

Freedom of Conscience and Religion

Section 15 of the Constitution guarantees freedom of conscience, and Section 16 stipulates that "everyone shall be entitled to profess privately and publicly any religious creed or to be without a religious denomination. . . ." In practice, however, churches are not allowed to have their own schools, and, in 1949, they were placed under the complete control of the State Office for Church Affairs. Clergymen are required to take a loyalty oath to the government and have been placed on the government payroll and under state authority. The State Office for Church Affairs is responsible for the development of church and religious life "in accordance with the Constitution and the principles of the people's democratic order." Hence, it supervises the teaching of religion, approves religious textbooks, censors the ecclesiastic press, and controls the charitable activities of the churches.

Priests may be appointed only with the consent of the government. Section 173 of the Criminal Code provides that "whoever performs ecclesiastical functions in a church or religious association without government consent shall be punished by confinement not to exceed three years. . . . Whoever, without governmental consent, appoints another for the performance of pastoral functions in a church or religious association, shall be punished by confinement for a period of one year to five years. . . ." Priests and bishops were jailed for their opposition to the new church legislation and for obedience to the Vatican. Monasteries were confiscated, and monks and nuns were dispersed or sent to forced labor camps. Any contact with the Vatican was declared a crime.

Freedom of Expression

Sections 18 and 21 of the Constitution guarantee freedom of expression and of the press. Section 22 stipulates that "the right to produce, distribute, publish, and exhibit, as well as to import and export motion pictures shall be reserved to the state. Broadcasting and television shall be the exclusive right of the state."

These constitutional provisions notwithstanding, criticism of the "people's democratic order" is considered an offense and is punished as such under the Criminal Code (Section 81). Law No. 184 of 1950 provides that the task of the press shall be to educate the people for socialism. Private individuals or enterprises are prohibited from publishing newspapers and periodicals under penalty of a fine not to exceed 250,000 crowns (about $5,000 at the official rate of exchange), or of confinement not to exceed six months. Under the Administrative Criminal Code, whoever manufactures or possesses any printing machine or multigraph shall be punished by a fine not to exceed 50,000 crowns, or by confinement not to exceed two months.

Under the provisions of Law No. 94, 1949, books and other nonperiodical literature may be published only according to a plan set up by the Ministry of Information, which also issues publishing licenses. Licenses may be granted to corporate bodies, but not to private individuals or enterprises. Distribution of printed matter is also regulated by the Ministry of Information. Any violation of these provisions may be punished by a fine not to exceed one million crowns and by confinement not to exceed six months.

Right of Assembly and the Right to Form Associations

Section 24 of the Constitution states that "the right to assembly and to form associations is guaranteed, provided that the people's democratic order is not threatened thereby." Nevertheless, all associations in existence before February 1948 were dissolved, or at least their non-Communist members were deprived of their functions. According to Section 25, "the interests of the employed persons in individual enterprises and offices shall be represented by the Uniform Trade Union Organization and its bodies." No other trade union organizations are permitted.

Personal Freedom

Section 2 of the Constitution guarantees personal freedom, which "may be restricted or withheld only on the basis of law." On October 25, 1948, personal freedom was restricted by the Law on Forced [illegible] It established regional boards consisting of three mem- [illegible] by the Ministry of the Interior, with the authority [illegible]ed labor camps "persons who are not less than 18 [illegible] that 60 years old, and who are physically and mentally [illegible] of working, but who evade work or threaten the people's [illegible]emocratic order or economic system. . . ." The boards were entitled to send such persons to a camp for a period of three months to two years. Moreover, the board could order that the convicted person be subject to further restrictions upon completion of his term. The forced labor camps are now regulated by the provisions of the new Criminal Code of 1950 and by the directives issued in its implementation.

The Criminal Code and the Code of Criminal Procedure provide that parole boards established at the Regional Courts may place a person convicted by a court in a forced labor camp for a period of three months to two years after he has served the full term of confinement imposed by the court (Sections 36 and 279). Prior to January 1, 1954, confinement in a forced labor camp could also be imposed as an independent penalty by the Penal Boards of the district People's Committees. Under Law No. 102 of 1953, these boards can now impose a sentence of correctional labor without confinement.

Equality

According to Section 1 of the Constitution, all citizens are equal before the law. The practical application of this law in the daily life of the Czechoslovak population reveals a different picture. An example of this was the rationing system. A proclamation of the Ministry of Domestic Trade denied ration cards to entire groups of the population, thus forcing them to make all their purchases on the free market at prices considerably above those of rationed goods. These groups included the village rich; private entrepreneurs (artisans, traders, craftsmen) and their families; absentees from work and their families; and retired civil servants who held important offices before 1945, and their wives or widows. The People's Committees were authorized to deny ration cards to all those whose state pensions were cancelled or reduced, to persons who were able to work but did not work, to private farmers who failed to deliver government quotas of agricultural products, and to members of agricultural cooperatives who failed to meet their compulsory delivery quotas (Proclamation of the Minister of Domestic Trade, *Uredni list,* No. 6, January 14, 1953).

These practices appear to be in agreement with the Marxian concept of equality, which has been described as follows:

Marxism considers equality not as equality in personal necessities and social conditions, but as the complete abolition of classes, i.e., (1) equal liberation of the working people from exploitation, as soon as the capitalists have been destroyed and their property expropriated; (2) equal abolition of private ownership of means of production, as soon as these means of production have been conveyed into the ownership of the entire community; and (3) equal duty of all to work according to their own abilities, and equal right of all workers to be paid according to the work done (socialist community). Thus, the Marxist viewpoint implies that the desires and needs of the people are not and cannot be equal in quality and quantity, whether in a period of socialism or of communism. . . . (Jan Fejes, "Februar" [February] in *Pravny obzor* [Law Review], No. 2, 1950.)

4. POLITICS AND POLITICAL ORGANIZATIONS

Curt Beck

Political Tradition Before 1945

Austro-Hungarian Period

Democratic traditions and political institutions antedated the attainment of political independence by the Czechs and Slovaks in 1918. A democratic interpretation of Czech history, the absence of an indigenous nobility, and the rise of a strong middle class in the latter part of the nineteenth century helped to make the Czech nationalist movement liberal and democratic. Frantisek Palacky, founder of the first Czech political party in the nineteenth century and leading statesman of the Czech National Revival period, linked the heroic phases of Czech history with the development of democratic ideas. Palacky's interpretation of Czech history was the main source of the political ideology of the country in the nineteenth and early twentieth centuries.

The growth and development of democratic ideas and political parties in Bohemia and Moravia were supported by a sizable middle class and large groups of industrial workers interested in stable political conditions and economic opportunity. In Slovakia and Ruthenia, however, economic and social conditions before World War I were less favorable to the growth of democracy. The differences between the Czech and Slovak stages of development became particularly marked following the Ausgleich of 1867. While the Czechs gained an increasing degree of political autonomy from Vienna, the Slovaks were victims of the Budapest policies of Magyarization, which aimed at suppressing Slovak nationalism and Slovak political life. While Czech schools prospered toward the end of the nineteenth century, Slovak schools were inferior and scarce, and after the 1870's, there were no Slovak schools at the intermediate and university levels. While both the Czech lands and Slovakia were essentially Catholic, the political conservatism of the Church had a stronger influence in predominantly rural Slovakia than in the more industrialized Czech lands.

Some of the parties of the Czechoslovak Republic had their origin in political parties which represented the Czech nation in the Austrian Reichsrat. At that time, the pattern of Czech political parties reflected a contest between radical and conservative groups, united by a common search for greater national rights. Three periods, significant in the development of Czech political parties, can be distinguished: the political dawn, 1848-49; the predominance of Czech conservatism, 1860-91; and the liberal era and rise of the mass parties, 1891-1914.

The 1848 revolution and its aftermath presented the first short-lived opportunity for political action. Czech political ambitions were expressed by two parties: the National Liberals and the Radical Democrats. The former had a conservative social and economic program and placed nationalistic before democratic objectives. The latter favored a more radical political and economic program combined with a flair for revolutionary tactics. The National Liberal Party was more influential and more powerful than its rival. With the restoration of the old regime in 1849, the activity of the Czech parties ended.

Political activity among the Czechs was not resumed until 1860, when the Imperial Council of Austria-Hungary was broadened to include some members selected by the diets of the "historic lands" of Austria. At first, a resurrected National Liberal Party, known as the "Old Czechs," was the only party representing the Czechs in the broadened Imperial Council. Its membership consisted of the nobility and wealthier merchants who associated themselves with the Czech national movement, as well as a few intellectual leaders. Predominantly conservative, the National Liberal Party also included some radical elements which, exasperated by the fruitless policy of the party, broke off on December 27, 1874, to form the National Freethinkers Party, soon known as the "Young Czechs." While the Old Czechs favored the Church, opposed measures which radically broadened the franchise, and pursued a policy of abstention from the Austrian Imperial Council, the Young Czechs favored an active policy to achieve national objectives, as well as liberal economic and political goals. The limited liberalization of the franchise in 1886, as well as the failure of the Old Czechs to advance significantly the objectives of the Czech national movement, led to the victory of the Young Czechs in the parliamentary elections of 1891.

During the period 1891-1914, the two-party system was replaced by a multiple party system. Several factors were responsible for this change. Lack of governmental responsibility of Czech parties prevented the development of "outs versus ins" rivalry. With all Czech parties in the opposition, competition developed for the most effective appeal to the various segments of the population. It became increasingly difficult for any one party to reconcile special interest groups under the pressure of economic development. Parties representing narrow segments of the population multiplied. They tended to espouse rigid ideological programs, such as Marxist, liberal, and so forth, rather than adjust their programs to political circumstances. New parties appealed to the masses, which assumed increasing importance after the introduction of universal suffrage in 1907. The Austrian Social Democrats became active among the Czechs in the late 1880's and 1890's, directing their appeal to all workers, regardless of nationality. In 1897, the Czech National Socialist Party was organized; it combined social democracy with Czech nationalism and an anti-German program. An Agrarian Party, organized in 1899, found strong support in the villages. The Catholic Christian Democratic Party, which defended the interests of the Catholic Church and of its hierarchy in spiritual, educational, economic, and political matters, was founded in 1896.

Before World War I, the Czech parties developed certain characteristics which made a lasting impression on party operations. Concentration of power in the hands of a few leaders resulted from the geographical situation, which required party leaders to act in the Vienna Reichsrat without first ascertaining the opinions of their distant constituents. The tendency of party leaders to speak for their membership without consultation became an accepted feature of party politics. Party newspapers became the main tie between leadership and party members.

The Czechoslovak Republic

World War I and independence changed the grouping of the Czech parties. The Social Democrats, National Socialists, and Agrarians underwent only minor changes, but several smaller parties joined together to form a new conservative party, the National Democrats. This party was an ideological descendant of the Young Czechs, concerned with nationalistic objectives, and professing pan-Slav and pro-Russian, but anti-Bolshevik sympathies. Several regional parties were fused into the Czechoslovak People's Party, safeguarding the interests of the Catholic Church. In May 1921, the left-wing elements of the Czechoslovak Social Democratic Party formed the Communist Party, which joined the Comintern the day of its founding. A Czech fascist party was active in the 1930's, but gained little popular support.

The Slovaks had no political parties at the end of World War I.

The Slovak National Party was a national, rather than a political organization. Shortly after the creation of Czechoslovakia, new Slovak parties sprang up and Czech parties extended their activities to Slovakia. The strong position of the Catholic Church in Slovakia enabled Slovak clergymen to wield political influence through the newly established Slovak People's Party which, after 1935, advocated Slovak separatism. After creation of the Slovak People's Party, the Slovak National Party became a predominantly Protestant party. The Slovak Agrarian Party, Social Democratic Party, and Communist Party were organized in Slovakia, but each coordinated its activities with its counterpart in the Czech lands. Other Czech parties were active in Slovakia with varying degrees of success.

The Social Democratic, People's, and Agrarian parties were also represented in the political organizations of the German minority. The German National Socialists (Sudetendeutsche Partei) was led in the 1930's by Konrad Henlein. The Hungarian, Ukrainian, Jewish, and Polish minorities in Czechoslovakia also organized political parties.

In the four parliamentary elections of the interwar period (1920, 1925, 1929, and 1935), none of the parties won a majority. Industrial workers were divided between two parties: the Communists and the Czechoslovak Social Democratic Party. White collar workers, teachers, government employees, and some skilled workers were attracted to the Czechoslovak National Socialists, National Democrats, and some smaller parties. The peasants divided their loyalty between the Agrarians and the People's Party. Businessmen were split among the Small Traders and Artisans Party, the National Democratic Party, and the Agrarians. The minorities voted for their national parties.

Coalition governments, which reflected the major shifts of public opinion, were necessary. In 1918-19, at the outset of Czechoslovakia's independent life, a conservative coalition, directed by the National Democratic Party, stressed a program of national unity. The local elections of 1919 indicated a shift in favor of the socialist parties. From 1919 to 1922, a coalition dominated by the Socialists enacted social reforms and moderate socialist economic changes. The 1920 parliamentary elections confirmed the socialist trend, but the creation of the Communist Party in May 1921 reduced the strength of the socialist parties and led to power a coalition which was dominated by the Agrarians and included all the other major Czech parties (1922-26).

The 1925 elections further weakened the socialist parties, while the strength of the Small Traders and the Czechoslovak and Slovak People's parties increased. In 1926-29, a coalition led by the Agrarians and backed by the Czechoslovak People's Party, but excluding the socialist parties, was in power. In 1929, the parliamentary elections indicated losses by the clerical party and gains by the Social Democrats and Czechoslovak National Socialists. A new coalition was formed, still led by the Agrarians, and including all major parties except the Communist. This government remained in office throughout the depression and the ensuing years of crisis created by Germany's aggressive policy.

From 1926 to 1938, some German parties were included in the various coalition governments. In the 1935 elections, the Nazi Sudetendeutsche Partei drew votes from all other German parties and became the second strongest party in Parliament, ranking next to the Agrarian Party. This created a major threat to Czechoslovak democracy in the years preceding Munich.

The nationality problem and the depression presented grave challenges to Czechoslovak democratic order in the interwar period. The Czechs and Slovaks, totalling about 66 per cent of the population, were under pressure to make concessions in the fields of education, government administration, and economic activity to the several minorities. The depression further emphasized these conflicts by arousing discontent with the *status quo,* and encouraging the minority parties who were advocates of change.

The organization of the Czechoslovak parties during the interwar period had considerable influence on subsequent developments. Each party had a strong concentration of power in the hands of the party leaders, who determined the policy of the coalition government; the party members in Parliament usually ratified this without dissent. Party leaders could strike dissident members from the party and deprive them of their seats in Parliament. Members of Parliament represented political parties rather than specific segments of the electorate.

After the Munich agreement of 1938, the Czechoslovak Parliament lost its influence on the government. Political parties were outlawed or disbanded. The German occupation ended the constitutional phase of the Czechoslovak state, weakened the foundation of its democratic order, and decimated its political leadership. The six-year lapse in legal political activity further impeded the restoration of a democratic state.

1945-1948

The Czechoslovak government in exile considered itself to be a legal continuation of the last government of independent Czechoslovakia. It was recognized by the British government on July 21, 1940, and was later recognized by the other Allied nations. The government in exile was headed by President Benes. Some pre-Munich political parties were represented in the State Council, an advisory body, and in the Cabinet.

Benes believed that the postwar policy of Czechoslovakia should be founded on cooperation with both the Soviet Union and the West. In pursuit of this policy, he concluded a treaty of friendship and mutual assistance with the Soviet Union on December 12, 1943. Benes also wanted to synchronize the activities of the Czechoslovak Communists, then in Moscow, with those of the government in exile in London, and to include some of the Moscow Communists in the London government. The Communists were unwilling to enter his government unless it were reorganized. Benes rejected this condition, but agreed to postpone the matter for later discussion. He agreed to the Communist demand for a program of economic and social change after the liberation, and approved Gottwald's proposal for the formation of People's Committees which would supplement the Parliament, although he had reservations on this point. Benes and Gottwald favored the cooperation of the Communists, Social Democrats, and National Socialists with the People's Party in a united National Front. Elections were to be held soon after the end of the war, preferably within six months. In the interval, a left-wing Social Democrat would head the government.

Benes and his government returned to Czechoslovakia in May 1945. They stopped first in Moscow, where Benes made further concessions to the Czechoslovak Communists, giving them key positions in the government. These concessions were partly due to Benes' realization that the United States, Great Britain, and Russia had decided at Teheran that Czechoslovakia would be in the Russian military zone. In 1944, the Slovak uprising had shown that no effective military aid could be expected from the West.

The agreements reached by Benes and the Communists in the 1943 and 1945 discussions formed the basis of the Kosice Program, ostensibly an agreement reached by the parties of the National Front on the policies to be pursued by the new Czechoslovak government upon its return home. Its most important features were the creation of the National Front coalition government and of the People's Committees which were to take over the functions of local and regional administration. The National Front consisted of the Czechoslovak and Slovak Communist parties (officially separate, but in fact a single party), the Czechoslovak Social Democrats, the National Socialists, the Czechoslovak People's Party, and the Slovak Democratic Party. For the first time, the Communist Party was included in a governing coalition. No party outside of the National Front was permitted to organize.

A party coalition had become a party directorate. The absence of opposition parties transformed the parliamentary system into a parliamentary dictatorship.

The creation of the National Front considerably improved the position of the Communists. They had the support of other parties in eliminating the opposition, especially in regard to the conservative Agrarian Party. The non-Communist parties believed they would gain votes by the dissolution of the rightist parties. Under the guise of national unity, the Communists compelled the other parties to follow their policies or else bear the blame for dissension within the National Front.

In the first postwar government, the Communists held the important Ministries of Interior, Agriculture, and Information. Communist agitation for the creation of local People's Committees was accepted by non-Communists because it professed to provide more democratic self-government. Before the other parties became organized on the local level, the Communists filled the political void left after the defeat of the Germans. With the support of the Red Army and the influence of their wartime resistance record, the Communists and their supporters were able to staff the majority of the new People's Committees. Elections to the People's Committees were not held until 1954, thus enabling the Communists to consolidate their position. By 1947, they held 57 per cent of the chairmanships of local People's Committees, 80 per cent of district People's Committees, and 100 per cent of provincial People's Committees.

In the 1946 parliamentary elections, the Communists received 38 per cent of the seats. With the aid of the Social Democrats, who were led by pro-Communist Zdenek Fierlinger, and who controlled 13 per cent of the parliamentary seats, the Communists were able to control the legislative body. Thus, from 1945 to 1948, Czechoslovakia was governed by the National Front coalition, of which the Communists were the most important element. Nevertheless, Czechoslovakia retained some characteristics of a democratic state: criticism of the government was possible, the non-Communist press was permitted to operate, and the courts, which were largely in non-Communist hands, protected the citizens against Communist abuse of power. The non-Communist parties worked against the objectives of the Communists and waited for another general election in which Communist strength would be reduced.

During this period, the Communists sought to consolidate their control of the labor unions and to win the support of peasants by granting them benefits and distributing the land taken from the expelled Germans. They claimed credit for all social benefits enacted under the National Front. They encroached steadily upon the private sector of the economy, carrying nationalization further than originally stipulated in the nationalization decrees of 1945. They invoked the power of the Soviet Union, stating that acts against the Czechoslovak Communists were acts against the Soviet Union itself.

In the fall of 1947, public opinion polls attested to the waning popularity of the Communist Party, a danger signal in view of the general elections to be held in summer 1948. The greater self-assurance of the democratic parties was a further concern to the Communist Party. Tension between the Soviet Union and the West was a deterrent to further Communist collaboration with other parties. The Czechoslovak government, which first unanimously agreed to participate in the July 1947 conference on the Marshall Plan, later reversed its decision under pressure from Moscow. This strained relations between the Communists and the other parties of the National Front.

The reorganization of the Slovak Board of Commissioners in October and November 1947 was an indication of coming developments. The Communists demanded the dismissal of several Slovak Democratic Commissioners, claiming that they plotted against the Prague government. The Communist Commissioners resigned and declared the Board dissolved. In violation of the Kosice Agreement of 1945, which stipulated that the Commissioners were to be selected by the Slovak National Front, the Communist Prime Minister of Czechoslovakia appointed new Slovak Commissioners. This strengthened the position of the Communists in Slovakia.

Communist Seizure and Consolidation of Power

Early in 1948, the non-Communist parties balked at the attempt of the Communist Minister of Interior to change the National Security Corps (SNB) into a Communist police force. Encouraged by the Communist loss in popularity, they decided to make this issue a rallying point for all non-Communist parties. They hoped to gain the support of the Social Democrats, who opposed a Communist police force. Defection of the Social Democrats from the Communists was considered possible after the fall 1947 shift in leadership, which replaced the radically pro-Communist Fierlinger by the more moderate Lausman. Without Social Democratic support, the Communists were in a parliamentary minority.

On February 13, 1948, the National Socialists, the People's Party and Slovak Democratic Party Ministers demanded that the Communist Minister of Interior rescind an order replacing certain police officials with trusted Communists. When this demand was not recognized, the Ministers of the three parties, stating failure to agree with the government, resigned.

The Communists labelled the resignation as an attempt of the "reaction" to seize power. They opposed the readmission of the resigning Ministers into another government, and hoped, through technical control of Parliament, to force the creation of a government excluding their opponents. They called for a revised National Front, including only those members of the National Front parties who repudiated the action of the resigning Ministers and representatives of mass organizations in agreement with the Communists. The support of the Social Democrats and the approval of President Benes, who had the power of accepting the Prime Minister and his Cabinet, were legally required for this action.

The Communists forced the Social Democrats to reinstate Fierlinger as their leader. Lausman played an equivocal role during the crisis, making it possible for Fierlinger to impose his wishes on the Social Democratic Party. The Social Democratic Party capitulated and agreed to assist the Communists in seizing control of Parliament.

In order to frighten Benes, the Communists called mass meetings of workers and peasants in Prague. Armed Communist trade unionists and factory militia units gave a threatening show of strength. Not accustomed to mass action on this scale, the other parties were bewildered. Benes, dreading civil war, was willing to compromise. With the threat of an armed mob in the streets, the Communists presented Benes with a new National Front Cabinet, including only Communists, Social Democrats, and Communist sympathizers from other parties and organizations. On February 25, 1948, Benes accepted the new Cabinet. The Communists assumed complete control of the government.

Parliament was inactive during the crisis. A purged legislative body was convoked on March 10, after the seizure of power by the Communists had been completed. Through the revolutionary action committees, the Communists liquidated their former opponents.

A new constitution was approved by the purged Parliament on May 9, 1948, and became effective one month later. President Benes refused to sign it, resigned from the Presidency on June 7, and died soon thereafter (September 3, 1948).

Parliamentary elections were held on May 30, 1948. They differed markedly from those held May 26, 1946, when the parties of the National Front competed for votes among the electorate by presenting separate lists of candidates. The 1946 elections determined the strength of the respective parties within the National Front. The electorate had at least a limited choice among the four parties of the National Front. In 1948, the voter could cast his ballot only for a single combined list of the National Front or cast a blank ballot. Furthermore, voters were urged to cast their ballots in public view to demonstrate their loyalty to the regime. The parties of the National Front were apportioned candidates on the basis of an agreement reached by party leaders several weeks before the elections. The Communist Party determined the percentages for all parties, and selected the candidates of the other parties. Thus, the 1948 elections transformed Parliament into an obedient instrument of the Communist Party.

On June 14, Klement Gottwald, chairman of the Communist Party, was elected President by the new Parliament. Zapotocky, number two man in the Party, became Premier. All top organs of government were in the hands of the Communist Party.

The non-Communist political parties were purged of all elements not in complete sympathy with the Communists and were then used as tools to reach those segments of the population which had formerly supported them. The Communist Party formally absorbed the Social Democratic Party on June 27, 1948, and the Slovak Communist Party on September 27, 1948. The reconstituted National Front thus became an organization headed by the vast Communist Party, comprising 79 per cent of representation in the National Assembly, and four small subsidiary parties: the (National) Socialist Party, 9 per cent; the People's Party, 7 per cent; Slovak Revival (the former Slovak Democratic) Party, 4 per cent; and the (Slovak) Freedom Party, 1 per cent.

Although the National Front functioned as an arm of the Communist Party, it was put to little use for several years. All electoral activity ceased until 1954, when the government organs, which were theoretically responsible to the electorate, were again subjected to elections. On May 16, 1954, elections to the People's Committees were held for the first time since 1945, when they had been chosen in the extraordinary circumstances surrounding the liberation of Czechoslovakia. On November 28, 1954, elections were held for the National Assembly, over six months after the terms of the deputies had expired.

The Communist Party

Membership

In comparison with the Communist parties in other countries, the membership of the Communist Party of Czechoslovakia (KSC) includes a relatively high percentage of the population. In 1953, the total population of Czechoslovakia was about 12,815,000; on June 11, 1954, the Communist Party claimed 1,489,234 members and candidates, or about 11.6 per cent of the total population (contrasted with 3.3 per cent in the Soviet Union in 1952). This percentage was even higher in August 1948, when it reached a peak of 19 per cent of the total population.

Even before World War II, the KSC had a relatively large membership and exhibited the external features of a regular parliamentary party, particularly during the days of the Popular Front. Czechoslovakia was the only East European country in which the Communist Party was permitted to operate legally during the entire period from World War I to the Munich Conference. In the immediate post-World War II years, the Communist attempt to seize power through a perliamentary majority encouraged further expansion of the Party membership. After the February 1948 coup, the KSC recruited many opportunists, which swelled its ranks to a peak membership of nearly 2,500,000.

The Communist Party has considered large membership a sign of weakness, except when used as evidence for the Party's claim of mass support. A large membership carries with it the threat of infiltration by anti-Communists, of loose discipline, and of potential opposition to authority emanating from the top. Since 1948, Party membership has been drastically reduced through a series of membership purges and screenings. This change is shown in the following chart of Communist Party membership in Czechoslovakia for selected years from 1946 to 1954:

Year	Membership
1946 (March)	1,159,164
1948 (October)	2,418,199
1949 (January)	2,311,066
1950 (September)	2,025,318
1951 (February)	1,677,433
1954 (June)	1,489,234

The membership loss has been even greater than these figures indicate, for the screenings are usually accompanied by new recruitments. In their drives for new members, the leaders of the KSC try to win the natural leaders in factories and on collective farms. By attracting men who play important roles in production, they hope to increase economic output. The Party also attempts to reduce the number of Party members with middle class background.

Party membership policy consisted of purging idealistic revolutionaries as well as opportunists who flocked to the Party between 1945 and 1948. These were to be replaced by men with fewer ideals but greater technical knowledge—men who could implement the Party's economic program.

Structure

With only minor exceptions, the structure of the KSC follows the pattern of the Communist Party of the Soviet Union. It is detailed in Party statutes, which enumerate the powers and functions of all Party organs, but do not limit or control the functions of Party officials. When desired by Party officials, provisions of the statutes are forgotten. The statutes are also subject to change at each Party congress, and recently they have been altered frequently. Nevertheless, they present a significant picture of the Party's operations.

The KSC is pyramidal in structure, with final authority held by a small group at the top. The Party pyramid falls into four layers, whose subdivisions correspond to the territorial divisions of the state. Each layer consists of a small committee which is responsible to a larger representative group (the congress, conference, or meeting), which meets infrequently. The representative group in each layer is chosen by the corresponding body in the subordinate layer immediately below it. On the lowest level, the representative group consists of an assembly of the total membership. Those at the top are insulated by indirect elections from the mass membership, but they are never completely out of contact. The channels of authority and command extend from the top down, rather than vice versa.

Relationships within the Party structure are known in Communist nomenclature as "democratic centralism." The definition of this term comprises several basic principles: election of all Party organs; accountability of elected organs to their electors; submission of the minority to the majority; and the unconditionally binding nature of decisions by higher organs upon lower organs. There is, however, no provision made for responsibility of the high Party organs to lower Party organs. The decisions of the higher organs are binding on the lower organs, while indirect elections leave the higher Party organs independent of control by the general membership. Emphasis on strict Party discipline contrasts with the lack of definition of the rights of Party members. For example, there is no guarantee of the right of Party members to challenge decisions reached by the leaders. Democratic centralism places major emphasis upon centralism, provides little scope for democratic action, and facilitates authoritarian behavior.

Basic Organizations. The grass-roots of the Party structure are the so-called basic organizations. They fall into two categories: functional and geographical. The former are centered around a Party member's place of employment and are called factory organizations (a generic term applying also to Party organizations in schools, offices, institutions, and machine tractor stations). The latter are based on the residence of a Party member. They are found mostly in rural areas, in villages, and, to a lesser extent, in cities, where they are known as street organizations. Formerly, membership in the two types of organizations often overlapped: a Communist was expected to be active in his local, as well as in his factory organization. Since 1953, a determined effort has been made to reduce the importance of geograpical organizations and to shift the emphasis to functional organizations. Since Party members are presumably engaged in productive work, it is thought more effective to use the place of work as the center of Party activity. The most important reasons for the shift are, however, economic and disciplinary. Increases in productivity can best be achieved by intensive Party activity among the workers. The KSC factory organization is intended to serve as a nucleus to which other workers are attracted and from which they receive impetus to fulfill and exceed work norms. Supervision of Party members is apparently easier in factory organizations, where their lives and views are open to inspection.

In some of the larger factories, organizations are subdivided into shop organizations and section organizations. The objective is to keep basic organizations small to insure greater effectiveness and easier control.

Activities on the local level fall into five categories:

1. Members must endeavor to improve their training in the fundamentals of communism as interpreted by the Party high command.
2. They must safeguard the security of the Party dictatorship by reporting suspicious activities.
3. They must spread among their non-Party neighbors the "Party line" regarding all aspects of domestic and foreign policy.
4. They must act constantly as the renovators of the Party's life blood by expelling "bad" elements and encouraging new members to enter.
5. In their factories and places of employment, they must see that the Party's economic goals are fulfilled and that the workers' morale is maintained at a high level.

City, District, and Regional Organizations. The city, district, and regional Communist organizations, i.e. the organizations on the intermediate level, differ from the basic organizations in their increasing remoteness from the general membership and in the manner in which their leaders are selected. Orders from above, conveyed through the secretaries of district and regional committees who are appointed on the next higher level, outweigh the "voice from below." City, district, and regional committee members have to be experienced Communists; their election requires approval by the higher Party leadership.

On this intermediate level, the importance of the committee increases and the representative group becomes merely an endorsing body. The committee meets much more frequently than the full conference. The existence of an executive group within the district and regional committee is another example of the concentration of leadership in the hands of a few trusted Communists. This elite guides the committee and does most of the work.

All-Party Congress. The top of the Party pyramid consists of several state-wide Party organs; these range from the largest, legally supreme, yet actually weakest top level organ, the All-Party Congress, to the small, all-powerful Political Bureau (Politburo). The All-Party Congress, elected by the regional conferences at their preceding meetings, is declared by Party statutes to be the supreme organ, but it is too large and meets too briefly to exert any real authority. Power is exercised by smaller organs, the Political Bureau and the Secretariat. Scheduled to meet at least once every four years, the Party Congress has met three times since World War II, in 1946, 1949, and 1954. These meetings are called to acquaint the Party masses with important changes, new objectives, and personnel replacements. Occasionally, as in 1952, Party conferences take the place of congresses. The former are less elaborately prepared and have less propaganda significance than the latter.

Central Committee. The agenda and policies of the Party congresses and national conferences are determined by the Central Committee, which, in 1954, consisted of 84 members and 28 alternates. The Central Committee is elected by the All-Party Congress and, theoretically, is responsible to it. It is the official ruling organ of the KSC when the Congress is not in session. It meets three or four times a year. The stated functions of the Central Committee are to direct all Party activities, to organize and direct the many Party institutions, and to "direct the work of the central state organs, of the National Front, and of public organizations through Party groups in those organs and organizations."

Political Bureau. The Central Committee is too large to carry out its functions and therefore delegates their execution to two smaller organs: a nine-man Political Bureau and a five-man Secretariat. Two alternates on the Political Bureau, called candidates, participate in meetings without a vote. They occupy an inferior position to the others in the hierarchy of power which controls the top policy-making body of the Party.

The Political Bureau was created at the Tenth Party Congress in June 1954, when it replaced the twenty-two man Presidium and the eight-man Political Secretariat. This arrangement follows Soviet practice, and the single executive organ provides a more accurate reflection of the power realities at the top of the pyramid. Real authority had never rested in the full membership of the Presidium but had been assumed by a small nucleus which consisted of the members of the Political Secretariat. The Political Bureau evolves policies and reaches basic decisions in all spheres of activity; these are then approved automatically by the Central Committee.

At the end of 1955, the nine full members of the Political Bureau of the KSC were Karol Bacilek, Rudolf Barak, Alexej Cepicka,[1] Jaromir Dolansky, Zdenek Fierlinger, Vaclav Kopecky, Antonin Novotny, Viliam Siroky, and Antonin Zapotocky. Ludmila Jankovcova and Otakar Simunek were the two candidate members. The biographies of the Political Bureau members (see page 418) show that power is in the hands of old Party men who have served in many capacities. A relative lack of formal education and frequent trips to Moscow are their common outstanding characteristics. The dominant group of old-timers have, however, accepted into their midst several men who possess specialized knowledge in such fields as economics or law.

Following the death of Slansky and of Gottwald, power in the Political Bureau was assumed by former close associates of Gottwald: Zapotocky, Novotny, and Siroky. These three now form the inner core of the Political Bureau, although several other members of the Political Bureau have at times figured in this inner core.

Secretariat. Party decisions are carried out by the Secretariat. The five members of the Secretariat (at the end of 1955, Jiri Hendrych, Bruno Koehler, Vratislav Krutina, Vaclav Pasek, and Antonin Novotny, who is also First Secretary of the Central Committee) act collectively to carry out the decisions of the Central Committee, which are in fact the orders of the Political Bureau. Individually they are in charge of the many sections of the Secretariat which roughly correspond with the branches of the government. These sections include international affairs, industry, finance and trade, agriculture, security, and so forth. Each of the sections supervises the Party work in a particular field on regional and district levels. The Secretariat employs a large staff which, together with the secretaries of

[1] Cepicka was formally dismissed from the Political Bureau on April 25, 1956, when he was also relieved of his positions of First Deputy Premier and Minister of National Defense.

the various city, district, and regional committees, forms the Party's "civil service."

The Secretariat is responsible for implementing the policies of the Political Bureau. However, in the past there have been instances of rivalries between the Secretariat and the Political Secretariat, the predecessor of the Political Bureau. Thus, Gottwald, who controlled the Political Secretariat, clashed with Slansky, who controlled the Secretariat. The 1951-53 purges involved to a large extent the reorganization of the top organs of the Party in such a way as to place the Secretariat (called the Organizational Secretariat from 1951 to 1954) in a subordinate position to the Political Secretariat. However, with the elimination of Rudolf Slansky from the Secretariat on September 6, 1951, Antonin Novotny, a man handpicked by the leaders of the Political Secretariat, rose to prominence in the Organizational Secretariat and eventually took over its control. He served as the link between the Political Bureau and the Secretariat, being the only man in 1954 to belong to both top level organizations. Novotny is responsible for selecting the other members of the Secretariat, none of whom are on the Political Bureau. He is thus designated as the senior member of the Secretariat, since the other members must communicate through him to be heard in the highest council of the Party.

The four junior members of the Secretariat (at the end of 1955), Jiri Hendrych, Bruno Koehler, Vratislav Krutina, and Vaclav Pasek, have all had long careers in the central Party apparatus as expositors of the Party's policy in different fields. They are frequent contributors to the Party press. Hendrych and Koehler appear to have been in disfavor for a while. They were connected with Slansky's Secretariat and had to re-establish their Party purity before regaining their present positions. Of the four, Koehler has the best known Party record. Krutina and Pasek appear to be new men whom Novotny promoted from the lower ranks of the Party, apparently in recognition of their Party reliability and devotion to Gottwald. Relatively little is known about either of these men.

Novotny is also First Secretary of the Central Committee. The Secretariat is usually dominated by the First Secretary, regardless of his official title. All the members of the present Secretariat are members of the Party's Central Committee, though this has not always been the case. Positions on the Secretariat have often been testing places, with only the successful candidates eventually serving on the Central Committee.

Central Auditing Commission. The only other organ, beside the Central Committee, directly responsible to the Party Congress is the

Central Auditing Commission. Its function is to audit the finances of all Party enterprises, and it has the right to exercise control over all Party organizations in economic and financial matters. Under the jurisdiction of the Central Auditing Commission are auditing commissions on the regional, district, and city levels with corresponding functions.

Party Control Commission. This organ, responsible to the Central Committee, examines Party members' and candidates' appeals against decisions of lower Party organs concerning Party penalties. It also conducts disciplinary investigations and proceedings in all cases referred to it by the Central Committee. The findings and decisions of the Party Control Commission are subject to the approval of the Central Committee.

Communist Party of Slovakia

The Slovak Communist Party has a special position in the formal structure of the KSC. Until the February 1948 coup, the Communist Party of Slovakia, while cooperating closely with the Communist Party of Czechoslovakia, was nevertheless formally independent. On September 27, 1948, the unification of the two parties was announced, but the Slovak Party did not lose its identity completely. As a concession to Slovak nationalist feelings, a special provision was incorporated in the statute of the KSC providing for a Slovak All-Party Congress, a Central Committee of the Slovak Communist Party, and a separate bureau and Secretariat of the Central Committee. In short, there exists in Bratislava a replica of the top organizational layer of the KSC. The Slovak Central Committee is, however, subordinate to that of the KSC in that it is required to carry out the decisions of the Central Committee of the KSC.

Developments Within the Party

Communist policy has passed through three distinct phases since February 1948. From February 1948 to February 1951, control over the organs of government and over the social, political, cultural, and economic institutions of the country was consolidated. From February 1951 to September 1953, the country was mobilized to meet the increased demands of the Soviet Union in connection with the Korean campaign. Since September 1953, a struggle for greater popular acceptance of an unpopular regime has been in progress. Each of these phases has called for revisions of policy and shifts in leadership of the KSC.

During the first phase, Party leadership had to change its revolutionary role into active statesmanship. Rivalries which had been submerged in the quest for power came to the surface. The dominant nucleus within the Presidium was formed by Party chairman Klement Gottwald, Party leader since 1929, with Antonin Zapotocky, leader of the trade unions, and a Slovak, Viliam Siroky. Rudolf Slansky, the Secretary General of the party, assisted by Josef Frank, Bedrich Geminder, Gustav Bares, and Marie Svermova, tried to use the Party Secretariat as a counterweight to Gottwald's dominant position in the Presidium. The Gottwald group appeared to have a more genuine working class background than the Slansky group. In February 1951, with the purging of Marie Svermova and Otto Sling, the era of outward harmony came to an end.

The second phase involved the destruction of Slansky and his friends. This period coincided with the increased demands imposed upon Czechoslovakia's economy by the Soviet Union. Responsibility for industrial shortages and economic discontent was blamed upon Slansky by Gottwald and his group. There were widespread purges of all economic, political, social, and artistic activity, culminating in the trial of Rudolf Slansky and thirteen "accomplices," November 20-27, 1952.

A new phase was started on September 15, 1953 with the announcement by Premier Siroky that emphasis was to be placed on the raising of living standards. Following the execution of Slansky and after the death of Gottwald on March 14, 1953, the leadership of the Party fell to some degree to a new group of Communist functionaries, who had not played important roles before February 1948. Antonin Novotny, First Secretary of the Central Committee, became the leading figure in Party affairs. He brought with him other functionaries who had risen in the Party apparatus: Rudolf Barak, Jiri Hendrych, Vratislav Krutina, Vaclav Pasek, Josef Tesla, and Jindrich Uher. However, Antonin Zapotocky, Viliam Siroky, Jaromir Dolansky, Karol Bacilek, and Alexej Cepicka, Gottwald's "old guard," retained key positions in the Party and government.

Mass Organizations

The term "mass organization" applies to all those organizations which seek to enroll the maximum membership in any activity lending itself to group action, such as sports, trade unions, and youth movements. The function of these organizations is to mobilize public opinion and to guide public activity in support of the aims and objectives of the Communist Party. Mass organizations are called voluntary organizations, but they are compulsory to a great degree and are regulated by legislation (Law of July 12, 1951, *Sbirka zakonu a narizeni republiky Ceskoslovenske* [Collection of Laws and Ordinances of the Czechoslovak Republic]).

A primary Party function is to oversee all mass organizations. Mass organizations are modeled upon the organization of the KSC, with a Communist Party group formed in practically every mass organization. The Party statute states that whenever three or more Party members are present in a mass organization, a Party group is formed whose task it is to strengthen the influence of the Party on the organization. Communist control is achieved through the appointment of important Party members to key positions.

The mass organizations can be divided into the following categories, based on the functions which they fulfill:

Economic: Revolutionary Trade Union Movement, Central League of Consumer Cooperatives;

Youth: Czechoslovak Youth League;

Women's affairs: Committee of Czechoslovak Women;

Military preparedness: League for Cooperation with the Army, Czechoslovak Sokol Community;

Civil defense and disaster: The Czechoslovak Red Cross;

Ideological propaganda: League of Fighters against Fascism, Czechoslovak Committee of the Defenders of Peace, Czechoslovak Society for the Propagation of Political and Scientific Knowledge;

Friendship with the Soviet Union: The Czechoslovak-Soviet Friendship League;

Advancement of science and technical knowledge: Various technical and professional organizations.

The Revolutionary Trade Union Movement is by far the most important mass organization. Its size alone (over 2,500,000 members) surpasses that of all other organizations. It is responsible primarily for the performance of production tasks specified in economic plans. Its main functions are to encourage an increase in the productivity of labor, to inform the government of essential needs of workers which must be satisfied if productivity is not to suffer, and to provide workers' recreation centers and spas.

The Czechoslovak Youth League, like the Soviet Komsomol, serves as an apprentice organization for the Communist Party. Its functions are to provide the Party with a pool from which young members may be chosen, to instill in the new generation a love for communism, and to undermine the authority of parents not susceptible to official propaganda. The age of the Youth League membership ranges from

15 to 25. Membership is large, since advancement is practically impossible for those who fail to join. Admission to universities, eligibility for state jobs, and almost all avenues of promotion are closed without Youth League membership, which is considered a sign of the young applicant's reliability.

The League for Cooperation with the Army is charged with training civilians in various fields which are useful from a military point of view. The scope of its activities is seen from a list of some of the organizations which it has absorbed: the People's Motoring Organization, the Voluntary League for People's Aviation, the League of Cyclists, the Central League of Carrier Pigeon Breeders, and the Czechoslovak League of Radio Amateurs.

Military preparedness also dominates athletic and sports activities. The Sokol organization, which has its roots in the Czech nationalist movement and dates from the second half of the nineteenth century, has traditionally been the leading organization for gymnastics and sports. Sokol was the most difficult organization for the Communists to infiltrate and control. Through repeated purges, it has been rendered "secure." It is used by the Communists to prepare Czech youth physically for combat.

The Czechoslovak Society for the Propagation of Political and Scientific Knowledge attempts to promote popular appreciation for Soviet ideas on science and religion. It seeks to undermine religious influences among the people.

One of the most important mass organizations is the Czechoslovak-Soviet Friendship League. This group had over 2,200,000 members in July 1952, which made it the second largest mass organization, surpassed in size only by the Revolutionary Trade Union Movement, and exceeding the membership of the Communist Party itself. The chief purposes of the Czechoslovak-Soviet Friendship League are to popularize Czechoslovakia's close ties with the Soviet Union, to solicit support for the foreign policy of the Soviet Union, to popularize the achievements of Soviet industry and science, to encourage imitation of Soviet methods, and to spread knowledge of the Russian language and of the Soviet Union. To accomplish these ends, the League has the customary intermediary organizational structure, as well as branches in towns, factories, and villages. The climax of the League's yearly activities is the "month of Czechoslovak-Soviet friendship," held each year from November 7, the anniversary of the Soviet revolution, until December 12, the anniversary of the 1943 Czechoslovak-Soviet treaty of friendship and mutual assistance.

5. THE GOVERNMENT

Curt Beck

The First Republic, 1918-1938

The Czechoslovak statesmen who participated in the formation of the Republic at the close of World War I were strongly influenced by French and Anglo-Saxon political concepts. These were applied to the concepts and institutions then existing in Austria-Hungary. As a result, considerable changes occurred in the top level of the new governmental structure, though at the lower levels, Austro-Hungarian traditions and practices remained largely unchanged.

Czech leaders endorsed the democratic principles of the American and French revolutions. French ideas and practices prevailed over Anglo-Saxon, however, because Czech leaders, with the notable exception of Thomas G. Masaryk, were better acquainted with French than with British and American political systems. French institutions were also more applicable to the existing situation in Bohemia and Moravia, where a multi-party system was firmly established by 1918.

The Constitution of February 29, 1920 provided that the National Assembly be the foundation of the governmental structure. The President of the Republic was elected for a seven-year term by the National Assembly. The President, in turn, selected the Prime Minister and his Cabinet, subject to approval by the National Assembly.

The National Assembly consisted of a Chamber of Deputies, and a Senate. The 300 members of the Chamber of Deputies were elected for six years, and the 150 Senators for an eight-year term. The length of these terms was not important, however, since all parliaments were dissolved before running their full course. Voters and candidates for the Senate were required to be somewhat older (26 and 45 years) than those for the Chamber (21 and 30 years), but both houses were elected by a direct vote and on the basis of proportional representation.

The power of the President was limited by the Cabinet. In practice, however, the President assumed a greater role than that stipulated by the Constitution, due to the impact of the two Presidents, Thomas

G. Masaryk and Edward Benes, who held office during the twenty years before Munich. Both men, especially Masaryk, were highly respected for their contributions to the establishment of the state. Their counsel was sought by party leaders of almost all political orientation.

The Cabinet was responsible to the National Assembly, and could be dissolved by the Chamber of Deputies through a vote of no confidence. In practice the Cabinet depended on the leaders of the parties of the coalition in power. Since no party ever held a majority in the National Assembly, it was necessary to form coalition governments. In order to preserve the stability of the coalition governments, the practice of consultation among the leaders of the coalition parties developed. Decisions were first reached by the directorate of party leaders and then translated into Cabinet action. This informal party directorate operated on a basis of political compromise and strict party discipline. Its decisions were binding on both the Cabinet and the National Assembly, since the party leaders of the directorate could control the deputies.

Thus the influence of the National Assembly was never as great as the 1920 Constitution intended. Instead, the existence of well disciplined political parties, in which the power was held by a small inner circle, created a situation in which the National Assembly could discuss government measures, but could not effectively challenge them. The presidents provided the only counterbalance to the parties, but they held this position on the strength of their personal influence, rather than by constitutional provision. Masaryk and Benes raised the prestige and power of the presidential office far above the anticipations of the framers of the 1920 Constitution.

The administration of justice was sufficiently removed from the executive and legislative branches of the government to assure the independent dispensation of justice. Judges were appointed for life by the President upon recommendation by the Cabinet. They could not be removed for political reasons. The courts were arranged in hierarchical order, culminating in a Supreme Court with jurisdiction over the entire country. Regular courts could not question the constitutionality of laws. This function belonged exclusively to the Constitutional Court, which, however, could not consider the constitutionality of a law unless it was requested by other courts or by the National Assembly. The Constitutional Court was never asked to perform this function, and thus there was no judicial check upon the legislature. A judicial check upon the executive branch of the government was more effective. This function was performed by the Supreme Administrative Court, which served as a board of appeal against decisions of administrative authorities. Courts could also question the legality of government ordinances.

With the disintegration of Austria-Hungary fresh in their minds, the framers of the Czechoslovak Constitution of 1920 sought to protect the state against centrifugal tendencies through creation of a centralized structure. On the other hand, they were concerned with minority demands for greater autonomy. Treaties protecting minority rights were an integral part of the peace treaties signed by Czechoslovakia and an important factor in encouraging the minorities to seek local autonomy. These conflicting tendencies were responsible for compromises effected in local and regional government.

There existed three levels of local government: the lands (Bohemia, Moravia-Silesia, Slovakia, and Ruthenia); the districts; and the villages, towns, and cities. The executive organs on all three levels acted as communication channels for decisions reached by the central government. However, certain areas of administration, such as the maintenance of roads and institutions, were under district or local administrative organs. Each of the three levels had a legislative and an executive branch. On the land and district levels, only two thirds of the membership of the legislature were elected by the people. The remaining third was appointed by the central government. The land and district legislatures could not effectively challenge the power of the executive appointed by the central government. On the local level, the elected legislative body could control the executive, but the power of the local administration was very limited. Local self-government was not developed to a significant degree, but, despite serious shortcomings, it was carried on fairly and efficiently.

The Slovaks, Ruthenians, and Germans were the most outspoken critics of the lack of land, district, and local autonomy. The Slovaks hoped to achieve a considerable measure of autonomy on the land level; the Czechs, on the other hand, felt that greater Slovak and Ruthenian autonomy would be feasible only after years of centrally controlled political education and economic development. The German population, living in the border territories and also dispersed in other parts of the state, appealed for greater district autonomy, as did the Hungarians and the Poles. These requests for autonomy were rejected by the Czechs primarily for strategic reasons. Since many Germans, Hungarians, and Poles were settled along the frontiers, the Czechs feared that in case of foreign attack, their defensive position might be weakened by grants of autonomy to the minorities.

The demand for local autonomy served twice as a pretext for destruction of the democratic order of the Czechoslovak state: in

1938-39 and in 1944-45. In 1938, demands for German autonomy within Czechoslovakia were stepping stones for the cession of the border areas to Germany, and later, for German occupation of Bohemia and Moravia. Slovak autonomy, granted on November 19, 1938, led to the creation of a Slovak satellite of Germany on March 14, 1939. Criticism of the "insufficient" democratic basis of local and regional governments also became one of the chief weapons with which the Communists during and after the war sought to undermine the central democratic institutions and seize power on the local level.

World War II and the Postwar Period, 1938-1948

Following destruction of the independent Republic, Czechoslovak political life was carried on in two centers, London and Moscow. In London, a government in exile was established by Benes. All changes in the legal framework of the state enacted after September 1938 were declared void on the ground that they had been forcibly imposed. Benes considered the 1920 Constitution still valid and organized his government according to it. Exceptions were made to meet the unusual circumstances of a government operating in exile. Although the President and the Cabinet ostensibly operated in collaboration with the State Council, which replaced the legislative representative body, in fact the government ruled by Presidential decree. The Czechoslovak government in exile was recognized by the United Kingdom, the United States, the Soviet Union, and other allied governments in 1940-42.

The fiction of Czechoslovakia's constitutional continuity was defended by Benes for both internal and international reasons. By legally recognizing only the *status quo ante,* Benes hoped for a guarantee from the Allies that Czechoslovakia would be reconstituted in its pre-Munich frontiers. The 1920 Constitution was also expected to ensure the survival of democratic government after the liberation of Czechoslovakia, since it would provide a set of stable principles. Benes planned to transfer his government in exile to Prague after the war, to re-establish the parliamentary machinery of government, and then to hold elections for a new National Assembly.

Benes might have realized his plan if Czechoslovakia had been liberated by Western armies. The Soviet Union, however, occupied a major part of Czechoslovak territory, and Benes was confronted with the plans of the Communist Party of Czechoslovakia. The Communists sought to control local governments and to gain an effective voice in the central government. The first objective was achieved through the creation of the People's Committees, and the second through the National Front.

The Communists were the first well organized group to appear in Czechoslovakia after the liberation. They were thus in a position to determine the outcome of local elections. Using this advantage over the disorganized liberal parties, they concentrated on furthering a plan for the reconstitution of Czechoslovakia's government from below. They demanded new local organs, the People's Committees, which would be directly responsible to the electorate and would have a large scope of action. This move was democratic in appearance, but the creation of entirely new local bodies in the chaotic conditions after liberation increased the power of the Communists and worked havoc with Benes' plan for the orderly reconstitution of democratic government.

The second major Communist objective, to achieve control over the central government, required obtaining control of the National Assembly. While the Communists expected to make major electoral gains, they were aware of the difficulties involved in a single party achieving a majority in the National Assembly. They intended to overcome this obstacle with the help of the National Front. Modeled on prewar coalitions, from which the Communists had always been excluded, the National Front was to consist of all parties opposed to fascism. It excluded some large prewar parties, in particular the Agrarian Party which, it was alleged, had played an equivocal role during the Munich crisis. The fact that the Communist Party had actually cooperated with the Germans from 1939 to 1941 was never officially mentioned. The National Front would control the National Assembly, and the Communists in turn would control the National Front.

In the post-liberation period, Communist strategy was more effective than that of the government in exile. While the Communists were determined to take full advantage of the emotionalism and prejudice of a people emerging from years of oppression, the people preferred to wait for the return of more stable conditions and judgment. The Communists stimulated the general mood of revenge against the collaborators, which enabled them to dispose of many opponents. They also benefited from the general impatience with slow-moving reforms.

The first major concession made by the Czechoslovak government in exile to the Communists was a constitutional decree issued by President Benes in London on December 4, 1944. The decree sanctioned the formation of People's Committees in the liberated territories and gave them the power to select delegates to the Provisional National Assembly.

In 1945, in Moscow, Benes made a second major concession, agreeing to reorganization of the government on the basis of the National Front. The extent of reorganization was revealed in Kosice on April 5, 1945. Benes remained President, but the Cabinet included only members of the National Front, with ministries distributed among the six parties of the National Front. However, the Communists achieved *de facto* control over the government through several political devices. They divided their party into the Communist Party of Czechoslovakia and the Communist Party of Slovakia. This gave them twice the number of Cabinet positions held by any other party. They brought several other Party members into the Cabinet, camouflaged as non-partisan specialists. They also obtained the most strategic ministries for achieving control: the Ministries of Interior, Agriculture, Information, Education, and Social Welfare. They gained indirect control over the Ministries of Industry, Foreign Affairs, and National Defense. The post of Prime Minister was held by Zdenek Fierlinger, a left-wing Social Democrat who has since become one of the leading Communists.

On April 5, 1945, the National Front published the Kosice Program, a broad plan of action in the political, economic, cultural, ethnic, and international fields. The most important aspects of this program were the significant role given to the People's Committees in rebuilding the country's government apparatus, and the extent of anticipated government control over the country's economy.

The Kosice Program was in fact a political mandate, because it presented to the people the only political organization legally permitted to operate in Czechoslovakia. Within the National Front, power was centered in the Central Committee, in which the Communist Party figured significantly. Thus, the Central Committee of the National Front assumed the role played in the pre-Munich Republic by the party directorate, without, however, being checked by opposition in the National Assembly.

In May 1945, the Czechoslovak government arrived in Prague. On October 28, 1945, a Provisional National Assembly met for the first time, selected largely by the National Front with the help of the People's Committees. Its primary function was to give legal sanction to the many governmental acts passed during the war and to make the necessary preparations for the election of a National Assembly, which would prepare a new constitution. The Provisional Assembly approved the nationalization decrees.

Parliamentary elections were held on May 26, 1946. The voters' choice was limited to parties of the National Front. The elections gave the Communists 38 per cent of the seats in the National Assembly and the Social Democrats 13 per cent. Under Zdenek Fierlinger's guidance, the Social Democrats voted with the Communists on most issues, thus giving the Communists control of the National Assembly. The Communists assumed the Prime Ministership (Klement Gottwald), but surrendered the Ministry of Education to the National Socialists (Jaroslav Stransky).

Thus, with the reconstitution of the government in 1946, the Communists were in a strong position, but they were not yet in control of state power. The Presidency was out of their reach, due to the popularity of Benes. The National Assembly was not fully in their control, as was evidenced by the protracted negotiations concerning the new constitution. The Cabinet was partially in their control, but the very fact that authority had to be shared, checked Communist designs. The Communist position in the Slovak Board of Commissioners was relatively weak due to the strength which the Slovak Democratic Party demonstrated in the 1946 elections. Communist influence was very strong in the People's Committees, but they had not yet succeeded in assuming the complete control necessary for implementation of their programs on the local level.

Non-Communists held the Ministry of Justice and attempted to restore the integrity of the judiciary and to make it a bulwark against Communist illegality. However, the usefulness of the courts against Communist attack was seriously impaired during the first few months after liberation: all parties associated justice with revenge on the Nazis and their collaborators, and thereby greatly weakened the effectiveness of the judiciary as a defender of civil liberties.

Until the summer of 1947, the Communists tried to achieve influence by cooperating with all those who were not actively anti-Communist and could be won over to a moderate Communist-directed policy. Drastic action began in the early fall of 1947, when the Communists decided that seizure of full control could not wait and that the political tide was turning against them. The Communist Ministry of Interior gave key positions in the police to trusted Communists, thus transforming it into a loyal arm of the Party. Other ministries were honeycombed with Communists in leading positions who could paralyze anti-Communist measures and further the Communist cause. This applied especially to the army. The autonomous government of Slovakia was overthrown on the basis of trumped-up conspiracy charges.

In the final crisis, the anti-Communists found themselves deprived of most of the instruments of state power. The Communists transformed a governmental crisis into a fight for the absolute control of the state, and, in the coup of February 1948, forced President Benes to accept the technically legal transformation of parliamentary government into a dictatorship of the Communist Party.

Government Structure under the Communists

After the Communist *coup d'état,* the National Front was reorganized, and, although other parties continued to be represented in the National Front, only those members who willingly followed Communist directions remained in the National Assembly. The new Cabinet consisted of Communists and Communist-approved members from the satellite parties. In the election held on May 30, 1948, there was no contest among the parties of the National Front. The election resulted in the elimination of any remaining "unreliable" members of the National Assembly. The Presidency was the last organ of government captured by the Communists. Benes resigned on June 7, 1948, and Klement Gottwald succeeded him on June 14.

The National Assembly

The function of the National Assembly under the Communists differs considerably from its former role. As long as several parties existed and party coalitions were subject to change, even control of the National Assembly by a party directorate did not stifle free expression of opinion and criticism. Discussions in the Assembly often rallied public opinion, which had an influence on the party leadership. Under Communist rule, the National Assembly was transformed into an agency used by the Party to transmit its decrees to the public.

Important policy decisions and pronouncements of the Central Committee of the Party, particularly those which involve the duties and obligations of citizens are enacted into law by the National Assembly. Thus, legislation bears the double imprint of Party and legislative approval. The function of the deputy is to popularize the laws passed by the National Assembly among his constituents. A deputy is also to transmit to the National Assembly the criticisms of his constituents, provided they deal with matters of technical implementation and do not question the basis of legislation.

In 1955, the National Assembly consisted of one house of 368 deputies, elected for a six-year term (the election of May 30, 1948 was not followed by another until November 28, 1954). Each deputy represented an election district of approximately 35,000 inhabitants. The occupational background of the deputies elected on May 30, 1948, and on November 28, 1954, were given as follows:

Occupational Background	1948	1954
Workers	57	95
Farmers	44	70
Employees of national and communal enterprises and associations	68	182
State and public employees	16	
Political and trade union workers and editors	47	
University professors, teachers, writers, lawyers, judges, doctors, scientists, and students	61	
Members of armed forces	6	21
Clergy	1	—
Total	300	368

Sources: Nova mysl (New Mind), VIII (October 1954), 1264; and *Rude pravo* (Red Right), December 16, 1954.

The National Assembly meets infrequently. In six years, from June 10, 1948, to the end of May 1954, the National Assembly held only 84 plenary meetings, as compared to 75 in 1932 alone. However, in those six years, 323 laws, as well as many acts and treaties, were passed or approved.

In 1954, the National Assembly had nine committees: economic planning, budget, constitutional law, agriculture, culture, public welfare and health, military affairs and state security, foreign affairs, and credentials. While these committees do not meet much more frequently than the plenum of the National Assembly, some discussion of the proposed legislation takes place in committee. The Communists state that in contrast to the discussions of the committees, the deputies in the plenary meetings of the National Assembly popularize the approved laws, explain to the workers their contents and significance, and thus mobilize the workers for the fulfillment of their assigned tasks. Since legislative work occupies little time, deputies are encouraged to keep their regular jobs and to implement among their fellow workers the application of the laws which the National Assembly has passed.

In the long intervals between legislative sessions, the work of the National Assembly is carried on by a twenty-four-member Presidium. Members of the Presidium are elected by the National Assembly for one-year terms. The Presidium is headed by the chairman of the National Assembly and several vice chairmen. It is permanently in session, and, as the directing committee of the National Assembly, it is responsible for affairs which lie within the jurisdiction of the National Assembly itself. It consists of representatives of the Communist Party and of other parties of the National Front, and it serves as a link between the Communist Party and the legislature. The chairman or one of the vice chairmen of the National Assembly has always been a member of the Presidium or of the Political Bureau of the Communist Party.

The President

The important position of the President in the present Czechoslovak government is a factor which distinguishes Czechoslovakia from most of the other Soviet-type states. In the First Republic, the Presidents had great political influence, although they had little constitutional power. When Benes resigned on June 7, 1948, the Communists did not diminish the importance of this position, but rather had the National Assembly elect the Communist leader, Klement Gottwald, to fill the vacancy. Gottwald sought to strengthen his position in the Communist Party and to increase his popular appeal. This decision deviated from the organizational pattern of the Soviet model, but it conformed to the leadership cult which was then strong in the Soviet Union. Gottwald became the Stalin of Czechoslovakia and took every top position. At the time of Gottwald's death, on March 14, 1953, the principle of collective leadership was not yet strong enough to interfere with the election of Antonin Zapotocky, number two man of the Communist Party, who assumed the Presidency on March 21.

Gottwald's powerful position as head of the state was based upon his chairmanship of the Party and his membership in the Political Secretariat, the Party's top policy-making organ. Zapotocky's present place in the hierarchy, while aided by the Presidency, is due to his prominent position in the Political Bureau of the Party. The principle of collective leadership is applied to party organs rather than to the government, since it is from the former that power is derived. Nevertheless, the importance of the Presidency is rather difficult to reconcile with collective leadership.

Under the Communist regime, the gulf separating the President and the Cabinet has been greatly narrowed. The President has in fact become a premier, senior grade. The Premier is subordinate to the President, and their respective tasks are determined by the Political Bureau of the Party. The lines of control lead from the President's office to the ministries. The President also devotes time to the ceremonial and propagandist functions of the Party.

Government

The 1948 Constitution defines the government as the Cabinet, consisting of the Premier and the other ministers. In fact, however, the Communists have established a new type of government. The ministries are not merely agencies providing services and exercising limited supervision over the life of the nation as in former times, but they are responsible for the operation of all phases of political, economic, and social life. The ministers no longer formulate policies, but, instead, act as the agents of the top policy-making body of the Communist Party.

The Communists have transformed the government apparatus of the First Republic into a Soviet-type instrument for administering a nationalized economy. They created a planning office and established separate ministries for the individual branches of the economy. They more than doubled the size of the pre-1948 Cabinet, convinced that the most effective method of controlling each segment of the economy was through a specialized ministry. Top government leaders became responsible for administrative details. Subdivisions of ministries (such as the ministries of industry, agriculture, and internal trade) into new ministries dealing with particular sections of the economy, reached its climax in 1952, a time of serious economic difficulties. However, on January 31, 1953, a Presidium of the government, consisting of the Premier and 9 Deputy Premiers (in March 1953 increased to 10, and in September reduced to 5), was created to act as a policy-making high command, free from details of administration. It determined general lines of action, but left implementation to the more than thirty ministers. Each member of the Presidium was assigned a special field in which he supervised the activities of the ministers. This attempt at more efficient top government supervision over the economy was also abandoned after a little more than a seven-month trial. On September 11, 1953, the Presidium was dissolved, and the proliferating trend reversed: many ministries were amalgamated into larger units. These changes in the structure of the government were enacted under the constitutional law of May 18, 1950, which gave the government power to create or abolish ministries, subject to the President's approval.

Positions in the government are occupied by Communists who frequently are members of the Party's policy-making organ, the Political Bureau, formerly the Political Secretariat. They formulate policies as Party leaders, and then announce their decisions as government policy. The government's powers are extensive. It proposes changes in the ministerial structure and appointments to important positions, which are then officially made by the President; it decides "all the more important matters of political nature"; it introduces bills in the National Assembly and supervises the Slovak government organs, as well as the administration of the entire country; and it issues numerous governmental ordinances. The government's delegated legislative power is much more important than that of the National Assembly.

Public administration has been a problem to government leaders, who complain about inadequate execution of government decisions, and about the excessive bureaucratization, which brings about the creation of numerous new agencies and the issuance of multitudinous decrees. The Communists have attempted to solve this problem through personnel shake-ups and by cutting down bureaucratic jobs.

Local Government

The People's Committees are the organs of government on the local, district, and regional levels. They administer local and municipal affairs and execute orders of the central government on the local level.

After World War II, the Communists used the People's Committees to seize control over the central government. However, once this control was achieved, the Communists lost interest in the Committees, which acquired new significance only in 1954, when the Communists started to use them to raise economic production. Since the People's Committees serve as the government's liaison with the people, it was important to make this contact as agreeable and effective as possible. The Communists therefore reorganized and restaffed the People's Committees.

On May 16, 1954, eight years after their establishment, elections were held for the People's Committees on the local, district, and regional levels. These elections presented the voters with the choice of voting for the Communist-selected National Front ticket or of casting a blank ballot. According to the provisions of 1954, the People's Committees on all three levels are to be elected every three years.

The elected bodies on the local, district, and regional levels have the responsibility of enforcing orders of the central government. Thus, more citizens who consider themselves responsible to the electorate take part in the enforcement of centrally determined measures, and more people have an incentive to see that the government's plans are fulfilled. The central government can also shift the blame for failures on the population and on the local boards it elected.

Government of Slovakia

Slovakia is in a special constitutional position. It possesses a legislature, the Slovak National Council, and an administrative body, the Board of Commissioners. Nevertheless, the actual degree of self-government exercised by the Slovaks is insignificant.

The Slovak National Council was established as the leading organ of the Slovak nation during the uprising against the Germans and the Slovak puppet state in 1944. It was the body which agreed to the Kosice Program on behalf of the Slovaks on March 27, 1945. This agreement provided for a considerable amount of Slovak autonomy within the framework of a restored Czechoslovak Republic. Since the military liberation of Slovakia antedated that of the Czech lands, circumstances early in 1945 resulted in the continuation in Slovakia of a measure of legislative and administrative autonomy from Prague. Once the Czechoslovak government had re-established itself in Prague, however, attempts were made to limit the power of the Slovak National Council. The Constitution of 1948 registered the changes which had taken place, transforming the Slovak National Council into an advisory body with few legislative powers and no control over Slovakia's administration. Section 96 of the Constitution enumerates fields in which the Council is permitted to legislate: national culture, education, public health, local administration, local transportation, industry, and small trade. Even in these fields, however, the Council must not interfere with national programs and plans; the Council may fill in only those gaps which are left by the central government.

The subordination of the Council to the central government is manifest in that all laws passed by the Council have to be signed not only by the Chairman of the Board of Commissioners and the Commissioner who is entrusted with carrying out the law, but also by the Premier at Prague. If the Premier refuses to sign the bill on the ground that it conflicts with the Constitution, or with constitutional laws, that it transcends its authority or interferes with the proper functioning of the economic plan, he must then present the bill to his Cabinet, which has the final authority to veto the bill.

Prior to the 1948 Constitution, the Council had the right to appoint the Board of Commissioners with the approval of the Cabinet. The political crisis in October and November of 1947, however, gave the central government an opportunity to interfere in the appointment of Commissioners. The 1948 Constitution then transferred the power of appointing Commissioners to the central government.

The Council can pass resolutions concerning the work of the Board of Commissioners. In matters which fall within the legislative scope of the Council, the Board is nominally responsible to the Council. However, only the central government can appoint and recall members of the Board, and it is difficult to detect how the Council could assert its voice in the Board.

The Constitution does not provide for regular spring and fall meetings of the Slovak Council as it does for the National Assembly.

The Council is called to meeting by the Premier who can also adjourn or dissolve it. It has met for ceremonial functions to commemorate the anniversary of the Slovak uprising, and for infrequent business meetings. Its organization resembles that of the National Assembly. It elects a presidium which performs a function similar to that of the Presidium of the National Assembly. Committees are less important than in the Assembly because there is less business to transact.

The first elections for the National Council under the 1948 Constitution were held on November 28, 1954, in conjunction with elections to the National Assembly. Before this election, the composition of the Council was determined by the National Front, which allocated seats to the National Assembly in Slovakia on the basis of the 1948 election returns.

The Board of Commissioners is more powerful than the Council, but less representative of Slovak autonomy. Its composition has changed several times. Its size has varied with the creation or abolition of corresponding ministries in Prague, although the changes have not always been identical with those in Prague. The Board of Commissioners is the chief executive body in Slovakia, carrying out laws passed by the Slovak Council and issuing directives in fields under its jurisdiction. It is also the agency through which orders are transmitted from the central government to lower administrative organs in Slovakia. This latter function is the more important.

The 1948 Constitution gave the Board of Commissioners in Slovakia jurisdiction over all fields, except national defense, foreign policy, and foreign trade. In 1948, the commissariats (offices of the members of the Board of Commissioners) generally paralleled the Czechoslovak ministries. Since then, economic commissariats have been added, in keeping with a similar proliferation of ministries in Prague.

In transmitting orders from the central government to the lower government organs in Slovakia, the Board supplements the six Slovak regional People's Committees and compounds the hierarchical structure. While the Board is clearly above the regional People's Committees, it does not completely break the direct line of authority between the central government and the Committees. This creates a certain amount of administrative confusion and inefficiency. Although the Board of Commissioners is appointed by the central government, its membership is made up of Slovaks. Thus, it acts as a transformer of Czech directives into Slovak administrative orders.

The Board of Commissioners does not fulfill this function in all fields, however. In some areas, the Czech ministries operate from Prague directly through the People's Committees and other administrative channels. The central government operated for some time without intermediary Slovak Commissioners in the fields of justice, national security, heavy industry, and state farms. In these fields, the central government did not want to risk decentralization.

The Judiciary

From 1945 to 1948, the administration of justice was one of the fields which escaped Communist control, but after the February 1948 coup, this situation changed quickly. Of the 1920 judicial structure, the 1948 Constitution preserves only the Supreme Court and the Administrative Court. A Supreme Military Court is the third top level court. The Supreme Court is at the summit of a hierarchy of lower courts. The Administrative Court was to continue its function of protecting the citizen against bureaucratic or governmental injustice.

The courts were to be filled by professional judges, appointed for life by the President upon nomination by the government, and by laymen, appointed for shorter periods by the People's Committees and the Cabinet. Thus, while the Constitution stated that the judiciary would remain separate from the executive, the independence of the judiciary was destroyed by political appointments to the benches.

On October 30, 1952, the National Assembly passed a constitutional law which centralized the judicial system. The Supreme Court became the last instance of appeal; beneath it were two levels of general courts, the regional courts and the people's courts, as well as special courts, including military and arbitration courts. Military courts were given a larger jurisdiction, including civilians involved in acts concerning the country's security. In an accompanying law, the responsibility of the courts was defined as "the protection of the social order and governmental structure of the Republic, of the building of socialism, and of socialist ownership."

The constitutional law of October 30, 1952, followed Soviet example in creating a Procurator General's Office. The Procurator General, appointed by the President upon nomination by the government, is also responsible to the government. His main task is to see that all laws are properly carried out and observed, both by government agencies and by private citizens, and to take action in all cases where he finds evidence of illegal activities.

Police, Para-Military, and Military Organizations

Although not mentioned in the Constitution, the pillars on which the power of Communist government lies and the instruments by which it controls the population are the police, the para-military, and the military organizations. In a totalitarian society, where political consensus is replaced by direct or indirect coercion, such organizations are of first importance and should be mentioned in connection with the implementation of government policy.

The Communists used the agencies of state security in the annihilation of all opposition after 1948. Internal security forces also play a role in the Communist plan to achieve set economic objectives. The regime's attempt to achieve high production without normal incentives for the workers, such as personal security, adequate real wages or improved social status, requires the use of threats backed by state power.

Internal Security Forces

The organization of internal security forces has passed through several stages since 1948. From February 1948 to May 1950, the security forces remained under the jurisdiction of the Ministry of Interior, headed by Vaclav Nosek. This Ministry was infiltrated by Communists before February 1948, and fell completely under their control after the coup. However, the Communist Party considered it too traditional an agency to cope with the special problems confronting a militant dictatorship embarked upon a social and economic revolution. A new ministry, the Ministry of National Security, was established on May 23, 1950, under Ladislav Kopriva and, later, Karol Bacilek. The prominence of these two men in Communist politics indicates the importance which the Party attached to the Ministry. For three years, from 1950 to 1953, the Ministry of Interior and the Ministry of National Security functioned side by side, the former concerning itself with the more traditional aspects of internal administration, while the latter assumed complete jurisdiction over security. On September 11, 1953, after the deaths of Stalin and Gottwald, the Ministry of National Security was abolished, and the security forces were again brought under the jurisdiction of the Ministry of Interior.

The Ministry of Interior and the Ministry of National Security operated on the regional, district, and local levels through the respective People's Committees. Security operations are the most important function of the People's Committees. The security department, which occupies a special position among the departments of the People's Committees, was organized to "defend and strengthen the people's democratic installations; enforce the fulfillment of planned economic targets, and protect the economy from criminal and other detrimental activities; combat exploitation; protect crops; execute the regulations on deportations, police supervision, and forced labor camps; supervise registration of the population; watch over the loyalty of citizens and keep delinquents in check; cooperate in the tasks connected with the defense of the country and protect the security of persons and property."

There exist several separate, though coordinate organs through which the security function has been carried out: regular police, frontier guards, internal guards, and, most important, state security forces.

Regular Police. The uniformed regular police (SNB) perform the customary policing functions: the maintenance of order and the enforcing of laws. It has, however, additional functions, such as supervision of forced labor camps and granting assistance to the secret police in the preparation of political trials. While most of the regular police forces are attached to People's Committees on the three levels, there exist also some special formations which are mobile and can be used anywhere in the country as the need arises. The uniforms of the regular police are distinguished by blue epaulets.

Frontier Guards. Two functions originally carried out by the regular police, border protection and factory protection, have been shifted to specially constituted organs. The protection of state frontiers was entrusted to the frontier guards on July 11, 1951. While the frontier guards resemble the regular police in many ways, they have special military characteristics. They are organized into military formations (i.e., brigades, battalions, companies, platoons, and squads), and function as auxiliary army units. This specially constituted guard was organized by the regime to curtail attempts to escape from the country and to diminish contacts with the outside world. Service in the frontier guards is counted toward the fulfillment of a citizen's military obligation. The frontier guards wear uniforms distinguished from the regular police by green epaulets and a collar insignia depicting a dog's head.

Internal Guards. The protection of factories and other economic installations was considered sufficiently important to warrant the creation of a new corps, the internal guard, on August 8, 1952. This corps combined functions previously carried out by the people's militia and the regular police. The people's militia, originally a corps of armed Communist workers entrusted ostensibly with protection of factories against "enemies of the working class" in the days before 1948, but actually a para-military arm of the Communist Party held in readiness for the coming struggle for state control, lost its original purpose and proved unsatisfactory when the Party began its program to increase production. Apparently, the regular police were not suited for this task either. A special force, the internal guard, was therefore created on the Soviet pattern. It was their duty to protect important industrial establishments against "attacks by thieves and diversionists." They were to cope with intentional or unintentional acts of industrial sabotage and to guard state property against theft, neglect, and any other form of waste and plunder. The internal guards wear uniforms with violet epaulets and collar insignia of a cogwheel with swords.

State Security Forces. The most important and the most feared organ with which the regime maintains its stranglehold is the state security forces (STB), or secret police. This branch is concerned with the protection of the state, not of the public. The secret police is responsible for ferreting out "hostile elements" and for safeguarding the position of the regime. It checks on government departments, as well as on factories, labor trade unions, and other mass organizations. The STB employs informers and supervises an espionage network, which reaches even beyond the frontiers of Czechoslovakia. STB units, like those of the SNB, are tied to the People's Committees on the local levels, with special STB squads available for use in any part of the state. Some members of the state security forces wear uniforms with red epaulets, but many are not uniformed.

The state makes great effort to recruit able young men devoted to the regime for its security forces and it offers special rewards to STB recruits. They enjoy special privileges and are paid relatively well. All the security organs are thoroughly trained and indoctrinated. The Party is careful to place its most trusted members in the key positions.

The power of security forces in a totalitarian country such as Communist Czechoslovakia is due to lack of public control over their operations, and the inability of citizens to protect themselves. The men who control the security forces hold a special position of strength, which creates mistrust on the part of other Communist leaders. The Communists have attempted to solve this problem by interweaving Party organizations in the security forces at all levels. Party leaders are subject to internal Party espionage, which seeks to prevent any one group from gaining complete control over the organs of power. With the help of this system, leaders who try to increase their power can be destroyed.

The Armed Forces

Development Before February 1948. While Czechoslovak armies have never been involved in a major military engagement on home territory, they have played an important role in the history of the

Czechoslovak state. The Czechoslovak army in exile was a key factor in bringing independence to Czechoslovakia in World War I. The role of the Czech and Slovak military units in Siberia in 1918 served the cause of a free Czechoslovakia. Czechoslovaks, captured by the Russians, but organized into independent military units in 1917, were in a strategic position from which to influence the course of the Russian civil war, Allied intervention in Russia, and the fate of their own nation. As the first foreign force on the side of the Allies engaged in warfare with the Bolsheviks, the Czechoslovak legions became a significant factor in Allied policy.

Similar, but smaller legions were also organized in Serbia, Italy, and France during World War I from among captured Czechs and Slovaks and from among those who lived in the West. The independent Czechoslovak state gave full recognition to the services rendered by these legions, and they were held in high public esteem. Legionnaires, particularly those from Russia, were an important factor in the army of the First Republic, as well as in the reconstituted post-1945 army.

There was considerable French influence in the Czechoslovak army prior to 1938. During World War I, Czechoslovak troops, including the legions fighting in Russia, were under the control of French military leaders. French influence in the Czechoslovak army was further strengthened by France's political and military interests in Central Europe after the war. French generals served as advisors to the growing Czechoslovak army in the twenties and thirties, and French military concepts became the basis of Czechoslovak military thought.

Following the rise of Hitler and the conclusion of a mutual assistance pact with the Soviet Union on May 16, 1935, the Czechoslovak army was prepared for a common Czechoslovak-Soviet war effort against Hitler's Germany. Anti-Bolshevik sentiments were played down. However, the army constituted under the First Republic was not put to a test in 1938. After the Munich Pact, the army was dissolved, though many of the remnants participated in the fight against Germany. Officers and soldiers went to Great Britain via Poland and France, and there joined the new army under the political leadership of the Czechoslovak government in exile. Other fragments of the army ended up in the Soviet Union, where a Soviet-controlled Czechoslovak battalion was formed. This expanded into an army corps, as many soldiers of the Slovak army deserted to the Russian side. Finally, some officers of the pre-Munich army joined the resistance movement and took an active part in the Slovak uprising in 1944 and the Prague uprising in the last days of World War II, in

May 1945. Out of these three elements, Czechoslovakia's army was reconstituted after the close of World War II.

The core of the reconstituted army was the Czechoslovak army corps organized in the Soviet Union under Soviet auspices. This was under the command of General Ludvik Svoboda, who was then nominally independent in politics, but who became a Communist Party member after the coup. Until 1948, some remnants of the "Western" army and of the domestic resistance movement remained an important part of Czechoslovakia's armed forces.

Even before the coup, the Communists had made considerable headway in their quest for control of the army. The Soviet Army was in control of most of Czechoslovakia until the end of November 1945, and thereafter remained a threatening force on Czechoslovakia's eastern, northern, and southern frontiers. Czechoslovakia's policy of friendly relations with the Soviet Union between 1945 and 1948 gave the Communists a further opportunity to curtail pro-Western influence in the army. Nevertheless, complete Communist control was not achieved, and later Communist reorganizations of the army indicate that the Communists were concerned with its loyalty.

Development After the Communist Coup. Communist policy since the coup has had two aims: to create a loyal army and to make this army an effective force in the event of an East-West conflict.

Loyalty means allegiance not only to the Czechoslovak Communist regime, but also to the Soviet Union. Creation of a loyal officer corps was among the most important measures to achieve this end. Since many officers in the higher echelons had a legionnaire background, supplemented by French indoctrination and service under British leadership in World War II, they were suspect to the Communists, who were inclined to eliminate such personnel. On the other hand, the Czechoslovak Communist leaders had no military experience and lacked men trained in military leadership. They were thus forced to rely on Party members placed in key positions to control officers of proven ability but uncertain loyalty. Many non-Communist officers remained in the Communist-controlled army, avowing their loyalty to the new regime. The Communists kept them only until Communist personnel replacements became available.

The Communists preferred officers of working class origin. In June 1954, Alexej Cepicka, Minister of Defense, claimed that as of January 1, 1954, 69.1 per cent of the officers were of working class origin, while 29.3 per cent were of peasant, white collar, or small trader background. Cepicka also claimed that the Party had sent more than 3,500 functionaries into the army. Of the high command, 61.7 per cent were Communist Party members. In all military formations and units, Party and Czechoslovak Youth League units were formed. Party control was exercised through the selection and indoctrination of new officers and the honeycombing of the army with Party functionaries.

Alexej Cepicka, son-in-law of Klement Gottwald, had replaced General Ludvik Svoboda in April 1950, and was responsible for consolidating Party control over the army. Cepicka held a high position in the Party, having previously brought the churches and the administration of justice under Communist control. He was dropped from the position of Minister of Defense in April 1956, and was replaced by Colonel General Bohumir Lomsky.

By reorganizing the officer corps and strengthening the position of the Party in the army, Cepicka greatly increased Soviet influence in the Czechoslovak army. Soviet officers were attached to Czechoslovak army units as specialists and advisors. The army became dependent on Soviet equipment, weapons, and ammunition. Czechoslovak training and operational practices were modeled on those of the Soviet Union; officers and men were indoctrinated with the need for closer Soviet-Czechoslovak friendship. Nevertheless, concern with the effectiveness of the army frequently led the Communists to tolerate officers of "politically doubtful background" in order to use their technical and military abilities. Training of army recruits was accelerated, and in June 1954, Cepicka claimed that the extent and scope of the training program had been greatly expanded. Joint maneuvers with other satellite armies, such as the Polish army, were occasionally undertaken.

To improve the effectiveness of the Czechoslovak army, the Communists have sought to create awareness of a military threat to Czechoslovak independence. The source of the threat is allegedly the United States, but the actual instrument of destruction is identified as a nationalistic, unrepentant Germany. The Communists hope that the traditional hatred of the Germans will provide the Czechoslovak army with sufficient motivating force and will overcome any latent dissatisfaction with the Communist regime or with the Soviet Union.

6. PROPAGANDA

Rudolf Sturm

The First Republic, 1918-1938

Goals and Techniques

Before World War II, Czechoslovak propaganda was primarily intended to supply information rather than to persuade or indoctrinate. The chief media of propaganda in this period were the press and the radio. Official use of mass rallies, lecture tours, or literary publications to promote governmental policy was inconceivable. If a play or a film with a political taint had appeared, the people would have ignored it and the press would have ridiculed it. A series of booklets and studies dealing with such subjects as the German minority in Czechoslovakia and the Italo-Abyssinian war, were published in the thirties by Orbis, the government publishing house, but these were designed for foreign consumption.

Before World War II, Czechoslovakia did not have a unified ministry or department dealing with propaganda. The Office of the Council of Ministers controlled the greater part of domestic information, while the Ministry of Foreign Affairs conducted Czechoslovak propaganda abroad. The Ministry of Education was in charge of a part of the cultural propaganda abroad and civic education at home. All three departments jointly governed Czechoslovak broadcasting. There were two government printing offices, one controlled by the Office of the Council of Ministers and the other by the Ministry of National Defense. On September 16, 1938, during the Munich crisis, President Edward Benes appointed former diplomat Hugo Vavrecka Cabinet Minister, with the purpose of unifying various information agencies into one Ministry of Information. Vavrecka remained in office only until the end of November and hardly had time to prepare a blueprint for the Ministry. With the inauguration of Emil Hacha as President, the idea was abandoned.

Press

In prewar Czechoslovakia, the main source of official news was *Ceskoslovenska tiskova kancelar* (Czechoslovak Press Bureau), a government agency controlled by the Office of the Council of Ministers. Its news was supplied to Czech and Slovak newspapers, and was also dispatched abroad. The *CTK,* as the agency datelined its releases, was supposed to be a self-supporting commercial enterprise, but never was.

The Office of the Council of Ministers published the daily newspaper *Prazske noviny* (Prague News); however, this had less influence on public opinion than the publications of the various political parties, which served as vehicles to support the government's domestic and foreign policy.

The Czechoslovak Communist press before World War II was in a separate category. The Communist Party opposed the government in every respect. Only after 1934, when Czechoslovakia established diplomatic relations with the Soviet Union, did the Communists support Czechoslovak foreign policy, including collaboration with the League of Nations, France, and the Little Entente. Their press in the middle thirties and until its abolition in 1938 followed the government line, especially in opposing Nazism and Fascism and in preparing the population for a defensive war with Germany.

Radio

The Czechoslovak Telegraph Act of April 23, 1923, declared that it was the exclusive right of the government to establish and maintain telegraphs, telephones, radiotelegraphs, and radiotelephones and that the Ministry of Posts and Telegraphs might grant licenses for the exercise of this right. During the same year, a private corporation, organized in Prague under the name Radiojournal, obtained a license from the government and began broadcasting. Two years later, the government became a partner in Radiojournal, owning 51 per cent of the capital, and was represented in the corporation by the Office of the Council of Ministers and the Ministries of Posts, Foreign Affairs, Education, and Finance. Owners of receiving sets were required by law to obtain licenses, which were granted by local post offices, and to pay a monthly fee of 10 crowns (about $0.35), which was collected by the Ministry of Posts.

Czechoslovak broadcasting expanded rapidly, and by 1938 there were eight stations which broadcast from early morning until late at night; the number of owners of radio receiving sets in 1938 exceeded one million. Beginning in 1925, Station Prague broadcast three times a week in German, which was later extended to a daily program, and in May 1938, when Station Prague II was completed, it devoted all its time to programs in German. Station Moravska Ostrava broadcast some of its programs in Polish; Bratislava and Kosice, in addition to their regular Slovak programs, broadcast in Hungarian; and Station Chust broadcast in Ruthenian and Ukrainian.

In an effort to strengthen the bond with Czechs and Slovaks living abroad, numerous programs were broadcast in Czech and Slovak over short wave. As the increasing importance of radio in foreign propaganda was realized, the government broadcast in several languages for listeners abroad.

Foreign Propaganda

The Czechoslovak government used the services of the Ministry of Foreign Affairs and the Ministry of Education for propaganda abroad. The Third Section of the Ministry of Foreign Affairs, endeavored to win favor for Czechoslovakia in the press of foreign countries, invited outstanding visitors from abroad, and published booklets and periodicals in several foreign languages. The Ministry assisted anti-Communist refugees from the Soviet Union and anti-Nazi refugees from Germany. It supervised the activities of press attachés, stationed in Czechoslovak legations in every important foreign country, and subsidized such organizations as the Czechoslovak Association for the League of Nations, and the Czechoslovak branch of the Coudenhove-Kalergi's *Paneuropa* movement.

The state publishing house, Orbis, controlled by the Ministry of Foreign Affairs, published a number of propaganda works in French, English, and other European languages as well as several periodicals, all designed for circulation abroad. A German daily paper, *Prager Presse;* a French weekly magazine, *L'Europe Centrale;* an English fortnightly, *Central European Observer;* and a Russian monthly, *Central'naya Europa* (Central Europe) were published by Orbis. The principal activities of the Ministry of Education in the field of foreign cultural relations and propaganda consisted in maintaining a Czechoslovak high school in Vienna; organizing and subsidizing an exchange program for high school students in France, Bulgaria, Yugoslavia, and elsewhere; subsidizing schools, libraries, and societies of Czechs and Slovaks in Austria, Yugoslavia, France, the United States, and other countries.

1938-1945

The Protectorate of Bohemia and Moravia

The Second Republic, from October 1938 to March 1939, represented the transition from a democratic regime to a totalitarian state. This transition found its expression primarily in propaganda. Shortly after the Munich Pact had been implemented by German occupation of the border territories, and Slovakia and Ruthenia became autonomous, the new government began to turn away from France, the Little Entente, the Soviet Union, and the League of Nations, declaring that these did not help Czechoslovakia in the Munich crisis, and that the new situation precluded the continuation of the old alliances. A new relationship with Germany was born. Nazism was no longer represented as an enemy. Western democracies, Jews, and Edward Benes were blamed for all the nation's woes. Several democratic papers and magazines were abolished, and others were compelled to toe the new pro-German line. All Czech political parties were absorbed, under German pressure, into two organizations, *Narodni jednota* (National Unity) and *Strana prace* (Labor Party). The Communist Party and its press were suppressed.

The German occupation of Prague in March 1939 and the establishment of the Protectorate of Bohemia and Moravia found the media of information, especially press and radio, well on the way toward Nazification. The two political parties then in existence were compelled to merge into one totalitarian party called *Narodni sourucenstvi* (National Union). The Commission for Press and Propaganda of this new body took over all the newspapers and magazines of former political parties. The German daily *Der Neue Tag* became the most influential paper of the Protectorate. The *CTK* was cut off from all outside communication and became a translation service for the dispatches of the German News Agency.

On the model of the German *Kraft durch Freude* and the Italian *Dopolavoro,* a new movement, *Radost ze Zivota* (The Joy of Life), was founded to organize recreation for the people while indoctrinating them with Nazism. The newly created Central National Union of Employees (NOUZ) and the Central Association of Czech Farmers were also used for the dissemination of Nazi propaganda. The Czech Union for Cooperation with the Germans was entrusted with an especially difficult task: to encourage Czech friendship for the Germans, and to popularize the righteousness of the Nazi cause and the good fortune of Europe in being offered Third Reich leadership. The League Against Bolshevism was another propagandist organization, conducting campaigns against Benes, the Freemasons, and the Bolsheviks, who were equally blamed for the downfall of the Czechs.

The most important among the official and semi-official organizations disseminating Nazi ideology was *Kuratorium pro vychovu mladeze v Cechach a na Morave* (Council for the Education of Youth in Bohemia and Moravia). Government Decrees No. 187 of May 28, 1942 and No. 189 of May 30, 1942 subjected all Aryan (non-Jewish) Protectorate nationals from 10 to 18 years of age to compulsory youth service, in which they would receive "physical, spiritual, and moral education." The management of the youth service was given to *Kuratorium* which, from 1942 to the end of the war, conducted thorough indoctrination of Czech youth either directly by organizing lectures, expositions, courses in German, discussions, and mass rallies, or in connection with various recreation projects, sports events, ski trips, and visits to picturesque regions of the Protectorate.

On January 15, 1942, the Protectorate's government issued Decree No. 14 establishing *Urad lidove osvety* (Office of People's Enlightenment) as a central department for "cultural-political matters." On June 15, 1942, its name was changed to *Ministerstvo lidove osvety* (Ministry of People's Enlightenment) and as such it functioned until the end of the war. The Ministry maintained rigid control over all mass communication media. The radio, although officially not under the Ministry, and the press, received detailed instruction as to what to say and what not to mention.

The Slovak State

The development of official information and propaganda in Slovakia after 1938 followed the pattern of that in Bohemia and Moravia, with only minor changes. Practically all media of mass communication were controlled or directly operated by *Urad propagandy* (Office of Propaganda). The Slovak People's Party absorbed all other political parties and became, next to the government, the standard-bearer of the Solvak state ideology. Both the government and the Party endeavored to persuade public opinion that the Czechs, Jews, and Bolsheviks were the real enemies of the Slovaks, while the Third Reich and Hitler were their benefactors; that the Slovak state was the fulfillment of the dreams and yearnings of every good Slovak; that after the Hungarian and Czech oppression there had come at last freedom for Slovakia; that German victory in the war was necessary; and that Slovakia would always remain at the side of Hitler's Germany. These tenets were propagated in *Slovak,* the Party's main organ, in *Gardista* (Guardsman), the daily paper of the Hlinka Guards (a para-military organization attached to the Party), and in all other Party periodicals. The same beliefs were disseminated by radio broadcasts and by pamphlets and books published or subsidized by the Office of Propaganda.

Most films shown during the war were of German and Italian production. *Slovfilm* (Slovak film company) made only documentary films and newsreels, which served as media of pro-Nazi propaganda. The Germans in Slovakia, like those in the Protectorate, had a privileged position. Their daily paper, *Grenzbote,* published in Bratislava, and German broadcasts on the Slovak radio, were of considerable importance. Nonconformist opinions were not tolerated by the government, except in some religious periodicals which were able to maintain a measure of independence. Literary production also remained relatively free of official interference.

The Czechoslovak Government in Exile

Czechoslovakia anti-Nazi emigres organized their own information service, first in France in 1939 through the Czechoslovak National Committee, and later in England through the government in exile. In Paris, even before the creation of the National Committee, a group of exiles started a news service, issued mimeographed bulletins, and supplied the French press with anti-Nazi articles on Czechoslovakia. In addition, a weekly magazine, *Cesko-slovensky boj* (Czecho-Slovak Struggle) was published in Paris. Broadcasts in Czech and Slovak were organized and beamed to Czechoslovakia over French radio stations; a periodical, *Nase vojsko* (Our Army), was published for Czechoslovak units in France; a French magazine, *L'Europe Centrale,* was issued as a continuation of the one published in Prague before 1939.

After the defeat of France in 1940, most of the Czechoslovak emigres transferred to England, where the Czechoslovak government in exile was set up, and a large information service was organized as part of the Ministry of Foreign Affairs. A similar department, called the Czechoslovak Information Service, was established in the United States.

In the emigres' propaganda and the government in exile information activities, a fourfold purpose is discernible:

First, to inform the Allies and the neutral countries of the resistance of the people in the Protectorate of Bohemia and Moravia and in the Slovak state against Nazism, the Germans, and their domestic collaborators; to persuade the Allied and other friendly governments that revocation of the Munich Pact and the re-establishment of Czechoslovakia within pre-Munich boundaries was a matter of justice and international necessity.

Second, to inform people at home of favorable developments abroad, of Allied successes, and German setbacks; to persuade them of the inevitability of Axis defeat; to encourage them to resist the enemy, both Germans and quislings.

Third, to mobilize the Czechs and Slovaks in the free world for the Allied war effort; to gain their support for the liberation movement, and to enlist the young for service in the Czechoslovak Army abroad.

Fourth, to prepare the atmosphere, both at home and abroad, for the necessity of orienting Czechoslovak foreign policy not exclusively to the West, as before 1938, but also toward the Soviet Union.

In England, the government in exile secured radio time from the BBC for broadcasts in Czech and Slovak beamed to Czechoslovakia. A fortnightly magazine, *The Central European Observer*, was issued for English-speaking countries, and a weekly, *Cechoslovak* (Czechoslovak), was published in Czech and Slovak. Lectures were organized throughout the United Kingdom, and close relations were maintained with the Czechoslovak Institutes in London and Edinburgh. A new *CTK* was set up in London, issuing bulletins in Czech, Slovak, and English, and a number of propaganda booklets and documents were published by the Ministry of Foreign Affairs. The Czechoslovak Army "somewhere in England" issued a mimeographed daily paper, *Nase noviny* (Our News), and the Ministry of National Defense in London published a magazine, *Vojenske rozhledy* (Army Review).

The Czechoslovak Information Service in the United States, operating from New York, published information bulletins in Czech and Slovak, English, Spanish, Yiddish, and Ruthenian. The New York office of the *CTK* supplied the Czech and Slovak language newspapers in the United States with daily releases. From 1940 until the end of the war, the Information Service broadcast news and commentaries in Czech and Slovak over Station WRUL for listeners in Czechoslovakia and for Czechs and Slovaks in Africa and South America. The Information Service also sponsored a number of lectures in the United States and Canada, subsidized publication of several books, and throughout the war maintained close relations with Czechoslovak-American organizations.

The attitude of the Communists among Czechoslovak emigres, until June 1941, was that of indifference toward the liberation movement abroad and the government in exile. However, with the Soviet Union's entry into the war, they began to participate in various propaganda activities of the Czechoslovak government in exile. In England, they published their own periodical, *Mlade Ceskoslovensko* (Young Czechoslovakia). In the Soviet Union they broadcast over Radio Moscow to Czechoslovakia, although it was a broadcast of the Soviet government rather than of the Czechoslovak Communists.

The Postwar Period

With the end of the war and the re-establishment of the Czechoslovak Republic, a complete change occurred. Government propaganda became the domain, with minor exceptions, of the Communist

Party, which geared it from the very beginning toward the sovietization of the country. Until 1948, the year of the Communist coup, a certain duality can be discerned in propaganda. The Communists clearly and unequivocally asserted that their—and the people's—goal was the transformation of Czechoslovakia into a socialist state, a "people's democracy." They declared that the main ally of Czechoslovakia was the Soviet Union, and that Czechoslovakia would remain forever at its side. The non-Communists also declared that the country must cooperate with the Soviet Union, but at the same time remain true to Western democracies. "Both the East and the West," was their key phrase. The Communists and the non-Communists alike were against Nazism and Fascism, in favor of the transfer of the Germans and Magyars from Czechoslovakia, and for strict observance of the demilitarization of Germany and its former allies.

Communist propaganda had to work against many odds: the traditional individualism of the Czech and Slovak people; the predominance of Catholicism; and the Western orientation of the country, which has exercised a strong influence throughout its modern history. An even more immediate reason for the populace to look West rather than East was the substantial material aid coming from numerous sources in the United States. The political impact of these one-way economic relations was difficult to combat.

On the other hand, several factors were helping Communist propaganda. Ever since 1848, pro-Russian sentiment had been strong among the Czechs and Slovaks, many of whom regarded the "Big Slavic Brother" as their natural and effective defender against the Germans. The anti-German feelings of practically everyone after 1945, the assertedly decisive role of the Soviet Union in defeating Germany, and the allegedly leading part of the Czechoslovak Communist Party in the underground movement during the war were additional factors which helped to influence many in accepting Communist propaganda. Disillusionment with France and England for their role in the Munich Pact also tended to turn the sentiments of the population from the West to the Soviet Union. The Communists also controlled practically all government media of mass communication, and the propaganda apparatus of the Communist Party was superior, both in numbers and in thoroughness, to that of the anti-Communist parties.

Since the 1948 coup, Czechoslovak propaganda has been dominated exclusively by Communist ideology and controlled by the Communist Party. All pretense of collaboration with the West, as well as tolerance of non-Communist ideologies in public life, have been eliminated. Sovietization of the country and obligatory admiration for everything Soviet were stepped up. Only the materialistic point of view in politics, literature, science, and the arts was proclaimed acceptable. Government and Party propaganda became inseparable, enlisting not only the usual media of mass communication, but also the whole government apparatus, trade unions, schools, mass organizations such as the Youth League, the Czechoslovak-Soviet Friendship League, the Peace Defenders' Committee, and the Women's Committee, the churches, and even history. Drives were conducted for increasing production in industry and agriculture, for farmers' cooperatives, and for improvement in work discipline. Campaigns were organized against capitalism and the West, especially the United States, against bourgeois nationalism and religious superstitions, against Thomas G. Masaryk, Edward Benes, and pre-Munich Czechoslovakia, against Czechoslovak refugees, the Free Europe Committee, and the Council of Free Czechoslovakia.

Government Apparatus

On April 2, 1945, President Benes issued Decree No. 1, providing that the Czechoslovak Republic was to be administered by sixteen Ministries, including the Ministry of Information. He appointed Vaclav Kopecky, an old-time Communist, Minister of Information. Within a short time, Kopecky had organized a vast propaganda machine, merging in his Ministry the Protectorate's Ministry of Public Enlightenment and several smaller units from the Ministries of Education and Foreign Affairs, and had assumed for it many new functions. In five out of the six divisions of the Ministry, he appointed as heads well-known Communist writers and poets.

The First Division of the Ministry of Information dealt with domestic information. It reviewed both the domestic and foreign press; published a daily newspaper and a weekly magazine in English; polled public opinion on various political, economic, and cultural questions; studied rumors circulating among the population; and maintained large archives of clippings, photographs, and documents.

The Second Division was charged with administration of the press. It licensed and supervised the periodical press; maintained an index of all Czechoslovak newspapermen; supervised the Union of Czechoslovak Journalists; jointly with the Ministry of Foreign Affairs, appointed press attachés to Czechoslovak embassies and legations abroad; supervised the *CTK*, and allocated newsprint to publishers of periodicals. The allocation of newsprint made it possible for the Ministry and thus for the Communist Party to determine and control the volume of circulation of each newspaper.

The Third Division licensed and supervised the publication of books; allocated paper to book publishers; supervised the government publishing house, Orbis; and collected and filed copies of all books published in Czechoslovakia, which publishers were required by law to deposit at the Ministry.

The Fourth Division had under its jurisdiction all matters pertaining to broadcasting, both domestic and foreign, including a vast monitoring service. The Fifth Division was charged with the production and distribution of films and with matters connected with movie theaters. The Sixth Division was responsible for cultural relations with foreign countries and with the Czech and Slovak societies in these countries. Among its functions were the promotion of Czechoslovak literature, music, arts, and folklore abroad, and the supervision of Czechoslovak cultural attachés, who were appointed by this division after consultation with the Ministry of Foreign Affairs. It was also responsible for acquainting the Czechoslovak public with the cultures of foreign countries.

A Commissariat of Information was created in Bratislava to deal with domestic propaganda in Slovakia. Communist and non-Communist influences were better balanced here than in Bohemia and Moravia, but after the 1948 coup, the Communists took over all media of mass communication previously controlled by their adversaries.

On January 31, 1953, the Ministry of Information was abolished. Its functions were taken over by the Office of the Council of Ministers, the Ministry of Education, and two newly created government agencies—the State Commission for Cultural Relations with Foreign Countries and the State Commission for the Arts. Vaclav Kopecky was appointed Deputy Premier, but remained the regime's mouthpiece in propaganda and arbiter in cultural matters. On September 11, 1953, a Ministry of Culture was established with Kopecky as its head. It assumed all the propaganda and cultural functions of the old Ministry of Information. Ladislav Stoll, a leading Communist theoretician, was appointed Minister of Culture and Ondrej Klokoc, a school teacher by profession and a prewar Communist became Commissioner of Culture.

An important role in the propaganda system is reserved to the Communist Party, which maintains a special section for agitation, propaganda, and culture (Agitprop) as part of its Central Committee. Until the 1948 coup, Agitprop worked more or less sub rosa, so that not even the staff of the Ministry of Information was aware of its connection with government propaganda.

Of great consequence in government propaganda is the Year of Party Schooling, which the Party conducts annually, usually from October through March, for training hundreds of new propagandists. It is interesting to note that since the coup the Party has used freely the term *propagandista,* while before 1948 propagandists were called "cultural-political workers." As a part of the Year of Party Schooling, main radio stations conduct a Marxism-Leninism "School of the Air" in weekly broadcasts. In all district towns, the Party maintains centers for the study and direction of Communist propaganda.

Press

The variety of daily newspapers and periodicals at the disposal of the Ministry of Information in 1945 was not considered adequate by the Communists. With the assistance of the Agitprop section, the Ministry started publishing a number of dailies, weeklies, and monthlies, disguised as organs of the trade unions, youth organizations, Farmers' Central Union, and the like. Thus, as early as 1945, the Communists controlled the majority of the press. The Party itself published from 1945 to the time of the coup the following daily papers: *Rude pravo* (Red Right) in Prague, *Rovnost* (Equality) in Brno, *Straz severu* (Guard of the North) in Liberec, *Nova svoboda* (New Freedom) in Ostrava, *Pravda* (Truth) in Bratislava, *Ciel* (Target) in Zilina, *Vychodoslovenska pravda* (East Slovakian Truth) in Kosice, and a Polish daily *Glos ludu* (People's Voice) in Tesin. The Communist-controlled Revolutionary Trade Union Movement published *Prace* (Work) in Prague and *Praca* in Bratislava; the Farmers' Union published *Zemedelske noviny* (Agricultural News) in Prague; the Youth Organization published *Mlada fronta* in Prague. The major non-Communist newspapers included the Czech Socialist Party's *Svobodne slovo* (Free Word), published in Prague and *Slovo naroda* (Word of the Nation), published in Brno; the Catholic People's Party's *Lidova demokracie* (People's Democracy), published in Prague and *Lidova obroda* (People's Regeneration), published in Brno; the Social Democratic Party's *Pravo lidu* (People's Right), published in Prague; and the Slovak Democratic Party's *Cas* (Time), published in Bratislava. The Czechoslovak Army published two nonpolitical dailies, *Obrana lidu* (People's Defense) in Prague and *Obrana ludu* in Bratislava. In addition, two democratic papers with no party affiliation were published in Prague: *Svobodne noviny* (Free News) of the Union of Cultural Organizations, and *Narodni osvobozeni* (National Liberation) of the Organization of Czechoslovak Legionaries of World War I.

Discounting the two neutral newspapers of the Army, during the crucial period from 1945 to 1948, the Communists had at their disposal twelve major newspapers, while the democratic forces had eight. The Communists' advantage over their opponents was further accentuated by the greater circulation of their newspapers and the larger format of two of them, *Rude pravo* and *Zemedelske noviny*.

About the same ratio prevailed between Communist and anti-Communist weeklies and monthlies. In addition, the *CTK*, controlled by the Ministry of Information, was headed by a Communist, Richard Slansky, brother of the then Secretary General of the Communist Party, Rudolf Slansky.

Two other types of Czechoslovak periodicals, factory papers and village papers, should be mentioned. *Rude pravo* reported on August 2, 1952 that more than 1,300 factories, plants, and mines published over two million copies of factory newspapers every month. The factory branch of the Communist Party is responsible for the political line in each of these organizations. Village papers, controlled by the Ministry of Agriculture, are periodicals published in every district for villages, collective farms, and individual farmers. Other important components of press indoctrination are the regional Party weeklies or semi-weeklies and the ideological and literary periodicals published by the Party or by various semi-official bodies.

The Party and the government see that everyone in Czechoslovakia receives reading material in his own language. There is the Polish daily paper, *Glos ludu,* and the Magyar daily, *Uj Szo* (New World) published in Bratislava. The Revolutionary Trade Unions issue twice a week *Aufbau und Frieden* for its German members, and semi-monthly *Democrazia Popolare* for Italian workers in Czechoslovakia. The Ministry of Education publishes two magazines for the German youth, *Freundschaft* and *Das rote Halstuch.* For the Ruthenian and Ukrainian speaking population, *Druzhno vpered,* a Ruthenian magazine, and *Dukla,* a Ukrainian quarterly for literature and the arts, appear.

Due to the shortage of newsprint after 1945, only 20 per cent of the space of any individual edition was permitted to be taken up by advertising. This ratio was lowered after 1948 to only 2.5 per cent. Economic considerations, among others, led the Communists to decrease the number of daily papers from 28 in 1948 to 20 in 1949 and to 13 in 1953. Many important newspapers and periodicals were abolished, and three periodicals of the Central Committee of the Communist Party, *Funkcionar* (Functionary), *Propagandista* (Propagandist), and *Slovo agitatora* (Agitator's Word), were discontinued in 1954 and superseded by the fortnightly magazine *Zivot strany* (Party's Life). The press of the Youth Organization does not seem to be affected by any economy measure. Besides the daily paper *Mlada fronta,* a host of juvenile periodicals are published on the model of Soviet children's periodicals.

The Communists pay attention to the organization of newspapermen. By Law No. 101 of May 28, 1947, dealing with the Union of Czechoslovak Journalists, only members of the Union are permitted to be employed as editors. The Union, supervised by the Ministry of Information, is given disciplinary powers over its members. During the 1948 coup, the Union barred from its ranks ninety-eight anti-Communist journalists in Prague and forty-five in Bratislava, so that they were not permitted to continue their work as editors. With their staunchest adversaries thus eliminated, the Communists forced the remaining opponents into submission by refusing to allocate news-print to their newspapers and by inducing the typesetters (whose union they controlled) to refuse to operate. Within ten days, the entire press was firmly in Communist hands.

On December 20, 1950, the National Assembly adopted a law stating bluntly that "the mission of the press is to assist in the building efforts of the Czechoslovak people and in their struggle for peace, and to collaborate in their education towards socialism." It further stipulates that the publication of newspapers cannot be the subject of private undertaking and is, therefore, limited to the government, political parties of the National Front, and similar official and semi-official bodies. No newspaper or periodical may be published without a license from the Ministry of Information. The Union of Czecho-slovak Journalists is assigned to see that editors fulfill their duties. The law reasserts that only members of the Union may be employed as editors, and that the Ministry of Information is to supervise the Union's activities.

On November 1, 1953, the Ministry of Communications took over distribution of the press of all political parties of the National Front. A special branch of the Ministry, called the Postal Service for Newspapers, is charged with home deliveries, sales at the stands, and all other distribution of newspapers and periodicals, collection of subscriptions, and drives for new subscribers.

Radio and Television

After World War II, there were two separate radio systems in Czechoslovakia, managed by the Ministry of Information and the Commissariat of Information: *Ceskoslovensky rozhlas* (Czechoslovak Broadcast) in Bohemia and Moravia, and *Slovensky rozhlas* (Slovak Broadcast) in Slovakia. From the time of the First Republic, they had functioned as separate corporations, with some of the shares in private hands, although their holders had no influence on programs. Shortly after the coup, Law No. 137 of 1948 unified both systems into one corporation, bearing the name *Ceskoslovensky rozhlas* (Czecho-slovak Broadcast).

There are fifteen stations broadcasting at present in Czechoslovakia, each devoting about 40 per cent of air time to direct propaganda, the rest of the time being taken up by music, folklore, non-political features, weather, and sport reports. Broadcasts beamed abroad are more than 90 per cent propaganda, music programs being only rarely included.

The price of an ordinary receiving set in Czechoslovakia is approximately one month's average salary. The government maintains the prewar licensing of all receiving sets, charging a fee equivalent to about $0.50 a month at the official rate. According to *Rude pravo* of December 17, 1952, there were then 2,717,000 receiving sets in operation in Czechoslovakia; the number is reported constantly growing.

A public address system is in operation in all cities and towns, and in most villages, as well as in all factories, mines, and larger government offices; loudspeakers are permanently installed on lamp-posts, street corners, and in large halls, among other places. The public address system broadcasts speeches by Party and government officials, invitations to join work brigades, announcements of progress in production quotas, and similar matters. Radio speakers are also installed in express trains.

Wired radio is an important device in Czechoslovak propaganda. It consists of programs sent by wire from a studio in Prague to a number of centrally located sub-stations, which in turn transmit by wire to individual listeners. Sets for receiving such broadcasts contain no mechanism except a single knob for turning the radio on and off and regulating volume. The press unanimously praises and recommends wired radio, stating that the quality of the transmission is excellent because there are no atmospheric disturbances, that no repairs are required, and that there are no bills for electricity (the network uses its own electricity). The fact that the listener has no opportunity to choose his favorite programs by dialing various stations is not mentioned. At present, Station Prague III is the center for wired radio programs, which do not differ much from the usual programs of other stations.

The government drive for the expansion of wired radio is quite intensive. From newspaper accounts at the end of 1955, it may be estimated that every city and major town possesses a wired radio sub-station, each reaching several hundred listeners. So far, there is no evidence that the authorities force holders of standard receivers to exchange them for wired radio sets or that standard sets are collected from those who now use wired radio sets.

The Czechoslovak Broadcast cooperates closely with broadcasts of the Soviet Union and the other Soviet bloc countries through specific radio agreements. On the basis of an agreement with the

Soviet Union, a 30-minute daily program called "Moscow Speaking" is broadcast over most Czechoslovak stations from 6:00 to 6:30 P.M.; it is a transmission in Czech and Slovak of selected programs of the Moscow radio.

Television in Czechoslovakia is limited to one station, with some 15,000 sets in and around Prague, according to *Rude pravo*, February 23, 1955. Another television transmitter is under construction in Ostrava, and still another in Bratislava for programs in Slovak. In 1955, the Prague television was on the air from Tuesday through Sunday, usually for 4 1/2 hours a day. Programs contain relatively less propaganda than those on the radio. A good amount of time is given to children's programs. The popularity of television has expanded rapidly and 1955 production was reported to have exceeded 17,000 sets. By 1960, annual output of television sets is to amount to 220,000 (*Rude pravo,* May 4, 1956).

Film

Until 1945, the two film companies in Czechoslovakia—one in the Czech lands and the other in Slovakia—were private undertakings with studios and laboratories in Prague, Barrandov, Hostivar, Zlin, and Bratislava. Both were nationalized by Presidential Decree No. 50 of August 11, 1945, which gave the government the exclusive right to manufacture films and project them in public, as well as to import and export films. The owners and managers of studios, laboratories, stocks of films, etc., were ordered to turn them over to the Ministry of Information, receiving no indemnity in return. Since 1945, the Ministry of Information has controlled the production and distribution of films in Bohemia and Moravia, while the Commissariat of Information has been in charge in Slovakia. In April 1948, both the Czech and Slovak units were merged into the Czechoslovak State Film Company.

Film is considered an important medium for education of the people toward communism, the presentation of Soviet examples, and the increase of production. The Ministry of Culture sees that "socialist" subjects and selected historical themes which foster Communist principles are used in screen plays.

The subjects and techniques of film production are decided by the Film Council. Its members are appointed by the Minister of Culture from among officials of the Party, the Ministry staff, officials of the Union of Czechoslovak Writers, and representatives of film directors, actors, and other groups. The Czechoslovak State Film Company also publishes a number of weekly and monthly periodicals.

An overwhelming majority of foreign films shown in Czechoslovakia are from the Soviet Union. Movie-goers, however, prefer American, English and French films. To remedy this situation, double-feature performances with one Soviet and one Western film were introduced. Since the audience would often attend only the Western film, it was subsequently announced that viewers would not be allowed to come in after the beginning or leave before the end of the double-feature performance.

Increased efforts have been devoted to bringing motion pictures to all rural communities which lack access to a theater. Since 1951, seasonal film festivals have been organized in the country's rural areas. In addition to this temporary expedient, a long-range program was launched to provide every community with a motion-picture theater. Following the annual International Film Festival at Karlovy Vary (Karlsbad), prize-winning Czechoslovak and foreign films are shown at "Film Festivals of the Workers" in all nineteen regional cities and other cultural centers. Motion-picture performances are also given in the open for workers of large plants or collective farms. Short films, connected with the work of the audience, are shown to acquaint workers with production targets and techniques of operation.

Agreements on the export and import of films, made by the Czechoslovak State Film Company, enable the government to send abroad some propaganda films. The program schedule of the Prague playhouses reveals that the number of films from the Soviet Union surpasses those imported from all other countries combined.

According to the Communist press, there were 3,450 motion-picture theaters in operation in Czechoslovakia in 1954, giving close to one million performances for 150 million spectators. In addition, there were some 6,500 projecting machines in use by various political, educational, and military organizations. In 1953, the Czechoslovak State Film Company manufactured twenty-four films, including nine in color as well as 481 short films; in 1954, twenty-two full length and 507 short films were made.

Other Propaganda Media

From 1945 to 1948, the Ministry of Information and the Communist Party made use of the services of a number of organizations in carrying out propaganda. Promoting closer relations with the West were such organizations as the American Institute, the Union of the Friends of the United States, and the Society for Cultural Relations with the United States; the Franco-Czechoslovak Society, the Scandinavian Society, the British Society, the British-Czechoslovak Friendship League, and several English clubs. Most of these societies were subsidized by the Ministry of Information.

Organizations fostering orientation toward the Soviet bloc were the Society for Cultural and Economic Relations with the Soviet Union, the Union of Friends of the Soviet Union, the Union of Friends of (Tito's) Yugoslavia, and several others. The expenses of these pro-Communist societies and clubs were defrayed by the Ministry of Information. Both groups organized exhibits of books, the arts, and folklore, and arranged lectures, song festivals, and plays.

A third group comprised organizations whose professed program was the fight against Nazism and Fascism: the Czechoslovak Anti-Fascist Society, whose declared objective was "to eradicate fascism on a scientific basis"; the Union of Liberated Political Prisoners, which, in addition to assisting former inmates of German camps and prisons, arranged lectures and expositions dealing with Nazism; various unions of the wartime partisans, many of whom were fanatical Communists; and a few other organizations of minor importance. Mass organizations, such as the Revolutionary Trade Unions, the Czechoslovak Youth League, and various Women's Committees, all of cardinal importance in Czechoslovak propaganda, are dealt with in Chapter 4. The Union of Czechoslovak Writers, a vital instrument in Communist long-range plans for indoctrination, is discussed in Chapter 9.

The 1948 coup brought the activities of all pro-Western societies to an end, while those of the pro-Soviet group were increased. Two new organizations appeared: the Czechoslovak-Soviet Friendship League, and the Czechoslovak Society for the Propagation of Political and Scientific Knowledge. Vaclav Kopecky, outlining the aim of the latter at the Society's constituent national congress in Prague on June 21, 1952, stated that it is to train the masses in the ideology of socialism; to propagate and popularize the scientific interpretation of socialism; to conduct a patient, yet persistent campaign of persuasion among those who still have reservations in regard to socialism; to explain the futility of American war propaganda and the peaceful intentions of the Soviet Union; to illustrate the unscientific nature of the Masaryk and Benes ideology; to promote Czechoslovak-Soviet friendship and strengthen the friendly relations of Czechoslovakia with the other people's democracies; and to fight against religious obscurantism, superstition, and the reactionary clergy (*Rude pravo*, June 22, 1952). The Society promptly began its activities with lectures, discussion groups, expositions, and drives for an increase in the circulation of Soviet periodicals. It sponsors books in which the recent history of Czechoslovakia has been rewritten in the Communist sense, and co-sponsors each year the Czechoslovak-Soviet Friendship Month. It also co-sponsors the annual "People's Film University," a series of courses in which documentary films are shown with the purpose of popularizing materialistic philosophy.

Sovietization

Transformation of Czechoslovakia into a Communist state, closely allied with the Soviet Union, has been the aim of the Communist Party and the Ministry of Information since 1945, as well as of the Ministry of Education and other governmental branches since 1948. Books promoting friendly relations between Czechoslovakia and the Soviet Union and describing the "thousand-year-old ties" between the two countries are published. Expositions of the arts, books, industrial and agricultural products of the Soviet Union, as well as hundreds of lectures on the Soviet way of life, are organized. Soviet Communist Party leaders, past and present, are brought to the Czechoslovak people through books, pictures, phonograph records, and all standard media of mass communication.

Particular attention is given to the Soviet press. May 5, the anniversary of the Russian Communist *Pravda's* first publication (in 1912) has been annually proclaimed the "Day of the Soviet Press." Contests on such subjects as "What the Soviet Press Has Given Me" or "Why I Read the Soviet Press" are conducted from time to time by newspapers or the Ministry of Culture, with prizes consisting of subscriptions to Soviet periodicals. In November 1953, an exhibition called "The Soviet Press Assists the Builders of Socialism" was shown in Prague and other Czechoslovak cities; it contained the originals, along with Czech and Slovak translations, of Soviet technical and scientific publications "which are of significant assistance in the work of our miners, metallurgy workers, and people in industry and agriculture" (*Rude pravo,* November 11, 1953).

The Czechoslovak Youth League conducts periodic campaigns to get new subscribers to Soviet youth publications. *Svobodne slovo* of May 6, 1953 revealed that 312 Soviet newspapers and magazines were received in Czechoslovakia, with a daily subscription of 289,000 copies; heading the list were *Pravda* and *Ogonek.* According to *Lud* of September 9, 1954, the number of Soviet periodicals was to increase in 1955 by some 200, including Ukrainian, Byelorussian, Uzbeck, Georgian, Lithuanian, and Latvian publications.

Soviet books play an equally important role in the scheme of sovietization. In all major cities, bookshops called *Sovietskaya Kniga* (Soviet Book) sell Soviet literature both in Russian and in translation. These books are much cheaper than other literature, as are phonograph records of Russian folk songs sold at the Sovietskaya

Kniga stores at one crown each (about 14 U. S. cents at the official rate), while other records cost 10 to 15 times as much. In 1952, a new device was introduced; *bibliobus,* a huge omnibus filled with Soviet books, visits schools, factories, and collective farms, giving exhibitions of Soviet books. According to *Rude pravo* of May 25, 1952, 1,500,000 copies of original Russian books were sold in Czechoslovakia in 1951, and 1,500 new Soviet titles were published in Czech and Slovak translation, with a total of over 21 million copies. Not even *Rude pravo* pretends, however, that all these millions of Russian books are read, nor does it mention the pressure by the Revolutionary Trade Unions, the Youth League, and the Party itself brought upon the populace to buy Soviet literature. Great quantities of these books have to be bought, especially by schools, the staff of various offices, and trade union libraries.

The main organization promoting the Soviet Union in Czechoslovakia at present is the Czechoslovak-Soviet Friendship League, a mass organization with two million members in 19,000 branches. Its chairman is Professor Zdenek Nejedly, one of the prewar Communist leaders. The League organizes political and cultural lectures and discussions about the Soviet Union, festivals of Soviet films, visits to and from the Soviet Union, and a score of similar activities. It published three weekly magazines, *SSSR v boji za mir* (USSR in the Struggle for Peace), *Svet Sovetu* (Soviet World) and *Svet socialismu* (World of Socialism), and several other periodicals. The Czechoslovak-Soviet Institute, which covers scientific and technological developments in the Soviet Union, publishes some twenty-four magazines for the Czechoslovak public.

Two institutions of higher learning which deal with Russian and Soviet affairs are the School of Russian Language and Literature in Prague and the Institute of Russian Language, Literature, and History of the USSR in Bratislava. Courses in Russian are given in practically all Czechoslovak schools; the study of Russian is compulsory starting with the fourth grade. In addition, various organizations conduct thousands of "people's courses" in Russian each year. The Ministry of Education publishes *Rusky jazyk* (Russian Language), a monthly magazine for teaching Russian in Czechoslovak schools. National conferences "on the importance of Russian" are held, and campaigns to induce Czechoslovak people to study Russian are organized. Even the Prague streetcars participated one year in this gigantic effort, displaying a letter of the Russian alphabet each week, so that the passengers could learn it while traveling to and from work. Russian is also taught by radio.

In November and December of each year, the sovietization campaign reaches its peak with the Czechoslovak-Soviet Friendship

Month. The month is usually opened by a celebration of the October 1917 revolution, on or about November 5, followed by lectures, meetings, round table discussions, contests, film festivals, concerts, theater performances, exhibitions, and many other undertakings designed to "sell" the Soviet Union to the Czechoslovak people. The most popular of these is the relay race "of peace and friendship," which is run in two columns over the whole territory of Czechoslovakia to the Soviet border. Each year an average of one million runners takes part in the race with more than two million spectators watching. The month is closed by a celebration of the anniversary of the Czechoslovak-Soviet Treaty of Friendship, Mutual Assistance, and Postwar Cooperation, which was signed in Moscow on December 12, 1943.

Propaganda Against the West and the Emigres

In propaganda campaigns against the West in general and the United States in particular, the Communists play up the present cooperation between the West and the Bonn government, counting on the traditional distrust of the Czechs for the Germans. They claim that the West is making an alliance with the Nazis, that American capitalists helped Hitler seize power in Germany, and that during the war, American industrialists were in league with the Germans and were making millions on the victims of Nazi imperialism. They say that American culture is concentrated in jukeboxes, comic strips, and gangster films, and that at best it is a business civilization, a worshipper of technology. The American way of life is described as the persecution of Negroes, purges of "progressive" books from libraries, stifling of academic freedom, perpetual strikes, and unemployment. Sport in the United States, wrote *Ceskoslovensky sport* (Czechoslovak Sport) on September 1, 1953, is famous for its brutality, shedding of blood, and even murders; football in particular is just a wild brawl devised for the basest instincts of both spectators and players; but all this is so because sport in the United States plays an important part in the "militaristic" education of American youth.

The behavior of American soldiers in Europe; Walter Reuther, the "worst breaker" of the working class and "darling of the automobile magnates"; Senator Joseph R. McCarthy and his "Hitlerite methods"; and the Vatican are other frequent subjects of Czechoslovak propaganda. At the time of the Korean war, germ warfare and bacteriological bombs were discussed almost daily, always coupled with attacks on the "Western imperialists." In April 1954, the exposition "Death Conquered by Life" was shown in Prague, containing "an American germ bomb" brought from Korea and other material on the effects of the atom bomb dropped on Hiroshima in 1945. Parades were organized in which school children carried placards reading: "We Shall Drive the American Thieves Out of Korea," or "If Truman Tries Something Against Us, We Will Tear Him to Pieces." Anti-American motion pictures, such as *Resist America, Help Korea* were shown throughout Czechoslovakia.

A specially violent campaign against the United States was launched in connection with the trial and subsequent execution of the atomic spies, Julius and Ethel Rosenberg. Both before and after their execution, numerous telegrams of protest were sent by various Czechoslovak organizations to Washington and to the American Embassy in Prague. They were all duly reported and commented upon in the Czechoslovak press. At Marianske Lazne, Hotel Sylva was renamed "Hotel of the Rosenberg Couple," and a street at Hradec Kralove was given the name "Rosenberg Couple Street." The book *Dopisy z domu smrti* (Letters from the Death House) was published in Prague in 1953, containing the Rosenbergs' correspondence and pictorial material. In 1954 and 1955, the play *Julius a Ethel* by Polish writer Leon Kruczkowski was given in several Czech and Slovak theaters. On April 18, 1954, Station Prague II broadcast the radio play *Manzele Rosenbergovi* (The Rosenberg Couple), by Maximilian Scheer. In all these propaganda outbursts, the United States was condemned for the "judicial murder," and the Rosenbergs were praised for their courage and perseverance "in the fight for peace."

The themes of anti-West propaganda vary with changing international developments. The United States, however, has always remained the arch-enemy, while England, France, Italy, and other democratic countries are usually described as American satellites. Use is made of United States Communists and fellow-travelers, particularly writer Howard Fast and singer Paul Robeson. A frequently repeated horror story is the allegation that United States bombers willfully destroyed the Skoda Works at Plzen just before the end of World War II to prevent a revival of Czechoslovak industry. Similar Anti-American sentiments are contained in Derek Kartun's book *USA 1953: The Truth Behind Eisenhower,* which was published in Czech translation in 1953 and received wide publicity.

The peace campaign has formed another regular feature of propaganda against Western democracies. The Movement of the Czechoslovak Defenders of Peace is an efficient instrument of the Soviet-sponsored World Peace Council.

Czechoslovak emigres have been the target of Communist propaganda ever since the 1948 coup. They are accused of having sold Czechoslovakia to Wall Street bankers, of preparing the return of the Sudeten Germans to Czechoslovakia, of planning a Central European federation on the model of the Austro-Hungarian Empire, and of desiring to impose the American way of life on the Czechoslovak people. The exiled leaders and the Council of Free Czechoslovakia are cursed for "selling" the rank-and-file refugees for service in the French Foreign Legion. The Free Europe Committee is attacked frequently for sending to Czechoslovakia the balloon-borne leaflets containing "lies and calumnies." Radio Free Europe, the BBC, Voice of America, and the Vatican Broadcast are charged with spreading enemy propaganda and with disrupting the peaceful development of Czechoslovakia.

Propaganda Abroad

To implement Czechoslovak propaganda abroad, the government uses the services of several of its departments and semi-official organizations, as well as the standard media of mass communication. As was noted earlier, the Ministry of Culture sends cultural attachés, and the Ministry of Foreign Affairs appoints press attachés, to all major countries. The task of the attachés is to watch the developments on the political and cultural scene and to influence the press, radio stations, film companies, book publishers, and educators in foreign countries. The attachés have at their disposal several foreign-language periodicals, which are published by the Czechoslovak government. As early as 1945, the Ministry of Information published *The Daily Review* for English-speaking countries, and the French monthly *Parallèle 50*. In 1946, *The Weekly Bulletin* appeared, which later changed its name to *The Czechoslovak Weekly*, and later still to *Czechoslovak Life*, under which title it is still published by the Ministry of Culture. The Ministry of Foreign Trade issues the monthly *Czechoslovak Economic Bulletin*. The fortnightly *Prague News Letter*, containing political and cultural news, is published by the Ministry of Culture. The government heavily subsidized the magazine *New Central European Observer*, which was sponsored in London by the British-Soviet Society until the end of 1952, when it was abolished. It is to be noted that the government never published a periodical in any language of the "people's democracies."

Radio Prague broadcasts in the following foreign languages: English, French, Italian, Serbo-Croatian, Slovene, Macedonian, German, Swedish, Norwegian, and Spanish. Broadcasts in English, Czech, and Slovak are beamed to the United States and Canada. Here, too, it should be noted that no broadcasts are made in the languages of the people's democracies (German programs of Radio Prague being beamed only to Western Germany). The opening announcement of the Czechoslovak foreign broadcasts is: "Prague Calling. This is the Voice of Peace from Czechoslovakia."

Considerable attention is given to Czechs and Slovaks living abroad. The Czechoslovak Foreign Institute, a semi-official branch of the Ministries of Culture, Education, and Foreign Affairs, is entrusted with watching over the "cultural needs" of people of Czechoslovak descent abroad. The weekly magazine *Ceskoslovensky svet* (Czechoslovak World) and the fortnightly bulletin *Domov* (Home) are mailed free of charge and without request. There are several Czech and Slovak language periodicals published outside of Czechoslovakia, to serve as vehicles of Communist propaganda. They are subsidized by the Czechoslovak government, usually in the form of paid advertisement, or subscription to a large number of copies.

For purposes of foreign propaganda, Czechoslovakia participates in all "progressive" international organizations, such as the World Federation of Trade Unions, the International Union of Students, the International Organization of Journalists, the World Federation of Democratic Youth, and the World Peace Council. The International Organization of Journalists had its seat in Prague until 1954, when it was transferred to Vienna. Prague is still the seat of the International Students' Union and the International Radio Organization.

When the remilitarization of Western Germany was negotiated in London and Paris in 1954, a nation-wide campaign against the ratification of the respective agreements was started in Czechoslovakia. The Revolutionary Trade Unions, the Czechoslovak Youth League, faculties of various schools, the Academy of Science, and even the Catholic bishops held meetings from which resolutions were sent to corresponding groups in Western countries, condemning the rearming of Germany and urging them to support the Soviet Union in its efforts "for a lasting peace." School children were made to write letters to children in France, England, Belgium, and other Western countries, asking them to urge their parents to stand up against the revival of German militarism.

The use of motion pictures in Czechoslovak propaganda abroad, though not very extensive, has been increasing in recent years. "Festivals of Czechoslovak Films" are organized in Soviet bloc countries on a regular basis. The International Film Festivals held annually in Karlovy Vary since 1946, are also intended to satisfy foreign rather than domestic propaganda needs. Since the idea of peaceful coexistence was introduced into East-West relations, Czechoslovak films have been shown in the West in increased numbers as part of a campaign for increased "cultural cooperation." In 1954 alone, Czechoslovakia participated in the Film Festival at Cannes, in the Festival of Documentary and Experimental Films at Montevideo, in the Seventh International Film Festival at Locarno, and in the International Congress of Popular Scientific Films in Rome. In the same year, motion picture exchange agreements were concluded with Swedish, Danish, and Finnish companies. In addition to the exchange of films, the drive for increased cultural cooperation has included exchange of visitors, students, art groups, and exhibitions. Special attention has been devoted to the Middle East countries, India, and Communist China.

In addition to official and semi-official channels for the dissemination of propaganda in foreign countries, the Czechoslovak government has made full use of non-official channels, such as various international gatherings of church, labor, and youth groups. Since the government approves or actually selects a delegation to any international gathering, only those favored by Communist authorities and expected to foster the regime's objectives are appointed. The task of these unofficial propagandists is not so much to serve as apologists for current Communist policies as to create favorable attitudes toward communism among groups which normally are hostile, indifferent, or inaccessible to official or semi-official propaganda. To this end, moderately critical attitudes on the part of such unofficial propagandists have been encouraged by the government. The best example is provided by the activities of Protestant theologian Josef Lukl Hromadka, Dean of the Jan Hus Theological Faculty in Prague, and head of the Czechoslovak delegation to the First Assembly of the World Council of Churches held in Amsterdam in 1948 and the Second Assembly in Evanston, Illinois, in 1954. Hromadka has been critical of both West and East, though far less of the latter. This has made him acceptable to some Protestant groups in the West, and it has served to create the illusion that freedom of thought and the right to dissent are respected in Communist Czechoslovakia.

Campaign for Exiles' Return

Ever since the Communists seized power in February 1948 and their democratic opponents began to leave the country in considerable numbers, the regime has been aware of the danger of these exiles as factors of adverse propaganda. It tries to discredit the exiles in Western countries where they found refuge, and even more in the eyes of the people at home. The most important means in this counter propaganda, however, are amnesties, which aim at inducing the exiles to return. In this plan, Czechoslovakia follows the example of the Soviet Union, which declared amnesty for White Russian emigres as early as 1922.

The first pardon for refugees was granted by the government and President Klement Gottwald in June 1948, five days after the latter's inauguration. From the regime's point of view, there were at least three reasons for the amnesty: first, to halt, or at least slow down, the exodus of refugees which, in the late spring of 1948, was assuming mass proportions; second, to offset the effects of the United States Displaced Persons Act of 1948, which contained a special quota of two thousand immigration visas for Czechoslovak escapees; third, to emphasize Gottwald's benevolence and to increase his popularity as President.

The results, if any, of this amnesty, which expired on September 19, 1948, are difficult to ascertain. An examination of the available Czechoslovak periodicals of 1948-49 does not reveal a single instance of a refugee availing himself of this pardon. Among the reasons for the complete failure of the first amnesty, the solidly anti-Communist and anti-Soviet sentiment in the West, which nurtured the hopes of many exiles for an early return to a liberated homeland, was probably the most important. Furthermore, at this early date, the hardships and frustrations of exile life had not yet wrought their corrosive influence. Finally, the Communist campaign for the exiles' return had not yet been sufficiently organized.

The second amnesty, proclaimed on May 9, 1955, remitted imprisonment penalties of those who had fled the country "under the influence of hostile propaganda," providing they returned to their homeland within six months. This pardon was preceded by a chain letter campaign conducted among the refugees in December 1954 and January 1955. Anonymous letters, hand-written in simple Czech, quoted sentimental Christmas poetry, described the present plight of escapees living in unfriendly foreign countries, evoked the beauty of the distant homeland, and invited the exiles to join *Hnuti exulantu pro navrat domu* (Exiles' Movement for the Return Home), *HEPND.* Recipients were requested to copy the letters and mail them to three refugee friends. Nearly every Czechoslovak refugee in Germany and Austria, as well as many exiles living in the Western hemisphere, received such letters, most of which were mailed from Vienna or West Berlin.

In February 1955, the chain letters were superseded by a mimeographed Czech bulletin called *HEPND,* distributed anonymously among refugees in camps and mailed to exiles living outside. This bulletin tried to create the impression that it was published by disillusioned refugees who wanted to return home. It was written in the unsophisticated style of the chain letters, containing no open Communist propaganda or even undertones of leftist ideology.

In the meantime, Communist agents in Camp Valka, near Nuremberg, West Germany, and in several other German and Austrian camps called meetings in which they attacked the Council of Free Czechoslovakia and the Free Europe Committee for "living on the refugees," and openly invited their audiences to return home. Letters were written by exiles' relatives in Czechoslovakia, either voluntarily or under pressure, urging their return. Thus, the psychological groundwork was well laid before the amnesty was proclaimed.

On June 2, 1955, in Prague, the Presidium of the National Front established the Committee for the Accommodation of Persons Returning to Czechoslovakia on the Basis of the Amnesty (Committee for Returnees). Miroslav Klinger, a Communist fellow-traveler, was appointed chairman. Shortly afterward, the June (No. 7) issue of the *HEPND* bulletin declared that its mission had been accomplished by the issuance of the amnesty and the creation of the Committee for Returnees, and that therefore it would cease publication.

On June 14, 1955, the Committee for Returnees began publishing a weekly newspaper in Czech and Slovak, *Hlas domova* (The Voice of Home). The newspaper is widely circulated by mail, free of charge throughout the West, and by Communist agents in refugee camps. It carries detailed instructions on repatriation procedure for refugees; information on eligibility (members of the Council of Free Czechoslovakia and the leading Czechoslovak employees of Radio Free Europe and the Voice of America are explicitly excluded); testimonials of the warm reception and favorable conditions found by returnees; personal appeals by families; severe criticism of exile leaders and their American sponsors; programs of Czechoslovak broadcasts beamed to the West; and articles on the achievements of Czechoslovak industry, agriculture, and cultural developments. Particular attention is given to sports events in Czechoslovakia apparently in an effort to appeal to the youth.

On November 15, 1955, *Hlas domova* published a front-page article by Miroslav Klinger, "The Road for Return Remains Open," which stated that although the amnesty expired on November 9, it would still be possible for refugees to return home upon individual application to Czechoslovak diplomatic representatives abroad. The extension of the pardon was also announced by President Zapotocky in his nation-wide speech on January 1, 1956.

Since August 1955, the Committee for Returnees has sponsored a special radio program for potential redefectors. It is called "The Song of the Native Land," and it is broadcast to the West over Station Prague I five times a week, containing news and feature stories about cultural life in Czechoslovakia and information pertaining to the amnesty.

Soon after the amnesty was proclaimed, the Czechoslovak Embassy in Washington, D.C., published advertisements in twenty American newspapers, including the *New York Times* and the *Washington Post*, calling the attention of Czechoslovak citizens to the pardon and inviting them to report to the Embassy for further details. Similar advertisements were published in the press in Canada, France, and other Western countries.

When a group of refugees returns to Czechoslovakia, the Communist officials hold a press conference, arrange a radio talk, and encourage a letter to the editor of a daily newspaper, denouncing the Western democracies, thanking Zapotocky for the amnesty, and praising the Czechoslovak government and life in general. In the second half of 1955, hardly a day passed without a broadcast concerning new returnees and their "sinister experience in capitalist states."

From May through the end of December 1955, the names of some 450 returnees were published in the Czechoslovak press. Conservative estimates, however, place the number of redefectors for that period at 600, since not all the names of returnees have been published. It is to be noted, in this connection, that, according to the American Fund for Czechoslovak Refugees, about 55,000 persons escaped from Czechoslovakia between 1948 and 1955.

Several reasons have induced the Czechoslovak regime to expend so much effort to bring escapees home. First, at a time when the Communists proclaim the possibility of coexistence, they cannot permit thousands of witnesses to remain in the West, proving by their very existence the falseness of their claims. The Communists want to disorganize the exiles, make them lose confidence in themselves, in their leaders, and in the Western democracies. Secondly, by winning redefectors from among the exiles and making propaganda out of their return, the government aims at destroying internal opposition by depriving it of its faith in the West and its hope in the political exiles.

Part III. The Society

7. CHURCH AND STATE

Vratislav Busek

Historical Background

Religion has played a prominent part in Czechoslovakia's cultural history and in its political development. Indeed, few nations' political fortunes have been so closely tied with their religious history as have those of the Czechs and Slovaks.

Christianity was introduced to the Czech and Slovak regions in the ninth century. Early in that century, the Slavs inhabiting the central part of present-day Czechoslovakia were united in a more or less independent principality of Great Moravia. The first missionaries, sent to Great Moravia by the German bishops of Regensburg, preached the Gospel in Latin. In 830, the first church was built in Nitra, and in 845, fourteen Czech tribal princes were baptized at Regensburg. The extension of German ecclesiastical organization into the Slavic lands, however, brought with it increased political pressure, which led the Moravian prince Rostislav to turn to Byzantium. In 863, he invited two brothers, Constantine (Cyril) and Methodius, to come to preach Christianity in his realm in a language his people could understand. Pope Hadrian II established for Methodius the Archbishopric on Pannonia, a step interpreted by the German bishops as a violation of their claims to ecclesiastical jurisdiction over this territory. The existence of an ecclesiastically and politically independent Slavic principality in an area where the interests of Byzantium, the Pope, and the Empire clashed, was short-lived. The German bishops reasserted their claims, and the disciples of St. Constantine and Methodius were expelled. They found a haven in Bulgaria, bringing with them the Church Slavonic (Cyrillic) alphabet which they had elaborated and perfected in Great Moravia and laying one of the foundations of Slavic culture in Eastern Europe.

The Magyar invasion towards the end of the ninth century dealt the final blow to Great Moravia as a political entity, brought the Slovaks, living east of the Carpathians, under the rule of the Magyars, and separated them from the Czechs. The long separation left its mark in the character and culture of both the Czechs and Slovaks and cast occasional shadows between them even after they had been reunited in the Czechoslovak Republic in 1918.

The introduction of Christianity into Bohemia did not take place without a struggle against native paganism, as was proved by the assassination of St. Wenceslaus (in 929) and of St. Ludmila. The acceptance of Christianity, however, spared the Czechs the fate of the Slavs settled along the Elbe River who were obliterated in their struggle against the Holy Roman Empire.

In 973, a bishopric was established in Prague. It was subordinate to the Archbishop of Mainz (Germany) until 1344, when the Archbishopric of Prague was founded. In 1063, the Bishopric of Olomouc was created in Moravia.

By the fifteenth century, the Czech nation had reached a relatively high level of cultural, political, and economic development. The University of Prague, one of the oldest in Central Europe (founded in 1348), had become a lively center of learning. The teachings of Wycliffe found an ardent exponent in Jan Hus, a religious reformer who preceded Luther by a century. His condemnation by the Council of Constance in spite of letters of safe conduct given him by Emperor Sigismund ("a word given to a heretic is not binding"), and his death at the stake on July 6, 1415, gave impetus to a powerful movement in Bohemia calling for reform of the Church. The Utraquist Church, giving laymen communion in both kinds, was established in Bohemia, and in 1436, its equality with the Catholic Church was formally recognized in the Basel Compacts. Though Pope Pius II declared the Compacts invalid in 1462, equal legal status of the Catholics and the Utraquists was temporarily guaranteed in the Czech lands by local laws.

The spirit of the Czech religious reformation was revived by Peter Chelcicky and the Union of Brethren, founded in 1457, which based itself on his teachings. The Union of Brethren was not recognized by the state, however, and its members were persecuted.

Gradually, under the presure of discrimination, some Utraquists returned to the Catholic Church. Others, known under the name of Neo-Utraquists, joined with the Union of Brethren and those professing Lutheranism, which had spread to Bohemia from Germany, in the so-called Czech Confession in 1575. In 1609, the signatories of the Czech Confession exacted from Emperor Rudolf II a patent granting them religious freedom. After the battle of the White Mountain (November 8, 1620), however, the Revised Bohemian Ordinance of 1627 and the Revised Moravian Ordinance of 1628 declared

Catholicism the sole religion of the state. The Czech Brethren, led by Jan Amos Komensky (Comenius), emigrated, and the nation, forcibly re-Catholicized, lost much of its spiritual vitality. The combination of political and religious absolutism produced in the Czech people a tendency toward religious lassitude and a strong anti-clerical sentiment masked by a veneer of conformity.

In Slovakia, the Reformation was not as utterly defeated as in the Czech lands. Here, relations between the Catholics and the Protestants were stabilized in 1606 by the Peace of Vienna, which guaranteed the Protestants religious freedom. By the Peace of Linz in 1645, the Protestants were divided into Lutherans and Calvinists, the latter preponderantly of Magyar nationality.

In the fifteenth century, many Hussites found asylum in Slovakia. Through them, Czech has survived as the liturgical language of the Slovak Protestants. Under the name of Moravian Brethren, the descendants of the Union of Brethren settled in Bethlehem, Pennsylvania, and Salem, North Carolina, at the beginning of the eighteenth century.

The period of Enlightenment brought religious tolerance to the Czech lands (the Austrian Toleration Patent of 1781) and, in a still greater measure, to Slovakia. The Hungarian laws XXVI and XXVII of 1790-91 granted the Protestant and Greek Orthodox churches the status of "accepted" denominations *(religiones receptae)*, i.e., parity with the Catholic Church. A century later (Law No. XLIII of 1895), the religion of all "accepted" churches was declared state religion in Hungary.

In the middle of the nineteenth century, liberalism began to assert itself in Austria. The stormy year of 1848 marked the beginning of the transition to a constitutional state. The toleration enjoyed by most of the churches during the period of enlightened absolutism was tacitly transformed into a liberal regime of "legal recognition," with the Catholic Church retaining its privileged status, formalized in the Concordat with the Holy See of 1855. However, the Concordat was *de facto* abolished by the Constitution of 1867. The spirit of liberalism was also reflected in legislation of the latter half of the nineteenth century which defined the status and operation of "recognized" churches and religious societies in detail. The Austrian laws (No. 64 of 1864; Nos. 44, 48, and 49 of 1868; Nos. 50, 51, and 68 of 1874; and No. 57 of 1890, *Imperial Codex*) and the Hungarian laws (No. XVII of 1867; No. LIII of 1868; Nos. XLII and XLIII of 1895; and No. XVII of 1916) served as the basis for Czechoslovak legislation after 1918.

By the time of the dissolution of the Austro-Hungarian monarchy, the following churches and religious societies had been "recognized" (either tacitly or by specific legislative acts) under Austrian law, and had established organizations in the Czech lands: the Catholic Church of all rites, the united Protestant (Lutheran and Reformed) Church, the Greek Orthodox Church, the Jewish Religious Society, the Evangelical Church of Brethren, and the Society of the Christians of the Old Rite. The organized denominations in Slovakia and Ruthenia, "accepted" under the Hungarian law, included the Catholic Church (Roman, Greek and Armenian), the Greek Orthodox Church, the Lutheran Church, the Protestant Reformed (Calvinist) Church, the Unitarian Church, and the Jewish Religious Society. The Baptist Religious Society and Islam of all rites were also recognized in Hungary (the former on the basis of Law No. XLIII of 1895, the latter by a special Law No. XVII of 1916), but had no established organization in Slovakia and Ruthenia.

Under Austrian and Hungarian law, "recognized" and "accepted" churches and religious societies were public corporations, supervised, supported, and protected by the state, enjoying full autonomy in internal matters. Only churches with full legal status were entitled to public practice of religion and other rights and privileges guaranteed by law or custom. Non-recognized denominations were considered legally nonexistent; their members were considered to have no religious affiliation and were entitled only to private practice of their cults. The conditions which a religious denomination had to satisfy to obtain legal recognition were specified in Austrian Law No. 68 of 1874 which applied in the Czech lands, and in Hungarian Law No XLIII of 1895, which applied in Slovakia and Ruthenia. Some religious sects were prohibited in both Austria and Hungary. These included the New Salemites, Johannites, the sect of New Jerusalem, and the cult of Pure Christianity. The Nazarene sect was prohibited in Austria, but it was tolerated in Hungary.

1918-1948

One of the first statutes of the Czechoslovak government declared Austrian and Hungarian laws, with the exception of the constitutional laws, effective within their former spheres of jurisdiction, pending amendment or repeal by subsequent Czechoslovak legislation (Law of 1918, No. 11, *Sbirka zakonu a narizeni republiky Ceskoslovenske* [Collection of Laws and Ordinances of the Czechoslovak Republic]). Churches and religious societies in Czechoslovakia thus continued to operate within the legal framework inherited from the Austro-Hungarian monarchy, and their status remained essentially unchanged until the Communist seizure of power.

In the first few years after World War I, a relatively strong drive for the separation of Church and State, and a resurgence of anti-Catholic sentiment developed in the Czech lands. The anti-Catholic sentiment stemmed partly from the memory of the Counter Reformation and partly from the fact that in Austria the Catholic Church had enjoyed the privileged status of State Church. Some of the latent resentment against the former Vienna government for its refusal to recognize Czech national and political aspirations was now channeled against the Catholic Church. A provision calling for separation of Church and State was incorporated into the original draft of the Czechoslovak Constitution. The subsequent parliamentary debate on the Constitution revealed, however, that the idea of separation of Church and State did not command a large following in the Czech lands and that it had practically no adherents in Slovakia. The article calling for separation was therefore stricken from the original draft without being replaced by other provisions. As a result, the Czechoslovak Constitution of February 29, 1920, bypassed the question of Church-State relations altogether and contained no provision concerning the status of churches and religious societies.

The Constitution guaranteed all inhabitants of the Republic "full and absolute protection of life and liberty, without regard to their origin, nationality, language, race, or religion" (Article 106); freedom of conscience and religious creed (Article 121); the right "to profess and practice publicly or privately any creed, religion, or faith whatsoever, so far as its exercise is not in conflict with public law and order and with good morals" (Article 122). All religious creeds were declared equal before the law (Article 124), and no one could be compelled either directly or indirectly to take part in any religious rite or ceremony except by virtue of paternal or guardian authority in the case of minors (Article 123). The rights specified in the Constitution were guaranteed to individual citizens and inhabitants of Czechoslovakia and not to churches and religious societies as such. Thus, technically, the public performance of religion ceased to be the monopoly of organized churches and religious societies.

Legislative changes during the interwar period were mainly concerned with a gradual transformation of the legal dualism inherited from the Austro-Hungarian monarchy into a uniform system of law effective throughout the country. Thus, laws of 1919, Nos. 320 and 362, and of 1924, No. 113, made both civil and religious marriage ceremonies optional throughout the Republic, either being declared sufficient to validate a marriage; removed certain obstacles to marriage based on canon law; and opened civil law divorce procedure to Catholics in both parts of the Republic (divorce was not allowed to Catholics under Austrian law, but was open to them under Hungarian law in Slovakia and Ruthenia). Law of 1922, No 226, and Cabinet Decree of 1925, No. 64, authorized the exemption of children from seven to fourteen from compulsory religious instruction at the request of their parents; the same provision also exempted children without religious denomination from compulsory attendance in religious classes. Perhaps the most important Czechoslovak legislative act concerning religion was Law of April 23, 1925, No. 96, which established uniform principles of inter-denominational law throughout the Republic. In Slovakia, it liberalized and simplified the procedure involved in a person's changing religious denomination or choosing a status "without religious denomination." The inter-denominational law granted to persons without religious affiliation and their societies, based on the constitutional right of assembly, the same rights legally guaranteed to recognized denominations and their members.

After the drive for the separation of Church and State had subsided, no further attempt was made to redefine the legal position of churches and religious societies within the state. The formal legal classification of religious denominations into "recognized," "accepted" *(religiones acceptae),* non-recognized, and prohibited was therefore maintained. However, in view of the constitutional guarantees of religious freedom to individuals rather than to churches and religious societies, this had little practical significance. The only government acts which bore directly on the status of churches were Law of 1926, No. 122, and Cabinet Decree of 1928, No. 124. "Recognized" or "accepted" churches and religious societies were divided into the so-called *kongrua* churches, in which the state paid direct supplements to clergymen's salaries and pensions, and the *dotation* churches, where the state paid a lump-sum subsidy to the churches, which were free to use it at their discretion. The churches and religious societies not included in either of these categories received special subsidies for administrative expenses. The "accepted" churches of Slovakia had a broad legal right to such special subsidies in the Law No. XX of 1848; the conditions of these special grants, however, were never defined.

The state did not examine the content of church norms, nor was the state placet (the traditional *placetum regium*) of ecclesiastical norms and decrees practiced in Czechoslovakia. Recognized churches and religious societies were not required to obtain special permission of state authorities for performance of any religious function or event conducted "in the usual manner." In most cases, the acquisition of property by churches and religious societies was not limited by law, but its management, alienation, and mortgaging were subject to supervision by state authorities. This supervision was quite close in the case of the Catholic Church throughout Czechoslovakia, and was practically nonexistent in the case of the Protestant churches in Slovakia. The appointment of higher church dignitaries and officials was subject to governmental approval (cf. the *modus vivendi,* below). The state also specified some of the qualifications for clergymen and church officials; among these were Czechoslovak citizenship, moral integrity, and certain educational standards.

All recognized churches and religious societies were accorded protection of the law against slander (*Criminal Code,* No. 111), blasphemy, and disruption of religious ceremonies (*Criminal Code,* Article 122; *Slovak Criminal Code,* Articles 190 and 191). In their public capacity, clergymen enjoyed the legal protection accorded to public officials; the same applied to documents issued by them, to their seals of office, and to all official property of the churches.

There were no special statutes concerning the clergy as a special estate. Czechoslovakia abolished the last special privilege of the clergy, i.e. its exemption from military service. Clergymen, however, were assigned, upon application, to auxiliary medical services and, upon completion of their tour of duty, to auxiliary reserve (Law of 1927, No. 147, *Collection*). Clergymen's dwellings were exempted from requisitioning for billeting troops, as were official ecclesiastical buildings (Law No. 93 of 1879; No. 100 of 1895; Law Nos. XXXVI of 1879, XXXIX of 1895, and 248 of 1920). Clergymen were exempted from serving as jurors; they could not be called as witnesses concerning what they had learned in confessions or under a vow of silence (Cabinet Decree of 1928, No. 8); and they could refuse to serve in tax commissions (Law of 1927, No. 76, *Collection*).

Though the supervision of education was declared the sole domain of the state (Czechoslovak Constitution of February 29, 1920, Article 120), churches and religious societies were guaranteed direct participation in religious instruction in public schools and the right to establish denominational schools. In Slovakia and Ruthenia especially, many denominational schools were maintained by the "accepted" Protestant churches. The state was obligated to contribute to the maintenance of these schools (Law No. XX of 1848).

The Catholic Church

For some years following the establishment of Czechoslovakia in 1918, relations between the state and the Catholic Church were marked by considerable strain, mainly as a result of the situation in Slovakia, where a large part of the Catholic clergy, particularly the upper hierarchy, was strongly pro-Magyar and viewed the creation of Czechoslovakia with apprehension. Many dignitaries of the Church who had held ecclesiastical posts in Slovakia withdrew to Hungary. Furthermore, the Czechoslovak-Hungarian frontier severed some Slovak dioceses from their ecclesiastical seats.

In 1919, all property of the Church held or administered by Church officials who refused to take an oath of loyalty to the Republic or who resided in Hungary was placed temporarily under the management of a governmental commission (Law of 1918, No. 64, *Collection*). This measure became a source of constant friction. A related controversy concerned certain nominating rights which the Austrian and Hungarian rulers had traditionally exercised as their prerogative (the so-called *nominatio regia*) and which the Czechoslovak government now claimed by succession. The Holy See, on the other hand, maintained that these rights had been granted only to specific ruling dynasties by formal treaties or concordats (cf. the allocution of Pope Benedict XV of November 21, 1921), and made several nominations which the Czechoslovak government refused to recognize. In addition, the Czechoslovak government did not allow Church dignitaries with seats in Hungary to exercise jurisdiction in the Slovak dioceses severed from their seats by the frontier. The relations between Czechoslovakia and the Vatican were further aggravated by mass exodus from the Church of both the clergy and laity—part of them joining the newly established Czechoslovak Church (see below), part joining the Protestant churches, and part remaining without any religious affiliation. All these problems were resolved by a *modus vivendi* between the Vatican and Czechoslovakia which went into effect on February 2, 1928 and which was implemented by the Papal bull of November 2, 1937, titled *Ad ecclesiastici regiminis incrementum.*

The *modus vivendi* stipulated that no part of Czechoslovakia would be subject to the authority of a foreign bishop. The Holy See and the Czechoslovak government were to agree upon a new delimitation of dioceses to coincide with Czechoslovakia's political frontiers. The management of Church properties by the government-appointed commission was declared temporary, and the board was subordinated to the Slovak Episcopate. Homes of monastic orders in Czechoslovakia were not to be subject to the authority of superiors residing abroad. The Holy See agreed that, prior to the appointment of archbishops, diocesan bishops, diocesan coadjutors *cum iure successionis,* and the army vicar, it would submit the candidates' names to the Czechoslovak government to assure the political acceptability of the Vatican's choice. Moreover, these prelates were to be Czechoslovak citizens. Following their nomination by the Holy See and prior to their assumption of office, the prelates were to take the following oath: "*Iuro et promitto sicuti decet Episcopum fidelitatem Reipublicae, necnon nihil me facturum quod sit contra salutem, securitatem, integritatem*

Reipublicae." The Czechoslovak government promised to bring legislation into conformity with the *modus vivendi.*

The Czechoslovak Church

Shortly after the birth of the Czechoslovak Republic in 1918, several new churches were established and other churches reorganized. The largest among the former was the Czechoslovak Church, founded January 8, 1920 at a meeting of the Club of Reformist Clergy, which split away from the Catholic Church. This new church was recognized in Bohemia and Moravia-Silesia by Law of 1920, No. 542. The Czechoslovak Church declared freedom of conscience (religious subjectivism) its guiding principle. It rejected celibacy of priests, and at its general congress on August 29-30, 1924, adopted its own order of consecration of clergymen, thus abandoning the principle of the sacramental character (apostolic succession) of bishops. On January 6, 1925, the church elected its first three bishops for the West Bohemian, East Bohemian, and Moravian-Silesian dioceses. The West Bohemian bishop, Dr. Farsky, was simultaneously elected Patriarch. By Law of 1925, No. 123, the Czechoslovak Church was recognized in Slovakia and Ruthenia. By 1930, its membership reached almost 800,000. The Church was quite heavily subsidized by the Czechoslovak government.

The Orthodox Church

Prior to World War I, there was no independent Eastern Orthodox Church organization in Czechoslovak territory. The small number of Orthodox in the Czech lands belonged administratively to the Viennese Orthodox congregation, which was subordinate to the Bishopric of Zadar in Dalmatia and the Metropolitanate of Cernauti in Bukovina. Members of the Orthodox Church in Slovakia and Ruthenia were considered a diaspora of the Serbian Orthodox eparchy of Buda in Hungary which provided their pastors. After World War I, the Orthodox ranks were increased by Czechoslovak legionnaires who had fought on the eastern front during the war and by a shift to Orthodoxy of a large number of members of the Czechoslovak Church in 1924.

In 1929, two Orthodox eparchates were established: one for the Czech lands (Decree of the Ministry of Education, No. 161, 192 of 1929) and the other for Ruthenia (Decree of the Ministry of Education, No. 161, 181 of 1929). The Orthodox congregations in Slovakia were administered by the Ruthenian eparchate. Prior to World War

II, the Czechoslovak Orthodox Church was subject to the jurisdiction of the Serbian Patriarchate in Belgrade. After World War II, it passed under the jurisdiction of the Patriarch of Constantinople. In the spring of 1946, the Moscow Patriarch sent the Archbishop and Metropolitan of Rostov and Taganrog, Jelevferij (Eleuterius), to Czechoslovakia with the rank of exarch for the purpose of uniting the Czechoslovak Orthodox Church with the Russian Church. This move was opposed unsuccessfully by both Archbishop Savatij of the Czechoslovak Orthodox Church and Maximus, the Patriarch and Archbishop of Constantinople. After the annexation of Ruthenia by the Soviet Union in 1945, the Orthodox in Slovakia (their number in 1946 was estimated at 70,000-80,000) were administratively assigned to the Czech eparchy.

Protestant Churches

Prior to the establishment of the Czechoslovak Republic, Protestants in the Czech lands, without distinction of nationality or creed, were organized in a single Austrian Protestant Church. Its status was defined in the Decrees of the Ministry of Cults and Education on December 15, 1891 (Law No. 4 of 1892, amended by a decree of July 24, 1913, No. 155). After 1918, it was reorganized into separate denominations along national lines. The Czech Protestants, at their Prague congress on December 17-18, 1918, established the independent Evangelical Church of Czech Brethren in Bohemia, Moravia, and Silesia. On May 26, 1928, this church was legally recognized in Slovakia and Ruthenia. The Evangelical Church of Brethren is to be distinguished from the Union of Brethren, a Czech Baptist society which did not apply for recognition.

In 1919, German nationals formed the German Protestant Church in Bohemia, Moravia, and Silesia. This church was organized on the basis of the Augsburg Confession and was approved by the Ministry of Education on July 7, 1924. Finally, the Protestants, who had formed the so-called Tesin (Teschen) Seniorate, founded the Lutheran Church of Eastern Silesia, which was recognized in 1923.

In Slovakia and Ruthenia, Protestants of both confessions, Augsburg and Calvinist, had independent organizations prior to World War I. The members of the Calvinist Church were for the most part Hungarians, while those of the Lutheran Church were predominantly of Slovak and German nationality. After the establishment of Czechoslovakia, the superiors of the Lutheran Church remained in Budapest, and the old constitution of the church was suspended in Slovakia. In 1919, the Slovak Lutherans organized an independent Lutheran Church in Slovakia (constitution approved by the Decree of the

Ministry of Education of December 27, 1922, No. 61 of 1923, *Collection*). The Calvinist Church in Slovakia retained its former organizational statutes. The Unitarian Church, which had been "accepted" in Slovakia and Ruthenia prior to World War I, was recognized in the Czech lands in 1930.

Jewish Religious Communities

The organization of the Jewish religious communities underwent no significant change during the interwar period. The Czechoslovak government, however, encouraged and assisted in the formation of higher organizational units based on nationality. As a top representative organization of the Jewish associations in the Czech lands, The Highest Council of Jewish Religious Societies in Bohemia, Moravia, and Silesia was established in Prague (approved by the Decree of the Ministry of Education, No. 97, 759/VI, dated September 3, 1927).

After World War I, the seats of the so-called central bureaus of the Slovak Jewish religious communities remained in Hungary. Seeking to eliminate all foreign influence, the government encouraged the establishment of a domestic central organization. The Ruthenian Orthodox societies first joined the Slovak Orthodox organization, but later they separated and formed their own association.

Numerical Strength of Individual Churches

The development of churches and religious societies during the first decade or so of Czechoslovakia's existence is reflected in Table 1, which shows the percentage distribution of the Czechoslovak population according to religious affiliation in 1921 and 1930. No comparable figures are available for any year following 1930. It can safely be assumed that the relative numerical strength of the various denominations did not change appreciably during the prewar decade. The published results of the 1947 and 1950 surveys do not include a breakdown of the population by religious affiliation.

The substantial decrease in Czechoslovakia's population in comparison with prewar years reflects mainly the withdrawal into West Germany of some 600,000 Germans during final phases of the war, the expulsion from Czechoslovakia of some 2,400,000 Germans in the immediate postwar years, and the annexation of Ruthenia (population approximately 750,000) by the Soviet Union in 1945. In 1947, Czechoslovakia and Hungary concluded an agreement under which 100,000 Magyars living in Slovakia were to be exchanged for an equal number of Slovaks living in Hungary; the agreement has been only partially carried out, and there is no reliable evidence on the numbers actually

Table 1. Distribution of Czechoslovak Population by Religious Denominations, 1921 and 1930
(in per cent)

	Czechoslovakia		Bohemia		Moravia-Silesia		Slovakia		Ruthenia	
	1921	1930	1921	1930	1921	1930	1921	1930	1921	1930
Total population:	13,613,172	14,729,536	6,670,582	7,109,376	3,335,152	3,565,010	3,000,870	3,329,793	606,568	725,357
Roman Catholic	76.29	73.54	78.20	74.78	89.51	85.83	70.92	71.61	9.09	9.55
Greek and Armenian Catholic	3.93	3.97	0.10	0.11	0.08	0.12	6.46	6.42	54.81	49.52
Protestant (all denominations)	7.28	7.67	3.69	4.58	4.52	4.89	17.68	16.69	10.38	10.23
Evangelical Church of Czech Brethren	1.72	2.02	2.22	2.82	2.51	2.55	0.08	0.18	0.05	0.13
Lutheran [a]	3.93	3.99	1.28	1.46	2.96	2.24	12.74	12.06	0.37	0.23
German Protestant Church	..	0.90	..	1.40	..	0.88	..	0.04	..	0.01
Lutheran Church of East Silesia	..	0.32	..	0.00	..	1.31	..	0.00	..	0.00
Slovak and Ruthenian Lutheran Church	..	2.77	..	0.06	..	0.05	..	12.02	..	0.22
Reformed (Calvinist)	1.53	1.49	0.03	0.02	0.02	0.03	4.82	4.38	9.94	9.77
Union of Brethren [b]	..	0.04	..	0.08	..	0.00	..	0.00	..	0.00
Baptist [b]	..	0.03	..	0.02	..	0.05	..	0.05	..	0.08
Union of Czech Brethren [b]	..	0.04	..	0.08	..	0.01	..	0.01	..	0.00
Methodist [b]	..	0.05	..	0.09	..	0.00	..	0.00	..	0.01
Other	0.10	0.01	0.16	0.01	0.03	0.01	0.04	0.01	0.02	0.01
Orthodox Church	0.54	0.99	0.11	0.21	0.06	0.27	0.10	0.27	10.06	15.44
Czechoslovak Church	3.86	5.39	6.56	8.70	2.57	4.53	0.06	0.35	0.03	0.31
Old Rite Christian	0.15	0.16	0.24	0.25	0.11	0.13	0.00	0.00	0.00	0.00
Other Christian	0.02	0.05	0.02	0.05	0.03	0.07	0.00	0.03	0.04	0.13
Jewish	2.60	2.42	1.20	1.07	1.36	1.16	4.53	4.11	15.39	14.14
Without religious affiliation	5.32	5.80	9.86	10.24	1.75	2.94	0.23	0.51	01.19	0.68
Unknown	0.01	0.01	0.02	0.01	0.01	0.01	0.02	0.01	0.01	0.00

Sources: Figures for 1921 are based on State Statistical Office, *Statisticky prehled republiky Ceskoslovenske* (Statistical Review of the Czechoslovak Republic) (Prague, 1930), pp. 10-11, Tables 8 and 9; those for 1930, on State Statistical Office, *Statisticka rocenka republiky Ceskoslovenske* (Statistical Yearbook of the Czechoslovak Republic) (Prague, 1937), p. 10.

Notes: [a] Breakdown for 1921 not available. [b] Data for 1921 not available.

transferred. The Jewish communities in Czechoslovakia were decimated during the war. While the Jewish population of the country was about 360,000 in 1938, it probably did not exceed 55,000 in 1945; by 1950, migration had reduced the Czechoslovak Jewish community to some 18,000.

The impact of these complex population changes upon the relative numerical strength of the various denominations in postwar Czechoslovakia is difficult to measure. Most of the Germans expelled from Czechoslovakia were Roman Catholic. The Slovaks repatriated from Hungary belong mainly to the Lutheran Church, while the Magyars who were returned to Hungary were mostly Calvinist. The annexation of Ruthenia by the Soviet Union reduced the strength of the Greek Catholic Church in Czechoslovakia by over 60 per cent, and that of the Orthodox Church over 75 per cent.

The Status of Churches under the Communist Regime

Until the Communist seizure of power in February 1948, there were no radical changes in the status of the churches. Some of the Catholic Church's estates were eliminated under the new Land Reform Act, drafted prior to February 1948. This act anticipated compensation of the Church for land expropriated by the state.

After February 1948, the Communist government launched a massive campaign to bring the churches under complete state control. Directed mainly against the Catholic Church, which embraces some three quarters of the population, the campaign passed through several phases. The first phase, which extended approximately to the middle of 1949 was marked by the regime's outwardly conciliatory attitude toward the Church, combined with measures designed to destroy its economic independence; the second phase, which lasted roughly until the beginning of 1951, was characterized by the regime's all-out offensive and culminated in the breakdown of the Church's open resistance; in the third phase, which extends to the present, the government is attempting to establish a schismatic Church and to convert it into a pliable instrument of domestic and foreign policy.

First Phase: February 1948–Summer 1949

On March 21, 1948, most of the land owned by the Church was confiscated under Law No. 46, but, contrary to the provisions of its initial draft, without compensation. It was left to the organs of local administration to reserve not more than 30 hectares of this land for the upkeep of the parish clergy. The expropriation also included the property of charitable institutions, hospitals, and monasteries. Following the ban on denominational schools (Law of April 1948, No. 95, *Collection*), all Catholic schools were seized and handed over to the Union of Czech Youth.

The confiscatory measures were tempered by the government's repeated assurances of good will toward the churches. Members of the government ostentatiously attended public religious ceremonies. Thus, on June 14, 1948, at a time when negotiations between the government and the Church were in progress, the entire Cabinet together with President Gottwald attended Mass celebrated by Archbishop Beran in St. Vitus Cathedral. The three principal issues concerned the fundamental attitude of the Church toward the Communist coup and the regime, Church property and Church schools. The discussions broke down mainly over the question of schools, as the Church strongly opposed surrendering its influence over education.

Second Phase: Summer 1949–February 1951

After the breakdown of negotiations early in 1949, the government launched its all-out attack to subjugate the Church. The strategy called for the accomplishment of several objectives: isolation of the Church from the Vatican and from the international Catholic community; isolation of the bishops from the rest of Church hierarchy; driving a wedge between Church and laity; and seizure of Church control by "patriotic" clergymen, i.e., those willing to cooperate with the government.

On July 13, 1949, the Vatican chargé d'affaires, Internuntius Verolino, left Prague. The government refused to grant an entry visa to his successor, Monsignor Bartoli. On March 16, 1950, the last member of the Papal Nunciature in Prague, Monsignor de Liva, was expelled from Czechoslovakia as *persona non grata.* On April 29, 1950, the Czechoslovak chargé d'affaires in the Vatican, Dr. Ilja Rath, closed the legation and left with his staff without any formal announcement. Diplomatic relations between Czechoslovakia and the Vatican were thus broken without formal severance.

Isolation of the bishops began with disbandment of the bishop's lay organization, Catholic Action, in the spring of 1949. On June 10, 1949, a new, "progressive" Catholic Action was created with the aid of "patriotic" clergymen. On June 19, 1949, this organization was declared schismatic by the Vatican, and all those who had assisted in founding it or had joined it voluntarily were excommunicated by the Holy See. On June 24, a Slovak Catholic Action Committee was founded. The ecclesiastical press was supressed. The Archbishops of Prague and Olomouc and all the bishops were placed under police surveillance and later interned in their residences. On June 28, 1949, the government issued three decrees: (1) public reading of pastoral letters and other communications from the bishops to the clergy or laity was prohibited without prior governmental consent, and violators were subject to arrest; (2) meetings of the clergy, patrons' councils, and committees responsible for the management of church property could be held only with explicit advance permission from the local People's Committees; and (3) all excommunication and suspension decrees were declared invalid. A separate decree of the Ministry of Interior threatened with arrest any person attempting to enforce an excommunication decree.

Communist Legislation. From October 1949 to July 1950, the government passed a series of legislative measures defining the status of churches. On October 14, 1949, the State Office for Church Affairs, headed by a Cabinet member, appointed by the President, was established as the central governmental authority over all churches and religious societies in the country (Law No. 217, *Collection*). Its powers extend to all ecclesiastical matters except church ritual: approval of ecclesiastical personnel and payment of their salaries; control of the administration and finances of churches, religious societies, and religious institutions, and supervision of their property; control of religious instruction in public schools, including the subject matter; supervision of ecclesiastical press; supervision of charitable and other activities of churches; and supervision of the international relations of churches and religious societies (Cabinet Decree of October 25, 1949, Law No. 228, Section 2). For Slovakia, a Slovak Office for Church Affairs was established in Bratislava. It is headed by a member of the Slovak Board of Commissioners who is appointed by the Cabinet in Prague.

On the regional, district, and local levels, the functions of the Office for Church Affairs are exercised by regional and district People's Committees, which are organs of local administration and act as agents of the Office. "Church secretaries" have been appointed within the People's Committee in each district town; they in turn appoint deputies in each of Czechoslovakia's fifteen thousand communities whose function is to serve as intermediaries between the Office for Church Affairs and the clergy. The deputies are responsible for the supervision of religious activities in their respective communities. Compulsory monthly meetings of the clergy, officials of the People's Committees, and members of Catholic Action in the district towns are to provide political re-education of Catholic priests.

The ancillary status of the churches is further defined by Law of

October 14, 1949, No. 218, and by Cabinet decrees Nos. 219-223. Law No. 218 specifies the government guarantees—as well as the government price—of the "economic security to be provided to the churches," which are now deprived of practically all independent sources of revenue. Decree No. 219 deals specifically with the Catholic Church.

Though this legislation declares all clergymen employees of the Church and not of the state, clergymen must satisfy "all general requirements for employment by the government." No clergyman may perform his duties without advance government consent. In the case of parish priests and other clergymen of lower rank, consent is granted by the regional People's Committee; in the case of dignitaries of chapters, chapter vicars, vicars-general, titular bishops, and abbots, approval must be granted by the Office for Church Affairs; appointment of archbishops, diocesan bishops, and apostolic administrators requires the placet of the Cabinet. Section 30 of Decree No. 219 is tantamount to vesting the appointive power in the government. It requires the consistories to publicize all vacant prebends in the official *List katolickeho duchovenstva* (Bulletin of Catholic Clergy), and to submit all applications to the government with a list of those applicants whom the consistory does not consider suitable for nomination; the consistory's rejection of a candidate "must be properly justified by reasons which are not in contradiction to the laws of the Czechoslovak Republic." From the remaining applicants, the government shall nominate its candidate to the Ordinary. If the Ordinary does not appoint this candidate within fourteen days, the office is automatically conferred upon the government nominee.

Government compensation has become the only regular source of income for the clergy. It is paid only to those clergymen and posts which have received government approval. The express consent of the government is required for the establishment of new ecclesiastical posts. In general, government compensation of the clergy corresponds to the salaries of public officials. It consists of basic salary, additional pay according to rank, and "efficiency bonuses" which are designed to reward the "exceptionally onerous work of a clergyman, his public activity, and his participation in the constructive endeavor of the working people." The basic annual salary at the time of the law's enactment was 36,000 crowns (720 U. S. dollars at the official exchange rate of 50 crowns for one dollar);[1] it was to be increased by 3,600 crowns for every three years of "creditable service," the number of such increases not exceeding twelve. To determine additional pay,

[1] After the 1953 currency conversion, wage salaries, bonuses, and other types of remuneration were generally adjusted at the rate of one "new" crown for five "old" crowns.

based on rank, all clergymen were divided into four categories: (1) independent pastors, clergymen in a supervisory function, and officials of consistories; (2) superiors of seminaries for the training of priests, teachers of theological schools, consistorial chancellors, consistorial executive secretaries, and resident canons; (3) dignitaries of chapters, vicars-general, chapter vicars, titular bishops and abbots; (4) archbishops, diocesan bishops, and apostolic administrators. The additional annual pay was 12,000 crowns for the first category to be increased by 12,000 crowns for each successive category. The "efficiency bonus" was not to exceed 2,000 crowns per month; the total annual amount of such bonuses was not to exceed 15 per cent of the basic salary plus additional pay. Clergymen are also entitled to travel expenses, provided their travel has been approved in advance by the appropriate People's Committee.

The government also undertook to defray maintenance of churches and ecclesiastical establishments which are not covered by other church revenues. Each diocesan consistory is required to submit consolidated budgets to the State Office for Church Affairs; these serve as the basis for the appropriation of funds to the diocese by the Office. The consistories are also required to submit annual inventories of their property. All church property and transactions involving church property are under government supervision. All private and public patronage of churches, prebends, and other ecclesiastical institutions was assumed by the government; obligations to contribute to churches, ecclesiastical communities, institutions, and foundations, based on patronage, other legal grounds, or long-standing customs, have ceased.

An oath of loyalty to the government is required of all clergymen. The oath reads: "I promise upon my honor and conscience to be loyal to the Czechoslovak Republic and to its people's democratic regime, and I will not do anything contrary to its interests, security, and integrity. As a citizen of a people's democratic state, I shall conscientiously perform all the duties inherent in my office, and I will do all in my power to support the constructive efforts directed towards the welfare of the people."

Law No. 218 specified penalties ranging up to a fine of 100,000 crowns (about $2,000 at the official rate of exchange) or six months' imprisonment. Some of these penal provisions were superseded by the new Criminal Code and Administrative Criminal Code of 1950. The performance of pastoral functions without governmental consent, or at a post other than that to which a clergyman has been appointed by the government, is subject to punishment by imprisonment not to exceed three years; church officials appointing others to ecclesiastical functions without governmental consent are punishable by imprisonment from one to five years (Criminal Code, Law No. 86, 1950, Section 173).

The regime's control over the teaching of religion in primary and secondary public schools was considerably tightened. Decree of 1949, No. 228, vested the Office for Church Affairs with "the regulation of religious instruction, approval of the syllabus, textbooks, equipment, and other devices, and the supreme supervision, in agreement with the Ministry of Education, Science, and Art, over the teaching of religion and over denominational educational institutions of any kind." According to Law No. 218, clergymen performing strictly ecclesiastical functions are required, without additional remuneration, to teach religion in schools where qualified teachers are not available. Cabinet Decree of July 14, 1950, No. 121, which regulates the salaries of lay teachers of religion, provides that "teachers of religion shall be appointed within the framework of the approved plan of employment after the church authority of the respective denomination has been heard." The appointment of lay teachers of religion thus completely passed into the hands of the State Office for Church Affairs, which is not obligated to observe the suggestions of church authorities. Regarding the qualifications for teachers of religion, the decree provides that "only a teacher who proves his higher political ability, higher special knowledge, and has had good results in his work shall be eligible to receive higher grades of the basic salary" (Section 4).

Another decree of July 14, 1950 (No. 112), abolished all existing theological faculties and seminaries and centralized Roman Catholic theological teaching in two divinity schools, one in Prague, the other in Bratislava. Both of these bear an identical name—The Roman Catholic Divinity School of Constantine and Methodius—which is intended to suggest the eastern links of Czechoslovak Catholicism and to underscore the regime's hostility toward the Vatican. Protestant theological instruction is conducted in three divinity schools, two in Prague and one in Bratislava. For the Orthodox Church, a divinity school has been established in Prague. The schools' deans are appointed by the Office for Church Affairs and are responsible to the Office for the activities of the faculty. Courses in Marxism-Leninism have been introduced as part of the curriculum.

The Domestic Relations Act of December 7, 1949 (Law No. 265, *Collection*) made civil marriage obligatory throughout the Republic, beginning January 1950; marriage in the church is not prohibited, but it has no legal validity. The act made divorce possible on grounds left to the discretion of the courts. The Civil Registry Records Act of December 7, 1949 (Law No. 268, *Collection*), transferred the function of keeping vital statistics records to the local People's Committees. This act implied no change in Slovakia. In the Czech lands, however, such records had been kept primarily by the churches. The statute required all churches to transfer such records to the People's Committees by January 1, 1950.

Capitulation of the Churches. On February 17, 1950, representatives of all churches and religious societies, including the Prague titular bishop, Antonin Eltschkner, took the prescribed oath of loyalty to the government. The Catholic bishops refused to take the oath at this time, though they authorized their clergy to do so; the Episcopate's authorization included bishop-coadjutors. One of the bishops of the Czechoslovak Church, Bohus Ciganek, refused to take the oath and resigned his office.

The government countered the Catholic bishops' refusal with intensified punitive measures. Mass arrests of the clergy, including high church officials, were followed by mass trials which extended throughout 1950 and 1951. The charges almost invariably included conspiracy against the regime and espionage; the sentences rarely ran below ten years' imprisonment. The trials were accompanied by a violent campaign against the Vatican, Archbishop Beran, the "seditious" bishops, and the clergy who remained loyal to such bishops. On April 13 and May 3, 1950, all remaining monasteries were closed. Some of them were converted into concentration camps for clergymen; some were transformed into "educational monasteries" for the political reorientation of monks and clergymen who had promised to cooperate with the regime; the remaining monasteries were sequestrated by the government and the Communist Party. High ecclesiastical administrative posts, vacated through arrest, death, or retirement of the incumbents, were filled with "patriotic" priests by the Office for Church Affairs. Given the Episcopate's authorization to take the loyalty oath, the ranks of the "patriotic" priests grew rapidly under the combined impact of fear and the enticement of the liberal compensation paid by the government to those willing to cooperate. This was especially true of the lower clergy, which had long known a life of extreme poverty. By the end of 1950, the government had filled most of the higher ecclesiastical posts with its own appointees and thus was in a position to run the Church without the bishops. On March 10, 1951, Archbishop Beran was banished from the capital; the Prague chapter elected Antonin Stehlik administrator of the Archbishopric. This act meant an automatic excommunication of all participating Church dignitaries, as the Vatican did not consider the Archbishopric vacant. On March 12, 1951, six of the twelve Czechoslovak bishops took the loyalty oath they had refused to take since November 1949; a month later, the seventh bishop took the pledge.

Third Phase: Formation of a Schismatic Church

Capitulation of the bishops meant the end of the Church's open resistance. Speaking on behalf of the bishops who had taken the oath, Bishop Carsky said: "We all recognize the state laws without reservation. . . . We shall pay no heed to penal sanctions of the Church against clergymen or laymen if such sanctions have been imposed for political reasons; we shall do our best to insure continued good relations between Church and State; we wish to support in all possible ways the constructive efforts of our working people and our people's democratic regime, because we know that . . . [they] are in accordance with the moral principles of our Holy Church. We also sincerely welcome the efforts of our people to preserve world peace." On April 17, 1951, one month after the loyalty oath, the bishops sent a telegraphic note to the French government protesting the ban on activities of the Secretariat of the World Peace Council. A similar protest against the French government's ban on the activities of other Communist front organizations—the Secretariat-General of the World Federation of Trade Unions, the International Federation of Democratic Women, and the World Federation of Democratic Youth—had been sent by the central committee of Catholic Action in the name of all Czechoslovak Catholics at the end of January 1951 (*Prace* [Work], February 2, 1951). The resolution of the central committee of Catholic Action, dated January 31, 1951, stated: "It is our aim that all citizens —Catholics above all others, as Christians—express their views concerning two basic questions of our times, namely the re-militarization of Western Germany and the traitorous activities of the [Czechoslovak] émigrés related to this question. The Catholic Action wants . . . to point out the role played by the Vatican in the struggle for peace, and to show what part the patriotic priests have in this fight and how they help to win it. . . ." Addressing a meeting of the Slovak Ordinaries in mid-April 1951, Bishop Lazik endorsed the demands of the World Peace Council and condemned "imperialistic American aggression in Korea, remilitarization of Western Germany, and war preparations in Western Europe." In a unanimous resolution, all present voiced their support of the World Peace Council's proposals and asked the five Powers to conclude a peace pact (*Rude pravo* [Red Right], April 15, 1951). A nationwide Peace Committee of the Roman Catholic clergy was organized with the aid of the "loyal" bishops in 1952.

Thus, with the Church completely isolated internationally, with her unity shattered by the actions of the "patriotic" clergy, and with the Episcopate's formal surrender to the state, the regime succeeded in transforming the Church into a tool of its domestic and foreign policy. Instead of their traditional role of spiritual guardians of the faithful, the priests were now forced, under close supervision of the regime's agents, to echo the Party line and to preach unquestioning obedience to the state. One of the clergy's main tasks, as defined by the regime, has been to foster the fulfillment of economic plans by exhorting the peasants to prompt delivery of their compulsory quotas of grain and other produce. Since the spring of 1951, establishment of a schismatic Church has proceeded apace. State-appointed, excommunicated diocesan administrators began reinstating excommunicated priests and inducing the clergy to sign resolutions condemning the Vatican.

The last problem confronting the state in its design to create a subservient schismatic Church in Czechoslovakia is the elimination of the hierarchical principle which vests ecclesiastical ruling power in the bishops—a principle essential to the unity of any religious organization based on dogmatic theology. Rather than attempting to arrogate the nomination of bishops, it seems that the government has decided to divest them of all power and do without them. On February 15, 1951, at a conference of general and chapter vicars from all over the country, Minister Plojhar, an apostate priest, urged that consistorial councils be reactivated and endowed with greater authority. This move initiated decentralization of power within the Catholic Church. A logical further step toward disintegration of authority within the Church would be to grant a formally decisive voice to the laity.

The regime can expect active support for its ecclesiastical policy from new priests who are being trained in the two divinity schools established in 1950. In 1945, Czechoslovakia had about 7,000 Catholic priests within her 15,000 communities. According to Vatican estimates, the Church-State conflict has resulted in the arrest of some 3,000 priests. As all institutions of higher learning, including theological schools, had been closed in the Czech lands during World War II, scarcely any priests were ordained in Czechoslovakia between 1945 and 1950. Thus, there are some 4,000 priests whose average age is over 55. According to the Communist press, each Catholic priest now serves from four to eight parishes. Under these circumstances, a schismatic Czechoslovak Catholic Church may be an accomplished fact within ten to twenty years.

The Catholic Church has borne the brunt of the regime's attack on the churches; it has also suffered the heaviest losses which attest to the strength of its resistance. In addition to some 43 per cent of the parish priests, all Church dignitaries who were unwilling to compromise have been removed from their posts. The Archbishop of Prague, Josef Beran; the Archbishop of Olomouc, Josef Matocha; the Olomouc titular bishop, Frantisek Tomasek; the Bishop of Brno, Karel Skoupy; and the Bishop of Ceske Budejovice, Josef Hlouch, have been interned. The Bishop of the Litomerice diocese, Stepan Trochta, and the Olomouc titular bishop, Stanislav Zela, have been sentenced to 25 years' imprisonment. The following received 20-year sentences: Abbot of the Tepla monastery, Herman Tyl; abbot of the Premonstratensian monastery, Jan Opasek; first secretary of the Prague Archbishopric, Jan Boukal; archdeacon of the Prague Archbishopric, Josef Cihak; both secretaries of the Olomouc Archbishopric, Josef Prasek and Josef Ryska; and canon of Prague Cathedral, Otokar Svec. In Slovakia, the Bishop of Spis, Jan Vojtassak, was sentenced to 24 years; auxiliary bishop of Trnava, Michal Buzalka, received a life sentence. The Bishopric of Banska Bystrica is being administered by State-appointed capitular vicar Jan Dechet, an excommunicated priest. Greek Catholic Bishop of Presov, Peter Gojdic, was sentenced to life imprisonment. Stefan Barnas and Basil Hopko, auxiliary bishops of Spis and Presov have also been imprisoned.

Non-Catholic Churches

Concurrent with the main campaign against the Catholic Church, the regime gradually destroyed the autonomy of non-Catholic churches. The Czechoslovak Church was the first to be brought under the regime's control because its administration had been virtually in Communist hands since the end of World War II. Immediately after the war, the representatives of the church were accused of collaboration with the Germans, and the church was placed under the administration of a central action committee, composed mainly of Communists. After February 1948, the committee placed the church in the service of the regime.

As in the case of the Catholic Church, the Communist government first severed all international connections of the remaining churches, particularly those associated with the World Council of Churches at Geneva, but subsequently authorized limited foreign contacts subject to government control. Numerical weakness and traditional dependence on the state for financial support placed the non-Catholic churches in an extremely difficult position; they were "outnumbered, isolated, and surrounded" from the moment of the Communist seizure of power. One of the regime's main strategems in bringing these churches into submission was to play on their latent hostility against the large and relatively wealthy Catholic Church. The congregational organization of most of these churches, particularly the Protestant, enabled the Communists to contrive clamorous "mass pressures from below" with more ease and effectiveness than in the case of the

Catholic Church, whose strict hierarchical system was centered in the Episcopate and the Vatican.

Intimidation, arrests, and other repressive measures soon broke the open resistance of the non-Catholic churches. The government disbanded the Association of Protestant Pastors and the Evangelical Union, confiscated parish houses and other church properties, forbade all activities other than worship proper to the churches, introduced strict censorship of religious publications, and placed church officials under close surveillance. In very few cases was the government able to enlist voluntary collaboration of the churches' legitimate representatives; collaboration was largely secured by removing dignitaries and officials and replacing them with men of "progressive" persuasion—a group analogous to the "patriotic" clergy of the Catholic Church. One notable exception has been the Protestant theologian and bearer of the Order of the Republic in recognition of his "struggle on behalf of peace," Josef Lukl Hromadka, who would discern no fundamental contradiction between Christianity and communism, and who seems to have voluntarily assumed the task of bridging the gap between them. So far, his views have failed to gain wide acceptance; this applies mainly to his own church, the Evangelical Church of Czech Brethren, which has tenaciously resisted both internal and external pressures to be transformed into a tool of the Communist state.

The Slovak Lutheran Church, which has played a prominent role in the nation's cultural and political history—a role far surpassing its limited numerical strength—steadfastly refused to surrender its spiritual independence. The government, however, forced the resignation of most of the leading dignitaries and officials and their replacement by men of its own choice. The list of those forced to resign includes Vladimir Cobrda, bishop of the church's eastern district; Fedor Ruppeldt, bishop of the western district; Peter Zatko, inspector general; and Ludovit Sensel, director of the church's press. Under governmental pressure and supervision, Jan Chabada, bearer of the Order of the Republic for his "struggle on behalf of peace" was "elected" senior bishop; another bearer of the same order, Andrej Ziak, was elected inspector general; and Andrej Katina and Julius Krcmery were elected bishops of the church's western and eastern districts, respectively. Several of the church's pastors were forbidden to perform pastoral functions and some were imprisoned. The church's publishing house Tranoscius was placed under state management, and the church's two periodic publications (*Cirkevne listy* [Church Bulletin], and *Evanjelicky posol zpod Tatier* [Evangelical Messenger from under the Tatras]) were placed in the charge of "progressive" editors. The church's administrative regions, the so-called seniorates, were newly delimited to enable a more effective control of contacts among them.

In 1950, the Greek Catholic (Uniate) Church was forcibly brought into the fold of the Orthodox Church. On April 28, 1950, Orthodox Exarch Jelevferij arranged a synod of self-appointed delegates of the Greek Catholic Church in Presov, who renounced their union with Rome and asked to be united with Moscow (*Svobodne slovo* [Free Word], May 25, 1950). On May 27, 1950, this change was formally recognized by the Czechoslovak government. On November 23, 1951, Alexius, the Patriarch of Moscow, raised the Czechoslovak Orthodox Church to the status of an autocephalous exarchate. On December 8, 1951, an assembly of bishops, clergy, and laymen convened in Prague to elect Jelevferij "Metropolitan of Prague and all of Czechoslovakia." Jelevferij was solemnly enthroned on December 9, 1951 (*Lidove noviny* [People's News], December 11, 1951). By this time, the Orthodox Church in Czechoslovakia was organized in the eparchies of Prague, Brno-Olomouc, Presov, and Michalovce and one Vicariate General in Kosice. In 1953, references to a fifth episcopal see at Trebisov appeared in the Communist press.

Campaign Against Religion

Parallel with its crusade against the various churches, the government has conducted an active campaign against religion in general. On June 21, 1952, the Society for the Propagation of Political and Scientific Knowledge was created in Prague. One of the principal purposes of this organization, according to Minister of Information Vaclav Kopecky, is "the struggle against religious obscurantism." The government's main target has been the younger generation, particularly children of school age. While being exposed to systematic antireligious instruction both in school and in various Communist youth organizations, pupils may attend religion classes only upon written request of their parents, and this is often withheld for fear of repercussions. Other favorite Communist devices in the campaign against religion have been the obstruction of religious services by professional hecklers or blaring local radio loudspeakers. Communist political parades are held in front of churches while religious services are in progress. Frequently, great pressure is applied on churchgoers to attend a political rally or "volunteer" for Sunday brigade work, rather than go to church. But, despite all this, church attendance in Czechoslovakia has increased conspicuously since the Communist seizure of power. Though it does not lend itself to a quantitative appraisal, this silent protest perhaps best vocalizes the true attitude of the Czechoslovak people toward their present regime.

8. EDUCATION

Ivo Duchacek

The First Republic, 1918-1938

Traditions

In Czech and Slovak history there has always been a close association between education and politics. The activities and popular esteem of college professors frequently extended beyond the walls of universities into the arena of politics. An impressive number of college professors attained high positions in the government following World War I. The President of Czechoslovakia, Thomas G. Masaryk, was a university professor, as were the Minister of Foreign Affairs (Edward Benes), the Vice Premier (Jan Sramek), the Minister of Finance (Karel Englis), and others. When Benes became President in 1935, he was succeeded in the Ministry of Foreign Affairs by Kamil Krofta, a university professor of history; a French writer at that time characterized Czechoslovakia as a "professorial democracy."

The association of universities with Czech political history dates back much further than the above reference may suggest. Many Czech writers represent the founding of Charles University as the culminating point of the medieval golden age of the kingdom of Bohemia. Charles University, founded by the Roman Emperor and King of Bohemia Charles IV in 1348 in Prague, was the first institution of its kind in Central Europe. Its clearly imperial and Western origin did not prevent the Communist Party of Czechoslovakia from trying to associate itself with the prestige and glory of Charles University during and after the celebration of its 600th anniversary in 1948.

Jan Amos Komensky (Comenius, 1592-1670) is another symbol of the traditional Czech link between political and educational aims. In Comenius, the Czechs possess a genuine prophet who anticipated the social and educational doctrines of the nineteenth century. In the wake of the Counter Reformation, Comenius left his native country and went into exile. He lived the rest of his life in Protestant countries of Western Europe (England, Sweden, and Holland). According to the views of this religious leader, educator, and politician, national education and the development of all individual national cultures were to merge as the means through which the peoples of the world would progressively eliminate war and find a peaceful and just universal commonwealth. The humane and religious quality of Comenius' philosophy does not prevent the Communists from appropriating his prestige for their purposes. In March 1956, the Central Committee of the Communist Party and the Czechoslovak government decided to start the publication of thirty-two volumes of Comenius' works. In Comenius' native town a monument will be erected. These decisions were made in order to celebrate the 300th anniversary of the publication of Comenius' work *Opera didactica omnia* in Amsterdam. The central organ of the Communist trade unions explained Comenius to its Communist readers on November 15, 1955, in the following manner:

> Comenius advocated universal compulsory education without social, racial, ethnic, or sex discrimination. His program could not be implemented in the feudal . . . or in the capitalist order as it touched upon the very foundations of class society. Only the Soviet Union and the People's Democracies were able to implement and further develop Comenius' principle of a uniform school system and universal education.

From the end of the seventeenth century until 1918, the destinies of the Czech political and educational programs remained interdependent. The education of Czechs and Slovaks was under the monarchic system of Austria-Hungary until the end of World War I. Many political struggles between the Czechs and Slovaks, on one hand, and the Austro-Hungarian government, on the other, revolved around education. The opposition of the Habsburg government to demands for popular education in the native Slavic languages was basically political: an increase in the number of Czech and Slovak schools, and thus in the number of Czech and Slovak-speaking intelligentsia, was viewed as a threat to the pre-eminence of the Austrian and Hungarian ruling classes, as well as a danger to the stability of the Empire's autocratic institutions. Although perhaps not originally, the Czechs and Slovaks finally viewed their struggle for improved Czech and Slovak schools in the same manner as their rulers; a struggle for cultural autonomy was equated with the struggle for political power. In this context, the Czech and Slovak struggle for education in the mother tongue was integrated with the Czech and Slovak political program of democracy, republicanism, and national independence; education became an end in itself, as well as a political weapon against foreign oppression and autocracy.

When Czechoslovakia became an independent nation in 1918, the educational system was placed under the direct control of the central government, which, according to the Constitution, was to be responsible and responsive to the will of the people. The Constitution of 1920 provided that "the supreme authority and control over all instruction and education shall be in the hands of the state." School funds and teachers' salaries were included in the state budget. A private school could be established only with authorization from a provincial board of education on recommendation from a local authority. Once established, a private school had to conform to the standards laid down for public institutions. The number of private schools has always been insignificant in Czechoslovakia. In 1921, in the Czech lands, there were 32 private institutions out of a total of 9,730 schools, and in Slovakia, there were 26 private schools, 797 public schools, and 2,386 denominational schools.

The aims of Czechoslovak education were described in 1930 by Minister of Education Ivan Derer:

> Education should be based on a national culture, for only through national culture may men participate in the world's cultural community. National education is also the principal means by which a student can use his abilities and his knowledge for the good of the whole human society. If national education is properly to fulfill its task, it must not—in its endeavor to create in the student a warm feeling for his own country—lead to an overestimation of his nation, or to the underestimation of other nations. Moreover, it must not limit the horizon of the educated man to the cultural field of his nation, for through knowledge and appreciation of other nations, he attains reliable criteria for the appreciation of his own. Respect for other nations, and above all the need for collaboration with other ethnic groups living in the same state, is to be associated with the love for one's own nation. Truly, national education should . . . develop national tolerance. . . . As regards the personality of the student, the secondary school should develop harmoniously his rational powers and mental abilities, not forgetting that proper intellectual development is also conditioned by the cultivation of physical qualities. . . . All phases of school education should be directed to the cultivation of the moral character of the student. . . . Moral education should begin by fostering self-control and moral habits aimed at building up solid ethical standards supported by rational reasoning. . . . The student should be educated to act independently, making moral decisions. . . . Instruction in religion . . . which brings the students into the ideological and moral circle of a certain faith should support the moral educational aims of the school. . . .

This educational directive put major emphasis on values which in the West have always been associated with enlightened democracy: individualism, humanitarianism, rationalism, and patriotism, with international overtones. In the above memorandum, one may also detect a marked stress, if not a mild warning, with regard to tolerance. The century-long struggle of the Czechs and Slovaks for national self-expression had obviously left an imprint. The new Czechoslovak state had been carved from the Habsburg multi-national empire in the name of national self-determination. Its population included several ethnic groups: Czechs and Slovaks, 66.91 per cent; Germans, 22.32 per cent; Hungarians, 4.78 per cent; and Ruthenians, 3.79 per cent. The transition from minority status, in which Czechs and Slovaks had lived for several centuries, to the status of Slavic majority with respect to the German and Hungarian minorities sometimes resulted in excessive nationalism and manifestations of intolerance. The Ministry of Education planned a fight against such tendencies, which were inconsistent with the humanitarian and democratic orientation of the new state.

Organization of Education

The highest authority in educational and cultural matters was the Minister of Education, who had to be an elected member of Parliament and, as a Cabinet Minister, was responsible to Parliament. His Ministry was responsible for the formulation of educational policy, the execution of educational laws, the preparation of the budget, and the authorization of expenditures. The Ministry supervised elementary, secondary, vocational, and university education. Administration of agricultural education was under the Ministry of Agriculture and military education under the Ministry of National Defense. National archives, museums, theaters, adult education, and public libraries, were controlled by the Ministry of Education. In communities with over two thousand people, a public library was compulsory. The Ministry also appointed school inspectors to examine, coordinate, and control the operation of the provincial, district, and communal boards of education. Legally recognized parents' councils were to advise and cooperate with school authorities. Two thirds of the members of the council were usually elected by the parents, and the remaining one third were teachers. The control of education by the people was thus assured in two directions: through the parents' councils and through the Parliament, to which the Minister of Education was accountable.

School attendance was compulsory from six to fourteen years of age. After five years in elementary school, a child could attend a four-year junior high school, which was an advanced elementary school where industrial, commercial, and agricultural subjects were emphasized. The curriculum in the junior high schools was similar to that of the American high schools which do not concentrate on preparing students for college. A child could also choose one of the five types of high schools which prepared students for universities or for institutes of technology. These schools provided students either with eight years of liberal education with emphasis on classical languages (Latin and Greek), or seven years of education stressing sciences and mathematics. Religious education in one of the seven denominations recognized and financially supported by the state was in principle compulsory, unless the child's parents requested exemption.

Czech and Slovak were the official languages of the Republic, and the government exercised the right to require students to learn them. However, the ethnic minorities of Czechoslovakia (Germans, Hungarians, Ruthenians, Poles, and even gypsies) had state-supported schools of their own, in which teaching was in their respective native tongues, with Czech or Slovak a compulsory second language. While German-speaking citizens were able to complete their whole education in their language (there was a German university in Prague and two German institutes of technology, one in Prague and the other in Brno), the Hungarian minority could receive only elementary and secondary education in their native tongue.

Universities. Prewar Czechoslovakia had four universities: Charles University (founded in 1348) and German University (1882) in Prague, Masaryk University (1919) in Brno, and Comenius University (1919) in Bratislava. Their functions and courses were similar to those of any American unversity. Universities were divided into five faculties (schools), headed by deans, who were elected by the professors. The five schools were Law, Medicine, Philosophy, Natural Sciences, and Catholic Theology. Each university was governed by a Rector (president) and an Academic Senate, composed of the deans and additional professor-members. Both the Rector and the Senate were elected by faculty members for one year. The Rector was selected from each of the schools in rotation.

The Academic Senate of the universities regulated and supervised all administrative, educational, and disciplinary matters. Although state-supported and state-controlled, Czechoslovak institutions of higher learning had a greater degree of autonomy than a state university in the United States usually has. The power of decision, which in the United States is often divided between the board of trustees and the faculty, was almost fully in the hands of the professor-administrators. Moreover, the annual change in the governing personnel of the universities prevented the emergence of an administrative hierarchy with an outlook different from that of the faculty.

The curricula of the universities were similar to those of American and English universities, except that Czechoslovak universities followed a completely different study of law. Unlike American study of law, which refers to earlier cases and decisions, Czechoslovak schools of law followed the tradition of Roman law, which resolves conflicts in terms of general and abstract principles. The Law School of Charles University, for example, required students to study not only the Czechoslovak codes, but also Roman private and constitutional law, canon law, central European history and law, philosophy of law, systematic philosophy, and international law and organization.

Specialized Institutions of Higher Learning. Czechoslovakia had seven institutions of higher learning, which emphasized engineering and natural sciences. Some of them were highly specialized, such as the Institute of Agriculture (founded in 1919) in Brno, and the Institute of Mines (1849) in Pribram. There were two Czech institutes of technology, one in Prague (1717) and the other in Brno (1919), and two German ones, in Prague (1803) and in Brno (1849). Like the universities, they were divided into different schools, including Chemical Engineering, Architecture, Mechanical and Electrical Engineering, and Building and Construction.

In addition to the two broad categories of institutions of higher learning (universities and technological institutes), there were other specialized institutions, such as the Protestant School of Divinity, School of Political Sciences and Journalism, Academy of Creative Arts, School of Music, War College, and Military College of Technology, and the German Academy of Music and Dramatic Arts.

All these institutions were supported and controlled by the state. The administrative and teaching personnel were employees of the government. Their salaries were determined, within the limits set by law, by the Ministry of Education, which also laid down regulations and requirements for teacher education and training, and issued prospective teachers' certificates.

Physical Education. Both within and without the school system, physical education was more important in Czechoslovakia than in most other countries. This was partly a result of educational philosophy, which put great emphasis on the beneficient influence of physical culture on the child's mind. Under Austro-Hungarian rule, the Czech athletic organizations became gathering places for Czech-speaking citizens, and gymnastics frequently was a pretext or a guise for political manifestation of Czech patriotism. The Czech athletic association of Sokols (Falcons) became the core of the patriotic movement in the last half of the nineteenth century. Under the Republic, gymnastic organizations increased and became diversified as a result of the close association between political parties and the athletic organizations. The Sokols, with 700,000 members, including women and children, were the largest. The Workers' Gymnastic Federation, ideologically linked with the Social Democratic Party, was the second largest. There was also a Catholic organization, Orel (Eagle), the Federation of Proletarian Physical Culture, organized by the Communist Party, several German sport associations, YMCA, YWCA, and numerous private sport clubs.

1939-1948

The close link between education and the political fate of the Czech people was symbolically demonstrated in 1939, a few months after the Nazi government had incorporated Bohemia-Moravia into the German Reich. As a reprisal for a patriotic demonstration, staged on November 17, 1939 by the students of Charles University in Prague, Nazi authorities closed all Czech institutions of higher learning, which remained closed until the end of World War II. Secondary and elementary schools were subjected to Nazi control; children continued to receive basic education in the Czech language, but the content was Nazi. As a consequence of this political and ideological pressure, some teachers and students were probably less dedicated to democracy, less immune to totalitarian pressures, and more ready to comply with the Communist streamlining of education than they would have been if the Communist coup of 1948 had followed a period of full freedom.

In Slovakia, which became a Nazi puppet state after March 14, 1939, institutions of higher learning remained open throughout World War II. A major change consisted in making all teachers, including those in private Catholic schools, employees of the state, although school facilities and buildings owned by private institutions remained in private hands. The large number of Slovak Catholic schools were nationalized by the Catholic-oriented, authoritarian government of the Slovak puppet state. After the war, government control of all Slovak schools continued, but the postwar government, composed of Communists and Protestant leaders of the Democratic Party, was less sympathetic toward the former Catholic schools. At that time, the school buildings became state property.

Following the six-year Nazi occupation, Czechoslovakia expelled more than four fifths of its German-speaking citizens. In the exuberantly nationalistic and revengeful atmosphere of 1945, all German elementary, secondary, and schools of higher learning were abolished. Former facilities of the German schools, including buildings, laboratories, and libraries, were transferred to Czech schools. This transfer was considered partial compensation for the six-year closing of Czech universities. After 1950, in line with the new Soviet approach to the German problem, some German elementary and secondary schools were reopened.

Developments under the Communists

The fundamental aim of Communist education is to provide the state with a new generation, whose aims, desires, and thinking are consistent with Communist political goals, and whose skills correspond to the production targets of economic plans. The schools must train the elite corps of administrators and managers needed by the state for the formulation and execution of policy. Thus, the educational system in Communist society is both an integral part of the economic plan and an instrument of political control.

Since the February 1948 coup, the Communist government has sought to bring Czechoslovak education into line with Marxist ideology and with Soviet institutions. It has subordinated the schools to a new, officially-sanctioned, educational philosophy. Marxism-Leninism is presented in the schools as a comprehensive and valid answer to all problems. Competing world views are introduced in the curriculum only to show how inadequate and false they are. According to the Communists, nothing but confusion and error are to be gained by subjecting the student to the traditional process of free discussion of competing world views.

The present educational system is based on the school law of April 24, 1953. Article 1 of this law expresses the Communist philosophy of education:

> Our schools must educate new socialist citizen-workers, farmers, and intelligentsia, well developed and perfectly prepared for the socialist society, which we are building. This goal can be attained only by schools which are closely linked with the great tasks of socialist building, with the political, economic, technological, and cultural developments of the country, and with national defense.

In accordance with this legal provision, education is permeated with political indoctrination, beginning with the first-grade reader in elementary schools and culminating with the curricula of universities.

Communist Indoctrination

The First Reader. The reader used in the first grade of elementary schools attempts to convince the child that he lives in a happy proletarian society. On August 16, 1951, *Mlada fronta* (Young Front), the daily publication of the Youth League, offered the following description of the contents of the first reader:

> Almost every page of the first reader shows our children the world of workers and farmers, the world in which there are no unemployed and in which there are people with new morality. On the first page of the reader, there is a picture of people returning from work. The father in this book is a worker. It is the workers of the glorious Soviet Union to whom we owe our freedom. Therefore, as the textbook shows, we raise the flag of the Soviet Union beside our own flag because the Soviet flag is the flag of our liberator, best friend, and protector. . . . The new reader not only familiarizes pupils with letters, but also has a far more important task: to educate pupils to become new citizens of our land, liberated from the last vestige of the old capitalistic morality; to enable boys and girls to enjoy great happiness in this Socialist and Communist epoch of our homeland, and to live in a world which will be free from all the horrors and the exploitation of people.

All elementary readers glorify manual labor. This emphasis was described by a Prague daily, *Lidove noviny* (People's News) on March 17, 1950:

> Manual labor was once a punishment and a threat to the children of the so-called better class . . . "one who will not study will have to go to work in the factories. . . ." Our schools are beginning to educate the children in another way. . . . Textbooks contain this type of teaching: "What will I be? From the time I was a little girl, I kept telling my mother that I would be a gardener. I will grow not only flowers and vegetables but also trees. I would like to know how to do it well, as the famous Michurin does it in the Soviet Union. . . ." Another example: ". . . If Peter wants to be a tractor driver, then I'll not only be a tractor driver but will drive a combine too. And what's more, I will go to a factory where they make those wonderful farm machines, and then Peter will see!"

Admiration for the Soviet Union. In all textbooks, the Soviet Union is glorified as the nation which surpasses the West in every field of human endeavor. In 1952, the Ministry of Education specified which pictures were to be hung in the classrooms. In addition to Czechoslovak Communist leaders, seventeen of the twenty-three acceptable names were Russian authors, philosophers, and politicians, such as Maiakovski, Gorki, Michurin, Pavlov, Pushkin, Tolstoy, Vyshinski, Molotov, and Zhdanov while the West was represented by a strange combination of Franklin D. Roosevelt, Karl Marx, Friedrich Engels, and Madame Curie. During the Korean War, many classroom walls in Prague were decorated by posters contrasting the United States with the Soviet Union: a poster with the caption "MacArthur Killing Women and Children" was paired with a poster depicting playing

Soviet children with the caption "The USSR—an Example for Us."

A fourth-grade reader elaborates the contrast between the capitalist and socialist worlds in the following manner:

> Uranium is a raw material for the production of radium and of atomic energy. Whereas in capitalist countries, particularly in the United States, they misuse atomic energy for promoting imperialistic aims, the Soviet Union uses atomic energy for the peaceful upbuilding of socialism. . . . In a capitalist society, industry produces luxury goods for the rich and inferior goods for the children of poor laborers. Here at home, production is designed . . . to increase the living standard of the working class by exclusive production of goods of the best quality. Under capitalism, all production is governed by the lust for profit. . . . In a time of depression the capitalists often destroy . . . food supplies just to keep prices high, while the unemployed suffer from hunger. . . . They produce food of less nutritious value for the miserably paid workers. In socialist industry, all production of food must be governed by the purpose of producing the best and most nutritious food for the working people.

Glorification of the Soviet Union and anti-West vituperation is not limited to the economic sphere, but extends to all fields, including geography. In 1952, Minister of Information Vaclav Kopecky made the following statement in an address to university teachers:

> In the interwar period, the Czechoslovak bourgeoisie based its entire educational system on the teaching of cosmopolitanism, directed toward Western ideology, toward Western science, and toward minimizing the culture of other nations, especially the Slavic. . . . We know that this cosmopolitanism was maintained after World War II and persisted even after February 1948 [Communist seizure of power]. . . . Presentation of geography, history, literature, physics, etc. was pro-Western. In geography, it was always maintained that the highest mountain in Europe was Mont Blanc, although in fact the highest mountain in Europe was Mount Elbrus in the Caucasian Range. There was hardly any teaching of the heights of mountains in Russia, of the expanse of the Soviet Union, of its great rivers . . . its national history and culture. . . . Lord Byron was always exalted while Pushkin, Shevchenko, Mickiewicz, and other great poets were suppressed. When they taught about military leaders, they spoke with awe about Napoleon, Wellington . . . but did not mention Suvorov. Speaking of admirals, they acknowledged Nelson but not Nachimov. . . . When they spoke of Jan Hus, our great man, they always included Wycliffe as his predecessor. . . . When they spoke of Comenius, they always intentionally emphasized his living in the West, as if he would develop his talent as an educator only during his exile in the West.

The study of Soviet institutions is now a permanent feature of Czechoslovak education. In a directive issued by the Ministry of

Education on August 20, 1951, the first objective in teaching third-grade civics is to "acquaint the student with the Soviet Union's constitution, its social and state organization, and its advantages as compared with the exploiting organization of the capitalist states." According to this directive, the study of Czechoslovakia (its Communist Party and economic structure) is relegated to second place. Coupled with the study of Soviet institutions is the study of the Russian language. Russian is an obligatory subject from the fourth grade. The circulation of Russian newspapers and magazines has been constantly increasing. According to *Svobodne slovo* (Free Word) of November 4, 1955, subscriptions to Soviet publications increased 100 per cent during the previous five years. The number of subscribers in 1955 was listed as 297,000, and over fifteen million copies of Soviet papers and magazines were distributed that year.

These impressive figures do not mean that Czechoslovak subscribers read the publications, since subscription is usually the result of manifold pressures. In addition to the compulsory teaching of Russian in schools, the Communists have organized voluntary Russian language courses for workers, administrators, and engineers. As these courses are organized within the framework of each enterprise, the individual worker can hardly avoid attending them. In 1952, over 300,000 workers from all levels had to attend these courses, making up some 19,000 study groups. There appears to be difficulty in fitting the Russian courses into the already heavy working schedules of the Czechoslovak workers. The Slovak trade union paper, *Praca* (Work), of November 9, 1955, reports that in some factories, workers' study groups have to meet at 4:30 A. M. as this is the only hour of the day when such meeting is possible.

A significant postscript to the overwhelming emphasis on the knowledge of the Russian language was offered at the close of the 1955 academic year by the official organ of Czechoslovak teachers, *Ucitelske noviny* (Teachers' News) of June 16, 1955:

> Final examinations gave us a great amount of satisfaction this year as they indicated a steady, although not dramatic progress in the knowledge of Russian. . . . The pupils were able to read a Russian text without difficulty and tried to have a correct accent and pronunciation. They had no difficulty in translating a completely unknown Russian text into Czech, but very often they made mistakes in their mother tongue.

Campaign Against Religion. Under Czechoslovakia's Communist regime, freedom of religion includes the right to agitate against religion as well as the right to practice religion. While all Czechoslovak schools ostensibly respect the right of parents and children to request instruction in the religion of their choice, the exercise of this right is discouraged. "Anti-religious education, i.e., the training of conscious and militant unbelievers, is an organic component of Communist education," wrote Andrej Pavlik, president of the Slovak Academy of Sciences, and translator of the official Soviet textbook on education (by I. A. Kairov) into Slovak. "Whenever possible," continues Pavlik, "the school should emphasize anti-religious movements in all subjects and should not be satisfied with making people indifferent to religion but should transform them . . . into militant atheists."

This campaign against religion, conducted by the Party, schools, and youth organizations, does not seem to yield results. The Communist press contains frequent references to the fact that students and teachers alike seemingly comply with the antireligious and scientific orientation of their studies, while in reality they remain "prisoners of unscientific views, religious illusions, and prejudices" (*Rude pravo* [Red Right], February 7, 1956).

Religious instruction, as well as education of the clergy and of religious teachers, is under severe pressure from Communist doctrine. Religious leaders who collaborate with the Communist regime try to fit Christianity within the doctrinal framework of Leninism. "Theological education and training of future priests must be directed toward fulfillment of a very serious duty: to support the building of a higher social order, which is based on a higher productivity of labor. Since the working classes, led by industrial labor, play an important role in building our fatherland . . . , theological doctrine, which aims at the knowledge and esteem of God, cannot stand idly by when a movement attempts to secure a happy life for men on earth" (Cyril Dudas, Dean of Catholic School of Theology in Bratislava, quoted in *Katolicke noviny* [Catholic News], October 2, 1955).

Communist Interpretation of History. A directive of the Central Committee of the Communist Party, dated May 28, 1951, indicates that one of the major objectives of the regime is to eradicate all historical references which link Czechoslovakia favorably with the West. On the other hand, certain aspects of Czechoslovakia's relations with the West, such as the crusades against Czech Protestants in the fifteenth century and the Munich Pact in 1938, are frequently depicted in the worst possible light. In contrast, ties with the Slavic East are glorified and represented as the best possible influence on Czech and Slovak history. With respect to the interwar period 1918-38, which many Czechs consider to be the golden age of their nation's history, the Communist Party directive says:

> It is necessary to expose clearly the bourgeois anti-people and anti-Soviet policy of the previous governments, and to show the truly reactionary policy of Thomas G. Masaryk and Edward Benes. In contrast, it is necessary to stress the progressive role of the Soviet Union in our history and the glorious struggle of the Communist Party of Czechoslovakia to shake off the yoke of oppression.

As long as Czechs and Slovaks yearn for conditions comparable to those that existed from 1918 to 1938, they will not give the present regime the loyalty it demands. Accordingly, the Communists are determined to root out all memories of a "golden age under capitalism."

Organization of Education

The Communist educational system is designed to accomplish three fundamental tasks:

1. A new intelligentsia must be created, which will accept unconditionally the principles of Marxism-Leninism and their application on the Soviet pattern. In this sense, education under the Communists becomes a major instrument of political thought control.

2. The new intelligentsia is to be oriented away from philosophy, law, and social sciences toward applied sciences. There has been a spectacular shift of emphasis in the structure of the school system toward specialized industrial schools and institutes of technology. Education is thus harnessed to the requirements of planned economy. particularly to the expansion and servicing of heavy industry. This is in accordance with the current Soviet-assigned role of Czechoslovakia as a workshop of the Communist world and a main supplier of machinery and technological skills to the underdeveloped neutral or Communist nations in Asia and Africa.

3. The class content of the new intelligentsia is to favor children of Communist officials, workers, and small peasants. The aim is to minimize the influence of parents and members of the old intelligentsia, educated in the pro-Western atmosphere of prewar Czechoslovakia, and to maximize the influence of Communist officials, Stakhanovites, and other groups who are favored by the new regime. This task, although seemingly simple, has encountered serious difficulties, as indicated in an article in *Svobodne slovo* of March 20, 1956:

> In disproportion with the social composition of our population, a relatively small number of young people from workers' and small peasants' families apply for admission to the institutions of higher learning. This is a very unhealthy phenomenon, and secondary schools as well as schools of higher learning have to make a maximum effort in the future to recruit students precisely from among those groups.

Elementary and Secondary Schools. In accordance with the education acts of 1948 and 1953, elementary and secondary schools are closely patterned on the Soviet system. Education is compulsory for all children between six and fourteen years of age. Attendance in kindergarten for children from three to five years of age is optional, but strongly encouraged. This serves two purposes: to expose a child to socialist influence as early as possible, and to enable recruitment of mothers for work, thus relieving the constant manpower shortage in industry. Minister of Education Zdenek Nejedly, speaking in the Czechoslovak Parliament on March 15, 1951, declared:

> It is a mistake to start training children late. We send them to kindergartens at the age of three. I remember that I was severely criticized in the West when I declared that we should have compulsory nursery schools, and that we should enroll children of rich parents as well. We must not leave the children at the mercy of anyone.

The school law of 1953 introduced a uniform school system, lowered the previous upper compulsory limit of school attendance from fifteen to fourteen years of age, and, in the field of secondary schools, placed the age for final examination at seventeen years, instead of the previous eighteen to nineteen years. The purpose of this reform was explained by the Minister of Education in an article in *Prace* (Work) on April 28, 1953.

> The new law speeds up the school training of our youth. . . . We must not lose time. Every year and every month which holds back our youth from work longer than is necessary is a pitiful loss. . . . Today's youth is much more advanced than it was before. Two years saved in school attendance represent a great capital for the republic.

The Communist reorganization of education created two broad categories of schools, one accessible to all, and the other reserved to carefully selected groups. The first category is composed of the following schools:

Schools	Age
Kindergarten	3- 5
Elementary schools (in small communities)	6-11
Junior secondary schools (8 grades, of which the first 5 are identical with elementary schools)	6-14
Apprentice schools or labor reserve schools (often attached to mines or industrial plants)	15-16

The second category of schools may be attended only by those who pass a test, which examines not only their academic knowledge but also their interest in building socialism, their attitude toward the Soviet Union, their motives and length of membership in the Pioneer or Czechoslovak Youth Organization, their proletarian origin, and the Party affiliation of their parents. This second group consists of the following schools:

Schools	Age
Senior secondary school (grades 9-11)	15-17
Selective vocational schools (e.g. pedagogy, industry, industrial arts, agriculture, forestry, social welfare, music, health, etc.)	15-17/18
Evening and correspondence education	no specification
Military and police schools	no specification

According to official statistics (State Statistical Office, *Statisticky obzor* [Statistical Review], No. 1 [1956], pp. 38-39), in 1955/56, 1,846,598 pupils attended compulsory elementary and secondary schools (grades 1-8), while 69,835 pupils were admitted to selective senior secondary schools (grades 9-11). Evening courses were attended by 26,423 students, and correspondence education by 6,982 people.

Universities. The Communists claim a total of forty institutions of higher learning: three universities, three institutes of technology, two institutes for economic studies, and thirty-two other institutions, most of them highly specialized. The total number of enrolled students was 48,534 in 1955/56. In addition, 19,767 students participated in higher education by correspondence, and 1,037 students attended evening courses. These figures indicate a considerable expansion, but the value of this expansion is questionable. The number of institutions of higher learning was increased partly by the territorial decentralization of universities formerly located in Prague and in Brno, and partly by the subdivision of many schools into narrowly specialized colleges. Moreover, most of the new schools were established without adequate instructors and facilities. Coupled with lowering the age of enrollment to seventeen years, these changes inevitably resulted in lower standards.

The former autonomy of state universities and institutes of technology was abolished by the Higher Education Act of May 1950. Under the Communists, control by the state and Party is absolute. Ministers of Education and Culture are always members of the higher organs of the Communist Party and of the government. Assisted by a newly created State Committee for Higher Education, they appoint rectors (presidents), deans, members of college councils (former academic senates), and professors. From below, all institutions of higher learning are under the control and pressure of Communist student organizations and university employees (clerks, cleaning women, janitors and other employees). Together with the deans and chairmen of different departments, the representatives of the students and university employees form "faculty councils," another instrument of pressure against the few non-Communist members of the teaching staff.

While the reorganized system of higher education is to train specialists in all fields, it is not expected, except in rare cases, to produce future members of the Party aristocracy. For this purpose, a Party University was established in September 1953, offering three-year courses and enjoying full university standing. It is under the administrative and financial control of the Central Committee of the Communist Party. Its function was described by the central organ of the Party, *Rude pravo,* on September 2, 1953:

> We need Party workers who see further than their desk; who are capable of solving, correctly and independently, urgent problems and of guiding others; who do not rely on some instinct and their own limited experiences, but are supported in their decisions and acts by profound knowledge of the laws of society, by the knowledge of the great experiences of our teacher, the Communist Party of Czechoslovakia, and the entire international workers' movement.

The reorganization of higher learning was accompanied by a marked shift toward engineering and other technical disciplines. The Czechoslovak economic plan, which puts great emphasis on heavy industry, mining, and production of machine tools, demands an increasing number of technicians, managers, engineers, and technological experts of all kinds. The educational system had to be adapted to this major task. Many specialized technical colleges are actually training schools for mining, metallurgy, chemistry, railroads, and textiles, and are closely associated with these industrial branches. However, these schools do not seem to attract a sufficient number of students. According to official statistics, 53.6 per cent of the total number of college students were registered at institutes of technology and technical colleges in 1955/56. The interests of young Czechs and Slovaks indicate a trend contrary to that of the regime, i.e. away from technology and toward the humanities. The organ of the trade unions, *Prace,* complained on November 5, 1955:

> Every year we are confronted with the same problem: masses of students apply to universities to study medicine, biology, and hu-

> manities, while technical disciplines stay unjustly neglected. In the study of medicine, we have usually three or four times more candidates than the universities can accommodate . . . and at the same time the lack of agricultural engineers is catastrophic.

Similar complaints can be found almost constantly in the Communist press. No reason is usually given for this lack of interest in technology, except for some obscure references blaming the lack of understanding and encouragement on the part of old-fashioned parents. It is possible that a partial explanation may be found in the desire of students to find careers which are less exposed to direct political and economic pressures and controls. The Slovak daily *Lud* (People) commented on this subject on March 1, 1956:

> The situation of our industry is serious, because of the lack of technicians, especially those with higher education. . . . It is a very grave problem that our youth do not show much interest in technical studies at the institutions of higher learning. There is no interest in mining, foundries, or the machine building industry. The interest in economic engineering . . . and in higher agricultural studies . . . is weak.

The same article stated that students graduating from secondary and vocational schools in spring 1956 were applying *en masse* for admission to the universities. At Comenius University in Bratislava, the number of applicants to the different schools for 1956/57 far exceeded the number of students the University can accommodate: in medicine, by 90 per cent; in pharmaceutical studies, by 130 per cent; in philosophy, by 190 per cent; and in natural sciences, by 110 per cent.

Conflict between the ambitions of the regime and those of the students does not end with registration and the assignment of students to schools. Students may refuse assignment to schools other than those of their choice, but they must then decide between the different kinds of apprentice or vocational schools, or between different kinds of manual work. Following graduation from the institutions of higher learning, graduates are assigned to specific areas or functions. According to the Minister of Manpower, Josef Tesla, speaking on February 1, 1956, "correct placement of our young people is not always in harmony with the personal interests of the youth. Only a systematic education of our youth and their parents can overcome this conflict between the interests of individuals and the needs of our economy."

A similar criticism concerning the unwillingness of graduates to take up state-assigned duties was voiced on February 14, 1956, in the law students' magazine, *Pravnik* (Lawyer):

> An implacable fight against the incorrect attitude of graduates toward state assignments is a precondition for correct placement of specialists. Often our students avoid taking up their assigned positions and try, through private channels, to find other positions. . . . A student whose college education necessitated considerable state expenditure must have a different attitude regarding his duties toward society.

Conclusion

Although Czechoslovakia has been subjected to the Communist system of education for only eight years, the effects clearly indicate the situation which lies ahead: a compartmentalized society in which only a small elite is trained to have an overall view and control of society while the majority is divided and subdivided into specialized groups of administrators, managers, technicians, engineers, builders, inventors and so forth.

The Communist system attempts to change the present pattern of superficial conformity, coupled with covert rebellion, at least into conformity *without* rebellion. Every step of the young, from nursery school to the first gainful occupation, is watched by the regime. Most pupils are organized in the Communist Pioneer movement, starting at the age of nine, and later join the Communist Youth League. In elementary school, pupils are introduced to their lifelong duty of active participation in the affairs of the socialist state. Every child must have a special "pupil's passport," in which his school record, participation in Pioneer organization, and socialist pledges are registered. Later, his participation in "voluntary" brigades, in Russian language courses, and in political class discussions, recorded in his personal file in the Communist Youth League, determine his qualification for further studies and scholarship.

The Communist effort to overburden the young with many extracurricular activities serves to alienate children from their families and to minimize the influence of the older generation. In some cases, Communist education has transformed children into informers which has led to the arrest of their fathers or mothers for alleged anti-state attitudes. In most cases, however, the bond between parents and children remains solid, and parents are able to correct the distorted views and information which the Communist school presents to their children.

In the spring of 1956 period of relaxation, which followed the Twentieth Congress of the Communist Party of the Soviet Union, parental influence on young generations seems to have paid rich dividends, despite the contrary and overwhelming pressure of the regime.

Student criticism of the Communist educational system and aims became quite open. This criticism was directed primarily against the many courses in Marxism-Leninism, the low standards of instruction, the absence of Western literature in university libraries, compulsory attendance at soporific lectures, and obligatory participation in extracurricular activities. There were also a number of frankly political demands, such as the request that the Soviet flag should not be displayed more prominently than the flags of other friendly nations. Significant of the impact of the democratic past on the Communist present exerted on the young by the older generation was a sign carried through the streets of Prague by the Charles University students on May 15, 1956, during their traditional May celebration (*majales*). Defiantly, it announced *urbi et orbi*, "We are young, but we remember a lot."

9. LITERATURE

Henry Kucera and Emil Kovtun

Czechoslovakia's geographical position on the "crossroads of Europe" and the problems of national survival which it brings are reflected also in its cultural history. While Czechoslovak culture is fundamentally Latin and Western, there is in it an underlying revolt against complete Westernization. Moreover, a conflict frequently appears between the concept of literature as an expression of the historical and national ambitions of the people, on one hand, and as a purely creative art, on the other. These conflicts, combined with other factors, created the traditional antinomies of Czech literature:[1] Western and Eastern orientation, Latin and Slavic heritage, cosmopolitanism and nationalism, universalism and self-justification.

Early Czech Literature

The Czech and Slovak peoples had no written literature prior to their first encounter with Christianity in the ninth century. Before the Czech language became the recognized literary medium, the liturgical languages of the early period, Church Slavonic, and later, Latin, were employed in written literature.

[1] Slovak was not codified and generally accepted as a literary language until approximately the middle of the nineteenth century, although some Slovak writings and attempts at establishing a distinct Slovak literary language date from an earlier period. From the middle of the fifteenth century to the middle of the nineteenth, Czech was used, especially among the Slovak Protestants, as the main medium of literary expression. Thus, while it is convenient to speak of Czech literature when discussing the period prior to the 1850's, it is necessary to bear in mind that this literature has at times originated in, or influenced, at least parts of the Slovak territory, and that several distinguished authors who wrote in Czech came from Slovakia. In this short survey, literature written in the Czech language is discussed under the heading of Czech literature, even when the authors were natives of Slovakia. Attempts at stabilizing a distinct Slovak literary language, and the literature following these successful efforts, are surveyed separately.

Brothers Constantine and Methodius, Greek scholars and missionaries, brought to Moravia (in 863) not only Eastern Christianity, but also the first Slavic literary language, the first Slavic alphabet, and the first church literature. Political and cultural developments in Czechoslovak territory soon interrupted the Church Slavonic liturgical and literary tradition. Nevertheless, much of it remained: realization that the national language was a suitable and dignified instrument for religious and literary expression led to national and Slavic consciousness—a factor of great importance in the subsequent periods of Czech history.

However, it was Latin culture which had a permanent influence on Czech literature. With the increasing predominance of Western Christianity in the last decade of the tenth century, Latin monopolized Czech literary life.

The Gothic period in the fourteenth century marked the first flourishing of literature in the Czech language; it encompassed all forms of medieval poetry and was characterized by a rich, cultured language and skillful poetic form. The Gothic period reached its peak in the second half of the fourteenth century, during the reign of Charles IV, a monarch who supported and encouraged scholarship and literary activity. Czech literature during the Gothic period had an independent character, showed little German influence, and brought a remarkable development in Czech poetry and prose.

The early Renaissance took only insecure roots in Bohemia, but the first ideas of religious reformation were received with much interest. A national meaning was soon added to the moral and social content of the Czech reformation movement, with emphasis on the Czech language in sermons, religious hymns, and the liturgy. The writings and proselyting talent of the fiery preacher of reformatory ideas, Jan Hus (1369-1415) introduced a new period of Czech history, one marked by heroism and tragedy. Hus contributed much as a modernizer of the Czech literary language and as a thinker and writer. He elevated the dialect of Prague into a literary language and created a new Czech orthography.

The Hussite wars interrupted all cultural contact between Bohemia and the rest of Europe, and were responsible for a temporary literary stagnation. Religious and military songs and hymns of the Hussite warriors, and polemic and tendentious literature represent the main production of this period. The greatest thinker of this period was Petr Chelcicky (1390-1460), whose return to the ideal of the simplicity of the apostolic church, and whose emphasis on "non-resistance to evil" represented a spiritual reaction against the warlike spirit of his times.

The Union of Czech Brethren, based on Chelcicky's philosophy, was founded in the middle of the fifteenth century, and played an important part in Czech literary life. In the following century, it gave to Czech culture Jan Blahoslav (1523-71), a literary critic, musical theoretician, historian, and translator of the New Testament. His translation became a part of the edition of the *Bible kralicka* (Kralice Bible), a masterpiece of the Czech language which remained the linguistic model for writers of the following centuries.

The defeat of the Czech anti-Habsburg opposition in the battle of White Mountain (1620) and the following period of Counter-Reformation brought about a gradual change in Czech literary life. The greatest figure of Czech culture in the seventeenth century is Jan Amos Komensky (1592-1670), known abroad as Comenius, who spent most of his adult life in exile and was the last bishop of the Czech Brethren. Comenius is the founder of modern educational methods, explained most comprehensively in his *Didactica Magna;* much of his energy was devoted to pansophic writings. Comenius' philosophy has many characteristics of the baroque spirit. His chief philosophical work is *Labyrint sveta a raj srdce* (The Labyrinth of the World and the Paradise of the Heart).

The seventeenth century saw the complete victory of the Catholic baroque in Bohemia, and inaugurated a period which the predominant school of Czech historians used to regard as the "dark age" of Czech culture. This viewpoint was revised by later research, which challenged the concept that the seventeenth and most of the eighteenth century represented a complete interruption of Czech literary tradition. The baroque period produced not only the patriotic historian Bohuslav Balbin (1621-88) and his followers, but also a flourishing folk literature and some remarkable works of baroque lyrics.

Czech Literature Before World War I

A new epoch in Czechoslovak cultural and political life was inaugurated at the end of the eighteenth century when the movement of National Revival aroused the cultural life of the land and drew literature into its service.

The Revival movement, at first an endeavor for a Czech linguistic and cultural emancipation from the tutelage of German Vienna, but later a more systematic program for economic and political liberation from Habsburg centralism, gradually penetrated into all strata of the population. The leading men during the early period of this movement devoted themselves to linguistic studies in an attempt to raise the prestige of the Czech language, study its relationship to other

Slavic tongues, and enrich it. Josef Dobrovsky (1753-1829) is the founder of comparative Slavic philology and of Czech literary criticism. Josef Jungmann (1773-1847) is the creator of modern Czech literary language, which he enriched by resurrected archaisms, many of his own neologisms, and borrowings from other Slavic tongues.

An effort was also made to create an ancient Czech literary tradition, an epos that would reflect the glorious past of the Czech nation. Vaclav Hanka (1791-1861) and Josef Linda (1789-1834) are believed to have been the authors of several literary forgeries, which purported to be manuscripts of the ninth to thirteenth centuries.

The Slavic consciousness which manifested itself in linguistic research, in translations from other Slavic languages, and in interest in Slavic folklore found its culmination in the works of Jan Kollar (1793-1852), a native of Slovakia. Kollar was the most ardent preacher of Slavic solidarity, a cultural Pan-Slavism influenced by Herder, idealistically conceived and without realistic political overtones. Kollar's contemporaries, Frantisek Palacky (1798-1876) and Pavel Josef Safarik (1795-1861), a native of Slovakia, entered literary life as poets and theoreticians of prosody. However, they were more prominent outside pure literature: Palacky, as author of the first modern Czech history, *Dejiny narodu ceskeho v Cechach a v Morave* (History of the Czech Nation in Bohemia and Moravia), and as a political writer and thinker, and Safarik as a student of Slavic archeology, philology, history, and literatures.

Soon, however, classicism, with its formal rigidity and idealistic philosophy, threatened stagnation in Czech literary creativity. The rejuvenation came, in the true spirit of romanticism, from folk poetry and its forms. Early Czech literary romanticism continued to build around the concepts of nationality, language, Slavic solidarity and reverence for the past, but it added to these concepts an active interest in the people, their songs, poetry, and folklore in general. The main representative of this movement was Karel Jaromir Erben (1811-70), who wrote verses of formal simplicity, inspired by mythology and the folklore demonism of nature and human passions, but who believed in the triumph of the pure and pious heart. The other main representative of Czech poetic romanticism, Karel Hynek Macha (1810-36), stands in sharp contrast to Erben. He is a poet of pessimism, metaphysical conflicts and anxieties, painfully aware of the duality of earthly life and the absoluteness of death. Macha, author of the famous poem *Maj* (May) and poet-revolutionary of Czech literature, was unappreciated by his contemporaries who were devotees of national romanticism. Two decades after his untimely death, he was finally recognized as one of the greatest personalities of Czech literature.

Economic developments and the political upheavals of the 1840's made it necessary to revise the idealistic character of the Czech National Revival. The first realistic criticism of Czech patriotism was the work of Karel Havlicek Borovsky (1821-56), one of the first outstanding Czech journalists. He emphasized realistic political efforts, rejecting historical sentimentalism and the Pan-Slavism sustained by Czech illusions.

The founder of modern Czech prose and the Czech village novel and short story was Bozena Nemcova (1820-62), author of the widely read, best-loved, and most optimistic book of Czech literature, *Babicka* (The Grandmother). However, the village short story did not lead to the realistic novel, and it is quite characteristic of Czech literature that its development in subsequent generations centered upon Czech poetry.

The literary generation of the 1860's found the struggle for national cultural survival successfully completed, but it faced new and more complex political and social problems. This "May generation" (named after the almanac *Maj* [May], where its program was proclaimed), which wanted to devote itself to contemporary problems and social realities, was influenced by the Hegelian left, and politically associated with the liberal-democratic movement. Although its members professed to be followers of Macha, they were inspired more by the poet's literary revolutionism than by his subjectivism and romanticism. The leading representatives of the "May generation" were poets and journalists, which is reflected in the literary production of the period. Among them, Jan Neruda (1834-91) stands out as the sceptic, ironic, at times bitter, but unquestionably significant poet. He was also a popular newspaper columnist, short story writer, and a literary and dramatic critic.

The generation which came to the fore in the last two decades of the nineteenth century illustrates the Czech antinomy of nationalism and cosmopolitanism. The national school, whose leading poet was Svatopluk Cech (1846-1908), revived most of the ideological values of the national movement from the beginning of the century. Its interest in the Czech past led to the flourishing of the historical novel. The best known writer of this genre was Alois Jirasek (1851-1930), author of many historical novels in which Hussite motifs predominate. Superior to Jirasek in artistic intensity and ability to experience psychological reality is Zikmund Winter (1846-1912), author of the masterpiece of the Czech historical novel, *Mistr Kampanus* (Master Kampanus).

Josef Vaclav Sladek (1845-1912), a translator of Shakespeare and Longfellow, and a poet of the Czech countryside, occupies a transitional position between the cosmopolitan and the national schools.

The cosmopolitan school evolved around Julius Zeyer (1841-1901) and Jaroslav Vrchlicky (1853-1912). The cosmopolitans, Western in orientation, supplemented the German influence on Czech letters by introducing French, Italian, and English authors, as well as new poetic forms. Zeyer was both a poet and a successful representative of the Czech psychological novel of the last century. Vrchlicky was the most versatile and prolific of Czech writers. Both in his original works and his numerous translations, he introduced to Czech literature a variety of metric forms, new subjects and ideas, and he enriched the Czech poetic language. He occupies a position of unequaled importance in Czech letters.

At the turn of the century, a new trend appeared in Czech culture: "critical" or "social" realism. Critical examination of older concepts and attitudes and preoccupation with social problems are its main characteristics. Thomas Garrigue Masaryk (1850-1937), a philosopher and anti-Marxian sociologist, and the leading political figure of modern Czech history, began to dominate Czech cultural and public life before the turn of the century. Masaryk added his own concepts of ethics to Comte's and Spencer's positivism, emphasizing moral revitalization of society, religious consciousness, and humanism. Besides his strong general influence on Czech cultural life, Masaryk's significance in the field of literature lies in his interpretation of the Czech National Revival movement, in his vigorous struggle against narrow nationalistic prejudice, and in his rejection of unrealistic Pan-Slavism.

Josef Svatopluk Machar (1864-1942), an uncompromising and aggressive polemicist, was the only true poet of "critical realism." The outstanding novelists of this genre were also extremely limited. In fact, it was the naturalist Karel Matej Capek-Chod (1860-1927), who exceeded all of his contemporaries, both in compositional skill and in popularity. He was a writer of penetrating insight into Prague society in all its social strata.

Some of the realistic and naturalistic poets and writers published works in both the prewar and postwar periods. This is also true of the founder of modern Czech literary criticism, Frantisek Xaver Salda (1867-1937), who follows Masaryk as one of the principal creators of the basic concepts of Czechoslovak culture. Inspired by French and English ideas of symbolism, Salda advocated art as an independent spiritual and creative activity, denying that it should serve Czech nationalism or any other ideology. To him, art is connected with the basic existence problems of the human personality. Salda was the arbiter of Czech literary taste and the interpreter of several literary generations and literary trends.

The partial disintegration of the traditional, regular, smoothly running dactylotrochaic verse was apparent before the turn of the century. In different forms and varying extent, free verse became the medium of the whole prewar poetic generation. As in other European literatures, impressionism and symbolism predominated. Antonin Sova (1864-1928) became the main impressionistic poet of Czech literature. The greatest Czech symbolist and perhaps the greatest modern poet of Czech literature was Otokar Brezina (1868-1929). Although he was a poet of vast intellect with theosophical interests and mystical philosophical leanings, his poetic work is founded on an exalted imagination, filled with metaphysical reflections of cosmic events and of human participation in these mysteries. In his poetry, the motifs of tragedy of existence alternate with optimistic faith in cosmic harmony. Although Jiri Karasek ze Lvovic (1871-1951) is usually listed as the original representative of Czech "decadence," several other poets of the generation born in the 1870's exceed him in artistic importance. This is especially true of Karel Hlavacek (1874-98), a poet of remarkable talent for sensitive symbolism, balladic form and exceptional melodiousness who has, in spite of his untimely death, won for himself one of the top places in Czech poetry. Other members of the same generation are less easily identifiable with specific poetic schools. Stanislav Kostka Neumann (1875-1947) abandoned his early individualism for socialistic collectivism and revolutionary pathos, and is now the "classic" poet for the Communist literary critics. Karel Toman (1877-1946), occasionally a nonmilitant socialist, was primarily a lyricist of unrhetorical verse and intense feeling, the poet of home, safely anchored in older Czech traditions. Petr Bezruc (1867-—) is a solitary bard of the Silesian borderland, preoccupied with the national and social motifs of his region. Frana Sramek (1877-1952) wrote balladic and sensual lyrics, and prose which was chiefly concerned with the erotic and emotional problems of youth. A rather isolated personality in Czech literature was Viktor Dyk (1877-1931), not only a poet of condensed and often abrupt verse frequently politically and socially inspired, and a writer of numerous ironic prose dramas, but also an ardently patriotic journalist and a conservative politician.

The new rise of Catholic poetry is represented by several authors, known as members of the Catholic Moderna. The most significant among them is Jakub Deml (1878-—), the author of soft lyrics, rhythmical prose, and autobiographical notes and polemics.

Slovak Literature Before World War I

The Czech lands and Slovakia were separated from the time of the downfall of the Great Moravian Empire and the Magyar conquest of its eastern part in the tenth century. The political subjugation of

Slovakia to Hungarian rule, interrupted only temporarily during the Hussite wars, did not terminate until the establishment of the Czechoslovak Republic in 1918. During these thousand years, Slovak life suffered greatly from the oppressive economic and cultural policy of the conquerors. Slovak survived as a spoken vernacular, but was not definitely established as a literary language until the middle of the nineteenth century.

The political separation of the Czech lands from Slovakia hampered, but did not entirely prevent Czecho-Slovak cultural contact. While most of the Slovak Catholics retained Latin as their means of literary communication up to the end of the eighteenth century, the Czech language used by the Protestants in their religious services and activities was, for a long time, the literary medium of many Slovaks.

The center of Slovak Protestants was in Bratislava; the Catholics congregated in the city of Trnava. There, the first attempts were made (aside from earlier sporadic ventures) to establish a distinct Slovak literary language in the last decade of the eighteenth century by Anton Bernolak (1762-1813), who selected the Western Slovak dialect as the basis of the new literary medium; his suggestions, not elaborated linguistically, did not take permanent hold.

The decisive step toward the establishment of a Slovak literary language was undertaken through the initiative of the Protestants. Ludovit Stur (1815-56) selected the central Slovak dialect as the basis for the Slovak literary medium. Beginning in the 1840's, several poets followed Stur and used the new literary language with great skill. The most outstanding among these were Andrej Sladkovic (1820-62), a poet of balladic epics which romantically treated domestic Slovak subjects; Samo Chalupka (1812-63), author of fiery patriotic verses, inspired by the forms of folk-poetry and songs; Janko Kral (1822-76), a wanderer, rebellious spirit, and melancholic poet; and Jan Botto (1829-81) who was strongly influenced by the Czech romantic Macha. Slovak prose, much slower in its development than poetry was pioneered by Jan Kalinciak (1822-71).

The Austro-Hungarian Compromise *(Ausgleich)* of 1867 and subsequent absolute Hungarian rule over Slovakia were hard blows to Slovak national ambitions. A policy of Magyarization was vigorously carried out, and Slovak opposition could be only defensive.

The writers and poets who were born around the middle of the century and who faced these adverse conditions, are traditionally classified by literary critics as "realists." This designation, however, is not entirely fitting in regard to the two great poets of these years, Vajansky and Hviezdoslav. Svetozar Hurban Vajansky (1847-1916) was a Russian-oriented advocate of Slovak traditionalism who consistently tried to combine high aesthetic criteria with the function of poetry in the Slovak national cause. Pavol Orszagh Hviezdoslav (1848-1921) is considered the greatest Slovak poet, acclaimed for the versatility of his works, his translations from European literatures, and his enrichment of the Slovak cultural horizon and literary language.

The first important realistic novelist was Martin Kukucin (1860-1928), founder of modern Slovak prose and teacher of later generations of writers, as well as author of many novels, short stories, and travel sketches.

Czech "critical realism" and Masaryk's influence reached Slovakia before the turn of the century when the periodical *Hlas* (Voice) (published from 1898 to 1905, and edited by Vavro Srobar and Pavol Blaho) became the focal point of the new generation. The "Hlasists" were advocates of common Czechoslovak statehood and opponents of Slovak separatist tendencies.

Among the writers of the Slovak Moderna, the new poetic school influenced by symbolism, the most significant was Ivan Krasko (1876-——), a rather pessimistic poet of melodious subjective lyrics, a seeker of new poetic and formal expressions. Janko Jesensky (1874-1945), closely bound to Slovak traditions and poetic forms of the nineteenth century, later turned to prose and achieved his greatest success with his novels, which appeared in the 1930's. Martin Razus (1888-1937) was a poet of fiery, often tendentious and rhetorical but impressive verse and, mainly after World War I, a writer of prose which attempts to analyze the ideological and social trends of postwar Slovak society.

Czech and Slovak Literature, 1918-1945

Czech Literature

While the pressures of war and the final struggle for Czechoslovak statehood were almost all-absorbing in their intensity during World War I, Czechoslovak cultural life displayed an atmosphere of relief and optimism almost immediately after the war. It was an era of new primitivism and vitalism, of humanistic reaction to the war, and of naïve faith in life. It was also a period of experimentation, of breaking with traditions, and of liberation from conventions. This atmosphere underwent a change in the late 1920's, and 1930's, when the threatening world situation, with the rise of Hitlerism across the border, brought about increasing pessimism and eventually a general expectation of catastrophe and war.

During the early postwar years, a radical reorientation of the general intellectual climate took place. The achievement of political independence had eliminated the need from reflecting the national struggle in artistic works and had freed Czechoslovak literature from much of its previous national tendentiousness. Czech nationalism was now replaced by internationalism. Ideas, trends, and models from abroad flooded into Czech literary life, and the literature of this period had an unmistakably cosmopolitan character. Various new literary trends from the West left a deep impact: expressionism, futurism, cubism, dadaism, and surrealism. The Russian revolution brought to Czechoslovakia the concept of proletarian poetry and literature as a means of social struggle.

Czechoslovak scholarship and science were striving to introduce modern concepts and to achieve world-wide recognition. The tradition of the previous century, which had found one of its main cultural tasks in the study of language and in its stabilization, was continued, and the work of the Prague Linguistic Circle (founded in 1926 by Roman Jakobson and Vilem Mathesius) and its structural linguistics has remained of lasting importance in modern philology.

For a short time, Czech poetry was preoccupied with social problems and motifs. The "proletarian poets" sought to make a vigorous break with individualism and expressed their need for identification with the masses. However, the trend away from "proletarian poetry" started soon. The new school of "poetism" represented a decisive step toward individualized lyricism and a break with the tradition of narrative poetry. Being a sort of *poésie pure,* poetism aspired to be a reflection of life, without any national or logical restrictions. Its intellectual content was minimal, the play of poetic images primary. While poetism was greatly influenced by dadaism, surrealism, and futurism, it also found theoretical justification in the structuralism of the Prague linguistic school, where poetic devices were analyzed primarily in view of their function in the organization of poetic works.

In the early 1930's, a reaction appeared against poetism, and some of its leading adherents abandoned it in search of more absolute values: a new personalism, a monumentalization of poetry, and the reintroduction of speculative and metaphysical motifs. At the same time, modern Catholic poetry emerged.

In prose, there was also a radical break with traditions. The loss of interest in the past accounts for the almost complete disappearance of historical subjects; when they do appear, they are completely lacking in the pathos and romantic nationalism of the traditional Czech historical novel. New historical criteria were formulated and a new interpretation of history accepted. The village short story and novel also passed from the scene, only to reappear later in the more psychologically sophisticated ruralistic novel. New forms are introduced, such as detective stories and novelettes.

The best known Czech novel of World War I was created by Jaroslav Hasek (1883-1923) in his *Dobry vojak Svejk* (The Good Soldier Schweik), which was translated into many foreign languages. In Svejk, a good-natured, innocent-looking Prague Czech who is inducted into the Austrian Army against his will, Hasek created a prototype of the Czech master of passive resistance against Austrian rule.

Of the generation which entered literature at the beginning of World War I, and shortly after it, two men, in many respects opposed in their philosophies and work, Karel Capek and Jaroslav Durych, are the leaders. Karel Capek (1890-1938), who was strongly influenced by pragmatism, was one of the most versatile and perhaps the best-known Czech authors abroad. Some of his works were written in co-authorship with his older brother, Josef Capek (1887-1945). In close contact with the political and social realities of his time, Capek was an admirer of Masaryk's philosophy, a pragmatic humanist and enemy of mechanization, an advocate of reason, and a defender of the individual against the abuses of collectivism.

A different personality is Jaroslav Durych (1886-——), founder of the youngest tradition of Christian spiritual art of Catholic character. His great contribution was the reintroduction of the historical novel into modern Czech literature in his *Bloudeni* (The Erring Quest). The conflict between the transcendental absolute and the relativity of man's earthly experience is always present in Durych's works.

Among the "proletarian poets," the greatest originality was achieved, in spite of his untimely death, by Jiri Wolker (1900-24), an impressively nonrhetorical poet, frequently occupied with social problems. Among the novelists of essentially Marxist and socialist orientation, the leading personality was Ivan Olbracht (1882-1952), a successful creator of modern realism.

While Karel Teige (1900-1952) was the principal theoretician of Czech poetism, Vitezslav Nezval (1900-——) was its main poet. A master of form and unexpected rhyme and of surrealistic metaphors, and an inventor of surprising images, Nezval was the true representative of "pure poetry," devoid of any rationalization. Also allied to poetism were the imaginative Konstantin Biebl (1898-1951), and Jaroslav Seifert (1901-——), the most popular poet of the recent generation. Seifert traveled the road from proletarian poetry to poetism, and eventually to a more formally traditional, melodious poetry, indicating his need for more absolute spiritual values.

This striving is even more apparent in several other leading representatives of this generation of poets, some of whom also had their beginnings in poetism. Among them is Frantisek Halas (1901-49), creator of a new form of Czech poetic language of the "naked word," devoid of all unsubstantial elements. His poetry expresses the pathos of human existence. Josef Hora (1891-1945), originally a socially inspired poet, later adopted a more moderate political outlook and became a spiritualist who reflects on basic metaphysical motifs, the dynamism of the universe and time. While Vladimir Holan's (1905——) poetry conveys the struggle with suffering, dread, and the betrayals of existence, Jan Zahradnicek (1905——) found a road from the despair of his earlier verses to a Christian concept of life and eternity and to a positive outlook on existence and nature. The melodious lyricist Frantisek Hrubin (1910——) is perhaps at his best when he writes about the Czech countryside and children's verses.

In prose, we find a unique master in Vladislav Vancura (1891-1942). His language draws on both popular and archaic elements and has at times a monumental effect. The village novel, in a psychologically sophisticated form which glorifies love of soil and country life as salvation from the decay of the city, is presented by the "ruralists" and writers allied to this school. The greatest artist among them is Frantisek Krelina (1903——).

Jan Cep (1902——), a leading Catholic author, also draws on subjects from village and country life, attempting to show the perspective of the divine plan which overshadows the confusions of sensual men and their inadequate reason (*Hranice stinu* [The Frontier of Shadow]). Zdenek Nemecek (1894——) draws the subjects for his novels from his extensive experience in foreign countries, which he interprets with a keen sense of observation and introspection (*New York zamlzeno* [New York–Foggy]; *Na zapad od Panonie* [West of Pannonia]). The novels of Egon Hostovsky (1908——) are distinguished by acute psychological insights and well organized structure (*Zhar* [The Arsonist]; *Dum bez pana* [House Without a Master]). (All three of these authors went into exile after the Communist coup.) The novels of Vaclav Rezac (1901——) are epically constructed with a great deal of compositional experimentation (*Cerne svetlo* [Black Light]). The Czech humorous short story and novel are represented in this period by the skillful journalist Eduard Bass (1888-1946) and by Karel Polacek (1892-1944).

In 1938-39, it appeared that the European history of freedom had come to an end. This danger was felt intensely by young writers who were striving to find a definite formulation of life's heroism appropriate to the times. Masaryk and Salda indicated the way with their example of individual heroism, strict self-discipline, and a synthesis of rationalism and religion.

The poetic generation which entered literature at this time and during the German occupation made its first appearance in *Jarni almanach basnicky* (Spring Poetic Almanac, 1940) and accepted the theoretical formulations of the leading literary critic, Vaclav Cerny (1905-—). An attempt at programmatic expression was made by one of the leading members of this group, Kamil Bednar in his *Slovo k mladym* (Word to Youth), published in 1940.

It is characteristic of this generation that it lacks a unifying ideological, social, political, or religious program. This is due mainly to its strong realization that any specific formulation of human relationships can be made only after the mysteries of the individual and the meaning of his existence have been explored. The influence of Kierkegaard and his philosophy of anxiety was of considerable importance for these poets. Kamil Bednar (1912-—) is a seeker of the ontological sense of human existence, at which he looks through the narrow opening of anguish and suffering. Ivan Blatny (1919-—) first wrote melodious and consoling lyrics, but later he abandoned his isolation from reality, and changed his verse to a rhythmically disconnected and almost fractional form. The most talented of this poetic generation was Jiri Orten (1919-41), who was killed at the age of twenty-two. He was a poet of the mystery of existence, which can be fully recognized only in death, a poet who, through despair and anxiety, tried to find self-knowledge.

German censorship limited the selection of prose subjects. As a result, a tendency toward the historical and psychological novel developed. Besides those of the older generation who continued to write in this genre, several new names appeared. The most important was Karel Schultz (1899-1943), whose remarkable descriptive novel of Michelangelo's life unfortunately remained unfinished. Jan Drda (1915-—), now one of the leading Communist authors and an outspoken advocate of socialist realism, published his first novel in 1940. Before his complete political subordination, he was a skillful writer of simple narrative.

Slovak Literature

After World War I, Slovak literature was slow in developing. Not until the early and middle 1920's did literary periodicals with new trends begin to appear. While efforts to build on the predominantly realistic literary tradition of the past continued, more writers turned toward the newer trends of symbolistic and postsymbolistic literary development. Czech literature had a deep impact in Slovakia, and all Czech literary fashions and trends, from proletarian poetry to Catholic spiritualism, appeared in Slovak literature. During World War II, the pro-fascist government of the Slovak state limited the freedom of literary expression. When the war ended, however, the prewar Slovak literary personalities again assumed leadership, and

Slovak literature had much the same character as in the late thirties, with the Catholic poets, the surrealists, and the socialist writers being most prominent. Two leading poets of the early postwar era are Jan Smrek (1899-—) and Emil Boleslav Lukac (1900-—), both of whom developed characteristic forms from their beginnings in symbolism. Among the prosaists, the expressionist Jan Hrusovsky (1892-—) and the writer of original and impressive style and composition, Jozef Ciger-Hronsky (1896-—), are significant. Around the literary magazine *Dav* (Throng) congregated Marxist and Communist writers and poets of the social revolt. The most significant among them was the poet Laco Novomesky (1904-—). The novelist Petr Jilemnicky (1901-49) was also preoccupied with social problems and contrasts of postwar Slovak life. The literary magazine *Mlade Slovensko* (Young Slovakia) united young authors who sought to break with Slovak traditions and to bring new themes and new forms to Slovak literature. Of these the most significant are Gejza Vamos (1901-—), the author of novels with intentionally provocative and shocking subjects and language, and Ivan Horvath (1904-—), a novelist of original composition. From the group around the literary magazine *Vatra* (Fire), mostly oriented toward Catholicism, came Milo Urban (1904-—), an analyst of Slovak village life.

Among the writers of the youngest Slovak literary generation, whose first works appeared in the late 1930's and during World War II, a distinct personality is Jan Kostra (1910-—), the most subjectivistic poet of new Slovak literature. The leading poets of Slovak surrealism are Rudolf Fabry (1915-—), Vladimir Reisel (1919-—), and Jan Brezina (1917-—). In the 1930's, the young Catholic poets also formed a literary group, finding their models in the poetry of Emil Boleslav Lukac and of Valentin Beniak (1891-—). The most significant of these young authors are Pavol Gasparovic-Hlbina (1908-—) and Rudolf Dilong (1905-—).

Czech and Slovak Literature since World War II

The existence of the coalition government in Czechoslovakia for almost three years after World War II assured a considerable degree of freedom of literary expression. However, even during these years political pressures were felt: friendship with the Soviet Union, the desirability of Soviet cultural influence, and basic socialist tenets were protected from criticism by unwritten taboos.

Culturally, the years 1945-48 had the character of a transitional era. The crisis of humanism in its social aspects became apparent. A new formulation of the idea of human freedom in relation to the new social reality brought about by the war appeared to be the main Czechoslovak cultural problem at the time when Communism attacked Czechoslovak cultural life.

After World War II, the group of prewar authors and the generation of 1940 were joined by several young poets who were predominantly under Hora's, Halas', and Orten's influence: Ladislav Fikar, Jiri Kolar, Vlastimil Skolaudy, Michal Sedlon, the Catholically oriented Ivan Slavik, and Zdenek Rotrekl. Thematically, many of the older and younger poets looked back to the agonies, terror, and catastrophies of the war. Verses inspired by revenge and hatred, by jubilation over liberation, and by the new social and political realities were frequent in the early postwar period. However, there is a marked difference between the year 1938, the beginning of trials and terror, which produced some superb poetic works in Czech literature, and the year 1945, the apparent end of these trials, when the poets limited themselves mostly to rhetorical descriptions of past catastrophies. More successful were those who looked into the future, even if it was with uncertainty. They were interested in a rebirth of the individual rather than in the rebirth of society. In this respect, the postwar verses of Ivan Blatny and of Ladislav Fikar are of special interest.

In 1946, the materialistically and socialistically oriented "dynamic-anarchistic" poetic group came into being. It was organized around the magazine *Generace* (Generation). J. M. Grossman was its main ideologist, Frantisek Listopad and Jaromir Horec its main poets. In the Moravian capital of Brno, a group of new surrealists with more constructive poetic tendencies appeared, with Ludvik Kundera as their main representative. In Slovakia, surrealism was still alive with several new names appearing: Stefan Zary, Julius Lenko, and Jan Rak.

In the early postwar years, poetry again predominated over prose. Among prosaists who spent the war in exile, Egon Hostovsky gained success by his novels, which were also published in English. Only a few significant new prosaists appeared, including the novelist and dramatist Jiri Mucha, as well as Jiri Valja, Bohuslav Brezovsky, Zdenek Urbanek, and several others.

Literature under the Communists

After the Communist coup in February 1948, literature was allowed only within strictly controlled limits. Systematic control was imposed in accordance with Marxist theory; it radically changed the character of Czechoslovak literature, which, in the past, was generally a part of West European culture.

The plan for uniformity and communization of literature was carried out in several phases. During the tense period 1945-48, when democracy could still function in Czechoslovak cultural life, the Communists, to their obvious surprise, were polemically pushed back when they attempted to gain cultural control by the propagation of "socialist realism." The Czech democrats fought this struggle on the basis of their humanistic and Christian traditions. The main representative of the opposition to Marxist intellectuals was Vaclav Cerny (1905-—), editor of the literary magazine, *Kriticky mesicnik* (Critical Monthly), and defender of Czech spiritual traditions against cultural dictatorship.

After February 1948, expulsion of liberal professors and students from the universities, the closing of publishing houses, the suppression of publications, and the arrest of scholars and writers paralyzed free discussion. In this respect, there is little similarity between developments in Czechoslovakia and the communization of literature in the Soviet Union after the Revolution, where the transition lasted for many years. Communist intervention in Czechoslovakia was fierce and sudden, and absolute state control over art was immediately enforced. The plan for the conversion to Marxism was simple: first, to eliminate all undesirable writers, scholars, and critics of the opposition (such as Jan Slavik, Jan Zahradnicek, Josef Palivec, Josef Knap, Bedrich Fucik, and Vaclav Renc); second, to unite the remaining and new writers in one organization; and, finally, to establish a set of values, norms, and aims for this Communist-directed institution.

In April 1948, at the Congress of National Culture, the Communists formulated their cultural program. Art, it was proclaimed, should become the "property of the people." Only social consciousness was to determine artistic creation, and only social practice should pass judgment on artistic forms. Since this was the first Communist interference, "socialist realism" was still presented as a concept broad enough to embrace some members of the literary avant-garde. However, the new ideological content of art was emphasized, together with a demand for destruction of all ideological radicalism and experimentation. The writer was asked to embrace unequivocally the realism of the "newly arisen class," and to oppose irrationalism, mysticism, and pessimism of "the destroyed bourgeois order." The writers were called upon to create a "classless art."

This formulation was too liberal for the Party to keep permanently; after consolidation of the Communists' political position, the Party turned to literature again. In March 1949, it ordered the dissolution of the Syndicate of Czechoslovak Writers, which had allegedly committed grave errors during the recent reform of literary life. The new Union of Czechoslovak Writers was founded. Jan Drda became its director in Bohemia; Milan Lajciak, and later Frantisek Hecko, in

Slovakia. New authoritative decrees were issued, the principles of the "only correct" evaluation of literary works were outlined, and the search for older "realistic classics" was begun.

An omen of worse things to come was the book of Josef Stefanek, *Ceska literatura po valce* (Czech Literature after the War) (1949), which programmatically classified contemporary Czech prose in two categories: progressive and reactionary. Stefanek presented socialist realism as the only admissible literary method. Attacks on the reactionary elements in the work of some contemporary and older writers, such as Frantisek Halas, Vladimir Holan, Jaroslav Seifert, and Rudolf Medek, appeared in Party publications. A new generation of leftist poets around the newspaper *Mlada fronta* (Young Front) was tolerated for a time, but was finally attacked. In January 1950, a new "legislator" appeared: Ladislav Stoll, a journalist and sociologist, later Minister of Culture and Art, an uncompromising Stalinist. His speech, "Tricet let boju za ceskou socialistickou poesii" (Thirty Years of Struggle for Czech Socialist Poetry), set the criteria for evaluation of Czech poetry. Only Jiri Wolker and S. K. Neumann were declared classics of modern Czech socialistic poetry, while Czech poetism, leftist in its political orientation, and the spiritual poetry of the 1930's were rejected. Of the poetists, Vitezslav Nezval and Konstantin Biebl were partially reinstated, as was Jaroslav Seifert, to a limited degree. Other poets were condemned: Josef Hora, Frantisek Halas, Kamil Bednar, and the theoretician of literature, Karel Teige.

In 1950, the purge reached Slovakia, where the "nationalist deviationists" were eliminated. A new trend was forced on Slovak literature, with emphasis on pro-Czech authors. Anti-humanistic writers became the protégés of the new regime. After some initial hesitation in 1948-50, the Masaryk tradition was declared inimical to the interests of the people. Stalin's attack on nonconformists in 1950 and the political offensive of 1951, which culminated in the execution of Slansky, gave Czechoslovak literature an entirely conformist form. The previous tolerance of some sort of independent Czechoslovak Communist art, in which the "liberal" writers were allowed to play a role, was now coming to an end.

The slogan of the anti-cultural offensive in 1951 was "struggle for Marxist aesthetics, linguistics, and literary criticism." During this campaign, Czech literary history and its outstanding representative, Arne Novak (1880-1939), came under attack. Novak's concept of objective aesthetic evaluation of a literary work in the perspective of historical traditions of the nation was denounced. All Western influences on modern Czechoslovak literary art were rejected. Rilke, Rimbaud, Gide, Apollinaire, Valéry, Mallarmé, and all of Western "literary decadence, pessimism, and mysticism" were victims. Masaryk's realism, with its cosmopolitan and basically Anglo-Saxon orientation (which was expressed in literature by Capek's pragmatism and by his idealization of the average democratic man), were declared treasonable. Even Frantisek Xaver Salda, founder of modern Czech literary criticism, was attacked because of his "aristocratic" criteria, his literary taste, and his neglect of the relation of aesthetics and morals. His mistakes were labelled "tragic," but not treasonable. The main center of attack was directed against the Czech linguistic and literary-historical school of structuralism, formulated in the Prague Linguistic Circle. The Communists attacked the evaluation of literary work as a structure of functional components, which is autonomous as artistic creation, claiming that it was an idealistic and formalistic concept, which strengthened cosmopolitan tendencies harmful to the proletarian revolution.

To replace the rejected national cultural heritage, the Communists introduced socialist realism, artistically concerned with the building of a planned and centrally managed society, with some coloring of Czech history.

The trend was initiated by the prominence given to the historical novels of Alois Jirasek. In June 1953, the Czechoslovak Academy of Sciences was established in Prague (officially decreed in November 1952) with a branch in Bratislava, designed to be the central organ of Czechoslovak scientific life.

In theory, socialist realism is the dogma of all Czechoslovak literary production since 1948. In fact, socialist realism is variable and depends upon the political situation; it has never been officially defined. According to Communist interpretation, literature is a sort of ideology which gives knowledge of life by reflecting reality. However, it is not an objective mirror because it includes the author's judgments and attitudes. Literary "recognition" of life is thus "conditioned" historically. Art is connected with class struggle and has a political basis, because every writer, being a member of society, must actively participate in the social struggle. Class ideology helps the artist to "reflect" life. The reflection must be "true," and truth is defined by the Party. Socialist realism does not strive for an objective reflection of reality, but wants to achieve a "true" picture of typical characters under typical circumstances. This implies an idealization of the hero, since the hero can only be someone who has gained the proper understanding of historical events, is engaged in the building of the new society, and perceives correctly its future.

Of the realists of the nineteenth century, only the "critical realists" are accepted today. Naturalists are rejected because they concentrated on mere registration of life, without expressing a critical evaluation. Cosmopolitanism, formalism, and naturalism are the worst crimes an author can commit. Revolutionary romanticism finds a place in socialist realism by connecting a "truthful" description of reality with "revolutionary phantasy," thus unveiling the "perspectives" of life. In practice, however, this is limited to such items as enthusiasm for increased production norms. Descriptions of private life and individual problems are replaced by interest in "collective labor." A man exists mainly as a manifestation of his work in the collective.

Thus, art is a system of propaganda and education, designed to influence the reader politically. The "beauty" of a work refers only to its social content. Without a "high ideology," there is no mastery.

Under these circumstances, there is no characteristic distinction between the literature written in Czech and Slovak, or between the works of authors of different generations. Socialist realism is an international blueprint for all Communist authors, and shows an organized tendency toward a monolithic tradition of ideology, genre, and subject matter.

Literature is still written by prewar Communist writers, but the activity of the postwar newcomers is increasing. These newcomers can be divided into three categories: the former editors of radical socialistic newspapers (Ludvik Askenazy, Alena Bernaskova, F. K. Sedlacek); the formerly unsuccessful second-rate writers (such as Frantisek Hecko and Vasek Kana); and the "worker-authors," by far the smallest group of socialistic writers, whose writing should prove that the popularization of culture has brought results. None of the non-Communist writers of the prewar period has published a new work of importance, though occasionally an isolated work appears. The majority of these authors write either children's verses, edit anthologies of classics, or translate from foreign literatures.

It is understandable why prose exceeds lyric poetry in the literary production of the years 1948-56, although it is contrary to the tradition of modern Czechoslovak literature. Lyric poetry can be subjected to socialist realism with only limited results. Current lyric poetry is often a hurried imitation of folk poetry. The poets are trying to imitate its spontaneity and to endow it with their aesthetic criteria. Poetry has a limited choice of themes: it may be patriotic and peace-promoting, or it may glorify constructive activity and socialist competition, the children of happy tomorrows, the Party, and, to a smaller extent, love. Czechoslovak metaphysical and intimate poetry perished entirely. Most of the Catholic poets were arrested.

Prose was integrated with greater success into Communist culture, but even the skillful Communist writers have not yet succeeded in picturing the new, positive Czechoslovak socialist hero. Prose production uses such literary forms as the *feuilleton, reportage,* or the short story, as well as *roman-fleuve,* an innovation in Czechoslovak prose. The latter are mostly trilogies dealing with the evolution of modern socialist man. Almost all of these novels, however, have so far reached only the epochs before the arrival of communism, and, while they purport to be histories, they are little more than collections of journalistic notes and editorial comments. There are three basic types of the new novel: the proletarian, the village, and the historical novel. There exist mostly stereotyped heroes of socialist realism, such as the shock-workers, the class enemy, the brigade workers, the absenteeist, the guardian of the border, the hesitating intellectual, and others. Negative heroes are increasingly frequent: the ardent listener to Radio Free Europe, the treacherous émigrés, or the inciters of popular opposition. The writers impose themselves yearly working quotas and challenge each other to competition. Authors frequently spend time in the factories, observing the "working process," in order to create "really living types."

A considerable difficulty for the Communists is the creation of new literary criticism. Currently, Czechoslovak Communist literature can look for judgment only to extra-literary authorities, such as Nejedly, Kopecky, and Stoll. The only significant Communist critic of the pre-1948 period, Bedrich Vaclavek, who is now dead, was severely criticized; the attitude toward Frantisek Xaver Salda is still vague. In literary theory, the leading authority appears to be Jan Mukarovsky, in spite of his structuralist past.

Women play a large role in Czech socialist prose. Marie Majerova (1882-—) published a new edition of her novel, *Nejkrasnejsi svet* (The Most Beautiful World), in which the positive, socialist class-hero appears for the first time. In 1951, Majerova published a collection of stories inspired by the events of the years 1938-49, *Cesta blesku* (The Path of Lightning), and in 1954 a collection of reports from the Soviet Union, *Vitezny pochod* (The Victorious March). Another Communist woman author of the pre-February years, Marie Pujmanova (1893-—), has become one of the most active supporters and glorifiers of the "new culture" in both prose and poetry. Her lyrical collections, *Verse z domova i ze sveta* (Verses from Home and from the World), *Vyznani lasky* (Declaration of Love), and *Miliony holubicek* (Millions of Doves), are a mixture of personal lyrics and campaign poems against "aggression in Korea," or in support of the "Stockholm peace declaration." Pujmanova has added two volumes to her novel, *Lide na krizovatce* (The People at the Crossroads). In these two volumes, *Hra s ohnem* (Play with Fire) and *Zivot proti smrti* (Life Against Death), the "end of capitalism" in Czechoslovakia is treated in the orthodox Communist manner.

Jarmila Glazarova (1901-—) who, before World War II, gained popularity with her novels of realistic narration, spent two and a half years after 1945 in the Soviet Union. Upon returning, she published *Leningrad,* a report on the history and reconstruction of this city, and *Dnes a zitra* (Today and Tomorrow), a collection of *reportage* from postwar Soviet and Czech life. The vigorous woman journalist, Alena Bernaskova, was one of the first writers to fulfill the demands of the regime for a new type of novel from the worker's life. Before writing her novel, *Cesta otevrena* (The Open Road), she spent time in a large factory in Northern Bohemia. In 1951, Bernaskova turned to drama in *Seherezada* (Scheherazade), and in 1953, to short stories (*Deti velke lasky* [The Children of Great Love]). Helena Dvorakova wrote a trilogy on the social development of a Prague suburb at the end of the nineteenth century, *Pad rodiny Bryknaru* (The Fall of the Bryknar Family), and then a novel about the settlement of the Czech border territory, *Ruku v ruce* (Hand in Hand). Similar subjects can be found in the novels of Anna Sedlmayerova, *Prekroceny prah* (The Crossed Threshold) and *Z prvnich rad* (From the First Lines).

Only a few men of the older generation have produced glorifications of the new epoch. To this group belong Karel Konrad, whose collection, *Prosa* (Prose), was published in 1953; Karel Novy a writer of village novels, who finished his trilogy, *Zelezny kruh* (The Iron Circle); and Frantisek Kubka who, in addition to short stories full of political and propaganda clichés (*Male povidky pro Mr. Trumana* [Small Stories for Mr. Truman]; *Picassova holubice* [Picasso's Dove]), writes histories of several generations of one family in which the transformation of Czech democrats into vigorous Communists is shown. The following volumes by Kubka have appeared: *Sto dvacet dni* (Hundred and Twenty Days), *Cizi mesto* (The Foreign City), *Vitr z hlubin* (The Wind from the Depths), and *Dedecek* (Grandfather).

Of the younger pre-February generation, best known is Jan Drda, the autocratic chairman of the Union of Writers. Drda wrote *Nema barikada* (The Mute Barricade), inspired by the fighting with the Nazi troops in 1945, and *Krasna Tortiza* (Beautiful Tortiza), a book of short stories. He has also written a play, *Romance o Oldrichu a Bozene* (The Romance of Oldrich and Bozena), in which an old Czech legend is transferred to a kolkhoz. Drda's importance lies in his function as intermediary between the Party and the writers.

Vaclav Rezac, also a writer with a liberal literary past, accepted the Marxist interpretation of social developments, and wrote the novel *Nastup* (Rallying the Ranks), and its sequel, *Bitva* (Battle), about the Czech industrial borderland. The problems of the communized village are the main themes of Pavel Bojar and Bohumil Riha, two writers of the new generation. Bojar concentrates on the social history of the South Bohemian countryside. He appears to be interested mostly in the change in people after they have entered agricultural collectives. Of a planned trilogy, two volumes have been published: *Jarni vody* (Spring Waters) and *Horke dny* (Bitter Days). Bojar also writes verses. Riha is praised for his "true observation" of the Czech village in the process of agricultural collectivization. He published two novels: *Zeme dokoran* (The Earth Wide Open) and *Dve jara* (Two Springs), as well as a collection of short stories, *Setkani pod lesem* (The Encounter below the Forest).

The most frequent theme in prose is that of the proletariat and the process of socialist construction. Adolf Branald, former train dispatcher, published two stories about the struggle of the railroad men against the Germans (*Severni nadrazi* [Northern Station] and *Lazaretni vlak* [Hospital Train]), and now writes semi-documentary descriptions of the origins of the proletarian movement (*Chleb a pisne* [Bread and Songs], and *Hrdinove vsednich dnu* [The Weekday Heroes]). Eyewitness stories about large construction works are contributed by F. K. Sedlacek in *Luisiana se probouzi* (The Mine Luisiana Awakens) and *Zavod ve stinu* (The Factory in the Shade), and by Josef Otcenasek, *Plnym krokem* (In Great Strides). T. Svatopluk, author of *Botostroj* (published in the 1930's), presents the fate of the workers in the Bata shoe factories in Zlin after nationalization in his new novel, *Bez sefa* (Without the Boss).

Aside from this standard Communist prose, there are numerous other works. Frantisek Kozik wrote a biography of the runner Emil Zatopek, *Vitez marathonsky* (The Winner of the Marathon), and Josef Sekera published a book dealing with the life of gypsies, *Deti z hlinene vesnice* (The Children from the Clay Village). The well-known author and film scenarist, Vladimir Neff, published a historical novel, *Srpnovsti pani* (The Srpnov Lords), while Vaclav Kaplicky also dealt with historical themes in *Ctveraci* (The Fourth Estate), and *Zelezna koruna* (The Iron Crown). Most productive among writers of shorter prose forms are Ludvik Askenazy and Jiri Marek. Askenazy, author of journalistic sketches on the West and the United States, published several collections of satirical stories, including *Kniha ostravskych povidek* (A Book of Ostrava Tales), *Vysoka politika* (High Politics), *Sto ohnu* (Hundred Fires), and *Nemecke jaro* (German Spring). Marek's main works are his satirical and socialistic stories: *Mladi bojovnici* (The Young Fighters), *Z cihel a usmevu* (From Bricks and Smiles), and *Nad nami svita* (Dawn Above Us).

As example for the new generation of Slovak writers, the Communist Party established Peter Jilemnicky (who died in 1949), the author of *Pole neorane* (The Unplowed Field), *Kompas v nas* (The

Compass in Us), *Vietor sa vracia* (The Wind is Returning), and *Kronika* (Chronicle), a literary record of the Slovak Uprising in 1944. The Party also acclaimed Frantisek Hecko, an unsuccessful prewar writer, and his socialistically realistic novel, *Drevena dedina* (The Wooden Village). A task similar to that being performed in Czech literature by Marie Pujmanova has been undertaken by Peter Karvas, who is writing a trilogy about the development of Slovak society during the last years of the democratic Republic. Karvas also published a novel, *S nami a proti nam* (With Us and Against Us), describing the battles of the partisan fighters in the Nitra region. The Slovak Uprising, generally, is a favored subject for a whole group of writers, among them Viera Markovicova, Katarina Lazarova, and Hela Volanska. The life of the Slovak factory workers and the villagers is the subject of works by Dominik Tatarka, Jozef Horak, Zuzka Zguriska, and Milos Krno. Of the older radical writers, Frano Kral is highly valued for his two books, *Cenkovej deti* (Cenkova's Children) and *Cesta zarubana* (Barred Road).

Lyric poetry during the period of 1948-54 shows a turn to a thematic monotony. In the framework of socialist realism, poetry must be filled with "constructive optimism," should not deal with private problems, and must picture "the working effort" of the whole nation. The poets are advised to write not only about everyday work, but also about "great historical events" of political character. They are urged to write "for the people," and to abandon the tradition of "formalism and naturalism."

The beginnings of socialist realism in Czech lyric poetry were marked by the tragic death of Frantisek Halas in 1949, who, the year before, had published his last collection, *V rade* (In Line), and by the suicide of Konstantin Biebl in 1951, the year his collection *Bez obav* (Without Fear) appeared. Vitezslav Nezval, on the other hand, a former surrealist and poetist, repented in time and offered his great technical and formal talent for producing socialist poetry. He has published several new collections, including *Veliky orloj* (The Great Steeple-Clock), *Z domoviny* (From Home), *Zpev miru* (The Song of Peace), and *Kridla* (Wings). Although the role of supreme arbiters in poetry seems to be played by Vitezslav Nezval and Jiri Taufer, considerable influence on young socialist poets is also exerted by Vilem Zavada, at one time a spiritualist poet, the author of *Povstani z mrtvych* (Resurrection) and *Mesto svetla* (The City of Light). Communist poetry can boast only two true poets of the younger generation: Josef Kainar (*Cesky sen* [The Czech Dream]) and Oldrich Mikulasek (*Horouci zpevy* [Burning Songs]), each of whom contributed a collection of verses. Once important poets now publish only occasionally. Jaroslav Seifert, who was severely criticized in 1949 for his *Zpev o Viktorce* (Song about Viktorka), now is organizing his *Dilo* (Works). At the end of 1954, he published tender verses, *Maminka* (Mother). Frantisek Hrubin (1910-—) who was greatly praised after World War II for his *Chleb s oceli* (Bread with Steel) and *Jobova noc* (The Night of Job), now writes mostly verses for children and occasional poetry. Kamil Bednar devotes most of his time to translating. Verses about love, transformed by the new outlook on life, are also written by Frantisek Branislav (*Milostny napev* [Love Tune], and *Krasna laska* [Beautiful Love]). Ladislav Stehlik published the collection *Pelynek* (Wormwood), and a novel in verse, *Marina Alsova.* Jan Pilar, formerly an idealistic poet, now writes verses to order; his last collection is *Hvezda zivota* (The Star of Life), verses about home, the fight for peace, and life among the workers. After a period of silence, some of the younger leftist intellectuals, who had been reproached for their "existentialist past," have reappeared: Ivo Fleischmann (*Pisen velikeho jara* [The Song of the Great Spring]), Vlastimil Skolaudy (*Ve jmenu zivota* [In the Name of Life], and *Usvit* [Dawn]), as well as Oldrich Krystofek. On the other hand, Ivan Skala, Jan Stern, and Stanislav Neumann belong to the proven activistic group, whose youngest wing has just entered poetry and accepted, without question, the principles of official Communist art. To this group also belong Pavel Kohout (*Verse a pisne* [Verses and Songs]), Jiri Ostas (*Zrani* [Ripening]), Miroslav Florian (*Cesta k slunci* [The Way to the Sun]), and Milan Kundera (*Clovek zahrada sira* [The Man—a Wide Garden]).

In Slovakia, a group of new young poets has taken over the poetic scene. Their leader, Milan Lajciak (1926-—), is the former chairman of the Union of Slovak Writers. His works are: *Sudruzka moja zem* (The Earth—My Comrade), *Pozdrav Stalinovi* (Greeting to Stalin), *Nenavidim a milujem* (I Hate and I Love), *Rano* (Morning), and *Vernost* (Fidelity). Other members of this group are Vojtech Mihalik and Ctibor Stitnicky. Of the older poets, Jan Smrek published his translations of the Hungarian romantic poet Petofi in 1953, and Jan Kostra, his collection *Javorovy List* (Maple Leaf); Pavol Horov, Andrej Plavka, and Jan Rak published verses about nature and factories.

Aside from the Communist literature published in Czechoslovakia, there also exists a Czechoslovak exile literature, created by poets and writers who fled the country after February 1948. It frequently originates under harsh material conditions in various countries, but it is an important and indivisible part of Czechoslovak culture, preserving the humanistic tradition. Several older as well as new authors are taking part in this effort. In 1954, Czech poets in exile published an anthology, *Neviditelny domov* (Invisible Home). Prose is represented by three major Czech authors, Jan Cep (*Cikani* [Gypsies]), Egon Hostovsky (*Pulnocni pacient* [Midnight Patient]), and Zdenek Nemecek (*Tvrda zeme* [Hard Land]), who were prominent before they left Czechoslovakia. With literature in Czechoslovakia subject to rigid control, this Czech and Slovak exile literature preserves the tradition of a free development of Czechoslovak letters.

10. PUBLIC HEALTH AND WELFARE

Harry Trend

Development of Social Security System

The First Republic

The pre-World War II Czechoslovak system of compulsory social insurance was built on the foundations established during the Austro-Hungarian period and taken over by the new Republic in 1918. Its chief aim was to protect workers against the economic consequences of old age and disability, death, illness and pregnancy, and occupational injuries. While all the basic types of social insurance available in Czechoslovakia during the First Republic had been introduced prior to World War I, both the range of benefits and the number of occupations and persons protected by compulsory social insurance were substantially increased during the 1918-38 period.

The system of social insurance prior to Munich was administratively divided into three separate branches: health (including pregnancy) insurance, accident insurance, and pension insurance. Insurance institutions were independent public legal persons, administering insurance funds separately from the rest of their property and under government supervision. The interest of the insured was safeguarded through extensive direct participation in the administration of insurance, but this administrative autonomy did not include the right to decide on the validity of claims to benefits. The latter function was reserved exclusively to independent insurance courts.

A major shortcoming of the system was its failure to provide unemployment insurance, though in the case of involuntary unemployment, the state-subsidized "Ghent" type of insurance was available to trade union members. Another major defect of the system was the multiplicity of insurance institutions dealing with the same hazards. In 1936, for example, the workers' health insurance program alone was administered by 295 insurance institutions. In agriculture, there

Note: A substantial part of this chapter is based on material compiled by Mr. Alois Rozehnal.

were 67 separate funds. The Public Employees' Sickness Insurance Fund was administered by three separate agencies. The Miners' Sickness Insurance was administered by special miners' benefit societies, and the salaried employees' scheme was administered by four insurance institutions. The old age pension program was somewhat better organized, but it also suffered from multiplicity of administrative organs and a lack of uniformity in administrative procedures. Moreover, there was a lack of uniformity in contribution rates, benefits, and qualifications for benefits.

The dispersed administration and non-uniformity in the pattern of contribution rates and benefits had their roots in the Austro-Hungarian period, when the individual institutions began to build their insurance funds. Subsequently, the differences in the wealth of individual institutions became the chief barrier to the establishment of an integrated social security system. Despite the multiplicity of social insurance institutions, however, there was a distinct trend toward a gradual centralization of social insurance administration. Thus, the major part of health insurance administration was concentrated in the health insurance branch of the Central Social Insurance Institute, while pension insurance administration was largely centered in the pension insurance branch of the General Pension Institute. Accident insurance administration had been centralized from the beginning in the Accident Insurance Institute, setting the pattern for the postwar unification of the entire social insurance system.

1938-1945

The period from Munich to the end of World War II was marked by a serious weakening of the social security system. As a result of the Munich Pact, the various social security institutions lost one third of their members and, after March 1939, only about one half of the previous membership of the Central Social Insurance Institute and other social security agencies remained.

Post-Munich developments varied with the changed political status of the different areas. In the territory annexed by Germany, the German social security system was introduced. In the Hungarian-occupied territory, including Ruthenia and certain parts of Slovakia, Hungarian legislation went into effect, though some features of the Czechoslovak system were recognized as legally binding. Slovakia established her own social security institutions. In the Czech lands, the pre-Munich social institutions were largely retained, but a number of changes were introduced, including improvements in workmen's compensation, aimed at neutralizing the workers' hostile attitude.

Since the increases in benefits were made without adequate increase in the income of the social insurance institutions, the solvency of the program was seriously undermined.

Developments after World War II

After the war, Czechoslovakia was faced with the problem of integrating the diverse social insurance institutions which had developed in the various parts of the country since Munich into a unified system. At the same time, a substantial extension of existing benefits was contemplated. With both these problems aggravated by postwar economic dislocations, particularly in the labor market and in the monetary system, a uniform national insurance program was not introduced until 1948. Under the new system, all social insurance institutions were nationalized and a large number of old institutions were abolished.

The national system of insurance was instituted by the National Insurance Act of April 15, 1948 (Law No. 99, *Sbirka zakonu a narizeni Republiky Ceskoslovenske* [Collection of Laws and Ordinances of the Czechoslovak Republic]). The statute provided for two basic types of insurance: pension or income insurance, and sickness and maternity insurance, the latter including both cash benefits and benefits in kind. Subsequent legislation modified the original statute, the most thoroughgoing revisions being introduced by laws of December 19, 1951, Nos. 102 and 103. The provisions of Law No. 102 stipulate that:

1. Pension insurance is separated from sickness insurance.
2. Pension insurance (including pensions for disabled servicemen and assistance to victims of the war and of fascist persecution) and supplementary pension insurance of all kinds are placed under a newly established State Pension Insurance Office.
3. Cash sickness benefits, layettes and domestic help, special medical care, and family allowances are placed in the charge of the Revolutionary Trade Union Movement, acting through the trade union locals.
4. Medical care for the insured, members of their families, and pensioners is provided by the public health service, excepting special medical care which is placed under the Revolutionary Trade Union Movement.

Basic Types of Social Insurance

The National Insurance Act of 1948 and subsequent provisions applying to members of agricultural cooperatives, self-employed, and unpaid family workers cover practically the entire labor force. However, the benefits, qualifications, and other aspects of pension insurance do not apply equally to all groups. Distinctions in benefits are made for the following three classes: employed persons, i.e. parties to a contract of employment; members of agricultural cooperatives of types III and IV (collective types); and self-employed persons, unpaid family workers, and members of agricultural cooperatives of types I and II (the least collectivized types). In effect, there are at least three separate insurance schemes rather than one national insurance program.

Old Age Insurance

The most comprehensive of these plans is the one applying to the category of "employed persons." In addition to employed persons who are parties to a contract of employment, the following occupational classes are generally on the same footing for the entire range of pension and sickness benefits: persons belonging to labor brigades operating for more than one week; agricultural workers who are part of forest labor brigades; members of the government, including the legislative bodies; young individuals over 15 years of age in reformatories; housekeepers of the clergy; officials of the People's Committees who carry on their official duties to the exclusion of another occupation; lawyers working in state legal advice offices; and members of religious groups working in health centers.

To qualify for old age benefits, the insured must have been covered in four out of five years preceding retirement, and must have reached 65 years of age if insured for less than 20 years, or 60 years if insured for 20 years or more. For miners, the age qualifications are modified: 55 years for those insured for at least 25 years in underground work, and for those insured for at least 35 years, of which 10 years were spent in underground mines; and 60 years for those insured for at least 15 years while working in the mines.

The total annual old age pension consists of three parts: (1) the base pension of 1,680 crowns (in 1953 currency); (2) an additional sum amounting to 20 per cent of the insured's average annual income in the last five or ten years prior to retirement, whichever is larger; and (3) service supplements. Service supplements are computed on the basis of average annual income and length of service, amounting to 0.4 per cent per year insured up to 20 years of service, 0.8 per cent per year beyond 20 years of service, and 2 per cent for each year of service beyond 60 years of age. A total of 28 per cent is granted as a service supplement minimum. Miners' service supplements are computed at the rate of 1.2 per cent per year for surface work, and 2 per cent per year for underground work.

Following the currency conversion of June 1, 1953, in which social security benefits were adjusted at the rate of five old crowns for one new crown (equal to about 13.9 U.S. cents at the official rate of exchange), old age and disability benefits were increased as indicated below (in crowns per month):

Amounts Previously Received	Increase
0 to 200	70
201 to 240	64
241 to 280	58
281 to 320	50
321 to 400	40
401 to 500	30
501 to 600	20

Disability Benefits

During the first year of disability, the individual is covered by the sickness insurance plan, with disability benefits beginning at the end of the year. To qualify for disability benefits, the individual must have lost more than one half of his earning power as a result of injury or permanent health impairment. In case of total disability due to occupational injury, the individual is entitled to two thirds of his annual income; in case of partial disability, this amount is reduced in proportion to the degree of disability. If the individual is 20 to 45 per cent disabled, he may apply for a lump sum settlement of his claim.

Supplements to Old Age and Disability Pensions

Housewife's Pension. The wife of a disabled employee is entitled to an annual pension of 1,200 crowns, provided she has been married to the insured for at least one year, is not gainfully employed, and does not receive an old age, disability, or widow's pension. The same applies to the wife of a worker who has reached the age of 65.

Dependent Children's Benefits. Old age and disability pension recipients are entitled to educational allowances for their children under 16 years of age. No distinction is drawn between legitimate and illegitimate children. The children's educational allowances paid in conjunction with old age and disability pensions are identical to those paid under the family allowance plan, which will be discussed below.

Survivors' Benefits

Under the National Insurance Act, widows, dependent children, and orphans of the insured are entitled to survivor benefits. The legality of the marriage does not affect the validity of the claim.

Widow's Pension. The widow is paid a benefit for the first year of her widowhood providing she was married to the insured at least one year at the time of his death, or at least two years if she married him after he had reached the age of 60. The minimum marriage requirements do not apply if the widow cares for a child. To be eligible for a widow's pension beyond the first year after the death of the insured, the widow must fulfill one of the following conditions: be an invalid; have reached the age of 45; have been married at least 15 years; or be responsible for a child entitled to a children's allowance. If the widow qualifies solely as a result of having been married for 15 years, the pension is 50 per cent of the old age or disability pension, less the potential service increments. Under the other three conditions, a minimum pension of 1,680 crowns is paid annually. Widows requiring constant care may receive increases up to 50 per cent of their pensions.

Children's Educational Allowances. The widow's pension is supplemented with dependent children's educational allowances, granted only if the child does not qualify for the orphans' pension discussed below. The amounts of allowances are similar to those received as supplements by the old age and disability pensioners. However, in the case of the widow a minimum of 60 crowns monthly is allowed for each child. Lump sum benefits for each child amounting to 10 per cent of the insured's average yearly income, are paid to the widow supporting the children if the death of the insured was a consequence of an occupational accident. The children's allowance may be increased up to 50 per cent if the child is in need of constant care and is over 7 years of age. Table 1 shows the changes in widow's pension and supplementary educational allowances for dependent children after the currency conversion of 1953.

Table 1. Change in Widow's Pension and Children's Educational Allowance, after the 1953 Currency Conversion (in 1953 crowns per month)[a]

Previous Widow's Benefit	Increase	New Benefits for Children: Number of Children	New Benefits for Children: Total Allowance
Up to 200	50	1	120
201 to 240	40	2	260
241 to 280	30	3	420
281 to 360	20	more than 3	160 additional for each child

[a] At the official Czechoslovak rate of exchange, one crown equals approximately 13.9 U.S. cents.

Orphan's Pension. Under the 1948 provisions, orphans, i.e., dependent children whose parents are both dead or who have been abandoned by the mother after the insured's death, were entitled to one half of the old age benefit, excluding the service supplements. A minimum orphan's pension, in terms of 1953 currency, amounted to 100 crowns per month. Following the currency conversion, the minimum was raised to 120, and the amounts paid previously were increased as shown below (in crowns per month):

Previous Benefit	Increase
Up to 120	60
121 to 160	40
161 to 200	20

Social Pensions

The National Insurance Act of 1948 also provided social (non-contributory) pensions for those citizens not covered by any part of the national insurance program. The social pensions are of two types: compulsory and non-compulsory. The compulsory pension is granted to an individual who does not receive any other pension and who is (1) over 65 years or disabled, and who had previously been employed in an activity which was subsequently covered by the national insurance program; (2) a widow over 65 years whose husband would have been covered by the 1948 statute; (3) an orphan whose father would have been covered by the 1948 statute. Non-compulsory social pensions are granted on the basis of need to individuals over 65 years, to invalids, and to widows with two or more dependent children. From 1948 to 1953, the aged, invalids, and widows were entitled to a pension of 1,680 crowns per annum; orphans received 1,200 crowns per annum (in 1953 currency). When both husband and wife qualify, the benefit is increased by 50 per cent. The changes made in social pensions after the 1953 currency conversion are indicated in Table 2.

Table 2. Social Pension Benefit Changes after June 1953
(in 1953 crowns per month)

Type of Social Pension	Amount of Increase	New Monthly Benefit
Old age, disability, or widowhood		
one entitlement	50	190
two entitlements	75	285
Orphan	50	150

Special Plans for Members of Agricultural Cooperatives, Self-Employed, and Unpaid Family Workers

A special system of old age, disability, and survivors' insurance was established for members of agricultural cooperatives, the self-employed, and unpaid family workers. This system, introduced on October 1, 1952, provided benefits for individuals complying with the minimum qualification requirements. Distinction is made between two groups: members of the highly integrated, kolkhoz-type of co-operatives, types III and IV; members of types I and II cooperatives, the self-employed, and unpaid family workers. The first of these groups is given the highest degree of protection in order to encourage this type of cooperative. To qualify for coverage as a member of agricultural cooperative types III and IV, the insured must be willing to work the minimum amount of work units required by the rules of the agricultural cooperative, and must not be a recipient of any other pension from a public source. The size of the old age and disability benefit is dependent upon the contribution rate stipulated in a contract between the insured and the cooperative. Monthly old age and disability benefits and the corresponding contribution rates for agricultural cooperative types III and IV are shown below (in 1953 crowns per month):

Benefit Rates[a]	Contribution Rate
160	14
200	26
250	40
300	54
350[b]	70
400[b]	88

[a] Following the currency conversion of June 1, 1953, the benefit rates were increased by 30 crowns.

[b] Applies to a minimum coverage of ten years; however, in no case can the insured receive less than 300 crowns monthly; coverage from four to ten years entitles the insured to proportionate increases over the minimum amount of 300 crowns.

A minimum monthly benefit of 160 crowns becomes effective when there is no contract between the member and the agricultural co-operative stipulating the benefit group chosen. Qualifications for old age benefits are the same as those set for national insurance, except that the recipient of an old age benefit must be totally disabled; if partially disabled, he must work according to his physical ability. This provision is indicative of the labor shortage.

Total permanent disability benefits are identical to those received under the old age provisions. Partial disability, to the extent of 50 per cent or more, entitles the individual to 60 per cent of the pension, providing he works to the extent of his physical abilities. Old age and disability pensions are supplemented by allowances for children up to 16 years of age. These allowances are identical to the insurance benefits covering regular employment contracts. Survivors' benefits are calculated on the basis of the pension to which the individual would have been entitled at the time of his death. The minimum allowance for a widow is 140 crowns and for an orphan 100 crowns per month. An educational allowance at the rate paid under national insurance is payable to the widow.

Benefits provided for the self-employed, unpaid family workers, and members of agricultural cooperative types I and II are generally less favorable than those paid to highly integrated agricultural cooperatives. The amount of old age or disability benefit is based on the "basic annual income" and the number of years of the insured's employment. The schedule of benefits is shown in Table 3.

Table 3. Monthly Old Age and Disability Benefits for Self-Employed, Unpaid Family Workers, and Members of Agricultural Cooperative Types I and II
(in 1953 crowns per month)

Annual Basic Income	Years of Insurance			
	4	6	8	10 or more
Up to 2,100	140	160	160	160
2,101 - 3,300	155	175	190	200
3,301 - 4,500	164	190	212	230
4,501 - 5,700	173	205	234	260
7,801 - 7,800	182	220	256	290
5,701 - 10,200	191	235	278	320
10,201 - 24,000	200	250	300	350

To qualify for old age pension, a self-employed person must either be unable to work or have the consent of the workers' council to retire. To obtain disability benefits, the individual must be totally disabled. The unpaid family worker's benefit cannot exceed that of the insured person for whom he worked, or that of a member of the agricultural cooperative types I and II. Survivors' benefits are calculated on the basis of the old age benefit, with a minimum of 120 crowns monthly for a widow and 80 crowns for an orphan. These minimum benefits are smaller than those paid to survivors of the members of the kolkhoz-type cooperatives. A decision of the State

Pension Insurance Commission permits a self-employed or unpaid family worker who joins a kolkhoz-type cooperative to receive the larger benefits granted to members of such cooperatives.

Workmen's Compensation

After 1948, the various workmen's compensation programs were gradually integrated in the general social security structure. The existing types and amounts of benefits in this social insurance category are discussed in the various sections of this chapter. Monetary benefits contingent on work injuries are discussed as part of disability and survivors' pensions, as well as under sickness benefits. Medical care is discussed in the section on non-monetary medical benefits.

Unemployment Insurance

The shift from "Ghent" unemployment relief to unemployment insurance dates largely from the period of World War II. A decree of the Reichsprotektor, issued March 29, 1940, provided an allowance for those "who are available for work." The unemployment benefit was in the form of allowances for attending training schools, for relocation to labor shortage areas, and for other purposes stimulating reemployment. With the acute labor shortage and universal labor duty under the Communists, unemployment insurance exists only on paper. The money collected for unemployment insurance has been utilized for financing non-monetary benefits, including vocational rehabilitation.

Family Allowances

Under a law of 1945 (No. 154, *Collection*), family allowances were granted to individuals insured against sickness, and benefits were paid by health insurance agencies. After a series of administrative changes, the administration of the family allowance program was transferred to the Revolutionary Trade Union Movement and on January 1, 1950, to the Central National Insurance Institute. Since 1949, the following individuals have been entitled to family allowances: employees insured under the national insurance law for sickness and maternity, with the exception of public employees whose salaries have been adjusted for dependents; individuals receiving health benefits or those in the care of institutions; women who qualify for maternity aid; armed forces personnel on active duty; and persons studying in recognized educational institutions.

To qualify as a dependent, a child, related by blood or adopted, must be under 16 years of age; if studying or engaged in vocational training, he (she) must be under 25 years. The child's income must not exceed 360 crowns in any calendar quarter. Family allowance schedules before and after the currency conversion of June 1, 1953, are shown in Table 4.

Table 4. Family Allowances in 1947-1949, 1949-1953, and after the 1953 Currency Conversion
(in 1953 crowns)

Number of Children	Monthly Allowance		
	1947-1949	1949-1953	Since June 1953
1	30	38	70
2	70	86	170
3	120	144	310
4	180	212	470
5	250	290	630
6	330	378	790
7	420	476	950
8	520	594	1,110
9	620	792	1,270
10	720	800	1,430
Each additional child	100[a]	108[a]	160

[a] Applies only to children over 10 years of age.

In the case of farmers, qualifications for family allowances are somewhat modified. Employees who own arable land in excess of 0.5 hectares or pasture land in excess of 2.0 hectares are disqualified. However, members of the kolkhoz-type cooperatives, and members of types I and II cooperatives, who joined the collective with a holding in excess of 0.5 hectares of agricultural land or 2.0 hectares of pasture land, are qualified for family allowances.

Sickness and Maternity Benefits

Sickness and maternity benefits, both monetary and non-monetary, are based on two laws of December 19, 1951 (Nos. 102 and 103, *Collection*). Monetary benefits and "special" medical care in convalescent homes, spas, and sanatoria have been placed under the Central Trade Union Council. Medical care benefits, including preventive medical care, are administered by the Ministry of Health.

All persons covered by the national pension insurance program are entitled to cash sickness benefits paid to the insured in his work establishment. Military personnel and members of work brigades are not entitled to cash sickness benefits. Pensioners who have worked continuously for at least three months prior to illness are entitled to the benefit for a maximum of 60 days. If the pensioner becomes ill due to an occupational injury or disease, he is entitled to cash sickness benefits for the same period as other workers.

In general, there is no specific qualifying period for the various cash allowances. Cash sickness benefits for the majority of the insured begin the day they are no longer entitled to wages or salary. In all cases, cash sickness benefits begin not later than the forty-third day of illness. The size of the benefit is correlated with the individual's average basic income for three months prior to his illness. The schedule of cash sickness benefits, corresponding to twenty-four wage classes established prior to 1953, is shown in Table 5.

Table 5. Cash Sickness Benefits
(in 1953 crowns)

Basic Income		Daily Allowance	Weekly Total Allowance as Percentage of Average Weekly Basic Income
Weekly	Monthly		
Up to 24	Up to 100	3	116.7
24 to 36	100 to 150	4	93.3
36 to 48	150 to 200	5	83.3
48 to 60	200 to 250	6	77.8
60 to 72	250 to 300	7	74.2
72 to 84	300 to 350	8	71.8
84 to 96	350 to 400	9	70.0
96 to 108	400 to 450	10	68.6
108 to 120	450 to 500	11	67.5
120 to 144	500 to 600	12.2	64.7
144 to 168	600 to 700	13.6	61.0
168 to 192	700 to 800	15	58.3
192 to 216	800 to 900	16.4	56.3
216 to 240	900 to 1000	17.8	54.6
240 to 264	1000 to 1100	19.2	53.3
264 to 288	1100 to 1200	20.6	52.2
288 to 312	1200 to 1300	22.0	51.3
312 to 336	1300 to 1400	23.4	50.6
336 to 360	1400 to 1500	24.8	49.9
360 to 384	1500 to 1600	26.2	49.3
384 to 408	1600 to 1700	27.6	48.8
408 to 432	1700 to 1800	30.0	48.3
432 to 456	1800 to 1900	30.4	47.9
456 to 480	1900 to 2000	31.8	47.6

The total cash sickness benefit is increased by 10 per cent if incapacitation lasts over 91 days, and by 15 per cent if it lasts more than 182 days. While receiving sickness benefits, the insured is still entitled to family allowances under the family benefit plan.

A lump sum maternity allowance of 500 crowns for each child is granted at the time of birth. In addition, an insured woman is entitled to cash sickness benefits for 18 weeks during the period of confinement, provided she does not continue working while she receives the benefit.

The majority of persons covered by the national pension insurance program are entitled to medical and hospital care. Exceptions include the self-employed and unpaid family workers who are entitled to these benefits only if the injuries were incurred at work in agricultural and forestry enterprises. Agricultural cooperative types III and IV have a choice of two alternative plans of medical care for their members: Plan A, providing limited care for a monthly payment of 8 crowns per member, and Plan B, providing full coverage for a monthly payment of 12 crowns per member. Children of members of the kolkhoz-type cooperatives who are under 15, or, if over 15, pursuing studies or vocational training, are also entitled to medical and hospital care. The wife may only qualify for such benefits in her own right.

Under the general program, non-monetary medical benefits include (1) out-patient care and medicines for one year; beyond this period the state continues to pay for the care only if the patient receives disability benefits; (2) in-patient care in public hospitals or other public institutions; and (3) special care in sanatoria, spas, or health resorts. Medical care includes a grant for a layette, dental care, prosthetics, and sterility aid.

Administration and Financing of Social Security Programs

In the First Republic, social insurance programs were administered by a large number of institutions. A major coordinating agency was the Central Social Insurance Institute, but a large number of social security agencies remained outside its jurisdiction. The complexity of the country's social insurance administration was further increased during World War II.

After the war, as the first step toward an integrated administrative structure, a provisional central insurance administration was established by a decree of the President of the Republic on September 29, 1945. In 1948, with the introduction of a uniform national program of social security, the administration of both pension and sickness insurance was temporarily vested in the Central National Insurance Institute, a nominally independent agency. The present system of social insurance administration, which will be sketched further in this section, is largely the result of a reorganization at the end of 1951. The objectives of the present social security administration policy are implicit in the following excerpts from a speech by Premier Zapotocky to the Central Trade Union Council on November 9, 1951, immediately preceding the reorganization of the social security administration:

> Our sickness and pension insurance system has been completely bureaucratic. It has lost touch with factories and workers. The insurance system still reflects the capitalist point of view, and the great new tasks in the building of socialism are entirely neglected. If this were not the case, absenteeism would not be increasing and insurance abuses would not be as frequent as they are today. Insurance matters are administered without regard to the interests of socialist production. Sickness insurance and its administration are not in close touch with working establishments, and they betray lack of understanding of the needs of production. The doctors also lack proper understanding of our production needs. . . . Very often they take the erroneous philanthropic and liberal view that the main objective is to provide relief for the individual. . . . Absenteeism has increased as a result of abuse of our sickness insurance system. . . . We must therefore reorganize sickness insurance in order to . . . eliminate the present bureaucratic defects and assist production. By so doing we shall help everyone, and we shall be able to advance more rapidly toward socialism . . . and a higher standard of living for our people.[1]

Administration of Pension Insurance

The law of December 19, 1951 (No. 102, *Collection*), which went into effect January 1, 1952, abolished the Central National Insurance Institute and, following Soviet practice, separated pension insurance from sickness insurance. The administration of pension insurance was placed under the newly established State Pension Insurance Office, while sickness insurance was integrated with the trade union structure. For the administration of the pension program in Slovakia, a Slovak Pension Insurance Office was established in Bratislava. Both these agencies were placed under the supervision of the State Pension Insurance Commission, whose chairman is the chief administrative officer of the State Pension Insurance Office. Members of the Commission are appointed by the Cabinet after consultation with

[1] Explanatory memorandum to Law of December 19, 1951, No. 102, *Collection.*

the Central Trade Union Council, the Association of Unified Agricultural Cooperatives, and the Association of Anti-Fascist Fighters.

At lower administrative levels, the activities of the former district offices of the Central National Insurance Institute were largely transferred to the councils of the district People's Committees. In 1953, additional duties were assigned to the councils. These included placement of individuals whose ability to work had been impaired as a result of occupational injuries, and administration of a welfare program for war victims.

Administration of Family Allowances and Sickness Insurance

Since 1952, sickness insurance and family allowance programs have been under the jurisdiction of the Central Trade Union Council. Administration of these programs is entrusted to the Central Sickness Insurance Administration, a separate agency established within the trade union organization. Funds for the social security programs are kept separate from other trade union funds. Initially, the income and expenditures of the trade unions' social security programs were not part of the state budget, though they were taken into account in the preparation of the state's financial plans. Subsequently, the financing of these programs became an integral part of the state budget.

Administration of the sickness insurance and family allowance programs is carried out by special insurance commissions in the individual production units. These commissions are part of the so-called works councils, representing labor in each production unit. This practice, facilitating the use of social security benefits as a means for tightening labor discipline, has caused strong resentment among the workers.

The 1952 administrative reorganization of Czechoslovakia's social security system was followed by a radical revision of judicial procedure in social security matters. The 1948 law had adopted the existing insurance court system in which decisions of district courts could be appealed to the Appellate Insurance Court and, in the final instance, to the independent Supreme Insurance Court. On December 30, 1953, this system was abolished, and a new appeal system was incorporated into the trade union structure. Notice of the claimant's right to appeal is served by the chairman of the insurance commission of the works council. The appeal must be submitted within 15 days after the claimant has received a written decision of the insurance commission. Upon appeal, the works council may review and reverse its original decision. If it fails to do so, the claimant may seek redress at higher echelons of the trade union organization, up to the central committee of the trade union which has jurisdiction over the entire industry or trade. Only then can appeal be made to regular courts.

Administration of Medical Services

Prior to the 1952 reorganization of the social security system, public medical services, both preventive and therapeutic, had been administered by the Central National Insurance Institute. On January 1, 1952, all property of the national insurance system used for medical care purposes was transferred to state ownership. Administration of medical services was entrusted to the Ministry of Public Health, which cooperates closely with trade union organizations and district and regional People's Committees.

The country is divided into geographic and industrial health sectors, each under a chief physician appointed by the district People's Committee. Each health sector serves 4,000-6,000 people, with the quality of medical service depending upon the classification of the particular sector. In general, the best medical services are available to extractive industries, particularly coal mines, and metallurgical and chemical industries. Administrative personnel and cultural and health workers are provided with the poorest medical care. Most of the country's large industrial establishments are equipped with infirmaries, consultation and treatment centers, polyclinics, and, in some cases, with hospitals. Smaller establishments, lacking their own medical facilities, are assigned to the nearest public medical service agency. The cost of medical care, both preventive and therapeutic, is borne by the industrial establishments, while the cost of installation and maintenance of medical equipment, instruments, and supplies, as well as the salaries of the medical staff, are paid by the health authorities.

Special medical care in sanatoria, spas, and convalescent homes is administered by the Central Trade Union Council. This type of care has been reserved primarily for outstanding workers, particularly those working under arduous conditions.

Financing the Social Security Programs

When the social security institutions were nationalized, the resources of the insurance system depended entirely on contributions and state subsidies. Though the original nationalization law of 1948 called only for employer contributions, employees were also required to share in contributions during a transitional period. Contributions varied with the employment category. Separate contributions were made for sickness and maternity insurance; old age, disability, and survivors' insurance; workmen's compensation; family allowances; and unemployment relief. Table 6 indicates the contribution rates prior to the revamping of the financial structure of the social security system at the end of 1952.

Table 6. Social Security Contribution Rates prior to 1952
(in per cent of wages)

Type of Insurance	Wage Earners (Except Civil Service) 1948	Civil Service Employees 1948	Civil Service Employees 1950	Self-Employed 1948	Family Workers 1948
Health and maternity	6.8	5[a]	6.8[b]	6.7	6.7
Pension (old age, disability, and survivors)	10.0	—	10.0	10.0	10.0
Workmen's compensation	1.0	1.0	1.0	—	1.0
Total insurance	17.8[c]	6	17.8[d]	16.7	17.7
Family allowance	4.0	—	—	—	—
Unemployment relief	1.0	—	—	—	—
Total social security	23.8	6	17.8	16.7	17.7[e]

[a] Entitled to sick leave, but not to cash sickness benefit.
[b] Employer contributed 4.8 per cent, employee 2 per cent.
[c] One-half contributed by employer, and one-half by employee.
[d] Employer contributed 15.8 per cent, employee 2 per cent.
[e] Total amount contributed by employer.

The law of December 11, 1952 (No. 76, *Collection*), introduced a new contribution system. Employees were no longer required to make direct contributions to the various social security programs. Instead, the wage tax was increased and a part of this tax was used for financing the national insurance program. Though the new wage tax was not specifically earmarked for social security financing, in June 1953 a minimum tax of 8 per cent on incomes above 400 crowns monthly seems to have accrued to the national insurance fund. The tax rate varies according to the number of dependents, marital status, degree of disability, age, and sex. A tax rate schedule for wage earners with two dependents is shown in Table 7.

Initially, state subsidies were contemplated for the national pension and sickness insurance programs. Since the wage tax loses its identity by becoming part of general revenue, it is impossible to determine to what extent social security programs are subsidized by the state.

Table 7. Tax Rates for Wage Earners with Two Dependents (per cent of wages in 1953 crowns)

Monthly Wage Rate	Tax Rate
0 - 200	no tax
201 - 300	5 per cent of wages
301 - 400	8 per cent of wages
401 - 600	32 crowns plus 10 per cent over 400 crowns
601 - 800	52 crowns plus 11 per cent over 600 crowns
801 - 1000	74 crowns plus 12 per cent over 800 crowns
1001 - 1200	98 crowns plus 13 per cent over 1,000 crowns
1201 - 1400	124 crowns plus 14 per cent over 1,200 crowns
1401 - 1600	152 crowns plus 15 per cent over 1,400 crowns
1601 - 1800	182 crowns plus 16 per cent over 1,600 crowns
1800 - 2000	214 crowns plus 17 per cent over 1,800 crowns
2001 - 2400	248 crowns plus 18 per cent over 2,000 crowns
2401 and over	320 crowns plus 20 per cent over 2,400 crowns

Employers are required to make a single contribution for all social security programs. The contribution rate is based on the total wage bill and varies according to the nature of the enterprise. The Government Ordinance of September 28, 1953 (Law No. 84, *Collection*), set the following contribution rates for the various categories of employers: 10 per cent of total wage bill of all organizations whose operations are financed through the national budget or whose net income reverts to the national budget; 3 per cent of total wage bill for the National Security Police (SNB); 15 per cent of total wage bill for private enterprises and all organizations not financed through the national budget (e.g., political parties, mass organizations, and voluntary associations); and 10 per cent of total wage bill for employers in the socialized sector who make use of military work brigades. In the last category one half of the contribution accrues to the armed forces, and the other half to the union administering the health insurance.

Another source of finance for the national insurance program has been provided by the funds accumulated by the various pension and sickness insurance institutions nationalized after 1948. At the end of 1950, the assets of the Central National Insurance Institute amounted to 7,813 million crowns (in 1953 currency). As of December 31, 1950, these assets were distributed among the various types of funds and reserves as follows:

Funds and Reserves	Million 1953 Crowns
Pension insurance reserve	5,569
Supplementary pension insurance reserve	259
Journalists' pension insurance reserve	29
Pension insurance relief fund	19
Sickness insurance reserve fund	753
Sickness insurance relief fund	64
Family allowance fund	1,120

Statistical Summary

The conflicting definitions and statistical data presented in Czechoslovak sources make it difficult to compile a series of consistent facts on the social security program. The data presented below have been gathered largely from periodicals reporting excerpts of speeches on social security. Table 8 presents a summary of the monetary benefits paid under the various insurance plans from 1945 to 1953.

Table 8. Monetary Benefits, 1945 and 1948-1953
(in million 1953 crowns)[a]

Type of Benefit	1945	1948	1949	1950	1951	1952	1953
Sickness, maternity, and other	....	....	876	1,003	1,275	1,443	1,523
Pensions	....	3,600	4,714	....	5,474	5,639	6,100
Family benefits (including maternity)[b]	1,003	1,334	....	1,442	1,660	1,685	1,828

Sources: Sickness, maternity, and other benefits, years 1945-1952, *Prace* (Labor), April 15, 1953; year 1953, budget estimate, *Rude pravo* (Red Right), April 24, 1953. Pensions, year 1948, based on *Rude pravo,* April 15, 1954; years 1949-1952, *Prace,* January 15, 1953; year 1953, budget estimate, *Prace,* April 15, 1953. Family benefits, years 1945 and 1950-1952, *Prace,* April 15, 1953; year 1948, based on *Rude pravo,* April 15, 1954; year 1953, *Rude pravo,* June 15, 1954.

[a] At the official Czechoslovak rate of exchange, one million crowns equals approximately $138,889.00.

[b] Includes children's benefits paid to parents, which amounted to 1,321 million crowns in 1952 (*Prace,* January 28, 1953), and 1,335 million crowns in 1953 (budget estimate, *Rude pravo,* April 24, 1953). On January 28, 1953, *Prace* reported that in 1952, a total of 2,385 million crowns was expended on all children's programs. Parents of 2,418,500 children received benefits.

Between 1952 and the end of 1953, there was a drop in the number of persons receiving pensions. In 1952, there were 1,817,488 pension recipients (*Prace,* November 15, 1953), while in 1953, total pensioners amounted to 1,809,000 (*Narodni pojisteni* [National Insurance], May 15, 1954). Table 9 shows a breakdown of the average number of pension recipients from 1949 to 1952, according to type of benefit.

Table 9. Average Number of Pension Recipients, 1949-1952

Type of Pension	1949	1950	1951	1952
Old age and disability	488,296	518,453	569,964	604,921
Widow and orphan	318,121	341,113	362,156	377,697
Accident disability	130,237	131,303	134,706	137,734
Social and other	99,056	244,253	302,201	312,186
Wife	2,257	35,712	59,824	73,747
Total	1,037,967	1,270,834	1,428,851	1,507,285

Sources: Prace, April 15, 1953, and November 15, 1953.

Of the 1,809,000 persons who received pensions at some time during 1953, 310,000 would not have qualified under the laws prior to 1948.

Health Service expenditures in selected years from 1946 to 1953 were as follows (in 1953 crowns): 1946, 363 million crowns; 1948, 1,127 million; 1952, 4,079 million; and 1953 (estimate), 4,960 million crowns (*Rude pravo,* April 24, 1953).

Total expenditures on health insurance, pension insurance, and family benefits for 1951-53 were as follows:

Year	Million 1953 Crowns
1951	9,707
1952	10,383
1953	10,480

Sources: 1951-52, *Rude pravo,* January 23, 1953; 1953, budget estimate, *Zemedelske noviny,* April 22, 1953.

On a per capita basis, 1951 expenditures were twenty times larger than those in 1937, and 1953 expenditures were about twenty-two times larger. These comparisons are made without any adjustment for changes in price level.

Conclusion

The introduction of national insurance marks one of the most significant developments in the field of social policy in post-World War II Czechoslovakia. The National Insurance Act of 1948 and supplementary legislation set forth a comprehensive social insurance program embracing nearly the entire population. However, like other measures introduced by the Communist government, the national insurance legislation has a distinct "class character," and its primary aim is to implement the government's economic and social policy rather than to provide social security. Furthermore, the broad scope of the national insurance program has been vitiated by discriminatory practices in the application of the law.

The eligibility for the various types of insurance, the range of benefits, and the contribution rates depend on the social status of the insured and his place in the productive process. The legislation favors the socialized sector as against the private sector, industry as against agriculture, heavy industry as against light industry, and higher types of agricultural cooperatives as against the lower types. Employers' health insurance contributions in the private sector amount to 15 per cent, in the socialized sector to 10 per cent, and in the police organization to only 3 per cent. Certain classes of the population are excluded from social insurance. Thus, health insurance does not extend to private entrepreneurs, private farmers, and farmers in lower types of agricultural cooperatives. According to Government Ordinance of April 17, 1953 (Law No. 22, *Collection*), pensions of individuals or of widows of individuals who played a prominent part in Czechoslovak political or economic life prior to February 1948 can be summarily discontinued.

The principal objective of the Czechoslovak national insurance program, as the explanatory memorandum to the Law of December 19, 1951 (No. 102, *Collection*) makes clear, is to stimulate the growth of production and to help shape a socialist society. In practice, the legal right to social insurance has been transformed into a privilege which is to be accorded only to "active builders of socialism . . . who fulfill their responsibilities, plans, and tasks, and who maintain political and trade union discipline" (*Rude pravo*, June 11, 1953).

Part IV. The Economy

11. THE ECONOMY, Retrospect and Prospect 1945-1960

Nicolas Spulber

From the standpoint of structural changes and of the development of the Czechoslovak economy, the postwar era, from 1945 up to 1960, can be conveniently divided into the following five basic periods: (1) the period of the first nationalization wave and of the preparation of planning, 1945-46; (2) the period of reconstruction and of the second nationalization wave, 1947-48; (3) the first Five-Year Plan, 1949-53; (4) the "new course," 1954-55; (5) the second Five-Year Plan, 1956-60.

During the early postwar period, nationalization was launched on a broad scale in industry and banking. By the turn of 1946, the state sector embraced 57.7 per cent of total industrial employment; in the consumer goods industries, the percentage of nationalization in terms of gainfully employed varied between 3 and 50 per cent; in the producer goods industries, this percentage varied between 50 and 100 per cent. While private capital lost considerable ground in the producer goods industries and in banking, it remained predominant in the consumer goods industries, in domestic and foreign trade, and in agriculture, where, despite an enlarged state sphere, small private ownership remained the rule.

The first economic plan, the two-year reconstruction plan, was established in 1946 in the conditions of the uneasy truce between the various economic and political forces of the country. The aims of the plan were to increase by 1948 total industrial output by 10 per cent above the prewar level, and to operate, during the same period, a shift in the industrial structure of the country in favor of the heavy industrial sector. Investments foreseen for the Two-Year Plan period were to approximate 70 billion crowns (at current prices), a sum roughly equal to one half the 1946 national income. Industry was to receive 38.4 per cent (25 per cent for heavy industry), transport 20.7 per cent, public services and housing 33.7 per cent, while agriculture was to obtain the lowest priority, namely 7.2 per cent of the total. Before the end of the reconstruction period, the unstable political truce was broken by the February 1948 *coup d'état* and the assumption of total power by the Communist Party. Immediately afterward, the scope of nationalization was rapidly extended, both in the spheres of production and in the distribution channels. By the turn of 1949, 96.4 per cent of those gainfully employed in industry were absorbed by the state sector, while the private sphere was correspondingly reduced to 3.6 per cent. Nationalization of wholesale trade reached 100 per cent, that of retail trade 54 per cent, and the share of the "socialist sector" (state and producers' cooperatives) in national income jumped to 61 per cent. Private property remained significant only in crafts and agriculture.

The first long-term plan, launched in the new conditions of almost exclusive state ownership outside agriculture, set far more ambitious goals than those of the reconstruction period. The goals were to increase industrial output by 57 per cent (heavy industry by 66 per cent) over 1948, to increase output of all key industrial commodities (coal, iron, steel, etc.), and to establish the "basis of socialism" through "all-round" development (i.e. development in all directions). In keeping with the Soviet model, the planners adopted a lopsided pattern: emphasis on industry in general versus agriculture; emphasis on metalworking in the heavy industrial sector versus other industries; emphasis on heavy machinery in the metalworking industry. In 1951, the over-all targets of the plan were raised again: industry was to double its 1948 output, and heavy industry was to reach the index 233 by the end of the plan. In order to achieve these goals, the share of investment was increased to over 20 per cent of the net material product (i.e., of the net national product excluding services). For the five-year period, according to official data, total investment reached a value larger than the net material product of 1951. The pattern of investment was adjusted to the scale of priorities, with industry receiving the highest priority (over 40 per cent of the total), and agriculture the lowest priority, some 8 per cent of total investments. As the plan unfolded, the sphere of state and collective ownership ("producers' cooperatives") was extended increasingly to the "small commodity" sectors: crafts, trade, and agriculture.

Toward the close of 1953, sharp imbalances appeared in the economy due to the heavy stress on industrial outputs, the processes of reorganization on collective lines of agriculture, and the fall in agricultural output. As these imbalances were apparent in the entire Soviet orbit, each country embarked upon a new policy called the "new course," which aimed at the correction of imbalances provoked by the first long-term plan, higher priorities for light industry and agriculture, limitation of the autarkic tendencies and of "all-round" developments, larger cooperation in the sphere of orbit trade and in planning the second long-term plans. However, before the end of the new course, new pressures built in the opposite direction: light industry was again reduced, while intra-orbit cooperation was limited to a narrower field than expected at the close of 1953. Agriculture retained its new, higher priority, but at the same time heavy industry remained the mainstay of planning. The new Five-Year Plan was prepared in these conditions. This plan was to start in Czechoslovakia and all the countries of the area (except Bulgaria) by January 1, 1956, and to extend up to December 31, 1960.

The economic balance sheet of the whole period 1945-55 is presented in detail in the following chapters. After an opening chapter on national income and product, the text examines the main economic sectors and branches: agriculture, mining, fuel and power, producer goods industries, consumer goods industries, foreign trade, domestic trade, banking and finance, and transportation and communications. The balance sheet uses official statistics as underlying data; there are in fact no other data for research in this field. In the opinion of the researchers, these data are deficient in many respects, due to the faulty system of collection and processing of basic data, the uncertainty regarding certain continuously shifting statistical definitions, the official method of withholding indispensable "linking" figures, the abusive utilization of percentage comparisons, and the impossibility, thus far, for independent observers to check many of the officially claimed performances. However, it is also the general consensus of the researchers that the data are significant and do lead to useful results, provided they are placed against the proper background and provided that their underlying definitions, often at variance with those commonly used in the West, are explained clearly.

It appears from the balance sheet of the whole period, that the economy has reached a given "speed" in respect to the growth of its income and product, to certain sector growth, and so on. Examination of the results poses a host of new problems, among which the most important are perhaps the following: Where is the Czechoslovak economy going after the broad structural changes carried out during the first long-term plan and the new course? Were the rates achieved during that period exceptional rates? Can this economy participate in a deep and wide division of labor within the Soviet orbit? Partial answers to these and other similar problems are given by the new Draft Directives for the second Five-Year Plan.

The Draft Directives of the new plan, published on May 4, 1956[1] (the plan was launched officially on January 1, 1956), foresee a total investment of 152.6 billion crowns (at January 7, 1955 prices), a sum stated to be 61.5 per cent larger than investment for the period 1951-55. The plan foresees an increase in the net national product of 48 per cent over the plan period, a rate somewhat lower than that outlined for the first Five-Year Plan, namely 59 per cent. The increases in income are to be due largely to increase in productivity: during the first Five-Year Plan, employment in the national economy was scheduled to increase by 17.1 per cent; this time the scheduled increase is to be about 7.2 per cent.

The basic growth pattern of the second Five-Year Plan is to be similar to that of the first long-term plan. As can be seen from Table 1,[2] the lopsided pattern is expressed in the scheduled increase of pro-

Table 1. Indices of Planned Gross Outputs During the Long-Term Plans and Actual Outputs for the First Five-Year Plan
(pre-plan period = 100)

Sector	Original Plan (1948)	Revised Targets (1951)	Actual Output (1953)	Second Plan (1956)
Industry	157	198	202	150
Producer goods	166	233	219	157
Consumer goods	150	173	180	140
Agriculture	137	153	114	130

Source: Data in following chapters, *passim; Economic Survey of Europe in 1955* (Geneva, 1956), p. 237; *Rude pravo,* May 4, 1956, Supplement.

ducer goods by 57 per cent. The rates are below those scheduled in the original draft of the first Five-Year Plan. As higher plateaus of development are reached, the rates of growth tend to fall. As can be seen from Table 2, while the annual rates for both producer and consumer goods have fluctuated substantially, there is a net tendency

[1] "Navrh smernic Ustredniho vyboru KSC pro sestaveni druheho petileteho planu rozvoje narodniho hospodarstvi CSR na leta 1956-1960" (Draft Directives of the Central Committee of the Czechoslovak Communist Party for the Second Five-Year Plan of Development of the Economy of Czechoslovakia), *Rude pravo,* May 4, 1956, Supplement.

[2] The upward bias of the indices of gross output and their limitations as a measurement of the performance of the economy are discussed in the introduction to Chapter 12.

toward a decline of the rate of growth, compared to the early years of the first long-term plan.

Table 2. Annual Rates of Growth of Gross Industrial Output

Sector	Actual Rates						Planned Rates	
	1950	1951	1952	1953	1954	1955	1956	1956-1960
Producer goods	16	23	27	5	4	....	9.8	10
Consumer goods	15	9	10	19	5	....	9.4	8
All industry	16	15	17	10	4	6	9.7	10

Source: Plan and plan fulfillment reports.

The new output targets for ten selected key commodities, including fuel and power, iron and steel, fertilizers, and cement, reveal the following interesting trends (see Table 3). In absolute terms, some targets are extremely high, far above the targets of the first Five-Year Plan or the outputs of 1955: e.g. electricity, brown coal, steel. Some other new targets are either below the unfulfilled goals of the first Five-Year Plan, e.g. iron ore, or slightly above these goals, e.g. bituminous coal. These data reveal that some bottlenecks, e.g. output of iron ore, bituminous coal, and coke (not shown in the table) might imperil realization of the new output targets. A close inspection of columns 2, 3, 4, and 5, reveals that many of the first Five-Year Plan targets remained only official directives which were not and could not be fulfilled in the prescribed time. In this light, many of the second Five-Year Plan targets should be considered as only rough orders of magnitude, and not as infallible guides to the actual product of the economy in 1960.

In the agricultural sphere, parallel to the extension of collectivization, the new Draft Directives foresee large increases in output: 22 per cent in bread grains, 126 per cent in increase in corn, 32 per cent in potatoes, and 11 per cent in sugar beets. The poor performance in agriculture during the first Five-Year Plan does not convey the impression that these targets can be reached while large institutional upheavals are being carried out in agriculture.

As in the first planned period, the new Draft Directives emphasize a more rapid development of Slovakia, whose total industrial and agricultural gross output should increase by 61.5 per cent and 39.8 per cent respectively, i.e. at a faster rate in both sectors than the national rate.

In summary, the new Draft Directives intend to place Czechoslovakia more firmly in the path of lopsided development of heavy

Table 3. Planned and Actual Production of Ten Selected Key Commodities

	1[a]	2[a]	3	4[a]	5	6[a]	7[a]	8	9[a]
	First Five-Year Plan 1949-1953					Second Five-Year Plan 1954-1960			
	Base:	Planned Increases[b]		Actual Increases		Base:	Planned Increases		1960
Commodity	1948	Absolute	Per Cent	Absolute	Per Cent	1955	Absolute	Per Cent	Targets
Electric power	7.5	5.2	69	4.9	65	15.1	10.3	68	25.3
Bituminous coal	17.7	9.6	54	2.6	15	23.2	6.1	26	29.3
Brown coal	23.6	12.2	51	10.8	46	38.8	19.0	49	57.8
Iron ore	1.4	3.7	264	1.1	79	2.5	1.1	46	3.6
Pig iron	1.6	1.4	87	1.1	69	3.0	1.8	60	4.8
Crude steel	2.6	1.9	72	1.8	67	4.5	2.1	46	6.5
Rolled products	1.8	2.1	116	1.2	73	3.1	1.4	47	4.4
Sulphuric acid	215.0	2.1	116	96.8	45	383.5	176.5	46	560.0
Nitrogenous fertilizer	31.3	33.1	106	6.3	20	60.5	80.5	133	141.0
Cement	1.6	1.7	102	0.7	40	2.9	1.6	56	4.5

Sources: As in Table 1.

[a] Electric power in million megawatt-hours; bituminous coal, brown coal, iron ore, pig iron, crude steel, rolled products, and cement in million tons; sulphuric acid and nitrogenous fertilizer in thousand tons.

[b] Revised targets.

industry, even though it is apparent this can be done only at a slower rate than during the first Five-Year Plan. No comprehensive division of labor in the orbit is chartered by the new plan. While the new directives refer in general to cooperation within the orbit, the only concrete example is the development of special rolling mills' products in Czechoslovakia. Broadly, the country is to continue to play in the orbit its role of producer of heavy goods, without neglecting domestic output of many products also made in neighboring countries.

12. NATIONAL INCOME AND PRODUCT

Nicolas Spulber

Conceptional Definitions and Problems

The total value of the income and product of a country can be established either by the summation of the incomes accruing to the factors of production during a year (income approach), or by the summation of the expenditure on the national product created during a year (product or expenditure approach). Distinct from the measurement of the two basic flows indicated above, a third way consists in the summation of the value added (or of the incomes originating), industry by industry, building up to a total covering the economy as a whole (income by "industrial origin," computed from the output or income side). These approaches should yield the same total after certain adjustments. The variations of this total from year to year, as well as the shifts in the share of its components, indicate both the performance of the economy as a whole and the ways in which its various parts are related to one another.

Numerous conceptual and statistical problems are involved in the definition of "incomes" and "national product" and, hence, in the establishment of national income computations. In the case of Czechoslovakia, two basic sets of data are available:

1. Summary estimates for the period 1929 to 1937, as well as more complete tabulations from 1937 through 1948, the latter computed at current prices on the bases of standard definitions prevailing in the West.

2. Global figures, in constant prices, for 1937-55, based on Marxist concepts and methodology.

The earliest estimate of the prewar Czechoslovak national income was made in the 1920's by R. Hotowetz on the basis of the calculations of F. von Fellner concerning the income and wealth of the Austro-Hungarian Empire.

After the Second World War, Milos Stadnik attempted to construct a framework of reference for the development of Czechoslovak income from 1929 to 1948. However, Stadnik presented only global figures for the period 1929 through 1937 (concerning Czechoslovakia in its pre-World War II frontiers) summary tabulations for the war years (for Czech lands only), and summary tabulations for the post-war reconstruction years, 1946 and 1947.[1] In the Stadnik computations, national income was defined as the aggregate of all payments for productive services rendered by labor, land, and capital, and corresponds closely to the standard definition of income "by distributive shares." Thus, it is comprised of (1) compensation for employment (wages and salaries); (2) income from agriculture (including consumption of his own produce by the farmer, valued at market prices); (3) entrepreneurial income (from industry, trade, and professions); (4) income from capital (including the rental value of owner-occupied houses); (5) savings of corporations; and (6) government income from public enterprises. The Stadnik definition contains only minor innovations as far as certain secondary items are concerned.

Stadnik presents tabulations of net national expenditure which follow basically the standard definition used in the West. They contain (1) private consumption expenditure on goods and services; (2) government expenditure; (3) net domestic capital formation; (4) net foreign investment; (5) minus indirect taxes, net of subsidies. Stadnik reduces this total, however, by the sum represented by the unfreezing of blocked accounts and includes, on the other hand, the free gifts of UNRRA as net foreign investment. This procedure has been rightly criticized in the West.

It should be noted that the estimates of Stadnik were used up to 1948 as official data. They serve as the underlying data of the Two-Year Plan and as the starting point for estimating both national income for 1948 and for the first Five-Year Plan (1949-53). While basically correct, these estimates convey a rather distorted picture of the Czechoslovak economy on the eve of the first Five-Year Plan: thus, they give the impression of full economic recovery in 1947, when the Czechoslovak economy was still below prewar levels in many key sectors.[2]

[1] Milos Stadnik, *Narodni duchod a jeho rozdeleni* (National Income and Its Division) (Prague, 1946), and *Ceskoslovensky narodni duchod a methody jeho zjisteni* (The Czechoslovak National Income and Methods of Its Computation) (Prague, 1947).

[2] Thus, according to Stadnik, national income in 1947 had increased to 194.4 billion crowns, or, at 1937 prices, to 62.3 billion, i.e. a level higher than that of a good prewar year, 1937, when national income reached 58.6 billion. There was a disastrous harvest in 1947, and the increase in national income was due only to the fact that the "public sector had grown disproportionately as against the prewar level." This example was subsequently used as an argument against the computation of income by the Western method, i.e. against the inclusion of services.

From 1949 on, new income series have been released both for 1937 and for post-World War II years, including the reconstruction period (1946 through 1948), on the basis of Marxist concepts and methodology, as they have evolved in the Soviet Union. This methodology postulates that national income includes only the income created in the production of material goods and of "productive services," valued at market prices. Material production has the following branches: agriculture, industry, construction, transport and communications, trade and catering, and miscellaneous. The services not directly related to production and distribution, i.e., nearly all personal and governmental services, are not included in national income.

National income is computed from the side of production. The gross yearly product is computed as the sum of the gross output (including duplications) in all the above-mentioned sectors of "material production." The total is obtained by multiplying quantities produced times market prices for each enterprise and for each sector. This total, in turn, is broken down as follows: cost of production (*c*), i.e., cost of materials and fuels, as well as depreciation allowances; wage bill and contributions to social security (*v*); "surplus value" (*m*), absorbed by the state in the form of the turnover tax and by the enterprises as "profit." The total $c+v+m$, while used as a key element in planning, is actually of very doubtful use as a measurement of the performance of the economy from one year to the next, since it disregards the fact that certain outputs of one industry are inputs of another. Official statistics in all Communist countries make a rather abusive use of the indices of the total final product, along with the national income figures as the measurement of the rate of development of the national economy.

From the total $c+v+m$, net material product is obtained, in its turn, by the subtraction of *c* and, hence, by elimination of duplications, is given as equal to $v+m$.

National income is divided (distributed) into a consumption fund (*C*) and an accumulation fund (*A*). The first comprises the outlay on consumer goods and material services of the population as a whole (personal consumption), as well as the material consumption of institutions, e.g. hospitals, state administration, armed forces, etc. (social consumption). Evidently, *C* is larger than *v*, since new redistributions of means occur in the broader framework determined both by all the transactions on goods and services and by the budget. Accumulation, which is correspondingly smaller than *m*, is equal to gross fixed investment (excluding equipment actually retired from utilization) but including current provisions for depreciation. The share of accumulation in national income is given only in percentages, while the total income produced in certain years can be derived only from officially released index numbers. A whole series of indispensable figures are not released (e.g. estimates of national income at current prices, estimates of personal consumption, etc.), and there is often doubt concerning the exact coverage and the comparability from year to year of the available information. All these elements, including the utilization of the price relations prevailing in prewar Czechoslovakia, the known deficiencies in collecting the basic data, and the incorrect valuation of new commodities entering into the stream of production as industrialization develops, place serious limitations on the validity of the data available.

This paper is based both on the data preceding the Marxist-type computations, such as the series of Dr. Stadnik, and on the official (Marxist-type) data, given in constant 1937 prices. The deficiencies of these later series, notably the valuation of new commodities, and the fact that we do not have any way of checking the official prices and indices used for deflating the computations in current prices after 1949, clearly imply (1) that the data presented below, the official data, have an upward bias which distorts up to an undeterminable point the rates of growth of total income, the importance of the various sectors, etc.; and (2) that the elements presented below must be considered with reservations. However, the analysis of these data underlines the main structural shifts in the Czechoslovak economy, the heavy drain of state investments, the pressure on consumption levels, and so on. In our opinion, the data are, hence, conducive to significant results.

Development of National Income

According to official postwar estimates in constant 1937 prices, Czechoslovakia reached and surpassed the 1937 income at the end of the reconstruction period, in 1948. However, this income was probably below that of the early 1930's. After 1948, progress continued to be rapid, and by 1953 the official index of national income attained 159, on the basis 1937 equals 100 (see Table 1). Due to the large changes in population caused by the war, the expulsion of the Germans, and the "cession" of Ruthenia to the Soviet Union, the index of per capita income appears lower in 1937 and higher in the early postwar years, than that of total income. The two indices run on closely parallel lines up to 1952; assuming a systematic growth in population, the index of total income starts to increase, for its part, more rapidly than the index of per capita income. Given the sharp fall in population compared to prewar, the per capita income looms very large compared to prewar: it appears to have doubled in 1953 (7,481 crowns, as against 3,717).

Table 1. National Income, 1937 and 1947-1954
(at 1937 prices)

Year	National Income (in billion crowns)	Index (1948 = 100)	Population (in millions)	Income per Capita	Index (1948 = 100)
1937	56.5	94.5	15,200	3717	76.7
1947	51.4	85.9	12,164	4225	87.2
1948	59.8	100.0	12,339	4846	100.0
1949	63.6	106.4	12,463	5103	105.3
1950	68.2	114.0	12,340	5526	114.0
1951	78.1	130.6	12,463	6266	129.3
1952	90.5	151.3	12,587	7261	149.8
1953	95.1	159.0	12,712	7481	154.4
1954 (Plan)	102.4	171.2	12,839	7907	163.1

Sources: National income for 1937 and 1949-51, Ministry of Foreign Trade, *Czechoslovak Economic Bulletin,* No. 238 (January 1, 1952), 12-14; for 1947, estimated in United Nations Economic Commission for Europe, *Economic Survey of Europe Since the War* (Geneva, 1953), p. 26; for 1948, *Sbirka zakonu republiky Ceskoslovenske 1951* (Collection of Laws and Ordinances of the Czechoslovak Republic 1951) (Prague, 1952), pp. 123-26; for 1952, *Uredni list republiky Ceskoslovenske* (Official Bulletin of the Czechoslovak Republic), No. 16 (1953); for 1953, *Nova mysl* (New Mind), No. 7 (1954), 814. Population for 1937-50, United Nations Department of Economic Affairs, *Demographic Yearbook 1952* (New York, 1952), pp. 97-98, 126-29; 1951-54 projections. Other figures, author's computations.

As far as Slovakia is concerned, its share in total income increased, according to official data, from around 13 per cent in 1937 to some 22 per cent in 1950, or, in real terms, more than 100 per cent over the prewar period (see Table 2).

Table 2. Income of Slovakia
(at 1937 prices)

Year	Per Cent of Total Income of Czechoslovakia	Income (in billion crowns)	Index (1937 = 100)
1937	13.4	7.57	100
1947	18.5	9.50	130
1950	21.9	14.93	202

Source: As in Table 1.

The substantial efforts made to increase the income share of Slovakia in total income have brought about appreciable changes in the relation of the regional per capita incomes as related to average per capita income. In 1937, the income per capita in the Czech lands stood at 113 and in Slovakia only at 57, related to the national average. In 1947, the index of per capita income in the Czech lands fell to 104, while that of Slovakia rose to 66, compared to the national average. Finally, in 1950, the index number of per capita income for the Czech lands rose to 108, while the index for Slovakia rose more rapidly, but only up to 78, related to the average (see Table 3).

Table 3. Regional Variations in Per Capita Income, 1937, 1947, and 1950 (at 1937 prices)

	Per Capita Income (in crowns)		Indices (1937 = 100)		National Average = 100	
Year	Czech Lands	Slovakia	Czech Lands	Slovakia	Czech Lands	Slovakia
1937	4202	2138	100	100	113	57
1947	4782	2792	113	130	104	66
1950	5995	4327	142	202	108	78

Source: Derived from Tables 1 and 2.

Structural Changes in National Income

The official figures imply a compound rate of growth of the net material product of 11 per cent during the first Five-Year Plan, with the highest yearly rates in 1951 and 1952 (14-15 per cent) and the lowest rate in 1953 (5 per cent). We will see immediately what these stepped-up rates of increase implied in regard to investment and consumption.

The data available on the national income by distributive shares for the period 1929-46 clearly reveal the substantial changes undergone by the Czechoslovak economy in the early postwar "reconstruction period," from 1946 to 1948, compared to prewar. As can be seen from Table 4, sharp declines are registered in the relative share of three types of income: income from capital, entrepreneurial income, and income from agriculture. (See also Tables I and II, pages 242 and 243.) The income from capital fell from a level of 6-7 per cent of the prewar income, to below one fourth of 1 per cent in 1947-48. Entrepreneurial profits fell from between 13-14 per cent in the prewar

Table 4. Shares of National Income by Category, Selected Years 1929-1948
(in per cent)

Category	1929	1930	1934	1935	1937	1946	1947	1948
Income of independent farmers	17.54	17.22	15.80	12.37	13.29	17.76	13.06	13.14
Rental value of farms	0.82	0.80	1.07	1.09	0.98	0.39	0.37	0.33
Income of forestry	0.85	0.52	0.13	0.15	0.60	0.09	0.20	0.15
Entrepreneurial profits in industry, trade, and professions	13.40	12.78	14.03	13.66	12.45	10.78	11.06	9.61
Wages and salaries	53.10	51.50	50.13	51.40	52.52	62.81	64.76	65.65
Income from capital	6.20	6.37	6.39	7.07	6.08	0.35	0.26	0.23
Rentals and subrentals	1.10	1.24	2.50	3.02	2.75	2.79	2.67	2.49
Other income								
Pensions and annuities	4.16	4.32	6.25	6.54	6.10	3.55	3.14	2.96
Undistributed profits	0.75	0.29	—	0.38	0.69	—	—	—
Profits of public enterprises	2.08	4.96	3.70	4.32	4.54	1.48	4.48	5.44
National income at factor cost	100.00	100.00	100.00	100.00	100.00	100.00	100.00	100.00

Sources: For 1929-46, Stadnik, *Ceskoslovensky narodni duchod a methody jeho zjisteni*, p. 40; for 1947-48, computed from data of the Czechoslovak Planning Office; *cf.* United Nations Statistical Office, *National Income Statistics, 1938-1948* (Lake Success, 1948), p. 60. For underlying data for 1937 and 1946-48, see Table I, p. 242.

period to 10-11 per cent in 1946-48. Finally, the income share of agriculture shows a rather steady declining tendency. From a level of over 17 per cent of the national income in 1929-30, this share fell to between 12 and 13 per cent in 1935-37; after a spurt in 1946 due to a sharp increase in agricultural prices, the income share of farmers fell to around 13 per cent in 1947-48.

Inversely, the strongest increases are registered, as could be expected, in the relative share of wages and salaries. This share rose from between 50 and 53 per cent of the total income in prewar years to 62-65 per cent of the total income of the 1946-48 period. The share of profits of public enterprises remained at the low level of about 5 per cent of the income in 1947 and 1948, a level comparable to that of certain prewar years, e.g. 1930, 1932, or 1935. The relative share represented by the profits of public enterprises ("accumulation") increased to five times its pre-1948 size only after the February 1948 *coup d'état,* and the complete reorganization of the Czechoslovak economy, its structure, price relations, and taxation system.

The following tabulations related to income give some indication of these structural changes in the period after 1948. As can be seen from Table 5, the socialist sector (i.e., state-owned enterprises and cooperatives) increased its share in the formation of the national income from 50.3 per cent before February 1948 to 92 per cent in 1953. The small commodity sector, i.e., the large part of the peasantry not organized in cooperatives and the remnants of private crafts and retail trade, as well as the capitalist sector (reduced by 1953 only to some so-called kulaks in the countryside) fell for their part from a share of 25 and 24.7 per cent, respectively, of the national income before February 1948, to a combined share of only 8 per cent in 1953.

Table 5. Shares of Income, by Sector, 1948 and 1953
(in per cent)

Sector	Before February 1948	End of 1948	1953
Socialist	50.3	61.4	92.0
Small commodity	25.0	25.0	8.0
Capitalist	24.7	13.6	
Total	100.0	100.0	100.0

Sources: For 1948, Ministry of Information, *La Tchecoslovaquie en marche vers le socialisme* (Prague, 1948); for 1953, *For a Lasting Peace, for a People's Democracy,* April 23, 1954.

If we consider the structure of the net material product by sector in 1937, 1948, and 1953 (Table 6), it appears that the share of agriculture fell from 23 per cent before the war to less than 18 per cent in 1948 and to about 13 per cent in 1953.[3] Reductions also occurred in the relative share of trade and catering, as well as of transport and communications. On the other hand, sharp increases were registered in the relative share of industry and building. Thus, according to these data, the relative share of industry increased from 53 per cent of the net material product in 1937 to 70 per cent in 1953. (See Table III, page 243.) In the combined net value of agriculture and industry, the share of agriculture fell sharply, from 30.4 per cent in 1937 to 22.1 per cent in 1948 and only 15.7 per cent at the end of the first Five-Year Plan.

Table 6. Net Material Product by Economic Sector, 1937, 1948, and 1953
(in per cent)

Sector	1937	1948	1953
Agriculture	23.2	17.6	13.0
Industry and handicrafts	53.2	61.9	70.0
Building	6.2	6.0	8.0
Transport and communications[a]	5.3	4.7	9.0
Trade and catering	12.1	9.8	
Total	100.0	100.0	100.0

Sources: For 1937 and 1948, *Czechoslovak Economic Bulletin*, No. 238 (January 1, 1952); for 1953, *For a Lasting Peace. . .*, April 23, 1954, and *Ceskoslovensky prehled* (Czechoslovak Review), Year II, No. 2 (February 1955).

[a] For 1937, communications are included in trade.

If we exclude the contribution of agriculture to the net material product, the nature of the shifts in the share of industry becomes clearer. (See Table 7.) The share of industry increased substantially at two decisive points: at the end of the reconstruction period (1948), and at the end of the first long-term plan (1953). The increase in 1948 is attributable to the reorganization of the industrial setup; the increase in 1953, to the completion of plant expansion called for by the plan. An indirect check on the accuracy of these figures can

[3] The 1953 estimate of the share of agriculture is based on the following indications: out of the 8 per cent of income outside the socialist sector, at the most 1-1.5 per cent was forthcoming from sectors other than agricultural (e.g. retail trade and crafts). As the private share in total agricultural output was about 50 per cent of the total, the share of agriculture can be estimated at some 13 per cent of the net material product.

Table 7. Shares of Industry and Building in Nonagricultural Net Material Product, 1937, 1948, and 1953
(in per cent)

Sector	1937	1948	1953
Industry	69.1	75.1	80.5
Building	8.0	7.3	9.2
All other	22.9	17.6	10.3
Total	100.0	100.0	100.0

Source: As in Table 6.

perhaps be obtained by considering the fluctuations in the contribution to the net material product of agriculture, industry, and of all the other sectors during the period 1948-53. As can be seen from Table 8, net agricultural output, at 1937 prices, remained below the prewar level during the whole period considered. The net output of agriculture attained only three quarters of the prewar level in 1948 and around 95 per cent of prewar in 1953. On the other hand, the net output of industry increased to around 115 per cent in 1948 and 220 per cent in 1953. These figures are parallel to the data concerning

Table 8. Indices of Net Material Product, by Sector, Selected Years 1937-1953
(1937 = 100)

Sector	1937	1948	1949	1951	1953
Agriculture	100	76	81	90	95
Industry	100	116	133	162	222
All other	100	86	96	130	121

Sources: For 1937-51, United Nations, *Economic Survey of Europe Since the War*, p. 26; for 1953, derived from *For a Lasting Peace. . .*, April 23, 1954.

increases in the gross output of industry in the country as a whole. The fact that these two series do not diverge might indicate that the corrected indices of gross output for the country as a whole do not exhibit an upward bias over the short span of time considered. The net output of all the other sectors taken together increased over the prewar level only after 1951. It should be noted, however, that large structural changes occurred in this group during the period under review; certain economic branches included in this group progressed, in fact, continuously in all these years (e.g. building), while others contracted sharply (e.g. trade).

Income, Gross Capital Formation, and Military Expenditure

There are two sets of official data concerning investment. The first is comprised of the percentages of "accumulation" in national income; the second, of data on realized investments.

The first set of data is presumably related to national income in current prices.[4] The second set of data, given at 1937 prices, can be related to our income series. According to these data, actual investment during the first Five-Year Plan reached a total of 83 billion crowns or close to 21 per cent of the total income (see Table 9). The peak of realized investment was reached in 1951, more than double the actual investment of 1949, the first year of the plan. While remaining at high levels, investment decreased, however, in the period of adjustment called the "new course," i.e. in 1953 and 1954. (See Table 9, Column 4.)

Table 9. "Savings" and Investment, 1949-1954

	1	2	3	4	5
	National Income	Realized Investment			
	(in billion crowns)	(in billion crowns)	(in per cent of income)	Index (1949 = 100)	Investment Index ÷ Income Index = 100
	63.6	10.11	15.9	100	100
	68.2	14.16	20.8	140	131
	78.1	18.31	23.4	181	147
	90.5	20.63	22.8	204	144
	95.1	19.82	20.8	196	132
-53	395.5	83.03	20.9	—	—
(plan)	102.4	20.00	19.5	198	123

urces: Column 1, as in Table 1; Column 2 for 1949-53, *Rude pravo* (Red Right), h 10, 1954; for 1954, United Nations, *Economic Bulletin for Europe* (Geneva), No. 1 (May 1955).

The relation of the index numbers of investment to the indices of income show even more strikingly the adjustment in the pace of investment during the "new course." The ratio of the two index

[4] The official percentages on accumulation are: 23.6 per cent of income in 1949, 22.3 per cent in 1950, 24.7 per cent in 1951, 24.3 per cent in 1952, 24.8 per cent in 1953, and 22.8 per cent in 1954.

numbers reaches a high point in 1951, decreasing quite clearly in the next two years, approaching the 1950 ratio. (See Table 9, Column 5.)[5]

By and large, the rate of actual (gross) investments during the first Five-Year Plan, namely around 21 per cent of national income, represents a very strenuous pace and a marked increase over the prewar period. According to prewar data, net investment in 1937 represented only a little over 6 per cent of the national income.

A comparison between total budgetary expenditure and both investment (i.e., total fixed investment at current prices) and military expenditure stresses again the continuous increases in state "accumulation" funds. As can be seen from Table 10, Column 2, the relative share of fixed investment in total expenditure rose steeply from around

Table 10. Shares of Gross Fixed Investment and Military Expenditure in Total Budgetary Expenditures, 1949-1953
(at current prices)

	1	2	3	4	5	6
		Fixed Investment		Military Expenditure		
Year	Total	In Billion Crowns	In Per Cent of Total	In Billion Crowns	In Per Cent of Total	Ratio of Column 4 to Column 2
1949	89.3	24.6	27.5	8.3	9.3	33.7
1950	131.6	48.2	36.6	13.0	9.9	27.0
1951	166.2	77.2	46.4	15.6	9.4	20.2
1952	323.5	92.0	28.4	22.4	6.9	24.3
1953	430.9	107.0	24.8	41.8	9.7	39.1

Sources: Budgets. Cf. Table IV, page 243.

[5] Both the planned and the actual capital-output ratios (i.e. ratios of investment to income showing the increment needed in the former in order to bring about an increase in the latter) are high, compared to intra-Soviet orbit countries and low, compared to the extra-orbit countries. This would suggest that larger investments, as related to a given increment in income, were needed in Czechoslovakia than in the other orbit countries. According to the first Five-Year Plan, the capital-output ratio over the whole plan period was to be 3.3. It apparently averaged less than that, namely 2.3, if the ratios are computed with a year lag between investment and output (e.g. ratio of investment of 1949 over increment in income in 1950). (In the short run, any generalization on the basis of this type of measurement is extremely risky; thus, any variation in aggregate income due to variations in the income from agriculture would cause substantial shifts in the capital-output ratios and thus impair the utility of this type of measurement from year to year.)

The surprisingly low rates, compared to the extra-orbit countries, could be explained—partially at least—as a result of the direction of investment in these countries (namely, their concentration on producer goods) and the suppression of a substantial part of the demand for private housing.

28 per cent in 1949 to over 46 per cent in 1951, and the percentage fell to around 25 per cent of the total expenditure only in 1953. Military expenditure increased appreciably from year to year, especially in 1953, even though its relative share remained the same, between 9 and 10 per cent of the total expenditure, except in 1952. The ratio of military expenditure to investment shows a rather sharp increase in 1953, when it reached a higher level than in any previous year.

If one considers that the budget covers both expenditure on the national economy and government expenditure proper, the following basic tendencies become apparent. During the first Five-Year Plan, 1949-53, the relative share of expenditure on the national economy increased systematically from year to year up to 1952, reaching in that year 67.2 per cent of total expenditure, compared to half this relative size in 1949. This share was reduced in 1953 to slightly less than 60 per cent of the total (see Table 11). As far as the government expenditures proper are concerned, the most outstanding features are the increase in the relative share of military expenditure—from 14 per cent in 1949 to 23.7 per cent in 1953—and the decrease of other items, particularly for administration and for the state debt.

Table 11. Pattern of Budget Expenditure, 1949-1953
(in per cent)

Category of Expenditure	1949	1950	1951	1952	1953
Expenditure on the national economy	33.6	38.4	49.3	67.2	59.1
Total, excluding national economy					
Cultural and social	....	62.8	59.4	58.5	64.6
Administration	16.0	17.3	19.3	18.9	10.6
Defense	14.0	16.0	18.5	21.1	23.7
Other[a]	....	3.9	2.8	1.5	1.1

Source: For underlying data see Table V, page 244.
[a] From 1950 on, state debt only.

The concrete weight of the military burden is hard to estimate. According to Czechoslovak data, 1951 defense expenditure, expressed in 1937 prices, "exceeded by about four times the amount spent on defense in 1937," the year of "the most intensive rearmament efforts of the pre-Munich Czechoslovakia."[6]

[6] *Hospodar* (Economist) (Prague), March 15, 1951, quoted by *Financial News Survey*, III, No. 40 (April 20, 1951), 320.

Income and Consumption

According to the data on net national expenditure available for 1937 and for the reconstruction period up to 1948, personal expenditure on goods and services declined sharply in 1948, compared to 1937. Indeed, it fell to around 72 per cent of the total expenditure, as contrasted to 82 per cent before the war. (See Table 12 and Table V, page 244.) The tabulation on net national expenditure reveals moreover a substantial increase both in government expenditure on goods and services (from 12 per cent to around 20 per cent in the postwar period) and in the net domestic capital formation (from a little over 6 per cent to close to 12 per cent in 1948).

Table 12. Net National Expenditure, 1937 and 1946-1948
(at market prices, in per cent)

National Expenditure	1937	1946	1947	1948
Personal expenditure on consumer goods and services	81.40	82.46	79.00	72.26
Current government expenditure on goods and services	12.56	23.41	19.02	18.95
Net domestic capital formation	6.35	0.57	6.26	11.82
Net foreign investment	–0.31	....	–1.46	–0.87
Less unfreezing of blocked accounts	....	–6.44	–2.82	–2.16
Total	100.00	100.00	100.00	100.00

Sources: Communication of the Czechoslovak Planning Office; United Nations, *National Income Statistics 1938-1948*, p. 58.

These trends were, of course, sharply accentuated during the first Five-Year Plan, up to 1953. According to the data concerning the division of the net material product (i.e., national income excluding services) between consumption and accumulation, in 1948 the share of consumption represented 61.9 per cent of the net material product, against 39.1 per cent for accumulation and "social" expenditures. By 1953, the relative share of consumption was brought down to 57 per cent of the net material product, against close to 21 per cent for investment and 22 per cent for government, defense, etc. With the launching of the "new course" policy in 1953, the share of consumption was scheduled to rise in 1954 to 62 per cent of the net material product. Thus, during the first Five-Year Plan, the relative share of consumption tended to diminish from year to year; the consumption fund available per capita increased, however, with the expansion of income, but, of course, at a far slower pace than that of total investment.

Using 1948 as a base (100), the total consumption fund increased to 147 and per capita consumption also to 147, while income is purported to have increased to 159 and investment to 196. Significant shifts also occurred in the specific situation of various consumer strata and, on the other hand, in the pattern of consumer expenditure. As far as certain consumer strata are concerned, official publications claim large increases in favor of the workers. Thus, real wages are supposed to have increased from 100 in 1939 to 162 in 1950; various computations based on official sources indicate, however, a fall in real wages during the first Five-Year Plan. As far as the pattern of consumption is concerned, a set of data from Czechoslovak sources for 1937 and 1946 indicate, as might be expected, quite substantial increases in the relative share of expenditure for food and clothing, while expenditure on rent, household goods, and miscellaneous declined, compared to prewar. According to another set of data compiled by the United Nations (and somewhat at variance with the former), these trends continued quite clearly during the first Five-Year Plan. (See Table VI, page 244.) The new pattern of consumer expenditure and the share assigned to consumption in national income suggest the following observation. Expenditure on consumer goods is evidently a function of both prices and quantities purchased. In Czechoslovakia, as in the whole Soviet bloc, consumer goods are heavily taxed. The tax applied essentially to these goods, the turnover tax, reaches up to, and even over, 80 per cent of certain retail prices. The heavier this tax, the higher the "share" of consumption in national income.

Concluding Remarks

The "new course" policy foresaw for 1954 a slight increase in the relative share of consumption in national income. With the lowering of total investment as a per cent of national income and the redistribution of this investment by increasing the shares of agriculture and of consumer goods industries, various new elements were liable to influence total national income, its growth and its distribution. However, after a short period, the emphasis was again placed on large investments in heavy industry; a slight priority was also extended to agriculture, while light industry was again reduced to the pre-"new course" level. It is to be expected now that during the second Five-Year Plan (1956-60), the basic trends observed during the first Five-Year Plan will be accented. The absolute share of consumption might eventually increase, given further income growth; however, this increase would occur only at a slow pace, as the emphasis has again been placed on expanding investment in heavy industry.

While international income comparisons are often misleading, the tradition remains strong in favor of the presentation of such figures.

Therefore, according to the official figures, referring to net material product only, income per capita increased in Czechoslovakia from \$244 in 1937 to \$336 in 1949 and \$492 in 1953.[7] Computation on the basis of national income, including services, gives for 1949 a per capita income of \$371 (at 1949 prices). Czechoslovak per capita income would thus remain higher than that of any other East-Central European country, but appreciably below the per capita income in northern or Western Europe.

To summarize, a rather rapid expansion in income appears to have been achieved in Czechoslovakia during the first Five-Year Plan, thanks to the systematic reduction of the share of consumption in total income and to the large allocation of investment to heavy industry. The terrible strain brought about by this stepped-up pace of industrialization and lopsided expansion finally forced the introduction of the "new course" at the close of 1953, a re-allocation of resources, and the slowing down of the rate of growth during the period of re-adjustment, 1953-55. Once this short period of adjustment was completed, unbalanced expansion of the Czechoslovak economy was resumed.

Supplementary Tables

Table I. Division of National Income, 1937 and 1946-1948
(in billion crowns)

Category	1937	1946	1947	1948
Income of independent farmers	7.7	27.6	25.4	28.0
Rental value of farms	0.6	0.6	0.7	0.7
Income from forestry	0.4	0.1	0.4	0.3
Entrepreneurial profits in industry, trade, and professions	7.3	16.7	21.5	20.5
Wages and salaries	31.0	97.6	125.9	139.9
Income from capital	3.5	0.5	0.5	0.5
Rentals and subrentals	1.6	4.3	5.2	5.3
Pensions and annuities	3.5	5.5	6.1	6.3
Profits of public enterprises	3.0[a]	2.4	8.7	11.6
National income at factor cost	58.6	155.3	194.4	213.1

Sources: For 1937 and 1946, Milos Stadnik, *Narodni duchod a jeho rozdeleni* (National Income and Its Division) (Prague, 1946), p. 181, and *Ceskoslovensky narodni duchod a methody jeho zjisteni* (The Czechoslovak National Income and Methods of Its Computation) (Prague, 1947), p. 40; for 1947 and 1948, computed from data of the Czechoslovak State Planning Office; *cf.* United Nations, Statistical Office, *National Income Statistics, 1938-1948* (Lake Success, 1948), p. 59.

[a] Includes undistributed profits of corporations.

[7] The rate of exchange used for the 1937 crown is 3.486 U.S. cents of 1937, or 6.577 U.S. cents of 1953.

Table II. Principal Components of National Income, 1937 and 1946-1948

gory	1937	1946	1947	1948	1937	1946	1947	1948
	(in billion crowns)				(in per cent)			
	2.2	5.0	5.9	6.0	3.8	3.2	3.0	2.8
me[a]	21.8	47.3	56.5	61.1	37.2	30.4	29.1	28.7
ies and pensions	20.0	51.1	62.2	66.0	34.2	32.9	32.0	30.9
es	14.6	52.0	69.8	80.0	24.8	33.5	35.9	37.6
onal income at factor cost	58.6	155.4	194.4	213.1	100.0	100.0	100.0	100.0

urce: As in Table I.

ncludes income from capital, profits of private entrepreneurs, liberal professions, pendent farmers, and profits of public enterprises.

Table III. National Product, by Sector, 1937, 1948, and 1953 (in billion crowns)

Sector	1937	1948	1953
Agriculture	13.1	10.5	12.4
Industry	30.0	37.0	66.6
Building	3.5	3.6	7.6
All other	9.9	8.7	8.5
Total	56.5	59.8	95.1

Sources: For 1937 and 1948, Ministry of Foreign Trade, *Czechoslovak Economic Bulletin,* No. 238 (January 1, 1952); for 1953, *For a Lasting Peace, For a People's Democracy,* April 23, 1954, and *Ceskoslovensky Prehled* (Czechoslovak Review), Year II, No. 2 (1955).

Table IV. Budget Expenditure During the First Five-Year Plan, 1949-1953

National Enterprises and Their Administration	Government Expenditure				Total Budget Expenditure
	Administration	Defense	Other[a]	Total	
	(in billion crowns)				
30.0	9.5	8.3	41.5	59.3	89.3
50.6	14.0	13.0	54.0	81.0	131.6
81.9	16.3	15.6	52.4	84.3	166.2
217.5	20.1	22.4	63.5	106.0	323.5
254.5	18.8	41.8	115.8	176.4	430.9
	(in per cent)				
33.59	10.63	9.29	46.49	66.41	100.0
38.45	10.64	9.88	41.03	61.55	100.0
49.28	9.81	9.39	31.52	50.72	100.0
67.23	6.22	6.92	19.63	32.77	100.0
59.06	4.37	9.70	26.87	40.94	100.0

urces: Budgets and reports on budget fulfillment.

te: From 1949 on, the Czechoslovak government established a new budgetary ture, unifying, on the one hand, the indirect taxes, and incorporating, on the other hand, the financial results of municipalities and nationalized banking institut (Profits of other nationalized enterprises were to be turned over to a fund administ by the investment bank.) Furthermore, the 1949 budget included a series of exp ture items excluded from the budgets which followed (e.g. funds for pro changes, expenditure for the equalization and regulation of prices, etc.). Thus, for the 1949-53 period, some of the budgetary headings and percentages are strictly comparable—especially, for instance, the heading "other."

[a] Cultural and social measures and state debt.

Table V. Net National Expenditure, 1937 and 1946-1948
(in billion crowns)

Expenditure	1937	1946	1947	1948
Personal expenditure on consumer goods and services	52.5	144.4	176.5	183.4
Current government expenditure on goods and services	8.1	41.0	42.5	48.1
Net domestic capital formation	4.1	1.0	14.0	30.0
Net foreign investment	–0.2	—	–3.3	–2.2
Less unfreezing of blocked accounts	—	11.3	6.3	5.5
Net national expenditure at market prices	64.5	175.1	223.4	253.8
Less indirect taxes minus subsidies	5.9	19.7	29.0	40.7
Net national expenditure at factor cost	58.6	155.4	194.4	213.1

Sources: Communication of the Czechoslovak State Planning Office, May 1949; cf. United Nations, *National Income Statistics, 1938-1948,* p. 60.

Table VI. Structure of Consumer Expenditure, Prewar, 1950, and 1953
(in per cent)

Commodity Group	Prewar	1950	1953 (second half)
Food	46.3	52.4	65.5
Clothing	11.2	18.7	15.4
Heat and light	7.0	4.0	3.4
Rent	15.9	3.8	3.0
Other (including household goods)	19.6	21.1	12.7
Total	100.0	100.0	100.0

Source: United Nations Economic Commission for Europe, *Economic Survey of Europe in 1953* (Geneva, 1954), p. 64.

13. AGRICULTURE

Ernest Koenig

Czechoslovakia possesses a relatively highly diversified agriculture reflecting the country's pattern of soil structure, topography, and climate (see Chapter 1). With growing industrialization, the relative importance of agriculture in the country's economy has diminished steadily since 1918. This trend has been particularly pronounced since the launching of the first Five-Year Plan (1949-53). Prior to World War II, Czechoslovakia was able to met nearly all its food requirements from domestic sources. Since the war, it has become increasingly dependent on imports. At the same time, significant changes have taken place in the pattern of ownership and size of agricultural production units.

The First Republic, 1918-1938

At the time of its establishment, Czechoslovakia comprised about one fourth of the population and about one fifth of the territory of the former Austro-Hungarian empire. According to the 1921 census, the agricultural population of Czechoslovakia (including Ruthenia) amounted to almost 5.4 million, i.e. to about 40 per cent of the total of 13.6 million. By 1930, the agricultural population had declined to about 5.1 million, or 34.6 per cent of the total of 14.7 million. Though no official data are available for a later period of the First Republic, it can be assumed that the agricultural population remained relatively stable during the thirties since, as a result of the depression, the normal flow of rural workers to urban centers was almost completely stopped.

The pattern of land utilization on the present territory of prewar Czechoslovakia was as follows: Agricultural land represented some 60 per cent of the total area and forest land accounted for over 30 per cent; the remainder consisted of unproductive land. About 74 per cent of the agricultural land was classified as arable. Table 1 shows the uitlization of arable land during the period 1933-37.

Table 1. Utilization of Arable Land, 1933-1937[a]

	Thousand Hectares	Per Cent
Cereals	3,399	59.4
Edible garden crops	772	13.5
Industrial crops	217	3.8
Seed crops	4	—
Forage crops	1,142	19.9
Vineyards and gardens	114	1.7
Fallow	78	1.6
Total	5,726	100.0

[a] Excluding Ruthenia.

During the interwar period, ownership of agricultural land was almost entirely in private hands. From 1919 to 1938, a moderate redistribution of land (the "First Land Reform") was carried out. Of a total acreage of land available for redistribution, amounting to 4,068,370 hectares (of which 1,313,721 hectares were arable), about 44 per cent were allotted to new owners, while about 45 per cent were returned to the original owners, the remainder being left undistributed as of January 1938. The extent of land redistribution and the resultant changes in the pattern of agricultural land ownership can be gauged from Table 2, which shows the distribution of agricultural land by size of holding before and after the land reform.

Table 2. Distribution of Agricultural Land by Size of Agricultural Holding Before and After the Land Reform

Size of Holding (in hectares)	Share of Total Agricultural Land Held		Number of Enterprises	Per Cent of Total
	Before Land Reform	After Land Reform[a]		
Less than 2	7.8	7.6	729,857	44.3
2 - 5	14.3	18.8	438,348	26.6
5 - 20	44.1	46.5	405,393	24.6
20 - 100	17.8	17.1	66,173	4.0
Over 100	16.0	10.0	8,833	0.5
Total	100.0	100.0	1,648,604	100.0

Source: Vladislav Brdlik, *Die sozialoekonomische Struktur der Landwirtschaft in der Tschechoslowakei* (Berlin, 1938), pp. 36 and 98.

[a] Refers to January 1, 1938.

According to the 1930 census, agricultural holdings under 50 hectares comprised 80.4 per cent of all agricultural land and 86.7 per cent of all arable land. The holdings under 50 hectares accounted for 87.4 per cent of total grain output, 67.6 per cent of sugar beet production, and 92.3 per cent of the potato crop. Furthermore, these holdings accounted for 89 per cent of the country's horses, 91.8 per cent of all cattle, 94 per cent of all pigs, 99.5 per cent of all goats, and 67.2 per cent of all sheep. Agricultural production was thus largely concentrated in small and medium size farms.

1945-1948

Czechoslovakia's agriculture suffered less during World War II than that of her neighbors in Central and Eastern Europe. In the aftermath of the war, however, profound changes took place in the social and economic structure of the country. Even before the Communist coup in February 1948, conditions in agriculture were radically different from before the war.

The loss of Ruthenia, which Czechoslovakia was forced to cede to the Soviet Union, reduced the total area of the country by about 9 per cent, but the consequent losses to agriculture were of little significance. Ruthenia represented only 4 per cent of the total arable area and only 7 per cent of the total agricultural land.

Losses in population were of far greater importance. The deportation of Czechoslovakia's German citizens reduced the population within the present boundaries by about 13 per cent, compared to 1930. The agricultural population declined by about 27 per cent between 1930 and 1947. In 1930, the per capita share of agricultural land was 0.55 hectares for the total population and 1.67 hectares for the agricultural population. In 1947, these ratios were 0.60 hectares and 2.16 hectares respectively. Thus, there was more land available to feed the population, but there were less people to till this land.

Land Redistribution

Immediately after World War II, Czechoslovakia launched a series of "land reforms" which had a profound influence on the development of agriculture. These "reforms" may be conveniently divided into three groups: "Land Transfer of 1945," "Revision of the First (i.e. post-World War I) Land Reform," and "New Land Reform." Viewed in retrospect, these land transfers were the prelude to the socialization of landed property. Public opinion, however, considered at least the first and most important of these changes as a sequel to the liberation of the territory, aimed at purging the population of all hostile elements (i.e., Germans, Hungarians, and Czech collaborators).

Land Transfer of 1945. The expulsion of the German population coincided with the expropriation of German property. With some insignificant exceptions, Germans, Hungarians, and all those who were considered traitors, regardless of nationality, were to be deprived of their land holdings. Actually, only a small proportion of Hungarian farms were expropriated. Most Hungarians were not expelled and retained their farms.

Farms and farm land gained by confiscation were to be distributed among persons of Slavic nationality, the amount not to exceed 13 hectares of agricultural land per recipient. Some agricultural land was to be given to villages and other public bodies, but practically none of the confiscated land was to be retained by the state for farming purposes. Beneficiaries of the land redistribution were to pay the state the value of one to two harvests from the allocated land, within a period of one to fifteen years; those who received buildings or building sites were to pay the value of one to three years' rent from such property within a period of one to fifteen years.

Confiscated forest land did not revert to private ownership. The state-controlled National Forest Administration was to acquire all forest holdings exceeding 100 hectares. Individual communities and some provincial bodies were to receive forest holdings of less than 100 hectares.

More than 80 per cent of the confiscated land was located in the border regions of Bohemia-Moravia. In the western part of the country, land transfer was practically identical with resettlement of the borderland. While farms situated in the interior of the country were often subdivided into small lots, those in the border regions, regardless of size, were taken over by new settlers. However, recipients of new farms or farm land did not receive title deeds immediately. The recipients were called national administrators and were entrusted with the management of farms and farm land as representatives of the nation: the implication was that farms would in due course become their personal property. However, by 1948, only about 60 per cent of the new settlers in Bohemia-Moravia had received ownership rights, and these rights applied only to holdings of 13 hectares or less. Farmers on holdings exceeding 13 hectares did not receive title deeds but continued as national administrators.

Since many of the new settlers in the borderland were either without farming experience or applied for land merely to gain property, without intention of permanent settlement, there was a continual flux to and from the borderland. Farms changed hands several times and were often abandoned altogether. The final results of the Land Transfer of 1945 are, therefore, difficult to establish. Some of the laws upon which it was based were not executed simultaneously in all parts of the country, and new "land reform" laws were enacted and executed before the 1945 Land Transfer had been completed. In Slovakia, for example, the land transfer based on 1945 laws was carried out only in 1948, merging with the land redistribution under way at that time.

Almost all Czechoslovak sources give contradictory data on the extent of the land transfer; approximate figures have therefore been compiled from a variety of sources. Figures for agricultural and forest land, confiscated under provisions of the Land Transfer of 1945, are as follows:

Confiscated Land	Thousand Hectares
Agricultural	1,772
Forest	1,251
Agricultural and forest	3,023

On the basis of 1933-37 land utilization within present boundaries, the confiscated land comprised 23 per cent of total agricultural land, 31 per cent of total forest land, and 26 per cent of total agricultural and forest land.

The same sources indicate the following allocation of confiscated agricultural land under the Land Transfer of 1945:

Allocation	Thousand Hectares
Private individuals, cooperatives, etc.	1,525
State Forest Administration	50
Communal and provincial administration	13
Airfields, military training grounds, etc.	82
Undetermined	102
Total	1,772

Confiscated forest land, amounting to 1,251,000 hectares under the Land Transfer of 1945, was allocated as follows: State Forest Administration, 1,115,000 hectares; provincial and communal administration, 136,000 hectares.

Revision of the First Land Reform. The land transfer, which began in 1945, was still under way when the Communist Party demanded a new "land reform." This demand was based on the allegation that the "First Land Reform," i.e. the land reform which had occurred in the interwar period, had not been executed in conformity with the original laws, that corruption had influenced the distribution of land, and that some of those whose land had been subject to confiscation had evaded the law. However, the demand for revision of the prewar land reform was less concerned with correcting past errors than with breaking the opposition of politically influential landowners, who represented an important obstacle to the policy of the Communist Party. Indeed, the law pertaining to the "Revision of the First Land Reform," after providing for revisions that applied properly to the "First Land Reform," contained a provision under which landed property of any kind, exceeding 50 hectares, could be expropriated "in case of urgent local need or if public interest demands it." This provision opened the way to confiscation of all landed property exceeding 50 hectares. Land obtained through this law was distributed among various groups: small farmers, in order to complement farms which were not self-supporting; farm workers and small farmers, for the creation of new farms; public corporations, workers, employees, and small tradesmen for building sites and gardens.

The Revision Bill was passed in 1947. Its execution, especially that of its more ambiguous provisions, met with strong resistance from the non-Communist parties. The political struggle centering upon this bill was one of the major issues in the political crisis that preceded the Communist *coup d'état* of 1948.

It is estimated that some 940,000 hectares of agricultural and forest land were expropriated under this bill. As far as is known, only 15 per cent of the confiscated land was distributed among private individuals. The number of beneficiaries amounted to about 100,000. The average share per recipient was 1.4 hectares of agricultural land.

"New Land Reform." After the Communist seizure of power, the so-called New Land Reform Act was passed. This law explicitly established the principle already implied in the Revision Bill of 1947, namely that private holdings may not exceed 50 hectares in size. All land holdings exceeding this size were confiscated and distributed among small farmers and workers. The "New Land Reform Act" also established another principle which stipulated that no person be permitted to own land which he did not work himself. There were some insignificant exceptions to this principle, but essentially it meant further encroachment upon private property. Although official sources indicated that as much as 500,000-700,000 hectares of land would be confiscated under this law, it is estimated that only about 130,000 hectares were affected by it. It is likely that none of this land has been distributed among private individuals.

About 4,100,000 hectares of agricultural and forest land have probably been confiscated in the course of the three "land reforms" during the period 1945-48. This represents about 35 per cent of the total agricultural and forest area in the country. About 1,665,000 hectares of agricultural land have been distributed among private individuals and private organizations, an average of 5.5 hectares per recipient.

Table 3 shows the number and area of agricultural and forest holdings in 1949, after the land transfers had been completed. The number of farms given in this table is not identical with the number of farm owners, since some farms were publicly owned and the legal status of many others had not been defined. Some farms were operated on private account, but by national administrators; others, though confiscated, were still managed by the original owners.

Table 3. Number and Area of Agricultural and Forest Holdings, by Size (Census of May 1949)

Size of Holding (in hectares)	Number of Holdings		Area of Holdings	
	In Thousands	Per Cent	In Thousand Hectares	Per Cent of Total
Less than 0.5	267,046	19.7	84,454	0.7
0.5-1	191,696	12.7	147,038	1.3
1-2	206,636	13.7	317,391	2.7
2-5	350,904	23.3	1,239,615	10.6
5-10	255,293	16.9	1,880,856	16.0
10-20	158,874	10.6	2,214,831	18.9
20-50	35,159	2.3	1,032,992	8.8
Over 50	11,489	0.8	4,810,264	41.0
Total	1,507,097	100.0	11,729,441	100.0

Source: State Statistical Office, *Statisticky zpravodaj* (Statistical Bulletin), XIII, No. 2 (Prague, 1950).

Although many private farms were taken by the state in the course of the land transfers, the number of independent farm operators increased. In Bohemia-Moravia, for example, the number of independent farm operators per thousand persons gainfully active in agriculture was larger in 1947 than in 1930. During this period, the number of agricultural laborers per thousand persons gainfully active in agriculture decreased by 33 per cent, and the ratio of agricultural laborers to independent farm operators fell by 48 per cent. Apart from the labor shortage arising from the deportation of the German population and the migration of the country population to the cities, the land transfers thus further increased the labor shortage in agriculture.

Other Measures Affecting Land Tenure

In 1946, a so-called Agricultural Tenancy Act was passed which aimed at fixing ceilings for land rents. Rents were to be based on net yields, as shown in the Land Register, and on actual harvest values obtained from rented land. Whenever whole farms were leased, the rent was not to exceed 3 per cent of the capitalized value of the leased property.

This act afforded great protection to tenants, but was wholly detrimental to the interests of landlords. It would have been of significance in prewar Czechoslovakia where, by 1930, about 8 per cent of all holdings were entirely leased and 36 per cent of all holdings partly owned and partly rented. Under conditions prevailing in the early postwar years, this act was less important: land was readily obtainable, and rent contracts could not be easily enforced, in view of the general uncertainty concerning property rights.

Another legislative measure pertaining to land tenure was the Act on Farm Inheritance and on the Prevention of Dividing Agricultural Land. This act, promulgated in 1947, was designed to limit the fragmentation of farm land through inheritance. Minimum limits were set for the division of a farm among the heirs of a deceased owner. Provisions regulating the subdivision of farms were based on the principle that farm land was to be subdivided only if the resulting smaller fields would permit efficient farming. The permitted minimum area was to be 0.5 hectare.

Before the war, few countries in Europe suffered more from land fragmentation than Czechoslovakia, where the average number of parcels per farm amounted to no less than thirty. This law, therefore, could have been of consequence before the war, but in 1947, when farm density had already declined, it was less relevant. Its beneficial effects were entirely overshadowed by the process of socialization, which set in two years later.

Allocation of Resources

In 1947, a Two-Year Plan was initiated. In agriculture, the plan sought to reach prewar levels of production by the end of 1948. Goals for crop and livestock production were given in detail, but the means of implementing the plan were not specified. No specific plans were elaborated for the various agricultural production regions, nor were plans assigned to individual enterprises. It was thought that the targets would be achieved through such indirect means as price policies, adjustments of the compulsory delivery quotas in force since the beginning of the war, and allocation of fertilizers, machinery, and manpower.

The Two-Year Plan in agriculture was not fulfilled. In 1948, national product again reached prewar levels and industrial production exceeded the prewar level by 17 per cent, but agricultural production was about 25 per cent below prewar. Unfavorable weather conditions contributed to the nonfulfillment of the agricultural plan, but faulty policies were equally responsible. Comparatively large amounts of commercial fertilizers, as well as numerous tractors and other agricultural machines, had been made available to farmers. However, the increase in productivity during this period did not compensate for the lack of agricultural manpower. The labor requirements of agriculture had been underestimated, and the agricultural labor force, instead of increasing as foreseen in the plan, showed a further decline during the period 1946-48.

Communist Agricultural Policies

Socialization

Collectives. One year after the *coup d'état* of 1948, the Communist government decided to proceed with the establishment of collectives. Both political and economic objectives were involved in the collectivization of agriculture. The main economic motives were the rationalization of agricultural production through introducing large scale farming, and an increase in the marketed share of agricultural output. Labor shortage in agriculture was to be overcome by mechanization, and the increasing demand for agricultural products, attendant upon industrial expansion, was to be satisfied by increased productivity.

Before 1948, Czechoslovakia had a well organized network of rural cooperatives, and the cooperative idea was deeply entrenched among the peasants. However, although practically all the known types of agricultural cooperatives were well developed, producer cooperatives were almost nonexistent, and the occasional attempts to organize them ended in failure. When the government proceeded to collectivize, it appealed to the cooperative tradition. It represented collectives as a logical, advanced stage of, rather than a radical departure from, the traditional cooperative movement. Indeed, the law which laid the groundwork for the establishment of collectives was called Act on Unified Agricultural Cooperatives, and a collective in Czechoslovakia is called "Unified Agricultural Cooperative."

Four types of collectives exist in Czechoslovakia, each representing a different degree of integration of work and property. In the early stages of collectivization, each of these types followed rather vague rules, but in 1953, a uniform charter was promulgated. However, even after the introduction of this charter, individual collectives exhibited significant deviations from the standard to which they are supposed to conform. As indicated below, there is a basic difference between types I and II (sometimes referred to as "lower types") and types III and IV ("higher types"). The former do not have much in common with collective agricultural production, but represent rather preparatory stages of collectivization. Peasants belonging to these collectives are more easily easily induced to join collectives of the higher types than peasants who have never belonged to any kind of collective. The main characteristics of each of the four types are outlined in the following summaries.

Type I

Neither land nor livestock is pooled. Machines are the only means of production which may become common property. For certain agricultural operations, which are collectively performed, income is distributed according to the work and services contributed by each member.

Type II

Land may be but need not be pooled. However, even if private property in land is maintained, sowing, plowing, and harvesting are performed in common, and all field operations are carried out as if the farms included in this type formed a single enterprise. Livestock is not collectivized, even if the boundaries of individual fields are abolished. Income is distributed in strict accordance with work and services contributed.

Type III

All land is pooled with the exception of a small private plot *(zahumenek)*, which may never exceed one hectare. All implements and farm buildings are pooled, except small tools, residential buildings, and stables needed for privately-kept livestock. Livestock is pooled but each member may retain one cow, three goats, two pigs, five sheep, and an indefinite number of poultry and rabbits. No compensation is paid for the land, but 80 per cent of the value of livestock, implements, and buildings is repaid, according to the ability of the collective. Upon withdrawal or expulsion from a collective, a member is to receive land equal in size to that with which he joined. However, the location of such land may be different from that of the original land. Up to 80 per cent of the value of buildings, implements, and livestock may be returned to a withdrawing member, after a deduction of compensation payments already made. The business of the collective is conducted by a general assembly of all members, with a board of managers elected by the general assembly. The work performed by members in the course of one agricultural year is measured in working units, or "work days." The annual sum of working units determines the personal income of members. However, up to 15 per cent of the collective's net cash proceeds may be paid in form of rent, according to the acreage contributed by individuals.

Type IV

This type resembles in every respect type III, except that all income is derived from work performed and no rent is paid.

As indicated in Table 4, collectivization reached a high point toward the middle of 1953. Thereafter, the number of collectives tended to decline.

Table 4. Growth of Collectives, Types II, III, and IV, 1949-1953

Date	Number of Collectives	Number of Households	Share of Total: Arable Land	Share of Total: Agricultural Land
			(in per cent)	
December 31, 1951	4,480	....	....	....
December 31, 1950	3,743	....	19.1	17.4
December 31, 1949	2,196[a]	....	15.9	15.1
December 31, 1952	7,819	289,401[b]	36.5	34.8
June 30, 1953	8,284	345,919	44.0	40.0

Sources: Czechoslovak Academy of Agricultural Sciences, *Za socialisticke zemedelstvi* (For a Socialist Agriculture), II (1952), III (1953), and IV (1954), various issues.

[a] All types.

[b] As of October 30, 1952. At this time there existed 7,280 collectives of types II-IV.

The percentage of collectives belonging to type IV reveals the attitude of peasants toward collectivization. At no time did the number of collectives of this type exceed 7 per cent of the total number. Even peasants who joined type III were reluctant to join type IV, as the latter abolishes all private property, while in type III, at least the identity of the original plots of land is preserved.

Lack of reliable data makes it difficult to judge the results of collective farming in production. It appears that collectives have had some success in grain production, chiefly due to the effects of land consolidation and to the application of modern machinery, which is primarily allocated to production of this kind. Collectives seem far less successful in the production of potatoes and sugar beets, which are of great importance in Czechoslovakia. These crops require a large labor force, but neither sufficient labor nor machine substitutes are available.

Livestock raising has been another weak point of collective farming. The relative inefficiency of collectives in animal husbandry is illustrated by a comparison of livestock density on collective farms with that on all farms (separate data for private farms are not available). In 1952, types III and IV collective farms had an average of 31.8 head of cattle and 40 hogs per 100 hectares of agricultural land, while the corresponding figures for all farms were 59.1 and 63.3, respectively. However, these figures are not an accurate index as they exclude the important fact that a large share of livestock owned by collectives is kept in the private stables of individual members and used for private profit. This greatly contributes to disrupting collective discipline, because the fodder supplies of the collective are diverted to private use and interest in collective work is diminished, since it is more remunerative to devote time to private farming than to work in the collectives.

The overall results of collective farming may be gauged from the fact that in 1952 only 14 per cent of all collectives belonging to types III and IV were able to pay their members the planned remuneration per working day (i.e., the share which members are to receive for work performed on the basis of the collective's plans). The great majority of members of collectives of these types received a much smaller income than planned or promised.

State Farms. Some state farms existed in Czechoslovakia even before World War II, but they consisted primarily of forest and pasture land: in 1936, only 38,000 hectares of a total of 500,000 hectares represented agricultural land. Before the war, state farms possessed some outstanding agricultural research centers, but they did not engage in commercial farming to any significant extent. As a result of the postwar land transfers, the number and area of state farms grew; by 1953, they covered about 10 per cent of the arable and 8.6 per cent of the agricultural area, that is, 522,000 hectares of arable and 630,000 hectares of agricultural land. Under the new regime, they were to be the leading agricultural enterprises, models of socialist large scale production.

State farms, like other farms in Czechoslovakia, are engaged in mixed farming, raising both crops and livestock. They also specialize in the production of certified seeds and plants, and they possess breeding and experimental stations for livestock. In the past, large farms were not important producers of livestock products, but state farms now lay heavy emphasis on this line of production. On many state farms, hog-breeding stations have been established, some of which are supposed to produce up to 30,000 pigs per year.

State farms enjoy priority in the allocation of machinery, fertilizers, and other means of production. They employ hired labor, which is organized in small groups and sections, each specializing in a particular line of production, such as mechanical operations, hog or cattle breeding, and crop production. Wherever possible, work is rewarded on the basis of achievement. Performance wages are measured according to the time spent on special operations, according to the quantity and quality of the harvest or on the basis of milk yields and slaughter weights of livestock. Among the state farms, two groups may be distinguished: the first includes farms which were large units in the past; the other includes farm units created through the amalgamation of many small farms. During the first years of the new regime, the former performed comparatively well, for changes in ownership were often not accompanied by changes in management. The latter showed unsatisfactory results from the beginning. The general difficulties of state farms increased when the internecine struggle that culminated in the Slansky trial led to extensive changes in management. Nevertheless, state farms are more important agricultural enterprises in Czechoslovakia than their limited area suggests, since their contribution to market supplies is comparatively higher than that of collective or private farms.

State Tractor Stations. The government at an early date decided to support the development of mechanization in agriculture. Machine-cooperatives were heavily subsidized, and even before 1948, State Machine Stations were set up to supply private peasants with the services of machinery and implements. The Law on Mechanization, passed in February 1949, created a new state-owned organization which took over the functions of the State Machine Stations and of private cooperatives. This new organization, State Tractor Stations, also called S.T.S., was to have a monopoly in the ownership of agricultural machinery. The private machine cooperatives and State Machine Stations were merged with them, and machinery belonging to private peasants was expropriated and included in the State Tractor Stations.

The State Tractor Stations' task is to work closely with collectives, providing them with the services of tractors, combines, threshers, and other heavy machinery, as well as participating in planning their work.

They also assist private farmers. State Tractor Stations may service state farms, but the latter possess their own machinery and this service is not frequently required.

According to official reports, by September 1953, there were 255 State Tractor Stations. These were organized in 2,277 tractor teams, possessing 18,911 tractors (in terms of 15 horsepower), 20,075 reaper-binders, 819 combines, and other heavy equipment. They performed 44 per cent of all field work done by collectives during 1953.

State Tractor Stations represent probably the weakest link in the triad, State Farms, Collectives, and State Tractor Stations. Frequent complaints of excessive under-utilization of equipment and lack of coordination between State Tractor Stations and private or collective farms indicate a low degree of efficiency.

Planning

With the inception of the first Five-Year Plan, planning in agriculture assumed the characteristics of all inclusive central direction of production. This was comparatively easy with regard to state farms and collectives, whose organization is based on planning. In the private sector, however, special methods had to be devised to make individual farms conform with central planning. An elaborate production plan for the entire country, drawn up by the central authorities, was broken down into regional and local plans; the plans designed for the villages were then in turn broken down and assigned to individual farms. These individual plans contained exact targets, stating the proportions of farm land to be sown to individual crops, the yields to be attained, and the quantity of fertilizers to be applied. The number of livestock at the end of the planning period, their quality, increases in slaughter weights, and milk yields were anticipated in the plan. Individual plans provided also for compulsory delivery quotas.

Enforcement of the plan on the farm level took the form of contractual agreements between each producer and the state. Thus, within narrow limits, the farmer had the possibility of modifying his assignments to coincide with his productive capacity. However, the system underwent considerable modification in the course of the first Five-Year Plan. Production and delivery goals were increased. Moreover, they were imposed without mutual agreement and regardless of the ability of individuals to comply. Only in the second half of 1953 were these rigid methods somewhat relaxed.

An exceedingly well organized system of agricultural statistics appeared to be one of the by-products of agricultural planning. Planning of individual farm production seemed to provide records of farm inventory, of livestock numbers, and of progress in production. However, resistance by the peasants to exaggerated demands led to great distortion in reporting and gravely disrupted agricultural statistics in general. Indeed, it appears that at present even the government has only vague information on many vitally important subjects, such as the amount of land under crops.

Allocation of Resources

To enable agriculture to reach the goals of the first Five-Year Plan, a considerable part of the total investment in agriculture was to be devoted to mechanization. Table 5 shows the increase in the number of tractors, which may be taken as an indicator of the progress made in mechanizing agricultural operations.

Table 5. Number of Tractors and Their Ratio to Agricultural Land, 1947-1953

Year	Number of Tractors (in thousand 15 HP units)		Hectares per Tractor
	Planned	Actual	
1947	14	14.5	505
1948	22	22.0	333
1949	27	27.1	270
1950	29	28.9	253
1951	35	....	....
1952	43	....	....
1953	50[a]	29.3	250

Sources: United Nations Economic Commission for Europe, *The European Tractor Industry in the Setting of the World Market,* 1952; *Zemedelsky pokrok* (Agricultural Progress), various issues, 1950; State Statistical Office, *Statisticky obzor* (Statistical Review), XXXIV, No. 5 (1954).

[a] The original goal was 45,000, but it was later revised to 50,000. Between 1948 and 1953 (original goal), there was to be a net increase of 23,000 tractors (30,000 tractors were to be supplied and 7,000 eliminated because of obsolescence).

Failure to reach targets for mechanization in agriculture grew even more serious as the agricultural labor force continued to decline throughout the Five-Year Plan. In 1947, there were in Czechoslovakia 2,207,000 persons active in agriculture, compared with 2,802,000 in 1930. The Two-Year Plan (1947-48) anticipated an increase of 250,000 for the country as a whole, but the increase did not materialize. The first Five-Year Plan allowed for a decrease of 5 per cent between 1949 and 1953. In 1953, however, it was reported that the agricultural labor force had declined by "20 per cent in recent years." Whatever the period referred to, it is certain that the planners miscalculated both the increase in productivity and the decrease in the agricultural labor force. It is obvious that labor shortage was one of the most important reasons for the failure of agriculture to reach prewar levels of production during the period under review.

Consumption of artificial fertilizers was low in prewar times, and during the immediate postwar years it exceeded prewar levels. At the end of the first Five-Year Plan, fertilizer consumption was much higher than at the beginning of the Plan, though it still fell short of planned goals. Consumption of fertilizer in prewar and postwar periods is illustrated in Table 6.

Table 6. Consumption of Commercial Fertilizers in Terms of Pure Nutrients, Selected Years 1933-1953
(kilograms per hectare of agricultural land)

Period	Nitrogen (N)	Phosphoric Acid (P_2O_5)	Potash (K_2O)
1933/34-1936/37	2.6	5.6	3.0
1946/47	3.4	4.9	9.3
1947/48	3.8	7.4	8.1
1948/49	4.8	7.7	3.3
1952/53 Plan	12.8	15.3	12.1
1952/53 Actual	7.6	10.7	9.0

Sources: State Statistical Office, *Statisticke informace* (Statistical Information), VI, No. 16 (1950); Viliam Siroky, speech at the Tenth Congress of the Communist Party of Czechoslovakia, June 1954.

The "New Course" in Agriculture

In the latter part of 1953, agricultural policies were sharply revised because many measures taken during the first Five-Year Plan had not been conducive to increased production. The highlights of the intended "new course" may be summarized as follows: It was conceded that private farms would continue to play an important role, though the resolve to proceed with collectivization was not abandoned. Collectivization, however, was to advance at a slower pace, in a more orderly way, and with greater material assistance on the part of the government. Since private farming was to stay, at least temporarily, the government promised to provide individual farmers with larger credit facilities. They were also to have a larger share in the allocation of means of production, and the peasantry as a whole was assured that more manufactured consumer goods would be made available. The government reduced compulsory delivery quotas for all farms, but continued to maintain, and even increased, discriminatory practices in the determination of quotas between private and collective farms. Finally, efforts to halt the drain on agricultural manpower were to be made, and special plans were prepared to increase agricultural production in the border regions.

Major Crops

The latest complete land utilization data are based on conditions prevailing in 1949. According to these data, arable and agricultural land in 1949 represented 91.5 and 94.6 per cent, respectively, of the 1933-37 average, within present boundaries. Arable land had decreased by about 500,000 hectares in comparison to prewar. (See map, page 263.)

Although 1949 data shown in Table 7 probably overstate the real extent of arable and agricultural land in that year, there is no doubt that land in use has declined since then. It is fair to assume that the area of land under crops decreased by another 200,000 hectares between 1949 and 1953. Moreover, some 5 per cent of the area actually under crops is probably outside government control, and therefore is neither subject to compulsory deliveries nor to planning.

Table 7. Land Utilization, 1949

Sector	Area	
	Thousand Hectares	Per Cent of Total
Arable land[a]	5,244	41.0
Permanent meadows and pastures	2,085	16.3
Total agricultural land	7,329	57.3
Forests	4,157	32.5
Other[b]	1,295	10.2
Total	12,781	100.0

Source: State Statistical Office, *Statisticke informace,* V, No. 35 (1949).
[a] Including gardens, vineyards, and some other land.
[b] Including 68,000 hectares whose use is undetermined.

The decline in arable land and the changes in the proportions of arable land used for individual crops resulted largely from the decrease in the agricultural population and the changes in land tenure consequent upon the land transfers. However, 1949 data given in Table 8 indicate the influence of the first Five-Year Plan.

Table 8. Area of Principal Crops Within Present Boundaries, 1949

Crops	Area (in hectares)	Index (1933-37 = 100)
Cereals		
Rye	709,563	83
Wheat	796,725	90
Barley	572,461	88
Oats	630,046	84
Corn	137,023	121
Other	5,141	....
Total	2,850,959	84
Pulses[a]	68,018	117
Potatoes	568,824	80
Sugar beets[b]	197,672	124
Oleaginous crops[c]	81,476	198
Industrial crops[d]	32,027	80
Forage crops[e]	1,161,729	102

Sources: As in Table 6, and State Statistical Office, *Zpravy* (Reports), 1933-38.

[a] Peas, beans and other pulses.
[b] Including sugar beet for seed.
[c] Rape, mustard, flax seed, soy beans, and others.
[d] Hops, tobacco, flax, hemp, and others.
[e] Including temporary meadows.

The first Five-Year Plan in agriculture aimed at an increase in both the area and production of all main crops, with the exception of bread grains and oil seeds. The area of bread grains was to decrease so that more land might be devoted to fodder production. The reduction of the area of oil crops was to be more than compensated by increased yields. Although production of bread grains was not to fall proportionately to the decline in the area, it was anticipated that larger grain imports would be required.

Neither the planned changes in area nor the planned increases in crop yields prevented attainment of the overall goals of the first Five-Year Plan. Indeed, the fact that the decline in arable area led to the exclusion of much marginal land and to concentration of production on better soils spoke in favor of its feasibility. The means of production which the government proposed to allocate to agriculture made the planned goals appear realistic. However, the policy of socialization, regimentation, and discrimination, as well as default in allocating the planned means of production, led ultimately to failure.

A comparison between the plan targets and the results achieved in 1953 does not show the degree of plan failure, since the original

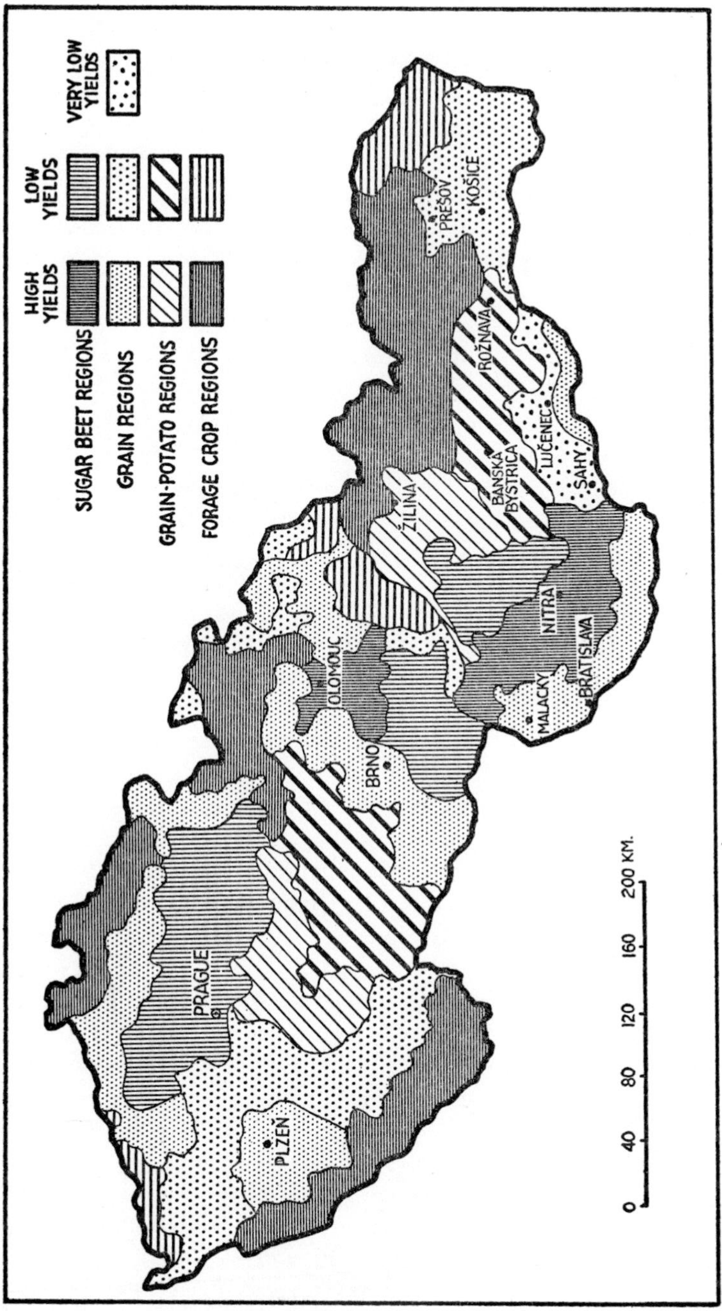

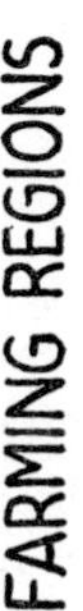

FARMING REGIONS

targets were subject to often unknown upward revisions in the course of the Five-Year Plan. However, it is highly significant to compare the average results of the plan period as a whole with prewar achievements. This comparison shows that among grains only barley exceeded prewar output. Wheat production was almost equal to prewar, but rye and oats were 27 and 25 per cent, respectively, below prewar levels. The production of sugar beets was practically equal to prewar, but that of potatoes was one fifth below the 1934-38 average. On the other hand, grain yields, with the exception of oats, increased, while those of sugar beets greatly declined. An index computed in terms of grain units shows that during the period 1949-53 the average output of the principal crops amounted to only 86 per cent of that attained in the period 1934-38.

Table 9. Production of Principal Crops, Selected Years 1934-1953, and 1953 Targets of the First Five-Year Plan

(area in thousand hectares, yields in metric quintals, production in thousand metric tons)

Crop	1934-1938[a] (average)	1949-1953[b] (estimated average)	1953 (original target)
Wheat			
Area	882	790	795
Production	1,513	1,496	1,558
Yield	17.1	18.9	19.6
Rye			
Area	978	635	560
Production	1,568	1,142	1,000
Yield	16.0	18.0	17.8
Barley			
Area	653	635	685
Production	1,109	1,160	1,266
Yield	17.0	18.2	18.5
Oats			
Area	748	605	615
Production	1,212	910	1,137
Yield	16.2	15.0	18.5
Potatoes			
Area	715	535	640
Production	9,635	7,510	9,755
Yield	135.0	140.0	152.4
Sugar beets			
Area	163	210	230
Production	4,664	4,690	6,706
Yield	286.0	223.0	291.6

[a] Prewar statistics for Czechoslovakia do not contain data for 1938. Such

data were published only during World War II in the Statistical Yearbooks of the Protectorate. The 1934-38 average is taken from FAO statistics.

[b] The 1949-53 average has been computed on the basis of data and information published in Czechoslovak publications.

Livestock

The first Five-Year Plan aimed at great increases in the number of almost all kinds of livestock, as well as at a considerably intensified utilization of animals. Table 10 shows available data on livestock numbers for selected years from 1934 to 1953.

Table 10. Livestock Numbers, Selected Years 1934-1953 (in thousands)

Livestock	1934-1938 (average)	1948	1953 Planned	1953 Actual[a]	1953 Index (1948 = 100)
Horses	664[b]	630	570	....	90
Cattle	4,297	3,276	4,400	4,064	134
Cows	2,384	1,862	2,350	2,149	126
Hogs	3,145	2,566	4,050	4,178	158
Breed sows	470	354	500	....	141
Sheep	404	386	600	1,019	155
Goats	529[c]	....	....	....	....
Hens	15,127[c]	13,000	18,500	20,210	142

Sources: 1934-1938, State Statistical Office, *Zpravy*, XII, No. 3 (1949), and XIII, No. 2 (1950); 1948, State Statistical Office, *Statisticky zpravodaj* (Statistical Bulletin), XI (1948) and XII (1949); 1953 plan, Ministry of Information, *The Czechoslovak Economic Five-Year Plan* (Prague, 1949); 1953 actual figures based on State Statistical Office, *Statisticky obzor*, XXXIV, No. 5 (1954); *Zemedelske noviny* (Agricultural News), January 27, 1953, and other periodicals.

[a] Author's estimates. Official statistics on livestock numbers are frequently contradictory, and only those have been selected which appeared reasonable in the light of prevailing conditions.

[b] 1936 only.

[c] 1937 only.

The 1953 planned increase in livestock numbers seems less ambitious if account is taken of the fact that livestock numbers in 1948 were abnormally low, due to the catastrophic drought of 1947. Only in the case of hogs, sheep, and hens did 1953 targets exceed prewar numbers to a considerable extent. Slaughter weight of cattle was to increase by 7 per cent, and that of hogs by 44 per cent. Production of beef was to increase by 52 per cent and pork by 77 per cent. However, even with this planned increase, beef production by 1953 would have still remained slightly below prewar, though pork production in 1953 would have exceeded the prewar level by 35 per cent, approximately in accordance with the increase in hog numbers. Considerable success in hog breeding induced the government to increase the targets for meat production. Total meat production by 1953 was to exceed the 1950 level by 50 per cent.

The goals of the first Five-Year Plan were attained or exceeded only in the case of hogs, sheep, and hens. With regard to all animals, the prewar average was approximately reached. However, utilization of livestock fell short of the planned goals, primarily for lack of fodder, but also because of the negative effects of socialization. In 1953, production of pork was probably some 20 per cent higher than in 1937, and egg production was probably also above prewar. Beef and veal output was probably slightly below prewar, while milk production was far below prewar levels.

Forestry

In 1950, almost all forest land was nationalized. Some small forests were under the administration of regional and communal bodies, and only insignificant forest tracts were in private hands. Since 1952, all forests (except those belonging to the military) have been under the control of the Administration of State Forests, which is attached to the Ministry of Forests and Lumber Industries. Timber cutting and processing is performed by individual enterprises, whose organization is similar to that of other firms in the nationalized industries.

Czechoslovakia's forests suffered during the war from destructive exploitation. Moreover, the loss of Ruthenia deprived the country of some of its richest forest lands. Before the war, the forest area of Czechoslovakia amounted to 4,489,000 hectares, 13 per cent of which was situated in Ruthenia. At present, the forest area is about 4,000,000 hectares (4,157,000 hectares according to the 1949 land utilization estimate).

The demand for forest products grew with the increase in industrial production. However, the diminution of the productive potential requires careful husbanding of the available resources, the annual net growth of trees being estimated at 23 per cent below prewar.

Planned timber cutting was to reach its highest level in 1949, with 11,670,000 cubic meters. Thereafter, it was to decrease as follows:

Year	Cubic Meters
1950	11,390,000
1951	10,990,000
1952	10,650,000
1953	10,300,000

Table 11 gives a breakdown of planned wood production during the first Five-Year Plan.

Table 11. Planned Wood Production, 1949-1953
(in million cubic meters)

Product	Quantity	
	Coniferous	Broadleaf
Roundwood	24.0	3.2
Sleepers	0.02	1.6
Pitprops	3.4	—
Pulpwood	7.7	1.1
Poles	0.6	0.2
Other industrial wood	0.1	0.4
Fuel wood	4.1	8.5
Total	40.0	15.0

Source: Ministry of Information, *The Czechoslovak Economic Five-Year Plan,* p. 36.

Data on wood production and consumption during recent years are very scarce. Partial estimates for 1950 are as follows (in cubic meters):

Plywood consumption	600,000
Plywood production	90,000
Roundwood cut	11,400,000

Fisheries

Fisheries play an insignificant role in Czechoslovakia's economy. Production is exclusively based on pond cultivation of fish since catches from streams and natural lakes are of little importance in total production. Total output may be estimated at about 4,500 metric tons per year. Carp, tench, pike, eel, and trout are among the most common species of fish. Before the war, most of the fish ponds of importance were on large private estates. Today, 80 per cent of all ponds are on state farms, with the total pond area amounting to about 50,000 hectares.

14. MINING

Vilem Brzorad

Czechoslovakia's mineral deposits are relatively poor. Though she has adequate supplies of coal, antimony, magnesite, mercury, uranium, graphite, kaolin and other clays, glass sands, limestone, and common building materials, her output of petroleum, iron ore, and other ferrous ores covers only a small part of domestic requirements. Domestic supply of most nonferrous metals is extremely limited or nonexistent. These crucial shortages have been the subject of increasing concern in recent years, particularly for the rapidly expanding metallurgical industry, which has had to meet practically all its needs from foreign sources.

Since the launching of the first Five-Year Plan (1949-53), the increase in the domestic output of minerals has been one of the government's prime objectives and it has often been pursued without regard to the costs involved. As part of the effort to increase the domestic supply of minerals, systematic prospecting and exploratory drilling have been conducted throughout the country. Though the results of these exploratory activities have not been published, fragmentary information indicates that no significant discoveries of new mineral deposits have been made in recent years. The location of Czechoslovakia's main mineral deposits is shown in the map on page 269.

Historical Background

Mining activity on the territory of Czechoslovakia can be traced back to prehistoric times when silver, gold, copper, and tin were mined. Al-Bekri, eleventh century Spanish-Moresque geographer, quoting Ibrahim Ben Yakub, an Arab-Jewish trader who visited Bohemia around 973, reported that Prague was a good market for buying gold and silver. By the thirteenth century, Bohemia had become one of the principal silver mining areas, with mining centered mainly around Jihlava and later around Kutna Hora. As early as 1249, the norms governing mining activity were embodied in a codex, *Iura*

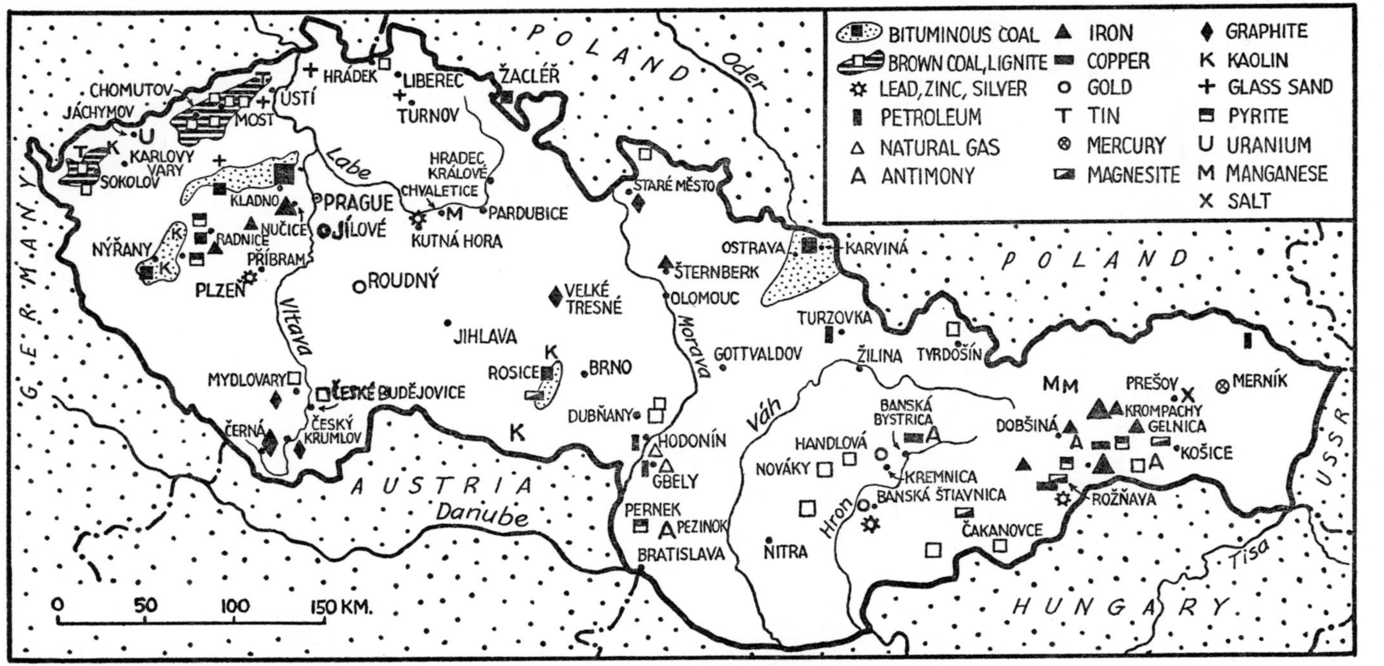

MINERAL RESOURCES

Montium et Montanorum. In 1300, another mining codex, *Ius Regale Montanorum,* was promulgated by King Wenceslaus II. This codex exerted a strong influence on the subsequent development of mining jurisprudence in Central Europe. In this period, the first miners' guilds were formed in Bohemia, mainly under the influence of German miners invited into the country by the King.

The Hussite wars and the Thirty Years War resulted in a decline of economic activity in the Czech lands. Mining of gold and silver never fully recovered, partly because of the depletion of some of the richest deposits and partly as a result of the discovery of overseas sources. Only Pribram and Jachymov, where silver was mined extensively, survived as important mining towns. Toward the close of the Middle Ages, the center of gold and silver mining shifted to Kremnica, Banska Bystrica, and Banska Stiavnica in Slovakia, where mining had been going on since the early Middle Ages. The mint established in Kremnica in the thirteenth century is still in operation.

With the coming of the industrial age, the exploitation of the country's iron ore and coal deposits soon overshadowed the mining of precious metals. In the eighteenth, and particularly the nineteenth century, large iron and steel centers developed in the coal regions of the Czech lands. While the country's comparatively small deposits of high grade iron ores were soon exhausted, the relative abundance of high quality coals of all varieties stimulated rapid expansion of metallurgical and other industries. This rapid industrial growth provided incentives for the exploitation of a variety of domestic industrial mineral deposits. The output of most of these minerals, however, was never sufficient to cover domestic requirements, and it had to be supplemented by imports. This situation has persisted with ever increasing intensity.

Developments prior to 1948

Before World War II, Czechoslovak mines were largely owned by private domestic companies. Both state ownership and foreign capital participation were relatively insignificant. Most bituminous coal, and ore mines were operated by metallurgical industries. Brown coal mines belonged mainly to independent coal mining and processing firms with some of the mines being operated by chemical concerns. Kaolin and clay quarries were largely owned by ceramic and porcelain industries. State ownership was limited to a small number of coal mines and some low grade nonferrous ore mines. As a rule, the latter operated at a loss, but they were kept in operation as a measure against unemployment.

State-owned mines were operated by the Ministry of Public Works. This Ministry also served as the government's agent for the supervision and enforcement of general standards of health, safety and other working conditions set forth in various statutes. It performed its supervisory functions through thirteen regional mining offices and through the so-called mining inspectorates, which were located in all mining centers.

During World War II, ownership of Czechoslovak mines passed largely into the hands of German firms. Control over production and distribution of minerals was vested in the planning office of the Reich's War and Armament Industry, and the operation of the mines was geared exclusively to the requirements of the German war machine.

By the Presidential Decree of October 24, 1945 (Law No. 100, *Sbirka zakonu a narizeni Republiky ceskoslovenske* [Collection of Laws and Ordinances of the Czechoslovak Republic]), the entire mining industry was nationalized and placed under the management of the General Directorate of Czechoslovak Mines, located in Prague, and the Provincial Directorate of Slovak Mines and Smelting Works, located in Bratislava. Overall control and supervision was vested in the Ministry of Industry. The nationalization act also provided for future compensation of the former owners of nationalized properties, but such compensation was never paid. The Communist coup took place before adequate provisions for reimbursement could be made, and the Communist government nullified the obligation.

Data on capital investment in the Czechoslovak mining industry for both the prewar and postwar periods are extremely fragmentary and vague. An illustration of the size of the mining industry and of its main branches in the immediate prewar and postwar periods is provided by Table 1, which shows the number of establishments, average number of workers, and the number of shifts worked in the industry's main branches in 1937 and 1946.

Prior to World War II, Czechoslovakia's mines, and particularly her major coal mines, had been mechanized to a fairly high degree. During the war, the country's stock of mining equipment and machinery was seriously depleted due to almost uninterrupted use, inadequate maintenance, and unavailability of replacements. Toward the end of the war and in the immediate postwar period, labor was increasingly substituted for worn out machinery in an effort to prevent major disruptions of production. As a result, productivity (measured by output per man-shift) rapidly declined. Though the level of employment in the mining industry in 1946 was substantially higher than in 1937, the 1946 output of most minerals lagged markedly behind the 1937 figures.

Table 1. Number of Establishments and Employment Level in Mining Industry, 1937 and 1946

Mining Branch	Number of Establishments		Average Number of Workers		Number o Shifts Work	
	1937	1946	1937	1946	1937	
					(in thousand	
Bituminous coal	80	89	43,392	58,410	11,945.5	15,6
Brown coal and lignite[a]	190	109	29,761	40,746	7,803.7	11,7
Iron ore	40	26	6,167	6,891	1,778.0	1,8
Other ores[b]	20	15	4,240	4,123	1,569.6	1,0
Other minerals	12	17	1,039	1,357	305.1	3
Total	342	256	84,599	111,527	23,401.9	30,6

Source: State Statistical Office, *Statistical Digest of the Czechoslovak Republic* (Prague, 1948), p. 56, Table 2.

[a] Lignite extraction accounted for an insignificant fraction of the totals in both

[b] Manganese, silver, lead, zinc, gold, copper, mercury, antimony, tin, and tur ores.

Postwar recovery of the mining industry proceeded at a slow pace. Except for UNRRA relief shipments of mining machinery, equipment, and auxiliary mining supplies, amounting to 10,810 gross long tons and valued at $6,300,000, the replacement of worn or obsolescent equipment and machinery was considerably retarded by extreme postwar scarcity of capital goods, which had to be strictly rationed among the principal branches of the economy. Another major impediment to the recovery of the mining industry was the acute postwar shortage of skilled workers, particularly coal miners. The shortage of skilled miners was due to several factors: first, at the end of World War II, a substantial number of experienced miners retired because of old age or left the mines for less strenuous occupations; second, a large number of Czech miners who had left Bohemia's brown coal regions following their annexation by the Germans in 1938, found other employment in other parts of the country and, after the war, did not return to their former occupation; third, most of the skilled miners of German nationality were forced to leave Czechoslovakia after the war with other expelled Germans; and finally, because of a general postwar shortage of industrial labor, particularly in the border regions, it was relatively easy to find more attractive jobs in other industries. This last factor was also chiefly responsible for the excessive labor turnover in the mining industry after the war.

The Two-Year Plan (1947-48) for the rehabilitation of the country's economy called generally for a 10 per cent increase above the 1937 level of output in all key sectors of production. Faced with relatively high output tasks on one hand and a serious shortage of capital equipment and skilled labor on the other, the mining industry had to resort to hiring large numbers of unskilled workers as well as to emergency expedients, such as the use of temporary labor brigades, to cope with bottlenecks in production. As a result, productivity rose extremely slowly from the low level of the immediate postwar period, costs of mining operations mounted rapidly, and the 1948 output targets were only partly fulfilled. Inadequate mechanization of the mines, the shortage of skilled miners, and the resultant low productivity have continued to pose serious obstacles to the development of the mining industry.

Developments after the Communist Coup

Since 1949, Czechoslovakia's requirements for industrial minerals of all varieties have rapidly mounted. With the exception of coal and a few minor metals, the bulk of the increased demand for minerals by the country's rapidly expanding heavy industry has had to be imported. To reduce Czechoslovakia's growing dependence on foreign countries, the government has made increased efforts to expand domestic mineral production. At the same time, imports from Western countries, which supplied the major part of Czechoslovakia's mineral requirements prior to the Communist coup, have been largely replaced by those from the Soviet Union and other Soviet orbit countries. By 1954, the Soviet Union accounted for 73.7 per cent of Czechoslovak imports of iron ore, 90.0 per cent of manganese ore, 71.8 per cent of copper, 93.9 per cent of aluminum, and 72.3 per cent of petroleum.

The pattern of development of Czechoslovakia's mineral resources in recent years clearly reflects the dominant position of heavy industry in the overall picture of economic development. Expansion of the output of those minerals essential to metallurgical, chemical, and construction industries has been fostered despite the low quality of most of the available deposits and the extremely high costs involved in their extraction. On the other hand, the country's comparatively high grade deposits of minerals, used primarily by consumer goods industries, have been relatively neglected. Furthermore, particular emphasis has been placed on the expansion of output of nonferrous metals in short supply in Soviet orbit countries (e.g., copper).

According to the original version of the first Five-Year Plan (Law of October 27, 1948, No. 241, *Collection*), total output of the mining industry in 1953 was to be 35 per cent above the 1948 level. In 1951, the initial target for coal output was raised another 19 per cent, and that for iron ore output 270 per cent (Government Ordinance of April 10, 1951, No. 33, *Collection*). No specific targets were given for other minerals in either the original or the revised version of the plan. Substantial modernization of the mining industry by electrification of the mines and large-scale mechanization of mining operations was also scheduled for the first Five-Year Plan period. Data on planned or actual investments in the country's mines have not been published; in available official sources, they are included in the overall category of total industrial investments. The size of the mining force was to increase from 137,000 in 1948 to 146,100 in 1953. With the planned mechanization of mining operations, significant increases in productivity were anticipated. As part of the drive to increase the domestic supply of minerals, a comprehensive survey of the country's mineral resources was to be undertaken, and 1,483 million crowns were allocated for this purpose; a separate appropriation of 264 million crowns was made for additional geological research.

The output targets of the first Five-Year Plan were largely set on the assumption that the mechanization and labor recruitment programs would be generally carried out as planned. However, the implementation of both these programs fell far short of the planned goals. Because of continuing heavy demand for capital goods on the part of all the expanding branches of industry, mechanization of the mines proceeded at a considerably slower pace than was anticipated. Some relief was provided by imports of mining machinery from the Soviet Union and Poland, but the imported machinery often required substantial adaptations to the conditions of Czechoslovak mines. Furthermore, in many cases, structural features of the country's mineral deposits and other technical obstacles prevented effective use of mining machinery. The labor recruitment drive was vitiated by the fact that the inflow of newly hired workers was offset by the continual efflux of workers from the mining industry. The high labor turnover was also largely responsible for the extremely slow rise in the average level of skill of the country's mining force. On the basis of fragmentary information, it can be estimated that as late as 1953 about one third to one half of Czechoslovakia's mining force consisted of unskilled workers. As a result of the slowdown in the mechanization program as well as the instability and low average efficiency of the labor force, actual output of most minerals has lagged behind the planned figures.

To compensate for the deficiencies in the supply of skilled labor, mining equipment, and machinery, the government has resorted to a variety of emergency measures, such as lengthening the workweek, the use of temporary work brigades, shock workers, forced labor, and obligatory overtime work. The government has also made a concentrated effort to reduce the high rate of absenteeism and labor turnover both by positive incentives and by penalties. Furthermore, since the early fifties, when most of the country's labor reserves had been absorbed by expanding industries, apprentice recruitment and training has received increased attention. As part of an overall industrial labor training program, training centers for apprentice miners have been established in all major mining regions and the recruitment of youth for work in the mines has been substantially stepped up.

To increase administrative efficiency, the management of mines has been partly decentralized, and the decision-making authority of lower administrative echelons, including plant managers, has been increased. In September 1951, coal and ore mines respectively were placed under the management of two newly established ministries, the Ministry of Power and Fuels, and the Ministry of Metallurgy and Ore Mines. The extraction of structural and building materials was placed under the Ministry of Building and Construction, and the extraction of glass sands, kaolin and clays, and other ceramic materials was placed in the charge of the Ministry of Light Industry. In 1953, planning of geological research and prospecting was concentrated in the newly created Government Commission for Geology, which was placed under direct government supervision. The former Geological Institute of the Czechoslovak Academy of Science, which was reorganized into the Central Geological Institute, was made directly responsible to the Premier. The Central Geological Institute carries out the actual research and prospecting on directives from the Government Commission for Geology.

Survey of Individual Minerals

Mineral Fuels[1]

Coal. According to American classification standards, the bulk of Czechoslovak coal falls in the bituminous and subbituminous class. The Czechoslovak system of classification, which is used in this chapter as well as throughout this handbook, distinguishes four principal ranks of coal on the basis of the degree of coalification: anthracite, bituminous coal, brown coal, and lignite. The two systems of classification are correlated in Table 2.

[1] This section, including the statistical tables, is largely based on Ladislav Stepan, *Coal Industry in Czechoslovakia, 1918-1955*, which will be published by Mid-European Studies Center, and on an unpublished manuscript on the Czechoslovak petroleum industry by the same author.

Table 2. Comparative Classification of Czechoslovak Coals by Rank

Czechoslovak Classification	Range of Equivalent ASTM Classifications[a]	
	Upper Group	Lower Group
Anthracite	Anthracite	Low volatile bituminous
Bituminous coal	Low volatile bituminous	Subbituminous B
Brown coal	High volatile A bituminous	Brown coal
Lignite	Lignite	Brown coal

Source: Stepan, *op. cit.* The classification is based on a statistical summary of physical and chemical properties of 4,460 samples from 184 mines.

[a] Reference is to the Standard Specifications for Classification of Coal by Rank of the American Society for Testing Materials (ASTM Designation: D 388-38), *1955 Book of ASTM Standards* (Philadelphia, 1955), Part 5.

In official reports on coal output, anthracite is included in bituminous coal production and, until very recently, lignite has been included in brown coal production. The principal reason for this procedure is that the country's anthracite deposits and output are very limited, and that lignite production has not yet been developed to any significant degree because of relative abundance of better quality coals. In 1954, for example, the production of lignite amounted to only 4.7 per cent of the combined output of brown coal and lignite.

Anthracite is mined in southern Bohemia, where small deposits occur in the vicinity of Ceske Budejovice and Sevetin, and in northwest Bohemia, north of Chomutov, near Brandov. Some anthracite is found west of Vlasim, near Semily, and in the vicinity of Cesky Brod.

Bituminous coals are found west and northwest of Prague in an arc extending from Plzen (Pilsen) to Kralupy on the Vltava; in northeast Bohemia around Zacler and Svatonovice; in northeast Moravia around Ostrava and Karvina; and in southwest Moravia in a narrow strip extending from Rosice near Brno to Oslavany. Small deposits occur in the vicinity of Lucenec in Slovakia.

Brown (subbituminous) coals are found in western and northwestern Bohemia in three separate basins extending along the Ore Mountains to the right bank of the Labe (Elbe), and in Slovakia in the neighborhood of Handlova. Small deposits occur in northern Bohemia, southern Moravia, and in Slovakia where brown coal is found in nearly all regions.

Lignite occurs jointly with brown coals in western Bohemia, and in the Handlova region in Slovakia. Deposits of lignite alone are found near Mydlovary and Cicenice in southern Bohemia, and around Hodonin, Kyjov, and Ratiskovice in southern Moravia. Small deposits occur in northern and northeastern Bohemia, Silesia, and central Slovakia.

There is considerable variation among the published estimates of Czechoslovakia's coal reserves. Furthermore, the available estimates make no clear distinction between "known" and "probable" reserves and, in most cases, the depth covered by the estimate is not specified. In 1937, the Czechoslovak State Geological Institute estimated the "known" and "probable" reserves of bituminous coal to the depth of 1,500 meters at 13,120,000,000 tons, and those of brown coal to a depth of 1,200 meters as 11,193,000,000 tons. These figures do not include the south Bohemia and south Moravian brown coal and lignite deposits, nor the small deposits of bituminous and brown coal scattered throughout the country. The most resent estimate, published in Miroslav Blazek's *Hospodarska geografie Ceskoslovenska* (Economic Geography of Czechoslovakia) in 1953, put the country's bituminous coal reserves at 12,000,000,000-13,000,000,000 tons and those of brown coal and lignite at 12,600,000,000 tons.

With the exception of small deposits of purely local importance, Czechoslovak coal resources are concentrated in five bituminous and six brown coal basins. The individual basins vary considerably in importance. The bulk of the country's bituminous coal output comes from the Ostrava-Karvina basin, which forms part of the large Upper Silesian coal deposits, while the major part of brown coal output is supplied by the North Bohemian basin. In 1947, the five bituminous coal basins contributed the following percentages to the country's total output of bituminous coal: Ostrava-Karvina, 79.5; Kladno-Rakovnik, 10.5; Plzen-Radnice, 4.6; Rosice-Oslavny, 2.7; and Zacler-Svatonovice, 2.5. In the same year, the percentages of total output of brown coal and lignite basins were: North Bohemian, 70.0; Sokolov and Cheb, 22.6; South Moravian, 2.5; Handlova, 3.3; and South Bohemian (including scattered small deposits), 1.6. The relative importance of the Ostrava-Karvina and the North Bohemian basins has increased still further in recent years; by 1953, the share of the former in the total output of bituminous coal had risen to 83.9 per cent, and that of the latter in the total output of brown coal and lignite to 72.0 per cent.

Some varieties of Ostrava-Karvina coals are well-suited for coking. They fuse well, contain a relatively small proportion of sulphur, ash, and volatile matter, and yield hard, solid coke. The Rosice-Oslavany coals have similar properties, but contain a higher proportion of sulphur. The coals from the Zacler-Svatonovice basin are generally less suitable for coking as they contain relatively large amounts of ash and volatile matter; and the Kladno-Rakovnik and Plzen-Radnice varieties are largely unsuitable for this purpose as they do not fuse well. However, in view of the relative shortage of high quality coking coals, inferior varieties have increasingly been used for coking. Furthermore, intensive experimentation has been in progress to develop a practical method for coking brown coals, particularly the high grade varieties of the North Bohemian basin. Since the end of World War II, brown coals of the North Bohemian basin have been increasingly used for gas manufacture. Furthermore, because of their high tar content, the North Bohemian brown coals are eminently suited for raw materials for numerous chemical industries, particularly the manufacture of synthetic fuels. Data on the output of coke and other coal products will be found in Chapter 15. Some basic properties of the principal varieties of Czechoslovak coals are presented in Table 3.

Nearly all Czechoslovak mines now in operation were opened prior to World War I. Since the early twenties, except for cyclical fluctuations and the period of World War II, the number of mines in operation decreased steadily as a result of mergers of existing mines and a gradual elimination of marginal mines. This applies particularly to the North Bohemian and Sokolov brown coal basins, where numerous shallow underground mines have been converted into large strip mines. Between 1921 and 1947, the number of bituminous coal mines fell from 175 to 79, and the number of brown coal and lignite mines from 266 to 103. Exact figures for the period after 1947 are not available. Although several new lignite mines have been opened in recent years, the downward trend in the number of mines, combined with a parallel increase in the scale of operations in the remaining mines, has continued.

Data on output of bituminous coal and brown coal and lignite in selected years from 1929 to 1955 as well as production targets for 1960 are presented in Table 4. All of the country's bituminous coal output comes from underground mines. Brown coal and lignite, on the other hand, has come increasingly from strip mines. In 1933, the share of strip mines in the total output of brown coal and lignite was about 20 per cent; by 1955, it had risen to 68 per cent.

Czechoslovakia has been both an exporter and an importer of coal. Until 1949, the initial year of the first Five-Year Plan, her coal output had been more than sufficient to cover domestic needs. Nevertheless, the high transportation costs involved in supplying the entire country from domestic sources have made it preferable to supply the coal requirements of some regions from less distant foreign sources. Conversely, Czechoslovakia has supplied part of the coal requirements of her coal producing neighbors. In addition, the country has been a traditional supplier of coal to Austria and Hungary, and of coke to Austria, Hungary, Romania, and Yugoslavia. In 1937, Czechoslovak bituminous coal exports amounted to some 2.2 million metric tons, while about 1.2 million tons were imported; brown coal exports

Table 3. Proximate Analysis and Some Elements of Ultimate Analysis of Czechoslovak Coals

Type of Coal and Place of Origin	Proximate Analysis[a]				Elements of Ultimate Analysis[b]		
	Moisture	Ash	FC and VM[c]	Upper Heat Value	H	C	S
	(in per cent)			(in thousand Calories)	(in per cent)		
Anthracitic coals of Ostrava	1-3	6-15	83-91	7.1-7.9	4.0-5.0	86-92	0.8-2.0
Coking coals of Ostrava-Karvina and Rosice-Oslavany	1-5	5-24	77-93	6.4-8.1	4.5-5.5	82-90	0.6-4.2
Bituminous coals of Zacler-Svatonovice	1-6	8-35	60-88	4.8-7.3	4.9-5.4	82-86	1.0-6.7
Gas coals of Ostrava-Karvina and Plzen-Radnice	3-10	5-20	75-92	6.1-7.8	5.3-5.9	80-85	0.5-2.0
Flaming coals of Kladno and Plzen	8-15	5-20	70-84	5.5-6.8	4.9-5.2	80-83	0.2-1.0
Flaming coals of Rakovnik, Slany, Radnice and Brasy	12-25	7-27	55-78	4.1-6.0	4.8-5.6	73-80	0.5-4.0
Bituminous coals from Radovce fields	5-9	14-28	64-82	4.9-6.4	4.3-5.5	77-86	2.5-3.4

Table 3. (con't.)

Type of Coal and Place of Origin	Proximate Analysis[a]				Elements of Ultimate Analysis[b]		
	Moisture	Ash	FC and VM[c]	Upper Heat Value	H	C	S
Brown pitch and glossy coals of North Bohemian basin	10-20	3-11	71-84	5.3-6.4	5.5-6.5	75-80	1.0-2.5
Ordinary brown coals of North Bohemian basin	25-35	3-20	50-72	3.4-5.5	5.3-6.4	69-77	0.3-2.5
Brown coals from Handlova region	13-17	6-20	65-80	4.6-5.8	5.3-5.7	71-73	0.9-1.9
Brown coals of Sokolov	30-45	3-15	48-64	3.4-4.9	5.1-6.5	68-76	0.5-3.0
Lignites of southern Bohemia and Moravia	38-52	8-23	38-48	2.3-3.2	5.0-6.2	62-69	1.0-4.0

Source: Stepan, *op. cit.*

[a] Samples "as received." [b] Dry, mineral-matter-free basis. [c] Fixed carbon and volatile matter combined.

Table 4. Output of Bituminous Coal, Brown Coal, and Lignite, Selected Years 1929-1955, and Targets for 1960 (in thousand metric tons)

Year	Bituminous Coal	Brown Coal and Lignite
1929	16,521	22,561
1933	10,627	14,968
1937	16,673	18,000
1941	21,071	22,440
1943	24,617	27,583
1945	11,716	15,356
1946	14,130	19,512
1947	16,216	22,362
1948	17,746	23,591
1949	17,003	26,526
1950	18,456	27,506
1951	18,277	30,200
1952	20,105	33,220
1953	20,341	34,325
1954	21,561	37,804
1955	22,100	40,700
1960 (Plan)	29,300	57,790

Sources: Data for 1929, State Statistical Office, *Statisticka rocenka republiky Ceskoslovenske, 1934* (Statistical Yearbook of the Czechoslovak Republic, 1934) (Prague, 1934), pp. 63-64; 1933, *ibid.* (1938 volume), p. 62; 1937, Ministry of Information, *Hospodarske dokumenty* (Economic Documents) (Prague, 1948), I, pp. 89-90; 1941-1945, State Statistical Office, *Prumyslove zpravy* (Industrial Reports), II, No. 15-16 (1947), p. 91; 1946-1950, United Nations, *Statistical Yearbook 1951* (New York, 1951), pp. 136-138; 1951, computed on the basis of data in *Rude pravo* (Red Right), January 27, 1952; 1952, based on *idem*, January 30, 1953; 1953, based on *idem*, February 24, 1954 and January 12, 1954; 1954, based on *Pravda* (Truth), February 3, 1955; 1955, State Statistical Office, *Statisticky obzor* (Statistical Review), No. 1 (1956), p. 39; 1960 plan, *Rude pravo*, May 4, 1956, Supplement.

(including briquettes) amounted to almost 2.0 million tons, while imports were insignificant. Expressed in terms of bituminous coal and including briquettes as well as coke, Czechoslovakia's 1937 coal trade balance showed an export surplus of some 3.2 million tons.

In the postwar period, the export surplus continued on a reduced scale until 1948. Since the launching of the first Five-Year Plan, Czechoslavakia's coal output has failed to keep pace with the rapidly mounting requirements of heavy industry. By 1954, the index of bituminous coal output, relative to 1937 (1937=100), had risen to 129 and that for brown coal and lignite to 210, while the corresponding index of total industrial production had increased to 230, and indices for crude steel and electric power output to 180 and 330, respectively. This situation has been further aggravated by a deterioration in the average quality of the coals mined. Despite the government's continued efforts to speed up the expansion of coal output, the gap between domestic coal supply and the rapidly increasing requirements of heavy industry has continued to grow. The gap has been largely filled by increased imports from Poland, combined with reduced exports and a curtailment of coal supplies to consumer goods industries and households. Since 1949, Czechoslovakia has been a net importer of coal. By 1954, her imports of bituminous coal from Poland can be estimated to have reached about 4 million tons.

The inability of the Czechoslovak coal industry to expand output at a rate sufficient to meet the growing industrial demand has been due to low productivity rather than inadequate size of the mining force. This is illustrated in Table 5, showing the number of workers as well as output per man-shift and output per man-year in the two sectors of the coal industry in selected years from 1929 to 1955.

Table 5. Number of Workers and Productivity in Coal Mining, by Sector, Selected Years 1929-1955

Year	Bituminous Coal Sector			Brown Coal and Lignite Sector		
	Number of Workers[a]	Output per Man-Shift	Output per Man-Year	Number of Workers[a]	Output per Man-Shift	Output Man-Ye
	(in thousands)	(in tons)		(in thousands)	(in tons)	
1929	58.5	1.009	282	40.9	1.938	551
1937	43.4	1.405	387	29.8	2.293	601
1946	58.4	0.906	243	40.7	1.657	478
1947	62.0	1.082	262	40.0	1.980	559
1948	63.0	1.086	282	38.0	2.229	621
1953	63.6	1.212	320	39.5	3.244	869
1954	64.0	1.217	337	40.0	3.491	945
1955	....	1.280	....	....	3.604	....

Sources: Number of workers: Year 1929, State Statistical Office, *Statisticka roc republiky Ceskoslovenske*, 1934, p. 63, Table AVI. Years 1937 and 1946, State Sta cal Office, *Statistical Digest of the Czechoslovak Republic, 1948, loc. cit.* Years 1947 1948, bituminous coal, United Nations, *Economic Survey of Europe in 1951* (Gen 1952), p. 157, Table 73; brown coal and lignite, estimates based on changes in ou and taking account of reported changes in productivity. Year 1953, bituminous based on *Rude pravo*, September 11, 1953; brown coal and lignite, same as 1947-1 Year 1954, bituminous coal, estimate based on fragmentary information in Czechosl press; brown coal and lignite, *Rude pravo*, January 9, 1955.

Output per man-shift: Year 1929, Georg Behaghel, *Kohle und Eisen in der Tsche slowakei* (Breslau, 1939), p. 58, Table VI. Years 1937 and 1946, calculated from in *Statistical Digest, loc. cit.* Years 1947 and 1948, bituminous coal, United Nat *Economic Survey of Europe in 1951*, p. 157, Table 74; brown coal and lignite, *podar* (Economist), January 25, 1951, and United Nations, *Quarterly Bulletin of* atistics for Europe, I, No. 3 (1952), p. 11. Year 1953, bituminous coal, based on *uhli* (Coal), V, No. 4 (1955), p. 113; brown coal and lignite, based on *Rude pravo,* ptember 11, 1953. Year 1954, bituminous coal, based on *idem,* November 1, 1954; own coal and lignite, based on *idem,* January 9, 1955. Year 1955, based on *Prace* abor), September 11, 1955.

Output per man-year was calculated from production figures in Table 4 and the ta on the number of workers in this table.

[a] Includes apprentices, but excludes supervisors and administrative personnel.

Petroleum. Czechoslovakia possesses only small deposits of crude petroleum. The largest of these, an extension of the Austrian Zistersdorf oil fields, extends from Malacky through Breclav and Hodonin to Prerov. Another oil field is located in the Flysch formation in eastern Slovakia, and still another in northwestern Slovakia. Despite intensive exploratory activities, no new deposits have been discovered in recent years. Data on Czechoslovak output of crude petroleum in selected years from 1937 to 1954 are shown in Table 6.

Table 6. Output of Crude Petroleum,[a] Selected Years 1937-1954
(in thousand metric tons)

Year	Output
1937	18.0
1942	36.3
1946	29.1
1947	40.0[b]
1948	49.0[b]
1949	60.0[b]
1950	102.0[b]
1951	119.0[b]
1952	181.0[b]
1953	196.0[b]
1954	202.0

Sources: Years 1937-1953, United Nations, *Statistical Yearbook 1955* (New York, 1955), p. 144; 1954, based on *Rude pravo,* February 3, 1955.

[a] Specific gravity 0.93.

[b] Estimate of United Nations Economic Commission for Europe.

Domestic production of crude petroleum covers only a small part of the country's requirements. In 1948, domestic production contributed only about 13 per cent of the country's estimated crude petroleum consumption of 410,000 metric tons. In addition to several refineries for processing domestic and imported petroleum, Czechoslovakia possesses a large synthetic fuel plant, which has supplied a substantial part of the country's requirements for motor fuels.

Natural Gas. Deposits of natural gas occur in the vicinity of Hodonin in southern Moravia and in western Slovakia. In 1946, the output amounted to 3.1 million cubic meters. In recent years, as a result of increased emphasis on the development of the country's natural gas deposits, the output has been substantially increased. According to *Ceskoslovensko v mapach* (Czechoslovakia in Maps [Prague, 1954], p. 14), the 1953 output was three times that of 1950.

Ferrous Metals

Iron. Iron ore deposits in Czechoslovakia occur in the following geological areas: the gneiss and schist formations of Bohemia; the pre-Cambrian formation of western Moravia; the Devonian formation of northern Moravia and Silesia; the Silurian basin of Bohemia; the Cretaceous formation of the Western Bezkydy range; the Lower Tatra region in Slovakia; the Slovak Ore Mountains; and the Kosice region of eastern Slovakia. However, only the Nucice-Zdice deposits in the Silurian basin of Bohemia, and the deposits in the Slovak Ore Mountains west of Kosice are economically important.

Probable reserves of the Nucice-Zdice district have been estimated at 334 million metric tons of crude ore, containing 117 million metric tons of iron. The deposits west of Kosice have been estimated at 30 million metric tons, with an iron content of 10 million tons. In addition to these deposits, Czechoslovakia possesses large reserves of low grade ores, with iron content of some 20 per cent, and very small deposits of high grade ores, with iron content as high as 70 per cent. The most recent estimate, published in 1953, puts the country's total iron ore reserves as of 1948 at 400-600 million metric tons.

Prior to World War II, Czechoslovak iron ore output was about equally distributed between the Czech lands and Slovakia. Since 1938, however, Slovakia's share has steadily increased. By 1952, it amounted to about 75 per cent of the country's total. However, productivity in Slovakia's iron ore mines has been substantially lower than in the Czech lands. In 1938, output per man-year in Slovakia's mines amounted to 183 metric tons, while in the Czech mines it amounted to 405 metric tons; in 1946, the corresponding figures were 153 metric tons for Slovakia and 307 metric tons for the Czech lands. The average for the country as a whole amounted to 231 metric tons in 1938 and to 163 metric tons in 1946. Despite postwar increases in productivity, Czechoslovakia's iron ore output per man-year has been considerably below that of Western countries.[2]

[2] In 1937, the average output of marketable iron ore per man-year in Czechoslovakia and selected Western countries was as follows (in metric tons): Czechoslovakia, 251; Germany, 440; France, 1,299; Sweden, 1,802; United Kingdom, 1,543; and United States, 2,823. (United Nations Economic Commission for Europe, *European Steel Trends in the Setting of the World Market* [Geneva, 1949], p. 48).

Most of Czechoslovakia's iron ore output comes from underground mines. This fact, combined with the relatively low average quality of Czechoslovak iron ores, inadequate mechanization of the mines, and shortage of skilled workers, greatly increases the industry's costs of operation. Data on the number of mines in operation and employment in 1937 and 1946 are presented in Table 1. By the end of the first Five-Year Plan, the number of mines was to increase to 45 and mining operations were to be substantially mechanized. Furthermore, by 1955, seventeen iron ore processing plants were to be constructed, mostly in Slovakia, to raise the efficiency of iron extraction. As was noted earlier, the mine mechanization program has lagged considerably behind the plan.

Data on Czechoslovakia's planned and actual output of iron ore in selected years from 1937 to 1960 are presented in Table 7.

Table 7. Planned and Actual Iron Ore Output and Iron Content, Selected Years 1937-1960
(in thousand metric tons)

Year	Ore Output		Iron Content
	Planned	Actual	Actual
1937	—	1,836.5	609
1941	—	2,199.6	697
1946	—	1,122.9	387
1947	1,498.6	1,363.5	460
1948	1,737.2	1,400.0	430
1949	....	1,500.0	480[c]
1951	....	1,800.0	540[c]
1953	1,400[a]-3,800[b]	2,300.0	690[c]
1954	2,500.0	2,342.0	690[c]
1955	....	2,500.0	....
1960	3,630.0	....	....

Sources: Planned ore output for 1947 from State Statistical Office, *Statistical Digest of the Czechoslovak Republic, 1948,* p. 87; 1948 figure from Law of October 25, 1946 (Two-Year Economic Plan Act), No. 192, *Sbirka zakonu a narizeni, 1946* (Collection of Laws and Ordinances, 1946); 1953 and 1954 figures from United Nations, *Economic Bulletin for Europe,* VI, No. 2 (1954), p. 102; 1960 figure from *Rude pravo,* May 4, 1956, Supplement.

Actual ore output figures for 1937, 1946, and 1947 from State Statistical Office, *Statistical Digest,* pp. 56 and 87; 1941 figure from Miroslav Turek, "Mining of Ferrous Metals in Czechoslovakia," unpublished Mid-European Studies Center manuscript; 1948 figure from United Nations, *Economic Survey of Europe in 1954,* p. 43; 1949 and 1951 figures from United Nations, *Quarterly Bulletin of Steel Statistics for Europe,* V, No. 3 (1954), p. 8; 1953 figure from United Nations, *Economic Survey of Europe in*

1954, loc. cit.; 1954 figure based on *Rude pravo,* February 3, 1955; 1955 figure based on *idem,* May 4, 1956, Supplement.

All data on iron content from United Nations, *Statistical Yearbook 1955,* p. 149.

[a] Original version of the first Five-Year Plan.
[b] Revised version of the first Five-Year Plan.
[c] Estimate of United Nations Economic Commission for Europe.

Czechoslovakia's domestic production of iron ore has been far short of the requirements of her iron and steel industries. Prior to World War II, about 50 per cent of the industries' needs had to be met from foreign sources, with Sweden the principal supplier. Since the war, more than 50 per cent of the rapidly increasing domestic demand for iron ore has had to be met from abroad, with the Soviet Union having replaced Sweden as Czechoslovakia's main foreign source of supply.

Manganese. Czechoslovakia's major manganese ore deposits occur at Chvaletice in eastern Bohemia, in the Bohemian Zelezne Hory (Iron Mountains), in the Ostrava region, and in the vicinity of Kysovce in Slovakia. In addition, several minor deposits without economic significance are scattered throughout the country.

No estimates on the country's total manganese ore reserves are available. Proved reserves in the Chvaletice district have been estimated at 10 million tons and the probable reserves at 20 million tons. The Chvaletice ore contains about 20 to 24 per cent iron, 12 to 14 per cent manganese, 20 to 24 per cent silicon, and 2.5 to 4 per cent phosphorus.

Data on production of manganese ore in selected years from 1929 to 1953 are shown in Table 8. In terms of metal content, domestic ore output covers only about 50 per cent of Czechoslovakia's requirements. In recent years, the bulk of the country's manganese imports has come from the Soviet Union.

Table 8. Manganese Ore Production, Selected Years 1929-1953
(in metric tons)

Year	Output
1929	96,529
1937	105,344
1946	73,232
1948	106,000
1950	168,000
1951	180,000
1952	231,000
1953	240,000

Sources: Year 1929, State Statistical Office, *Statisticka rocenka republiky*

Ceskoslovenske, 1932, p. 90; 1937 and 1946, *idem, Statistical Digest of the Czechoslovak Republic, 1948,* p. 56; 1948, Deutsches Institut fuer Wirtschaftsforschung, *Wochenbericht,* September 11, 1953, p. 148; 1950-1953, United Nations, *Quarterly Bulletin of Steel Statistics for Europe,* V, No. 3 (1954), p. 50.

Iron Pyrites. In view of the relative scarcity of domestic iron ore deposits, iron pyrites have increasingly been used for iron manufacture. Czechoslovakia's largest deposits are located at Smolnik in the Slovak Ore Mountains. Additional deposits occur west of Prague, in the vicinity of Plzen, in the Chvaletice region, and in the Low Tatra Mountains. Czechoslovak iron pyrites contain on the average 40-42 per cent sulphur, 30-40 per cent iron, and 0.5-2 per cent copper. By smelting, the yield of iron is raised to 55-65 per cent.

Data on the volume of reserves are not available. Production data for selected years from 1929 to 1951 are shown in Table 9. Domestic production has supplied only a small part of the country's requirements. In 1948, the last year for which data on imports are available, Czechoslovakia imported 252,000 metric tons of crude and 29,000 tons of smelted pyrites.

Table 9. Output of Iron Pyrites, Selected Years 1929-1951
(in metric tons)

Year	Output
1929	23,005
1937	18,361
1946	7,895
1948	15,000[a]
1951	25,000[a]

Sources: Year 1929, State Statistical Office, *Statisticka rocenka republiky Ceskoslovenske, 1932, loc. cit.;* 1937 and 1946, *idem, Statistical Digest of the Czechoslovak Republic, 1948, loc. cit.;* 1948 and 1951, Turek, *op. cit.*

[a] Estimated output.

Precious Metals

Through centuries of exploitation, the once rich deposits of gold and silver on Czechoslovak territory have been largely depleted. The remaining gold deposits located in central Bohemia and the Slovak Ore Mountains are of little economic significance, as are the silver deposits of Jihlava, Kutna Hora, Stribro, and Jachymov in Bohemia, and of Kremnica and Banska Stiavnica in Slovakia.

Nonferrous Metals

Although most nonferrous metals occur in Czechoslovakia, only antimony, mercury, and uranium ore deposits are suitable for economic exploitation. The deposits of copper, tin, lead, and zinc, which have been mined for centuries, have been largely depleted, and the deposits of other metals are either too small or inferior in quality. As a result, the major part of the country's requirements has had to be imported. Prior to the Communist seizure of power, the bulk of Czechoslovakia's imports of nonferrous metals came from Western countries. Since the Communist coup and the ensuing reorientation of Czechoslovakia's foreign trade, a concentrated effort has been made to increase domestic output of nonferrous metals, most of which are in short supply in Soviet orbit countries. In addition to more intensive exploitation of the existing mines, the increase has been achieved by the reopening of mines formerly abandoned as unprofitable, and by the tapping of inferior deposits.

Copper. Czechoslovakia's largest copper deposits are found in the eastern part of the Slovak Ore Mountains. Smaller deposits occur near Trutnov and in other localities on the slopes of the Giant Mountains, in the Czech Ore Mountains, in Central Bohemia, and in Moravia. The ore mined at Nizne Slovinky in the Slovak Ore Mountains contains 3 per cent copper, 20 per cent iron, and 40 grams of silver and 2 grams of gold per metric ton. The Kraslice ore from the Czech Ore Mountains contains up to 30 per cent of copper, but its deposits are very small.

Because of the low grade of the existing deposits, copper mining in Czechoslovakia has been extremely costly. Prior to World War II, as was pointed out earlier, it was maintained by the government mainly as a relief measure against unemployment. In recent years, with the Western sources of supply ruled out and the Soviet bloc sources narowly limited, copper ore mining has been expanded without regard to cost. Available data on copper ore production are presented in Table 10.

Lead and Zinc. The largest Czechoslovak deposits of lead and zinc, accompanied by silver, copper, antimony, and other metals, are located at Pribram in Bohemia. Other deposits occur at Jachymov in the Czech Ore Mountains, where zinc was discovered during World War II, and at Banska Stiavnica, Plesivec, and Kremnica in Slovakia.

Czechoslovak lead, zinc, and silver ores contain on the average about 2 per cent lead, 0.3 per cent zinc, 0.2 per cent antimony, 0.15 per cent copper, 0.172 per cent silver, and small amounts of gold.

The Czech ores are richer in lead, silver, and antimony, while the Slovak ores contain more zinc, copper, and gold.

Data on lead, zinc, and silver ore output are shown in Table 10. The lead and zinc content of the ores mined in Czechoslovakia in selected years from 1937 to 1950 is shown below (in metric tons):

Year	Lead	Zinc
1937	3,900	2,000
1945	1,100	100
1946	2,200	300
1950	4,000	400

Source: Bruno Kiesewetter, *Statistiken zur Wirtschaft Ost- und Sued-osteuropas* (Berlin, January 1955), I, 28.

Tin and Tungsten. Czechoslovakia's only known deposits of tin ore (cassiterite) are located in the Czech Ore Mountains. The deposits had been largely depleted and abandoned prior to 1914, but because they contain some tungsten, several mines were reopened during World War I and most of them were closed again at the end of hostilities. The mines were again reopened during World War II and have been kept in operation. The casserite ores contain on the average 0.32 per cent tin, 0.21 per cent tungsten, 0.19 per cent copper, 0.01 per cent lead, and 0.001 per cent molybdenum. Data on tin and tungsten ore production are shown in Table 10.

Antimony. This is Czechoslovakia's most abundant nonferrous metal. It is produced in sufficient quantities to yield substantial surpluses for export. Prior to World War II, the country produced about one third of Europe's total output, and 6-8 per cent of the world's total. Today, Czechoslovakia is the largest antimony producer among Soviet orbit countries.

Major deposits of antimony ores occur in the Slovak Ore Mountains. Minor deposits are located at Pribram in central Bohemia, in western Bohemia, and in northern Moravia. Most of the ores contain about 9-10 per cent of antimony, though in some cases metallic content runs as high as 53 per cent. Figures on antimony ore production are shown in Table 10.

Mercury. Czechoslovakia's deposits of mercury ores are sufficient to supply domestic needs as well as to provide some surpluses for export. The bulk of mercury output is obtained as a by-product of copper and iron pyrite processing at Koterbachy in the Slovak Ore Mountains. In addition, small deposits of mercury ore (cinnabarite) are located at Mernik in eastern Slovakia. In 1937, output of mercury amounted to about 95 metric tons and in 1946 to 29 metric tons. In recent years, the 1937 figure has probably been exceeded. Data on mercury ore output are shown in Table 10.

Magnesium. Substantial deposits of magnesite ($MgCO_3$) are located between Lucenec and Kosice in Slovakia. In addition to these deposits where magnesite occurs in crystalline form, deposits of amorphous magnesite, associated with serpentine ($H_4Mg_3Si_2O$), are found in southern Bohemia. Dolomite, another potential source of magnesium, is found in several places throughout the country, particularly in Slovakia.

Prior to World War II, only small quantities of magnesium metal were produced, and most of the domestic output of magnesite was used in chemical and cement industries and as a refractory material. A major part of the country's magnesite output was exported, and most of the special types of magnesium metal, such as those required in the production of light metal alloys, were obtained largely through imports. Since the Communist coup, domestic production of magnesium metal has increased substantially above the prewar level. Data on magnesite output are presented in Table 10.

Uranium. Up to the end of World War II, which marked the beginning of an intensive search for uranium ore throughout the world, Czechoslovakia's deposits at Jachymov in the Czech Ore Mountains were the only known in Europe. In 1945, control over the Jachymov uranium ore deposits, the largest in Europe, was assumed by the Soviet Union, and exhaustive prospecting for new deposits was initiated. Since the end of the war, new mines have reportedly been opened in the Pribram silver, lead, and zinc mining district, and additional uranium ore deposits were discovered on both sides of the Brdy range, in the Vimperk-Rejstejn-Kasperske Hory area in the Sumava Mountains, at Kasejovice near Blatna, and in the Giant Mountains. Data on the size of the country's uranium reserves are extremely scant, as all information pertaining to the deposits and their exploitation has been surrounded with utmost secrecy. A 1953 estimate put the metal content of Czechoslovakia's uranium ore deposits at 1,500 metric tons.

Between 1922 and 1937, the output of U_3O_8 averaged 19.6 metric tons, the output of pitchblende being 2.5 to 3 times as much. Maximum production, reached in 1936, totalled 32 metric tons of U_3O_8, while the minimum production, in 1922-23, was about 10 metric tons. The pre-World War II output of radium amounted to 3.52 grams in 1929 and to 4.15 grams in 1937. The number of workers in the Jachymov mines varied between 300 and 400 during the prewar period. Data on postwar output, all of which has been shipped to the Soviet

Union, are not available. The size of the present mining force in the Jachymov mines, which is composed largely of forced laborers, has been estimated at several tens of thousands.

Table 10. Output of Nonferrous Ores, Selected Years 1937-1953 (in metric tons)

'ype of Ore	1937	World War II Peak Output Year[a]	1947	1948	1950	1953
'opper	117,780[b]	161,039	80,000[c]	120,000[c]	....	
ead, zinc, and silver	168,967	202,734	167,052[d]	142,514	....	294,450[d]
ntimony	18,187	59,332	44,598	....	....	....
lagnesite	....	....	173,300	....	173,000[d]	....
lercury	5,359	....		5,000[d]	....	....
in and tungsten	....	160,203	87,306	....	....	....

Sources: Copper ore: Years 1937 and 1939 (World War II peak output year) from iroslav Turek, "Mining of Nonferrous Metals in Czechoslovakia," unpublished Mid-uropean Studies Center manuscript, 1952; years 1947 and 1948, Law of October 25,)46 (Two-Year Economic Plan Act), *loc. cit.*

Lead, zinc, and silver ore: Year 1937, State Statistical Office, *Statistical Digest of e Czechoslovak Republic, 1948, loc. cit;* years 1941 and 1947, Vladislav Paulat, 'rimary Nonferrous Metal Industry in Czechoslovakia," unpublished Mid-European udies Center manuscript, 1953; years 1948 and 1953, Miroslav Blazek, *Hospodarska ografie Ceskoslovenska* (Economic Geography of Czechoslovakia) (Prague, 1953), rt I, p. 114.

Antimony ore: Year 1937, State Statistical Office, *Statistical Digest of the Czecho-vak Republic, 1948,* p. 75; year 1943, Turek, *op. cit.;* year 1947, Paulat, *op. cit.*

Magnesite ore: Year 1947, United Nations, *Statistical Yearbook 1953,* p. 132; year 50, United States Department of the Interior, *Minerals Yearbook 1951* (Washington, C., 1954), p. 1630.

Mercury ore: Year 1937, State Statistical Office, *Statistical Digest of the Czecho-vak Republic, 1948,* p. 56; year 1943 and 1948, Turek, *op. cit.*

Tin and tungsten ores: Year 1944, Turek, *op. cit.;* year 1947, Paulat, *op. cit.*

[a] Copper ore, 1939; lead, zinc, and silver ores, 1941; antimony ore, 1943; mercury , 1943; tin and tungsten ore, 1944.

[b] Refers to 1938.

[c] Planned output.

[d] Estimate.

Nonmetallic Minerals

Czechoslovakia possesses rich deposits of ceramic materials, structural and building materials, and some refractory, as well as industrial and manufacturing materials. On the other hand, the country completely lacks such important fertilizer minerals as potash and phosphates. With the loss of Ruthenia in 1945, Czechoslovakia also lost most of her salt deposits.

Kaolin and Clay. Abundant deposits of high quality kaolin occur at Sedlec in the Karlovy Vary region, and at Horni Briza and Dobrany in the Plzen region. Minor deposits are found in northwestern Bohemia and in Moravia. Prior to World War II, annual production fluctuated between 220,000 and 500,000 metric tons, with a substantial part of the output destined for export. In 1937, about 236,000 tons were shipped abroad. In 1948, production amounted to 766,000 metric tons, of which about 70,000 were exported. No later data are available. In view of the decreased importance of the ceramic industry since the launching of the first Five-Year Plan, production of kaolin is not likely to have increased after 1948.

Deposits of refractory clays and argils are also abundant, with those of the Rakovnik area in western Bohemia being the most important. In 1947, output amounted to 428,700 tons.

Feldspar. Major deposits of high grade feldspar are located in the area of Domazlice in southwestern Bohemia, and smaller deposits occur in southeastern Bohemian and in Moravia. Postwar production has been sufficient to meet domestic requirements.

Glass Sands. Major deposits of glass sands are found in northern and northwestern Bohemia; minor deposits occur in central Bohemia. Prior to World War II, domestic glass sands were mainly used for the manufacture of industrial glass. Fine grain sands for the production of high quality glass were largely imported from Saxony, even though substantial domestic reserves of high grade sands were available. In 1937, imports amounted to 121,235 metric tons, while domestic production may have been about twice as high. In the postwar period, the volume of imports has been insignificant, and domestic output has risen substantially above the prewar level. In 1948, output of glass sands amounted to 346,800 tons.

Limestone. Abundant deposits of high grade limestone are found all over the country, particularly in the vicinity of Prague, in northern Bohemia, in northwestern Moravia, and in western Slovakia. The prewar annual output was estimated at over 3 million metric tons. This figure was substantially exceeded in recent years.

Salt. Having lost her relatively large Ruthenian salt deposits, Czechoslovakia now possesses only minor salt beds located in the Presov area in eastern Slovakia. Prior to World War II, domestic output of edible salt was almost sufficient to meet domestic demand, but large quantities of salt for industrial and agricultural purposes had to be imported. Since 1945, the bulk of the country's requirements has had to be imported. In 1937, production amounted to 165,898 metric tons; of this amount, only 18,413 tons were supplied by salt mines located within the country's present territory; no edible salt was imported in that year, while imports for industrial purposes amounted to 188,414 tons. In 1947, domestic production was 16,562 tons. In 1948, 192,121 tons of edible salt and 227,867 tons of industrial salts were imported.

Graphite. Czechoslovakia is one of the world's largest graphite producers. Her major deposits are in the vicinity of Ceske Budejovice in southern Bohemia; minor deposits occur in northwestern Moravia and Silesia, and in Slovakia. The carbon content of the deposits varies from 25 to 88 per cent. In 1929, Czechoslovakia produced 23,651 tons of crude, and 14,399 tons of finished graphite; in 1937, the corresponding figures were 5,144 and 5,024; and in 1946, 5,108 and 1,668. In 1948, production of crude graphite amounted to 15,000 tons, and 1950 output was estimated at 36,000 tons. As in the case of coal, Czechoslovakia has been both an exporter as well as importer of graphite, with exports as a rule exceeding imports. In 1929, exports amounted to 9,889 and imports to 5,821 tons; in 1937, the corresponding figures were 2,880 and 3,535; and in 1948, 1,249 and 718.

Other Nonmetallic Minerals. The country has ample supplies of granite, marble, sandstone, syenite, slate, trachyte, travertine, and other building stones. Mineral pigments are extracted in northwest Bohemia and in the Slovak Ore Mountains; though some pigments are produced in sufficiently large quantities to enable exports, others have to be imported. Small deposits of sulphur occur in the Czech-Moravian Highlands and in the Slovak Ore Mountains. Sulphur has been largely obtained as a by-product of iron extraction from pyrites. Prior to World War II, its output amounted to about 9,000 tons annually. Low quality asbestos deposits are found in Slovakia, where prewar output was estimated at 1,000 tons. Gypsum is found in Moravia-Silesia and in Slovakia, with 1948 output amounting to 91,000 tons. Small quantities of chalk are extracted in several localities throughout the country. Talc is present mainly on the sites of the magnesite deposits, but no domestic production has been reported. The deposits of mica, asphalt, and corundum are also too limited for economic exploitation.

Czechoslovakia is rich in mineral springs, which occur mainly in northwest and northeast Bohemia, and in western and central Slovakia. Among the best known are the springs of Karlovy Vary (Karlsbad), Marianske Lazne (Marienbad), and Frantiskovy Lazne (Franzensbad)in northwestern Bohemia and Piestany in western Slovakia.

15. FUEL, POWER, AND PRODUCER GOODS INDUSTRIES

Vilem Brzorad

Introduction

Czechoslovakia is the most highly industrialized country of the Soviet orbit, possessing a greatly diversified industrial structure which comprises nearly all the main branches of both heavy and light industry. While most industrial branches were established prior to World War II, both the size and the structure of industry have been substantially altered in recent years. Since the launching of the first Five-Year Plan, the capacity and output of heavy industry have been raised considerably above prewar levels, the greatest increases being registered in the extractive industry, electric power production, primary metal production and machine building. Furthermore, numerous new lines of production have been developed, particularly in heavy engineering and chemical industries. On the other hand, productive capacity of some consumer goods industries, which occupied a prominent place in Czechoslovakia's economy prior to World War II, has been reduced considerably below prewar levels. A major aspect of the country's postwar industrial expansion has been the industrialization of Slovakia, which has been carried out partly by transfer of industrial plants from the Czech lands and partly by the development of Slovakia's industrial resources.

The importance of industry for Czechoslovakia's economy, and its rapid postwar growth, can be gauged from the data presented in Table III, page 243, Chapter 12, "National Income and Product." In 1937, when net material product was valued at 56.5 billion crowns, industry accounted for about 53 per cent, agriculture for 23 per cent, and building, transport, and trade for the remaining 24 per cent. By 1953, with the value of net material product increased to 95.1 billion crowns (at 1937 prices), the share of industry had risen to 70 per cent, that of agriculture had dropped to 13 per cent, and that of building, transport and trade to 17 per cent. The 1953 index of industrial production, on the basis 1937=100, stood at 220, the index of agricultural production at 94, and that for building, transport, and trade at 120.

With postwar expansion confined largely to producer goods industries, the structure of Czechoslovak industrial production has changed significantly. According to official figures, the share of producer goods in gross industrial output increased from 57.8 per cent in 1937 to 62.3 per cent in 1953, while the corresponding share of consumer goods decreased from 42.2 to 37.7 per cent.[1] During the same period, production of electricity rose from 4.1 to 12.4 billion kilowatt-hours, production of coal of all varieties from 34.7 to 54.7 million tons, and that of crude steel from 2.3 to 4.4 million tons. Between 1948 and 1953, the share of machine building industry in gross industrial output increased from 17 to 28 per cent.

The pattern of postwar industrial growth reflects the radically altered domestic economic policy since the Communist coup as well as Czechoslovakia's role in the economic development of other Soviet orbit countries. Since her absorption into the Soviet sphere, Czechoslovakia has become a major supplier to her Soviet bloc partners of industrial machinery and equipment, including machine tools, complete equipment for electric power plants, chemical and food processing plants, agricultural machinery, transportation equipment, and other products of machine building industry. Parallel with the reorientation of foreign trade, the structure of exports has radically changed. In 1937, machinery accounted for only 6.4 per cent of the country's total exports; by 1953, its share had risen to 40 per cent. During the same period, the share of consumer goods fell from 36.8 to 15 per cent.

Historical Background

Industrial activity on Czechoslovak territory began in the twelfth and thirteenth centuries with the development of gold and silver mining in both the Czech lands and in Slovakia. The first manufacturing industries developed largely from local arts and crafts scattered in the mountain regions, with a substantial part of the capital and entrepreneurial skill provided by German settlers invited into the country

[1] These figures are based on a recent reclassification of industries, with several branches that produced consumer goods before the war now included in the producer goods category. The figures thus overstate the prewar share of producer goods and understate the magnitude of the change. Another set of figures, based on the classification of industries in effect prior to the first Five-Year Plan, will be found in Chapter 16.

by the king and given numerous political and economic privileges. Since the beginning of the modern era, the Czech lands have far outstripped Slovakia in industrial development, mainly as a result of their more favorable geographical location, richer endowment with industrial raw materials and resources, better transport system, and more favorable political position within the Austro-Hungarian empire. While the economy of the Vienna government favored concentrated industrial development of the Czech lands, Slovakia, under the tutelage of Budapest, remained undeveloped, serving mainly as a source of cheap labor and raw materials for the industries in the Hungarian lowlands.

As early as the twelfth century, beer was manufactured in the Czech lands not only for domestic consumption but for export as well. Lesser quality textiles, manufactured in Bohemia and Silesia, also found their way to foreign markets. In the fifteenth century, the first glass manufacture was opened in the Sumava region of Bohemia, but the center of the glass industry soon shifted to northern and northeastern Bohemia. By the end of the eighteenth century, paper and porcelain industries had been developed, the latter particularly in the Karlovy Vary region where excellent deposits of kaolin and clay were available. At the same time, a highly diversified textile industry began to develop in northern and northeastern Bohemia, and in the Humpolec, Krnov, and Brno regions. In the nineteenth century, numerous industrial plants for the processing of agricultural products sprang up throughout the Czech lands.

Abundant deposits of high quality coal in the Czech lands stimulated the development of heavy industry in the second half of the nineteenth century. Thus, the Ostrava-Karvina region, where large reserves of coking coal were available, became the center of ferrous metallurgy, processing iron ore from the Slovak Ore Mountains, from Styria in Austria, and from Poland and Sweden. Other centers, utilizing iron ore from the Nucice-Zdice region southwest of Prague and imported ores, developed in Plzen, Rokycany, and Kladno. At the same time, metal fabricating industries were established in Plzen, Prague, and Brno. In response to the demand of these industries, extraction and processing of copper and other ferrous metals were introduced. Production of textile machinery was developed in the north Bohemian centers of textile manufacture, and that of agricultural machinery in Central Bohemia and at Prostejov in Moravia.

Modern chemical industry was established early in the nineteenth century at Plzen, and in the middle of the century at Usti nad Labem (Aussig an der Elbe). Unlike the metallurgical and engineering industries, which became increasingly dependent on foreign sources of raw materials, the chemical industry possessed an excellent domestic raw material base in the North Bohemian, Cheb, and Falknov (now Sokolov) brown coal basins.

Once established, with their market extending throughout the Austro-Hungarian empire, the industries of the Czech lands grew at a rapid pace. By 1914, the Czech lands produced 86 per cent of the empire's total output of bituminous coal, 84 per cent of brown coal, 60 per cent of metallurgical products, and 75 per cent of chemical products. Their share in the output of light industries, particularly consumer goods, was even more impressive as they produced the empire's total output of porcelain, 92 per cent of glass, 92 per cent of sugar, 92 per cent of malt, 57 per cent of beer, 70 per cent of leather, and 75 per cent of paper.

Slovakia, on the other hand, remained largely a raw material supplier for the building and manufacturing industries of Hungary. Her main products included agricultural raw materials, timber, and a variety of minerals. In 1913, Slovakia's mines accounted for 57.7 per cent of Hungary's total output of iron ore, 67.2 per cent of iron pyrites, 63.0 per cent of copper ore, 56.4 per cent of antimony ore, and 71.3 per cent of manganese ore. Except for a small metallurgical industry, which processed part of the domestic output of mineral ores, Slovakia's manufacturing industry was limited to a few small textile factories, paper mills, and agricultural processing plants.

Developments Prior to 1948

The First Republic

After the breakup of the Austro-Hungarian empire, Czechoslovakia found herself with an industrial capacity far in excess of domestic requirements. While many industries in the Czech lands had been equipped to meet the demand of a population of 50 million, the elimination of the former Austrian, Hungarian, and German trade outlets (partly because of the serious postwar economic disruptions, partly because of their altered economic policies, and partly because of their hostility toward the new Republic) reduced their market largely to the domestic population of about 13.5 million. Continued operation of these industries at capacity depended on their ability to sell the major part of their output on foreign markets. The necessity for a radical expansion of Czechoslovakia's exports was further intensified by the fact that some industries were completely dependent on raw material imports from other countries.

The readjustment of Czechoslovak industries to the new market situation was accomplished with relative speed and without major dislocations. According to an official estimate, during the period 1919-36, about 60 per cent of industrial production was marketed abroad.

While Czechoslovak exports during the interwar period included substantial amounts of heavy industrial products, it was mainly the light industries that were dependent on foreign markets; thus, Czechoslovakia exported about 90 per cent of her production of glass and china, an equal percentage of her furniture production, 75 per cent of beer, 73 per cent of sugar, and 70 per cent of textiles.

The post-World War I readjustment in the established lines of production was marked by an increasing concentration of production in large-scale enterprises, with marginal firms being either eliminated or merged with larger ones. This readjustment process was substantially eased by a simultaneous development of new lines of industrial production, giving rise to numerous new small-scale enterprises, and resulting in a further diversification of the country's industrial structure. Furthermore, competition was partly eliminated by cartel agreements regulating both prices and production quotas, and by the establishment of central sales agencies for the main products of Czechoslovak industry in both domestic and foreign trade. At the same time, substantial modernization was undertaken to increase efficiency to a point where the industries could successfully compete on world markets. The trend toward concentration of production in large-scale establishments was particularly pronounced in heavy industries, such as mining and the production of steel and chemicals, and it was further intensified during the depression of the thirties. The major part of heavy industry was controlled by a few large vertical combines which possessed their own sources of fuel, power, and raw materials, as well as processing and manufacturing plants. These included the Skoda Works at Plzen; the Poldi Works at Kladno and Chomutov; the Vitkovice Mines, Steel and Iron Corporation; the Mining and Iron Works of Prague; and the Prague Iron Company.

Ownership of Czechoslovak industry was largely in private hands, with exclusive state ownership confined to tobacco, salt, and saccharine production. In addition, the state owned a small number of coal mines, several nonferrous ore mines, and one steel mill, which were operated by the Ministry of Public Works. Furthermore, the state participated in the ownership of armament producing industries, particularly in the Skoda Works at Plzen. Except for this direct participation in production, state intervention in industry was limited to inspection of working conditions, such as health and safety measures, and to enforcement of standards set forth in various statutes.

Although most of the capital invested in Czechoslovak industry was of domestic origin, foreign capital investment, particularly French and British, was fairly substantial. The French Schneider-Creusot financial group owned about half of the shares of the Mining and Iron Works of Prague and a large part of the shares of the Skoda

Works at Plzen. British capital was invested in several Czechoslovak banks, which, in turn, were the country's principal industrial investors. In addition, Allied Insurance, Ltd. of London owned the entire Vitkovice Mines, Steel and Iron Corporation. In 1938, the French-owned shares were sold to Czechoslovak investors, mainly banks. The participation of German and Austrian capital was relatively insignificant. German banks had limited investments in the glass, china, textile, and other light industries of northern Bohemia, which were largely owned by Czechoslovak citizens of German nationality.

While the basic pattern of location and structure of Czechoslovak industry remained essentially unaltered until World War II, a marked expansion of heavy industry, both in volume and range of products, took place during the interwar period. The largest increases were registered in metallurgy and in engineering and chemical industries. The new lines of production introduced during the interwar period included electrical machinery and equipment, transportation equipment, motor vehicles, bicycles, radio receivers, precision instruments, synthetic fibers, rubber tires, and pharmaceutical products. The stress on heavy industry became particularly pronounced after the depression of the early thirties which demonstrated the extreme vulnerability of the country's light industries, which were largely dependent on foreign markets; the heavy industries were hit far less severely and recovered far more rapidly than the light industries. Another factor stimulating the expansion of the heavy industries in the thirties was the rapidly deteriorating international political situation, which led to an increased demand for armaments.

Slovakia's industrial development during the interwar period was seriously handicapped by two factors: the existence of excess productive capacity in the Czech lands, particularly in the light industries for which relatively favorable conditions obtained in Slovakia; and the lack of an adequate fuel base, which posed a serious obstacle to the development of heavy industry. As a result, there was little inducement for industrial activity in Slovakia. In the post-World War I period of readjustment, Slovakia's limited industrial capacity was actually temporarily reduced, since her small textile, leather-working, food processing, and metallurgical plants could not compete with the relatively efficient industries of the Czech lands in the sharply restricted postwar market. While many marginal industrial firms in the Czech lands were also eliminated, their workers were more easily absorbed than in Slovakia, where alternative employment opportunities were quite narrowly limited. After a brief period of recovery, the depression of the early thirties hit Slovakia's light industries with extreme severity. It also completely eliminated her small metallurgical industry.

The government sought to encourage economic activity in Slovakia in three ways: first, by improvement of the transport system to stimulate trade, and by other public construction projects to increase the income of the local population; second, by tax incentives, favorable railroad freight rates, and other measures to stimulate local manufacturing activity; and third, by development of Slovakia's health resorts and large-scale promotion of tourist trade. However, despite a marked expansion of industrial activity, Slovakia continued to lag far behind the Czech lands in industrial growth. On the eve of World War II, less than one quarter of the population of the Czech lands derived their livelihood from farming, while the corresponding figure for Slovakia was still over one half. In 1937, Slovakia's share in gross industrial production amounted to only 8 per cent.

World War II

The German occupation and the harnessing of the Czechoslovak economy to the needs of the German war machine produced far-reaching changes in the ownership, organization, and structure of Czechoslovak industry. By seizure of the country's main financial institutions, amalgamation of its leading industries with large German concerns, confiscation of some industrial establishments and forced sale of others to German firms, and by placement of all industries under the supervision of German officials, Germany established complete control over all key industries.

After the outbreak of the war, authority over industrial production and allocation of all strategic resources were vested in the Planning Office of the Reich's War and Armament Industry. With Czechoslovak industry geared to the German war economy, a mass shift toward heavy industry, particularly armament production, took place. Mining of coal, iron ore, nonferrous ores, and nonmetallic minerals was expanded to unprecedented levels. Several new lines of heavy industrial production were introduced, including the manufacture of synthetic motor fuels from brown coal, for which a giant plant with a projected annual capacity of one million tons was built at Horni Litvinov near Most. While exact production data for the war period are unavailable, the extent of the wartime shift toward heavy industry is illustrated by the changes in employment in the various branches of industrial production. Between 1937 and 1944, the size of the labor force in the mining industry increased from 92,850 to about 156,000. Employment in iron and steel production and metal fabricating industries increased from 362,000 to 769,000, and in chemical industry from 56,000 to 102,000. At the same time, some 440,000 workers were transferred to Germany to relieve the Reich's acute ıdustrial labor shortage. In Czechoslovakia, the necessary manpower vas obtained partly by conscription of labor and partly by sharp urtailment of consumer goods production. The textile industry, which mployed about 250,000 workers in 1937, was almost completely losed down during World War II. The operation of glass, ceramic, nd leather industries was also radically curtailed.

War damage to Czechoslovak industry was estimated at 345 billion rowns at prewar prices (about 11.5 billion dollars at the prewar ate of exchange). The list of the country's major industrial plants amaged by bombing included most of the oil refineries, the synıetic motor fuel and chemical plants at Horni Litvinov near Most, ıe Skoda Works at Plzen, and the Vitkovice iron, steel, and engineerıg works. The transport system was also seriously disrupted. Most f the war damage, however, had been caused by reckless use of apital equipment, deliberate destruction by the retreating Germans, nd looting by both the German and Soviet armies, rather than by irect military action. Another legacy of war was the disruption of ıe labor market, which resulted partly from mass exodus of workers om industries to which they had been forcibly assigned during the ar and partly from the expulsion of Germans from Czechoslovakia. rom 1944 to 1945, the number of industrial workers fell from about .5 million to 1.16 million. Mining, metallurgy, metal fabricating, and hemical industries suffered the greatest losses of manpower.

945-1948

The postwar reconstruction period brought another series of radical hanges in the ownership and organization of industry. The basic rinciples of the country's postwar political, social, and economic olicy were set forth in the Kosice Program of February 1945, which alled for the confiscation of all property owned by the Germans and ıeir collaborators, nationalization of all key industries and financial nd credit institutions, and the introduction of planned economy. The ationalization program was implemented by four decrees of the resident on October 24, 1945 (Law Nos. 100, 101, 102, and 103, *birka zakonu a narizeni republiky Ceskoslovenske* [Collection of aws and Ordinances of the Czechoslovak Republic]). Mining, elecic power production, primary metal production, armament industry, nd other industries classified as essential were nationalized comletely, regardless of the size of the individual plants. In the remainıg industries, only establishments above a certain size (measured y the number of workers, which varied from 120 to 500, depending n the industry) were to be taken over by the state. In practice, owever, many smaller industrial enterprises were nationalized under a supplementary elastic clause of the nationalization decrees whicl made any industrial establishment subject to expropriation if sucl an action were "in the public interest." The decrees provided fo compensation of the former owners of nationalized properties. Al though some foreign owners were partly reimbursed, no compensatio was paid to Czechoslovak citizens as the Communist *coup d'éta* took place before adequate provisions for the settlement of thei claims could be made, and the Communist government revoked th obligation.

The nationalized industrial establishments, except those processin food, were placed under the management of the Ministry of Industry The vertically organized industrial concerns were broken up, and th individual establishments, now called "national enterprises," wer reorganized into several industrial groups, according to the type o product. Each of the industrial groups in the Czech lands was place under the control and supervision of a General Directorate in Prague while Slovakia's industries were placed under Provincial Directorate located in Bratislava. The decision-making authority was centralize in the Ministry of Industry or in the Directorates, which were th Ministry's executive organs. The authority of individual plant man agers was quite narrowly limited. By the end of 1947, the nationalize sector comprised some 47 per cent of all industrial establishment and about 80 per cent of the country's total industrial labor force

Economic planning was introduced at the same time as nationaliza tion of key industries. Initially, planning was entrusted to two govern ment agencies, the Economic Council, which had been in existenc since August 25, 1945, and the State Planning Office, which wa established on November 23, 1945 (Law No. 145, *Collection*). Th Economic Council was to draft broad economic programs for th entire country and to submit them to the government for approval while the State Planning Office, with its Slovak branch, the Stat Planning and Statistical Office in Bratislava, was to work ou government-approved projects in concrete detail. At the same time as a first step toward centralized control of industrial investmen activity, all investment funds (i.e., depreciation allowances, profits reserves, etc.) of state-owned enterprises were consolidated in th National Economy Fund, which was to serve as a channel for th reallocation of investment funds in accordance with government di rectives. However, since the national enterprises were authorized t continue borrowing both short-term and long-term funds from variou financial institutions, the National Economy Fund never became a effective device for the control of industrial investment activity. Both the planning and financing of the country's economic activity wer basically revised after the Communist coup.

In the immediate postwar period, Czechoslovakia's industrial recovery was substantially speeded up by UNRRA deliveries, which were valued at 261 million dollars, including about 72 million dollars' worth of transport equipment, fuel, industrial machinery, and raw materials. Additional help was provided by foreign credits, amounting to about 150 million dollars, which Czechoslovakia secured in the West, particularly in the United States, United Kingdom, and Canada. From the earliest days of postwar reconstruction, priority in the allocation of manpower, energy, and other productive resources was given to heavy industries, while little was done to speed the rehabilitation of consumer goods industries, particularly those dependent on raw material imports and traditionally producing for export to Western countries. Though the emphasis on speedy reconstruction of heavy industries stemmed partly from the urgent need for replacement of obsolescent transport and industrial equipment, it was also prompted by Czechoslovakia's altered political and economic situation. The postwar shift in Czechoslovakia's foreign trade from Western countries to those of Eastern and Southeastern Europe, which was strongly fostered by the Communists for political reasons, called for a change in the commodity structure of exports from consumer goods to the products of heavy industry. While the non-Communist members of the Czechoslovak government viewed the implications of this shift with alarm, they found some comfort in the prospect of replacing Germany as a major supplier of heavy industrial products to the countries of Eastern and Southeastern Europe.

After the initial period of basic reconstruction, the rehabilitation program was embodied in the Two-Year Plan (1947-48), which was enacted on October 25, 1946 (Law No. 192, *Collection*). Broadly, the plan called for reactivation of industrial capacity, without major new investments. By the end of 1948, gross industrial production was to be 10 per cent above the 1937 level, but its structure was to differ substantially from that of the prewar period. While the output of producer goods, in most cases, was to exceed the 1937 level by more than 10 per cent, consumer goods production was to remain below prewar figures. Brown coal production was to exceed the 1937 figure by 33 per cent, bituminous coal output by 6 per cent, electric power by 80 per cent, and motor vehicles by 79 per cent; production of locomotives was to increase four times, that of railroad cars eleven times, and that of tractors fifteen times. Out of the planned total industrial investment of about 25 billion crowns, earmarked largely for replacement, some 80 per cent were to be allocated to heavy industry. By 1948, the industrial labor force was to reach its prewar size. Average productivity per worker was thus to be 10 per cent higher than in 1937. Since average output per worker in 1946 was only about 70 per cent of the prewar figure, the plan in effect called for a 40 per cent increase in productivity during the period 1947-48.

According to official sources, the 1948 index of gross industrial output relative to 1937 was 108. This figure would indicate that the overall production target was broadly achieved. However, the output of some basic commodities, including coal, iron ore, industrial and agricultural machinery, transport equipment, fertilizers and other chemicals, fell short of planned goals. The serious drought in 1947 resulted in a critical shortage of agricultural products, necessitating increased imports of foodstuffs instead of industrial raw materials. The change in the structure of industrial production between 1937 and 1948 is reflected, up to a point, in the 1948 indices of gross output of producer and consumer goods, relative to 1937, which stood at 125 and 80 respectively.

Developments after the Communist Coup

Organization of Industry

Within a few months after the Communist seizure of power, control over productive resources was centralized in the hands of the state, and the economy was cast into a framework of institutions of the Soviet type. On May 1, 1948, in a second sweep of nationalization, all industrial establishments employing over fifty people were nationalized. As a result, only 5 per cent of the total labor force was left within the private sector. Ownership of industry as of May 1, 1948 is shown in Table 1.

Table 1. Ownership of Industrial Establishments, May 1, 1948

Ownership Status	Number of Firms	Number of Employees (in thousands)
Nationalized	3,329	907.7
Confiscated	8,410	392.4
State owned[a]	306	18.4
Communal	375	6.2
Cooperative	862	13.2
Private	6,108	73.4
Total	19,390	1,410.2

Source: New Central European Observer, II, No. 2 (1949), 121.

[a] Refers to establishments owned by the state prior to nationalization.

During the first Five-Year Plan (1949-53), the private sector in industry, as well as in other spheres of economic activity except agriculture, was virtually eliminated by further nationalization. At the end of 1953, publicly owned enterprises accounted for 99.6 per cent of industrial production, 99.8 per cent of building and construction, 100 per cent of transport services, 99.7 per cent of trade, and 45.4 per cent of agricultural production.

With all but an insignificant number of productive establishments under direct control of the state, centralized economic planning of the Soviet type was rapidly introduced. On February 22, 1949, responsbility for economic planning was centralized in a newly established State Planning Office, the existing planning agencies being simultaneously abolished (Law No. 60, *Collection*). The Chairman of the State Planning Office was made a member of the Cabinet of Ministers. At the same time, the State Planning Commission was created as an advisory board to the Chairman. The existing State Statistical Office was placed under the Chairman's authority. In Bratislava, the Slovak Planning Office and the Slovak Planning Commission were established as subordinate organs of the State Planning Office in Prague.

To insure effective control over the operations of individual enterprises, "control by the crown" was instituted in 1950. Financing of current operations of individual production units was concentrated in the local branches of the State Bank, each enterprise being required to maintain an account with but a single branch. Detailed accounts of transactions of the individual enterprises, kept by the local branches of the State Bank, were to serve as evidence of their performance. Since January 1952, the flow of investment funds has been channeled through the state budget and their allocation has been controlled by the Investment Bank, which was established in 1948.

In the first postwar years, particularly after the second phase of nationalization in 1948, the Ministry of Industry, which was responsible for the operation of nearly all industrial establishments, grew into a vast bureaucratic machine, bogged down under its own weight. To increase the tractability of this giant administrative apparatus, a long series of reorganizations has been carried out. In January 1951, the Ministry of Industry was divided into two independent ministries for heavy and light industries, respectively. The general and provincial industrial directorates were abolished. In September of the same year, the Ministry of Heavy Industry was split into five independent administrative departments. On January 31, 1953, in a basic reorganization of the Czechoslovak Cabinet, the number of industrial ministries was further increased. At the same time, the ministries were completely divested of policy-making authority and were transformed into production management organs responsible to the Cabinet Presidium, composed of the Premier and his deputies. Subsequently, the number of industrial ministries was again reduced. As of 1954, their complete list included the following: Fuel and Power, Metallurgy and Ore Mines, Chemical Industry, Engineering (in charge of all machinery production, including electrical machinery and precision instruments), Building and Construction, Forestry and Timber Industry, Light Industry (including all light industrial branches except food processing), Food, Transportation, and State Economy (supervising all industrial activity performed directly by the state, as distinguished from that of national enterprises). In most industries, the individual enterprises have been organized into trusts and these, in turn, into syndicates, which are directly responsible to the appropriate ministry.

The centralized system of economic planning and industrial administration placed the managers of individual enterprises within a rigid framework of controls, which extended not only to major aspects of operation, such as production policy, determination of wages and prices, or appointment of key administrative and technical personnel, but to a host of minor matters involving day-to-day operations as well. Furthermore, in matters nominally left to their discretion, the plant managers often had to face the interference of local Communist Party and trade union organs. Gradually, as the defects of the system of industrial management were unmistakably reflected in lagging output, execution of some policies was left to the discretion of the trusts, directors of enterprises, or managers of individual plants. Furthermore, the authority of plant managers and other executives was somewhat strengthened, and the interference of Party organs reduced, as "politically reliable" Communist-trained executives replaced formerly indispensable, but suspect, "bourgeois" experts.

Industrial Policy and Industrial Growth

Since the launching of the first Five-Year Plan on January 1, 1949, Czechoslovakia's economic development has been marked by continued expansion of basic and heavy industries, relatively slow growth of consumer goods industries, and near stagnation of agriculture. According to the original version of the plan, enacted into law on October 27, 1948 (Law No. 241, *Collection*), total industrial production in 1953 was to be 57 per cent higher than in 1948, at the same time, producer goods output was to rise 70 per cent and consumer goods production 50 per cent. On April 10, 1951 (Law No. 33, *Collection*), these relatively moderate targets were revised upwards, with increased emphasis on a further expansion of producer goods output. The revised targets, expressed in terms of indices relative to 1948, called for total industrial production to increase to 198, with producer goods output rising to 230 and consumer goods output to 170.

While the revised version anticipated substantial production increases for all branches of basic and heavy industry, it placed particular emphasis upon the expansion of machine building. Next largest increases were planned for the chemical and metallurgical industries. The policy established by the revised plan has been followed without any significant changes. The revision, adopted after the establishment of the Council for Mutual Economic Assistance in Moscow and after the outbreak of the Korean war, reflected increased Soviet demands upon the productive potential of Czechoslovak industry. It also indicated the economic role Czechoslovakia was to play within the Soviet orbit. According to an authoritative Soviet source, Czechoslovakia was to participate in "a socialist division of labor, under which all the democratic countries, forming a united camp, supplement each other economically, each of them . . . developing its economy according to its national resources, domestic needs, and the demands of the entire international democratic market. . . . Czechoslovakia will be an exporter of machine tools, spare parts, textile machinery, tractors, as well as of complete production units for food, textile, footwear, and chemical industries."[2] To facilitate coordination of economic planning within the Soviet orbit launching of the second long-term plans in the orbit countries (except Bulgaria) was synchronized with the Soviet sixth Five-Year Plan. Accordingly, in 1954 and 1955 the Czechoslovak economy operated on the basis of annual plans.

In the original version of the first Five-Year Plan, a total of 336.2 billion crowns at 1948 prices (6.72 billion dollars at the official rate of exchange) was allocated to investment in all branches of the economy. The ratio of gross investment to national income was to increase from about 20 per cent in the initial year to about 30 per cent in the final year of the plan. Planned distribution of investment among the various economic sectors is shown in Table 2.

Out of the total of 336.2 billion crowns allocated under the original plan, 219 to 235 billion crowns were earmarked for net investment, the balance representing planned replacement expenditures. Heavy industry (including building industry) was to receive 106.5 billion crowns (2.11 billion dollars), i.e. about 78 per cent of all industrial investment and about 32 per cent of the total for the economy.

In 1951, the total investment target for the first Five-Year Plan was raised to 558 billion crowns at 1950 prices, i.e. about 400 billion

[2] A. Chistyakov, "Razvitie ekonomicheskogo sotrudnichestva stran sotsialisticheskogo lageria" (Growth in Economic Cooperation among the Countries of the Socialist Camp), *Kommunist*, No. 15 (1954), pp. 4, 5, and 7.

crowns (8 billion dollars) at 1948 prices. Investment in heavy industry was to be raised to 185 billion crowns (3.70 billion dollars) at 1948 prices, i.e. to 46 per cent of the total for the economy. Since excess capacity existed in many light industries, it may be assumed that no appreciable investment increases were planned for this sector. Heavy industry was thus to receive about 85 per cent of all industrial investment allocations.

Table 2. Planned Distribution of Investment Expenditure in the First Five-Year Plan, 1949-1953[a]

Economic Sector	Type of Expenditure: Equipment	Type of Expenditure: Construction	Sector's Total	Sector's Share in Total Investment
	(in billion crowns at 1948 prices)			(in per cent)
All industry	91.2	45.3	136.5	40.6
Heavy industry	....		101.9	30.3
Building industry	3.9	0.7	4.6	1.4
Light industry	..	...	30.0	8.9
Agriculture	15.0	11.8	26.8	8.0
Transport and communication	29.8	23.1	52.9	15.7
Trade	3.1	1.9	5.0	1.5
Housing	—	39.3	39.3	11.7
Social, health, and cultural services	14.2	14.4	28.6	8.5
Public administration[b]	6.0	41.1	47.1	14.0
Total	159.3	176.9	336.2	100.0

Sources: Ministry of Information, *Government Memorandum on the Five-Yea[r] Act,* quoted from *News from Behind the Iron Curtain,* II, No. 11 (1953), 37. F[igures] for heavy and light industries based on United Nations, *Economic Survey of E[urope] in 1955* (Geneva, 1956), p. 236.

[a] Initial version.

[b] Roads, bridges, and other public projects are included under "public admi[nistra]tion" expenditures.

Actual investment during the first Five-Year Plan fell short of planned goals. In heavy industry, realized investment amounted to 128 billion crowns (2.56 billion dollars), i.e. 69 per cent of the planned total of 185 billion; in light industry, 18 billion crowns (0.306 billion dollars), i.e. about 60 per cent of the estimated target of 30 billion crowns (0.6 billion dollars) were actually invested; and in the economy as a whole, the actual investment of 338 billion crowns (6.76 billion dollars) fell 15 per cent short of the target of 400 billion

More than one quarter of total industrial investment during the first Five-Year Plan went into the machine building industry, whose capacity was expanded by the construction of twenty-four new plants. The industry's stock of automatic and semi-automatic tools was increased by 40 per cent. During the same period, twelve large electric power plants (six hydroelectric and six thermal) were put into operation, with additional plants under construction. The capacity of the metallurgical industry was expanded by the addition of six blast furnaces (bringing the total to twenty), nine open-hearth furnaces, and eight electric furnaces. Production capacity for the manufacture of special steels, ferroalloys and nonferrous metals was also substantially expanded, and new lines of production were introduced. Furthermore, the construction of a giant metallurgical combine at Kuncice in Moravia was reported well under way by the end of the first Five-Year Plan; its completion was announced in 1955. In the chemical industry, both production capacity and the range of products were also substantially expanded.

The pattern of growth of Czechoslovak industry and the emphasis on heavy industry during the first Five-Year Plan are illustrated in the tabulation below, showing the 1953 indices of production for all branches of industry relative to 1948:

Industrial Branch	1953 Production Index
	(1948 = 100)
Electric power	210
Fuel	142
Ore mining	162
Metallurgy	202
Machine building	324
Chemicals	238
Building materials	196
Glass	121
Ceramic	128
Wood processing	168
Paper	152
Printing	125
Textiles	150
Leather	119
Food processing	185

Source: State Statistical Office, *Statisticky obzor* (Statistical Review), XXXIV, No. 2-3 (1954), 111.

The 1953 output in most of the major branches of industrial production fell substantially short of the revised target figures. The important causes were the lack of correspondence between the raw material base and the rate of expansion of industrial capacity, acute shortage of labor, and failure to complete planned investment projects on schedule. The output of coal, vital to all industries, lagged persistently behind the plan, and coal imports were insufficient to close the growing gap between domestic production and the rapidly increasing requirements of the expanding heavy industry. Reserves of industrial manpower were largely exhausted in the first half of the five-year period. The large increases in production scheduled for the second half of the plan could thus be obtained only by substantial increases in productivity which, however, failed to materialize. The impact of lagging productivity on total output was offset to some extent by lengthening the workweek, compulsory overtime work, and unremunerated work on Sundays and holidays, but these measures led to a serious deterioration of workers' morale and a further impairment of efficiency. Compulsory measures as well as positive incentives to increase the labor force in the key branches of heavy industry soon drained the light industries and agriculture of their already inadequate labor supply, and led to increased shortages of food and other consumer goods. Pressure for speed in production, combined with inadequate maintenance and repair of capital equipment, resulted in frequent breakdowns in operation. Some resources allocated to new investment projects were wasted, as the projects were abandoned before completion. Thus, construction of a giant metallurgical combine in the vicinity of Kosice in eastern Slovakia was abandoned when only half completed. The combine was to produce one million tons of steel a year, and construction required a labor force of 10,000.

By 1953, the numerous bottlenecks and dislocations in the economy led the government to realize that the high rate of expansion of heavy industry, called for by the revised version of the plan, could not be maintained without expansion of its fuel and raw material base, of the stock of housing in industrial centers, and of the supply of food and other consumer goods. Accordingly, the investment program was somewhat modified. Total investment scheduled for the year was to be reduced by about 16 per cent, while investment allocations to basic industry, particularly coal mining and ore extraction, housing construction, and agriculture were to be increased. The shortage of manpower in agriculture was to be relieved by a shift of some industrial workers back to agriculture. At the same time, the production targets set for 1954 for the main branches of heavy industry implied a reduction in the rate of growth of output well below the average rate for the Five-Year Plan period.

The growth of output of major producer goods between 1948 and 1953 is shown in Table 3, which also shows the original and revised targets of the first Five-Year Plan and the goals of the annual plan for 1954.

Table 3. Planned and Actual Output of Selected Producer Goods, 1948, 1953, and 1954

modity	Unit of Measurement	1948 Actual	1953 Original Plan	1953 Revised Plan	1953 Actual	1954 Plan
ninous coal	million tons	17.7	20.8	25.0	20.3	22.0
n coal	million tons	23.6	32.2	35.8	32.8	37.1
	million tons	5.6	8.0	8.0	8.5	9.3
ore	million tons	1.4	1.4	3.8	2.3	2.5
e oil	thousand tons	49.0	240.0	306.0	196.0	212.0
ric power	million MWh	7.5	11.2	12.3	12.4	13.9
gas	billion cubic meters	0.6	2.9	2.9	0.9	....
ron	million tons	1.6	2.7	3.0	2.8	3.0
e steel	million tons	2.6	3.5	4.5	4.4	4.6
d products	million tons	1.7	2.5	3.8	2.9	3.3
oad wagons d coaches	thousand	11.0	7.7	....	12.5	....
r vehicles	thousand	13.2	24.0	32.8	20.9	....
romotors to 25 KW	thousand	448.0	890.0	890.0	623.0	....
hate tilizers	thousand tons	387.0	438.0	514.0	477.0	571.0
te tilizers	thousand tons	161	220.0	330.0	193.0	230.0
ent	million tons	1.6	2.6	3.4	2.3	2.8
	million tons	0.9	1.3	1.3	1.1	1.3
s	billion	0.9	1.3	....	1.3	1.5
glass	thousand tons	131.0	114.0	....	147.0	....

urce: United Nations, *Economic Survey of Europe in 1954*, p. 43.

The "new course" signified no basic change in industrial policy. It merely meant a recognition of the limitations to a sustained rapid growth of heavy industry, posed by the available supply of basic materials and manpower, as well as the rate at which additional industrial capacity could be put into operation. After a brief slackening in the rate of expansion of producer goods output, combined with an increase in consumer goods and agricultural production, the emphasis on producer goods was again resumed, though on a somewhat reduced scale. This is illustrated in the last two columns of Table 4, showing the annual rates of growth of producer and consumer goods output from 1950 to 1954, as well as the targets for 1955 and 1956. The table also shows indices of gross output of industry from 1949 to 1955 and, for purposes of comparison, corresponding indices of agricultural production. In 1948, output of agriculture stood about 25 per cent below the prewar figure, and by 1955, it may have barely reached the prewar level.

Table 4. Indices of Gross Industrial and Agricultural Production, 1949-1955, and Annual Rates of Growth of Producer and Consumer Goods Output, 1948-1956

Year	Industrial Production Index (1948 = 100)	Agricultural Production Index (1948 = 100)	Annual Rates of Growth: Producer Goods (per cent of previous ye[ar])	Consume[r] Goods
1949	116.7	110.2	....	...
1950	134.3	113.3	16	15
1951	154.6	114.8	23	9
1952	186.1	112.4	27	10
1953	202.8	112.4	5	19
1954	212.0	113.3	4	5
1955	231.5	126.3	9[a]	9[a]
1956 (plan)	....	....	10	7

Sources: Industrial and agricultural production indices, Academy of Sciences of USSR, *Voprosy Ekonomiki* (Economic Problems), No. 3 (1956), pp. 162 and [...] industrial indices were recomputed to 1948 base. Annual rates of growth of prod[...] and consumer goods output, United Nations, *Economic Survey of Europe in 1*[...] p. 228.

[a] Planned output.

A further substantial expansion of heavy industries, particularly the machine building, metallurgical, and chemical industries, is contemplated during the second Five-Year Plan (1956-60). According to the draft directives, published on May 4, 1956, total industrial production during the period 1956-60 is to increase 50 per cent, while producer goods output is to rise 57 per cent and consumer goods output 40 per cent. Total industrial investments are to amount to 152.6 billion crowns (about 21.2 billion dollars) at July 1, 1955 prices.

Industrialization of Slovakia

Both the original and the revised version of the first Five-Year Plan called for rapid industrial development of Slovakia through the transfer of some industrial plants from the Czech lands and through development of local resources. This policy was prompted partly by a desire to reduce the disparity in economic development between the western and eastern parts of the country, partly by the existence in Slovakia of relatively large labor reserves, and partly by considerations of military and political strategy. While the transfer of some heavy industrial plants, including armament factories, from the Czech lands to Slovakia was supposed to improve military security, the transformation of Slovakia from a rural to semi-industrial region was to strengthen the regime's political position in the area.

According to the initial version of the first Five-Year Plan, the volume of gross industrial production in Slovakia was to increase 75 per cent between 1948 and 1953, while heavy industrial production was to double. These targets were radically increased in the revised version, which called for the index of industrial production relative to 1948 to increase to 268 and that of producer goods output to 400. By 1953, Slovakia's share in Czechoslovakia's gross industrial output was to increase to 19.6 per cent.

During the period 1949-53, Slovakia accounted for the following percentages of Czechoslovakia's investment expenditures:

Year	Total Investments	Industrial Investments
1949	25.5	20.7
1950	27.9	22.2
1951	28.7	23.8
1952	27.9	24.8
1953	26.2	24.9

Source: State Statistical Office, *Statisticky obzor,* XXXIV, No. 4 (1954), p. 205.

During the same period, the index of Slovakia's gross industrial production rose to 236 (1948=100), while the corresponding indices for producer and consumer goods output increased to 253 and 216, respectively. The 1953 index of electric power production stood at 195, fuel extraction at 252, ore mining at 161, metallurgical production at 354, engineering production at 470, chemical production at 253, rubber manfacture at 322, building materials output at 215, glass production at 157, timber output at 118, wood processing at 213, and paper production at 126. Most of these large relative increases represent only small increases in absolute terms. Absolute figures on Slovakia's production of various industrial commodities are generally unavailable.

The progress of Slovakia's industrialization relative to the Czech lands is illustrated in Table 5, showing Slovakia's share in the country's total gross industrial production in 1937 and in the period 1948-53.

Table 5. Slovakia's Share in Czechoslovak Gross Industrial Production, 1937 and 1948-1953

Year	All Industry	Producer Goods	Consumer Goods
1937	8.0	7.3	8.9
1948	13.9	13.1	15.0
1949	13.9	12.4	15.9
1950	14.9	13.5	16.8
1951	15.2	14.1	16.8
1952	15.6	14.6	17.3
1953	16.2	15.2	18.0

Source: Ibid.

Survey of Individual Industries

Fuel and Power

Nearly 95 per cent of all energy in Czechoslovakia is derived from coal, which represents the country's principal solid fuel. Liquid fuel production is relatively small, and hydroelectric potential is also limited. The limit of feasible exploitation of this potential has been put as about 8,500 million kilowatt-hours, annually. Czechoslovakia is the largest European producer of uranium ore, but the total output is shipped to the Soviet Union. The structure of Czechoslovak consumption of sources of energy in 1937-38 and 1950 is shown in Table 6.

Table 6. Gross Consumption of Sources of Energy, 1937-1938 and 1950 (in thousand metric tons of bituminous coal equivalent)

Source of Energy	1937-1938	1950
Solid fuels	24,694	35,720
Liquid fuels	625	810
Natural gas	2	...[a]
Hydroelectric power	390	720
Total	25,711	37,250[a]

Source: United Nations, *World Energy Supplies in Selected Years, 1929-1950*, September 1952, pp. 62-63.

[a] The 1950 output of natural gas, in terms of bituminous coal equivalent, was not large enough to affect the total significantly.

Data on output of solid fuels, crude oil, natural gas, and pre-World War II figures on uranium ore mining are presented in Chapter 14. This section will briefly survey the manufacture of coke, crude oil refining, synthetic motor fuel production, gas manufacture, and electric power production.

Coke Manufacture. The manufacture of coke dates from the middle of the nineteenth century. It has been largely concentrated in the Ostrava-Karvina basin, where the bulk of the country's bituminous coal deposits is located, and its growth has closely paralleled the development of metallurgical industry in the area. As of 1955, thirteen coke plants were in operation; eleven of these were located in the Ostrava-Karvina basin, one in the Rosice-Oslavany basin, and one at Kladno. Except for one plant built in 1952 in conjunction with a new metallurgical combine at Kuncice in the Ostrava-Karvina basin, all the country's coke plants were built prior to World War II, though their capacity has been substantially expanded since the launching of the first Five-Year Plan. A large number of additional coke oven batteries has been installed directly in metallurgical plants, and there has been a marked tendency to shift coke production to the latter, where high quality coke-oven gas can be utilized for firing blast furnaces.

While the demand for coke has rapidly mounted as a result of the expansion of the metallurgical industry, coke exports, particularly to Hungary and Romania, have also substantially increased. In 1937, Czechoslovakia exported about 950,000 metric tons of coke, while during the first Five-Year Plan average annual exports amounted to some 1,300,000 tons. Between 1948 and 1955, coke output increased 55 per cent, while bituminous coal production rose only 31 per cent. The shortage in the domestic supply of coking coals has necessitated increased bituminous coal imports from Poland, amounting to about 4 million tons by the end of the first Five-Year Plan. At the same time, intensive search for a workable method of coking brown coal has been conducted to ease the acute shortage of bituminous coking coal.

About 10 per cent of coke output comes from gas works, where coke is obtained as a by-product. In addition to coke manufactured from bituminous coal, Czechoslovakia produces large quantities of brown coal semi-coke, which is obtained as a by-product of synthetic fuel manufacture at Horni Litvinov near Most. Data on production of coke and semi-coke in selected years from 1937 to 1955, as well as planned production for 1960, are shown in Table 7.

Table 7. Production of Coke and Brown Coal Semi-Coke, Selected Years 1937-1955 and Planned Output in 1960
(in thousand metric tons)

Year	Coke	Brown Coal Semi-Coke
1937	3,528	—
1944	4,941	....
1948	4,522	1,094
1953	6,513	2,023
1955	7,020	2,400[a]
1960 (plan)	8,630	....

Sources: Data for 1937-1953 and 1955 figure for brown coal semi-coke from Ladislav Stepan, *Coal Industry in Czechoslovakia, 1918-1954,* to be published by Mid-European Studies Center. Figures for 1955 and 1960, *Rude Pravo* (Red Right), May 4, 1956, Supplement.

[a] Estimated output.

Crude Oil Refining. Prior to World War II, Czechoslovakia possessed thirteen oil refineries, which were almost entirely dependent on imports of crude oil and semi-finished products. In 1937, domestic production of crude oil amounted to only 18,000 metric tons, while 484,700 metric tons were imported. Most of the oil refineries were severely damaged during World War II, and postwar reconstruction proceeded very slowly, as the production of liquid fuels was concentrated in the synthetic fuel plant built by the Germans during the war.

Information on postwar output of oil products is scanty. In 1952, total annual consumption of oil products was estimated as 780,000 metric tons. Of this amount, some 300,000 tons may have been processed by domestic oil refineries, the remainder being supplied by the synthetic motor fuel plant near Most and by imports.

Synthetic Fuel Production. Synthetic motor fuels are manufactured by hydrogenation of brown coal tar which, in turn, is obtained by low temperature carbonization of brown coals from the North Bohemian and, to a smaller extent, Sokolov basin. Because of their high content of tar, amounting to 17-18 per cent on dry basis, these coals are well suited for synthetic fuel production. They represent the best raw material available in Europe for this purpose, and deposits are sufficiently large to insure an adequate supply in the foreseeable future. This may have been a decisive factor behind Germany's insistence, during the negotiations of the Munich Pact, upon the annexation of all but a small part of the North Bohemian coal region. Immediately following the occupation of the territory in the fall of

1938, the Germans began to build a giant plant at Horni Litvinov near Most, with a projected annual production capacity of one million tons of motor fuels. By May 1944, when the plant was first damaged by bombing, capacity had reached some 450,000 tons. The projected capacity was never realized. By the end of 1944, production was stopped and it was not resumed till after the war.

In 1945, the plant fell to the Soviet Union as war booty. It was turned over to the Czechoslovak government as compensation for the Jachymov uranium ore mines, which the Soviet Union appropriated. By 1946, the plant, named the Stalin Works, was sufficiently rebuilt to permit annual production of 120,000 metric tons of motor fuels. The revised version of the first Five-Year Plan called for expansion of the plant's synthetic fuel production capacity to 525,000 tons. Expansion is still in progress, with the Stalin Works being built into the largest chemical combine in Europe for processing brown coal. In addition to synthetic motor fuels, such as low and high octane gasoline, kerosene, gas oil and fuel gas, the plant produces large amounts of nitrogen, hydrogen, phenol, sulphur, pyrocatechin methanol, formaldehyde, carbon dioxide, and other chemicals.

Official data on synthetic motor fuel production have not been released. Output by the end of the first Five-Year Plan was estimated at 350-400 thousand tons, and by 1955 it may have risen to about half a million tons. The latter figure would seem to be in accord with the 1955 figure for total output of motor fuels published in *Rude Pravo* on May 4, 1956 (810,000 tons), representing the total output of oil refineries.

Manufactured Gas. The first gas works was built in Prague-Karlin in 1847. Brno, Plzen, Slany, and other large towns soon followed Prague and the gas-making industry spread rapidly in the Czech lands. Prior to World War II, there were eighty-five gas works in Czechoslovakia, fifty-one located in Bohemia, twenty-seven in Moravia, and seven in Slovakia. Data on the number of gas works in the postwar period are not available.

In recent years, with the rapidly increasing production of coke, coke-oven gas has been rapidly gaining in importance as a general utility gas, while the various producer gases and those obtained as by-products in industrial operations (e.g., blast furnace gas and the gas originating in the manufacture of synthetic motor fuels) are utilized almost exclusively by the industry as fuel or for further processing. Czechoslovakia's output of manufactured gas (produced in gas works and coke plants) in selected years from 1937 to 1954, is shown in the following tabulation. Gas produced in gas works represents slightly over 10 per cent of the total.

Year	Output of Manufactured Gas
	(in million cubic meters)
1937	1,446
1944	2,048
1948	2,172
1953	2,841
1954	2,974

Source: Stepan, *op. cit.*

Electric Power Production. Prior to World War II, over 90 per cent of Czechoslovakia's electric power came from thermal plants. Because of the postwar coal shortage, increased stress has been placed on utilization of the hydroelectric power potential, which was estimated at 1,500,000 horsepower, Bohemia accounting for 600,000 horsepower, Moravia-Silesia for 120,000, and Slovakia for 775,000. Czechoslovakia's postwar economic development has been marked by a rapid rate of electrification. In 1955, production of electricity was double that of 1948, and 3.66 times as high as in 1937. Per capita output of electricity rose from less than 300 kilowatt-hours in 1937 to 1,000 kilowatt-hours in 1953. By 1960, per capita production is to increase to 2,000 kilowatt-hours.

During the first Five-Year Plan, six large hydroelectric plants were put into operation, the largest among these on the Orava, Vah, and Chrudimka rivers. In 1954, another large power plant, located at Slapy on the Vltava River, was completed. Early in 1955, seven major hydroelectric projects were reported under construction, and by 1960, nine additional hydroelectric plants are to be built. Due to the simultaneous rapid expansion of the capacity of thermoelectric plants, the share of hydroelectric plants in the total output of electricity had risen to only 13 per cent by 1954. This proportion is to increase to 20 per cent by the end of the second Five-Year Plan.

The country's largest thermoelectric plants are located at Ervenice in the North Bohemian brown coal basin and in the Ostrava-Karvina bituminous coal basin. Major recent additions include the plants at Hodonin in southern Moravia and at Zemianske Kostolany in Slovakia, both utilizing local lignite deposits, and the plants in the Krkonose Mountains of Bohemia, using brown coal from the North Bohemian basin. On the basis of an agreement with Poland, Czechoslovakia shares the output of a large thermoelectric plant which she helped to build in the Polish Silesian coal basin. A similar agreement with Hungary calls for joint construction and exploitation of a large hydroelectric power station on the Danube in the vicinity of Komarno, but the project is still in the blueprint stage. Czechoslovakia's power transmission network is based on a 220,000-volt main transmission line extending from the Ervenice thermal plant in northern Bohemia to Nove Mesto nad Vahom in western Slovakia, which is to become the center of the Vah hydroelectric power system.

Data on production of electricity in selected years from 1937 to 1955 and planned production in 1960 are shown in Table 8. In view of the country's relative coal shortage and limited hydroelectric potential, plans for the period beyond 1960 call for the development of atomic energy plants as a main source of electric power. According to the Czechoslovak delegate to the International Conference on the Peaceful Uses of Atomic Energy in Geneva in 1955, Czechoslovakia is to produce 40-45 billion kilowatt-hours of electricity in 1965 and up to 100 billion kilowatt-hours in 1975. In 1965, atomic energy is to account for about 20 billion kilowatt-hours, and in 1975 for about 60 billion.

Table 8. Production of Electric Power and Installed Capacity, Selected Years 1937-1955 and 1960 Plan

Year	Production	Installed Capacity
	(in million kilowatt-hours)	(in thousand kilowatts)
1937	4,115	1,870[a]
1943	6,660	. . .
1945	4,457	2,464
1948	7,400	2,740
1953	12,363	3,700[b]
1955	15,080	. . . .
1960 (plan)	25,340	. . . .

Sources: Production: 1937 and 1945, State Statistical Office, *Statistical Digest of the Czechoslovak Republic, 1948* (Prague, 1948), pp. 59 and 87; 1943, Jan H. Wszelaki, *Fuel and Power in Captive Middle Europe* (New York, 1952), p. 41; 1948, United Nations, *Economic Survey of Europe in 1953* (Geneva, 1954), p. 272; 1953, Ministry of Fuel and Power, *Energetika* (Energetics), IV, No. 6 (1954), 256; 1955 and 1960 plan, *Rude pravo*, May 4, 1956, Supplement. Installed capacity: 1937 and 1945, United Nations, *Statistical Yearbook, 1953* (New York, 1953), p. 273; 1948 and 1953, Ministry of Information, *Prvni ceskoslovensky petilety plan* (The First Czechoslovak Five-Year Plan) (Prague, 1949), p. 75.

[a] Refers to 1936.

[b] Planned output.

Primary Metal Industry

The beginnings of the modern metallurgical industry date from the second half of the nineteenth century, though smelters and forges based on local supplies of iron ore and charcoal had existed in the Plzen, Beroun, and Ostrava regions since the Middle Ages. The development of the industry was prompted largely by the relatively abundant deposits of high quality coal, while the limited domestic supply of metallic ores had to be increasingly supplemented by imports. With the rapid expansion of the metallurgical industry in recent years, Czechoslovakia's dependence on ore imports has greatly increased, despite the government's determined efforts to expand domestic output of ferrous and nonferrous ores (see Chapter 14).

Czechoslovak metallurgical production is concentrated in the Ostrava-Karvina and Kladno districts. Secondary metallurgical centers are located at Chomutov in northwestern Bohemia, Plzen, and Rokycany in western Bohemia, Zdar in Moravia, and Brezno and Tisovec in Slovakia.

Ferrous Metallurgy. Prior to World War II, the bulk of output of iron and steel was produced by three companies: the Vitkovice Mines, Steel and Iron Corporation at Ostrava-Vitkovice, the Prague Iron and Steel Company at Kladno and Kraluv Dvur, and the Mining and Iron Works at Trinec and Bohumin. Smaller but highly specialized were the Mannesmann Pipe Rolling Mills at Chomutov and Svinov, and the Poldi Works at Kladno, specializing in the production of fine steels. In addition, there were a number of small establishments. The Ostrava and Kladno regions produced 95-98 per cent of the total output of pig iron and 80-85 per cent of crude steel and finished products. The industry's total labor force (including workers, apprentices, and administrative personnel) in 1937 amounted to 24,800.

Except for nationalization of the industry and the increase in size, the prewar pattern of location and specialization has remained relatively unchanged. Most of the metallurgical plants were undamaged by war, and the industry's recovery proceeded rapidly. By the end of the Two-Year Plan, the output of iron and steel had reached the prewar level. Since the launching of the first Five-Year Plan, the industry's capacity has been substantially enlarged by additions to the existing plants, as well as by the construction of a giant metallurgical combine at Kuncice near Ostrava, which has an annual production capacity of one million tons of steel. The industry's total labor force by the end of the Five-Year Plan has been estimated at 62,000.

Data on pig iron and crude steel production in selected years from 1937 to 1955 and production targets for 1960 are shown in Table 9. The growing gap between pig iron and steel production has been due to the increasing use of scrap iron for steel production.

Table 9. Pig Iron and Crude Steel Production, Selected Years 1937-1955 and 1960 Plan
(in thousand metric tons)

Year	Pig Iron	Crude Steel
1937	1,675	2,301
1943	1,706	2,565
1948	1,600	2,600
1953	2,800	4,400
1955	2,990	4,480
1960 (plan)	4,780	6,540

Sources: Data for 1937, State Statistical Office, *Statistical Digest of the Czechoslovak Republic, 1948*, pp. 58 and 87; 1943 (World War II peak production year), pig iron, United Nations, *Statistical Yearbook, 1953*, p. 228; steel, United Nations, *Economic Survey of Europe in 1948* (Washington, D. C., 1949), p. 212; 1948 and 1953, United Nations, *Economic Survey of Europe in 1954* (Geneva, 1955), p.43; 1955 and 1960, *Rude pravo*, May 4, 1956, Supplement.

Nonferrous Metallurgy. Despite extremely limited domestic reserves of most nonferrous metals, Czechoslovakia has long possessed a highly diversified nonferrous metallurgy, based largely on imported ores. Since the Communist coup and the subsequent embargo on strategic material exports by Western countries, Czechoslovakia has become dependent on nonferrous ore imports from the Soviet orbit countries, particularly the Soviet Union. In recent years, efforts have been made to expand domestic output of nonferrous ores, and to use substitutes for metals in short supply. Thus, ferroalloys are frequently replaced by ferromanganese, copper is increasingly being replaced by aluminum, and in general, whenever practicable, metals are replaced by glass, plastics, and other nonmetallic materials.

Data on the production of various nonferrous metals in selected years from 1937 to 1952 are shown in Table 10. Figures on the limited output of ferroalloys and minor metals are largely unavailable. A major item omitted from the table is the production of aluminum, which has been recently introduced on a relatively large scale, with the bauxite imported from Hungary and Russia. In 1955, production of crude aluminum amounted to nearly 25,000 tons. By 1960 it is to increase to 56,000 tons.

Table 10. Output of Nonferrous Metals, Selected Years 1937-1952
(in metric tons)

Year	Antimony	Copper	Lead	Mercury	Zinc	Tin[a]
1937	1,429	.... [b]	5,063	94.8	7,773	1,760
1943	2,249	....	4,000	....	9,540	....
1947	1,434	5,954[c]	8,227	26.5	1,964	....
1948	....	6,500	7,900	28.0	3,300	1,100
1950	2,000	7,500	....	50.0	....	1,300
1952	....	9,000	....	....	....	1,600

Sources: Antimony: 1937 and 1947, State Statistical Office, *Statistical Digest of the Czechoslovak Republic, 1948,* pp. 58 and 87; 1943, United Nations, *Statistical Yearbook, 1953,* p. 128; 1950, United States Department of the Interior, *Minerals Yearbook, 1951* (Washington, D. C., 1954), p. 1630. Copper: 1937 and 1947, *Statistical Digest,* pp. 58 and 87; 1948-1952, United Nations, *Economic Survey of Europe in 1954,* p. 266. Lead: 1937 and 1947, *Statistical Digest,* pp. 58 and 87; 1943 and 1948, United Nations, *Statistical Yearbook, 1951,* p. 258. Mercury: 1937 and 1947, *Statistical Digest,* pp. 58 and 87; 1948 and 1950, Bruno Kiesewetter, *Statistiken zur Wirtschaft Ost- und Suedosteuropas* (Berlin, 1954), p. 34. Zinc: 1937 and 1947, *Statistical Digest,* pp. 58 and 87; 1943, United Nations, *Statistical Yearbook 1954,* p. 237; 1948, State Statistical Office, *Prumyslove zpravy* (Industrial Reports), IV, No. 28-29 (1949). Tin: United Nations, *Statistical Yearbook 1954,* p. 284.

[a] Refers to industrial consumption.

[b] Black copper, 1,078 metric tons; cement copper, 2,180 metric tons; refined copper, 935 metric tons.

[c] Refers to "copper and its alloys."

Metal Fabricating

Metal fabrication occupies by far the most prominent place within the country's industrial structure. While most of the existing branches of the metal fabricating industry were developed prior to World War II, their productive capacity as well as the number of products have been radically increased in recent years. The greatest increases have taken place in the production of industrial, agricultural, and transport machinery and equipment. At present, Czechoslovakia's major lines of production include the following: mining and metallurgical machinery and equipment; electric power machinery; machine tools; textile machinery; leather, chemical, and food processing machinery and equipment; transport machinery and equipment; agricultural machinery and implements; and river craft. In addition, the country possesses a relatively well developed armament industry, and a growing electrotechnical equipment and precision instrument industry. The scope of Czechoslovakia's metal fabricating industry is illustrated in the tabulation below, listing the main products and the location of the principal plants. Some plants producing mainly consumer goods, but easily convertible to producer goods manufacture are included.

Major Products	Location of Major Plants
Armaments and heavy industrial equipment	Plzen, Prague, Brno, Strakonice, Dubnica nad Vahom
Central heating equipment	Prague, Plzen, Decin, Kolin, Horovice, Olomouc, Marianske Udoli
Metal furniture	Prague, Plzen, Duchcov, Lysa nad Labem, Hradec Kralove, Ostrava, Gottwaldov
Household implements	Ceske Budejovice, Plzen, Horovice, Brno, Frydlant, Prague, Chrudim, Filakovo, Bratislava
Water pumps	Prague, Vysoke Myto, Olomouc-Lubin, Hradec Kralove
Locomotives	Plzen, Prague, Slany
Rolling stock	Prague, Koprivnice, Studenka, Brno, Ceska Lipa
Automobiles, airplanes, and motorcycles	Prague, Mlada Boleslav, Koprivnice, Strakonice, Povazska Bystrica
River craft	Komarno, Prague, Usti nad Labem
Tractors	Brno, Mlada Boleslav, Kosmonosy
Machine tools	Prague, Brno, Plzen, Olomouc
Textile machinery	Liberec, Brno, Krnov, Tyniste nad Orlici
Agricultural machinery	Roudnice nad Labem, Brandys nad Labem, Mlada Boleslav, Jicin, Prerov, Prostejov, Olomouc, Bratislava
Sewing machines	Opava, Sobeslav, Boskovice
Typewriters	Brno
Refrigeration equipment	Kolin
Electrical machinery	Prague, Kolin, Pardubice, Brno, Ostrava, Pribram, Usti nad Labem, Decin
Cables and electric wires	Kladno, Bohumin, Bratislava
Fire extinguishers	Prague, Vysoke Myto, Olomouc-Lubin, Hradec Kralove
Watches	Brno, Sternberk, Cheb
Optical instruments	Prague, Brno, Rumburk, Prerov

During the first Five-Year Plan, the output of the machine building industry reportedly increased 3.3 times, and its share in gross industrial production rose from 16 per cent in 1948 to 26 per cent in 1953.

In value terms, at 1948 prices, this would amount to a rise from about 46 billion crowns in 1948 to 151 billion crowns in 1953. The largest relative increases (expressed as 1953 indices relative to 1948) were reported in the output of the following types of machinery: steam turbines, 460; diesel engines, 420; machine tools, 270; hydraulic presses, 300; mining equipment, 350; mine cars, 600; cranes, 870; and turbo-compressors, 500. Absolute data on the output of individual products are fragmentary. Some of the available figures for 1948 and 1953 are given in Table 3, page 311. Additional data on the output of selected products of the machine building industry in 1937, 1948, and 1955 are shown in Table 11. No data are available on current armament production. In 1944, when armament production in Czechoslovakia reached its wartime peak, a total of about 200,000 persons were employed in the industry. It is evident that the postwar expansion of heavy industry, and particularly machine building, has substantially increased the country's armament production capacity.

Table 11. Output of Selected Products of Machine Building Industry, 1937, 1948, 1955, and Production Targets for 1960

Product	Unit of Measurement	1937	1948	1955	19 (Pl
Steam locomotives	unit	74	308	....	
Electric locomotives	unit	....	....	33	2
Diesel locomotives	unit	....	....	217	3
Trucks	unit	4,000	7,400	10,533	15,8
Passenger cars	unit	12,600	17,800	12,500	55,0
Tractors	unit	207	9,100[a]	12,304[a]	28,3
Agricultural machinery[b]	million crowns	300	1,526	545	9
Electric motors	megawatt	....	....	1,314	2,3
Diesel engines	thousand horsepower	....	....	797	1,2
Machine tools	unit	5,500	11,814	15,680	27,3
Ball and roller bearings	thousand	....	....	14,250	28,5
Machinery for chemical industry	ton	....	....	29,070	75,0
Rolling mill equipment	ton	....	....	15,470	41,0
Cement plant equipment	ton	....	....	7,410	22,0
Textile machinery	million crowns	....	....	56[c]	27
Food processing machinery	million crowns	....	....	131[c]	38
Precision instruments, optical laboratory and medical equipment, and office machines	million crowns	....	....	545[c]	97

Sources: For 1937: Steam locomotives, United Nations, *Statistical Yearbook 19*

p. 241; trucks and passenger cars, United Nations, *Economic Survey of Europe in 1948* (Geneva, 1949), p. 281; tractors, Kiesewetter, *op. cit.*, p. 40; agricultural machinery, Kiesewetter, *Die Wirtschaft der Tschechoslowakei seit 1945* (Berlin, 1954) p. 22; machine tools, United Nations, *Economic Survey of Europe in 1953*, p. 272. For 1948: Steam locomotives, Kiesewetter, *Statistiken*, p. 39; trucks, passenger cars, tractors, and machine tools, United Nations, *Economic Survey of Europe in 1953*, p. 272; agricultural machinery, Kiesewetter, *Die Wirtschaft*, p. 22. For 1955 and 1960, *Rude pravo*, May 4, 1956, Supplement.

[a] In 15-horsepower units.

[b] Data for 1937 and 1948 in current prices; those for 1955 and 1960 in prices of July 1, 1955. Expressed in U.S. dollars, at the official rate of exchange, the series would run roughly as follows: 1937, 10 million; 1948, 30.5 million; 1955, 75.7 million; 1960 (plan), 134.7 million.

[c] In prices of July 1, 1955.

Chemical Industry

The Czechoslovak chemical industry developed relatively late. Prior to World War I, the competition of large German concerns, which supplied the major part of Czechoslovak requirements for chemicals, discouraged the development of domestic chemical enterprises. Another adverse factor was the lack of certain basic chemical raw materials, particularly pyrites, industrial potassium, sodium salt, and phosphates. After 1918, with outside competition partly removed, the industry began to expand. By 1937, it employed about 56,000 persons. Its main products during the interwar period included sulphuric acid, sodium compounds, chlorine, products of coal tar and wood distillation, enamels, paints, varnishes, lacquers, synthetic fertilizers, pharmaceuticals, photographic films, and a wide range of additional products requiring a relatively high degree of processing. During World War II, the industry's size was nearly doubled by the addition of a giant synthetic motor fuel plant in Horni Litvinov near Most.

During the first Five-Year Plan, production of chemicals increased nearly 2.5 times. The range of products has been greatly increased by the utilization of the by-products of synthetic fuel manufacture, as well as by the development of additional lines of production. These include primarily synthetic products, such as the polyamids and polyvinyl chloride, which are used as substitutes for nonferrous metals, synthetic fibers, and synthetic leather. By 1955, a synthetic rubber plant was to be constructed. The production of pharmaceuticals was also substantially expanded. Since the end of World War II, the manufacture of several types of modern drugs, including penicillin has been introduced. A complete penicillin manufacturing plant was given Czechoslovakia in 1946 as part of the UNRRA assistance program.

Production of artificial fertilizers, basic chemicals, and dyes and paints is concentrated largely in Usti nad Labem, Prague, Plzen, Hradec Kralove, Ceske Budejovice, Pardubice, Brno, Ostrava, Gottwaldov, Handlova, and Bratislava. Plastics and synthetic fibers are produced at Lovosice, Gottwaldov, Senica, and Svit near Poprad. The manufacture of photographic materials is located at Hradec Kralove, Cesky Brod, Prague, and Brno, and the production of explosives in the Pardubice area.

The output of selected chemicals in various years from 1937 to 1955 and the 1960 production targets are shown in Table 12.

Table 12. Production of Selected Chemicals, Selected Years 1937-1955, and 1960 Plan
(in thousand metric tons)

Product	1937	1948	1953	1955	1960 (Plan)
Sulphuric acid	166	215	312	384	560
Sodium hydroxide	. . .	37	61		
Nitrogenous fertilizers[a]	23	31	38	61	141
Phosphate fertilizer[b]	48	60	74	98	156.5
Polyvinyl chloride	—	—	. . . .	3	9
Rayon filament yarn	4	5.2	9.6	48.5[d]	66.6[d]
Rayon staple fiber	0.3	18	27[c]		

Sources: Sulphuric acid, sodium hydroxide, nitrogenous and phosphate fertilizers and polyvinyl chloride: 1937-53 United Nations, *Economic Survey of Europe in 1954,* p. 266; 1955 and 1930, *Rude pravo,* May 4, 1956, Supplement. Rayon filament yarn and staple fiber: 1937-53, United Nations, *Statistical Yearbook 1954,* p. 198; 1955 and 1960, *Rude pravo,* May 4, 1956, Supplement.

[a] In terms of nitrogen content.
[b] In terms of plant nutrient.
[c] Refers to 1952 output.
[d] Refers to total output of artificial fibers.

Building Materials Industry

Czechoslovakia possesses adequate supplies of nearly all mineral building materials. Cement is produced throughout the country, with the largest plants located at Kraluv Dvur near Prague, Cizkovice in the North Bohemian industrial region, Malomerice near Brno, Stramberk and Hranice in northern Moravia, and Hornie Srnie, Stupava, Ladce and Lucka in Slovakia. Industrial ceramic production is concentrated in the Plzen-Rakovnik area, where both clay and coal deposits are available. The main products include fireproof and acidproof materials, walling and flooring tiles, crucibles and fusing pans for glass works, and chemical stoneware. A large part of the porcelain industry of the Karlovy Vary region, which manufactured high quality consumer goods prior to World War II, has been converted to the production of industrial porcelain. Industrial glass production is concentrated in the Teplice-Sanov area of the North Bohemian basin.

Output of some of the major products of the building materials industry in selected years from 1937 to 1955, as well as the targets for 1960 are shown in Table 13.

Table 13. Production of Building Materials, Selected Years 1937-1955 and 1960 Plan

roduct	Unit of Measurement	1937	1948	1953	1955	1960 (Plan)
ement	million tons	1.3	1.6	2.3	2.9	4.5
me	million tons	0.9	0.9	1.1	1.5	2.3
dustrial porcelain	thousand tons	5.9[a]	7.6			....
icks	billion	1.1	0.9	1.3	1.7	2.7
ate glass	thousand tons	....	130.9	146.6		....
ate glass	million cubic meters	....	....	....	21.1	26.5

Sources: Cement, lime, bricks, and plate glass: 1937-53, United Nations, *Economic rvey of Europe in 1954*, p. 266; 1955 and 1960, *Rude pravo*, May 4, 1956, Supple- ent. Industrial porcelain: 1937, State Statistical Office, *Statisticka rocenka republiky skoslovenske 1938* (Statistical Yearbook of the Czechoslovak Republic 1938) rague, 1938), p. 93; 1948, State Statistical Office, *Prumyslove zpravy*, III, No. 28- (1948).

Woodworking, Paper and Allied Industries

Czechoslovakia's forests, extending over four million hectares or nearly one third of the country's total area, provide a wide base for a diversified wood processing industry. Large sawmills are located in the Sumava, Krkonose, Jeseniky and Bezkydy regions, and in the Klatovy, Ceska Trebova, Tesin, Zilina, and Liptovsky Hradok districts. Small sawmills are found in all parts of the country. Particularly well developed is the production of railway ties, telegraph poles and other impregnated wood products, which is concentrated mainly in Sobeslav in southern Bohemia. Also well developed is the production of packing case, parquet flooring, plywoods, veneers and furniture. Paper and cellulose manufacture is concentrated mainly in Plzen, Nejdek, Vetrno near Cesky Krumlov, Hostinne, Svoboda on the Upa river, Vrane on the Vltava river, Olsany, Tesin, Zilina, Martin, and Slavosovce. Output of basic wood, paper and allied products in selected years from 1937 to 1954 is shown in Table 14.

Table 14. Output of Wood, Paper and Allied Products, Selected Years, 1937-1954

Year	Lumber (thousand cubic meters)	Plywood (thousand cubic meters)	Veneer (thousand square meters)	Railway Ties (thousand cubic meters)	Newsprint (thousand metric tons)	Paper Other than Newsprint (thousand metric tons)	Cellulose (thousand metric tons)
1937	2,850	34	8,400		49	208	270
1948	3,010[a]	71	11,300	196	45	215	235
1950	....	90	....		50	244	270
1953	....	111.5[b]	15,200[b]	1,620[b]	60	257	320[b]
1954	....	....	....		65	265	....

Sources: Lumber, newsprint, and paper: United Nations, *Statistical Yearbook 1955*, pp. 227, 230 and 231. Plywood, veneer, and railway ties: 1937, Rudolf Perina, "Timber and Woodworking Industry in Czechoslovakia," unpublished manuscript (1952); 1948, State Statistical Office, *Prumyslove zpravy, III* (1948), No. 28-29; 1950, United Nations Food and Agriculture Organization, *European Timber Trends and Prospects* (Geneva, 1953), p. 160; 1953, Ministry of Information, *The Czechoslovak Five-Year Plan Act.* Cellulose: 1937 and 1950, United Nations, *Statistical Yearbook 1953*, p. 200; 1948, State Statistical Office, *Prumyslove zpravy*, III (1948), No. 28-29; 1953, Ministry of Information, *The Czechoslovak Five-Year Plan Act.*

[a] Includes 2,800,000 cubic meters of softwood and 210,000 cubic meters of hardwood.

[b] Original plan target figures.

16. CONSUMER GOODS INDUSTRIES

DEVELOPMENTS BEFORE 1948

Industries which participate in consumer goods production have traditionally held a prominent position in Czechoslovakia. During the entire interwar period and as late as 1948, consumer goods output represented more than one half of the total value of Czechoslovak gross industrial production.

Many of these industries are old and have developed out of village crafts. Some, such as the manufacture of textiles, glass, beer, and sugar, are among the oldest and best developed in Europe. Czechoslovakia inherited practically all these production branches from the Austro-Hungarian monarchy in 1918, when the Czechoslovak Republic was established. Since nearly 60 per cent of all Austro-Hungarian industry was located on Czechoslovak territory, with extremely heavy concentration of consumer goods manufacture, it is not surprising that after World War I, the country retained a large share, including 80 per cent of the textile, 92 per cent of the sugar, 92 per cent of the glass, and 100 per cent of the ceramics industries of the empire.

Czechoslovakia thus became heir to industrial capacities which had served a much larger and more populous territory and which greatly exceeded its domestic requirements. In such items as textiles, glass, and porcelain, 20 per cent of the output during the 1930's were usually sufficient to supply domestic demand, leaving some 80 per cent for export. A somewhat similar, although not so drastic situation, existed in leather, footwear, gloves, and sugar manufacture.

Maintenance of production in plants whose output exceeded domestic demand not only gave rise to a compelling need to export, but also determined the composition and direction of Czechoslovak foreign trade. Czechoslovak exports during the period before World War II were composed primarily of finished consumer goods, with textiles providing a full third of the total export value. Metal-working products, sugar, and leather goods usually followed textiles in that order, comprising the largest branches of the export trade. The majority of exports in these years went to the old markets of these industries in the territory of the former Austro-Hungarian Empire and in various Western European countries.

In contrast to the highly developed branches of production, a few consumer goods industries suffered from underdevelopment. Such was the case in some branches of agricultural processing, especially in food canning and freezing, dairy products, and artificial fats manufacture. In the two first-mentioned, large scale industrial manufacture was negligible even as late as 1948, and most production was confined to households.

Despite their prominent position in the Czechoslovak industrial structure, many of the largest consumer goods industries lacked domestic raw materials and had to depend nearly exclusively upon imports. In the case of textiles, the most important raw material, cotton, had to be imported entirely, since cotton cannot be grown domestically. Similar deficiencies existed in wool, hides, and tobacco. Practically all these raw materials were imported from the West.

Several branches of consumer goods industries were, however, adequately supplied with domestic raw materials of excellent quality. Rich deposits of high-grade china clay and sand, together with highly skilled craftsmen, made Czechoslovak glass and porcelain famous throughout the world. The quality of Czechoslovak hops and malting barley contributed to the brewing of excellent beer. Extensive cultivation of sugar beets was the basis for one of the largest sugar refining industries in Europe.

Practically all manufacturing enterprises were privately owned. Cooperatives were also important, especially in the agricultural processing sector. Small crafts production participated to a considerable extent. For instance, in the agricultural processing branch, about 80 per cent of the total employment consisted of workers in small workshops, and about one half of the employees in glass manufacture worked in their homes. State ownership was limited to a few state monopolies, of which the tobacco monopoly was the most remunerative. A number of enterprises were financed in part by foreign capital, chiefly German, Swiss, British, and Dutch.

Most consumer goods industries were located in the Czech lands, Bohemia and Moravia, with only relatively minor concentrations in Slovakia. This situation was reversed only in the case of tobacco processing.

While consumer goods industries are generally highly vulnerable during wartime, due to the emphasis then given to armament and capital goods production, Czechoslovak industries in this field were particularly jeopardized because of their extreme dependence on imports of raw materials. It is therefore not surprising that the damage they suffered during World War II as the result of conversions to war productions, deterioration of equipment, and lack of investment, was substantially greater than in other branches of production.

During the interwar period, the world-wide depression increased competition on the world market. International cartel agreements limiting production in such fields as textiles and sugar production became more common, and a portion of the excess capacity in existence before World War II was eliminated through failure to reactivate plants after the end of hostilities. A further reduction of capacities in practically all consumer goods industries was effected by the Communists following the February 1948 *coup d'état.*

Main Trends in Communist Policy

The process of nationalization of industry developed in Czechoslovakia in two distinct stages. The first phase was carried out on the basis of a decree issued by the President of the Republic in October 1945: it embraced only the largest enterprises, primarily those employing from 150 to 400 persons. The second stage was initiated in 1948, immediately after the Communist *coup d'état.* The bulk of industrial enterprises was nationalized, leaving outside the state sphere only those plants employing less than 50 persons. However, subsequent denials of raw materials and credit and absorption of their labor into nationalized enterprises forced the private owners left outside the nationalized sphere either to abandon operation of their plants or to join the state-controlled "socialized sector," i.e., national, communal, or cooperative enterprises.

By 1953, with the exception of a few independent tailors, cobblers, and other craftsmen, and the smallest flour mills, owned mainly by aged people with no other means of subsistence, all consumer goods production was nationalized under the control of two ministries, the Ministry of Light Industry and the Ministry of Food Production.

Exclusive ownership of the main industrial enterprises enabled the Communist government to alter substantially the old Czechoslovak economic structure within a rather short period. Starting with the first Five-Year Plan (1949-53), and particularly after the revision of the plan in 1951 (following the outbreak of war in Korea), emphasis was laid on an increase in producer goods output. The planners scheduled a marked decrease in plant capacities available for consumer goods production, especially in textiles, ceramics, glass, milling, and alcoholic beverages manufacture. A number of plants were dismantled or closed, and generally only negligible investments were authorized in the remaining plants, making modernization or replacement of equipment practically impossible. In addition, labor was absorbed into the heavy industries, despite the fact that many consumer goods industries already had suffered heavy labor losses as a result of the expulsion of the Germans after World War II. Plants which were left in operation were fused into large "national enterprises," consisting in some cases of as many as one hundred formerly independent plants. A number of plants were moved from the western border areas into the less industrialized regions of Slovakia.

As a result of this shift in emphasis, consumer goods industries lost their leading position in the Czechoslovak industrial structure. At the end of 1953, their output constituted an estimated 47 per cent of the gross industrial output, in contrast to a share of 55 per cent in 1948.[1]

While capacities in most branches of the consumer goods industries were thus heavily reduced, some branches, particularly those of significance to the armed forces were to be expanded beyond their prewar level. This expansion was envisaged notably for some food-processing industries, such as freezing and canning of food, cold storage, and dairies.

In other branches of production, in addition to contraction of capacity, the type of product was changed from decorative or luxury articles to technical commodities for use in other industries. Thus, in glass and porcelain production, the plan provided for reducing production of decorative glass and utility porcelain in favor of increased manufacture of technical glass and electrotechnical porcelain. At the same time, in all lines of production an effort was made to reduce the number of types produced to a few basic lines, which were standardized in many instances according to Soviet specifications.

Finally, a serious effort has been made to increase the domestic supply of raw materials. The production of artificial fibers has been increased to compensate for shortages of cotton and wool. Plastics have been utilized instead of hides and leather. Generally, wherever practicable, substitutes have been used instead of raw materials in short supply.

[1] According to recent Czechoslovak claims, consumer goods output dropped from about 42 per cent of gross industrial production in 1948 to about 38 per cent in 1953. However, these figures are based on a redefined concept of the consumer goods category. Figures used in this text conform with the Czechoslovak definition of consumer goods in effect in 1949 (cf. *Statisticky zpravodaj* [Statistical Bulletin], XII, No. 5-6 [1949], p. 187), which served as the basis for the preparation of the first Five-Year Plan.

Although in some consumer goods industries the volume of output has been maintained at about prewar levels, lack of investment and failure to modernize and replace outdated equipment has taken its toll. Breakdowns of equipment and production stoppages due to inadequate maintenance have been frequent. In the textile industry, some of the machinery in use was 70 years old at the end of World War II. In many cases, at the end of the first Five-Year Plan in 1953, some industries were in much worse condition than after the war.

Production in the Principal Consumer Goods Industries

Textiles and Clothing

Czechoslovak textile and clothing manufacture, which represented the largest single branch of industrial manufacture in the 1930's currently ranks third, following the machine building and agricultural processing sectors. By the end of 1953, it represented 11 per cent of the total gross industrial output. It employed 16 per cent of the total industrial labor force, a substantial drop from the prewar period, when it employed some 29 per cent of industrial workers. Within the branch itself, some 78 per cent of the value of output consists of textiles, while clothing manufacture represents the remaining 22 per cent.

The industry is old, its beginnings dating back to the second half of the eighteenth century. It reached its peak in the period preceding and immediately following World War I. Throughout the interwar period, the majority of its enterprises consisted of relatively small plants. Many of these were forced out of business during the Great Depression as a result of loss of markets and inability to replace obsolescent equipment. During World War II, the industry was again hit hard. Many plants were either closed or were converted to other types of production.

The industry was traditionally concentrated in the northern and northwestern border regions of the country. Other relatively minor concentrations were in the areas around Brno in Moravia and the Ruzomberok-Zilina area in Slovakia. Some centers of specialized production were in Prostejov and Prague (clothing), Novy Jicin (hats), and Varnsdorf (knitwear and hose).

The Communist government has closed a number of plants and transferred others to Slovakia and other underdeveloped regions of

Czechoslovakia. The northwestern Bohemian region thus lost in importance, while the Brno-Boskovice region in Moravia relatively gained. Finally, new textile manufacturnig areas were established in Gottwaldov (formerly Zlin) and other localities in Moravia (Nove Mesto na Morave, Straznice, Velka nad Velickou), in southern Bohemia (Pisek, Prachatice, Trebon), and in Slovakia (Banska Stiavnica, Dolny Kubin, Puchov, Spisska Nova Ves, Liptovsky Svaty Mikulas). Likewise, Trencin in Slovakia has reportedly developed into one of the country's largest clothing manufacture centers.

Clothing products manufacture represents the largest sector of the Czechoslovak textile industry, followed by wool and linen textile manufacture. In 1937, cotton manufacturing had over 3.5 million spindles, one-third of which were installed in the Liberec region of Bohemia. At that time, Czechoslovakia was the largest manufacturer of velvets in the world and exported 90 per cent of her production. By 1946, the number of spindles had decreased to 2.2 million, with only 1.3 million in operation.

Throughout the interwar period, the industry had to depend heavily on imports of raw materials, primarily cotton and wool. About 80 per cent of the textile raw material requirements were covered by imports. On the other hand, as much as 80 per cent of the industry's output was usually destined for export. Foreign trade in textiles during this period normally amounted to as much as 30 per cent of Czechoslovak imports and exports, representing the largest foreign trade category.

After 1948, the textile industry faced serious difficulties, due to inability to import certain raw materials from the West, especially cotton, the bulk of which had previously been imported from the United States, Egypt, and the East Indies. This situation developed, even though considerable quantities of cotton and wool were made available after 1948 by the Soviet Union, which is now Czechoslovakia's largest supplier of raw materials. However, Soviet raw materials are reported to be of inferior quality and therefore difficult for Czechoslovak machinery operation.

The general shortage of imported raw materials was partly offset by increased production of artificial fibers, which was practically nonexistent prior to World War II. Two artificial fiber maunfacturing plants are said to have been erected during the first Five-Year Plan. Official reports claim that the country now produces rayon, nylon, and glass fibers.

The output of textiles and clothing in selected years from 1936 to 1953 is shown in Table 1.

Table 1. Production of Textiles and Clothing, Selected Years 1936-1953

Item	1936	1937	1946	1947	1948	1949	1950	1953 (Plan)
(in thousand metric tons)								
Cotton yarn[a]	41.2	88.7	....	54.7	68.1	75.8	....	114.2
Wool yarn	15.9	27.2	....	29.5	32.0	35.4	....	41.8
Cotton, linen and silk fabrics	....	55.7[b]	....	36.4[b]	59.6	54.1	....	104.7[c]
Woolen fabrics	7.8	17.2	....	19.6	23.8	25.8[d]	....	30.2[e]
Rayon filament yarn	3.4	4.0	3.1	4.4	5.2	5.6	5.4	11.0
Rayon staple fiber	—	0.3	9.4	14.5	18.0	20.5	20.6	25.0
Knitwear	13.8	7.4	9.1	....	....	....	....	25.7
(in million pieces)								
Men's outer garments	....	....	....	....	....	3.4	....	3.8
Women's dresses	....	....	....	....	....	3.8	....	6.9
Work clothes	....	....	....	....	....	3.9	4.6	5.4

Sources: 1936-1950 actual output of cotton yarn, wool yarn, rayon filament yarn, and rayon staple fiber, United Nations, *Statistical Yearbook 1954* (New York, 1954); for cotton, linen and silk fabrics, and woolen fabrics, United Nations, *Statistical Yearbook 1949-1950;* for knitwear, men's outer garments, women's dresses, and work clothes, State Statistical Office, *Statisticky zpravodaj* (Statistical Bulletin), No. 1 (1950); 1953 plan targets, Ministry of Informaton, *The Czechoslovak Economic Five-Year Plan,* p. 31.

[a] From 1937, includes vicuna and tire cord yarn.

[b] Cotton fabrics only.

[c] Actual production reported as 439 million meters, estimated equivalent to 71,500 metric tons.

[d] Also reported as 47.8 million meters.

[e] Actual production estimated at 28,600 metric tons.

At the end of the first Five-Year Plan (1953), over-all production of the textile and clothing industry was only some 17 per cent above the prewar level, and had failed to reach the planned target. The postwar output index varied as follows (1937=100):

Year	Index
1946	49.3
1947	59.6
1948	76.5
1949	83.0
1950	90.0
1953	**117.0**
1953 (Plan)	139.0

Leather and Footwear

Leather and footwear production also declined considerably in importance after World War II. During the interwar period, leather and footwear ranked fourth among Czechoslovakia's exports.

Despite the industry's traditional dependence on imports of raw materials (to the extent of about 80 per cent), it ranks among the world's five largest footwear producers. This was due primarily to the rapid development of a modern and efficient shoe manufacturing industry by the Czech manufacturer Bata. During the interwar period, his enterprise in Zlin (now Gottwaldov), produced half of the footwear output of the country. It was the largest shoe manufacturing plant in Europe and the second largest in the world. Currently, this branch of manufacture is reported to provide only 2.2 per cent of gross industrial production. The industry now employs 3 per cent of the total industrial labor force, while in 1930 its share was 6 per cent.

Manufacture in this industry includes processing of raw hides and the output of such products as shoes, luggage, small leather articles, and gloves. Before World War II, Czechoslovakia ranked second only to France in the manufacture of leather gloves.

Processing of hides is located primarily in the eastern and central regions of Bohemia and the upper Vah valley in Slovakia. Shoe manufacture is heavily concentrated in Gottwaldov, with important secondary centers in Partyzanske (formerly Batovany) in Slovakia and in the areas of Ledec and Trebic. The pre-World War II footwear production areas in eastern Bohemia were liquidated in 1945 due to obsolescence of equipment. Glove manufacture, formerly an important cottage craft industry, which in 1937 exported 9.4 million pairs of gloves (6.3 million to the United States and the United

Kingdom), is concentrated in and to the south of Prague, as well as in northwestern Bohemia.

Communist policies introduced after 1948 also affected this branch very unfavorably. Stress on producer goods output, restriction of imports of raw materials from the Balkans, France, and Turkey, and the loss of Western markets caused a contraction of several lines of production to levels which barely satisfy the planned demand of the country and of the Soviet bloc.

The effort to eliminate dependence on Western raw materials has emphasized the substitution of plastics and domestic leather for imported hides. As a result, the quality of manufactured commodities has deteriorated substantially. By 1951, it was claimed officially that dependence on Western imports had been practically eliminated. At the same time, however, it was acknowledged that faulty and leaky shoes were being produced and that domestic leather was suitable only for the production of work gloves.

Output of leather and rubber footwear for selected years is shown below:

Year	Million Pairs
1937	55.0
1948	64.4
1953 (original plan)	72.5
1955	63.3

Sources: 1937 and 1948, United Nations, *Statistical Yearbook 1954*, p. 225; 1953 plan, Ministry of Information, *The Czechoslovak Economic Five-Year Plan*, p. 31; 1955, *Rude pravo*, May 4, 1956, Supplement.

Glass and Ceramics

The glass and ceramics industries are currently of minor importance in the Czechoslovak industrial structure. They are estimated to employ some 3 per cent of the total industrial labor force. The glass industry alone was reported to employ 2 per cent of all industrial workers at the end of 1953, compared to 7 per cent in 1930. The gross value of production in these industries in 1953 accounted for about 1.5 per cent of the total gross industrial output and that of the glass industry alone for 0.9 per cent.

Both industries are old, especially glass production, which can be traced back to the eleventh century. Their expansion was virtually completed before World War I. They began to decline in efficiency after 1918, and their output gradually diminished. The process of deterioration was hastened considerably after World War II.

Between 1914 and 1928, the number of porcelain factories decreased from 60 to 40. At present, there are 15 national enterprises in this field. In the glass industry, some 1,600 smaller plants were closed after the expulsion of the Germans following World War II. The approximately 1,200 remaining factories were then amalgamated into 17 national enterprises. The industry is concentrated in its traditional location in the northern and northwestern regions of Bohemia, despite transfers of a number of plants to central and eastern Slovakia.

In 1948, the industries employed some 51,000 workers, of which 36,000 were in glass manufacture. The majority of skilled workers in both glass and ceramics manufacture used to be Germans, and both industries suffered after their expulsion. Czechoslovak authorities claim that this loss of skilled labor has been offset by intensive training of Czech and Slovak workers, but the quality of the product appears to have deteriorated.

Both industries produced decorative and utility articles which played an important part in Czechoslovak foreign trade prior to the Communist *coup d'état*. During the interwar years, some 70 per cent of production was exported. In the case of glass, these exports amounted to nearly 7 per cent of the total value of exports in 1937. Since the raw materials for both glass and ceramics industries come almost exclusively from domestic sources, the foreign exchange earning capacity of these industries was substantial and very important to the state. The majority of exports during this period were directed to the West, with the United States and United Kingdom the most important customers. By 1953, the share of glass in Czechoslovak exports had dropped to 3.1 per cent. Due to the absence of demand for decorative lines of production in the Soviet orbit, the Communist regime curtailed such production and converted plants to manufacture of technical lines, such as glass fibers, laboratory and packing glass, electro-technical porcelain, and tiles.

Considerable research effort was initiated in an attempt to utilize glass and ceramics as substitutes for some alloys and nonferrous metals in short supply. It is claimed that molten basalt tubes are now being used instead of manganese steel for drilling in mines, and glass tubing was reportedly installed in dairies and refineries. Although definite priority is given to this type of production, some decorative glass and porcelain in the form of cut glass costume jewelry and fine china are still being manufactured to supply a fraction of the former extensive Western markets.

Current glass production can be divided into three basic categories: hollow glass, such as bottles, containers, scientific glass, and tableware; sheet glass, including window, safety, structural, rolled wire, polished, and mirror glass; and small glassware, such as costume jewelry, Christmas ornaments, lenses, signal glass, tubes, and buttons. Volume of production in these categories for selected years is shown in Table 2.

Table 2. Glass Production, Selected Years 1937-1953
(in thousand metric tons)

Type	1937	1946	1947	1948	1949	1953 (original plan)
Hollow glass	115.0	81.0	120.0	128.4	132.2	137.1
Sheet glass	107.0	96.5	126.3	130.9	135.5	113.7
Small glassware	11.7	5.7	8.4	8.5	9.9	9.5

Sources: 1937-1949, State Statistical Office, *Statisticky zpravodaj,* XII, No. 7-8 (1949), and *idem, Statistical Bulletin of Czechoslovakia,* No. 7 (1948); 1953, Ministry of Information, *The Czechoslovak Economic Five-Year Plan,* p. 30.

Agricultural Processing Industries

The output of agricultural processing industries at the end of the first Five-Year Plan represented 19.8 per cent of the value of Czechoslovak gross industrial production, ranking as the second largest industrial branch, immediately following the machine-building sector. The postwar de-emphasis of consumer goods production is well expressed in this figure, since its share of total industrial output decreased from some 27 per cent in 1937 to 24 per cent in 1948 and was planned to drop to about 22 per cent at the conclusion of the first Five-Year Plan in 1953. Constant underfulfillment of planned targets evidently reduced its share even below the planned figure. The planned development of various sectors of this industry is demonstrated in Table 3.

The industry, which has been completely nationalized since 1950, is under the management of the Ministry of Food Industry. Within the Ministry, seven Main Administrations (*hlavni sprava*) are in charge of the industry's various branches. There are Main Administrations for sugar and candies, alcohol, canned foods and starch, beer, mills and bakeries, meat and fish, and milk and fats. Four national enterprises are outside this structure, being managed directly by the Minister of Food Industry: Czechoslovak Deep Freezing Plants, Czechoslovak Tobacco Industry, Czechoslovak Salt Industry, and Cutisin (production of casings). A provincial organization, the Slovak Food Industry, manages the industry in Slovakia.

Table 3. Gross Value of Actual and Planned Output of Agricultural Processing Industries
(in billion crowns)

Branch	Actual Value 1948 (estimate)	Planned Value 1953 (original plan)	1953 (revised plan)
Sugar	8.7	10.2	12.5
Alcohol	5.3	5.6	....
Beer and malt	5.7	9.6	....
Milling	3.6	4.7	....
Other food	34.5	61.8	....
Tobacco	12.1	12.8	....
Total	69.6	104.7	121.5
Gross industrial output	288.0	454.0	550.0
Agricultural processing (per cent of total)	24	23	22

Sources: Ministry of Information, *The Czechoslovak Economic Five-Year Plan,* p. 32 and 33; Government Ordinance of April 10, 1951 (plan revision), No. 33, *Sbirka zakonu a narizeni Republiky ceskoslovenske* (Collection of Laws and Ordinances of the Czechoslovak Republic).

As of 1950, the Ministry was in charge of 189 national enterprises, which usually consisted of one central and a number of affiliated plants. The division of enterprises among the branches of production was as follows:

Industry	Number of Enterprises
Sugar	100
Alcohol	15
Beer and malt	23
Milling	18
Artificial edible fats	6
Chocolate and candy	17
Fruit and vegetable canning	2
Meat processing	2
Fish processing	2
Food freezing	1
Dairies	3
Total	189

These 189 enterprises represented an amalgamation of some 1,667 former privately-owned plants, 395 confiscated properties, and 34 state-owned enterprises. In addition, some 22,600 small food processing workshops in the Czech lands and an undisclosed number of such small units in Slovakia were also socialized. These were either merged with the national enterprises or formed into cooperative and communal enterprises. In other words, the new national enterprises consisted in some instances of 100 or more former food processing plants or small shops. As of 1950, the division into the national, communal, and cooperative forms of organization within the "socialized sector" was reported as follows:

Enterprises	Per Cent
National	72
Communal	12
Cooperative	16
Total	100

Source: State Statistical Office, *Statisticky zpravodaj,* XII, No. 5 (1950).

There was, however, practically no difference in the structure of these organizations.

Latest available data indicate that as of 1948, some 116,000 persons worked in these industries. This amounted to 7.6 per cent of the total industrial labor force, a situation practically identical to that of 1937, when 7.5 per cent of the total industrial labor was employed in these branches. Some 31 per cent of the employees were women, a proportion higher than in other industrial sectors. The government planned to increase this ratio further in order to release men for employment in heavy industries. Because of the seasonal nature of many of these manufactures, a substantial influx of labor customarily occurs during the peak of the season. Thus, for instance, in the sugar industry the number of workers increases about fourfold as a result of the influx of seasonal labor.

While several branches of the Czechoslovak food processing industries, such as sugar, beer, malt, milling, alcohol, and tobacco were highly developed, others, such as dairies and plants for food preservation, were not. As already indicated, it is to these latter branches that the Communist planners assigned the bulk of capital investment, notably for the construction of dairies and deep freezing and cold storage plants, primarily in Slovakia. Planned outlay in other branches was to remain negligible. Data on actual investment by branches have not been made public.

Despite basically well-developed food processing industries,

Czechoslovakia was a net importer of processed foods prior to World War II, and appears to have remained an importing country up to the present.

Among the most important branches of Czechoslovak agricultural processing industries are the manufacture of sugar, alcohol, beer and malt, dairy products, flour, and tobacco. These are discussed below under separate headings.

Sugar. In Czechoslovakia, sugar is manufactured from domestically grown sugar beets. About 80 per cent of the sugar beet crop is utilized for the manufacture of sugar.

The industry is old, dating back to 1812, and it is heavily concentrated in the sugar beet producing regions of the Czech lands. Out of 105 plants in operation in 1947, only ten were located in Slovakia. There are two types of sugar plants: raw sugar factories, and plants combining sugar production with sugar refining. In 1947, there were 55 of the former and 50 of the latter type of plants in Czechoslovakia, a significant drop from a total of 160 plants in existence in the 1925-30 period.

The peak of production was reached during the early post-World War I period, when the annual output amounted to some 1,200,000 tons of raw sugar. More than half of the output was exported. Subsequently, due to the introduction of international control, both production and export volume decreased. Some 200,000 tons were exported annually in the period immediately preceding World War II. Because of its foreign exchange earning capacity, sugar was often referred to as "white gold."

The prewar peak of output was not reached until 1953. According to official statistics, production of sugar in 1949-50 amounted to 602,000 tons. The first Five-Year Plan originally called for an annual output of 790,000 tons of refined sugar by 1953. This goal was increased in the 1951 plan revision to some 970,000 tons. However, as late as 1955, actual production amounted to no more than 656,800 tons according to official figures released in May 1956. As for exports, the current volume appears to be between 200,000 and 250,000 tons. The bulk of exports is evidently directed to the Soviet Union and its captive states. As early as 1948, the Soviet Union became the sugar industry's largest foreign customer, having received some 70,000 tons in that year; this was more than half of Czechoslovakia's 1948 sugar exports.

Since only minor investments, primarily for maintenance purposes, were contemplated under the first Five-Year Plan, it appears that the government expected to achieve higher production with the existing equipment and without any noteworthy expansion. The industry's production of refined sugar in selected years from 1935-36 to 1955 is shown below:

Year	Thousand Metric Tons
1935/36	486.9
1936/37	604.4
1945/46	396.9
1946/47	533.2
1947/48	313.4
1948/49	564.3
1949/50	602.3
1952	590.0
1953	637.0
1955	656.8

Sources: State Statistical Office, *Prumyslove zpravy* (Industrial Reports), II and III (1947 and 1948); State Statistical Office, *Statisticky zpravodaj,* XIII, No. 1 (1950); United Nations, *Economic Survey of Europe in 1954* (Geneva, 1955), p. 266; *Rude pravo,* May 4, 1956, Supplement.

Alcohol. The bulk of the alcohol produced in Czechoslovakia is manufactured from agricultural products, primarily potatoes, molasses, grain, fruit, and maize. In the pre-World War II period, there were two types of alcohol distilleries: agricultural distilleries, which were small plants with an annual production not exceeding 1,500 hectoliters, mainly processing potatoes; and industrial distilleries, which were large plants, utilizing primarily molasses. Furthermore, some alcohol was produced by fruit distillers.

Alcohol manufacture is located primarily in the Czech lands. According to available data, out of a total of 652 distilleries in existence in 1949, nearly 70 per cent were located in Bohemia and Moravia; some 6,000 workers were employed in this branch of production. Any distinction between the two forms of manufacture mentioned above was eliminated in the process of nationalization, when the alcohol distilleries were fused into fifteen national enterprises.

In addition to the two types of alcohol distilleries, there were some 952 plants producing alcohol from fruit and manufacturing various brandies and liqueurs. Their most common product was *sliwowitz* (plum brandy). In this field, the Communist government planned a most drastic elimination and concentration; out of 952 plants, only 185 were to remain in operation by 1953.

The output peak was achieved in the 1934-37 period, when about 100 million liters of pure alcohol were produced annually. Since 1932, alcohol has been mixed with gasoline and utilized as motor fuel.

About one half of total production was consumed in this manner. According to the first Five-Year Plan, no more than 69,000,000 liters were to be produced in 1953. On the basis of reported plan fulfillment indices, it has been estimated that actual production in 1953 amounted to about 65,000,000 liters. Pure alcohol production figures for selected years from 1935/36 to 1953 are shown below:

Year	Million Liters
1935/36	101.36
1936/37	99.24
1946/47	53.88
1947/48	26.88
1948/49	49.69
1950	56.10
1953 (plan)	69.00

Sources: 1935-49, State Statistical Office, *Prumyslove zpravy,* II and III (1947 and 1948), and *idem, Statisticky zpravodaj,* XIII, No. 1 (1950); 1950, United Nations, *Economic Survey of Europe in 1953,* p. 272; 1953 plan, Ministry of Information, *The First Czechoslovak Economic Five-Year Plan.*

Beer and Malt. Brewing of beer is one of Czechoslovakia's oldest and most renowned industries. Its beginnings date back to the ninth century. It has long been a popular beverage in Czechoslovakia, particularly in the Czech lands, and is often referred to as "liquid bread." Among such beers as those produced in Plzen (Pilsen) and Ceske Budejovice (Böhmisch Budweis) are world renowned, practically the entire beer production was consumed domestically. In 1937, less than 2 per cent of the output was exported.

The prewar peak of production of 1,160 million liters was attained in 1930. In 1937, a total of 830 million liters was produced in 380 breweries. Due to obsolescence of equipment and uneconomical production, a number of breweries did not reopen after World War II. According to latest figures, only 254 breweries were active in 1947. Of these, only 5 per cent were located in Slovakia. The industry in 1947 employed 14,505 workers. In 1949, the country produced 970 million liters, and ranked fifth among the beer manufacturers of the world.

Under the Communist regime, the industry, which is completely nationalized, was to increase production to some 1,300 million liters by 1953. With the exception of reactivation of an idle brewery in Slovakia, this output was to be realized in existing plants. The planned goals appear to have been achieved.

The beer produced is of the light type (8-10 saccharometric degrees) and utilizes domestic raw materials (malt and hops), which are of excellent quality. The malt is manufactured by the breweries themselves or obtained from individual malting plants. In 1947, there were 167 malt producers, of which 135 represented malt producing breweries. This was less than half of the 368 malt producers in existence in 1937. Nationalization fused all manufacturers into two national enterprises.

In the 1930-35 period, the country exported some 80,000 tons of malt annually, nearly 40 per cent of its production, and was the largest malt exporter in Europe. By 1948, exports had dropped to some 15,000 tons. (See Table 4.)

Table 4. Production of Malt and Beer, Selected Years 1936/37-1953

Year	Beer	Malt
	(in million liters)	(in metric tons)
1936/37	828	198,253
1946/47	857	85,794
1947/48	816	118,600
1948/49	930	165,800
1950	1,076	....
1953	1,183	....

Sources: 1936-49, State Statistical Office, *Prumyslove zpravy*, II and III (1947 and 1948), and *Statisticky zpravodaj*, XIII, No. 1 (1950); 1950 and 1953, United Nations, *Economic Survey of Europe in 1953*, p. 272.

Milled Products. The Czechoslovak milling industry developed from small village mills. It processes primarily wheat, rye, barley, and oats. Pulses are milled by a minor number of plants.

The capacity of this industry, which in 1937 consisted of 8,339 mills, was far in excess of domestic requirements. By 1947, the number of plants had been reduced to 5,586, of which 3,889 were located in the Czech lands. The industry then employed some 20,000 workers. Even in this reduced number of plants, available capacity was only about 30 per cent utilized. The vast majority of mills operated on a contractual basis, processing grain for individual clients.

Under the first Five-Year Plan, a further radical concentration of capacities was planned. It is estimated that as a result of the elimination of smaller, less economical mills, about one half of the 1947 capacity still exists. In the remaining plants, only the most essential maintenance and some electrification was to be carried out.

The output of milled wheat and rye, which constitutes the bulk of the milled products, is listed in Table 5.

Table 5. Production of Milled Wheat and Rye, Selected Years 1935/36-1953
(in thousand metric tons)

Year	Milled Wheat	Milled Rye
1936/37	1,326.7	1,077.8
1948	817.2	661.2
1949	691.0	378.0
1953 (plan)	600.0	267.0

Sources: 1936-49, as in Table 4; 1953 plan, Ministry of Information, *The Czechoslovak Economic Five-Year Plan,* p. 33.

Tobacco Products. Since 1918, this branch of manufacture has been a state monopoly, representing before 1945 the only production performed exclusively by the state. In 1950, the monopoly was transformed into a national enterprise to bring its structure into conformity with other nationalized industries.

The industry had 12 plants in 1946, with the majority located in the less developed regions of Slovakia. It employed 3,287 workers that year, two thirds of whom were women. The industry depends heavily on imports of tobacco; 44 per cent was imported from outside the Soviet bloc as late as 1950. However, it was planned to restrict the sources of imports to the orbit countries by 1952.

More than one half of the tobacco industry's production consists of cigarettes, which absorbed the following proportion of raw materials: 39.5 per cent in 1949; 55.4 per cent in 1950; 64.7 per cent in 1951; and 70 per cent in 1952 (planned). Cigarettes produced in Czechoslovakia are of the oriental type. Four-fifths of their production consists of one brand.

In 1951, the industry still worked in one shift, indicating excess of installed capacity. Output of tobacco products is listed in Table 6.

Table 6. Output of Tobacco Products, Selected Years 1937-1953

Year	Cigars (in millions)	Cigarettes (in millions)	Tobacco (in metric tons)
1937	149	11,716	7,133
1948	51	12,984	3,220
1949	....	11,945	
1953 (plan)	60	11,700	3,700

Sources: 1937-49, United Nations, *Statistical Yearbook 1954,* p. 184; 1953 plan, Ministry of Information, *The Czechoslovak Economic Five-Year Plan,* p. 33.

Dairy Products. This industry is among the few agricultural processing branches assigned relatively large investments for expansion purposes. During the interwar period, production in dairies was inadequate, and only about 15 per cent of the total milk production was channeled through the dairies in 1937. At that time, the country had a total of 772 dairies, the majority of which were small creameries. Larger dairies existed only in urban centers. Although some specialties of the industry, such as the Olomouc cake cheese (*syrecky*) and Slovak soft cheese from sheep's milk (*bryndza*) were exported, Czechoslovak dairy product imports were invariably higher than exports throughout the interwar period.

Despite the fact that several large cooperative dairies were constructed during the German occupation, the prewar number of plants was reduced to 374 by 1947. Of these, only 72 were located in Slovakia. The employment that year was, however, reported at 11,500 workers, nearly double the number of employees in 1937, which indicates that the remaining plants were substantially larger than those closed.

The Communist regime planned the construction of an additional 35 dairies under the first Five-Year Plan. According to official plan fulfillment reports, only 30 dairies were constructed. This suggests that some 400 dairies were in existence in Czechoslovakia at the end of 1953. Also reported was the construction of five milk drying plants; no information was released on the planned construction of nine cheese producing plants. Judging from scattered references in the daily press, it nevertheless appears safe to conclude that some of these were completed.

Despite the addition of these capacities, the dairy industry generally failed to meet the planned 1953 goals. Part of this failure was undoubtedly due to the fact that Czechoslovak milk production remained far below prewar levels.

A comparison of planned and actual output of milk and butter in selected years from 1937 to 1953 is presented in Table 7.

Table 7. Output of Milk and Butter, Selected Years 1937-1953

Year	Milk		Butter	
	Actual	Planned	Actual	Planned
	(in million liters)		(in thousand metric tons)	
1937	4,330	—	14.3	—
1946	2,570	—	25.8	—
1947	2,340	2,560	19.1	47.5
1948	2,500	3,240	23.0	50.0
1953	3,200	4,890	34.0	48.7[a]

Sources: Actual output data for 1937-47, State Statistical Office, *Statisticky zpravodaj*, XII, No. 3 (1949); 1948 and 1953, United Nations, *Economic Survey of Europe in 1954*, p. 43; 1947 and 1948 plan targets, *The First Czechoslovak Economic Plan;* 1953 plan, Ministry of Information, *The Czechoslovak Economic Five-Year Plan Act.*

[a] Original target, raised to 52,000 metric tons in the 1951 plan version.

17. FOREIGN TRADE AND FINANCE

Development Before 1948

Although never prominent in foreign trade on a world-wide basis, Czechoslovakia during the interwar period developed into the principal industrial and trading country in Central Europe, next to Germany. In this period, Czechoslovakia's foreign trade represented about 1.5 per cent of the world trade turnover. Considering the extent of Czechoslovak territory and the size of its population, this small figure represented a substantial exchange of goods. In 1937, the last year before Munich, the country's foreign trade represented some 26 per cent of national income, and in 1948, the year of the Communist *coup d'état,* the corresponding figure was 35 per cent.

After a brief period of adjustment to the new market situation following World War I, the peak of Czechoslovak foreign trade was reached in the 1928-29 period, immediately prior to the Great Depression. In 1928, the value of Czechoslovakia's exports amounted to 21.2 billion crowns and that of imports to 19.2 billion, resulting in an active trade balance of 2 billion crowns. Except for 1932, excess of exports over imports was the rule throughout the interwar period, although Czechoslovakia did not need to seek a net export balance since her foreign debt was insignificant. From 1932 until the outbreak of World War II, Czechoslovak foreign trade showed an almost uninterrupted rise. The value of Czechoslovak imports and exports, and the net balance of trade in selected years during the interwar period, are shown in Table 1.

Throughout the interwar period, over one half the imports consisted of industrial raw materials and semi-finished products, primarily those for the textile and leather industries. On the other hand, nearly three quarters of the country's exports was composed of finished goods, with textiles the leading commodity.

Broken down in a somewhat different manner, approximately one third of imports consisted of textile raw materials, of which cotton usually accounted for as much as one half. Another third was taken up by foodstuffs and agricultural products, mainly bread grains, fruit, vegetables, and tobacco. The last third was composed of fuels (coal and crude oil), iron ores, nonferrous metals, and chemicals. In exports, finished textile products amounted to about one third of the total (of which cotton goods represented about one half). Footwear, another product of light industry, represented some 6 per cent of the country's exports. One sixth of total exports consisted of foodstuffs, mainly sugar, barley, malt, hops, fruit, and beer. Another sixth was composed of fuels (coal, coke, and coal briquettes), metals, and minerals. The remainder—approximately one fourth—of exports was about equally divided among machinery and equipment, glass, and china.

Table 1. Czechoslovak Foreign Trade, Selected Years 1922-1937[a]
(in million crowns)

Year	Imports	Exports	Balance
1922	13,436	19,510	+6,074
1924	15,855	16,981	+1,126
1926	15,277	17,755	+2,478
1928	19,191	21,205	+2,014
1930	15,712	14,472	+1,760
1932	7,487	7,343	—144
1934	6,382	7,280	+898
1936	7,909	8,008	+ 99
1937	10,981	11,974	+993

Sources: 1922-1936, State Statistical Office, *Annuaire statistique de la Republique Tchecoslovaque* (Prague, 1938); 1937, United Nations, *Statistical Yearbook 1949-1950* (New York, 1950), p. 356.

[a] Merchandise only, excluding currency and precious metals.

The country's relatively large imports of coal prior to World War II may appear surprising, since Czechoslovakia possesses large coal deposits. The high transportation costs involved in supplying the entire country from domestic sources, however made it preferable to meet the coal requirements of some regions from less distant foreign sources, notably Poland and Germany. Despite large imports, Czechoslovakia remained throughout this period a net exporter of coal.

The trade pattern sketched in the preceding paragraphs remained essentially unchanged throughout the prewar years. Only one basic change developed between the earlier post-World War I years and the period immediately preceding World War II. In an attempt to develop a more self-sufficient economy, a trend characteristic of practically all European countries at that time, Czechoslovakia raised her domestic agricultural production. This resulted in a drop of bread grain imports from about one million tons in 1928 to some 200,000 tons annually during the period 1934-38.

Throughout the interwar period and as late as 1947, the major part of Czechoslovak trade was conducted with other European countries. In 1928, some 70 per cent of Czechoslovak imports came from this source (76 per cent in 1947), while exports to other European countries amounted to about 84 per cent (81 per cent in 1947).

Among the largest European suppliers during the interwar period were Germany (about 24 per cent), the United Kingdom (4.5 per cent), and France (4 per cent). Some 30 per cent of imports originated from overseas, with the United States supplying more than one third (12 per cent of total imports). The largest import item from the United States was cotton.

On the export side, Germany again figures as the largest customer (23 per cent), followed by Austria (15 per cent), continuing trading practices which originated under the Austro-Hungarian monarchy. The United Kingdom imported 7 per cent. The only major customer overseas was the United States, which also purchased 7 per cent of Czechoslovak exports. Among the principal commodities exported to the United States were costume jewelry, glass, china, and leather goods. Trade with the Soviet Union was negligible, amounting to only 1 per cent of the total trade turnover.

During the entire interwar period all trade was in private hands, and there was a gradual shift to markets outside the former Austro-Hungarian territory. The Western and overseas countries, which were the main suppliers of raw materials, were also steadily developing into principal purchasers. The diversification of markets enabled the country to build up its gold and foreign currency reserves, since, except for Germany, trade with these countries was not conducted through clearing accounts.

This favorable development was disrupted by World War II. The first postwar years, however, were marked by the country's rapid progress towards recapturing its former position. With the help of UNRRA deliveries (valued at 260-270 million dollars), which began flowing in immediately after the war, and credits obtained in Western countries, combined with the initiative of the leading private trading companies, Czechoslovakia's foreign trade soon recovered to a level close to "normal."

As Table 2 shows, the commodity structure of Czechoslovakia's foreign trade in the first postwar years differed only slightly from the prewar pattern. The difference reflects mainly wartime emphasis on the production of heavy industrial goods to the detriment of agricultural production; also reflected in the figures is the uncompleted process of rehabilitation, as well as the drought of 1947.

Table 2. Commodity Structure of Foreign Trade, 1937 and 1947
(in per cent of total)

Commodities	Imports 1937	Imports 1947	Exports 1937	Exports 1947
Live animals	1.9	0.3	0.1	0.1
Foodstuffs	11.0	19.0	8.2	11.0
Raw materials and semi-finished products	57.4	57.3	19.8	15.0
Finished products	29.7	23.4	71.9	73.9

Source: State Statistical Office, *Statistical Digest of the Czechoslovak Republic, 1948* (Prague, 1948), p. 97.

During 1947-48, the country continued to rebuild its world-wide trade relations. The Scandinavian countries replaced Germany as Czechoslovakia's major trading partners. While the Soviet Union's share of the total trade turnover increased five or six times relative to the prewar period (amounting after the war to about 6 per cent of the total), it remained substantially below that of the other major European countries. As late as 1947, some 61 per cent of imports and 68 per cent of exports were with European countries, excluding the Soviet bloc, but including Yugoslavia. The structure of Czechoslovak foreign trade by countries of origin and destination in 1937 and 1947 is shown in Table 3.

Table 3. Czechoslovakia's Major Trading Partners in 1937 and 1947
(in per cent of total)

Area	Imports 1937	Imports 1947	Exports 1937	Exports 1947
Europe	69.1	76.4	74.1	80.8
Soviet Union	1.1	6.7	0.8	4.9
Germany	17.4	1.0	15.0	1.8
United Kingdom	6.3	11.7	8.6	6.4
Denmark	0.5	2.8	0.6	2.4
Norway	1.2	2.3	1.6	2.0
Sweden	3.8	6.9	3.4	7.3
France	5.3	3.5	3.8	3.1
Asia	9.1	3.4	7.0	5.4
Africa	5.0	3.9	3.9	3.7
Western Hemisphere	15.3	15.7	14.3	9.5
United States	8.8	10.2	9.2	4.4
Australia	1.3	0.6	0.6	0.4
New Zealand	0.2	0.0	0.1	0.2

Sources: Data for 1937, State Statistical Office, *Statistical Digest of the Czechoslovak Republic 1948*, pp. 95-96; data for 1947, *Ceskoslovenska statistika* (Czechoslovak Statistics) (Prague, 1947).

Thus, up to the Communist *coup d'état* in February 1948, Czechoslovakia continued to gravitate toward the West. This observation is borne out by Czechoslovakia's original decision to participate in the Marshall Plan.

Communist Foreign Economic Policies

It was in the realm of foreign economic relations, about eight months prior to the Communist *coup d'état,* that Czechoslovakia and the world at large learned that the Soviet Union would not tolerate independent action on the part of any country within its sphere. In 1947, Czechoslovakia was in a precarious situation. As a result of a severe drought, nearly half the agricultural production was lost, necessitating large imports of foodstuffs. Nationalization of foreign property in accordance with the President's decrees of 1945 resulted in sizeable foreign indebtedness, as the country accepted liability for the compensation of foreign owners. Czechoslovakia's own foreign investments in neighboring Central and East European countries were lost because of the nationalization carried out in these countries, and the gold and foreign currency holdings of the National Bank were extremely low. In view of this situation, Western countries gradually grew more hesitant to grant Czechoslovakia credits. Czechoslovakia, therefore, found the invitation to participate in the Marshall Plan extremely attractive. In June 1947, after having officially expressed her intention to participate in the Marshall Plan, she was forced to withdraw at the order of the Soviet Union.

After the Communist coup of February 1948, Czechoslovakia's trade with the West was severely restricted and the country was assigned the task of becoming a major supplier of investment goods to the Soviet bloc, a position formerly held by several Western countries, and one for which the Czechoslovak economy was ill equipped. Czechoslovakia was required to expand and develop her heavy industry (steel, power, metal working, machine building) to the detriment of her traditional light industries. Deliveries of heavy industrial products were to be counterbalanced by deliveries of food and raw materials from the orbit. These structural changes in the Czechoslovak economy were soon reflected in the foreign trade structure. The leadership of light industrial exports ceased, and the share of heavy industrial exports increased almost threefold between 1947 and 1951. As of 1953, machinery alone constituted 40 per cent of all goods exported. Imports of cereals increased more than sevenfold, the strong rise in agricultural imports resulting from the de-emphasis of agriculture.

While in 1937 only some 12 per cent of total Czechoslovak trade was conducted with countries now in the Soviet orbit (including Communist China, excluding Yugoslavia), in 1953, 78 per cent of the trade was with this area, marking a full reversal of the prewar pattern. The shift away from the free world markets was not completely the result of Soviet pressure, because Czechoslovakia faced growing buyers' resistance in many of her former Western markets, particularly in the United States. While the motivation in many instances was primarily political, Czechoslovakia's failure to fulfill export obligations on time, deterioration of quality of her products, and her lack of adjustability to commodity trends on the Western markets played an important role. Moreover, Czechoslovak foreign trade, which was fully nationalized by 1949 and organized into some 20 foreign trade state monopolies under the control of the Ministry of Foreign Trade, became highly inflexible and difficult to engage in on the part of free world buyers.

Despite the tendency within the orbit to restrict the flow of trade to the non-orbit area, the Communists recognized that the area's deficiency in certain raw materials and equipment precluded complete isolation from the rest of the world. On the part of Czechoslovakia, this led on one hand to dumping practices in several Western markets in an effort to gain the hard currencies necessary for the purchase of deficient goods. On the other hand, in the case of imports, it resulted in attempts to circumvent the trading restrictions imposed by the Western countries after 1948.

The recent attempts to increase Czechoslovak trade relations with underdeveloped countries of the Near and Far East and Latin America, as well as other extra-orbit countries show that Czechoslovakia remains interested in the development of her extra-orbit trade. The goods being offered in exchange for foodstuffs and raw materials are preponderantly capital goods. The extent of such deliveries, however, is likely to be relatively minor.

Figures on present Czechoslovak holdings of gold and foreign exchange are not available. It is nevertheless safe to assume that with the severe restriction of trade with the West, such resources have diminished considerably. Acute shortage of such holdings seems to have developed as early as mid-1949, when the regime established special stores (*darex*), to sell to the population goods formerly destined for export against payment in foreign currency or precious metal. Trade with the orbit is conducted through clearing accounts and does not involve foreign exchange, since trade deficits are made up by additional deliveries of goods.

Foreign trade, like all other economic activity, is planned. Planning functions in this case are carried out by the State Planning Office, with the assistance of the Ministry of Foreign Trade. The latter, which is in charge of implementing planned tasks, assigns detailed execution to the various trade monopolies under its control. Under this system, all protective devices (tariffs, exchange controls, quotas) are of little importance.

Survey of Foreign Trade under the Communists

Only limited statistical data are available on the extent and regional distribution of foreign trade under the Communists. The value of imports and exports and the resulting trade balance between 1946 and 1951 are shown in Table 4.

Table 4. Value of Foreign Trade, 1937 and 1946-1951
(in million crowns)

Year	Imports	Exports	Balance
1937	10,981	11,974	+ 993
1946	10,308	14,283	+3,975
1947	28,920	28,550	— 370
1948	37,869	37,653	— 216
1949	39,400	40,308	+ 908
1950	34,320	36,700	+2,380
1951	48,650	42,400	—6,250

Sources: 1937, from Table 1; 1946, State Statistical Office, *Statistical Digest of the Czechoslovak Republic 1948,* p. 96; 1947-1948, Ministry of Foreign Trade, *Mesicni prehled zahranicniho obchodu republiky Ceskoslovenske* (Monthly Review of Foreign Trade of the Czechoslovak Republic) (Prague, 1947 and 1948); 1949-1952 United Nations, *Direction of International Trade,* various issues, 1949-1952.

The regional distribution of trade since 1948, which is shown in Table 5, indicates a sharp redirection of the flow of trade away from Western Europe toward the Soviet orbit.

The changes in the composition of trade were equally drastic. While no comprehensive data have been released since 1949, it was reported that between 1937 and 1953 the share of textiles in total exports declined from 25.1 per cent to 6.8 per cent. Glass dropped from 6.6 per cent to 3.1 per cent during the same period. In general, heavy industrial products replaced light industrial commodities as the leading components of export trade.

Table 5. Direction of Foreign Trade, 1937 and 1946-1952
(in per cent of total)

	Imports			Exports		
	Soviet Orbit[a]	Rest of Europe	Non-European West	Soviet Orbit	Rest of Europe	Non-European West
7	11.2	58.3	30.5	12.9	62.6	24.5
6	24.8	61.1	14.1	19.5	66.9	13.6
7	15.0	61.4	23.6	13.3	67.8	18.9
8	29.0	60.4	19.6	31.3	48.6	20.1
9	44.2	32.7	23.1	46.7	26.2	17.1
0	54.5	25.3	20.2	54.8	29.2	16.0
1	59.6	19.0	21.4	61.4	21.1	17.5
2	70.6	29.4		68.2	31.8	

ources: As in Table 4.
Including Communist China; excluding Yugoslavia and Eastern Germany.

Trade with the Soviet Orbit

Since the launching of the first Five-Year Plan, Czechoslovakia's trade with the Soviet orbit has grown rapidly. This growth is illustrated by the tabulation below, showing the 1949 and 1954 indices of the volume of Czechoslovakia's trade with the Soviet Union and the European orbit countries (1948=100):

Country	1949	1954
Soviet Union	157.3	320.7
Poland	134.3	180.2
Romania	147.8	102.0
Hungary	140.3	310.1
East Germany	212.0	695.8
Bulgaria	141.0	209.3
Albania	100.0	316.0

Source: Richard Dvorak, "Vneshnaia Torgovlia Chekhoslovakii" (Foreign Trade of Czechoslovakia), *Vneshnaia Torgovlia* (Foreign Trade) XXV, No. 2 (1955), p. 8.

According to official claims, trade with the Soviet orbit in 1953 represented 78 per cent of Czechoslovakia's total foreign trade turnover. The individual countries accounted for the following percentages:

Country	Per Cent
Soviet Union	35.5
Poland	12.4
Romania	9.0
Hungary	8.8
East Germany	7.5
Bulgaria	3.6
Albania (estimate)	1.2

Source: State Statistical Office, *Planovane hospondarstvi* (Planned Economy), No. 10 (1954), pp. 652-653.

Czechoslovakia's exports to the orbit countries include mainly metallurgical products, industrial machinery, and equipment. Her principal imports are industrial raw materials, particularly metallic ores, metals, and grain.

Intra-orbit trade is currently performed within the broad framework of long-term (five-year) agreements which Czechoslovakia concluded with practically all orbit countries. Most of these initial agreements expired at the end of 1955, the last year before the launching of the second Five-Year Plan. In 1956, five-year plans, as well as trade agreements of the countries within the Soviet orbit, except Bulgaria, were synchronized. Since all Soviet orbit countries have planned economies, these agreements form an integral part of their economic plans. Within the general framework of long-term agreements, specific trade agreements are negotiated each year.

Broad coordination of intra-orbit trade apparently rests with the Council of Mutual Economic Assistance (CEMA), which was established in Moscow in January 1949 under Soviet control and in which all the Soviet orbit countries are represented. The post-World War II growth of the Soviet orbit's share in Czechoslovak foreign trade is illustrated in Table 6.

Table 6. Participation of Soviet Orbit Countries in Czechoslovakia's Foreign Trade, Selected Years 1947-1953 (in per cent of total)

	Share of Soviet Orbit	Share of Soviet Union	
Year	In Total Turnover	In Imports	In Exports
1947	13.8	6.8	4.9
1950	54.7	29.7	25.0
1952	71.8	36.4	31.0
1953	78.0	37.8	27.4

Source: Ministry of Foreign Trade, *Zahranicni obchod* (Foreign Trade), VIII, No. 10 (1953).

Trade with the Soviet Union. Since 1948, the Soviet Union has been Czechoslovakia's most important trading partner, absorbing about one half of Czechoslovak trade with the bloc. The initial Czechoslovak-Soviet five-year trade agreement of December 1947 provided for Czechoslovak annual exports in the value of 5 billion crowns (one hundred million U. S. dollars at the official exchange rate of 50 crowns to one dollar) and imports amounting to some 6 billion. This volume has been substantially increased since then. In autumn 1948, an increase in goods exchange to 18 billion crowns was negotiated. The Soviet Union was to increase substantially its deliveries of industrial raw materials, particularly minerals. In addition, Czechoslovak imports were to include 10,000 tons of cotton, 300,000 tons of wheat, 25,000 tons of meat, and 25,000 tons of fats. In return, the Soviet Union was to receive foundry products valued at some 1.2 billion crowns, heavy industrial products amounting to one billion crowns, cotton fabrics valued at 750 million crowns, rubber goods valued at 690 million crowns, footwear, paper, glass ceramics, and other manufactured goods. In February 1950, a new addition to the long-term agreement was negotiated, according to which Soviet deliveries of cereals, metallic ores, and industrial metals were to be raised further.

On November 3, 1950, about two years before the expiration of the 1947-52 five-year agreement, a new five-year agreement for the period 1951-55 was concluded. This stipulated a goods turnover increase of 150 per cent above the 1948 level. Compared to average deliveries in the 1947-48 period, the Soviet Union's exports of iron ore were to increase by 250 per cent, those of aluminum by 300 per cent, and copper by 400 per cent. In 1954, the Soviet Union accounted for the following percentages of Czechoslovakia's main raw material and food imports: iron ore, 73.7; managanese ore, 90.0; copper, 71.8; aluminum 93.9; petroleum, 72.3; synthetic rubber, 84.8; cotton, 80.5; wool, 37.3; grain, 93.6; and butter, 81.7. Soviet deliveries of grain reportedly amount to about a half of domestic consumption.

In addition to industrial raw materials and food items, Soviet exports to Czechoslovakia in recent years have included agricultural combines, caterpillar tractors, coal mining combines, excavating machinery, road building machinery and special machine tools. Czechoslavakia's exports to the Soviet Union consist largely of finished goods, particularly the products of the country's machine building and metallurgical industries (plant equipment, machine tools, electrical machinery, locomotives, electric motor-coaches, refrigeration equipment, petroleum drilling equipment, river craft, pipes, rails, cables, etc.), as well as light industrial products such as textiles, footwear, and sugar. In addition, exchange of technical information and services of industrial technicians has also taken place on an increasing scale in recent years.

Trade with Poland. Czechoslovakia's economic relations with Poland contain several features which merit special mention. Besides the usual five-year trade agreements calling for Czechoslovak deliveries of such commodities as rolled steel products, industrial machinery and equipment, automobiles, tractors, and footwear, in exchange for Polish coal, paper, zinc, chemicals, electric power, mining machinery and equipment, food and other products, additional agreements were concluded on economic cooperation in the field of transport, joint industrial development, and exchange of technical and scientific information. One of the first results of these agreements was a project for joint construction of a 150 million kilowatt power plant on the Polish-Czechoslovak border. Poland is to construct the plant and provide coal for its operation, while Czechoslovakia is to bear half of the construction costs and to deliver the necessary machinery. After the completion of the project, Czechoslovakia is to receive electric power equivalent to 300,000 tons of coal annually for the adjacent industrial region of Ostrava-Karvina. Under supplementary agreements, Poland also made available to Czechoslovakia port facilities in Szczecin and free navigation on the Oder for 30,000 tons of cargo annually.

Trade with East Germany. Czechoslovak trade with relatively highly industrialized East Germany has shown a pattern of exchange of both semi-fabricated as well as fabricated commodities. Czechoslovakia's principal exports to East Germany are metallurgical coke, steel, chemicals, industrial machinery, kaolin, yarn, textiles, footwear, hops, malt, food, motorcycles, furniture, and leather goods; her main imports from East Germany are printing, textile, and wood-working machinery, mining and construction equipment, chemicals, fertilizers, photographic supplies, and watches.

Trade with Other East-Central European Countries. In recent years, Czechoslovakia has figured prominently in the industrialization program of Romania, Hungary, Bulgaria and Albania as a major supplier of industrial machinery and equipment in exchange mainly for industrial raw materials and food.

Exports to Romania include mainly machine tools, rolled steel, equipment for the chemical industry, and coke. In addition, Czechoslovakia is to supply all the equipment and machinery required for the implementation of the Romanian ten-year plan for electrification. In return, Romania supplies Czechoslovakia with crude petroleum and petroleum products, corn and grain, timber, and other raw materials.

The list of Czechoslovak exports to Hungary includes machinery and equipment for electric power production and for chemical, leather, textile, and food processing industries, tractors and other agricultural machinery, metallurgical coke, coking coal, timber, cellulose, newsprint, and magnesite. Czechoslovakia's imports from Hungary include agricultural products (wheat, rye, corn, rice, meat and meat products, fats, fish, eggs, fruit and vegetables) industrial raw materials (asphalt, paraffin, pharmaceutical raw materials, petroleum, and brown coal) as well as trucks and electric motor-coaches. Furthermore, in a special agreement aimed at the development of the aluminum industry in both countries, which was signed in 1951, Czechoslovakia agreed to supply Hungary with machinery, equipment, and electric power, in exchange for Hungarian bauxite.

Bulgaria receives from Czechoslovakia mainly industrial machinery and equipment, coke, motor vehicles, railroad equipment and rolling stock, as well as some industrial raw materials. In exchange, Czechoslovakia receives grain, tobacco, iron ore, fertilizers, chemicals, fruit, and vegetables.

Exports to Albania include industrial machinery, rolled steel, chemical products, paper and paper products, and some consumer goods. Imports include mainly chromium ore, asphalts, furs, fruit, and medicinal herbs.

Trade with Communist China. Czechoslovakia's first trade agreement with Communist China was signed in 1950. In 1953, Czechoslovakia accounted for about 29 per cent of Communist China's trade with the European countries of the Soviet bloc. Main articles of export to Communist China include metallurgical products and machinery, particularly equipment for electric power stations and sugar refineries, machine tools, hoisting equipment, dredging machinery, diesel motors, large capacity trucks, and telecommunication equipment, as well as chemical and paper products. In return, Czechoslovakia imports primarily iron ore, nonferrous metals, raw materials for textile and leather industry, vegetable oils, rice, tea, spices, and fruit.

Trade with the Rest of the World. By 1953, Czechoslovak trade with the non-orbit area was at its lowest point, amounting to only 23 per cent of the country's total trade turnover. The steady decrease of Czechoslovak trade with non-orbit countries is evident from the figures in Table 7.

Despite strong pressure within the orbit tending to absorb Czechoslovak disposable resources, Czechoslovakia has attempted to maintain contact with its old partners in the West to a greater degree than the other orbit states. Thus, Czechoslovakia was the only country among the captive states which remained a member of GATT (General

Agreement on Tariffs and Trade), the International Monetary Fund, and the World Bank. At the end of 1954, she was expelled from the two latter organizations for failure to comply with their charters.

Table 7. Czechoslovakia's Share in World Trade, Excluding Intra-Orbit Trade, 1948-1953
(in per cent of total)

Year	Czechoslovak Exports	Czechoslovak Imports
1948	.89	.75
1949	.73	.64
1950	.57	.42
1951	.41	.36
1952	.31	.33
1953	.30	.30

Source: Ministry of Foreign Trade, *Zahranicni obchod,* IX, No.4 (1954).

In value terms, Czechoslovak trade with the West in 1951 amounted to about 250 million 1937 US dollars, approximately 62 per cent below the prewar level. Principal exports to this area consist of traditional Czechoslovak commodities, mainly sugar, malt, hops, glass, as well as some products of her metalworking industries, and vehicles. The majority of imports is composed of raw materials (iron ore, wool), machinery and equipment, instruments, pharmaceuticals, and chemicals.

By 1951, no single West European country was a principal trading partner of Czechoslovakia. Her largest West European partners in 1951 are listed in Table 8.

Table 8. Czechoslovakia's Principal Trading Partners in Western Europe, 1951
(in million current US dollars)

Country	Czechoslovak		
	Imports	Exports	Turnover
Sweden	26.3	21.6	47.9
Austria	23.8	21.7	45.5
Switzerland	22.1	17.0	39.1
West Germany	20.8	17.0	37.8
United Kingdom	10.8	25.5	36.3
Benelux countries	17.1	8.4	25.5
France	9.9	11.2	21.1

Source: United Nations, *Direction of International Trade,* 1952, various issues.

As Table 9 shows, the most drastic decline in trade occurred with overseas countries, particularly with the United States, which in 1937 was Czechoslovakia's second ranking partner on a world-wide basis.

Table 9. Czechoslovak Trade with the United States, 1949-1952 (in million current US dollars)

Year	Imports	Exports	Balance
1949	21.6	19.9	— 1.7
1950	10.1	26.5	+16.4
1951	1.0	23.5	+22.5
1952	0.02	1.50	+ 1.48

Sources: United Nations, *Direction of International Trade,* 1949-1953, various issues.

During this period, the most important Czechoslovak export articles to the United States were textiles, nonmetallic minerals, glass, china, semiprecious stones, and chemicals (primarily coal derivatives). These items amounted to about two thirds of all exports in 1950. The largest import was cotton, totaling about one half of all imports in 1950. Since 1950, cotton has not been imported from the United States.

A considerable part of the decrease in Western trade has been due to an export licensing system introduced by the United States in 1948 and later adopted by other Western countries. The effects of this system, which amounted to an actual embargo on a number of goods, were felt especially after the start of the war in Korea and caused Czechoslovakia to introduce a costly program of research for substitutes for unavailable raw materials.

In an effort to offset the effects of trade restrictions, Czechoslovakia has attempted to increase its trading relations with several underdeveloped areas of the Middle and Far East and Latin America. In the Near East, Egypt is prominent as a supplier of cotton. Czechoslovak imports from this country, amounting to 27 million US dollars during 1951, are greater than those from any other non-orbit country. In September 1955, a trade agreement was signed providing for the exchange of Egyptian cotton for Czechoslovak armaments. Data on the volume of these deliveries have not been published.

Trade with Southeast Asia (India, Pakistan, Malaya, and Indonesia) allegedly grew some 65 per cent between 1949 and 1951. As of the beginning of 1954, Czechoslovak sources claimed that Czechoslovakia imported 50 per cent of Indian iron ore exports. Malaya is a source of rubber and tin, while Australia is the principal purchaser of Czechoslovak manufactured goods in the area.

In Latin America, Argentina and Brazil represent the two major Czechoslovak partners, exporting raw materials in exchange for Czechoslovak finished goods.

Most non-orbit trade is conducted on the basis of one-year trade and payments agreements, which usually stipulate the overall values and commodity quotas involved. There are also some long-term (usually five-year) agreements, which provide the framework for prospective goods exchange, with specific details negotiated annually. By these agreements, the signatory government is committed to grant only export and import licenses for goods in quantities listed. For the Western partner, actual performance under the agreement is left to the individual private companies, which negotiate the terms of delivery, quality, and price with the Czechoslovak export monopolies. Payments are effected through a clearing account, which usually provides for a minor reciprocal credit. Imbalances outstanding at the end of a period are settled according to the agreement provisions, either in gold or agreed currency, or by additional commodity deliveries.

Many trading partners in the West are willing to negotiate this type of trade agreement because of their desire to receive compensation for their nationalized property, as portions of Czechoslovak export earnings are usually set aside for this purpose.

Finance

Apart from minor amounts of credit resulting from the trade agreements discussed above, Czechoslovakia does not now possess any credits in the West. Only fragmentary information is available on credits granted within the orbit.

While it is reasonable to assume that small clearing credits, similar to those in the West, exist in orbit trade agreements, the only specific information indicates that Czechoslovakia received a short-term loan from the Soviet Union in 1947, amounting to about 24 million US dollars to finance the purchase of large quantities of grain following the 1947 drought. The loan was repayable in 1949. Subsequently, during the 1948 negotiations with the Soviet Union, Czechoslovak sources reported another loan in gold and foreign currency amounting to some 120 to 200 million US dollars, allegedly to enable Czechoslovakia to meet its obligations toward Western countries and to make the rejection of the Marshall Plan offer more palatable.

Although statistics on the Czechoslovak postwar debtor-creditor position are lacking, circumstantial evidence indicates that the country has become a net debtor, in contrast to the prewar situation. After World War II, Czechoslovak gold and foreign exchange assets decreased substantially. Her foreign investments, totaling some 160 million US dollars before World War II were lost either through nationalization (e.g. in Romania and Yugoslavia) or because of migration from Czechoslovakia of nationals holding the investments.

Data on the Czechoslovak foreign debt, which consists of obligations dating back to World War I, are likewise not available for more recent years. Latest reported information on Czechoslovak foreign obligations is listed below (in million US dollars):

Year	Long-Term	Short-Term
1945	355.4	25.9
1948	376.1	82.3
1949	323.2	53.0 (approximately)

Nationalization of Foreign Assets

Deterioration of Czechoslovak foreign financial relations with the West, prior to the Communist coup, was largely due to the nationalization of foreign assets. Nationalization of both domestic and foreign property started in 1945, on the basis of legislation contained in the Presidential Decree of October 1945, and continued after February 1948. As a result, Czechoslovak foreign indebtedness increased and the Western countries concerned, mostly the largest trading partners, grew more and more reluctant to grant credits which would further increase Czechoslovak indebtedness.

Czechoslovakia generally recognized the compensation claims of these countries. Up to the present, compensation agreements for nationalized property have been negotiated with the United Kingdom, France, Belgium, Luxembourg, Switzerland, and the Netherlands. A major exception, where no compensation agreement has been reached, is the United States. In the case of Sweden, most claims were negotiated privately by the Swedish companies concerned. In all other cases, payment was usually tied to trade agreements and was met from Czechoslovak export surpluses. Claims usually involve personal property, real property, patents, licenses, and franchise contracts.

The approximate value of the claims or negotiated settlements is listed in Table 10.

Table 10. Foreign Claims Against Nationalized Properties
(in million US dollars)

Claimant	Amount of Claim or Settlement	Method of Payment
United Kingdom	22.4	From export surplus; in 18 annual installments.
France	10.6	No definite settlement as yet; payments effected from export surpluses.
Switzerland	16.5	6.5 million US dollars paid in 1948; balance in 20 semiannual installments from export surplus.
Belgium	1.0	Unknown.
Netherlands	5.0	In 10 annual installments; some claims settled privately.
Sweden	29.0	Bulk settled privately.

Source: Compiled from various trade agreements between Czechoslovakia and the countries listed.

Balance of Payments

No information is available on the Czechoslovak balance of payments after the Communist accession to power. Comparison of the 1937 balance sheet with that of 1948, however, indicates a deterioration of the Czechoslovak postwar position. In the prewar period, the merchandise trade balance was usually more than sufficient to offset any deficit in the invisible item on the current account. Net deficits on the current account during this period usually resulted from payments of insurance, foreign representation, commissions, license fees, and so forth. Receipts for transportation of goods in transit and for foreign travel usually showed a credit balance.

Since World War II, there has been a strong increase in Czechoslovak transportation and insurance costs, while receipts from these sources declined, increasing the total deficit on the invisible account. At the same time, export surpluses were not sufficient to cover these charges, resulting in a passive balance on the current account. The 1948 deficit was met by drawing on various loans and by net sales of gold. As for private capital, the net inflow in 1937 amounted to nearly 10 million US dollars, while in 1948 only 2 million US dollars entered the country.

Gold and Foreign Exchange Holdings

During the interwar period, Czechoslovakia was able to accumulate adequate gold and foreign exchange reserves, which in 1938 totaled some 137 million US dollars. The German occupation and financing the war effort dissipated more than one half of these assets. After 1938, all gold deposited in Prague was seized by the Germans and utilized for their war operations; some 29.8 million US dollars in gold on deposit in London was placed at the disposal of the Czechoslovak government in exile.

At the end of World War II, there remained no more than 52.8 million US dollars in gold and foreign currency holdings.

Figures released by Czechoslovak authorities for several postwar years indicate that the country never regained the level of its prewar holdings (see Table 11).

Table 11. Gold and Foreign Exchange Holdings of the Czechoslovak National Bank, Selected Years 1937-1949
(in million US dollars)

Year	Gold	Foreign Exchange	Total
1937	92.2	16.8	109.0
1938	94.6	42.7	137.3
1945	35.1	17.7	52.8
1946	11.5	94.3	105.8
1947	18.9	77.0	95.9
1948	17.0	66.7	83.7
1949	....	....	60.1

Sources: International Monetary Fund, *International Financial Statistics,* No. 12 (1950), and Zivnostenska Bank (Prague), *Monthly Bulletin,* January 1949.

A seemingly favorable increase in foreign exchange holdings appears to have developed in 1946. However, 78.6 million US dollars of the total reserve that year was in nonconvertible currencies. A steady decrease in holdings occurred thereafter, especially following the Communist coup.

The last detailed breakdown of the National Bank foreign exchange holdings is available for September 30, 1947. At that time, the total amounted to 18.9 million US dollars, divided as follows: bullion in vaults, 1.6 million; gold seized by Germany during occupation and recovered by Allied forces, 14.3 million; gold on deposit with Bank of International Settlement, Basel, 3.0 million.

It is evident that the largest part of the Czechoslovak gold holdings listed above is not actually a holding, but represents a claim against the pool of gold recovered in Germany by the Allied forces and held by the Allied Tripartite Gold Commission in Brussels. The latter has the Czechoslovak claim under consideration, along with the claims of other states whose gold reserves were taken to Germany during the war.

Exchange Rates

Through stringent exchange controls introduced during the 1930's, the period of world-wide depression, Czechoslovakia succeeded to a considerable degree in maintaining the stability of her currency. Throughout the interwar period, the Czechoslovak crown generally followed the trend set by the US dollar. The gold content of the crown, which stood at 44.58 milligrams in 1934, was reduced to 37.15 milligrams in 1936. In relation to the US dollar, this represented a ratio of 1 crown to 4.2 cents or 3.5 cents, respectively. The latter exchange rate was maintained up to the time of World War II. Throughout these years, sale of foreign exchange to the National Bank was compulsory and both export and import trade was subject to licensing.

After World War II, the currency reform of 1945 again revalued the crown, which was made equal to two US cents. This rate was accepted by the International Monetary Fund. Foreign trade licensing and limitation of transfers of domestic currency abroad helped to maintain the official exchange rate, although illegal black market trading usually showed the US dollar at five or six times the official rate.

The second postwar currency conversion of June 1953 raised the gold content and tied the crown to the ruble at a rate of 1.80 crowns to 1 ruble. The relationship to other currencies was determined through the ruble and resulted in the exchange rate of 1 crown to 14 US cents.

18. DOMESTIC TRADE, BANKING, AND FINANCE

Edward Ames

Developments Before 1948

Prewar Institutions

The prewar Czechoslovak financial structure was characterized by considerable regional differences in degree of development. Within the more developed Czech lands (including the German areas), there was a wide variety of well-developed financial institutions. Some idea of the difference in the financial development of the two parts of the country is provided by the comparisons in Table 1.

Table 1. Loans and Credits in Financial Institutions in the Czech Lands and in Slovakia, End of 1937
(in million crowns)

	Czech Lands	Slovakia	Total
Long-term loans	28,038	1,016	29,054
Short-term loans	14,644	1,322	15,966
Current account credit	20,666	1,427	22,093
Total	63,348	3,765	67,113

Source: State Statisitcal Office, *Statistical Digest of the Czechoslovak Republic, 1948* (Prague, 1948), p. 80.

There were four main types of credit institutions: commercial banks, financial institutions owned by provinces and municipalities, credit cooperatives, and the government-owned Postal Savings Bank. The commercial banks were set up under Austrian or, in the case of the Slovak banks, Hungarian law, as amended in 1924. They were licensed and audited by the Ministry of Finance, and were required to issue savings deposit books and to maintain minimum reserves. Control of interest rates by law began in 1935, after a period of agreements among the banks. The Czechoslovak commercial banks, like those of neighboring countries, had important investments in industrial enterprises, which in many cases they controlled. Most of the larger banks were partly owned by foreign interests. The Czechoslovak government owned about one third of the stock of four banks, which together possessed about a quarter of all the capital of the commercial banks. This stock, however, appears to have been acquired to relieve shortages of funds during crises, rather than as an instrument of control.

There were originally six provincial banks, established in the provinces of Bohemia, Moravia, and Silesia during the late nineteenth century. By the 1930's their number had been reduced by merger to four, of which one, Zemska Banka (The Land Bank of Bohemia) held 60 per cent of the total assets. After 1928, the boards of these banks were appointed by the national government rather than by the provinces. Their capital consisted of irredeemable bonds; most of their assets (in contrast to those of the commercial banks) were in long-term loans, particularly to municipalities, in railroads and public utilities, and in securities.

The savings banks were originally private institutions, but in 1920, with two exceptions, they were converted into municipal institutions. After 1934, they were subject to reserve requirements. The remainder of their assets was invested in government securities, mortgages, and municipal loans, or deposited with the commercial banks.

Cooperative credit associations provided credit to agriculture and to small business. There were various legal types, though all were subject to uniform controls over interest rates, audit, and so forth. There were twenty-two federations of credit associations, based upon linguistic, religious, and political groupings in the population.

Central banking functions were shared by several institutions. The National Bank was the bank of issue; it was a private institution, but the government held one third of its stock and appointed a third of the directors, as well as the governor of the bank. The Postal Savings Bank was the fiscal agent and depository of the government. In addition, after 1931, it received savings deposits. In common with the prewar Austro-Hungarian postal savings system, of which it was a successor, it operated a checking service through the giro system; this was the method by which moderate-income families usually made check payments. The monthly turnover of Postal Savings payments in 1937 was 29 billion crowns, compared to 10 billion through the Prague, Brno, and Bratislava clearing houses combined, and 22 billion through the National Bank. The assets of the bank consisted mainly of short-term government securities; the bank usually acted as head of syndicates in charge of government security issues. Finally, the Rediscount and Lombard Institute was established in 1934 and charged with receiving the required reserve accounts of commercial banks, savings banks, and insurance agencies. The Institute, which was administered by the Zemska Bank, invested these funds, together with borrowings from the National Bank, in government securities, with the dual objective of providing liquid resources for the banking system and of ensuring the marketability of government securities.

The National Bank tended to have only an indirect role in supplying reserves to the banking system, since open-market operations were actually conducted by the Rediscount Institute, even though the funds were provided by the National Bank.

The Occupation Period

The territories severed from Czechoslovakia by the Munich Pact were incorporated directly into Germany in 1938, and their financial institutions were absorbed by equivalent German institutions. The National Bank and the Postal Savings Bank were divided into separate institutions for the Protectorate of Bohemia-Moravia and for Slovakia in 1939. The Rediscount Institute, operating solely in the Protectorate, was not divided. In 1939, when the partition was completed, separate currencies were set up: the crown (designated K, in place of the Czechoslovak crown, Kc) in the Protectorate, and the Slovak crown (designated Ks) in Slovakia. The gold and foreign exchange reserves of the National Bank of Bohemia-Moravia and of the National Bank of Slovakia (successors to the National Bank of Czechoslovakia) were transferred to the Reichsbank. Initially, the two currencies were established on a parity; the exchange rate of the Czech crown with the Reichsmark, however, was set at 10:1, while that of the Slovak crown was set at 11.62:1. The cross-rate between the two crowns was maintained at 1:1, however, until the German-Czech customs frontier was abolished on October 1, 1940. At that time, the cross-rate dropped to K 10=Ks 11.62.

The wartime period was characterized by an extremely rapid expansion of the money supply, particularly after mid-1941. The cause of the expansion was the extraordinarily large accumulation of Reichsmark balances by banking institutions, reflecting the requisitioning of goods by the German authorities as well as the remittances of large numbers of Czechoslovak workers sent to work in German industry. In Bohemia-Moravia, the note circulation increased from 6.3 billion crowns at the end of 1939 to 40.5 billion in June 1945, and the deposits of the National Bank grew from 1 billion to 26.5 billion. All assets of the Bank other than Reichsmark assets declined from 10 billion to 5 billion, while the Reichsmark assets grew from nothing to 91 billion. In Slovakia, the increase in Reichsmark assets was less pronounced (this region having less to offer the German war effort), accounting for only 60 per cent of the increase in note circulation. On the other hand, the Slovak government had to borrow more from the central bank than did the Protectorate, so that the expansion of central bank credit was about equally rapid in the two parts of the country.

The other banks were subjected to a variety of pressures during the occupation. The separation of the "Sudeten" territories had a considerable effect upon the number of branches of the large commercial banks; the savings banks, municipally owned, were affected mainly through their absorption into the Reichsmark currency area. Under the anti-Semitic legislation of the period, some consolidation of the commercial banks was carried out. The Kreditanstalt der Deutschen and other banks owned by Sudeten German interests were the beneficiaries of much of the reorganization. Immediately before the occupation, the powers of the Ministry of Finance to regulate and reorganize the banking system had been greatly strengthened. In 1941-42, this regulatory apparatus was transformed into a Central Federation of Banking, which exercised regulatory powers over the banks in the manner of the trade associations favored by Nazi policy within Germany. The Federation itself was dominated by German personnel.

The large increase in central bank credit led to a very great expansion in the deposits of commercial banks (see Table 3). At the end of 1945, sight liabilities of those banking institutions for which data are available had increased from 23 billion to 126 billion crowns, while savings deposits rose from 18 to 87 billion. Only a small part of this increase seems to have been invested or loaned out. The cash resources of the banking system rose by 112 billion; security holdings rose only 26 billion, while 29 billion of savings bank assets were in blocked Reichsmarks. These last were probably the assets of banks in the Sudeten territories. Loans increased by only 2 billion crowns. The increase in security holdings probably represented mainly borrowing by the puppet governments, which borrowed a total of almost 46 billion crowns from all sources. Of the Slovak borrowings of 12 billion, probably half came from the Slovak National Bank. However, very little of the 33 billion borrowed by the Protectorate came from the National Bank of Bohemia-Moravia. In the absence of any large non-bank market for these securities, the banks probably absorbed most of the balance.

It is not possible to give an accurate description of price movements during the war, partly because of the absence of data on Slovakia, and partly because the official price indices for Bohemia-Moravia probably do not take into account changes in black market prices or the prices of goods sold directly in towns by the rural popu-

Slovakia,[a] 1939-1945 (in million crowns)

Year[b]	Province	Assets			Liabilities			
		Gold and Foreign Exchange	Reichsmark Assets	Other Assets	Notes	Deposits	Other Liabilities[c]	Balance Sheet Totals
1939	Bohemia-Moravia	2401	—	7645	6345	1054	2125	10046
	Slovakia	57	—	1730	1392	208	87	1787
1940	Bohemia-Moravia	2285	6947	1908	6453	1560	2584	11140
	Slovakia	108	398[d]	1641	1657	207	181	2147
1941	Bohemia-Moravia	2299	12844	1405	9398	2800	3805	16548
	Slovakia	97	845[d]	1697	2023	147	364	2639
1942	Bohemia-Moravia	2243	17299	1337	14089	1666	4581	20879
	Slovakia	78	1575[d]	1915	2742	177	541	3568
1943	Bohemia-Moravia	2290	34220	1359	24073	3210	10042	37869
	Slovakia	116	1900[d]	2466	3532	291	542	4482
1944	Bohemia-Moravia	2315	56851	5679	34879	6435	22975	64845
	Slovakia	62	3500[d]	5501	6489	1676	751	9036
1945	Bohemia-Moravia (June)	2304	91046	2748	40539	26548	28453	96098
	Slovakia (March 7)	63	3600[d]	7591	7570	2905	653	11254

Sources: National Bank of Bohemia-Moravia, *Monthly Bulletin* and periodic balance sheets (Prague, 1939-1945); Bank for International Settlements, National Bank of Slovakia Balance Sheets in the *Central Bank Balance Sheet Series* (Basel, Switzerland, 1939-1945).

[a] It is probably not admissible to add the two to obtain a total for Czechoslovakia (excluding the "Sudeten" territory), since the exchange rates were not on a par. On the other hand, the exchange rates do not necessarily reflect the actual changes in purchasing power of the two currencies. In the circumstances, it is probably best to leave the two series separate.

[b] Except for 1945, refers to end of December.

[c] Excluding capital accounts, which make up the entire difference between the sum of the liabilities listed here and the balance sheet totals.

[d] Estimated from balance sheet detail published by the Bank for International Settlements.

Table 3. Consolidated Balance Sheets of Selected Czechoslovak Financial Institutions, 1940 and 1945
(in million crowns)

	Commercial Banks		Provincial Banks		Savings Banks		Total	
	1940	1945	1940	1945	1940	1945	1940	1945
Assets								
Cash	459	440	188	189	168	677	815	1306
Deposits with financial institutions	1565	40827	517	31455	2379	44373	4461	116655
Loans and bills	8097	13978	8261	7771	8100	4809	24458	26558
Securities	8297	22208	5942	14337	5237	9277	19476	45822
Participations	623	1531	—	—	39	22	662	1553
Other assets	786	1538	252	1231	762	2121	1800	4890
Blocked Reichsmarks	—	—	—	—	—	29477	—	29477
Liabilities								
Savings deposits	4550	13403	1411	2773	11763	70843	17724	87019
Sight liabilities	12811	63718	6923	46297	2937	16309	22671	126324
Bonds	210	221	5935	3834	262	115	6407	4170
Capital and other	2256	3180	891	2079	1723	3489	4870	8748
Balance sheet totals	19827	80522	15160	54983	16685	90756	51672	226361

Sources: Czechoslovak National Bank, *Monthly Bulletin*, various issues.

lation. These, of course, are not covered in the official indices. The indices, however, indicate increases of 40 per cent in weekly wages, and of 56 per cent in the cost of living (probably measured in official prices). Available price and wage indices for the period from 1940 to April 1944 (1939=100) are shown in Table 4.

Table 4. Price and Wage Changes in Bohemia-Moravia, 1939-1944
(Index 1939 = 100)

Year	Wholesale Prices	Cost of Living	Construction Costs	Weekly Wages
1940	125	123	131	124
1941	136	144	148	132
1942	141	156	150	137
1943	143	153	148	139
1944 (April)[a]	145	156	149	140

Source: Statistisches Jahrbuch fuer das Protektorat Boehmen-Maehren, 1942-1944.

[a] Later wartime data are not available.

The Transition Period, 1945-1948

In 1945, Czechoslovakia had three principal problems in the monetary sphere: unification of the currency, by eliminating the separate systems existing in the former Protectorate, in the German-annexed territories, and in Slovakia; control of inflation; and re-establishment of a banking system.

In addition to the central bank notes, which had rapidly expanded, the Czechoslovak currency included Protectorate notes (10 billion crowns were outstanding in June 1944, the last date for which information is available), as well as German currency (in the "Sudeten" territories) and occupation currency of both German and Czech-Soviet occupation forces. These various currencies were taken out of circulation in a currency conversion in October 1945, which re-established a Czechoslovak crown (abbreviated *Kcs* to distinguish it from the prewar crown, *Kc,* and the wartime crowns, *K* and *Ks*). This conversion took place on a 1:1 basis. In order to limit the purchasing power of individuals and hence the inflationary trend, limitations were put upon the actual currency paid. Individuals were allowed to receive only 500 crowns, and enterprises could draw only one month's payrolls. Balances above these figures were placed in special blocked accounts. Although payrolls had to be met in new currency, transfers among blocked accounts were permitted until the end of 1945 to meet obligations incurred prior to the conversion (including tax liabilities). These transactions were supposed to cease at the end of the year.

The currency conversion necessitated the blocking of large amounts of assets and deposits, and in effect the books of the National Bank and other financial institutions were started afresh. Until mid-1947, however, the pre-conversion accounts were continued on the books of the various banks, and movements in the various accounts (see Table 5) indicate that there was deblocking of about 23.6 billion crowns during 1946, and of about 10.4 billion during the first half of 1947. The accounting of these deposits has not been well explained, and there is some divergence between the data on blocked deposits and monthly estimates by the National Bank, which cannot be explained by known changes in the volume of blocked assets.

At the same time that the currency conversion took place, the commercial banks were nationalized. The nationalization decree provided that compensation for the holders of stocks in the commercial banks should follow the general rules laid down in the general law on nationalization. The banks were to be managed by a committee consisting of a chairman, vice chairman, and five members. Two of the members were to be elected by the staff of the bank, subject to approval of the Minister of Finance; the remainder were to be appointed by the Minister of Finance. These new regulations amounted basically to a continuation of the control functions of the Ministry as established under the Protectorate. The principal difference was that the individual banks, instead of being privately owned and subject to a federation of the Nazi type, were now state owned and subject to very similar control by the Ministry of Finance. For the early postwar period, therefore, the banking system consisted, as before, of a central bank which had relations with commercial banks on much the same formal basis as in the late 1930's or the war period.

Analysis of the balance sheets of the banks is complicated by the fact that the banks (other than the National Bank) do not distinguish clearly between blocked assets and deposits and those which were free. It is possible, however, to give some indication of the course of the money supply, and of the principal factors affecting it (see Table 5). The note circulation increased steadily from the level of 28.2 billion at the end of 1945, and passed the wartime peak of 52 billion (May 1945) in the last quarter of 1947. At the same time, current accounts rose from 11.5 billion to 54 billion. This level, however, was still below the 70 billion of (blocked) current accounts existing at the end of 1945. The rise in note circulation was thus more marked, by comparison with wartime developments, than the rise in deposits. The increase in the money supply was principally due to an increase in bank credit and to unblocking the preconversion deposits. Savings deposits increased from almost nothing right after the conversion to a total of 27.5 billion at the end of 1947, and these were the main factors offsetting the inflationary effect of the credit expansion.

Table 5. Factors Affecting Money Supply, 1946-1947
(in million crowns)

	Level at End of			Change During	
	1945	1946	1947	1946	1947
ıey Supply					
rency in circulation	28,197	46,577	61,699	+18,380	+15,122
rent accounts	11,501	42,471	54,327	+30,970	+11,856
Total	39,698	89,048	116,026	+49,350	+26,978
tors Affecting Money Supply					
ding by National Bank	3,520	7,899	17,436	+ 4,379	+ 9,537
ding by other banks	83,246	114,943	128,284	+31,697	+13,341
ings deposits	796	15,209	27,466	—14,413	—12,257
d and foreign exchange	2,645	5,279	4,793	+ 2,634	— 486
cked deposits	257,936	234,361	—	+23,575[b]	+10,443[b]
ıer				+ 1,478	+ 5,610

ources: Czechoslovak National Bank, *Monthly Bulletin,* 1945-1947, various issues.
Sign indicates effect on money supply.
These are the net decreases in blocked deposits for 1946 and the first half of 1947. *Monthly Bulletin of the National Bank* indicates an average monthly release of 50 million (21,000 per year) in 1946, but only 3,680 in the first half of 1947. In 1947, blocked deposits were transferred to the Currency Liquidation Fund. According to the National Bank, only 78 million were unblocked during the last half r. It is not possible to reconcile these two sets of figures.

Domestic Trade and Finance Since 1948

The Communist *coup d'état* of February 1948 was followed by an extensive reorganization of the entire economic structure of the country; the numerous changes in trade and financial policies described below were thus a part of much broader changes. They involved a transformation of domestic institutions into replicas of Soviet institutions. These administrative changes, however, are more than a slavish copying of Soviet practices. The first Five-Year Plan (1949-53) adopted in the fall of 1948, and accelerated in 1951, would in any case have necessitated important modifications in the financial structure established in 1945.

Reorganization of Trade

The internal trade policy of Czechoslovakia is closely connected with price, investment, and monetary policy, as well as with the general attitude of the government toward the various social groups. The government's objective was in part to hold down the prices received by producers. In the case of agriculture, the policy aimed at eliminating private agriculture; in the case of industry, it aimed at holding down the funds available for wage increases, or for unauthorized investment.

Retail Trade. This sector has been almost completely socialized. While in 1946, about 88 per cent of all retail trade was in private hands, by 1949 the private share had dropped to 46 per cent, and by 1952 had almost vanished. The socialized stores in the urban areas are primarily state owned. In the rural areas, they are mainly consumer cooperatives in form, although they are in fact dominated by local government agencies and the Ministry of Trade. The function of the rural stores is not confined to selling goods to the farm population, for they also purchase farm goods remaining in the possession of farmers after the completion of compulsory deliveries. To some extent, the sales to farmers by these stores seem to be conditional upon sales of farm produce by farmers to the stores.

Wholesale Trade. The nationalization of wholesale trade followed a pattern slightly different from that of the nationalization of industry. Most of the wholesale firms were nationalized only after the February 1948 *coup d'état.* From 1945 to 1948, the organization of wholesale trade was not at first materially affected, since the nationalized enterprises in the industrial sphere did not lose their organizational identity immediately. In the earliest phase of nationalized trade, the principal change affected agriculture, primarily as a result of the development of the compulsory deliveries system.

Until the end of 1951, wholesale trade was carried on by a large number of organizations: the purchasing and sales organizations of the General Directorates of the Ministry of Industry, the nationalized wholesale trade enterprises, wholesale trading organizations of the Ministry of Trade, the cooperatives (these purchased and distributed goods for retail trade), and so forth. Late in 1951, however, in connection with the reorganization of industry and the abolition of the General Directorates, each industrial ministry was given a special purchasing and a special sales organization, in which the wholesale trading operations (other than in agriculture and consumer goods) were concentrated.

Beginning in 1950, the nationalized wholesale trading organizations made use of "material balances" as their planning method. The plan of that year involved the establishment of flow charts for some 2,000 commodities, indicating export surpluses and import requirements as well as the industries and enterprises which were to receive allocations. However, the system seems to have had two principal technical defects from the government's point of view. First, it did not take sufficient account of the actual course of output, and was thus unrealistic. Second, it seems to have left more room for bargaining than the planning authorities liked. By bidding up prices of materials, enterprises of relatively low priority in government plans were able to obtain unduly large amounts of scarce goods, thus impeding the development of industries which the government wished to expand.

The reorganization of 1951, by separating all wholesale trading functions from producing enterprises and placing them under ministries, sought to eliminate the "bargaining process," which had been criticized by the authorities. The new distribution agencies were supposed to determine the requirements of enterprises on the basis of technological requirements implied by the annual plans. Beginning with the 1953 plan, the determination of the material requirements per unit of output (or "coefficients" in technical language) was assigned to the State Planning Office, thereby providing the last step in the centralization of wholesaling operations. The wholesale organizations of the producing ministries thus came to carry out mainly technical distribution functions, and in the main resemble similar wholesaling functions in the Soviet Union.

Reorganization of Banking

After the *coup d'état* of February 1948, the Czechoslovak government adopted a series of laws affecting the banking system, in order to simplify the banking structure, and to establish banking practices which would facilitate the diversion of resources out of the consumer sector and into the investment categories stressed in the first Five-Year Plan. In all of these matters, Czechoslovak legislation closely resembles that of the Soviet Union, although it was not until 1950 that a complete similarity of formal structures was achieved.

Central banking was dealt with in the laws concerning the National Bank and the Postal Savings Bank. These two decrees specified that the National Bank was to act as a bank of issue, and to control the note circulation, while the Postal Savings Bank was to be a central bank, supervising and regulating the commercial banks, in which the deposits of enterprises were to be concentrated. There was thus still at this stage a duality in the central banking apparatus, which was not overcome until 1950.

The National Bank during 1948 seems to have moved in the direction of becoming exclusively a bank of issue, although it also handled foreign exchange operations. The note liabilities of the bank increased from 58.5 to 72 billion crowns, while the deposits of banks (in practice almost the only deposits) declined from 7.3 billion to 2.0 billion. The increase in note circulation was entirely the result of increased discounting, which rose from 13.7 billion at the end of 1947 to 25.3 billion at the end of 1948, while other assets remained either stable or declined.

The Postal Savings Bank, on the other hand, was empowered to accept deposits from banks and insurance companies, and also to issue credits to them, a function which might hitherto have been the province of the National Bank. The bank was authorized to deal in securities insofar as this might relate to its central banking functions, and was to collaborate with the National Bank in preparing financial plans. Banks and insurance companies were required to transfer their deposits to the Postal Savings Bank in accordance with instructions of the Ministry of Finance. The Bank was in effect controlled by the Ministry of Finance, which appointed its Managing Committee of nine members.

The transfer of these interbank deposits began in December 1948. In November 1948, the Postal Savings Banks had 1,638 million crowns of interbank deposits, compared to 33,943 million held by other banks; in December, Postal Savings deposits were 10,258 million, compared to 19,298 billion for other banks; and in November 1949 (the latest date for which information is available), Postal Saving deposits were 15,801, compared to 7,449 for the other banks. In this way, the Postal Savings Bank came to hold the bulk of the liquid assets of the banking system. The effect of this increase in the role of the Postal Savings Bank can be ascertained from Table 6, which shows the increasing concentration of payments in the Postal Savings Bank during 1949, the last year for which data are available.

Table 6. Structure of Payments Turnover in the Banking System, 1946-1949
(in per cent of total clearings)

Principal Components	1946	1947	1948	June 1949	November 1949
Bankers' accounts with National Bank	41	37	39	35	28
Clearing Associations	8	11	12	8	—
Postal Savings accounts	51	52	49	57	72

Sources: Czechoslovak National Bank, *Monthly Bulletin,* 1946-49, various issues.

The separation of investment from commercial banking was achieved through measures affecting both the enterprises and the banks. As far as the enterprises were concerned, a decree of March 1948 provided that funds made available to them might be used only for the specific purposes for which they had been authorized. In particular, loans for financing current operations or for financing construction were to be made from separate banks specializing in that type of loan. Enterprises were not allowed to transfer the proceeds of loans between each other, carry out barter transactions, or extend credit to each other from their own funds. In order to control these provisions, it was specified that all payments among enterprises must be made through the appropriate bank, and that enterprises could draw currency only on the basis of instructions of the Ministry of Finance. The purpose of this legislation resembled that of similar Soviet legislation, namely, to ensure that funds designated for construction were not devoted to inventory financing, and vice versa.

In December 1948, it was decreed that payments for construction must be made through deposits in the Investment Bank, and that all other transactions must go through two commercial banks—Zivnostenska Bank in the Czech lands, and Tatra Bank in Slovakia. While an enterprise might, in some cases must, have an account in each bank, it might use the Postal Savings System only to the extent that its banks permitted it to make payments through their accounts. Finally, enterprises were not permitted to have giro accounts in the National Bank.

The Investment Bank was established through a merger of several other banks, mainly the Provincial Banks (although, since these had previously absorbed several commercial banks, its ultimate origin is not so simple). The purpose of the bank was "to carry out the financing and monetary control of equipment investments, the granting and taking over of long-term loans, whether by way of emission or not, and for purposes other than capital equipment, as well as the performance of services for the Fund of the Nationalized Economy." In practice, this meant that all construction funds were to be channeled through the Bank, whether these came from the budget (as happened after 1951), or from the resources of enterprises financing construction through non-budgetary funds.

The commercial banking system was reorganized in January 1948 by the merging of all commercial banks in the Czech lands into the Zivnostenska Bank, and those in Slovakia into the Tatra Bank. An act of July 1948 gave the Ministry of Finance exclusive competence and control over them, with power to determine their activities, as well as to reorganize and merge them. The Minister was given power to appoint the members of the Board of Directors of the banks.

Other banking institutions were reorganized by the same act. All the credit cooperatives, district agricultural loan offices, savings banks, and private banks in a community were merged into a single savings and loan bank, referred to as a "People's Banking Institution." District savings and loan institutions performed central banking functions for the local institutions, and a "People's Banking Central Office" was established in Prague to carry out the functions of the various central banking offices of the former associations. At the end of 1952, these institutions were renamed State Savings Bank offices in a reorganization of the system which seems to be of only administrative importance.

The final step in the consolidation of the banking system came with the establishment of the State Bank in March 1950. This act provided for the merging of the National Bank, the two remaining commercial banks (Zivnostenska and Tatra), and the Postal Savings Bank. With this act, the last formal distinction between Czech and Slovak banking ceased, and the Czechoslovak banking system came to resemble in detail the Soviet banking system. The State Bank has the function of controlling both notes (formerly the province of the National Bank) and deposits (formerly the province of the Postal Savings Bank).

Prices, Taxes, and Investment

The basic feature of the first Five-Year Plan was an expansion of investment in heavy industry. In August 1948, almost all of the remaining private enterprise outside of agriculture was nationalized. The problem henceforth was to select an appropriate method of financing capital construction in heavy industry. The decision made by the Czechoslovak authorities was to permit the establishment of a price structure analogous to that of the Soviet Union. Since wage payments tended to increase without corresponding increases in the availability of consumer goods, the authorities could have raised either income taxes (a politically unpopular move), or consumer goods prices as a means of absorbing popular purchasing power. The latter course was chosen. This, however, involved the establishment of a dual price system, in which goods were sold off ration at prices well above the level of rationed goods prices. Since the rationing system discriminated increasingly against "bourgeois elements" in the cities, while unrationed prices competed with and held down prices received by "bourgeois elements" in the rural areas (peasants selling in the free market), this decision suited the general distribution policy of the government.

The considerable amount of profit accruing to the state from these transactions was transferred into the budget by means of the "general tax," introduced at the beginning of 1949. This tax is virtually the same as the Soviet turnover tax. Its name distinguished it only from the older Czechoslovak turnover tax, which represented a small uniform levy on all transactions, a kind of sales tax common throughout continental Europe. Some idea of its importance as an element of state revenue is shown by a comparison of revenue in the first half of 1949 with that in the corresponding period of 1948. In 1949, the general tax provided 28.9 billion crowns of revenue, compared to 18.7 billion from all other sources combined, and compared to a total revenue of 23.6 billion in the first half of 1948.

The general tax served to control investment, as well as to limit purchasing power. It prevented the high prices of consumer goods from leading to high profits in consumer goods industries. Had such profits been allowed to accumulate, it would have been difficult to limit investment in these industries and to stimulate investment in the capital goods industries. By diverting funds out of consumer goods industries and into the budget, the state was able to finance the capital goods industries.

These policies greatly increased the level of investment and of consumer goods prices. The magnitude of investments is clearly indicated by the increase in budget appropriations on the economy, which rose from 42 billion crowns in 1949 to 255 billion in 1953. Even if allowance is made for large increases in costs, planned investment in 1953 was substantially higher than in 1949. Income from the general tax rose to a level of 292 billion crowns, or two thirds of total planned revenue, in 1953.

Consumer goods prices seem also to have risen steadily. According to a United Nations study, the cost of living index in 1952 was about 700 per cent of 1937, or about 215 per cent of June 1948. Prices of unrationed goods in 1952 were about 3.7 times as high, on the average, as the prices of rationed goods.

Despite the increase in prices, shortages of consumer goods were continuously evident after 1950. While in part these reflected inefficiencies in the distribution system (which indeed was continuously under attack in the press), the major reason was an excess of consumer demand at the prevailing prices. In most Soviet orbit countries, such a condition has led to flow of currency from the cities to the rural areas. However, Czechoslovakia has been a food-importing country, so that this phenomenon apparently did not occur.

At the end of May 1953, the government announced a currency conversion, the obvious purposes of which were threefold: to liquidate large holdings of currency which had been the result of unsatisfied consumer demand in previous years; to eliminate rationing and multiple pricing by lowering the level of wages relative to prices; and to re-establish the general level of wages and consumer prices at about the 1940/41 level. The details of this conversion are discussed below. It may merely be noted that this conversion, which was very similar to others conducted within the Soviet orbit after 1947, had the apparently unexpected effect of injuring the city population more than that of the rural areas, because of the unusual pattern of currency holdings mentioned above. Moreover, the conversion affected the lower-income groups more than the high-income groups, some of whom may actually have benefited in terms of the wage-price ratio changes. As a result, disturbances broke out in a number of cities. Although these were soon quelled, they apparently led the government to reconsider its investment programs and to take steps to increase the supply of consumer goods. The success, and indeed the seriousness of these endeavors, have been difficult to measure in view of the generally negative reaction to the conversion itself.

Money Supply

Data on the money supply are available only through 1949. As noted below, bank legislation of 1948 tended to create two banking centers: the National Bank, which, as bank of issue, supervised the note circulation; and the Postal Savings Bank, which was in charge of controlling the remaining commercial banks (all of which were nationalized) and of taking over banking operations under the new system of financing non-banking enterprises.

The note circulation in 1948/49 seems mainly to have varied with the level of discounting and other short-term credit issued by the National Bank. The functions of the bank as a center of liquid reserves for the banking system were gradually suppressed. Movements in other accounts of the National Bank seem roughly to have offset each other and the movement of commercial bank reserves.

The principal factors affecting the note circulation during the period 1947-49 are shown in Table 7.

The decline in the note circulation in 1949 probably reflects, in part at least, the opening of state stores selling unrationed goods. Restrictions on the holding of currency by enterprises went into effect in March 1948. Thereafter, wage payments tended to be the main factor increasing, and retail sales the main factor decreasing, the note issue. Since both employment and wage rates rose in 1949, the decrease in note circulation is explainable by an increase in the value (not necessarily the volume) of retail transactions.

Table 7. Factors Affecting Note Circulation, 1947-1949
(in million crowns)

	Level at End of			Change[a] During	
	1947	1948	1949	1948	1949
circulation	58,539	71,997	66,626	+13,458	—5,371
and foreign exchange	4,793	4,187	3,004	— 606	—1,183
unts, advances and securities	17,436	30,233	25,067	+12,797	—5,166
ther National Bank assets	65,659	48,201	46,893	—17,458	—1,308
deposits in National Bank	7,316	2,039	895	+ 5,277	+1,144
ther National Bank liabilities	21,240	7,790	6,324	+13,450	+1,416

urces: Czechoslovak National Bank, *Monthly Bulletin,* 1947-49, various issues.
ign denotes effect of change on note circulation.

The level of current account deposits rose from 42 billion at the end of 1946 to 54 billion at the end of the following year. During 1948, it dropped by 1 billion, but in 1949 it more than doubled, reaching a total of almost 117 billion in November. All but 8 billion crowns of this increase of 63 billion was in Postal Savings Bank accounts. This last increase cannot be explained in terms of any change in economic conditions. While the volume of clearings through the Postal Savings System rose, the velocity of turnover of deposits dropped sharply. It may probably be concluded that the rise was mainly of accounting significance. In 1948, enterprises were forbidden to extend credit to each other. If the credit formerly granted by enterprises was all transferred to the Postal Savings Bank (and this is the sense of the legislation), this would increase current accounts of enterprises (as they divested themselves of their receivables) and bank credit, even if no change in the total volume of credit (non-bank and bank combined) had taken place.

The very extensive growth in the liquid assets of enterprises, however, must have been a factor contributing to the shortages which developed after 1950 throughout the economy. Unless some budgetary device was used to take these funds away from enterprises (no such device is known), there can hardly have been any effective limitation on the liquidity of enterprises, particularly in the presence of price controls.

Both prices and wages showed decided upward movements after 1948, in contrast to the period 1946-48. During the earlier period, monthly wages had increased over 35 per cent, while the cost of living dropped by 4 per cent. In 1952, monthly wages had increased a further 43 per cent, but prices had more than doubled, according to available estimates. The increase was in the main due to higher prices of unrationed goods. Prices of unrationed goods were at about the 1946 level, or perhaps 6 per cent above 1948. The nominal purchasing power of wages had declined by 32 per cent, and was slightly below the 1946 level. (The ordinary concept of "purchasing power," as measured by the ratio of prices to wages, must here be used cautiously. To the extent that people have income which they are willing, but not able to spend, because of goods shortages, a measure such as this overstates real purchasing power.)

Tables 8, 9, and 10 show the volume of credit during the period 1946-49, cost of living indices in selected years from 1945 to 1953, and money wages from 1946 to 1953, respectively.

Table 8. Indicated Volume of Credit, 1946-1949
(in million new crowns)

	1946[a]	1947[a]	1948[a]	1949[a]
Postal Savings Bank				
Savings deposits	877	1,777	2,453	2,557
Interbank deposits	2,466	2,239	10,258	15,801
Current account liabilities	13,057	10,945	16,514	72,146
Total	16,400	14,961	29,225	90,504
Other Banks				
Savings deposits	14,332	25,689	31,180	34,070
Current accounts	29,414	43,382	36,817	44,667
Total	43,746	69,071	67,997	78,737
less: interbank deposits[b]	12,534	9,555	12,297	16,696
Net deposit liability	31,212	59,516	55,700	62,041
Indicated credit by all banks other than the National Bank[c]	47,612	74,477	84,925	152,545
Public debt[d]	18,190	28,129	32,808	31,071[e]
All other	29,412	46,348	52,117	121,474

Sources: Czechoslovak National Bank, *Monthly Bulletin*, 1946-49, various issues.

[a] December data for 1946-1948; November data for 1949. November 1949 was the last month for which the National Bank published these series.

[b] Interbank deposits with the National and Postal Savings banks.

[c] Total deposits of the Postal Savings Bank, plus net deposit liabilities of other banks.

[d] Total public debt incurred after liberation. It is here assumed that it was all held by banks other than the National Bank.

[e] June.

Table 9. Cost of Living Indices
(1937 = 100)

Expenditures	1945	1946	June 1948	1952	Post-Conversion Prices June 1953 old crowns	new crowns
Food—rationed	160.4	341.9	330.6	372	849[a]	170[a]
unrationed	—	—	—	2,020	1,246[b]	249[b]
Clothing—rationed	239.0	402.3	409.8	696	882[a]	176[a]
unrationed	—	—	—	1,210	855[b]	171[b]
Rent	124.4	124.4	128.2	137	254 (Rent and Heat and light)	51 (Rent and Heat and light)
Heat and light	172.3	273.7	294.3	307		
Other	272.9	491.4	440.4	745	641	128
Total	187.3	340.6	328.5	702	737	147
rationed	—	—	—	349	638[a]	128[a]
unrationed	—	—	—	1,306	907[b]	181[b]

Sources: 1945-48, Czechoslovak National Bank, *Monthly Bulletin,* 1945-48, various issues; 1952-53, United Nations, *Economic Bulletin for Europe* (Geneva, first quarter 1954). The two series are not necessarily based upon the same commodity coverage, since not all prices are reported in 1952-53; they apparently also differ from official (classified) Czechoslovak prices indices, which are probably based upon a postwar family budget pattern.

[a] The post-conversion prices of goods which had been rationed.

[b] The post-conversion prices of goods which either had not previously been rationed or of rationed goods also available for sale without ration coupons.

Table 10. Expansion of Money Wages, 1946-1953

Year	Average Monthly Wage in Industry		Average Hourly Wage in Industry	Industrial Employment	Other Non-Agricultural Employment[a]	Estimated Monthly Wage Bill[c]	
	Workers	Employees				Industry[b]	Total[c]
	(in old crowns)		(in old crowns)	(in thousands)		(in billion old crowns)	
1946	2663	4343	12.91 (Feb.)	1158	2134	3.1	8.8
1947	3218	5038	16.29 (May)	1273	2033	4.1	10.6
1948	3611	5378	17.23 (Feb.)	1345	2000	4.9	12.1
1949	3829	5658	18.12 (Mar.)	1415	....	6.4	13.1
1950	4543	6259	19.84 (Feb.)	1466	....	6.7	15.3
1951	4979	6476	22.12 (Feb.)	1524	....	7.6	17.1
1952	5200	....	....	1550	....	8.1	18.0
1953	5633	....	....	1618	....	9.1	19.8

Sources: 1946-49, based on State Statistical Office, *Statisticky zpravodaj* (Statistical Bulletin), 1946-49; 1949-53, compiled from Ministry of Foreign Trade, *Czechoslovak Economic Bulletin,* various issues.

[a] Average of monthly data. For 1948, the average for the first 6 months; thereafter, publication of the series on total employment ceased.

[b] Employment times average worker's wage.

[c] Assuming employment outside industry was 2,000,000 in 1949 and 1,900,000 thereafter, and that the average wage outside industry was the same as that in industry.

The Currency Conversion of June 1953

On June 1, 1953, the Czechoslovak government undertook a second currency conversion (the first one took place in October 1945). From an internal point of view, there were two basic conversion rates: 5 old crowns for one new crown, and 50 old crowns for one new crown. The favored rate applied to (1) current accounts of enterprises; (2) the first 5,000 crowns of individual savings deposits; (3) an amount equal to one month's payroll in the case of private enterprises; (4) the first 5,000 crowns of the "indivisible funds" of Types III and IV agricultural cooperatives; and (5) the first 300 crowns of currency of individuals holding ration cards.[1] The 50:1 rate applied to all other holdings of currency by individuals and enterprises. Savings deposits and the deposits of agricultural cooperatives were treated on a sliding scale, depending upon their size. Various annulments of debt and readjustment of insurance policies took place simultaneously, and are discussed separately. Rationing was abolished at the time of the conversion, with the prices of rationed goods raised and those of unrationed goods lowered so as to provide a single price system in the consumer goods markets. This new level of prices was cut by 80 per cent, as were money wages (in the case of wages, minor adjustments were made in favor of low-paid workers). Since people with low wages spent a larger proportion of their income on rationed goods than did people with high wages, the unification of prices would naturally tend to benefit high-income groups and harm low-income groups. This tendency was in part offset by wage increases given lower income groups. However, computations made by United Nations economists indicate that the tendency was not overcome by actual wage changes. As Table 11 shows, the low-income group suffered losses in purchasing power ranging up to 20 per cent, while high-income groups made gains of up to 29 per cent.

An expansion of the Czechoslovak currency sufficient to cause a collapse of the internal distribution system, in the absence of a currency conversion, is not to be explained on the grounds of deficit budgetary financing, since the budget after 1948 seems to have been in balance or shown a surplus. An expansion of credit by the State Bank throughout this period and declines in consumer goods availabilities are better explanations of the conversion. It is known that in late 1952 the government adopted measures to strengthen credit controls by the State Bank, and *Rude pravo* of December 15 and 28, 1953, complained of continuous increases in inventories throughout

[1] "Bourgeois elements" had been deprived of ration cards under earlier legislation to force them to make all their purchases at high unrationed-goods prices.

the year. These increases would have been impossible had effective credit controls existed.

Table 11. Impact of June 1953 Currency Conversion on Working-Class Family Expenditures, at Various Levels of Income

Weekly Family Income	Income Spent on Rationed Goods	Money Income	Cost of Living	Real Income
(in new crowns)	(in per cent)	(June 1953, in per cent of 1952)		
121	100	146	183	80
182	77	131	157	83
242[a]	58	123	136	90
363	39	118	113	104
484	29	115	102	113
726	19	112	91	123
968	15	111	86	129

Source: United Nations, *Economic Bulletin for Europe* (first quarter 1954), p. 6.

[a] The source incorrectly states that the average wage for all industrial workers was 242 crowns per week. This figure actually refers to the 1952 level, converted to new crowns. The corresponding 1953 figure would be 263 crowns. This point has been clarified by correspondence with the authors of the article in question.

The shortage of consumer goods beginning in 1950 resulted primarily from the investment program, which diverted resources into construction, and from an upward pressure on wages. With increased purchasing power reaching the population at a time when resources were being diverted away from consumer goods production, an increase in note circulation could have been avoided only by increased consumer goods prices. This is true because consumer spending in state stores is the main way through which notes are returned to the banking system. (It was partly to increase this inflow of notes that the government had introduced the "free" market and the general tax at the beginning of 1949.)

The currency conversion involved price policy because it was accompanied by the abolition of rationing and the establishment of a single level of prices above the former level of rationed prices and below the former level of free (unrationed) prices. The Czechoslovak authorities had established stores selling unrationed goods at the beginning of 1949, but they apparently felt that prices in these stores were too low to absorb the available money incomes of the population. Equilibrium could have been restored either by raising the level of free prices, while maintaining the level of rationed goods prices, or by unifying prices at a level sufficiently high to hold demand to the level of available goods. Since the unrationed goods stores were officially justified as a means of holding down prices in the black market, with which these stores competed, the former possibility was not acceptable. The latter, according to Premier Zapotocky, in a speech on June 10, 1953, would have meant raising the level of prices above the price level existing in the unrationed stores, which for the same reasons would have been unacceptable. The alternative was to reduce the amount of currency outstanding, so as to reduce current demand. It would then become possible to unify prices at a level below the former level of unrationed prices.

It may be supposed that the monetary purpose of the conversion of the currency was (1) to eliminate accumulated unspent currency earned in the past, and (2) to reduce it further to a level consistent with the readjusted price and wage levels. Had only the first objective existed, old notes would have been exchanged for new at the rate of 10:1. Since prices and wages were to be reduced to 20 per cent of their former levels, the conversion ratio would have to be 50:1. With regard to the first part of the conversion, it might be concluded that the existing note circulation was about 10 times as great at the time of the conversion as it would have been if consumers had no accumulated cash savings and were currently spending all of their current earnings.[2] With regard to the second, 80 per cent reduction in retail prices probably served to reduce the level of prices to roughly the levels prevailing in 1940/41, at the beginning of the German occupation, but before wartime inflation was far advanced.

Government Finance and Fiscal Policy

The changes in the financial structure and practices of the nationalized enterprises, as explained above, would have increased the importance of the state budget after 1948, even if there had been no change in the level of actual expenditures on investment or armaments. Actually, both of these increased sharply, the former beginning with the introduction of the first Five-Year Plan in 1949, and the latter beginning especially in 1952. A further technical increase in the scope of the budget occurred in 1953, as various social services were brought into the budget.

It has already been noted that money wages showed a steady upward tendency over this period. This increase took place at a time when price controls at the factory level were in force. It is likely, judging from repeated complaints in the press, that costs tended to

[2] This discussion ignores the 300 crowns which ration-card holders could exchange at a rate of 5:1. The amount of currency involved here would have been small, probably not in excess of 1 or 2 billion crowns (compared to a note circulation exceeding 70 billion in early 1950).

rise, and that extensive subsidization of heavy industry took place. For this reason, budgetary "expenditures on the economy," which technically include many items other than investment, may probably be taken to measure roughly the cost of investments, including subsidization. However, a portion of this investment would, in the budgetary procedures of other countries, be considered as a military allocation, since the construction of armament plants not actually operated by the armed forces is treated as a civilian, rather than a military program.

Beginning in 1949, actually budgetary expenditures are not available in any adequate breakdown. Recourse must be had to planned figures, which are at least illustrative of the orders of magnitude involved. Table 12 shows such a breakdown. The 1953 budget was issued before the currency conversion took place, and it may be recalled that the conversion reduced all prices by 80 per cent. The actual data for the year would thus be partly in preconversion prices and partly in postconversion prices. Moreover, during the latter part of the year, some relaxation of the construction program took place, as part of the general shift in Soviet policy following Stalin's death and the disturbances in East Germany.

Table 12. Planned Budgetary Income and Expenditures, 1949-1953
(in billion crowns)

Items of Income and Expenditure	1949	1950	1951	1952	19
Total Income	89.3	131.9	166.5	324.3	43
Income from the socialized sector	....	....	....	280.5	33
Turnover (general) tax[a]	50.9	67.0	107.8 }	262.2	29
Deductions from profit	12.2	....	41.6 }		
Direct and wage taxes	....	....	9.3	20.1 }	3
Other taxes	....	....	.... }	13.6 }	
Administrative revenues	....	....	.... }		
Social and cultural services	3.8	....	....	9.3	5
Defense and security agencies	0.3	....	....	0.8	
Total Expenditures	89.3	131.6	166.2	323.5	43
Expenditures on the economy	21.3	42.1	87.1	217.5	25
Social and cultural	25.9	50.3	47.6	58.8	11
Defense and security	8.3	9.6	10.5	22.4	4
Administrative	....	....	16.3	20.1	1
State debt reserves	....	....	4.7	4.7	
Surplus	0.0	0.3	0.3	0.8	

Sources: Bruno Kiesewetter, *Die Wirtschaft der Tschechoslowakei seit 1945* (B 1954), p. 28.

[a] From 1949 to 1952 called "general tax."

[b] Of which 60 billion crowns was for new investment; 37 billion crowns more to be provided from profit and depreciation funds of enterprises.

Czechoslovakia is unique among the Soviet orbit countries in that she has not had an internal loan of the more or less involuntary type common elsewhere. On the other hand, the government has not attempted to operate at a surplus, as might have been expected of a country in which inflationary pressures were strong. The postwar public debt had risen to a peak of about 33 billion crowns by the end of 1948. Publication of data stopped in June 1949, when it was 31 billion. These bonds were repudiated at the time of the 1953 currency conversion, together with all other securities and the deposits blocked in 1945. It would appear, therefore, that the Czechoslovak government does not recognize any internal debt.

19. TRANSPORTATION AND COMMUNICATIONS

Vaclav E. Mares

General Comments

The development of Czechoslovakia's transportation system has been strongly influenced by the country's geographic setting as well as by its economic and political history. Though these factors are closely interrelated and though their specific effects cannot be appraised with any degree of accuracy, their most conspicuous features deserve special mention.

Location has undoubtedly been the most significant among the geographic factors, and it is responsible to a great extent for the unevenness in development of transport facilities between the western and the eastern parts of the Republic. The Czech lands, located in the center of Europe, have been an important hub of transcontinental traffic since the Middle Ages. Under the Austro-Hungarian monarchy, their position between the imperial capital of Vienna and the seaports and industrial regions of Germany as well as the western regions of Poland fostered the construction of long-distance transportation facilities. Relatively rapid industrialization of the Czech lands, which began early in the nineteenth century, provided additional impetus and encouraged the growth of a local transport network. Slovakia, on the other hand, traditionally played only a minor role in international traffic. Her location in the predominantly rural zone of Central Europe, combined with her economic underdevelopment, did not provide adequate incentives for the construction of modern facilities. Systematic development of Slovakia's transportation did not begin until after 1918, when she became one of the constituent parts of the Czechoslovak Republic. As a result of the political reorganization of Central Europe following World War I, Slovakia's role in international traffic substantially increased. Since the end of World War II, this role has been further enhanced as a result of rapid industrialization and the radical shifts in the direction of trade of the Central and East European countries.

Topography is another geographic factor that has contributed to the disparity in the development of transportation in the two parts of the country. Surface configuration in the Czech lands, particularly in Bohemia, has been more favorable to the construction of an integrated transport network than in Slovakia. While in both parts of the country abrupt changes in relief have occasionally posed serious construction problems for all types of transportation, major natural obstacles exist primarily in Slovakia. Though the engineering problems involved in surmounting these obstacles are not greater than those in other mountainous regions of Europe, inducements for the construction of transport facilities entailing large outlays have been lacking.

Czechoslovakia's political history has also left its mark on the country's transport system. The network of roads, railroads and waterways that Czechoslovakia inherited in 1918 had been part of a transportation system designed to serve the interests of the Austro-Hungarian monarchy and it reflected the political and economic dualism of the monarchy. It was ill suited and inadequate for the needs of the new Republic. Modern transport facilities in the Czech lands had been planned and built under close supervision of the Austrian government. Vienna was the nodal point of all the main lines of communication in the Austrian-controlled provinces, and Prague was a secondary center for local Bohemian lines. Slovakia's meager facilities, on the other hand, largely converged on Budapest. They had been planned with the close supervision of the Hungarian government in an effort to tie the "upper province" more firmly to the Hungarian capital. Thus, Czechoslovakia's principal problem in the field of transport was to integrate the inherited facilities into a system corresponding to the country's political boundaries and to improve the means of transport in her underdeveloped regions. This meant primarily the construction of new lines of communication between the western and the eastern provinces, and the building of additional facilities in the latter.

Post-World War II Changes and Communist Policies

The growth and pattern of commercial transportation is illustrated in Table 1, showing the volume of freight and the number of passengers transported by the main carriers in 1937, 1948, 1951, and 1953. In freight traffic, the railroads' share decreased from some 78 per cent in 1937 to about 72 per cent in 1953, while the proportion of freight carried by road increased during the same period from about 17 to 25 per cent of the total. The participation of waterways decreased slightly from over 4 per cent to about 3 per cent. The volume of freight carried by airlines and the number of passengers transported by waterways were insignificant.

Table 1. Freight and Passenger Traffic, Selected Years 1937-1953

Year	Freight Traffic (in million metric tons)			Passenger Traffic (in millions)		
	Railroads (1)	Roads (2)	Waterways (3)	Railroads (4)	Roads (5)	Airlines (6)
1937	69.5	15.5	3.9	264.0	75.0	0.1
1948	74.8	22.4	2.4	415.0	252.2	0.2
1951	112.3	....	4.6	540.0	....	....
1953	129.2	44.8	5.8	548.0	500.0	0.334

Sources: Data for 1937 and 1948, except as noted, based on State Statistical Office, *Statisticky zpravodaj* (Statistical Bulletin) XII, No. 11 (Prague, 1949); figure for 1948, col. (5), State Statistical Office, *Prumyslove zpravy* (Industrial Reports), III, No. 28-29 (Prague, 1948), p. 196, from Adam Rudzki, *East-Central European Transportation* (Washington, D. C., 1955), p. 28. Data for 1951, col. (1), Rudzki, *op. cit.*, p. 20; col. (3) computed from *Doprava* (Transportation), III, No. 5 (Prague, 1955); col. (4), I. M. Maergoiz, *Chekhoslovakiia* (Moscow, 1954), p. 147. Data for 1953, col. (1), Rudzki, *op. cit.*, p. 20; col. (2) *ibid.*, p. 27; col. (3) computed from *Doprava, loc. cit.;* col. (4) based on *Rude pravo* (Red Right), April 15, 1954; col. (5), Rudzki, *op. cit.*, p. 28; col. (6) based on *Rude pravo, loc. cit.*

In passenger transport, the railroads' share, measured by the number of passengers carried, decreased from about 78 per cent in 1937 to approximately 52 per cent in 1953, while that of roads increased correspondingly. The participation of the remaining carriers amounted to only a negligible fraction of the total in both periods.

The figures in Table 1 take no account of distances involved, and tend to exaggerate the growing importance of road traffic in recent years. The postwar increase in road traffic has been largely confined to short distances, with practically all long-distance traffic handled by railroads. Measured in terms of ton-kilometers and passenger kilometers, the dominant position of railroads did not change significantly. As late as 1951, their share in freight and passenger traffic amounted to 94 and 80 per cent respectively; corresponding figures for road carriers in that year were 2 and 20 per cent; waterways comprised 4 per cent of freight traffic, while in passenger traffic their share was practically nil.

Because of large war losses of rolling stock and equipment (see Table 3) and the unavailability of replacements, railroads were under great strain in the immediate postwar years of economic rehabilitation. Though prewar performance in freight transport, measured in terms of ton-kilometers, was slightly exceeded in 1947 (see Table 4), this was achieved only at the cost of a further rapid deterioration of facilities. Highways and highway bridges suffered comparatively less, with wartime destruction limited to some of the eastern regions of the country. Furthermore, postwar relief deliveries quickly restored Czechoslovakia's stock of motor vehicles. Water transport was the slowest to recover. As late as 1948, waterways handled less than two thirds of the freight they had carried before the war. Their slow recovery was due, on the one hand, to war destruction of port installations along the Labe (Elbe) and to mines floating in the Danube, which endangered shipping for years, and, on the other, to the reorientation of the country's foreign trade.

When they seized power, the Communists inherited the unfinished task of postwar reconstruction as well as the problem of equipping the country's railroads for the increased eastbound traffic that resulted from the radical shift of Czechoslovakia's foreign trade policy. New construction projects, which this change in trade policy necessitated (the doubling of track on existing eastbound lines and other improvements of east-west connections), had not been completed even as late as 1955. As a result, eastbound traffic has imposed a great strain on facilities and the personnel servicing them.

In road transport, the Communist government has emphasized the development of short-distance motor transportation to supplement long-distance rail and water freight traffic, and has eliminated the prewar construction projects of highway turnpikes. A similar stress has been placed on the development of short-distance passenger transport, especially that for commuters. This sector has shown the largest relative increases, enabling the railroads, without substantial expansion of facilities, to carry considerably more freight.

In the case of waterways, largely as a result of the reorientation of trade, emphasis has been shifted from the Labe-Vltava system to the Danube and the Oder systems.

Despite greatly increased demands upon transport facilities, stemming mainly from rapid industrial expansion, Communist transport policy has been marked by an absence of major new investments. This applies even to projects which would facilitate implementation of Czechoslovakia's new trade policy, emphasizing trade relations with the Soviet Union and other countries of the Soviet orbit, e.g., additional railroad construction in Slovakia, the building of an east-west turnpike, improvement of navigation on the Danube, or construction of the long projected Danube-Oder-Labe canal. With industrial expansion high on the list of priorities, investment resources have been allocated primarily to heavy industry.

Individual Sectors of the Transportation System

Railroad Transport

Historical Introduction. Czechoslovakia's railroad history began in 1804 with a plan for linking the Vltava and Danube basins by horse- or bullock-drawn vehicles running along wooden lines. In 1823, a track for transportation of goods and passengers was put into operation between Ceske Budejovice in southern Bohemia and Mauthausen, near Linz in Austria.

The first steam-powered railroad was built, by sections, between 1839 and 1848 in Moravia. It ran from Breclav along the Morava River, through the Moravian Gate, and along the Oder River to Ostrava-Bohumin. Called Ferdinand's Nordbahn (Northern Railroad), it was part of a trunk line connecting Vienna with Cracow. Its importance greatly increased after the mid-century, when development of the Silesian coal fields and industries began on a large scale. Almost simultaneously with the main line, several important branch lines were built, extending from Breclav to Brno, from Prerov to Olomouc, and from Ostrava to Opava. In 1845, the Olomouc branch was extended westward through Ceska Trebova to Prague. In 1849, the line Brno-Ceska Trebova was put into operation, connecting the capital of Moravia with Prague. In 1851, the line Prague-Decin-Dresden was built along the Labe River, giving the Bohemian capital access to the seaport of Hamburg. Ten years later, Prague was connected with Bavaria by a line running through Plzen and across the northern tip of the Sumava ranges to Nuremberg. The basic pattern of rail transport in the Czech lands was thus established within a span of two decades in the middle of the nineteenth century.

Between 1855 and 1880, as a result of financial difficulties, the Austrian government's interest in railroad development faded, and numerous concessions to build and operate railroads were granted to private entrepreneurs. Rapid industrialization of the western and northern regions of the Czech lands stimulated private construction of railroads in these regions. The rail network of the Kladno and Plzen bituminous coal basins, the North Bohemian brown coal basin the Sudeten region, and the Ostrava bituminous and steel producing region dates largely from this period. In the predominantly agricultural south, on the other hand, railroad construction proceeded at a much slower pace.

After 1880, the Austrian government's interest in railroad building and operation was resumed. However, though railroad development in the Czech lands during the period 1880-1914 was quite lively, new construction was largely limited to secondary lines in the neglected rural regions.

Slovakia's railroad development prior to World War I centered on two main lines: Kosice-Bohumin and Bratislava-Zilina. The first was a private venture connecting eastern Slovakia's iron ore deposits and limestone quarries with the Silesian coal mines and foundries. It was put into operation in 1869. The Bratislava-Zilina railroad, running for most of its length along the Vah River, was built by the Hungarian government between 1873 and 1889. Except for these two main lines and their branches, the Slovak railroad network built prior to World War I was oriented toward Budapest. Slovakia's rail connections with the Czech lands were limited to the Kosice-Bohumin line in the north, the Trencin-Bylnice line through the Vlara Pass in the White Carpathians, and the Bratislava-Breclay-Brno line in the south.

Before the Communist Coup. After 1918, railroad development centered upon three principal objectives: the building of additional lines across the White Carpathians to provide more adequate east-west connections; construction of new lines in Slovakia to facilitate fuller economic development; and improvement of the network in the Czech lands.

By the time of the dismemberment of Czechoslovakia following the Munich Pact, this program had been only partly completed. Rail links between the Czech lands and Slovakia were strengthened by two new lines across the White Carpathians—one running from Horni Lidec to Puchov and the other from Veseli nad Moravou to Nove Mesto nad Vahom—and by the improvement of the Vlara Pass line from Bylnice to Trencin. In Slovakia, four lines were added: Cervena Skala-Margecany, running in an east-west direction through Slovakia's main mining region; Zvolen-Krupina, connecting the southern farm lands with the mining and timber region of Central Slovakia; Handlova-Horna Stubna, providing additional access to Slovakia's only major brown coal and lignite basin; and Vajany-Uzhorod, connecting eastern Slovakia with the capital of Ruthenia. In addition to these standard gauge lines, the trackage of narrow gauge lines was also noticeably increased, particularly in the Slovak timber regions. Improvements in the Czech lands consisted mainly in doubling some single track lines.

All of these additions were made prior to 1930. With the Great Depression, railroad construction virtually ceased. Table 2 summarizes some of the basic data on the distribution of railroads among Czechoslovakia's provinces on the eve of Munich.

Table 2. Distribution of Railroads among the Four Provinces, 1938

Province	Population	Area	Length of Railroads[a]	Percentage of Total Length	Length of Railroads per 100 km² of Area	Lengt Railrc per 1, Inhabi
		(in square kilometers)	(in kilometers)		(in kilometers)	(in kilome
Bohemia	7,108,376	52,062	6,791	50	13.04	.95
Moravia-Silesia	3,565,010	26,808	2,864	21	10.68	.80
Slovakia	3,329,793	49,029	} 3,942	29	6.39	.97
Ruthenia	725,357	12,617				
Total	14,728,536	140,508	13,597	100	9.68	.92

Sources: Population data from Harriet Wanklyn, *Czechoslovakia* (New York, 19 p. 327. Figures for area and length of railroads from State Statistical Office, *Statis rocenka republiky Ceskoslovenske, 1937* (Statistical Yearbook of the Czechoslovak public, 1937) (Prague, 1937), pp. 1 and 120. Data on length of railroads are for 1934.

[a] Refers to main and secondary lines, both standard and narrow gauge; light industrial railways are excluded.

Some 2,000 kilometers of the country's railroad lines were double tracked. Seventy-one per cent of the railroads' total length were concentrated in the Czech lands. Average density of rail network (measured by the length of railroads per square unit of area) in the Czech lands was almost twice as high as in the eastern provinces. With average density for the country as a whole amounting to nearly 10 kilometers per 100 square kilometers of area, Czechoslovakia ranked fourth in Europe, preceded only by Belgium, Great Britain, and Germany.

Throughout the interwar period, railroads were largely steam powered, with only about 1 per cent of the lines electrified. Ninety-eight per cent of the railroads' operating length were standard European gauge (1,435 meters), the remaining 2 per cent being narrow gauge (0.75 meters). Most of the railroads belonged to and were operated by the state. Privately owned railroads accounted for 18 per cent of the total mileage, but only 3 per cent of the country's railroads were both owned and operated privately. Railroads constituted the largest state enterprise in Czechoslovakia. They were administered by the Ministry of Transport through eight regional railroad directorates.

The structure of freight traffic during the prewar period was relatively stable. About one third of the total consisted of coal and coke; building stone, lumber, and sugar beets accounted for another third; the remaining third consisted of various farm products, ores, machinery and other finished products.

On the basis of the nationalization decrees promulgated at the close of World War II, all railroads passed under state ownership. The most pressing task facing the railroad administration was to repair the war damage and to restore orderly and efficient service. The extent of this damage and of postwar recovery and expansion are illustrated in Table 3, showing the railroads' rolling stock for selected years from 1937 to 1953.

Table 3. Railroad Rolling Stock, 1937-1953

Year	Locomotives	Coaches	Freight Cars
1937[a]	4,111[b]	10,391[c]	95,896[d]
1946	3,375[e]	7,614[f]	62,177[g]
1948	3,080	9,747	72,035
1953 (estimate)	3,200	10,500	over 120,000

Sources: 1937 and 1946, State Statistical Office, *Statistical Digest of the Czechoslovak Republic 1948* (Prague, 1948), p. 72; 1948, United Nations, *Statistical Yearbook 1949-1950* (New York, 1950), p. 290; 1953 estimates for locomotives and coaches, Rudzki, *op. cit.*, p. 18; number of freight cars estimated on the basis of data in Ministry of Transport, *Zeleznice* (Railroads), No. 1 (1954) p. 1.

[a] All figures for 1937 include Ruthenia.

[b] Comprises 4,091 steam and 20 electric locomotives.

[c] Includes 544 self-propelled coaches of which 7 were powered by steam, 12 by electricity, and 525 by diesel engines.

[d] Comprises 2,869 mail and luggage cars, 32,979 box cars, and 60,048 flat cars.

[e] Comprises 3,353 steam and 22 electric locomotives.

[f] Includes 494 self-propelled coaches, of which 11 were powered by steam, 11 by electricity, and 472 by diesel engines.

[g] Comprises 855 mail and luggage cars, 18,373 box cars and 42,949 flat cars.

After the Communist Coup. During the first years following the Communist seizure of power, the administration and operation of railroads remained unchanged. However, in 1952, a special Ministry of Railroads was created, and Soviet administrative and operational methods were introduced. The new approach proved to be unsuccessful and, after several minor reorganizations, the Ministry of Railroads was abolished in 1954 and railroads were again placed under the Ministry of Transport.

The new orientation of foreign trade substantially increased the demands upon railroads in both export and import traffic. With most of the country's export industries located in the border districts of the Czech lands, transport requirements were relatively small as long as some 75 per cent of Czechoslovakia's foreign trade was with Western countries. With the change of the main flow of trade to the east, the average length of haul per ton increased from 145 kilometers in 1937 to 233 kilometers in 1948. In 1948, though the total volume of Czechoslovakia's foreign trade was still 22 per cent lower than in 1937, the ton-kilometer figures in import and export traffic were 28 per cent above their 1937 level. In addition, the rapid industrial expansion under the first Five-Year Plan substantially increased transport requirements. By 1953, the combined domestic and foreign freight traffic, measured in ton-kilometers, was more than twice that of 1937. Passenger traffic, measured in passenger-kilometers, increased almost 2.5 times in the same period. The growth of railroad freight and passenger traffic, in both absolute and relative terms, from 1937 to 1953 is shown in Table 4.

Table 4. Railroad Freight and Passenger Traffic, 1937 and 1946-1953

	Freight Traffic		Passenger Traffic	
Year	In million ton-kilometers	Index (1937 = 100)	In million passenger-kilometers	Index (1937 =
1937	10,620	100.0	8,850	100.0
1946	9,268	87.3	13,190	149.0
1947	11,423	117.0	14,655	165.6
1948	12,690	119.6	18,160	205.2
1949	14,500	136.5	19,000	214.7
1950	16,700	157.3	21,200	239.5
1951	19,200	180.8	....	....
1952	20,400	192.1	21,500	242.3
1953	22,000	207.2	21,556	243.6

Sources: Data for 1937-1948, United Nations, *Statistical Yearbook 1949-1950*, p. Freight traffic figures for 1949-1953, Rudzki, *op. cit.*, p. 20. Passenger traffic figure 1949 and 1950 estimated on the basis of fragmentary information published in Cze slovak press; those for 1952 and 1953 from Rudzki, *op. cit.*, p. 24.

To cope with the rapidly growing transport requirements, construction of several new lines was undertaken. Carrying out one of the prewar projects, and utilizing some local dead-end lines, the Communist government has completed a new line between Brno and Havlickuv Brod (formerly Nemecky Brod), which establishes a new connection between Brno and Prague. This line, which is some 120 kilometers in length, will somewhat relieve the pressure on the main line between Prague and Ceska Trebova. Another new line, about 18 kilometers in length, running between Vizovice and Horni Lidec in eastern Moravia, was still under construction in 1955. It is an extension of the Horni Lidec-Puchov line built in the interwar period. Finally, the construction of a third new line, connecting Roznava and Turna nad Bodvou in eastern Slovakia, reportedly was also completed.

To meet the transport needs stemming from increased freight traffic with the Soviet Union, the track of the Bohumin-Kosice railroad, the main line leading to the Czechoslovak-Soviet frontier, was to be doubled throughout. By the end of 1954, about half of this project had been completed. New transloading facilities and installations for the switching of railroad car axles from standard European to Russian wide gauge have been built at the frontier station of Cerna nad Tisou. (See map, page 403.)

A third track connecting Prague with Kladno was still under construction in 1955. This line is the main artery of coal supply to the capital.

As of 1955, the Prague-Ceska Trebova and the Zilina-Spisska Nova Ves sections of the main east-west railroad—each about 165 kilometers long—were in the process of electrification. The Zilina-Spisska Nova Ves segment is to be operated by power generated by the new hydroelectric plant in the Orava region. In contrast to the few existing electrified lines operated by direct current at 1,500 volts, the new line will use direct current at 3,000 volts.

The main objective of major electrification projects has been to relieve the growing pressure on the coal supply. The same purpose is to be served by a substantial increase in the number of locomotives and coaches propelled by diesel engines. In 1954, it was reported that there were over a thousand self-propelled coaches and locomotives equipped with diesel engines.

On the whole, despite the pressing need for more extensive railroad transport facilities in the postwar period, the reconstruction and expansion program has proceeded at a slow pace. Restoration of damaged railroad stations, bridges, tracks, and workshops appears not to have been completed until 1950 or 1951. While the estimated number of freight cars in 1953 exceeded the 1937 stock by about one quarter, the number of locomotives in that year was still more than 20 per cent below the 1937 level (see Table 3). The substantially increased performance of railroads in the postwar years has been due largely to the introduction of higher capacity freight cars, overloading, employment of more workers, and an exacting system of rewards and penalties for railroad personnel. According to Czechoslovak data, the average load carried per freight car rose from 724 metric tons in 1937 to 1,321 metric tons in 1952.

The growing operational difficulties of the overburdened Czechoslovak railroads stem from a variety of causes. Some of the main problems can be traced to inferior construction. Among the railroads built by the Austrian government, only the main lines dating from the middle of the nineteenth century were built according to high standards. In the case of secondary lines, which were built largely in the second half of the nineteenth century, these standards were considerably relaxed as a result of financial difficulties of the Austrian government. Inadequate maintenance was an added factor. The period after World War I, aggravated by numerous readjustment problems and the effects of the depression, was too short for substantial improvement of the physical condition of the railroads. Serious maintenance problems have been the result. Furthermore, failure to reinforce the structure of track and bridges on several secondary lines has prevented their use by heavier locomotives.

During World War II, the country's railroads suffered from reckless exploitation and drastically limited maintenance. War damage and deliberate destruction of railroad facilities by the retreating German armies exacted a further toll. Due to inadequate postwar repairs and new construction, the country's railroad system has been taxed far beyond the limit of economical use. With large-scale expansion of facilities highly unlikely in view of the Communist transport policy, the prospect for the country's railroads suggests increasing operational difficulties during the second Five-Year Plan.

Road Transport

Prague has been a focal point of European communications since the fourteenth century, but some transcontinental trade routes crossed present Czechoslovak territory long before that time. Most early transcontinental routes ran in the north-south direction. Among these, the ancient road through the Moravian Gate (sometimes called the amber road), provided an easy natural passageway between the plains of northern Europe and the Danube valley, and played a prominent role both as a commercial and military route. Complementary to these early trunk lines were the roads connecting the trading centers within the country. A number of seigneurial roads, built and maintained by peasant serfs, linked medieval castles and forts. In the eighteenth

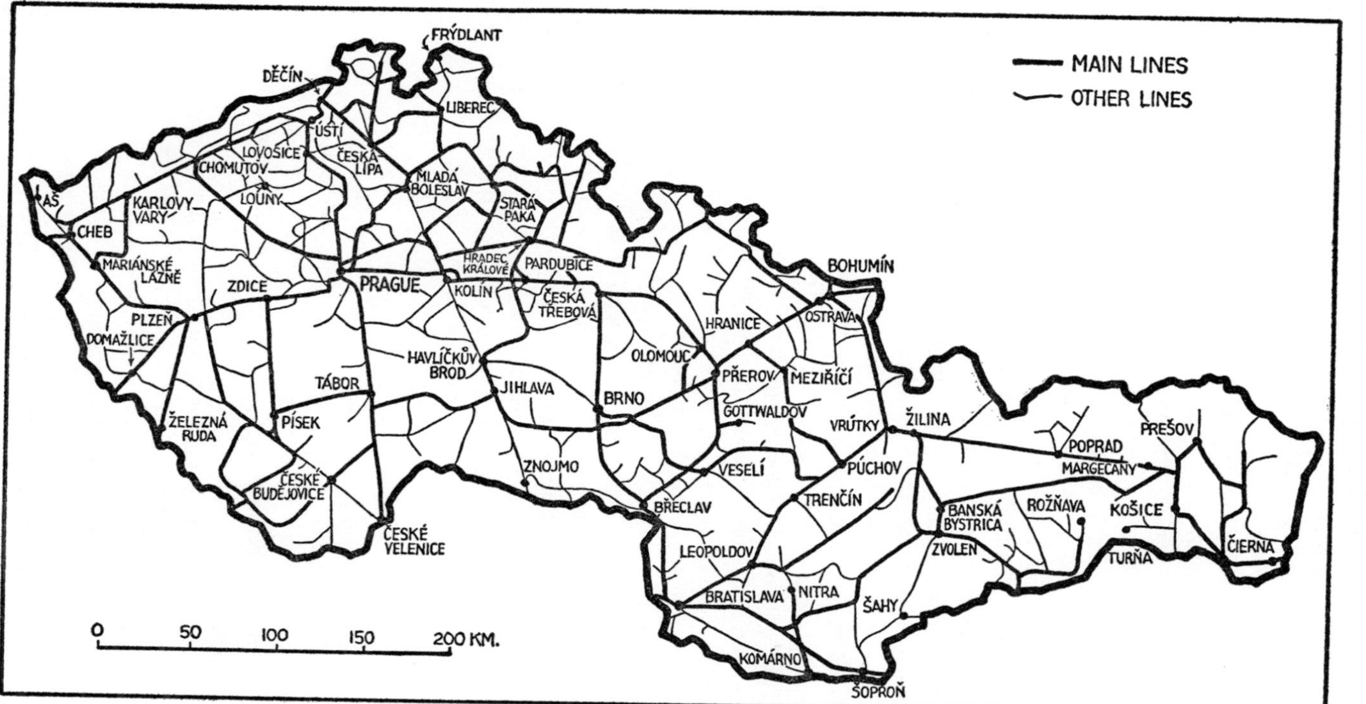

RAILROAD TRANSPORTATION

century, with the development of regular postal services, new post roads were added. Finally, in the nineteenth and twentieth centuries, military roads completed the network of various special purpose roads.

As in the case of railroads, the road network Czechoslovakia inherited from the Austro-Hungarian monarchy reflected the uneven development of the western and eastern provinces, and was highly inadequate for the country's needs. Hard surface roads were practically non-existent. Prior to 1918, there had been no coordination in road building between the western and eastern parts of the country, and no adequate road connections. With very few exceptions, roads were technically unsuitable for motor traffic.

Despite serious natural obstacles, particularly in Slovakia and Ruthenia, the road network was markedly improved and expanded during the interwar period. A number of main and secondary roads were broadened and paved with stone, concrete, or asphalt. Bridges were rebuilt or reinforced, numerous connections between Moravia and Slovakia were constructed, and road density in the latter was substantially increased. New secondary roads built in the southeastern lowlands of Slovakia and in Ruthenia stimulated local trade and economic development as they provided easy access to town markets where agricultural products commanded higher prices. The opening of Slovakia's mountain regions, on the other hand, stimulated the development of tourist trade. The plan to build two turnpikes—one traversing the country from west to east and the other from north to south—was precluded by the outbreak of World War II.

In the first postwar years, construction was restricted to repair of war damage, particularly rebuilding of destroyed bridges. In more recent years, road building activity has been insignificant. The only improvement anticipated by the first Five-Year Plan was the hard-surfacing of some 5,000 kilometers of roads.

Data on the distribution of the three main types of roads (state highways, district roads, and communal roads) among the country's provinces in 1936 and 1946 are shown in Table 5. As was noted earlier, no significant additions to the existing road network have been made since 1946.

Information on road surfacing is available for the prewar period and for state highways only. In 1937, about 65.6 per cent of state highways had all-weather surfacing; this figure includes 31.4 per cent of highways with heavy surface of concrete or stone, 10 per cent with medium surface, and 24.2 per cent with lightly coated surface. The remaining 34.4 per cent of state highways were largely covered with rolled dirt.

Table 5. Distribution of Roads, by Provinces, 1936 and 1946[a]
(in kilometers)

	State Highways		District Roads		Communal Roads		Total	
ince	1936	1946	1936	1946	1936	1946	1936	1946
tal	14,000	36,660	47,153	27,030	—	—	37,132	39,085
kia	8,033	8,380	—	—	—	—	15,988	16,225
via-Silesia	1,513	9,242	14,475	6,983	6,680	6,347	14,713	14,727
mia	4,454	19,038	32,678	20,047	6,680	6,347	67,833	70,037

urce: State Statistical Office, *Statistical Digest of the Czechoslovak Republic*, , p. 71.

ll data for present boundaries. In 1936, Ruthenia's roads extended over some) kilometers.

Stock of Motor Carriers. Prior to World War II, Czechoslovakia's stock of motor vehicles substantially exceeded that of her neighbors, with the exception of Germany. The country's automobile industry, with an estimated annual production capacity close to 40,000 vehicles, met practically all domestic requirements and exported motor vehicles to other countries of the Danubian basin, the Near East, and some overseas countries. The large number of motor vehicles, relative to the country's size and population reflected to some extent the high standard of living in prewar Czechoslovakia. In 1937, the number of passenger cars in Czechoslovakia (including Ruthenia) exceeded 90,000, while the combined total for Poland, Romania, Bulgaria, and Hungary amounted to only 66,000; in the same year, Czechoslovakia had over 28,000 trucks, while the four countries together had only 18,000. In recent years, however, these disparities have been substantially reduced.

Data on Czechoslovakia's stock of motor vehicles in 1937, 1948, and 1950 are presented in Table 6. Official figures for more recent years have not been published. The relatively high figures for 1948 reflect the acquisition of motor vehicles abandoned by the retreating Germans, as well as UNRRA, U. S. Army surplus, and other postwar relief deliveries, which raised Czechoslovakia's stock of trucks and passenger cars well above the prewar level. The number of buses, on the other hand, seems to have lagged behind the prewar figure for several years. In 1946, only some 2,800 obsolescent buses were in active service, with a substantial number of additional vehicles immobilized because of lack of spare parts. As a result, trucks were extensively used for passenger transport. Exact figures on the stock of buses and trucks after 1946 are not known because official statistics list only their combined totals (see Table 6). Though the number of buses appears to have increased considerably above the 1937 level in recent years (with some trucks being shifted from passenger to freight transport as a result), the increase has apparently been insufficient to meet mounting requirements for passenger transport. As for the number of trucks, there is some evidence that no substantial net additions were made between 1950 and the end of the first Five-Year Plan. The plan emphasized proper maintenance of the existing stock of vehicles rather than a net increase in their number. Furthermore, the steeply rising average daily load transported, and the average daily distance covered by motor carriers in recent years suggest that the rapidly growing volume of freight and passenger traffic has been met by more intensive use, rather than expansion of, the available stock of carriers. As for passenger cars, their number has probably dropped well below the 1948 level as a result of wear and the extremely high price of new cars.

Table 6. Stock of Motor Vehicles, 1937, 1948, and 1950[a]

Year	Trucks and Buses	Passenger Cars
1937	30,406[b]	84,844
1948	63,000	105,000
1950	65,000	....

Sources: Data for 1937, State Statistical Office, *Statisticka rocenka republiky Ceskoslovenske, 1938* (Statistical Yearbook of the Czechoslovak Republic, 1938) (Prague, 1938); data for 1948, United Nations, *Statistical Yearbook 1949-1950,* p. 301; figure for 1950, United Nations, *Statistical Yearbook 1953* (New York, 1953), p. 305.

[a] All figures pertain to present boundaries.

[b] Total for 1937 includes 27,311 trucks and 3,095 buses.

Freight Traffic. Prior to World War II, Czechoslovakia was the only country of Central and Eastern Europe (not including Germany) in which road transport played a relatively important role. However, road transport was and has remained largely local in scope and supplementary to, rather than competitive with, the railroads. In 1937, the average length of haul per ton of freight was 22 kilometers, compared with 145 kilometers for the railroads. By 1948, the figure for railroads had increased to 233 kilometers, while that for roads remained relatively unchanged. Railroad freight rates for short hauls usually exceeded trucking charges by comparatively wide margins.

During the prewar period, the bulk of trucking was handled by private operators, the share of state-owned carriers being negligible.

Under the nationalization decrees of 1945, only about 16 per cent of the trucking services were transferred to state ownership; the firms accounting for the remainder were too small to be affected by the decrees. Only in 1948, after the Comunist coup, were all trucking firms nationalized and, with a few exceptions, merged in The Czechoslovak Motor Transport, National Enterprise; the exceptions were a small number of minor firms placed under the management of communal enterprises.

Both the Two-Year Plan (1947-48) and the Five-Year Plan (1949-53) called for substantial increases in motor freight traffic relative to the prewar level. The rapid postwar growth in the volume of motor freight traffic was illustrated in Table 1. By 1948, the final year of the Two-Year Plan, freight tonnage transported by road had risen above the 1937 level by almost 45 per cent; and by 1953, the last year of the first Five-Year Plan, it was double that of 1948. Motor freight traffic has been limited to short-distance hauls, while long-distance hauling has been largely handled by the railroads. As a result, the large increase in motor carriers' share in the total volume of freight (from some 17 per cent in 1937 to about 25 per cent in 1953) tends to exaggerate the relative importance of motor freight carriers in the postwar period, and, conversely, to underrate the relative importance of railroad carriers. In terms of freight turnover, measured in ton-kilometers, motor carriers have played a comparatively minor role, accounting for only about 2 or 3 per cent of the total.

The rapidly growing postwar demand for trucking services seems to have been largely met by more intensive utilization rather than an increase of the supply of trucks. This is well illustrated by the following figures, showing the average daily load (in metric tons), as well as the average daily run (in kilometers) per truck during the period of the first Five-Year Plan:

Year	Average Daily Load	Average Daily Run
1949	4.7	48.1
1950	7.3	61.4
1951	8.5	62.2
1952	12.5	74.7
1953	15.7	86.1

Source: Rudzki, *op. cit.*, pp. 28-29.

Passenger Traffic. The development of passenger transport services has closely paralleled that of motor freight traffic. Prior to World War II, about 75 per cent of commercial passenger traffic was handled by private operators. State-owned carriers, which were operated as an adjunct to state railroads, accounted for the remainder. In 1945, following the promulgation of the nationalization decrees, the state's share in the volume of passenger transport increased to 68 per cent. In 1948, the remaining 32 per cent were absorbed by communal transport enterprises.

The volume of passenger traffic in 1937, 1948, and 1953 is shown in Table 1. By 1948, the number of passengers transported by road was almost 3.4 times that of 1937, and by 1953 (on the basis of the estimate in Table 1, which puts the actual figure 50 million below the original target of the first Five-Year Plan), it had risen to 6.7 times the 1937 volume. According to recent claims in the Czechoslovak press, the number of passengers transported by motor carriers in 1954 was over 600 million, i.e. more than eight times the 1937 figure. The number of regular bus routes reportedly increased from 700 in 1937 to 1,500 in 1948, 1,322 in 1951, and to 3,540 in 1953. Their total length was reported to have increased less rapidly, amounting to 43,700 kilometers in 1953 (a comparable figure for 1937 is not available).

The steep rise in passenger motor traffic in the postwar period can be traced to several causes. In the immediate postwar years, with many segments of railroad lines temporarily out of commission because of war damage, motor carriers were called upon to supplement the disrupted railway services. The rehabilitation and rapid expansion of the country's economy, combined with an acute shortage of housing in industrial and mining centers, swelled the number of regular daily commuters. Extensive use of labor brigades to cope with frequent bottlenecks in production, particularly in coal mining, has been another major factor. Numerous Communist Party conferences and political mass meetings in district towns and regional centers, political indoctrination courses, and recreation programs for workers also substantially added to the volume of passenger motor traffic.

Recent increases in the number and capacity of buses in operation have been inadequate to offset the growing strain on the available facilities. While in 1949 the average daily load per bus was 263 passengers and the average daily run was 103 kilometers, by 1953 these averages had increased to 336 and 121, respectively. Furthermore, a substantial volume of passenger traffic is borne by trucks. Thus, the steep postwar rise in Czechoslovakia's passenger motor traffic strongly suggests a simultaneous deterioration in saftey standards and passenger comfort.

Water Transport

Waterways have played a relatively minor role in Czechoslovakia's domestic traffic, though they have figured quite prominently in the country's foreign trade in certain commodities. Czechoslovakia controls only the upper reaches of some of the major European waterways, and only three of her rivers are navigable: the Vltava (Moldau), which runs its full course within Czechoslovak boundaries; the Labe (Elbe), which provides access to Germany's North Sea port of Hamburg; and the Danube, which links Czechoslovakia with the other countries of the Danubian basin and the Black Sea. The Oder, which has its source in northern Moravia and provides access to Czechoslovakia's free zone in Poland's Baltic Sea port of Szczecin, can accommodate only small vessels within its Czechoslovak segment. However, with the postwar reorientation of the country's foreign trade, increasing stress has been laid on the expansion and improvement of traffic on the Oder as well as on the Danube.

The greatest shortcoming of water transport facilities stems from the fact that the major waterways are not connected, but form independent segments of international water routes. The construction of the projected artificial waterway linking the Danube, the Oder, and the Labe would be of major significance for both Cezchoslovakia and Poland[1] as well as for most of the other Central and East European countries. Such a waterway would integrate the country's navigable rivers into a single network and provide a link between the Black Sea on one hand, and the North and Baltic seas on the other. The Danube-Oder-Labe canal has been in a blueprint stage for over fifty years. Though its construction has posed no serious technical problems, and despite the fact that all governments which have exercised jurisdiction over the Czechoslovak territory for the past fifty years (including the present Communist government) have unequivocally endorsed it, actual work on the project has never been started.

The Labe-Vltava Waterway. Both the Labe and the Vltava flow through rich farm, mining, and manufacturing regions of Bohemia and have been important in their economic development. Commercial traffic on both these rivers began on a major scale with the rapid expansion of mining and manufacturing in the nineteenth century. The Vltava has traditionally served as a waterway for domestic traffic, while foreign trade freight has been largely carried by the Labe. The internationalization of the Labe and the creation of a Czechoslovak free zone in the port of Hamburg after World War I greatly increased this waterway's significance.

Unsatisfactory conditions for navigation have necessitated the adoption of a permanent improvement program on both rivers (dredging the river bed, construction of levees, locks, and dams, etc.). Both rivers are fully navigable for some 220-260 days a year. Traffic comes

[1] The Oder segment of the canal would have to be extended about 30 miles into Polish territory to a point from which the river is fully navigable.

to a virtual halt during the winter when the rivers freeze and again in the summer when the water level drops.

Prague can be reached from Hamburg by steamers and cargo boats up to 1,000 tons for a period of about six months a year. It can be reached by smaller craft for an additional two months. The remainder of the year, when the water level is usually around or below 120 centimeters, the river can be used only for downstream (northbound) traffic by smaller vessels.

The structure of freight, particularly that carried by the Labe, has been highly diversified. Downstream cargo on the Labe consists chiefly of brown coal, building stone, sugar, fruit, malt, hops, glassware, textiles, leather goods, farming machinery, and other industrial products; upstream cargo is mainly composed of iron ore, metals, glass sands, phosphates, and crude oil. On the Vltava, downstream cargo includes timber, stone, building materials, and some farm products, while upstream freight consists mainly of coal, fertilizers, and some industrial products.

Prior to World War II, the Labe-Vltava route accounted for almost two thirds of Czechoslovakia's water-borne traffic, with the Danube accounting for the bulk of the remainder (see Table 7). Postwar rehabilitation of traffic on the Labe-Vltava waterway proceeded at a very slow pace, both because of the war damage to shipping facilities and the postwar reorientation of Czechoslovak foreign trade policy, which called for a rapid expansion of Danube and Oder river traffic. By the end of the first Five-Year Plan, the Labe-Vltava waterway accounted for only 42 per cent of the country's river freight, and as late as 1954, the volume of cargo conveyed by this route was still below the prewar level.

The Danube Waterway. From Devin to Szob, a distance of over 100 miles, the Danube forms the southern boundary between Czechoslovakia and Hungary. Bratislava and Komarno, the two Danube ports on Czechoslovak territory, have been trading centers since Roman times.

The Danube flows from highly industrialized Germany, through nearly as highly industrialized Austria and Czechoslovakia, into the predominantly agricultural countries of Hungary, Yugoslavia, Bulgaria, and Romania. The river carries a relatively light cargo (manufactured goods) downstream, and a relatively heavy cargo (grain, petroleum, and minerals) upstream; this somewhat anomalous pattern of traffic strongly influenced the freight rate policy of Danubian shipping firms. During the first Five-Year Plan, a significant change occurred in the pattern of downstream traffic. Czechoslovakia started to send downstream substantial quantities of uranium ore destined for the Soviet Union. On the other hand, she received from the Soviet Union large quantities of iron ore which she had previously imported from other sources.

The Danubian port of Bratislava is Czechoslovakia's largest river port. Its transshipment volume in 1937 amounted to 883,000 tons and, as the figures in Table 7 suggest, by the end of the first Five-Year Plan, had risen to about three times the prewar figure. Komarno, the country's second largest river port and the site of Czechoslovakia's largest shipyards, accounts for the remaining volume of traffic.

By 1937, Danube shipping represented about 32 per cent of Czechoslovakia's river traffic. After almost complete disruption during the immediate postwar period, recovery proceeded at a relatively rapid pace, and by 1948 the volume of freight reached the prewar figure. During the first Five-Year Plan, the volume of cargo increased 2.7 times, and by 1953 the Danube waterway accounted for about 58 per cent of Czechoslovakia's river traffic.

The Oder Waterway. The importance of the Oder waterway lies in the fact that it connects the industrial and coal mining regions of Upper Silesia with the Baltic Sea. Its usefulness for the Czechoslovak coal mining and industrial region of Ostrava is small because of the limited navigability of its Czechoslovak segment. As was noted earlier, the river is fully navigable only from the Polish town of Kozle, which lies about 30 miles beyond Czechoslovakia's frontier. Czechoslovak coal and coke from the Ostrava region and Swedish ores, the main items of Czechoslovakia's foreign trade conveyed by the Oder waterway have to be carried to and from Kozle by rail. Construction of the projected canal, linking the Oder with the Danube and the Labe, would remove this serious limitation.

Floating Stock and Freight Traffic. As a result of war destruction and postwar requisitioning of river craft by Soviet authorities, the number of vessels was reduced far below the prewar level. In 1937, the number of tugs in operating condition amounted to 81 and that of barges to 947; in 1948, despite some restitution of river craft by Soviet authorities, the corresponding figures stood at 29 and 296, respectively; in addition, there were some 70 barges which could be returned to service after some repair. Exact data for more recent years are not available, but the relatively slow recovery of river traffic would seem to indicate that as late as 1950 the county's floating stock was still below 1937 capacity.

Data on the voume of Czechoslovak river traffic, presented in Table 7, show clearly the postwar shift from the Labe-Vltava to the Danube waterway. Separate figures for the Oder waterway are available for the period 1937-48 only. Since 1948, traffic on the Oder has been reported jointly with that on the Labe-Vltava waterway.

Table 7. Volume of River Traffic, Selected Years 1937-1954
(in thousand tons)

<table>
<tr><th>Year</th><th>Labe-Vltava</th><th>Oder</th><th>Danube</th><th>Total</th></tr>
<tr><td>1937</td><td>2,489</td><td>138</td><td>1,262</td><td>3,889</td></tr>
<tr><td>1945</td><td>706</td><td>—</td><td>112</td><td>818</td></tr>
<tr><td>1946</td><td>1,007</td><td>—</td><td>494</td><td>1,501</td></tr>
<tr><td>1948</td><td>1,153</td><td>48</td><td>1,262</td><td>2,442</td></tr>
<tr><td>1950</td><td colspan="2">1,872</td><td>1,715</td><td>3,587</td></tr>
<tr><td>1951</td><td colspan="2">2,307</td><td>2,329</td><td>4,636</td></tr>
<tr><td>1952</td><td colspan="2">2,384</td><td>3,055</td><td>5,439</td></tr>
<tr><td>1953</td><td colspan="2">2,435</td><td>3,396</td><td>5,834</td></tr>
<tr><td>1954</td><td colspan="2">2,439</td><td>3,378</td><td>5,817</td></tr>
</table>

Sources. Data for 1937-1948 from State Statistical Office, *Statisticky zpravodaj, loc. cit.;* data for 1950-1954 based on *Doprava, loc. cit.*

Air Transport

Air transport in Czechoslovakia began some thirty-five years ago. Compared with the other branches of transportation, it has shown the slowest rate of development. In 1918, there was only one airfield on Czechoslovakia's territory, located in Cheb, in the western tip of Bohemia. Between 1918 and 1923, airfields were constructed in Prague, Bratislava, and Kosice. The first regular service, connecting Prague with Strasbourg and Paris, was established in 1920 by a Franco-Romanian corporation, with some participation of Czechoslovak capital. Subsequently, the flights operated by this company were extended to include Warsaw, Vienna, Budapest, Belgrade, and Istanbul.

In 1923, the first domestic air route was established between Prague and Bratislava. It was operated by the newly created, state-owned Czechoslovak State Airlines (Ceskoslovenske statni aerolinie, CSA). In 1924, the flight was extended to service Kosice, and in 1926 the city of Brno.

In 1927, a private airline corporation, the Czechoslovak Air Transport Company (Ceskoslovenska letecka spolecnost, CLS), was founded. The Zlin Air Transport Company (Zlinska letecka spolecnost, ZLS), a small company owned by shoe manufacturer Bata, completed the list of Czechoslovak airlines operating before World War II. In 1927, domestic air connections were extended to Marianske Lazne (Marienbad), in 1928 to Uzhorod, the capital of Ruthenia, in

1931 to Karlovy Vary (Karlsbad), in 1935 to Piestany, Hradec Kralove, Ostrava-Opava, and Zlin, and in 1937 to Liberec.

In 1928, Czechoslovak airlines established international connections, the first with Rotterdam, followed by the Berlin-Prague-Vienna route. Between 1930 and 1938, air connections were established with Yugoslavia, Switzerland, Romania, France, the Soviet Union, Hungary, Belgium, Italy, and Finland. During the same period, the number of foreign-owned airlines servicing Czechoslovakia gradually increased to ten.

By 1933, the CSA operated eighteen aircraft, the CLS fourteen, and the ZLS from six to eight. Most of these aircraft had a single motor and a capacity of five to eight passengers. The main air routes, however, were serviced by aircraft with two or three motors, with a maximum capacity of twenty-five passengers. Beginning in the early thirties, airfields were improved by the installation of modern safety devices and night illumination equipment.

During World War II, Czechoslovak territory was serviced exclusively by the German Lufthansa. After the war, resumption of air traffic was considerably delayed by the lack of aircraft and necessary equipment. In 1946, the Czechoslovak State Airlines, re-established as a state monopoly, resumed operations with a few salvaged, obsolete JU-52's. Subsequently, several American DC-3's were secured from Allied war surplus and adapted for civilian use. When air transportation was resumed in 1946, the CSA possessed about eight JU-52's, thirty DC-3's, and six Douglas-47 cargo aircraft.

Prewar density of the Czechoslovak air transport network was surpassed by the end of 1946; scheduled domestic flights included Prague, Brno, Bratislava, Sliac, Kosice, Ostrava, Olomouc, Piestany, Zilina, and Karlovy Vary, and international connections covered Zurich, Strasbourg, Brussels, Rotterdam, London, Copenhagen, Oslo, Stockholm, Warsaw, Belgrade, and Bucharest. In 1947, domestic services were extended to Presov, Poprad, Zlin, Marianske Lazne, Liberec, and Ceske Budejovice, and international services to Zagreb, Zadar, Budapest, Berlin, Rome, Athens, Istanbul, Ankara, Cairo, and Lydda. In 1948, immediately prior to the Communist coup, the towns of Trencin and Kromeriz were added to the domestic network, and international connections were expanded to Sofia, Göteborg, Helsinki, Beirut, and Nice. This point marked the peak in Czechoslovakia's air transport development.

After the 1948 *coup d'état,* flights to countries outside the Soviet orbit were sharply curtailed. In 1949, air connections with Lydda, Beirut, and Istanbul were discontinued. In 1950-51, all CSA air services involving the overflight of West Germany were cancelled as a result of the revocation of Czechoslovakia's overflight permit due to her aircrafts' violations of the allocated air corridors. Domestic services were also sharply reduced. In 1955, according to official Czechoslovak sources, only Prague, Brno, Bratislava, Kosice, Ostrava, Gottwaldov (formerly Zlin), Olomouc, Poprad, Sliac, and Presov were provided with air connections. In the same year, the list of the Czechoslovak State Airlines' scheduled international flights included only the capitals of the Soviet bloc countries (including the Soviet Union), Denmark, Sweden, Finland, Austria and the city of Berlin. In addition, since early 1955, the CSA has shared the Prague-Paris route with Air France. All other air connections with the Western countries have been provided by Western airlines. In 1955, Swissair provided three flights a week between Zürich and Prague, and the Dutch KLM provided the same number of flights between Amsterdam and Prague; the latter company also operated one flight per week between Prague, Beirut, and Cairo. The Belgian Sabena operated three flights a week between Brussels and Prague.

In 1950, the CSA reportedly owned about fifty aircraft. Figures for more recent years have not been published.

Some data on the volume of passenger air traffic were included in Table 1. Additional available data are presented in Table 8, showing both the scheduled as well as the total traffic in selected years from 1937 to 1953. The figures indicate that about half of the total distance flown was accounted for by unscheduled flights. They also reflect the curtailment of air transport services after 1948 and a slight upturn by the end of the Five-Year Plan.

Table 8. Air Traffic, Selected Years 1937-1953

Year	Number of Flights[a]	Distance Flown		Passenger Turnover		Freight Turno	
		Scheduled	Total	Scheduled	Total	Scheduled[b]	To
		(in 1,000 km)		(in 1,000 Passenger-km)		(in 1,000 ton-k	
1937	11,954	1,888	3,672	9,235	18,576	228	5
1948	18,114	5,878	9,648	55,254	91,008	2,811	5,0
1951	....	2,373	....	26,100	....	663	...
1952	....	1,624	....	17,862	....	486	..
1953	....	1,689	13,600[c]	20,541		600	..

Sources: All data for scheduled services from United Nations, *Statistical Yearbc 1954* p. 315; all total traffic data from State Statistical Office, *Statisticky zpravodaj, l. cit.*

[a] Refers to total number of flights.

[b] Includes the following mail cargo turnover (in thousand ton-kilometers); 18 1937; 480 in 1948; 120 in 1951; 76 in 1952; and 87 in 1953.

[c] Refers to target figures of the original version of the Five-Year Plan; subsequ developments which are discussed in the text made the achievement of the tar impossible.

Postal, Telephone, and Telegraph Communications

The first regular postal service, established in 1527 in the territory of present-day Czechoslovakia, served exclusively the king and his court. In the seventeenth century, the city of Prague had regular postal connections with five European capitals: London, Paris, Brussels, Rome, and Vienna. Postal services were first operated as a franchise by some aristocratic families, but in the eighteenth century they were taken over by the state. At the end of the nineteenth century, these services were organized under the Ministry of Post, Telegraph, and Telephone. In addition to the regular postal and telecommunication services, the ministry operated a postal money order system, an important public service in a country where the use of checking accounts was not common.

In 1918, Czechoslovakia inherited a postal organization from the Austro-Hungarian monarchy. While the mail and postal money order services could be used without major adjustments, the telegraph and telephone lines did not correspond to the needs of the new state. As in the case of railroads, most of the lines ran in a north-south direction, whereas west-east connections were lacking in many cases.

In 1938, after twenty years of systematic investments (particularly in long-distance west-east trunk lines), the system was well adjusted to the country's needs and the quality of service was up to Western standards. During the interwar period, telegraph and telephone services were modernized and extended overseas, and communications by telephone and wireless telegraph expanded rapidly. Direct long-distance telephone connections gradually replaced the older form of communication by telegraph.

In 1937, there were 4,473 post offices in the country; the total length of communication wires amounted to 140,000 kilometers; there were 4,689 telegraph stations, i.e., one station for every 31 square kilometers of territory and for each 3,400 inhabitants; the length of local telephone lines was 20,000 kilometers; trunk lines measured 19,000 kilometers; there were more than 150,000 telephone subscribers, 42,000 of whom were in Prague; the annual number of telephone calls amounted to 250 million. Nevertheless, telephone service continued to be a privilege of the densely populated urban areas; among Czechoslovakia's 15,034 communities, only 2,808 had telephone connections. The number of radio receivers exceeded the one million mark shortly before World War II.

After World War II, the country's postal, telephone, and telegraph services continued to expand. By the end of 1948, the number of communities with telephone connection increased to 10,247, i.e. to over 68 per cent of the total. In the Czech lands, the proportion of communities with telephone service rose to 73 per cent and in Slovakia to 51.4 per cent.

The number of radio receivers also rapidly increased in the postwar period. By 1948, their total reached 2,108,000 as compared with 1,034,000 in 1937; the Czech lands alone accounted for 1,877,000 receivers in 1948 as against 928,000 in 1937.

The Communist government thus inherited an efficient postal and telecommunications system which was adequate for the needs of the country. Only fragmentary information is available on developments following the Communist coup. By 1953, according to an official claim, all the country's communities had been provided with telephone connection. In the same year, the number of telephones reportedly stood 44 per cent above the 1948 level; this would indicate a total of about 450,000. The number of radio receivers reportedly amounted to 2.7 million, i.e. one radio receiving set for each 4.7 inhabitants.

Appendix

BIOGRAPHICAL SKETCHES
of Leading Figures of the Communist Regime

Curt Beck

The present alignment of Communist Party and government leadership in Czechoslovakia is largely an outgrowth of the Gottwald-Slansky conflict, which is briefly reviewed in the two introductory biographical sketches of Gottwald and Slansky. These sketches are followed by short biographies of the leading Czechoslovak Communists, arranged in alphabetical order.

Gottwald and Slansky

Klement Gottwald (1896-1953) was born November 23, 1896 in the village of Dedice in Moravia, of Catholic Czech peasant parents. At twelve, he was sent by his mother to Vienna to learn the carpenter's trade. While in Vienna, he came under the influence of the Social Democratic Party. He returned to the Czech province when he was eighteen, trained not only in carpentry, but fairly well acquainted with literature and politics. In addition, he had acquired fluency in German. After serving in World War I, he worked at his trade and took part in political activities among his fellow workers. In 1921, he joined the newly formed Communist Party and participated in professional Party activities. He was active as editor of a small provincial Communist newspaper and must have distinguished himself, because he was elected to the Central Committee of the Party in 1925. He won recognition for his propaganda work and became head of the Central Committee's Agitprop section—the section dealing with agitation and propaganda.

Gottwald's reputation spread beyond local Communist circles and he became active in the international Communist movement. In 1928, he was elected to the executive committee of the Sixth Congress of the Comintern, which was held in Moscow. His rise to prominence coincided with, and was helped by, that of Stalin. With the added prestige of Moscow approbation, Gottwald set out to wrest control from the "right" wing of the Czechoslovak Communist Party, which was headed by Jilek. He succeeded in this at the Fifth Party Congress, held in Prague in 1929, when he was elected General Secretary of the Party. Gottwald was a strong proponent of the Popular Front and took a leading role in drafting the Popular Front policy at the Seventh Comintern Congress in Moscow in 1935. He was also elected deputy to the National Assembly in Prague the same year.

After World War II, which he spent in Moscow, Gottwald devoted his primary attention to increasing Communist influence in the government. He assumed several offices in post-World War II governments. He was Deputy Prime Minister from April 1945 to July 1946; Prime Minister from July 1946 to June 1948; and President from June 1948 to March 1953, when he died. The time required by his government office forced him to abandon his Party administrative duties and to limit himself to general policy supervision. Hence, at the Eighth Party Congress in March 1946, Gottwald was elected Party Chairman, relinquishing the Party Secretaryship to Rudolf Slansky. However, in the Communist *coup d'état* of February 1948, Gottwald played the leading role.

Rudolf Slansky (1901-52) was born July 31, 1901, in Nezvestice, near Plzen. He was of Jewish Czech middle-class background. His father was a small village trader.

Slansky was educated at the Plzen Commercial Academy. After World War I, he went to Prague and associated with leftist intellectuals, becoming a member of the so-called Marxist Club and joining the Communist Party in 1921, when it broke off from the Social Democratic Party. He became active in Party affairs, engaging in youth activities and later in Party journalism. He rose quickly in the Party hierarchy, and was chosen a member of the Presidium and Politburo at the Fifth Congress in 1929, the same time Gottwald became General Secretary. His selection was undoubtedly based upon his support of the Gottwald faction in the struggle which preceded the Congress. Like Gottwald, he was also elected to the Czechoslovak National Assembly in 1935. After Munich, as one of the Czechoslovak Communist leaders who were considered indispensable, he was sent to Moscow, where he spent most of the war. There he participated in the March 1945 discussions between Benes and the Communists concerning the organization of the postwar government. While Gottwald concerned himself with the government, Slansky took over the administration of Party affairs. This situation was confirmed at the Eighth Party Congress, held in March 1946, when Gottwald assumed the newly created position of Party Chairman and Slansky took over the post of General Secretary.

The accusation made against Slansky at his trial, November 20 to 27, 1952, that he strengthened his position within the Party by placing his men in crucial positions within the Party apparatus, appears plausible. Until the Communist victory of February 1948, the battle for the conquest of the government pushed internal Party contests into the background. Men of such different types as Gottwald and Slansky played equally important roles in the period 1945-1948. That early phase required spellbinders and mass organizers, such as Gottwald, as well as adroit schemers, such as Slansky, who could outmaneuver opponents in one organization after another. However, once the Communist goal of power had been achieved, the hitherto latent rivalries could no longer be ignored. The exercise of government power required agreement on a positive program.

Both Gottwald and Slansky approached the showdown with certain assets. Gottwald enjoyed the support of the majority of the members of the Political Bureau. He was backed by such old timers as Zapotocky, Siroky, Bacilek, and Dolansky, as well as by his son-in-law, Cepicka. He was in control of the top policy-making organ and of the government. However, Slansky had established control over the Party apparatus and was rapidly infiltrating key governmental organs with men loyal to him. As far as popular support was concerned, Gottwald and Zapotocky were better known and could act as men of the people, whereas Slansky and his friends could be portrayed as "cosmopolitan," Jewish, or German, and could in other ways be designated as alien and un-Czech. However, in the last analysis, the contest within the Czechoslovak Communist Party could only be won by that faction which gained the support of the Soviet Union. A widely spread view pictured Slansky as enjoying Moscow's confidence. It was reasoned that Slansky, having fewer national Czech ties than Gottwald, would be more acceptable to Moscow than the latter, who had exhibited Titoist tendencies. However, the factor which finally determined Moscow's attitude appeared to have been the desire to back the group more likely to succeed in building up the Czechoslovak economy to the point where it could provide the Soviet economy with needed products. It should also be remembered that Gottwald had furthered Stalin's Comintern policies from 1928 onward—an ample indication of loyalty to Moscow.

Gottwald engineered Slansky's downfall methodically. Some of the more unpopular men whom Slansky had placed in influential positions (e.g., Otto Sling, Regional Secretary of the Brno region, and Bedrich Rejcin, division general, Deputy Minister of National Defense, and Chief of Military Intelligence) were accused of Party excesses. Lacking sufficient power to halt these accusations, Slansky participated in some of the preliminary purges. Once the purges were in full swing and it had become clear that the Party organization was deeply involved in a crisis of confidence, it was relatively simple for Gottwald to point to Slansky as the source of all trouble. It had been Slansky's responsibility to maintain a functioning Party organization, and he apparently had failed. Slansky was demoted in the Party on September 6, 1951, and his arrest was announced November 27, 1951. Having himself participated in the purges of his assumed friends, he was isolated when his turn came. Once his name was identified as an evil influence in the Party, he became a convenient scapegoat for all the regime's mistakes. Everything from inefficient Party administration to the insufficient electricity supply was blamed on him. Slansky's career reached its end with the trial of November 20-27, 1952, when he was charged with treason, sabotage, and espionage. His sentence, death by hanging, was carried out on December 3, 1952.

This left Gottwald in undisputed control of the Party and government. Gottwald, as Party Chairman had absorbed the functions of the General Secretary on September 6, 1951. However, upon returning from Stalin's funeral (March 5, 1953), he died suddenly on March 14, 1953, leaving his associates in firm control of the Party and the government.

BACILEK, KAROL: Member of the Political Bureau of the Central Committee of the KSC[1] and of the Political Bureau of the Central Committee of the KSS;[2] First Secretary of the Central Committee of the KSS.

Born: October 2, 1896, in Chotanky, Bohemia; of poor parents.

Career: Bacilek's education was limited to elementary school, which he left in his early teens to become a locksmith's apprentice. At fourteen, he moved to Prague, where he became a metal worker. He served in World War I and was imprisoned for carrying on Communist agitation among the troops. After the war, he became active in the Social Democratic Party, leaving it to join the Communist Party when the latter was founded in 1921. He worked on the railroad in Slovakia, but apparently spent most of his time in political activities, which resulted in his dismissal. In the late twenties, he rose in the Party organization while working in various Slovak districts. The practical experience gained in these activities was supplemented in 1934-35 by a year's study at the Lenin School in Moscow.

In 1939, Bacilek left for the Soviet Union, where he spent most of the war. He was not among the Czechoslovak émigré leadership which had congregated at Moscow. Instead, he went to the provinces, working for a while in the Stalingrad Tractor Factory. In 1941, he joined the Soviet Army, eventually fighting with partisan units in Poland. He participated in the Slovak uprising, and from that time on held a prominent position in the KSS. He was elected Secretary General of the KSS in 1944, but was later reduced to Deputy Secretary General. At the Ninth Party Congress of the KSC, which was held in May 1949, Bacilek was elected to the Central Committee. At the meeting of the Central Committee, which on September 6, 1951 decided to demote Slansky from his top Party post, Bacilek was elevated to the Presidium and to the Political Secretariat (called the Political Bureau since June 1954). It thus appears that Bacilek, like Novotny, was a man whom Gottwald placed in the highest Party councils to strengthen his own position.

In the central government Bacilek served variously as Deputy Premier (for six months in 1953), Minister of State Control, and, from January 1952 to September 1953, as Minister of National Security, a post which gave him control of the secret police. This was of great importance at the time when the Slansky and related purges were in progress. Gottwald probably reasoned that Bacilek, whose main activity had concerned Slovakia, would be more ruthless in eliminating Slansky men in the Czech territories than any Party man with close personal ties in Bohemia and Moravia. If this is a correct interpretation of Bacilek's role, it is not surprising that the conclusion of the Slansky-Gottwald feud was followed in September 1953 by Bacilek's return to his Slovak bailiwick. He was appointed First Secretary of the Central Committee of the KSS, filling the post equivalent to that which Novotny occupies in the KSC. Bacilek acts as Novotny's agent in Slovakia.

[1] Communist Party of Czechoslovakia.

[2] Communist Party of Slovakia.

BARAK, RUDOLF: Member of the Political Bureau of the Central Committee of the KSC; Minister of the Interior.

Born: Place and date are unknown, though the date was probably between 1905 and 1910.

Career: Very little information concerning his family background, education, and past activity is available. He first appeared in a high position in December 1952, when he was named a candidate to the Central Committee of the KSC by the National Party Conference. At that time, it was announced that he was chairman of the Regional People's Committee of Brno. It is probable that his reputation in the Party was earned through outstanding work on the regional level. The strong administrative machine in the Brno region, which effectively quelled the riots following the currency conversion (June 1953), is credited to Barak's organizational efficiency.

On March 25, 1953, four days after Zapotocky's elevation to the Presidency, Barak was made Deputy Premier. Six months later, he was relieved of this post and made Minister of the Interior. He was elected to the Central Committee in June 1954 at the Tenth Party Congress and, immediately after the Congress, was elected a full member of the Political Bureau.

CEPICKA, ALEXEJ: Member of the Political Bureau of the Central Committee of the KSC; First Deputy Premier; Minister of National Defense.

Born: August 18, 1910, in Kromeriz, Moravia; son of a letter carrier.

Career: Cepicka's rise to power paralleled that of Bacilek, but the two men, who between 1951 and 1953 were almost always bracketed together, came from entirely different backgrounds and displayed different methods of operation. Cepicka attended Charles University, where he received a Doctorate of Law in 1935. He did not join the Communist Party until 1938, though he claims that during his student years he was a leader of Communist student organizations. After completing his studies, he worked as a candidate for the bar in an attorney's office in Ostrava. Investigated for financial irregularities in the middle 1930's, he was stricken from the list of candidates by the Chamber of Advocates in Brno.

After the outbreak of World War II, he joined the Communist underground in Ostrava. He was arrested in 1942 and spent the rest of the war in the German concentration camps at Oswiecim (Auschwitz) and Buchenwald. After the war, he returned to Kromeriz and became chairman of the local People's Committee. He was elected to the Constituent National Assembly in May 1946 and was one of the Communist Party representatives on the Constitutional Committee. There is considerable evidence that Cepicka was involved in the attempted plot on the lives of three non-Communist ministers, Jan Masaryk, Petr Zenkl, and Prokop Drtina, in 1947. Cepicka became the Minister for Internal Trade in 1947 and established close relations with Gottwald, whose daughter Martha he married in July 1948.

After the coup, Cepicka became Minister of Justice and piloted through the Cabinet and National Assembly a legislative measure entitled the Law Concerning the Protection of the Republic, as well as acts to reorganize the profession of law and the judiciary, to replace the established courts by Communist-dominated people's courts, and new civil, criminal, and procedural codes. In addition to being Minister of Justice, he was Secretary General of the Central Action Committee of the National Front and head of the State Office for Church Affairs. His reputation as trouble shooter had been well established by this time, and he was given the crucial task of transforming the army into an effective support of the Soviet Army. He assumed the job of Minister of National Defense in 1950. In 1950, he received the rank of Army General, though he had no previous record of military services. His successes as reorganizer of non-Communist agencies into bulwarks of Communist strength earned him promotion to the Political Bureau (then the Presidium) on September 6, 1951. In 1953, he became First Deputy Premier.

Cepicka was formally dismissed from his positions of First Deputy Premier, Minister of National Defense, and Political Bureau member on April 25, 1956. He was removed for having fostered "the cult of the individual," especially in the army.

DAVID, VACLAV: Member of the Central Committee of the KSC; Minister of Foreign Affairs.

Born: September 23, 1910, in Studeny, district Ledec nad Sazavou in Bohemia; of a laborer's family.

Career: David is one of the younger Communist leaders who was brought in by Novotny, but who does not belong to the Political Bureau. He attended a business academy, from which he graduated in 1929. He was active in Communist youth organizations and, in 1935, joined the Communist Party. Throughout the war, he remained in Czechoslovakia and participated in the underground. After the war, largely on the reputation which he had gained in the resistance, he rose in Party ranks, eventually becoming a district leader and playing an important role in the National Assembly, to which he was elected in 1945. He became a member of the Central Committee in 1946 and a member of the Presidium in 1949. In 1951, he was picked by Novotny to help in the reorganization of the Secretariat. In February 1953, he stepped out of the Party apparatus to assume the job of Minister of Foreign Affairs, a post he still holds.

DOLANSKY, JAROMIR: Member of the Political Bureau of the Central Committee of the KSC; First Deputy Premier.

Born: February 25, 1895, in Prague; of well-to-do parents.

Career: Dolansky is one of the few Communist leaders from a comparatively wealthy background. He encountered few difficulties in his search for a good education, which he completed with a Doctorate of

Law from Charles University. While at the University, he was drawn into left-wing political activities, and in 1921 he joined the Communist Party. In 1923, he was elected a member of the Central Committee of the KSC. He was elected to the National Assembly in 1925, and has served in it ever since. He concentrated on economic matters, contributing articles on the subject to the Party press. In the Jilek-Gottwald conflict of the twenties, Dolansky sided with Gottwald. A member of the Communist underground, Dolansky was arrested and sent to the German concentration camp at Sachsenhausen during World War II, where a close friendship with Zapotocky was cemented. He went to Moscow after his release, and did not come to Prague until 1945.

Dolansky rose quickly again in Party leadership: from 1945 to 1946, he was Deputy Secretary General of the Party; in 1946, he was re-elected to the Party's Central Committee, and was given the post of Minister of Finance in the July 1946 government headed by Gottwald. After the coup, he was placed in charge of a special economic planning section within the Party, and in April 1949, became chairman of the State Planning Commission. He also became a member of the Party's Secretariat in 1949. He was appointed Deputy Premier in charge of coordinating the economic ministries in 1951, and has been First Deputy Premier since 1953.

Dolansky's over-all task of coordinating the domestic economy is supplemented by his task of linking Czechoslovakia's economy with that of the other captive states and the Soviet Union. He has been a representative on the Council for Mutual Economic Cooperation. He is one of the few intellectuals in the Party leadership.

DURIS, JULIUS: Member of the Central Committee of the KSC; Minister of Finance.

Born: March 9, 1904, in Rovany, near Lucenec, in Slovakia; son of a shoemaker who later became a schoolteacher.

Career: Duris studied law in Prague and in Paris, but never achieved a university degree. Sometime during the period 1926-28, he also received training in Moscow. He became a member of the Party in 1927, and during the Party's internal struggle in the late twenties, he adhered to the Gottwald group. His early experience in the Party was that of journalist and agitator. He spent the years 1929-32 in France as editor of a Communist publication, *Rovnost* (Equality) for Slovak émigrés; he was expelled by the French government in 1932. Upon his return to Slovakia, he worked as editor of the Communist *Ludovy Dennik* (People's Daily) until 1934, when he was elected deputy to the Slovak Provincial Assembly. At that time, he also became a member of the Land Committee of the KSC and Secretary of the Bratislava (capital of Slovakia) regional division of the Party.

After Slovakia's separation from Czechoslovakia, Duris participated in the underground, becoming a member of the three-man Central Committee of the KSS. He was imprisoned in 1941 and did not reappear on the political scene until 1945, when he joined the Czechoslovak government in exile on its return through Kosice.

In 1945, he became a member of the Central Committee and of the Presidium of the KSS, remaining in the former position until April 1955, and in the latter until July 1954. Since 1949, he has been a member of the Central Committee of the KSC.

Duris' government career has fluctuated considerably. In the first postwar government, he held the position of Minister of Agriculture, from which he was demoted by Gottwald in 1951 for lack of competence. After his demotion, Duris was assigned the chairmanship of the Slovak Board of Commissioners, a position he held until his reinstatement into the Czechoslovak government during its reorganization in September 1953. As an initial step to his reinstatement, he was appointed Minister of Forests and Timber Industry in February 1953. Seven months later, he was promoted to Minister of Finance, a post of high rank which he still holds.

FIERLINGER, ZDENEK: Member of the Political Bureau of the Central Committee of the KSC; Chairman of the National Assembly.

Born: July 11, 1891, in Olomouc, Moravia; son of middle-class parents.

Career: Fierlinger graduated from the Commercial Academy of Olomouc in 1910, and worked in Tsarist Russia as representative of a bicycle firm from that time until the outbreak of World War I.

In 1915, he became an officer with the Czechoslovak Legion in Russia. In 1918, he was transferred, with the rank of colonel, to the Czechoslovak Army in France. He collaborated closely with Benes, and after the war entered the diplomatic service, becoming Chief of the Czechoslovak Mission in France. Benes, who was Foreign Minister, thought highly of Fierlinger's services and rewarded him with many outstanding assignments in the diplomatic service.

Aside from being in charge of various sections of the Foreign Ministry, Fierlinger held the following foreign assignments: Minister to the Netherlands, 1921-24; Minister to Romania, 1924-25; Minister to the United States, 1925-28; Minister to Switzerland and Permanent Delegate to the League of Nations, 1928-32; Minister to Austria, 1932-36; Minister to the Soviet Union, 1937-38. Ever since his sojourn in Tsarist Russia, Fierlinger seems to have had an attachment to that country. He was actively concerned with the signing of the Czechoslovak-Soviet Mutual Assistance Pact of 1935. After the Munich Agreement, he stayed in Moscow without diplomatic status until 1940. Finally, upon eviction by the Soviet government, he joined Benes's government in exile in London.

When the Soviet Union renewed relations with Czechoslovakia in 1941, Benes sent Fierlinger to Moscow as Czechoslovakia's Minister and later Ambassador. While Benes favored cooperation with the Soviet Union up to a point, Fierlinger advocated unequivocal and irrevocable collaboration. Fierlinger was instrumental in the preparation and signing of the Soviet-Czechoslovak Alliance Treaty in 1943, thus crowning with success his wartime efforts.

After the war, Fierlinger turned to the field of domestic politics. He became a leader of the Social Democratic Party and made it his task to lead that party toward ever closer cooperation with the Communist Party. He also played an important role in the government, becoming the first Prime Minister after liberation. Following the 1946 elections, Fierlinger had to be satisfied with the post of Deputy Prime Minister. After a short period (November 1947–February 1948) of exile from leadership of the Social Democratic Party, Fierlinger recaptured his position during the days of the February 1948 coup. Once the Communists had achieved complete control over the government, Fierlinger led the purged Social Democratic Party to complete union with the Communist Party in June 1948. As a reward, he became a member of the Presidium of the Communist Party. However, his usefulness to the Communist cause had declined, and he had to be content with less important governmental positions.

Since 1945, he has held a variety of government and Party posts, having been twice Deputy Prime Minister, Minister of Industry, Chairman of the State Office for Church Affairs, member of the Presidium of the Central Action Committee of the Party, and delegate to various Communist conferences in the Soviet Union and the captive countries. In 1953, he became Chairman (Speaker) of the National Assembly and, in 1954, he was elected to the Political Bureau of the Central Committee of the KSC.

His position is probably due, at least in part, to the regime's effort to placate Social Democratic elements, and he presumably wields very little power.

HARUS, JAN: Chairman of the Control Commission of the KSC.

Born: July 12, 1892, in Polnicka, near Pribyslav; son of a weaver.

Career: Harus is an old-time Communist who has always been at the outer reaches of Party power. He received only elementary education, and then became a glass worker. He participated in the founding of the Communist Party in 1921. Since 1925, he has been a member of the Central Committee of the KSC. He has also attended Comintern meetings in Moscow and has been a deputy in Czechoslovakia's National Assembly since 1925, with several interruptions in service. Due to illegal activities in the thirties, Harus had to flee to the Soviet Union, where he worked as a glass blower. During the war, he assumed an important role in the Moscow group of Czechoslovak émigrés. After the war, he became active in the Party apparatus, finally reaching a top position in 1951 as Chairman of the Party's Control Commission, the organ which handles irregularities in the Party apparatus.

HENDRYCH, JIRI: Member of the Secretariat of the Central Committee of the KSC.

Career: Hendrych was a member of Slansky's Secretariat, and appears to have suffered from the reorganization of the Secretariat following

Slansky's arrest in 1951. His name was little heard when Novotny first assumed control, and he only gradually re-emerged from obscurity after his Party purity had been re-established.

JANKOVCOVA, LUDMILA: Candidate Member of the Political Bureau of the Central Committee of the KSC; Deputy Premier.

Born: 1897; of middle-class family.

Career: Jankovcova is a graduate of the Commercial Academy of Prague. Before World War II, she was active in social welfare work and in politics. During the war, she worked in the underground trade union movement. The death of her husband, a professor, at the hands of Nazis, embittered her, and was probably one of the factors which pushed her toward greater extremism. After the war, she was active in the Social Democratic Party, siding with Fierlinger in the crucial days of February 1948. She was elected to the Communist Party's Presidium and, in June 1954, became the first woman candidate member of the Political Bureau of the KSC. She is also a Deputy Premier in the central government.

KOEHLER, BRUNO: Member of the Secretariat of the Central Committee of the KSC.

Born: July 16, 1900, in Nove Mesto pod Smrkem, district of Frydlant, in northern Bohemia.

Career: At the age of fourteen, Koehler took a job in the printing house of the German Social Democratic Party. He soon associated himself with the left wing of the Party; when the Czechoslovak and German Communist parties were established in 1920, he was one of the founding members of the German component, which was then led by Karl Kreibich. Soon after the merger of the two Communist parties in Bohemia, Koehler gained an important position in the Party machinery, and, in 1921, he was a delegate for the Party at the Third World Congress of the Communist International. He was one of the leading figures in the Czechoslovak League of Young Communists and worked as a member of its central secretariat in Prague and Karlovy Vary. In 1924, he was made Secretary of the Communist Party in the Ostrava region, and two years later went to Moscow for political training.

During the late twenties and the thirties, he supported Gottwald in his fight against the "Trotskyites." In 1935, he became a member of the Czechoslovak Parliament. After Munich, he left Czechoslovakia for France, but in 1941 went to Moscow, where he joined the Gottwald group. After the war, he was kept in the background, due to the nationalist anti-German policy of the Party. He was sent to the eastern sector of Berlin as a liaison officer with the German Communists and the German Unity Party. Meanwhile, his wife was Gottwald's private secretary.

Koehler returned to Prague in 1947 and took part in the Communist coup of February 1948. He participated in the purge of Marie Svermova, being one of the three members of a special commission appointed by the Party Presidium to investigate Svermova, Sling, and Clementis. In July 1951, he was one of the officials of the Central Committee charged with carrying out the transfer of 77,500 administrative workers to productive work. In April 1952, he attended the first city conference of the Communist Party in Prague as the "representative of the Central Committee."

Since the purge of Bedrich Geminder as a Slansky accomplice in 1951, and the relegation to relative obscurity of Karl Kreibich, Bruno Koehler has been the outstanding Sudeten German Communist in high Party ranks. In more recent years, he has concerned himself primarily with Party administrative matters.

KOPECKY, VACLAV: Member of the Political Bureau of the Central Committee of the KSC; Deputy Premier.

Born: August 27, 1897, in Kosmonosy, Bohemia; son of a tradesman, grandson of a famous puppeteer.

Career: Kopecky has been Czechoslovakia's Goebbels, his field of concentration centering upon propaganda and cultural affairs. He studied at the Law Faculty of Charles University, but did not obtain his degree. He participated intensely in Marxist student activities, however, and was one of the founders of the Communist Party in 1921. He has probably belonged to the Party's Central Committee since its inception.

Before World War II, he was active in Party journalism and in 1929 became editor-in-chief of *Rude pravo* (Red Right), the official organ of the Communist Party. In this year, he was also elected to Czechoslovakia's National Assembly. In 1936, he was identified as being in charge of communications between the Czechoslovak and the Soviet Communist parties.

During World War II, he worked in Moscow as editor of the principal Czechoslovak Communist newspaper in exile. He was appointed Minister of Information and Culture in the first postwar government, which rank he held until 1953, when he became Deputy Premier and Minister of Culture. Remaining in this latter position until late 1954, he undertook the major task of replacing symbols of freedom and democracy with those of Communist authoritarianism.

A member of the supreme organs of the Communist Party of Czechoslovakia since 1935, he has played an active role in international communism, including a trip to Communist China in 1952. He held membership in the Presidium and the Political Secretariat (appointed December 6, 1951), and has been a member of the Political Bureau of the KSC since its organization in June 1954.

NEJEDLY, ZDENEK: Minister without Portfolio.

Born: February 10, 1878, in Litomysl, Bohemia; of middle-class family.

Career: Nejedly received his Doctorate of Philosophy from Charles University before World War I, and, after the war, taught there as a full professor of music history. He also published several scholarly books and articles on Czech composers and statesmen. Equally interested in politics and music, he went to Spain at the age of fifty-nine to participate in the Civil War. When the Germans occupied Czechoslovakia, he fled to Moscow, where he became very active in Communist organizations. After the war, it fell to him as Minister of Education in the postwar Czechoslovak government to reorganize the educational system along Communist lines. In 1946, he became a member of the Central Committee, and in 1949 he joined the Presidium. He holds the rank of Minister without Portfolio in the present government.

Nejedly's scholarly reputation has been of value to the Communists, lending a certain aura of respectability to the regime's educational policies.

NOVOTNY, ANTONIN: Member of the Political Bureau of the KSC; First Secretary of the Central Committee.

Born: December 10, 1904, in Letnany, near Prague; son of a bricklayer.

Career: Novotny received elementary education and was then trained as a locksmith. In his youth, he became active in political affairs, joining the newly created Communist Party in 1921. For years he worked as a minor Party functionary. His work in the Party and in non-Party organizations, such as sports groups and consumer cooperatives, earned him sufficient Party reputation to be chosen a member of the Central Committee before World War II. In 1935, he was a member of the Czechoslovak delegation to the Seventh Congress of the Comintern in Moscow. However, he was not sufficiently important in the Party to be chosen to spend the Second World War in Moscow.

In 1941, he was arrested by the Germans and imprisoned in the concentration camp at Mauthausen. Upon liberation, he emerged as Secretary of the Regional Party Organization in Prague, thus occupying one of the most important positions in the Party. When Slansky established control over the Party Secretariat and when some regional Party secretaries, such as Sling, joined the Slansky camp, Novotny's importance increased since he was the most powerful regional Party Secretary to remain loyal to Gottwald. Gottwald rewarded Novotny by assigning him the duties which Slansky had executed before his fall. On September 6, 1951, the date of Slansky's demotion, Novotny was brought into the top Party organization as a member of the newly formed Organizational Secretariat. On December 6, 1951, a few days after Slansky's imprisonment, Novotny became a member of the highest Party organs, the Presidium and the Political Secretariat. It was clear that Novotny was Slansky's successor in operating the Party organization, although Gottwald had formally assumed Slansky's duties on September 6, 1951.

Upon Gottwald's death, Novotny was officially charged with the direction of the Party Secretariat. He was made Deputy Premier early in 1953, a position which he relinquished in September of that year, when "collective leadership" was installed. On September 14, 1953, it was announced that he had been made First Secretary of the Central Committee of the KSC (ergo, head of the Secretariat). In these promotions, Novotny followed the pattern set by Nikita Khrushchev in the Soviet Union after Stalin's death. In June 1954, he was elected to the Political Bureau.

Novotny has occupied a variety of roles in the supreme organs of the KSC since 1951—the time of Slansky's purge. It is safe to rank him as the number two man in the Communist hierarchy, second only to Zapotocky. His great power in Czechoslovakia is primarily due to his control of the Party apparatus.

PASEK, VACLAV: Member of the Secretariat of the Central Committee of the KSC.

Career: Very little known about Pasek. He appears to be one of the men whom Novotny promoted from the lower ranks of the Party apparatus, apparently in recognition of his Party reliability and devotion to Gottwald.

SIMUNEK, OTAKAR: Candidate Member of the Political Bureau of the Central Committee of the KSC; Minister of the State Planning Office.

Career: Simunek is a newcomer to the top ranks of the Party. Little is known about him except that he was formerly active on the regional Party level.

SIROKY, VILIAM: Member of the Political Bureau of the Central Committee of the KSC; Member of the Central Committee of the KSS; Premier.

Born: May 31, 1902, in Bratislava; son of a railroad worker.

Career: Siroky had very little formal education, and started to work as a railroad laborer at the age of thirteen. He soon became interested in politics, joined left-wing activities, and became a member of the Communist Party in 1921, when he was nineteen years old. He was sufficiently active in the Party to become a delegate to the Sixth Comintern Congress in 1928. He was elected to the Central Committee of the Party at the same Congress (1929) at which Gottwald assumed control over the Party. Like Gottwald and Slansky, he was elected deputy in the Czechoslovak National Assembly in 1935. In 1938, he was placed in charge of the Communist Party of Slovakia, but he had to leave the country. After a brief stay in Moscow and Paris, he clandestinely returned to Slovakia in 1941. He was soon arrested, and spent the major part of the war in prison. Early in 1945, he escaped and returned to Moscow, where he took part in the March 1945 discussions with Benes concerning the organization of the postwar Czechoslovak government.

He became Deputy Prime Minister in the first postwar government. As Chairman of the KSS (1945-53), and also as Chairman of the Presidium of the KSC, he first sought to capitalize on Slovak demands for autonomy in local matters. However, after the Communists had gained control of the central government, he reversed his position and concentrated on integrating Slovakia into the Republic on a centralist basis, and on condemning "outmoded concepts of bourgeois nationalism." In 1950, he assumed the position of Foreign Minister in the central government. Upon Zapotocky's elevation to the Presidency, Siroky succeeded to the Premiership on March 21, 1953. Despite his position in the central government, it is apparent from his speeches that Slovakia remains one of his special concerns. Not until Bacilek was selected as First Secretary of the KSS in September 1953 did Siroky surrender some of his prerogatives as Communist expert on Slovakia.

At the time of the Eleventh Congress of the KSS in April 1955, he relinquished his position on the Political Bureau of the KSS, due to the pressure of his duties in the KSC and government; he still remains on the Central Committee of the KSS as well as the Political Bureau of the KSC.

Siroky, number three man in the Party hierarchy, owes his position to control of the government and the influence which he wields among Slovak Communists.

TESLA, JOSEF: Member of the Central Committee of the KSC; Minister of Manpower.

Born: February 22, 1905, in Ostrava; son of a miner.

Career: Tesla attended elementary school and became a lathe operator. In the twenties, he was active in various Communist-dominated mass organizations, such as the youth movement and trade union activities. In the thirties, he rose in the Party organization, and he was sent to Moscow for training in 1935-36. During World War II, he was in a German concentration camp. He was elected to the National Assembly in October 1945, and continued his work on the regional Party level and in the central Party organization. Upon the fall of Slansky, it became his task to supervise Party work in industry. This meant primarily encouraging greater production and eliminating the flaws which developed in the administration of the economic plan. Since 1953, he has been the Party's chief supervisor of trade unions, continuing his attempt to increase the productivity of labor. Tesla is another of the younger Communists catapulted into prominence at the time of Novotny's rise to power.

UHER, JINDRICH: Member of the Central Committee of the KSC; Minister of Food Industry.

Born: June 18, 1911, in Predmerice, near Hradec Kralove; son of a locksmith who himself became a Party functionary at the founding of the Communist Party in 1921.

Career: Uher had little education, but was active as a laborer in Communist-controlled activities from his earliest youth. He spent the war in German concentration camps. After the war, he rose in the Party apparatus. He was elected to the Central Committee in 1946, dropped in the 1949 elections, but appointed a candidate member in 1952 and re-elected a regular member in 1954. Active in various regional Party organizations, he specialized in agricultural matters, though he had little experience in this field. In 1953, he was placed in charge of the Ministry of Agriculture, and in 1954 was appointed to his present post, Minister of Food Industry.

ZAPOTOCKY, ANTONIN: Member of the Political Bureau of the Central Committee of the KSC; President of the Republic.

Born: December 19, 1884, in Kladno, Bohemia; son of a tailor who became a founder of the Social Democratic Party.

Career: Zapotocky had no formal education and worked as a stonecutter. In 1900, at the age of sixteen, he joined the Social Democratic Party and, following in his father's footsteps, became an active Party worker. He also assumed a leading role in his trade union.

After World War I, he was one of the left-wing members of the Social Democratic Party instrumental in founding the Communist Party. He assumed a leading position in the new party, serving on the Executive Committee of the Comintern and attending the various Comintern Congresses held in Moscow in the twenties and thirties. After 1925, he also served in the Czechoslovak National Assembly. Though older than Gottwald and more experienced than Slansky, he was gradually pushed into the background, probably because of a certain lack of personal forcefulness. On his attempt to leave Czechoslovakia in 1939, he was captured by the Germans and spent World War II in the German concentration camp at Sachsenhausen.

Upon the liberation of Czechoslovakia, he assumed leadership of the entire trade union movement, which had been unified under the Germans. As Chairman of the Central Trade Union Council, he played a crucial role from 1945 to 1948, mobilizing the workers to full support of the Communist Party, and thereby facilitating the February coup. With membership in both the Presidium and the Political Secretariat, he ranked as number three man in the Party. He was appointed Deputy Premier in February 1948 and Premier in June 1948. He resigned from the Central Trade Union Council in 1950, at which time he was serving on the Presidium of the Central Committee, in a special fifteen-man Economic Council attached to the Presidium, and as Premier. Gottwald's death in March 1953 opened the way to Zapotocky's becoming President.

Perhaps more than any other leading figure in Communist Czechoslovakia, Zapotocky symbolizes the old school revolutionary. Long after the extreme left had changed its policies and tactics, Zapotocky's speeches still reflected in some measure the earlier revolutionary zeal. Zapotocky speaks frankly, frequently shocking the Party and country with unpleasant realities. It is probably not too inaccurate to assume that his many blunt and perhaps unorthodox speeches meet with a readier reception than the countless trite tirades of his comrades. It is also likely that his pre-eminent position within the Party and the government stems from the respect he enjoys as an "elder Communist statesman," rather than from his skill in Party politics.

A BRIEF CHRONOLOGY, 1944-1956

1944

April 8

Soviet Army reaches Czechoslovak frontier.

August 22

France repudiates Munich Agreement in joint French-Czech declaration signed in London.

August 25

Government in exile names delegation to organize administration of liberated territory. Frantisek Nemec, leader of the delegation, arrives in Moscow.

August 29

Slovak uprising against German occupation and the Slovak puppet government of Jozef Tiso breaks out at Banska Bystrica.

September 17

Congress of Slovak Communist Party is held at Banska Bystrica. Karol Smidke and Gustav Husak, the only delegates, assume the positions of chairman and vice-chairman, respectively. Slovak Social Democratic Party is merged with Slovak Communist Party.

September 21

London government announces the creation of the first Czechoslovak Army in Slovakia, commanded by General Rudolf Viest.

October 18

Soviet Army enters Ruthenia along a 171-mile front, pushing through seven passes of the Carpathians.

October 27

Soviet Army occupies Uzhorod, capital of Ruthenia.

October 28

Frantisek Nemec and his delegation establish headquarters in Chust, Ruthenia.

November 11

Ruthenian People's Committee in Uzhorod sends telegram to London government requesting immediate incorporation of Ruthenia into Soviet Ukraine.

November 29

Czechoslovak plan to transfer two million Germans from Czechoslovakia to Germany is approved by Soviet Union.

1945

March 17

President Benes and members of the provisional government arrive in Moscow. Conferences between Benes, Czechoslovak Communists in Moscow, and members of the Slovak National Council establish framework for new provisional government.

March 22

Valerian Zorin, former chief of the Soviet Foreign Ministry's Section for the Balkans and Central Europe, is appointed Ambassador to Czechoslovakia.

April 3

Benes and members of provisional government arrive in Kosice from Moscow.

April 5

National Front announces the Kosice Program, setting forth basic policies for Czechoslovakia's postwar government. Official aims of the program were: to follow the Soviet Union closely in foreign affairs; to strengthen relations with the United States, Britain, and France; to recruit and organize a new army; to take judicial action against all collaborators; to outlaw the Agrarian Party and the Slovak People's (Catholic) Party; to grant autonomy to the Slovak nation; and to take action against citizens of German and Hungarian nationality who could not prove their loyalty to Czechoslovakia from 1939 to 1945.

May 5

Prague uprising against German occupation.

May 6

United States military forces occupy Plzen. Karlovy Vary-Budejovice line agreed upon as boundary between American and Soviet forces.

May 9

Soviet tanks enter Prague. German resistance breaks.

May 10

Provisional government returns to Prague. National Council of the Resistance voluntarily dissolves.

June 17

Czechoslovak Army occupies German districts of Kladsko (Glatz), Hlucinsko (Hlutschin), and Ratibor; government claims their inclusion in frontier adjustments.

June 22

Government issues decree expropriating all land held by Germans, Hungarians, and Czech collaborators, a measure affecting 270,000 farms comprising 6,240,600 acres.

June 29

Fierlinger and Molotov sign treaty in Moscow providing for the incorporation of Ruthenia into the Soviet Union.

July 23

Presidential decree nullifies all German and Hungarian legislation affecting Czechoslovakia.

September 9

Five hundred and thirteen trading companies and 2,475 industrial firms, employing 800,000 persons, are nationalized.

October 14

Provincial councils of Bohemia and Moravia elect 200 deputies to Provisional National Assembly: 40 Social Democrats, 40 National Socialists, 40 Communists, 40 People's Party, 40 non-party organizations. Fifty Slovak Democrats and 50 Slovak Communists had been elected previously in Slovakia.

October 24

Presidential decree nationalizes: (1) all industries directly exploiting natural resources; (2) key heavy industries; (3) certain large enterprises in food and beverage industries; (4) banks and insurance companies.

December 1

United States and Soviet armies complete withdrawal from Czechoslovak territory.

1946

January 20

Slovak Labor Party is established in Bratislava.

February 27

Czechoslovak-Hungarian population exchange agreement signed in Budapest providing for exchange of 100,000 Hungarians (of total 600,000) in Slovakia for Slovaks in Hungary, on basis of equal numbers and equal compensation.

March 28-30

Eighth Congress of Czechoslovak Communist Party in Prague.

April 1

Communist Party Chairman Klement Gottwald announces Party membership exceeds one million.

April 8

Slovak Minister of Interior, Julius Viktory (Communist), announces the arrest of 5,000 persons in governmental anti-fascist "clean-up" campaign.

May 2

Karl Hermann Frank, wartime chief of the "Protectorate of Bohemia and Moravia," is sentenced to death.

May 25

General election held, in which Communists poll 38 per cent, National Socialists 18 per cent, People's Party 16 per cent, Social Democrats 13 per cent, and Slovak Democrats 14 per cent of the total vote. Vote in Bohemia and Moravia is a victory for the Communists, but in Slovakia, 60 per cent voted Slovak Democrat. Thus, National Assembly is made up of a left bloc of Communists and Social Democrats, holding 152 seats, and a right and center bloc of People's Party, Slovak Democrats, and National Socialists, holding 148 seats.

May 31

Communists call general strike in Bratislava as protest against victory of Slovak Democratic Party in general elections. Communist public demonstrations demand dissolution of Democratic Party. Rioting and fighting put down by troops and police.

June 19

New Constituent National Assembly unanimously elects Edward Benes President for third term.

July 3

Klement Gottwald, leader of the majority party (Communist), forms a new government consisting of 9 Communists, 4 National Socialists, 3 Social Democrats, 4 Slovak Democrats, and 3 People's Party members—a total of 16 Czechs and 7 Slovaks. Slovak Board of Commissioners retain its Communist chairman, but is reorganized in favor of Slovak Democrats in a 2:1 ratio, instead of 50-50 Communist-Democrat division of provisional government.

July 26

Moscow Conference between Gottwald, Masaryk, Clementis, and Stalin, Molotov, Vishinsky, and Mikoyan results in (1) expression of sympathy for Czechoslovak demands on Hungary; (2) Soviet credit for reconstruction of Czechoslovak Army; (3) Soviet cession to Czechoslovakia of synthetic oil plant built by Germans at Most during the war and other German plants left in Czechoslovakia (in compensation for monopoly of Czechoslovak uranium ore exploitation granted to the Soviet Union in a separate secret agreement signed in October 1945; see below, June 7, 1948); (4) Soviet recognition of property rights of former Czechoslovak citizens in Soviet zones of Austria and Germany; (5) agreement to replace provisional trade agreement by a long-term treaty "which would reflect Czechoslovak needs in connection with her Two-Year Plan"; (6) Soviet-Czechoslovak air communications agreement.

August 26

United States suspends remaining $40,000,000 of $50,000,000 credit to Czechoslovakia for purchase of US war surplus in Europe, and discontinues Export-Import Bank negotiations for additional $150,000,000 loan. Anti-Americanism of Czechoslovak press and stalling on compensation for American-owned nationalized property stated as primary reasons for suspension.

September 30

The National Front agrees to postpone elections to the People's Committees indefinitely, owing to the exigencies of the Two-Year Plan. It also agrees to refrain from attacks on ministers engaged in execution of the plan.

October 5

Paris Peace Conference meeting approves Czechoslovak request for a Danubian bridgehead opposite Bratislava. Minority problem to be settled by bilateral negotiations between Hungary and Czechoslovakia.

October 15

Government adopts Two-Year Economic Plan providing for increased production in every sector, and for the transfer of some industrial plants from the Czech lands to Slovakia.

October 29

Final organized transfer of Germans from Czechoslovakia, completing total of 1,415,000 transferred to US Zone and 750,000 to Soviet Zone. One hundred thousand remained in Czechoslovakia.

1947

March 10

Czechoslovak-Polish Treaty of Friendship and Mutual Assistance is concluded, on request of Soviet Union. Supplementary protocol calls for the resolution "of all territorial questions of both countries . . . on the basis of mutual agreement, within two years," and for mutual economic and cultural reconstruction.

April 18

Jozef Tiso, President of wartime Slovak Republic, executed by hanging.

May 5

People's War Crime Courts are dissolved and replaced by ordinary courts.

June 11

Emergency government meeting considers Communist charge of "reaction" against Slovak Democratic Party.

July 7

Czechoslovak government unanimously votes to send a delegation to the Paris Economic Conference, and to decide subsequently on its future attitude towards the Marshall Plan (announced June 8).

July 10

Upon telephone instruction from Gottwald in Moscow, Czechoslovak Cabinet decides to refuse invitation to Economic Conference in Paris, to avoid "an act directed against the Soviet Union and our other allies."

July 12

Czechoslovak Soviet Five-Year Trade Treaty is signed.

September 11

Minister of Industry Lausman announces that a bomb attempt on the lives of Foreign Minister Masaryk, Minister of Justice Drtina, and Deputy Prime Minister and leader of National Socialist Party Zenkl has been prevented.

October 8

The arrest of 235 persons on charge of conspiracy against the state is announced officially. Included in the arrest was Otto Obuch, secretary to Jan Ursiny, Deputy Prime Minister and member of the Slovak Democratic Party.

October 15

The Danubian bridgehead area is formally ceded to Czechoslovakia by Hungary under Article I of the Hungarian Peace Treaty.

October 19

Social Democratic Party declares it will not amalgamate with any other party in Czechoslovakia.

October 30

Premier Gottwald announces the resignation of Deputy Prime Minister Ursiny.

October 31

Communist members of the Slovak Board of Commissioners unsuccessfully demand appointment of non-party Commissioners to replace the Slovak Democratic Commissioners of Interior and Justice. Communist Chairman of Slovak Board of Commissioners, Gustav Husak, announces the resignation of the five Communist Commissioners and the dissolution of the Board.

November 5

One hour strike of 300,000 (180,000 according to *New York Times*) factory workers is called by Slovak Trade Union Council in support of the dissolution of the Slovak Board of Commissioners and its reconstitution with members of the Revolutionary Trade Union Movement, resistance organizations, and Slovak Peasants' Union.

November 14

New Slovak Board of Commissioners appointed. Slovak Democrats lose their majority in favor of Slovak Freedom Party.

November 16

Congress of Social Democratic Party at Brno elects Bohumil Lausman to replace Zdenek Fierlinger as chairman.

November 18

Police announce arrest of 206 persons connected with conspiracy in Slovakia.

November 21

Ministry of Justice and court of Olomouc intervene in police investigation of bomb plot against Drtina, Masaryk, and Zenkl, arresting six. Ministry of Interior accuses Minister of Justice of interfering with police investigation; Minister of Justice replies that police information was false and that his own investigation has revealed punishable acts that will be prosecuted.

November 25

Prague Cabinet is reorganized: Tymes (Social Democrat) succeeds Fierlinger as Deputy Prime Minister, and Jankovcova (Social Democrat) succeeds Lausman as Minister of Industry. Stefan Kocvara succeeds Ursiny as Deputy Prime Minister on latter's resignation in connection with alleged revolutionary plot of the Slovak Democratic Party.

November 29

Membership in Czechoslovak Communist Party reaches 1,250,000, as against 85,000 in 1939.

December 11

Czechoslovak-Soviet trade agreement signed: Czechoslovakia to receive 40 per cent of grain requirements, 25 per cent cotton, 10-15 per cent wool and iron ore from Soviet Union.

1948

February 12

Cabinet majority instructs Minister of Interior Nosek to stop packing police force with Communist officials.

February 17

Foreign Ministers of Czechoslovakia, Poland, and Yugoslavia meet in Prague to consider their joint interests regarding Germany. Bi-zonal arrangement in Western Germany condemned as violation of Yalta and Potsdam.

February 18

Communist Party manifesto issued charging non-Communist parties with plotting against the National Front and calling workers and "all democratic and progressive elements" to resistance under Gottwald's leadership.

February 19

Soviet Ambassador Zorin arrives in Prague, ostensibly to discuss wheat agreement contained in Soviet-Czechoslovak pact.

February 21

National Socialist, People's Party, and Slovak Democratic ministers withdraw from Cabinet on request of their party leadership.

February 22

Gottwald addresses Communist mass trade-union demonstrations in Wenceslaus Square, calling for a new National Front of "progressive" elements of all parties and organizations, early elections, and the establishment of action committees.

February 23

Ministry of Interior charges National Socialist Party with plotting armed revolution; issues warrant of high treason against Ursiny, leader of Slovak Democrats; and suspends passports of Czechoslovak citizens for travel abroad.

February 24

Action committees throughout nation taking charge of government offices, factories, schools, newspapers, etc. Editors of *Svobodne slovo, Lidova demokracie,* and *Svobodne Noviny* are expelled from positions. Czech Socialist Students' Club is raided, and several students arrested.

February 25

Benes accepts ministerial resignations and Prime Minister Gottwald's new Cabinet list. University students' march to Hradcany Castle is dispersed by police.

February 26

Joint American, French, and British statement condemns Czechoslovak Communist Party for usurping power in Czechoslovakia. Soviet Ambassador Zorin departs.

February 27

New Cabinet sworn in by President Benes. Twelve Communists, supported by eleven crypto-Communists, compose new government.

March 10

Suicide of Jan Masaryk, Foreign Minister, is announced. Official explanation of death is made by Minister of Interior to National Assembly: "Telegrams of 'recriminations' from Britain and America must have caused depression and disturbed his mind."

Czechoslovak delegate to United Nations, Jan Papanek, requests investigation of Communist coup and charges the Soviet Union with violating the Czechoslovak-Soviet treaty of 1943 and United Nations charter. Request is refused as not complying with proper form of government communication.

Slovak Revival Party is established to replace Slovak Democratic Party.

Gottwald presents government program to National Assembly, calling for further nationalization, break-up of large farms and estates, credits to farmers and small enterprises, completion of measures projected in 1945, and enactment of a new constitution.

March 19

Vladimir Clementis is appointed Foreign Minister.

March 25

Law on "Reactivation of Retribution and People's Courts" is passed by National Assembly; prosecution of wartime collaborators to be resumed until end of year.

April 9

Minister of Social Welfare announces that 4,800 persons (excluding exiles), have been affected by political purges, of which 1,432 have been placed in "new jobs."

April 13

Cabinet approves electoral law (passed in National Assembly on April 16) allowing the voter a choice between the official single list or a blank ballot. Local action committees are granted power of disfranchising persons who have "transgressed against the Republic and its democratic institutions."

April 21

Uniform School Law is passed by National Assembly.

April 26

Law nationalizing enterprises with 50 or more employees.

April 28

Law nationalizing the building industry, radio broadcasting, and apartment houses.

May 5

Announcement of prearranged allocation of seats in National Assembly: Communists, 211; Social Democrats, 25; Socialists, 26; People's Party, 23; Slovak Revival Party, 12; and Slovak Freedom Party, 3.

May 9

National Assembly adopts new constitution by unanimous vote.

Association of Czechoslovak Legionnaires, Association of National Resistance, Union of Liberated Political Prisoners, Association of Czechoslovak Soldiers of World War II, Union of Czechoslovak Partisans, and Union of

Prague Barricade Fighters vote to merge into new unified organization, Union of Fighters for Freedom, to "put all forces, experience, and tradition of our fight at the disposal of the People's Democratic Republic."

Communist Party membership total officially put at 2,000,048.

May 30

Election of new National Assembly; official report announces 89 per cent of votes cast for single list.

June 7

Former Chairman of Foreign Relations Committee of the Czechoslovak National Assembly, Ivo Duchacek, reveals in London that a secret treaty, signed in October 1945, gave exclusive control of Czechoslovak uranium mines at Jachymov to the Soviet Union.

Benes resigns Presidency. Gottwald's letter of acceptance terms Benes "co-creator of the new order."

June 9

Gottwald, as President *pro tempore,* signs new constitution.

June 10

Central Committee of the Communist Party approves nomination of Gottwald as President and Zapotocky as Premier.

June 14

National Assembly unanimously approves Gottwald President and Zapotocky Premier.

Slovak Board of Commissioners is installed.

June 19

Father Josef Plojhar, Minister of Health, and several other Catholic clergymen who stood as election candidates are suspended from ecclesiastical functions by Catholic Church.

June 27

Announcement of formal fusion of Communist and Social Democratic parties into the Communist Party.

July 15

Communist Party Presidium announces that mass recruiting of new members is to cease in favor of "individual recruitment" by Party. Membership has reached 2,300,000—one out of every three citizens of voting age.

July 21

National Assembly passes bills providing for (1) merging of all cooperatives into the Central Union of Cooperatives, headed by a presidium appointed by the Minister of Social Welfare; (2) share of net profits of factories to be used by a united fund of the working people for social needs; (3) compulsory assignment of workers for work periods over one year; (4) commercial enterprises to be set up and administered as independent legal bodies by People's Committees; (5) state guarantees of credit for persons settled in "Sudeten lands."

August 5

Ministry of Industry announces nationalization of 93 per cent of all Czechoslovak industry. Of the 4,300 enterprises nationalized since 1945, 2,000 have been nationalized in last two months. Two hundred fifty-one state trusts are to be established by amalgamation of nationalized enterprises.

September 3

Edward Benes dies.

September 27

At meeting of Central Committee of Slovak Communist Party in Bratislava, Chairman Viliam Siroky announces merger of Slovak Communist Party with Czechoslovak Communist Party.

October 25

Law on Forced Labor Camps, sponsored by Minister of Interior, is passed by National Assembly, to be applied against those "who refuse to work properly."

October 27

The Five-Year Plan Act is promulgated.

November

Czechoslovak Youth League conducts investigation of university enrollment lists to check reliability of student body.

December 3

Government decree abolishes the provinces of Bohemia, Moravia, and Slovakia, replacing them with 19 administrative regions (*kraje*).

December 12

Czechoslovak-Soviet trade agreement for 1949 signed in Moscow. Total trade between the two countries to be 45 per cent above 1948.

December 22

Law on "Popularization of the Judicial System" is passed by National Assembly; lay judges are introduced at court benches on all levels.

1949

January 25

Council for Economic Mutual Aid (CEMA), comprising the Soviet Union, Czechoslovakia, Poland, Romania, Hungary, and Bulgaria, is established in Moscow.

February 22

Law on Economic Planning is passed by National Assembly.

May 25-29

Ninth Congress of Communist Party of Czechoslovakia is held in Prague.

June 12

Archbishop Beran issues pastoral letter branding new Catholic Action Committee "schismatic" and instructing Catholic clergy to boycott all government organizations and publications professing to be "Catholic."

June 19

Archbishop Beran's service in St. Vitus Cathedral interrupted by 250 members of Workers' Militia.

July 7

Government issues text of new church law, applying to all denominations, which requires government sanction of all church appointments; closes ecclesiastical offices to those convicted in civil courts; provides for salaries of priests to be paid by the state; and introduces state inventory and control of church property.

August 8

Archbishop Beran sends letter to State Prosecutor protesting government interference in internal affairs of the Church, denial of his personal freedom, and official failure to prevent or investigate the Communist demonstration in St. Vitus Cathedral on June 19.

August 14

Roman Catholic bishops meet in Trnava and draw up memorandum to government, asking for government recognition of Papal authority in Church affairs, and cessation of state prosecution of priests for high treason when carrying out Vatican decrees on excommunication.

August 28

Minister of Justice accuses Beran and bishops of maintaining subversive network of espionage and sabotage.

September 9 and 10

Approximately 300 Catholic clergymen are arrested for infringing Church Law.

October 14

State Office for Church Affairs is established by law. Acts regulating clergymen's salaries and requiring them to take loyalty oath to the state are passed.

October 15

Government explains arrest of past two weeks (amounting to at least 10,000 businessmen, shopkeepers, professional men, army officers, priests, dissident Communists, and government officials), as resulting from evidence brought forth on Titoism in Czechoslovakia at the Rajk trial in Hungary.

October 25

Alexej Cepicka appointed Director of State Office for Church Affairs.

December 7

New marriage law and family code is passed by National Assembly. Divorce permitted only if marriage does not fulfill "social function."

1950

January 10

Government bans sale of all books published in Czechoslovakia before May 5, 1948.

January 22

Government announces 98.2 per cent of all Catholic priests have taken oath of allegiance prescribed in the Church Law. No bishop is reported to have taken the oath.

February 15

Government appoints Dean Jan Dechet diocesan administrator.

February 18

Titular Bishop Antonin Eltschkner takes loyalty oath before Cepicka (first bishop to do so).

Pope excommunicates Dechet for accepting appointment from lay authorities.

March 14

Clementis resigns as Minister of Foreign Affairs and is replaced by Deputy Premier Viliam Siroky.

April 5

Ten leading members of the Premonstratensian, Jesuit, Redemptorist, Franciscan, and Dominican Orders are sentenced to long prison terms on charges of conspiring with foreign powers to overthrow the government.

April 18

Government confiscates most monastic houses and restricts members of ecclesiastical orders to the few that remain.

April 19

Czechoslovak government demands closing of United States Information Service offices in Prague and Bratislava, and recall of American Embassy's press attaché.

April 21

United States agrees to comply with Czechoslovak demand to recall press attaché, but repudiates charges against him, and orders retaliatory closure of Czechoslovak consulate in Chicago by May 1.

April 25

Cabinet reshuffle. Minister of National Defense Ludvik Svoboda named Minister of Physical Education and Deputy Premier; Minister of Justice and head of State Office for Church Affairs Alexej Cepicka named Minister of National Defense; Stefan Rais named Minister of Justice; and Zdenek Fierlinger, head of State Office for Church Affairs.

May 5

Government dismisses Gustav Husak, Chairman of the Slovak Board of Commissioners, and Ladislav Novomesky, Commissioner of Education. Karol Bacilek is appointed Chairman.

Government replaces Chief of Staff General Drgac with General Jaroslav Prochazka, head of army political education branch.

May 12

Government closes British Information Office and British Council offices in Czechoslovakia in protest against BBC broadcasts.

May 13

United States closes Czechoslovak consulates in Cleveland and Pittsburgh and orders reduction of Czechoslovak diplomatic staff in the US commensurate with reduction in US Embassy staff in Czechoslovakia.

May 23

Ministry of State Security is created, headed by Ladislav Kopriva.

May 24-27

Ninth Congress of Slovak Communist Party is held in Bratislava. Siroky's address charges Clementis, Husak, Novomesky, and Smidke with "bourgeois nationalism." All four make statements of "self-criticism," which are not accepted by the Congress, and none of them is re-elected to the Central Committee, though all retain Party membership.

June 23

East German-Czechoslovak agreement on the final resettlement of Germans from Czechoslovakia.

July 12

New Criminal Code is passed by National Assembly, to become effective August 1, 1950.

September 2

Trial of alleged Yugoslav spy ring. Yugoslav Vice Consul at Bratislava is sentenced to life imprisonment.

September 19

New Civil Code is approved by government, to become effective January 1951.

November 3

Czechoslovak-Soviet five-year trade agreement for 1951-55, is announced. Trade is to exceed 1948-50 level by 50 per cent.

1951

January 10-16

Trial in Bratislava of three Catholic bishops on espionage and treason charges.

February 21-24

Meeting of Central Committee of Communist Party in Prague. Otto Sling, Marie Svermova, and Vladimir Clementis are denounced as major traitors in plot to seize power by violent means, and to replace Gottwald and Slansky with group hostile to the Soviet Union.

Deputy Secretary General Frank announces results of fourth screening of Party membership since liberation: 169,544 Communists have been expelled from the Party since September 1, 1950; intensive screening of members is to be a permanent feature of Party discipline. Membership (including candidates) is now 1,677,433, compared with 2,311,066 in May 1949, and 2,418,199 on October 1, 1948.

March 9

Minister of Defense Alexej Cepicka announces that Major General Bedrich Reicin and Lieutenant Colonel Josef Kopold (son-in-law of Marie Svermova) have been revealed as traitors.

March 10

Archbishop Beran banished from Prague and fined for "negative attitude" toward government Church laws.

Five-year economic agreement signed with Poland.

May 12

Government decree authorizes school matriculation commissions to direct all children leaving school at 14 into any branch of industry or agriculture.

June 29

Government decree orders transfer of 77,500 administrative workers to "productive jobs."

July 4

William N. Oatis is sentenced to 10 years' imprisonment, escaping a death sentence only by "spontaneous confession" and "aid in uncovering work of other espionage agents."

July 11

New law on Defense of State Frontiers assigns basic responsibility to Ministry of State Security.

September 6

Central Committee approves reorganization of the Communist Party:
The post of Secretary-General abolished, and duties transferred to Party Chairman;
New Political Secretariat set up, consisting of Gottwald, Zapotocky, Siroky, Slansky, Dolansky, Bacilek, and Cepicka;
Novotny, Frank, Bares, David, Hendrych, and Bastovansky elected to new Organizational Secretariat, headed by Gottwald;
Bacilek and Cepicka elected to Presidium to replace Svermova and Smrkovsky.

September 7

Official announcement of Cabinet reshuffle.
Deputy Premier and Minister of Physical Education Ludvik Svoboda, and Minister of Social Welfare Erban "relieved of their posts";
Slansky appointed Deputy Premier in place of Svoboda;
Jan Sevcik, Deputy Premier, appointed Minister of Physical Education;
New Ministry of Manpower replaces Ministry of Social Welfare;
Jaroslav Havelka, formerly Deputy Minister of Church Affairs, appointed Minister of Manpower;
Ministry of State Control created, with extensive powers in economic field; Bacilek appointed Minister;
Ministry of Heavy Industries abolished and five new ministries created: Fuel and Power (Vaclav Pokorny), Foundries and Ore Mines (Jan Bilek), Chemical Industry (Jozef Pucik), Heavy Engineering (Augustin Kliment), and General Engineering (Josef Jonas);
Josef Nepomucky appointed Minister of Agriculture, succeeding Julius Duris; the latter replaced Bacilek as Chairman of Slovak Board of Commissioners.

September 25

Anatol Lavrentiev is announced as new Soviet Ambassador to Czechoslovakia.

October 19

Central Committee of the Slovak Communist Party meets in Bratislava. Chairman Siroky takes over duties of former Secretary-General Stefan Bastovansky; Jan Pull, Koloman Mosko, Milos Gosiorovsky, and Bastovansky become Secretaries of Central Committee.

November 27

Announcement of arrest of Rudolf Slansky for "conspiracy against the state."

December 6

Meeting of Central Committee is addressed by Gottwald on Slansky issue. Central Committee (1) expels Jarmila Taussigova-Potuckova from Control Commission and elects new five-man Commission; (2) elects Antonin Novotny to Presidium; (3) elects Novotny and Vaclav Kopecky to Political Secretariat.

1952

January 17

Diocesan peace committees of Catholic clergy hold meetings in several Slovak regions. Catholic priests to "extend their help in the socialization of the countryside." Participants "acquaint themselves" with the new parish boundaries, altered to conform with district boundaries.

January 23

Ladislav Kopriva, Minister of National Security, is relieved of post upon "own request." Karol Bacilek is appointed to replace him. Jan Harus takes over Bacilek's office as Minister of State Control.

March 1

Brno conference of scientific workers appeals to all Czechoslovak scientists, in the "spirit of socialist patriotism and humanism," to aid in stamp-out all traces of Western orientation in science.

March 23

Czechoslovakia informs Israel that Mordecai Oren, visiting leader of Socialist Mapam Party, has been arrested in matter involving state security.

April 1

State Office for Church Affairs announces that Josef Hlouch, Bishop of Ceske Budejovice, has been fined and removed from his diocese for his "negative attitude toward Church laws." Vicar General Joseph Buchta is elected Capitular Vicar of the diocese by St. Nicholas Chapter in Ceske Budejovice.

May 21-22

Constituent Congress of the Society for the Dissemination of Political and Scientific Knowledge meets in Prague; Minister of Information Kopecky explains the aims of the society, stressing the fight against "religious obscurantism, religious superstition, and reactionary clerical thought."

November 20-27

Trial of Rudolf Slansky and thirteen accomplices. Slansky is charged with treason, sabotage, and espionage, and is sentenced to death by hanging.

1953

January 31

Basic government reorganization is carried out: a Presidium, consisting of a Premier and nine Deputy Premiers, is established as an "inner cabinet" to supervise the activities of the individual Ministries, which are divested of policy-making authority and transformed into executive organs of the Presidium.

February 5

Gottwald appoints Vaclav Ales Procurator General (Chief State Prosecutor).

March 9

Gottwald, Bacilek, and Cepicka attend Stalin's funeral.

March 14

Gottwald dies in Prague.

March 21

The National Assembly elects Antonin Zapotocky President of the Republic; Zapotocky immediately appoints Viliam Siroky Premier.

March 25

Zapotocky appoints Oldrich Beran and Rudolf Barak Deputy Premiers, and Josef Reitmajer Minister of Foundries and Ore Mines, replacing Jan Bilek, who is relieved for "reasons of health."

April 16

Premier Siroky submits program of his Cabinet to National Assembly.

May 15

President Zapotocky grants clemency to William N. Oatis, who is immediately released from prison.

May 30

A law providing for currency conversion and the abolition of rationing, effective June 1, is announced officially.

United States lifts some restrictions imposed on trade with Czechoslovakia after the Oatis trial in 1951.

June 15

President Zapotocky attends Congress of the Slovak Communist Party, which elects a new Central Committee. A new Presidium is chosen by the Central Committee.

June 18

The Slovak National Council passes an act establishing the Slovak Academy of Sciences.

July 1

A government ordinance, introducing heavy punishment for absenteeism and unauthorized changes of employment, is enacted.

July 6

Public opinion forces the Cabinet to cancel the ordinance concerning punishment of absenteeism.

September 28

President Zapotocky appoints Josef Urvalek (State Prosecutor in the Slansky trial) presiding judge of the Supreme Court.

September 29

Gustav Kliment, chairman of the Central Trade Union Council, is granted prolonged sick leave at the Council's tenth plenary session. Josef Tesla is elected First Secretary and entrusted with the Council's direction during Kliment's absence.

October 10

It is officially announced in Prague that the diplomatic missions of the Czechoslovak Republic in Berlin and of the German Democratic Republic in Prague have been transformed into embassies.

1954

January 4

The International Bank for Reconstruction and Development announces that Czechoslovakia's membership has been suspended for failure to pay $625,000 owed on its capital subscription.

January 22

The Presidium of the Supreme Soviet recalls Ambassador Bogomolov from Prague and appoints Nikolai Pavlovich Firiubin his successor.

January 28

Marie Svermova is sentenced to life imprisonment as a Slansky accomplice, following a three-day trial before the criminal division of the Supreme Court.

February 25

Cabinet approves three draft bills concerning the organization, jurisdiction, and elections of the People's Committees.

March 3

National Assembly approves the bills concerning the People's Committees.

March 13

The Ministry of Foreign Affairs sends a protest to the United States government, concerning the penetration of Czechoslovak air space by two US military aircraft on March 12, 1954.

March 23

Government sends note to the United Nations, insisting the UN questionnaire on forced labor is "illegal," and refusing to supply answers.

April 24

The four-day trial of Gustav Husak, former chairman of the Slovak Board of Commissioners, and four other former leading Slovak Communists results in a life sentence for Husak and long-term prison sentences for the other defendants.

May 16

Elections to the People's Committees are held. An editorial in *Rude pravo* proclaims anyone who does not vote for the candidates of the National Front an "enemy of the Republic."

May 19

The Central Election Commission announces the results of the People's Committee elections, admitting that about 7 per cent of the voters refused to cast their votes for the National Front candidates.

June 15

At the Tenth Party Congress, a nine-man Political Bureau (Politburo) is created, replacing the twenty-two man Presidium and the eight-man Political Secretariat.

June 29

Former Deputy Premier Jan Sevcik is sentenced to 18 years' imprisonment for treason, sabotage, endangering state property, and pilfering national property.

July 2

A plenary session of the Central Committee of the Communist Party of Slovakia elects a Political Bureau, consisting of nine regular members and two candidate members.

July 23

Stepan Trochta, Bishop of Litomerice, and three Roman Catholic priests receive long-term prison sentences at two-day trial in Prague.

November 28

Elections to the National Assembly and the Slovak National Council result in an "overwhelming victory" for the National Front candidates.

November 29

Premier Siroky heads Czechoslovak delegation at conference on "European Security" in Moscow.

December 12

Following election of the new National Assembly, President Zapotocky appoints a new Cabinet. Zapotocky appoints his second Deputy, Vaclav Pleskot, to replace Colonel General Frantisek Janda, as chairman of the State Committee for Physical Training and Sports.

December 17

In connection with the election of the new Slovak National Council, the government appoints a new Board of Commissioners.

1955

January 21

Orthodox Bishop Kliment and Orthodox Vicar-Bishop Jan of Prague take the loyalty oath before Deputy Premier Kopecky.

February 4

President Antonin Zapotocky declares cessation of the state of war and resumption of peaceful relations between Czechoslovakia and Germany.

May 1

A gigantic monument to Stalin is unveiled in Prague by Deputy Premier Kopecky.

May 9

A decree of amnesty is promulgated as part of the celebration of the "tenth anniversary of the liberation of our nation by the glorious Soviet Army." This amnesty remits penalties previously imposed on defectors, providing they return to the Republic within six months of the day of the amnesty.

May 11

"Conference of European States to Safeguard Peace and Security in Europe" opens in Warsaw. The Soviet Union and seven captive states participate; the Chinese People's Republic is represented by an observer.

May 24

The National Assembly in Prague approves the Warsaw Treaty of Friendship, Cooperation, and Mutual Help, concluded on May 14 between the Soviet Union and the seven captive countries.

June 2

The Presidium of the Central Committee of the National Front establishes a "committee to care for persons who return to Czechoslovakia on the basis of the amnesty"; Miroslav Klinger is appointed chairman and Vojtech Daubner deputy chairman.

July 6

The cabinet publishes a declaration on the delivery of armaments to Slovak Board of Commissioners.

October 2

First announcement in Czechoslovak press of the Czechoslovak-Egyptian Arms Agreement, providing for the exchange of Egyptian cotton for Czechoslovak armaments.

October 4

The Cabinet publishes a declaration on the delivery of armaments to Egypt, rejecting the "international campaign" by which the Egyptian government "should be compelled to cancel the agreement."

November 15

The National Front committee in charge of returnees announces that measures have been taken to enable refugees to return home without being punished after expiration of the amnesty of May 9, 1955.

December 2

The Czechoslovak government recognizes Austria's permanent neutrality.

1956

April 25

Alexej Cepicka is formally dismissed from his posts as First Deputy Premier, Minister of National Defense, and member of the Political Bureau, for having fostered "the cult of the individual," particularly in the army.

April 26

Colonel General Bohumir Lomsky is appointed to replace Cepicka.

May 4

Draft Directives for second Five-Year Plan are published.

May 15

In their traditional May celebration (*majales*), students of Charles University express open dissatisfaction with the government's administrative and educational policies. A resolution drafted by the students is presented to the Party's Central Committee, the Youth Union, the Ministry of Education, and the National Assembly. The resolution demanded establishment of a factual press and radio, abolition of the "index" of prohibited foreign literary and philosophical works, an end of jamming of Western radio broadcasts, publication of parliamentary debates and critical comments, and less adulation of the Soviet Union. It also demanded an answer to the questions of the ownership and management of the Jachymov mines and uranium resources.

May 28

Fourth trainload of armaments is dispatched to Egypt from the Klement Gottwald Iron Works at Vitkovice.

TREATIES AND AGREEMENTS, 1943-1956

Compiled by Jindrich Nosek

Date and Place of Signature	Cosignatories	Type of Treaty	Published or Reported in[1]
November 9, 1943, Washington, D. C.	General treaty	Agreement on United Nations Relief and Rehabilitation Administration	SZ, No. 149, 1945
December 12, 1943, Moscow	Soviet Union	Treaty of Friendship, Mutual Aid and Postwar Cooperation	SZ, No. 11, 1946
December 7, 1944, Chicago	General treaty	Convention on international civil aviation	SZ, No. 147, 1947
February 26, 1945, London	UNRRA	Agreement concerning relief and rehabilitation for Czechoslovakia	SZ, No. 149, 1945
March 1, 1945, Ottawa	Canada	Financial agreement	UNTS, II, No. 185
May 16, 1945, Brussels	Belgium	Agreement on repatriation of displaced nationals	UNTS, II, No. 119
June 26, 1945, San Francisco	General treaty	Charter of the United Nations, and Statute of the International Court of Justice	SZ, No. 30, 1947

[1] Abbreviations denote the following sources: SZ, *Sbirka zakonu a narizeni republiky Ceskoslovenske* (Collection of Laws and Ordinances of the Czechoslovak Republic); UNTS, United Nations, *Treaty Series;* BTS, H. M. Stationery Office, *Treaty Series;* ZO, Ministry of Foreign Trade, *ZahrBanicni obchod* (Foreign Trade).

Date and Place of Signature	Cosignatories	Type of Treaty	Published or Reported in
June 26, 1945, Ottawa	Canada	Amendment to financial agreement of March 1, 1945	UNTS, II, No. 185
June 29, 1945, Moscow	Soviet Union	Treaty concerning cession of Ruthenia	SZ, No. 186, 1946
August 8, 1945, London	Great Britain, United States, France, Soviet Union, *et al.*	Agreement on prosecution and punishment of major war criminals	SZ, No. 164, 1947
September 27, 1945, London	United States, Belgium, Denmark, France, *et al.*	Agreement concerning the establishment of European Inland Transport Organization	UNTS, II, No. 35
October 16, 1945, Quebec	General treaty	Constitution of United Nations Food and Agriculture Organization	SZ, No. 127, 1946
November 1, 1945, London	Great Britain	Agreement relating to money and property situated in Czechoslovakia and in the United Kingdom which have been subjected to special measures in consequence of enemy occupation of Czechoslovakia.	SZ, No. 85 1947
November 1, 1945, London	Great Britain	Monetary agreement	UNTS, I, No. 62

November 5, 1945, Paris	General treaty	Amendment of Constitution of the International Labor Organization	SZ, No. 98, 1947
December 8, 1945, Paris	France	Supplementary protocol to the declaration concerning scientific, literary and educational relations	UNTS, I, No. 701
December 13, 1945, Oslo	Norway	Monetary agreement	UNTS, I, No. 280
December 21, 1945, Paris	Albania, United States, Australia, Belgium, Canada, *et al.*	Accord on reparations from Germany, on the establishment of Inter-Allied Reparation Agency, and on restitution of monetary gold	SZ, No. 150, 1947
December 27, 1945, Washington, D. C.	General treaty	Agreement on International Monetary Fund	SZ, No. 68, 1946
December 27, 1945, Washington, D. C.	General treaty	Agreement on International Bank for Reconstruction and Development	SZ, No. 69, 1946
January 3, 1946, Prague	United States	Air transport agreement	UNTS, I, No. 84
January 4, 1946, London	General treaty	Agreement on establishment of the European Coal Organization	SZ, No. 156, 1946
January 24, 1946, Prague	Poland	Agreement concerning air communications	UNTS, I, No. 363
February 12, 1946, Prague	Poland	Agreement on mutual return of property removed after outbreak of war	UNTS, I, No. 364

Date and Place of Signature	Cosignatories	Type of Treaty	Published or Reported in
February 27, 1946, Budapest	Hungary	Agreement on exchange of population	SZ, No. 145, 1946
April 3, 1946	Belgium and Luxemburg	Payments agreement	ZO, No. 10, 1954
April 12, 1946, Moscow	Soviet Union	Agreement on mutual deliveries of goods	SZ, No. 157, 1945 and No. 79, 1947
May 9, 1946, Belgrade	Yugoslavia	Treaty of Friendship, Mutual Aid, and Cooperation	SZ, No. 168, 1946
June 28, 1946, Ottawa	Canada	Amendment to financial agreement of March 1, 1945	UNTS, I, No. 662
July 22, 1946, New York	General treaty	Constitution of World Health Organization	SZ, No. 189, 1948
July 25, 1946, Moscow	Soviet Union	Agreement establishing air services	UNTS, I, No. 409
July 27, 1946, London	General treaty	Accord concerning German-owned patents	SZ, No. 75, 1947
July 29, 1946	France	Payments agreement	ZO, No. 10, 1954

October 9, 1946, Montreal	General treaty	Partial revision of conventions adopted by General Conference of International Labor Organization at its first twenty-eight sessions	UNTS, Vol. 66, Annex A, No. 583
October 16, 1946, Rio de Janeiro	Brazil	Trade treaty and payments agreements	SZ, No. 1, 1947
November 14, 1946, Washington, D.C.	United States	Agreement on commercial policy	UNTS, I, No. 94
November 15, 1946, Prague	Yugoslavia	Agreement concerning valorization of customs rates	SZ, No. 226, 1946 and No. 27, 1948
November 16, 1946, London	General treaty	Constitution of United Nations Educational, Scientific, and Cultural Organization	SZ, No. 196, 1947
December 5, 1946, Ankara	Turkey	Trade and payments agreements	SZ, Nos. 54 and 152, 1947
December 18, 1946, Berne; January 18, 1947, Prague; February 7, 1947, Berne	Switzerland	Agreement concerning nationalized and confiscated property in Czechoslovakia	*Recueil Officiel Suisse,* 1948, p. 547
January 2, 1947, Montevideo	Uruguay	Trade and Payments agreement	ZO, No. 2, 1947
January 29, 1947, Dublin	Ireland	Agreement on air transport	UNTS, I, No. 411

Date and Place of Signature	Cosignatories	Type of Treaty	Published or Reported in
February 7, 1947, Prague	Belgium and Luxemburg	Trade and payments agreement	ZO, No. 4, 1947
February 8, 1947, Neuchatel	General treaty	Agreement on preservation and restoration of industrial property rights affected by World War II	SZ, No. 167, 1947
February 10, 1947, Paris	Soviet Union, Great Britain, United States, Australia, *et al.*, and Hungary	Peace treaty with Hungary	SZ, No. 192, 1947
February 10, 1947, Paris	Soviet Union, Great Britain, United States, Australia, *et al.*, and Bulgaria	Peace treaty with Bulgaria	SZ, No. 207, 1947
February 10, 1947, Paris	Soviet Union, Great Britain, United States, Australia, *et al.*, and Finland	Peace treaty with Finland	SZ, No. 208, 1947
February 10, 1947, Paris	Soviet Union, United States, Great Britain, Australia, *et al.*, and Romania	Peace treaty with Romania	SZ, No. 209, 1947

February 10, 1947, Paris	Soviet Union, Great Britain, United States, China, *et al.*, and Italy	Peace treaty with Italy	SZ, No. 5, 1948
February 19, 1947, Prague	Great Britain	Agreement for supply of certain aircraft and equipment to Czechoslovakia	BTS, No. 60, 1947
February 25, 1947, Belgrade	Yugoslavia	Trade Agreement	UNTS, I, No. 1539
February 27, 1947, Bombay	India	Agreement on money and property in Czechoslovakia and British India which have been subjected to special measures in consequence of enemy occupation of Czechoslovakia	SZ, No. 86, 1947
March 3, 1947, Warsaw	Poland	Treaty of Friendship and Mutual Aid	SZ, No. 154, 1947
March 5, 1947, Ankara	Turkey	Agreement on air communications	UNTS, I, No. 214
March 6, 1947, Prague	Belgium	Cultural agreement	SZ, No. 41, 1949
March 8, 1947, Berne	Switzerland	Agreement on exchange of goods	ZO, No. 7, 1947
March 19, 1947, Brussels	Belgium	Agreement concerning nationalized and confiscated Belgian property	UNTS, I, No. 341

Date and Place of Signature	Cosignatories	Type of Treaty	Published or Reported in
March 20, 1947, Prague	Norway	Agreement on exchange of goods	UNTS, I, No. 460
April 15, 1947, Prague	Romania	Protocol on exchange of goods	ZO, No. 11, 1947
April 22, 1947, Sofia	Bulgaria	Agreement on exchange of goods	ZO, No. 11, 1947
April 27, 1947, Belgrade	Yugoslavia	Cultural agreement	SZ, No. 155, 1947
May 3, 1947, Prague	Norway	Supplementary protocol to agreement of March 20, 1947	ZO, No. 11, 1947
May 14, 1947, Copenhagen	Denmark	Agreement on air services	UNTS, I, No. 413
May 19, 1947, Santiago	Chile	Trade agreement	ZO, No. 12, 1947
June 16, 1947, London	Great Britain	Cultural convention	BTS, No. 82, 1947
June 20, 1947, Sofia	Bulgaria	Cultural agreement	SZ, No. 148, 1948
July 2, 1947, Prague	Italy	Trade agreement on basis of most-favored-nation clause	ZO, No. 10, 1954

July 2, 1947, Buenos Aires	Argentina	Trade and financial agreement	ZO, No. 14, 1947
July 3, 1947, London	Great Britain	Supplement to monetary agreement of November 1, 1945	BTS, No. 57, 1947
July 4, 1947, Prague	Poland	Agreement on economic cooperation	SZ, No. 10, 1948 and No. 9, 1949
July 4, 1947, Prague	Poland	Cultural agreement	SZ, No. 259, 1948
July 5, 1947, Paris	General treaty	Universal Postal Convention	SZ, No. 243, 1948
July 17, 1947, London	General treaty	Supplementary protocol to the accord of July 27, 1946, concerning German-owned patents	SZ, No. 258, 1948
July 25, 1947, Prague	United States	Agreement concerning settlement of certain war accounts and claims incident to operations of United States Army in Czechoslovakia	UNTS, I, No. 1223
August 8, 1947	New Zealand	Agreement on mutual release of sequestrated monetary assets	SZ, No. 71, 1948
September 1, 1947, Prague	Netherlands	Agreement on air services	UNTS, I, No. 495
September 4, 1947, Belgrade	Yugoslavia	Agreement concerning sequestrated and nationalized Czechoslovak assets in Yugoslavia	UNTS, I, No. 1540
September 5, 1947, Prague	Romania	Cultural agreement	SZ, No. 149, 1948

Date and Place of Signature	Cosignatories	Type of Treaty	Published or Reported in
September 10, 1947, Berne	Switzerland	Provisional agreement on air services	UNTS, I, No. 518
September 24, 1947, Copenhagen	Denmark	Trade and payments agreement	ZO, No. 20, 1947
October 2, 1947, Atlantic City	General treaty	International Convention on Telecommunications	SZ, No. 18, 1949
October 3, 1947, Lake Success	United Nations	Agreement on activities of the United Nations International Children's Emergency Fund in Czechoslovakia	UNTS, I, No. 816
October 15, 1947, Stockholm	Sweden	Agreement on air services	UNTS, I, No. 683
October 20, 1947, Prague	Finland	Trade agreement	ZO, No. 21, 1947
October 30, 1947, Geneva	General treaty	General Agreement on Tariffs and Trade	SZ, No. 59, 1948
October 30, 1947, Prague	Sweden	Protocol on exchange of goods	ZO, No. 23, 1947
November 1, 1947	Hungary	Trade agreement	ZO, No. 22, 1947

Date and place	Country	Agreement	Source
November 26, 1947, Ottawa	Canada	Supplementary financial agreement	UNTS, I, No. 662
November 27, 1947, Caracas	Venezuela	Trade treaty	SZ, Nos. 86 and 226, 1948
December 11, 1947, Moscow	Soviet Union	Trade and navigation treaty	SZ, No. 31, 1949
December 16, 1947, Bucharest	Romania	Trade and payments agreements	ZO, No. 2, 1948
January 22, 1948, London	New Zealand	Agreement concerning credits for financing purchases of wool	UNTS, I, No. 264
February 5 and March 4, 1948, Copenhagen	Denmark	Trade agreement	SZ, No. 154, 1948
February 10, 1948, Prague	Netherlands	Agreement on exchange of goods	ZO, No. 4, 1948
February 11, 1948, Stockholm and March 11, 1948, Prague	Sweden	Exchange of notes modifying the agreement on air services of October 15, 1947	UNTS, Vol. 53, Annex A, No. 683
March 4, 1948, Oslo	Norway	Trade agreement	SZ, Nos. 156 and 255, 1948
March 4 and April 6, 1948	Spain	Agreement on the valorization of customs rates	SZ, Nos. 159 and 230, 1948

Date and Place of Signature	Cosignatories	Type of Treaty	Published or Reported in
March 5, 1948, Brussels	Albania, United States, Australia, Belgium, *et al.*	Supplementary protocol to the accord of December 21, 1945 on German reparations	SZ, No. 43, 1949
March 11, 1948, Prague	Iceland	Agreement on exchange of goods	ZO, No. 7, 1948
March 14, 1948, Belgrade	Yugoslavia	Air transport agreement	UNTS, I, No. 421
March 23 and March 27, 1948, Warsaw	Poland	Agreement on the valorization of customs rates	SZ, Nos. 157 and 262, 1948
March 23, 1948, Berne	Switzerland	Fifth supplementary protocol to the trade treaty of February 16, 1927	SZ, No. 160, 1948
March 24, 1948, Havana	General treaty	Protocols modifying certain provisions of the General Agreement on Tariffs and Trade	SZ, Nos. 211, 212, and 216, 1948
April 5, 1948, Warsaw	Poland	Agreement on cooperation in social policy and social administration	SZ, Nos. 260 and 261, 1948
April 5, 1948, Prague; and May 28, 1948, Copenhagen	Denmark	Agreement modifying the accord of May 14, 1947 relating to air services	UNTS, I, No. 413

April 7, 1948, Canberra	Australia	Agreement to amend the trade treaty of August 3, 1936	SZ, No. 153, 1948
April 7, 1948, Prague	Greece	Agreement on the valorization of customs rates	SZ, No. 158, 1948
April 7, 1948, Prague	Bulgaria	Trade and payments agreement	ZO, No. 8, 1948
April 10, 1948, Prague	Yugoslavia	Supplementary agreement to the Treaty of Commerce and Navigation of November 14, 1928	SZ, Nos. 155 and 256, 1948
April 23, 1948, Prague	Bulgaria	Treaty of Friendship, Cooperation and Mutual Aid	SZ, No. 178, 1948
April 25, 1948, Prague	Bulgaria	Agreement concerning provisional arrangement of economic relations	SZ, No. 163, 1948 and No. 4, 1950
April 29, 1948, Brussels	Belgium and Luxemburg	Agreement on exchange of goods	ZO, No. 10, 1948
May 18, 1948, Prague	France	Supplementary agreement to the Treaty of Commerce of July 2, 1928	SZ, No. 170, 1948 and No. 38, 1950
May 24, 1948, Prague	Yugoslavia	Trade agreement	UNTS, I, Nos. 1539, 1542, 1544, and 1545
June 24, 1948, The Hague	Netherlands	Supplement to trade agreement of January 20, 1923	SZ, No. 227, 1948 and No. 71, 1951
July 3, 1948, Brussels	Belgo-Luxemburg Economic Union	Supplementary agreement to the Treaty of Commerce of December 28, 1925	SZ, No. 228, 1948 and No. 10, 1951; UNTS, I, No. 997

Date and Place of Signature	Cosignatories	Type of Treaty	Published or Reported in
July 21, 1948, Bucharest	Romania	Treaty of Friendship, Cooperation and Mutual Aid	SZ, No. 130, 1949
July 21, 1948, Bucharest	Romania	Agreement concerning provisional arrangement of economic relations	SZ, No. 327, 1948
July 22, 1948, Vienna	Austria	Trade and payments agreement	ZO, No. 15, 1948
July 28, 1948, Prague	Norway	Protocol concerning exchange of goods	UNTS, I, No. 460
August 6, 1948, Paris	France	Agreement on exchange of goods and compensation for nationalized property	ZO, No. 17, 1948
August 18, 1948, Belgrade	Soviet Union, Bulgaria, Hungary, Romania, Ukraine, and Yugoslavia	Accord concerning navigation on the Danube	SZ, No. 241, 1949
September 11, 1948, Sofia	Bulgaria	Agreement on social policy and social administration	SZ, No. 177, 1949
September 14, 1948, Geneva	General treaty	Second Protocol of Rectifications to the General Agreement on Tariffs and Trade	UNTS, I, No. 814

September 14, 1948, Geneva	General treaty	Protocols modifying some provisions of the General Agreement on Tariffs and Trade	SZ, No. 175, 1949
September 16, 1948, Prague	United States	Agreement on settlement of lend-lease and some other claims	UNTS, I, No. 1224
September 22, 1948, Prague	Denmark	Trade agreement	ZO, No. 19, 1948
September 25, 1948, Berne	Switzerland	Trade and payments agreement	ZO, No. 20, 1948
October 12, 1948, Paris	France	Agreement on social security	SZ, No. 215, 1949
October 16, 1948, Helsinki	Finland	Agreement on exchange of goods	ZO, No. 21, 1948
October 29, 1948,	Austria	Agreement on exchange of goods	ZO, No. 10, 1954
November 4, 1948	Great Britain	Agreement extending the monetary agreement of November 1, 1945	UNTS, Vol. 81, Annex A, No. 62
November 20, 1948, Prague	Hungary	Five-year (1949-1953) agreement on exchange of goods	ZO, No. 23, 1948
December 8, 1948, Paris	General treaty	Convention on Prevention and Punishment of the Crime of Genocide	SZ, No. 32, 1955
December 31, 1948 and January 3, 1949, London	Great Britain	Agreement extending the monetary agreement of November 1, 1945	UNTS, Vol. 82, Annex A, No. 62

Date and Place of Signature	Cosignatories	Type of Treaty	Published or Reported in
January 21, 1949, Warsaw	Poland	Treaty on mutual legal relations in civil and criminal matters	SZ, No. 89, 1949
February 4, 1949, Moscow	Soviet Union	Protocol concerning mutual deliveries of goods	ZO, No. 7, 1949
February 16, 1949, Prague	Iceland	Agreement on exchange of goods	ZO, No. 8, 1949
February 28 and March 2, 1949, London	Great Britain	Agreement extending the monetary agreement of November 1, 1945	UNTS, Vol. 82, Annex A, No. 62
March 1, 1949, Belgrade and Prague	Yugoslavia	Trade and payments agreements	UNTS, I, Nos. 1546 and 1547
March 3, 1949, Prague	Great Britain	Agreement on mutual upkeep of war graves	UNTS, I, No. 1104
March 12, 1949, Prague	Albania	Trade and payments agreement	ZO, No. 12, 1949
March 29, 1949, New Delhi	India	Agreement on exchange of goods	ZO, No. 14, 1949
March 30, 1949, Prague	Uruguay	Agreement on exchange of goods	ZO, No. 11, 1949

March 30, 1949, Prague	Norway	Protocol on exchange of goods	UNTS, No. 460
April 1, 1949, Prague	Bulgaria	Agreement on social insurance	SZ, No. 5, 1950
April 16, 1949, Budapest	Hungary	Treaty of Friendship, Cooperation, and Mutual Aid	SZ, No. 212, 1949
April 23, 1949, Prague	Hungary	Agreement concerning provisional arrangement of economic relations	SZ, No. 197, 1949
May 4, 1949, New York	General treaty	Protocol amending the International Agreement for Suppression of White Slave Traffic of May 18, 1904 and the International Convention for Suppression of White Slave Traffic of May 4, 1910	UNTS, Vol. 92, Annex A, No. 446
May 6, 1949, Helsinki	Finland	Agreement concerning provisional arrangement of economic relations	SZ, No. 291, 1949
May 10, 1949, The Hague	Netherlands	Agreement on exchange of goods	ZO, No. 21, 1949
June 29, 1949, Moscow	Soviet Union and Finland	Protocol on tripartite clearing among Czechoslovakia, Soviet Union, and Finland	ZO, No. 28, 1949
July 9, 1949, Prague	Turkey	Trade and payments agreement	ZO, No. 29, 1949
July 13, 1949, Helsinki	Finland	Air transport agreement	UNTS, I, No. 779

Date and Place of Signature	Cosignatories	Type of Treaty	Published or Reported in
July 16, 1949, Prague	Austria	Protocol on exchange of goods and payments	ZO, No. 31, 1949
August 12, 1949, Geneva	General treaty	Final Act of the diplomatic conference convened for revision of the Geneva Convention of July 27, 1929 for the Relief of the Wounded and Sick in Armies in the Field; of the Hague Convention of October 18, 1907 for the Adaptation to Maritime Warfare of the Principles of the Geneva Convention of July 6, 1906; of the Convention concluded at Geneva on July 27, 1929 relative to the Treatment of Prisoners of War; and for the Establishment of a Convention for the Protection of Civilian Persons in Time of War	SZ, No. 65, 1954
August 13, 1949, Annecy (France)	General treaty	Protocols modifying some provisions of the General Agreement on Tariffs and Trade	SZ, No. 292, 1949
August 18, 1949, London	Great Britain	Agreement on sterling payments	UNTS, I, No. 1155
September 19, 1949, Geneva	General treaty	Convention on road traffic	UNTS, I, No. 1671
September 28, 1949, London	Great Britain	Trade and financial agreement	UNTS, I, No. 1156

September 28, 1949, London	Great Britain	Agreement on compensation for British property, rights, and interests affected by Czechoslovak measures of nationalization, expropriation, and dispossession	UNTS, I, No. 1157
September 28, 1949, London	Great Britain	Agreement relating to settlement of certain intergovernmental debts	UNTS, I, No. 1158
October 10, 1949, Annecy (France)	General treaty	Protocol of terms of accession to the General Agreement on Tariffs and Trade	SZ, No. 292, 1949
October 21, 1949, Frankfurt	West Germany	Trade and payments agreement	ZO, No. 44, 1949
October 28, 1949, Prague	Finland	Trade and payments agreement	ZO, No. 45, 1949
November 9, 1949, Mexico City	Mexico	Trade treaty	SZ, No. 91, 1950
November 30, 1949, Prague	Belgium and Luxemburg	Agreement on exchange of goods	ZO, No. 49, 1949
December 3, 1949, Budapest	Hungary	Agreement on exchange of goods	ZO, No. 50, 1949
December 17, 1949, Copenhagen	Denmark	Trade and payments agreements	UNTS, I, Nos. 961 and 962
December 22, 1949, Tirana	Albania	Trade agreement	ZO, No. 53, 1949

Date and Place of Signature	Cosignatories	Type of Treaty	Published or Reported in
December 22, 1949, Prague	Switzerland	Trade and payments agreement	ZO, No. 53, 1949
December 30, 1949, Prague	Pakistan	Trade agreement	ZO, No. 2, 1950
January 9, 1950, Berlin	East Germany	Trade and payments agreement	ZO, No. 2, 1950
March 20, 1950, Prague	Israel	Trade and payments agreement	ZO, No. 12, 1950
March 27, 1950, Prague	Bulgaria	Trade agreement	ZO, No. 13, 1950
March 30, 1950, Prague	Sweden	Protocol on exchange of goods and payments	ZO, No. 14, 1950
April 5, 1950, Prague	India	Trade agreement	ZO, No. 14, 1950
May 17, 1950	Brazil	Trade and payments agreements	ZO, No. 10, 1954
May 19, 1950, Prague	Iceland	Trade agreement	ZO, No. 21, 1950
June 2, 1950, Prague	France	Supplement to payments agreement of July 29, 1946	ZO, No. 23, 1950

June 14, 1950, Peiping	China	Trade and payments agreements	ZO, No. 25, 1950
July 8, 1950, Bucharest	Romania	Special trade and payments agreement	ZO, No. 29, 1950
October 20, 1950, Prague	Mexico	Payments agreement	ZO, No. 43, 1950
October 20, 1950, Helsinki	Finland	Trade and payments agreement	ZO, No. 44, 1950
November 3, 1950, Moscow	Soviet Union	Agreement on deliveries of goods for the period 1951-1955	ZO, No. 12, 1951
November 4, 1950, Prague	Norway	Protocol on exchange of goods	UNTS, II, No. 460
November 4, 1950, Prague	Norway	Supplementary protocol to the monetary agreement of December 13, 1945	UNTS, II, No. 280
December 28, 1950, London	Great Britain	Agreement amending the Sterling Payments Agreement of August 18, 1949	UNTS, I, No. 1792
March 1, 1951, Prague	Albania	Agreement on deliveries of industrial equipment by Czechoslovakia in the period 1951-1955	ZO, No. 10, 1951
March 3, 1951, Budapest	Hungary	Treaty on Legal Assistance in Civil and Criminal Matters	SZ, No. 85, 1951
March 13, 1951, Moscow	Soviet Union	Protocol concerning supplementary deliveries in 1951, and protocol to the November 3, 1950 trade agreement	ZO, No. 14, 1951

Date and Place of Signature	Cosignatories	Type of Treaty	Published or Reported in
March 16, 1951, Stockholm	Sweden	Trade agreement	ZO, No. 12, 1951
April 21, 1951, Torquay	General treaty	Torquay Protocol to the General Agreement on Tariffs and Trade	SZ, No. 51, 1951
April 26, 1951, Warsaw	Poland	Trade and payments agreement for the period 1951-1955	ZO, No. 19, 1951
June 4, 1951, Prague	East Germany	Trade agreement	ZO, No. 23, 1951
July 14, 1951, Prague	Bulgaria	Trade and payments agreement for the period 1951-1955	ZO, No. 29, 1951
October 24, 1951, Prague	Egypt	Trade and payments agreement	ZO, No. 41, 1951
February 28 and March 3, 1952, London	Great Britain	Extension of Sterling Payments Agreement of August 18, 1949	UNTS, II, No. 991
April 4, 1952, Copenhagen	Denmark	Trade agreement	UNTS, I, No. 1792
April 4, 1952, Copenhagen	Denmark	Supplementary protocol to the payments agreement of December 17, 1949	UNTS, Vol. 133, Annex A, No. 962

April 29, 1952, Bonn	West Germany	Payments agreement	ZO, No. 10, 1954
May 6, 1952, Peiping	China	Cultural agreement	SZ, No. 104, 1952
July 11, 1952, Brussels	General treaty	Universal Postal Convention	SZ, No. 5, 1954
July 12, 1952, Beirut	Lebanon	Trade agreement	SZ, No. 64, 1953
July 24, 1952	Uruguay	Payments agreement	ZO, No. 10, 1954
July 30, 1952, Damascus	Syria	Trade agreement	SZ, No. 65, 1953
July 31, 1952, Rio de Janeiro	Brazil	Trade agreement	*Diario Oficial* of Brazil, No. 227, Sept. 30, 1952
August 1, 1952, London	Great Britain	Agreement extending the Sterling Payments Agreement of August 18, 1949 for a period of three years	UNTS, II, No. 1155
August 28, 1952, Teheran	Iran	Trade and payments agreements	ZO, No. 10, 1954
September 2, 1952, Rio de Janeiro	Argentina	Trade agreement	ZO, No. 10, 1954
February 21, 1953, Prague	Romania	Trade agreement for 1953	ZO, No. 3, 1953

Date and Place of Signature	Cosignatories	Type of Treaty	Published or Reported in
February 23, 1953, Prague	Albania	Trade and payments agreement for 1953	ZO, No. 4, 1953
February 24, 1953, Prague	Hungary	Trade agreement for 1953	ZO, No. 3, 1953
March 17, 1953, Prague	Poland	Trade and payments agreement for 1953	ZO, No. 4, 1953
March 20, 1953, Prague	East Germany	Protocol to the trade agreement of December 1, 1951	ZO, No. 4, 1953
March 31, 1953, New York	General treaty	Convention on Political Rights of Women	SZ, No. 46, 1955
May 3, 1953, Peiping	China	Trade agreement	ZO, No. 5, 1953
May 16, 1953, Sofia	Bulgaria	Protocol on exchange of goods and payments in 1953	ZO, No. 5, 1953
June 25, 1953	Denmark	Trade and payments agreement	ZO, No. 10, 1954
July 3, 1953, Vienna	Austria	Protocol on exchange of goods	ZO, No. 7-8, 1953
August 31, 1953, Prague	Iceland	Trade agreement	ZO, No. 9, 1953

September 16, 1953, London	Great Britain	Protocol on exchange of goods	ZO, No. 10, 1953
October 17, 1953	Paraguay	Payments agreement	ZO, No. 10, 1954
November 17, 1953	Norway	Payments agreement	ZO, No. 10, 1954
November 17, 1953, New Delhi	India	Trade and payments agreement	ZO, No. 11, 1953
November 24, 1953, Berne	Switzerland	Trade treaty	SZ, No. 50, 1954
December 22, 1953, Brussels	Belgium and Luxemburg	Trade agreement	ZO, No. 1, 1954
February 1, 1954, Athens	Greece	Trade and payments agreements	ZO, No. 2, 1954
February 13, 1954, The Hague	Netherlands	Trade agreement	ZO, No. 2, 1954
February 17, 1954, Prague	Finland	Trade and payments agreement	ZO, No. 2, 1954
February 17, 1954, Prague	Austria	Protocol on exchange of goods	ZO, No. 2, 1954
March 6, 1954, Berlin	East Germany	Agreement on trade and payments in 1954	ZO, No. 4, 1954

Date and Place of Signature	Cosignatories	Type of Treaty	Published or Reported in
April 13, 1954, Prague	Bulgaria	Treaty on Legal Assistance in Civil and Criminal Matters	SZ, No. 57, 1954
April 14, 1954, Prague	Albania	Agreement on trade and payments in 1954	ZO, No. 4, 1954
April 15, 1954, Moscow	Soviet Union	Protocol on deliveries of goods in 1954	ZO, No. 4, 1954
April 27, 1954, Prague	China	Agreement on trade and payments in 1954	ZO, No. 5, 1954
May 7, 1954, Paris	France	Trade agreement	ZO, No. 5, 1954
May 22, 1954, Prague	Bulgaria	Protocol on exchange of goods in 1954	ZO, No. 6, 1954
May 24, 1954, Prague	Switzerland	Protocol on exchange of goods	ZO, No. 6, 1954
June 9, 1954, Prague	Norway	Agreement on exchange of goods	ZO, No. 6, 1954
July 8, 1954, Prague	Indonesia	Trade and payments agreements	ZO, No. 7-8, 1954
July 21, 1954, Bucharest	Romania	Agreement on exchange of goods and payments in 1954	ZO, No. 9, 1954

August 22, 1954	Afghanistan	Trade and payments agreement, concluded for four years with automatic extension clause	ZO, No. 10, 1954
August 31, 1954, Reykjavik	Iceland	Trade and payments agreements, concluded for three years with automatic extension clause	ZO, No. 9, 1954
September 10, 1954, Prague	Brazil	Trade and payments agreement	ZO, No. 9, 1954
November 11, 1954, Prague	Lebanon	Protocol on exchange of goods	ZO, No. 11, 1954
December 13, 1954, Oslo	Norway	Trade agreement	ZO, No. 12, 1954
January 20, 1955, Prague	Austria	Protocol on exchange of goods	ZO, No. 1, 1955
February 25, 1955, Prague	East Germany	Protocol on goods exchange and payments	ZO, No. 3, 1955
February 26, 1955, Moscow	Soviet Union	Agreement on air traffic	ZO, No. 3, 1955
March 5, 1955, Prague	Greece	Protocol on exchange of goods in 1955	ZO, No. 3, 1955
April 20, 1955, Prague	Soviet Union	Protocol on mutual deliveries of goods in 1955	ZO, No. 4, 1955
April 29, 1955, Prague	Belgium and Luxemburg	Trade and payments agreement	ZO, No. 5, 1955

Date and Place of Signature	Cosignatories	Type of Treaty	Published or Reported in
April 1955, Sofia	Bulgaria	Protocol concerning exchange of goods in 1955	ZO, No. 5, 1955
April 22, 1955, Prague	Albania	Trade agreement	ZO, No. 5, 1955
May 5, 1955, Prague	Romania	Agreement on goods exchange and payments in 1955	ZO, No. 5, 1955
May 14, 1955	Albania, Bulgaria, Hungary, East Germany, Poland, and Soviet Union	Treaty of Friendship, Cooperation, and Mutual Aid	SZ, No. 45, 1955
May 26, 1955	Denmark	Agreement on exchange of goods and payments	ZO, No. 6, 1955
June 5, 1955, Prague	Hungary	Trade and payments agreement	ZO, No. 6, 1955
June 25, 1955, Prague	France	Trade agreement	ZO. No. 7, 1955
July 19, 1955, Cairo	Egypt	Trade and payments agreement	ZO, No. 9, 1955

August 10, 1955, Hanoi	Vietnam	Trade and payments agreement for 1955	ZO, No. 9, 1955
August 29, 1955, Stockholm	Sweden	Trade and payments agreement	ZO, No. 9, 1955
September 12, 1955, Montevideo	Uruguay	Trade and payments agreement	ZO, No. 10, 1955
September 24, 1955, Prague	Iceland	Protocol on exchange of goods	ZO, No. 10, 1955
November 11, 1955, Prague	China	Trade and payments agreement for 1956	ZO, No. 11, 1955
December 14, 1955, Prague	Soviet Union	Protocol on mutual deliveries of goods in 1956	ZO, No. 12, 1955
February 6, 1956, Prague	East Germany	Agreement on mutual deliveries of goods and payments in 1956	ZO, No. 2, 1956
February 2, 1956, Athens	Greece	Protocol on goods deliveries in 1956	ZO, No. 2, 1956
February 14, 1956, Helsinki	Finland	Trade agreement for 1956	ZO, No. 2, 1956
February 16, 1956, Prague	Yugoslavia	Trade agreement for 1956	ZO, No. 2, 1956

BIBLIOGRAPHY

GENERAL

Bartlett, Vernon. *East of the Iron Curtain.* New York, 1949.

Betts, R. R. *Central and South East Europe 1945-1948.* London, 1950.

Beuer, Gustav. *New Czechoslovakia and Her Historical Background.* London, 1947.

"Ceskoslovensko" (Czechoslovakia), in *Masarykuv slovnik naucny* (Masaryk Encyclopaedic Dictionary), Vol. I, p. 1925. Prague, 1925.

Council of Foreign Relations. *Political Handbook of the World.* New York, 1936-53.

Czechoslovak Ministry of Foreign Affairs. *Czechoslovakia Fights Back.* Washington, 1943.

Czechoslovakia–Old Culture and New Life at Crossroads of Europe. Prague, 1947.

Dallin, David J. *The New Soviet Empire.* New Haven, 1951.

Friedman, Otto. *The Break-up of Czech Democracy.* London, 1950.

Hosak, Ladislav. *Nove ceskoslovenske dejiny* (New Czechoslovak History). Prague, 1947.

Janda, Bohumil, ed. *Ceskoslovenska vlastiveda* (Czechoslovak Encyclopaedia). Prague, 1929-30. 10 vols.

Kann, Robert A. *The Multinational Empire.* New York, 1950.

Kapras, Jan, Bohumil Nemec, and Frantisek Soukup, eds. *Idea Ceskoslovenskeho statu* (Idea of the Czechoslovak State). Prague, 1936. 2 vols.

Kerner, Robert, ed. *Czechoslovakia.* Berkeley, 1945.

Kerr, Walter. *Behind the 'Iron Curtain.'* New York, 1947.

Polisensky, J. V. *History of Czechoslovakia in Outline.* Prague, 1947.

Ripka, Hubert. *East and West.* London, 1944.

Schmidt, Dana Adams. *Anatomy of a Satellite.* Boston, 1952.

Seton-Watson, R. W. *A History of the Czechs and Slovaks.* London, 1943.

Slovak Academy of Arts and Sciences. *Slovenska vlastiveda* (Slovak Encyclopaedia). Bratislava, 1943. 5 vols.

Taborsky, Edvard. *Czechoslovak Democracy at Work.* London, 1945.

———. *Nase vec* (Our Cause). Prague, 1946.

Thomson, Samuel Harrison. *Czechoslovakia in European History.* 2nd ed. Princeton, 1953.

Vesely, Jaroslav, ed. *Encyclopédie Tchécoslovaque.* Prague, 1923.

Wanklyn, Harriet. *Czechoslovakia.* New York, 1954.

Warriner, Doreen. *Revolution in Eastern Europe.* London, 1950.

Land and Population

Barton, Paul. *La communauté Européenne de détente: le drame de l'emigration dans la guerre froide*. Paris, 1954.

Blazek, Miroslav. *Hospodarska geografie Ceskoslovenska* (Economic Geography of Czechoslovakia). Prague, 1953. 2 vols.

Bohac, Antonin. "Obyvatelstvo v Ceskoslovenske republice" (The Population of the Czechoslovak Republic), in *Ceskoslovenska vlastiveda* (Czechoslovak Encyclopaedia). Prague, 1929.

Bohac, Antonin, *et al.* "Obyvatelstvo Ceskoslovenske republiky" (The Population of the Czechoslovak Republic), in *Atlas republiky Ceskoslovenske* (Atlas of the Czechoslovak Republic). Prague, 1935.

Ceskoslovensko v mapach (Czechoslovakia in Maps). Prague, 1954.

Czechoslovak Republic. State Statistical Office. *Recensement de la population de la République Tchécoslovaque, effectué le 1er décembre 1930.* Prague, 1934-39. 4 vols.

Frumkin, Gregory. *Population Changes in Europe Since 1939.* New York, 1951.

Koncek, Mikulas and Michal Luknis, eds. *Geographica Slovaca.* Bratislava, 1949.

Korcak, Jaromir. *Geopoliticke zaklady Ceskoslovenska. Jeho kmenove oblasti* (Geopolitical Structure of Czechoslovakia. Its Tribal Regions). Prague, 1938.

Maly politicky atlas sveta (Small Political Atlas of the World). Prague, 1954.

Prigrada, Anthony. *Danube Waterways.* New York, 1953.

Rudzki, Adam. *Roads, Waterways, and Seaports of Captive Europe.* New York, 1954.

"Satellite Demography," in *News from Behind the Iron Curtain,* Vol. IV (May 1955).

Stefanek, Anton. "Zaklady sociologie Slovenska" (Elements of the Sociology of Slovakia), Part III, "Demografia" (Demography), in *Slovenska vlastiveda* (Slovak Encyclopaedia). Bratislava, 1944.

United Nations. *Demographic Yearbook.* New York, 1949-55.

United States. Bureau of the Census. *The Population of Czechoslovakia* (International Population Statistics Reports, Series P-90, No. 3). Washington, 1953.

History and Politics

Barton, Paul. *Prague à l'heure de Moscou: Analyse d'une démocratie populaire.* Paris, 1954.

Benes, Edvard. *Memoirs. From Munich to New War and New Victory.* London, 1954.

———. *Svetova krise: Kontinuita prava a nove pravo revolucni* (The World

Crisis: the Continuity of Law and the New Revolutionary Law). Prague, 1946.

———. *Uvahy o Slovanstvi* (Thoughts on Slavism). London, 1945.

Berdych, Frantisek. *Obrana statu a nase politicke strany* (Defense of the State and Our Political Parties). Prague, 1938.

Bloss, Esther. *Labor Legislation in Czechoslovakia, with Special Reference to the Standards of the International Labor Organization.* New York, 1938.

Bokes, Frantisek. *Dejiny Slovenska a Slovakov od najstarsich cias po oslobodenie* (History of Slovakia and Slovaks from Ancient Times until Liberation). Bratislava, 1946.

Bolton, Glorney. *Czech Tragedy.* London, 1955.

Boura, F. *O ustave 9. kvetna* (The Constitution of May 9). Prague, 1951.

Budnik, Josef. *Prozatimni statni zrizeni Ceskoslovenske republiky* (Provisional Political Organization of the Czechoslovak Republic). Prague, 1947.

Busek, Vratislav. *Pouceni z unoroveho prevratu* (The Lesson of the February Coup). New York, 1954.

Busek, Vratislav, J. Hendrych, K. Lastovka, and V. Mueller. *Ceskoslovenske cirkevni zakony* (Czechoslovak Ecclesiastical Laws). Prague, 1931.

Clementis, Vlado. *Slovensko a Evropa* (Slovakia and Europe). Prague, 1938.

Cobban, Alfred. *National Self-Determination.* London, 1945.

Communist Party of Czechoslovakia, Central Committee. *Protokol IX. radneho sjezdu Komunisticke strany Ceskoslovenska* (Minutes of the Ninth Regular Congress of the Communist Party of Czechoslovakia). Prague, 1949.

The Constitution of the Czechoslovak Republic. With Introduction by Jiri Hoetzel and V. Joachim. Prague, 1920.

Crankshaw, Edward. *Cracks in the Kremlin Wall.* New York, 1951.

Czechoslovak Republic. *Declaration of Independence of the Czechoslovak Nation by Its Provisional Government.* New York, 1918.

———. *Nationalization in Czechoslovakia.* Decrees of the President of the Republic of October 24, 1954 on the nationalization of mines and some industrial enterprises, some enterprises of the food industry, joint-stock banks, and private insurance companies. Prague, 1946.

———. *Rodinne pravo* (zakon zo dna 7. dec. 1949, cis.265 Sb. 1 vyd.) (Family Law; Law of December 7, 1949, No. 265 of the Collection of Laws, 1st ed.). Bratislava, 1953.

———. Ministry of Foreign Affairs. *Four Fighting Years.* London, 1943.

———. Ministry of Information. *Czechoslovakia on the Road to Socialism.* Prague, 1949.

———. Ministry of Information. *Deset let parlamentni retrospektivy: od Narodniho Shromazdeni r. 1935 k Prozatimnimu Narodnimu Shromazdeni r. 1945* (Ten Years of Parliamentary Retrospection: From the National Assembly of 1935 to the Provisional National Assembly of 1945). By Vladimir Zadera. Prague, 1948.

———. Ministry of Information. *Zakony nasi pozemkove reformy* (Laws

Concerning Our Land Reform). By Jiri Kotatko. 1st ed. Prague, 1945.

———. Ministry of Information and Public Culture. *The Constitution of the Czechoslovak Republic.* Translated from the Czech by F. D. Stein. 2nd ed. Prague, 1948.

———. Ministry of Information and Public Culture. *Funkce prava v hospodarskem planovani* (The Function of Law in Economic Planning). By Arnost Chmelar. Prague, 1949.

———. Ministry of Justice. *Obcansky soudni rad* (Civil Procedure Code). Prague, 1950.

———. Ministry of Justice, Law Institute. *Pravnicka prirucka* (Law Manual). Edited by Vladimir Rolenc. Prague, 1954.

———. Ministry of National Defense. *Dvacet let ceskoslovenske armady v osvobozenem state* (Twenty Years of Czechoslovak Army in the Liberated State). Prague, 1938.

———. Ministry of Social Welfare. *Twenty Years of Social Welfare in the Czechoslovak Republic.* Prague, 1938.

Derer, Ivan. *Slovensky vyvoj a Ludacka zrada* (Slovak Development and the Treason of the People's Party). Prague, 1946.

Dolezal, Jiri. *Slovenske narodni povstani; prispevek k jeho vzniku a pruhehu* (Slovak National Uprising; a contribution to the study of its origin and development). Prague, 1954.

Drucker, A. "The Czechoslovak Legal Council," *Law Journal,* No. 92, p. 363 (November 14, 1942) London.

Duchacek, Ivo. "The February Coup in Czechoslovakia," *World Politics,* Vol. 2, No. 4, pp. 511-32 (July 1950).

———. "The Strategy of Communist Infiltration: Czechoslovakia, 1944-1948," *World Politics,* Vol. 2, No. 3 (April 1950).

———. *The Strategy of Communist Infiltration: The Case of Czechoslovakia.* New Haven, 1949.

Erhart, Josef. *Ustavni pravo a obecna cast spravniho prava* (Constitutional Law and General Administrative Law). Prague, 1935.

Fierlinger, Zdenek. *Demokracie a otazka narodnostni* (Democracy and the National Question). Prague, 1931.

———. *Ve sluzbach CSR* (In the Service of the Czechoslovak Republic). Prague, 1947-48. 2 vols.

Friedman, Otto. *The Breakup of Czech Democracy.* London, 1950.

Gadourek, I. *The Political Control of Czechoslovakia; A Study in Social Control of a Soviet Satellite State.* Leiden, 1953.

Goldman, Josef. *Czechoslovakia: Test Case of Nationalization.* Prague, 1947.

Gottwald, Klement. *O ceskoslovenske zahranicni politice* (Czechoslovak Foreign Policy). Prague, 1948.

———. *Selected Speeches and Articles, 1929-53.* Prague, 1954.

———. *Vybrane spisy* (Selected Works). Prague, 1954-55. 8 vols.

Graham, Malbone W. *New Governments of Central Europe.* New York, 1924.

———. *New Governments of Eastern Europe.* New York, 1927.

Grospic, Jan. *O pravech obcanu v lidove demokratickem state* (Civil Rights in the People's Democratic State). Prague, 1954.

Gsovski, Vladimir. *New Codes in the New Slavic Countries* (Poland, Czechoslovakia, Yugoslavia). Washington, 1934.

Hartmann, Paul. *Die Politische Partei in der Tschechoslowakischen Republik, eine Juristische Studie.* Brunn, 1931.

Hoch, Karel. *Les partis politiques en Tchécoslovaquie.* Prague, 1936.

Hoetzel, Jiri. *Ceskoslovenske spravni pravo* (Czechoslovak Administrative Law). Prague, 1934.

International Labour Office, Committee on Freedom of Association, Eighth and Tenth Reports. *Trade Union Rights in Czechoslovakia.* London, 1953.

Janowsky, Oscar I. *Nationalities and National Minorities.* New York, 1945.

Jaszi, Oscar. *The Dissolution of the Habsburg Monarchy.* Chicago, 1929.

Josten, Josef. *Oh, My Country.* London, 1949.

Klapka, Vladimir. *Nova organizacia sudov a prokuratury* (New Organization of the Courts and of the Procurator General's Office). Bratislava, 1953.

Kopecky, Vaclav. *30 let KSC; vzpominky na zalozeni KSC a hlavni udalosti jejiho vyvoje* (30 Years of the KSC; Recollections of the Founding of the KSC and of the Chief Events in Its Development). Prague, 1951.

Korbel, Pavel. *Parliamentary Elections in Czechoslovakia.* New York, 1952.

———. *The Supreme Organs of the Communist Party of Czechoslovakia.* New York, 1952.

Korbel, Pavel and V. Vagassky. *Purges in the Communist Party of Czechoslovakia.* New York, 1952.

Korkisch, F. "Die Verfassungsrechtliche Entwicklung in der Tschechoslowakei bis zur Verfassung vom 9 Mai 1948," *Zeitschrift fur auslandisches offentliches Recht und Volkerrecht,* Vol. XIII, No. 3 (March 1951), Stuttgart and Koln.

KSC v boji za svobodu (Communist Party of Czechoslovakia in the Fight for Freedom). Prague, 1949.

Kunosi, Alexander. *The Basis of Czechoslovak Unity.* London, 1944.

Lausman, Bohumil. *Kdo byl vinen?* (Who Was Guilty?). Vienna, 1953.

Lettrich, Jozef. *History of Modern Slovakia.* New York, 1955.

Malypetr, Jan, Frantisek Soukup, and Jan Kapras. *Armada a narod* (The Army and the Nation). Prague, 1938.

Mandak, O. *Statni zrizeni CSR* (The Constitution of the Czechoslovak Republic). Prague, 1951.

Mares, Vaclav E. "Czechoslovakia Under Communism," *Current History,* Vol. 26, No. 154 (June 1954).

Masarykova Universita. *Problemy nove ceskoslovenske ustavy* (Problems of the New Czechoslovak Constitution). Brno, 1947.

Meyer, Peter *et al. The Jews in the Soviet Satellites.* Syracuse, 1953.

Moody, Joseph N., ed. *Church and Society.* New York, 1953.

Narodny Front. Ustredny akcny vybor (National Front. Central Action Committee). *Nase nove obcianske pravo.* Prejavy prednesene v plene

Narodneho Shromazdenia dna 25. oktobra 1950 (Our New Civil Code. Addresses delivered at the National Assembly, October 25, 1950). Edited by Vaclav Chvatal and Milos Parma. Prague, 1950.

National Committee for a Free Europe. *Cistky v Komunisticke strane Ceskoslovenska* (Purges in the Communist Party of Czechoslovakia). New York, 1952.

Necasek, Frantisek, ed. *Dokumenty o protisovetskych piklech ceskoslovenske reakce;* z archivniho materialu o kontrarevolucni cinnosti Masaryka a Benese v letech 1917-1924 (Documents on the Anti-Soviet Conspiracy of Czechoslovak Reaction; archive materials demonstrating counterrevolutionary activities of Masaryk and Benes during the years 1917-1924). Prague, 1954.

Nejedly, Zdenek. *Klement Gottwald v boji za osvobozeni CSR* (Klement Gottwald in the Struggle for the Liberation of the Czechoslovak Republic). Prague, 1949.

Nemec, Ludvik. *Church and State in Czechoslovakia.* New York, 1955.

Neuman, Alois. *Novy pravni rad v lidove demokracii* (New Legal Order in a People's Democracy). Prague, 1952.

Odlozilik, Otakar. "Bohemian Protestants and the Calvinistic Churches," *Church History,* Vol. VII, No. 4 (December 1939).

Peiser, Werner. *Land ohne Freude.* Zurich, 1949.

Peroutka, Ferdinand. *Budovani statu; ceskoslovenska politika v letech poprevratovych* (The Building of a State; Czechoslovak Politics in the Postwar Years). Prague, 1934-36. 4 vols.

Peska, Zdenek. *Ceskoslovenska ustava a zakony s ni souvisle* (The Czechoslovak Constitution and Laws Related to It). Prague, 1935. 2 vols.

———. *Dokumenty k ustavnim dejinam ceskoslovenskym 1938-1946* (Documents for the Czechoslovak Constitutional History 1938-1946). Prague, 1947. 2 vols.

Pool, Ithiel de Sola. *Satellite Generals.* Stanford, 1955.

Pravda velike doby. Reportaze z triceti rocniku Rudeho prava (The Truth of a Great Era. Selected articles published during the last 30 years in *Rude Pravo).* Library of Rude Pravo, Vol. 21. Prague, 1950.

Rais, Stefan. *Nova organisace soudu a prokuratur, posila socialisticke zakonnosti* (New Organization of Courts and Offices of the Government Attorneys—A Reinforcement for Socialist Legality). Prague, 1952.

Reimann, Pavel. *Dejiny komunisticke strany Ceskoslovenska* (History of the Communist Party of Czechoslovakia). Prague, 1931.

———. *Komunizmus a moralka* (Communism and Morality). Bratislava, 1949.

Ripka, Hubert. *Le Coup de Prague: Une révolution préfabriquée.* Paris, 1949.

———. *Czechoslovakia Enslaved: The Story of the Communist Coup d'Etat.* London, 1950.

Roessler, Fritz. *Die Slovakei zwischen Gestern und Heute.* Dresden, 1943.

Rotnagl, Josef. *Cesi a Slovaci* (Czechs and Slovaks). Prague, 1945.

Russkaia Narodnaia Rada, Uzhorod. *Zakonoproiekt tsentral 'noi Russkoi Narodnoi Rady o konstitutsii avtonomnoi Podkarpatskoi Rusi* (Draft Constitution for an Autonomous Ruthenia, Submitted by the Russian National Council). Uzhorod, 1937.

Sander, Fritz. *Grundriss des tschechoslovakischen Verfassungsrechtes.* Reichenberg, 1938.

Schwebl, R. "Legislation in Exile," *Journal of the Society of Comparative Legislation,* 3rd ser., No. 24, pp. 120-24 (November 1942) London.

Seton-Watson, Hugh. *The East European Revolution.* London, 1952.

Seton-Watson, R. W. *The New Slovakia.* Prague, 1924.

Seton-Watson, R. W., ed. *Slovakia Then and Now.* Prague, 1931.

Shuster, George N. *Religion Behind the Iron Curtain.* New York, 1954.

Sidor, Karol. *Slovenska politika na pode Prazskeho Snemu* (Slovak Policy in the Prague Parliament). Bratislava, 1943.

Skilling, Gordon H. "People's Democracy, the Proletarian Dictatorship, and the Czechoslovak Path to Socialism," *The American Slavic and East European Review,* Vol. X (April 1951).

Slovnik verejneho prava ceskoslovenskeho (Dictionary of Czechoslovak Public Law). Compiled by Emil Hacha, Antonin Hobza, Jiri Hoetzel, Frantisek Weyr, Karel Lastovka, and Jiri Havelka. Brno, 1929-38. 5 vols.

Sobota, Emil. *Zmeny ustavy republiky cesko-slovenske; ustavni zakony o autonomii Slovenske zeme a Podkarpatske Rusi* (Changes of the Czecho-Slovak Constitution; constitutional laws on the autonomy of the Slovak land and of Ruthenia). Prague, 1939.

Sobota, Emil, Jaroslav Vorel, Rudolf Krovak, and Antonin Schenk. *Ceskoslovensky president. Statopravni instituce a jeji zivot* (Czechoslovak President. The Constitutional Institution and Its Development). Prague, 1934.

Spacil, Bedrich. *Pece statu o cirkve* (Government Care of Churches). Prague, 1951.

Stivin, Josef. *Rudy prapor zavlaje, 1878-1938. Strucne dejiny csl. socialne demokraticke strany* (The Red Flag Will Wave On High, 1878-1938. A Brief History of the Czechoslovak Social Democratic Party). Prague, 1938.

Storm, Walter. *The Crisis in Czechoslovakia.* Prague, 1948.

Sverma, Jan. *Ceska otazka ve svetle marxismu* (Czech Question in the Light of Marxism). Prague, 1933.

Svoboda, Alois, Anna Tuckova, and Vera Svobodova. *Jak to bylo v unoru* (How It Was in February). Prague, 1949.

Taborsky, Edvard. "The Czechoslovak Judicial Council: A Bold Attempt at Solving the Problem of Administrative Justice Abroad," *Modern Law Review,* No. 6, pp. 143-48 (April 1943) London.

———. *Nase nova ustava* (Our New Constitution). Prague, 1948.

Tobolka, Zdenek, ed. *Ceska politika* (Czech Politics). Prague. 6 vols.

Tobolka, Zdenek V. *Politicke dejiny ceskoslovenskeho naroda od r.1848 az do dnesni doby* (Political History of the Czechoslovak Nation from 1848 until the Present). Prague, 1932-37. 4 vols.

Ustava 9. Kvetna (The Constitution of May 9). Prague, 1948.

Vesely, Jindrich. *O vzniku a zalozeni KSC* (The Origin and Founding of the Communist Party of Czechoslovakia). Prague, 1952.

Vyzkumny ustav osvetovy, Praha (Research Institute of Public Culture, Prague). *Narodni vybory organy moci pracujiciho lidu* (People's Committees, organs of the working people's power). Prague, 1954.

Weyr, Frantisek. *Soustava ceskoslovenskeho prava statniho* (The System of Czechoslovak Constitutional Law). 2nd ed. Prague, 1924.

Weyr, Frantisek and Zdenek Neubauer. *Ustavni listina ceskoslovenske republiky, jeji zneni s poznamkami* (The Constitution of the Czechoslovak Republic, Its Text with Annotations). Prague and Brno, 1931.

Witz, Karel. *Ceskoslovenske pracovni pravo* (Czechoslovak Labor Law). Prague, 1954.

Wiskemann, Elizabeth. *Germany's Eastern Neighbours. Problems Relating to the Oder-Neisse Line and the Czech Frontier Regions.* Oxford, 1956.

Zapotocky, Antonin. *Boj o jednotu odboru* (Struggle for the Unity of the Trade Unions). Prague, 1950.

———. *Nova odborova politika* (New Trade Union Policy). Prague, 1948.

Zeiss, R. and I. Kliment. *Spravni rizeni* (Administrative Procedure). Prague, 1937.

Zinner, Paul. "Marxism in Action, the Seizure of Power in Czechoslovakia," *Foreign Affairs*, Vol. 28, No. 4 (July 1950).

———. "Problems of Communist Rule in Czechoslovakia," *World Politics*, Vol. IV, No. 1 (October 1951).

Zizka, Vaclav. *Bojujici Ceskoslovensko* (Fighting Czechoslovakia). Kosice, Prague, 1945.

Culture

Bittner, Konrad. *Das Slowakische Schrifttum der Nachkriegszeit.* Munich, 1939.

———. *Das Tschechische Schrifttum der Nachkriegszeit.* Munich, 1939.

Bobek, Wladyslaw. *Prehladne dejiny slovenskej literatury* (Survey of the History of Slovak Literature). Bratislava, 1939.

Bor, Jan E. *Poezia povojnoveho Slovenska* (Poetry of Postwar Slovakia). Trnava, 1934.

Bujnak, Pavel. *Strucne dejiny literatury ceskoslovenskej* (Brief Outline of Czechoslovak Literature). Banska Stiavnica, 1923.

Buzek, Kamil. *Uvod do pravni organisace narodniho skolstvi v RCS* (Introduction in the Legal Organization of National Schools in the Czechoslovak Republic). Prague, 1931.

Caplovic, Jan. *O studiu starsej literatury slovenskej* (The Study of Older Slovak Literature). Bratislava, 1953.

Cerny, Vaclav. *Boje a smery socialisticke kultury* (Struggles and Trends in Socialist Culture). Prague, 1946.

Chrobak, Dobroslav. *Rukovat dejin slovenskej literatury* (Survey of the History of Slovak Literature). Prague, 1936.

Evans, F. Bowen, ed. *Worldwide Communist Propaganda Activities*. New York, 1955.

Gotz, Frantisek. *Strucne dejiny literatury ceske* (Brief History of Czech Literature). Brno, 1927.

Harkins, W. E. *Anthology of Czech Literature*. New York, 1953.

———. *The Russian Folk Epos in Czech Literature 1800-1900*. New York, 1951.

Harkins, W. E. and Klement Simoncic. *Czech and Slovak Literature* (Slavic Bibliography Series, Columbia University). New York, 1950.

Hrabanek, Jan. *Ceskoslovenske pravo tiskove* (Czechoslovak Press Law). Edited by A. Milota. Prague, 1933.

Jakobson, Roman. "The Kernel of Comparative Slavic Literature," in *Harvard Slavic Studies*, Vol. 1. Cambridge, 1953.

———. *Zaklady ceskeho verse* (Basis of Czech Verse). Prague, 1926.

Jakubec, Jan. *Dejiny literatury ceske* (History of Czech Literature). Revised edition. Prague, 1929-34. 2 vols.

Jakubec, Jan, and Arne Novak. *Geschichte der Tschechischen Literatur*. Leipzig, 1907 and 1913.

Jelinek, Hanus. *Histoire de la littérature tchéque*. Paris, 1930-35. 3 vols.

Kral, Josef. *O prosodii ceske* (On Czech Prosody). Prague, 1923-38. 2 vols.

Krcmery, Stefan. *Prehlad dejin slovenskej literatury a vzdelanosti* (Survey of the History of Slovak Literature and Culture). Turciansky Sv. Martin, 1920.

Lutzow, Franz. *A History of Bohemian Literature*. London, 1899 and 1907.

Machal, Jan. *Dejiny ceskeho dramatu* (History of Czech Drama). Prague, 1917 and 1929.

Mraz, Andrej. *Dejiny slovenskej literatury* (History of Slovak Literature). Bratislava, 1948.

———. *Die Literatur der Slovaken*. Berlin, Prague, Vienna, 1942.

Mukarovsky, Jan. *Kapitoly z ceske poetiky* (Chapters from Czech Poetry). Prague, 1948-49. 3 vols.

Nosek, Vladimir. *The Spirit of Bohemia*. London, 1926.

Novak, Arne. *Dejiny ceskeho pisemnictvi* (History of Czech Literature). Prague, 1946.

———. *Strucne dejiny literatury ceske* (Brief History of Czech Literature). Edited by R. Havel and A. Grund. Olomouc, 1946.

———. *Die tschechische Literatur aus der Vogelperspektive*. Prague, 1923.

Novak, Arne and Josef Novak. *Prehledne dejiny literatury ceske* (Survey of the History of Czech Literature). Olomouc, 1936-39.

Patzakova, A. J., ed. *Prvnich deset let ceskoslovenskeho rozhlasu* (The First Ten Years of Czechoslovak Broadcasting). Prague, 1935.

Polak, Karel. *Ceskoslovenska literatura, 1890-1935* (Czechoslovak Literature, 1890-1935). Prague, 1936.

———. *Literatura a socialismus* (Literature and Socialism). Prague, 1946.

Prazak, Albert. *Dejiny slovenske literatury* (History of Slovak Literature). Prague, 1950.

Reissmann, Otto. *Ceskoslovenske pravo rozhlasove* (Czechoslovak Broadcasting Law). Prague, 1936.

Ripellino, Angelo Maria. *Storia della poesia ceca contemporanea.* Rome, 1950.

Salda, Frantisek X. *Krasna literatura ceska v prvnim desetileti republiky* (Czech Belles-Lettres in the First Decade of the Republic). Prague, 1930.

———. *Kriticke glosy k nove ceske poesii* (Critical Comments on New Czech Poetry). Prague, 1939.

———. *Moderni literatura ceska* (Modern Czech Literature). Prague, 1909 and 1920.

———. *O nejmladsi poesii ceske* (Newest Czech Poetry). Prague, 1928.

Selver, Paul. *Czechoslovak Literature, an Outline.* London, 1942.

———. *Masaryk, a Biography.* London, 1940.

———. *Otokar Brezina, a Study in Czech Literature.* Oxford, 1921.

Smrek, Jan, ed. *Slovenska literarna a umelecka pritomnost* (Slovak Contemporary Literature and Creative Arts). Prague, 1931.

Souckova, Milada. *A Literature in Crisis.* New York, 1954.

———. "The First Stirrings of Modern Czech Literature," in *Harvard Slavic Studies,* Vol. II. Cambridge, 1954.

———. "Marxist Theory in Czech Literature," in *Harvard Slavic Studies,* Vol. I. Cambridge, 1953.

Stoll, Ladislav. *Face to Face with Reality.* Translated by Stephen Jolly. Prague, 1948.

———. *Tricet let boju za ceskou socialistickou poesii* (Thirty Years of Struggle for Czech Socialist Poetry). Prague, 1950.

Strakhovsky, Leonid I., ed. *A Handbook of Slavic Studies.* Cambridge, 1949.

Stransky, Rudolf. *Democracy and Education.* Prague, 1938.

Svaz ceskych novinaru (Union of Czech Journalists). *Newspapers and Newspapermen in Czechoslovakia.* Prague, 1947.

Union des Journalistes Libres de l'Europe Centrale et Orientale. *La presse derrière le rideau de fer.* Paris, 1948.

Vaclavek, Bedrich. *Ceska literatura XX. stoleti* (Czech Literature of the Twentieth Century). Prague, 1947.

Vasica, Josef. *Ceske literarni baroko* (Czech Literary Baroque). Prague, 1938.

Vilikovsky, Jan. *Pisemnictvi ceskeho stredoveku* (Literature of the Czech Medieval Period). Prague, 1948.

Vlcek, Jaroslav. *Dejiny ceske literatury* (History of Czech Literature). Prague, 1892-1914, 1931, 1940, 1951. 4 vols.

———. *Dejiny literatury slovenskej* (History of Slovak Literature). Turciansky Sv. Martin, 1890, 1923, 1933.

Vlcek, Jaroslav, ed. *Literatura ceska devatenacteho stoleti* (Czech Literature of the Nineteenth Century). Prague, 1902-7, Vols. I, II, III/1 and III/2. Revised edition by Jan Jakubec. Prague, 1911-17. 2 vols.

Wellek, Rene. Entries on Czech and Slovak Literature in *Columbia Dictionary of Modern European Literature*, edited by H. Smith. New York, 1947.

———. "Modern Czech Criticism and Literary Scholarship," in *Harvard Slavic Studies*, Vol. II. Cambridge, 1954.

———. "The Two Traditions of Czech Literature," in *Slavic Studies*. Ithaca, New York, 1943.

Za socialistickou skolu (For the Socialist School). Bratislava, 1950.

Zieris, K. F. *The New Organization of the Czech Press*. Prague, 1947.

Economics

Ames, Edward. "Soviet Bloc Currency Conversions," *American Economic Review*, Vol. XLIV (June 1954).

Bata, Jan A. *Budujeme stat pro 40,000,000 lidi* (We Are Building a Country for 40,000,000 People). Zlin, 1938.

Braibant, Guy. *La Planification en Tchécoslovaquie*. Paris, 1948.

Brdlik, Vladislav. *A Short Survey of Agriculture in Czechoslovakia*. Prague, 1938.

———. *Die sozialoekonomische Struktur der Landwirtschaft in der Teche-choslowakei*. Berlin, 1938.

Cihar, Julius. *Narodohospodarsky Atlas Ceskoslovenska* (Economic Atlas of Czechoslovakia). Prague, 1928.

Czechoslovak Republic. *Slovenske podohospodarstvo* (Slovak Agriculture). Bratislava, 1946-50.

———. Ministry of Agriculture. *Dvacet let ceskoslovenskeho zemedelstvi, 1918-1938* (Twenty Years of Czechoslovak Agriculture). Prague, 1938.

———. Ministry of Information. *The Czechoslovak Economic Five Year Plan*. Prague, 1949.

———. Ministry of Information. *Prvni ceskoslovensky plan; sbirka projevu a dokumentu o dvouletem hospodarskem planu* (The First Czechoslovak Economic Plan; a collection of addresses and documents concerning the Two-Year Economic Plan) 2nd ed. Prague, 1946.

———. Ministry of Information and Public Culture. *The First Czechoslovak Economic Plan*. Law No. 241 of October 27, 1948 and Cabinet Message. Translated from the Czech by F. O. Stein. 1st ed. Prague, 1949.

———. Ministry of Information and Public Culture. *Pozemkova reforma v Ceskoslovensku* (Land Reform in Czechoslovakia). Prague, 1949.

———. National Bank. *Deset let Narodni banky ceskoslovenske* (Ten Years of the Czechoslovak National Bank). Prague, 1937.

———. State Planning and Statistical Office in Bratislava. *Statisticka prirucka Slovenska* (Statistical Handbook of Slovakia). Bratislava, 1948.

———. State Statistical Office. *Statistical Digest of the Czechoslovak Republic*. Prague, 1948.

———. State Statistical Office. *Statisticka rocenka republiky Ceskoslovenske*. Prague, 1930-38.

———. State Statistical Office. *Zpravy Statniho uradu statistickeho republiky Ceskoslovenske* (Reports of the State Statistical Office of the Czechoslovak Republic). Prague, 1947—.

Dewar, Margaret. *Soviet Trade with Eastern Europe, 1945-1949*. London, 1951.

Fabry, V. *Zemedelske zakony republiky Ceskoslovenske* (Agricultural Laws of the Czechoslovak Republic). Prague, 1949.

Fellner, F. von. "Das Volkseinkommen Osterreichs und Ungarns" (The National Income of Austria and Hungary), *Statistische Monatschrift*, Vol. XXI (1916).

Fiala, Ctibor. *Zeleznice v republice Ceskoslovenske. Historie a vyvoj* (Railroads in the Czechoslovak Republic. History and Development). Prague, 1932.

George, Pierre. *L'Economie de l'Europe Centrale Slave et Danubienne*. Paris, 1949.

Goldman, Josef and J. Flek. *Planned Economy in Czechoslovakia*. Prague, 1949.

Gottwald, Klement. *Zaklady prvni petiletky* (Foundations of the First Five-Year Plan). Prague, 1948.

Hertz, F. O. *The Economic Problem of the Danubian States. A Study in Economic Nationalism*. London, 1947.

Hotowetz, R. *Nase hospodarstvi roku 1926 a jeho dalsi vyvoj* (Our Economy in 1926 and Its Further Development). Prague, 1927.

Hubacek, Josef. *Tuha paliva Ceskoslovenske Republiky* (Solid Fuels of the Czechoslovakian Republic). Prague, 1948.

Kiesewetter, B. *Die Wirtschaft der Tschechoslowakei seit 1945*. Berlin, 1954.

Kriz, A. and V. Mares. *The Iron and Steel Industry in Czechoslovakia*. Prague, 1930.

Mares, Vaclav E. "The Disrupted Czech Economy," *Current History*, Vol. 24, No. 142 (June 1953).

Meisner, M. *Weltmontanstatistik* (World Mining Statistics). Stuttgart, 1932 and 1939.

Roubik, Frantisek. *Z ceskych hospodarskych dejin* (Excerpts from Czech Economic History). Prague, 1948.

Shimkin, Dmitri B. *Minerals, a Key to Soviet Power*. Cambridge, 1953.

Stadnik, M. *Ceskoslovensky narodni duchod a methody jeho zjisteini* (The Czechoslovak National Income and Methods of Its Computation). Prague, 1947.

———. "Konstrukce narodniho duchodu v CSR" (The Construction of National Income in Czechoslovakia), *Socialni revue* (Social Review), July 1947.

———. *Narodni duchod a jeho rozdeleni* (National Income and Its Division). Prague, 1946.

———. *Narodni duchod a narodni spotreba v Ceskoslovensku v roce 1946* (National Income and National Expenditure in Czechoslovakia in the Year 1946). Prague, 1947.

United Nations. *Direction of International Trade*. New York, 1948-52.

———. *Statistical Yearbook*. New York, 1948—.

———. *World Economic Report, 1949-50*. New York, 1951.

———. Economic Commission for Europe. *Economic Survey of Europe*. Geneva, 1948—.

United Nations Food and Agriculture Organization. *European Agriculture*. Geneva, 1954.

———. *Yearbook of Food and Agricultural Statistics, 1952*. Rome, 1953.

United States. Department of Interior. Bureau of Mines. *Minerals Yearbook 1951*. Washington, 1954.

———. War Department. Civil Affairs Handbook Series. *Czechoslovakia*. Washington, 1944.

Vesely, Jaroslav, ed. "Industrie et Commerce" in *Encyclopedie Tchécoslovaque*. Prague, 1923.

Zimmermann, E. W. *World Resources and Industries*. New York, 1951.

CONTEMPORARY PERIODICALS

Ceskoslovenska akademie ved, Historicky ustav (Czechoslovak Academy of (Journal). Prague.

Ceskoslovenska akademie ved, Historicky ustav (Czechoslovak Academy of Sciences, Historical Institute). *Ceskoslovensky casopis historicky* (Czechoslovak Historical Journal). Quarterly, Prague.

Ceskoslovenska akademie ved, Kabinet ekonomie (Czechoslovak Academy of Sciences, Department of Economy). *Politicka ekonomie* (Political Economy). Quarterly, Prague.

Ceskoslovenska akademie ved, Kabinet pro kartograffii (Czechoslovak Academy of Sciences, Department of Cartography). *Kartograficky prehled* (Journal of Cartography). Quarterly, Prague.

Ceskoslovenska akademie ved, Ustav pro ceskou literaturu (Czechoslovak Academy of Sciences, Institute for Czech Literature). *Ceska Literatura* (Czech Literature). Quarterly, Prague.

Ceskoslovenska akademie ved zemedelskych (Czechoslovak Academy of Agricultural Sciences). *Za socialisticke zemedelstvi* (Socialist Agriculture). Semimonthly, Prague.

Ceskoslovenska obchodni komora (Czechoslovak Chamber of Commerce). *Czechoslovak Economic Bulletin*. Monthly, Prague.

Ceskoslovenska strana lidova (Czechoslovak People's Party). *Lidova demokracie* (People's Democracy). Daily, Prague.

Ceskoslovenska strana socialisticka (Czechoslovak Socialist Party). *Svobodne slovo* (Free Word). Daily, Prague.

Ceskoslovensko-sovetsky institut (Czechoslovak-Soviet Institute). *Praha-Moskva* (Prague-Moscow). Monthly, Prague.

Ceskoslovensko-sovetsky institut, Sekce spolecenskych ved (Czechoslovak-Soviet Institute, Section of Social Sciences). *Sovetska veda: stat a pravo* (Soviet Science: State and Law). Six issues a year, Prague.

Ceskoslovensky ustav zahranicni (Czechoslovak Foreign Institute). *Ceskoslovensky svet* (Czechoslovak World). Weekly, Prague.

Communist Party of Czechoslovakia, Central Committee. *Lidova sprava* (Local Government). Semimonthly, Prague. Ceased publication in 1952.

———. *Nova mysl* (New Mind). Monthly, Prague.

———. *Tvorba* (Construction). Weekly, Prague.

———. *Zivot strany* (Party Life). Semimonthly, Prague.

Communist Party of Czechoslovakia. *Rude pravo* (Red Right). Daily, Prague.

Communist Party of Slovakia. *Pod zastavou socialismu* (Under the Banner of Socialism). Semimonthly, Bratislava.

———. *Pravda* (Truth). Daily, Bratislava.

Czechoslovak Republic. Central Administration of Czechoslovak State Railways. *Vestnik* (Gazette). Prague.

———. Commissariat of Agriculture. *Rolnicke noviny* (Agricultural News). Semiweekly, Bratislava.

———. Commissariat of Information and Public Culture. *Dnesne Slovensko* (Slovakia Today). Quarterly, Bratislava.

———. Commissariat of Interior. *Narodne vybory* (People's Committees). Semimonthly, Bratislava.

———. Commissariat of Interior. *Uradny vestnik* (Official Gazette). Bratislava.

———. Office of the Government Presidium. *Narodni vybory* (People's Committees). Weekly, Prague.

———. Ministry of Agriculture. *Zemedelske noviny* (Agricultural News). Daily, Prague.

———. Ministry of Culture. *Osvetova prace* (Cultural Work). Biweekly, Prague.

———. Ministry of Education. *Pedagogika* (Pedagogy). Ten issues a year, Prague.

———. Ministry of Education. *Predskolni vychova* (Preschool Education). Monthly, Prague.

———. Ministry of Education. *Vestnik* (Bulletin). Three issues a month, Prague.

———. Ministry of Finance and the Czechoslovak State Bank. *Finance a uver* (Finance and Credit). Ten issues a year, Prague.

———. Ministry of Foreign Trade. *Czechoslovak Economic Bulletin.* Monthly, Prague.

———. Ministry of Foreign Trade. *Zahranicni obchod* (Foreign Trade). Weekly, Prague.

———. Ministry of Interior. *Uredni list Ceskoslovenske republiky* (Official Gazette of the Czechoslovak Republic). Prague.

———. Ministry of Interior. *Za socialisticky stat* (For a Socialist State). Bimonthly, Prague.

———. Ministry of Justice, Institute of Law. *Socialisticka zakonnost* (Socialist Legality). Ten issues a year, Prague.

———. Ministry of Justice, Institute of Law. *Soudce z lidu* (Lay Judge). Monthly, Prague.

———. Ministry of Labor and Social Welfare. *Socialisticka prace* (Socialist Labor). Monthly, Prague. Includes a supplement: *Vestnik,* official bulletin of the Ministry.

———. Ministry of Transportation. *Doprava* (Transportation). Monthly, Prague.

———. National Assembly. *Sbirka zakonu a narizeni republiky Ceskoslovenske* (Collection of Laws and Ordinances of the Czechoslovak Republic). Prague.

———. State Planning Office. *Cenove zpravy* (Price Reports). Weekly, Prague. Ceased publication in 1951.

———. State Planning Office. *Planovane hospodarstvi* (Planned Economy). Monthly, Prague.

———. State Planning and Statistical Office, Bratislava. *Zpravy* (Reports). Monthly, Bratislava.

———. State Statistical Office. *Prumyslove zpravy* (Industrial Reports). Monthly, in both Czech and English, Prague. Ceased publication in 1949.

———. State Statistical Office. *Statisticke informace. Rada 8. Prumyslova statistika* (Statistical Information. Series 8. Industrial Statistics). Prague.

———. State Statistical Office. *Statisticky obzor* (Statistical Review). Monthly, Prague.

———. State Statistical Office. *Statisticky zpravodaj* (Statistical Bulletin). Monthly, in Czech and French. Prague. Ceased publication in 1949.

———. Supreme Court. *Sbirka rozhodnuti ceskoslovenskych soudu* (Collection of Decisions of Czechoslovak Courts). Ten issues a year, Prague.

———. *Uradne noviny* (Official Gazette). Official gazette for Slovakia. Bratislava.

Hospodar (Economist). Weekly, 1949-51, Prague.

Jednota ceskoslovenskych pravnikov v Bratislave (Association of Czechoslovak Lawyers in Bratislava). *Pravny obzor* (Law Review). Monthly, except July and August, Bratislava.

Slovansky vybor Ceskoslovenska (Czechoslovak Slavic Committee). *Slovansky prehled* (Slavic Review). Monthly, Prague.

Slovenska akademia vied (Slovak Academy of Sciences). *Ekonomicky casopis* (Economic Journal). Four issues a year, Bratislava.

———. *Historicky casopis* (Historical Journal). Quarterly, Bratislava.

———. *Slovensky narodopis* (Slovak Ethnography). Quarterly, Bratislava.

Slovenska akademia ved, Ustav slovenskej literatury (Slovak Academy of Sciences, Institute of Slovak Literature). *Slovenska literatura* (Slovak Literature). Quarterly, Bratislava.

Svaz ceskoslovenskych spisovatelov, Slovenska sekcia (Union of Czechoslovak Writers, Slovak Section). *Kulturny zivot* (Cultural Life). Monthly, Bratislava.

Svaz ceskoslovenskych spisovatelu (Union of Czechoslovak Writers). *Literarni noviny* (Literary News). Weekly, Prague.

———. *Novy zivot* (New Life). Monthly, Prague.

Ustredni rada odboru (Central Trade Union Council). *Odborar* (Trade Unionist). Biweekly, Prague.

Ustredni svaz obchodu (Central Union of Commerce). *Ceskoslovensky obchod* (Czechoslovak Commerce). Weekly, Prague.

Index

Note: Numbers in italics refer to maps and tables.

UNIVERSITY LIBRARY
NOTTINGHAM